MW00830371

AIRLINES OF THE UNITED STATES

SINCE 1914

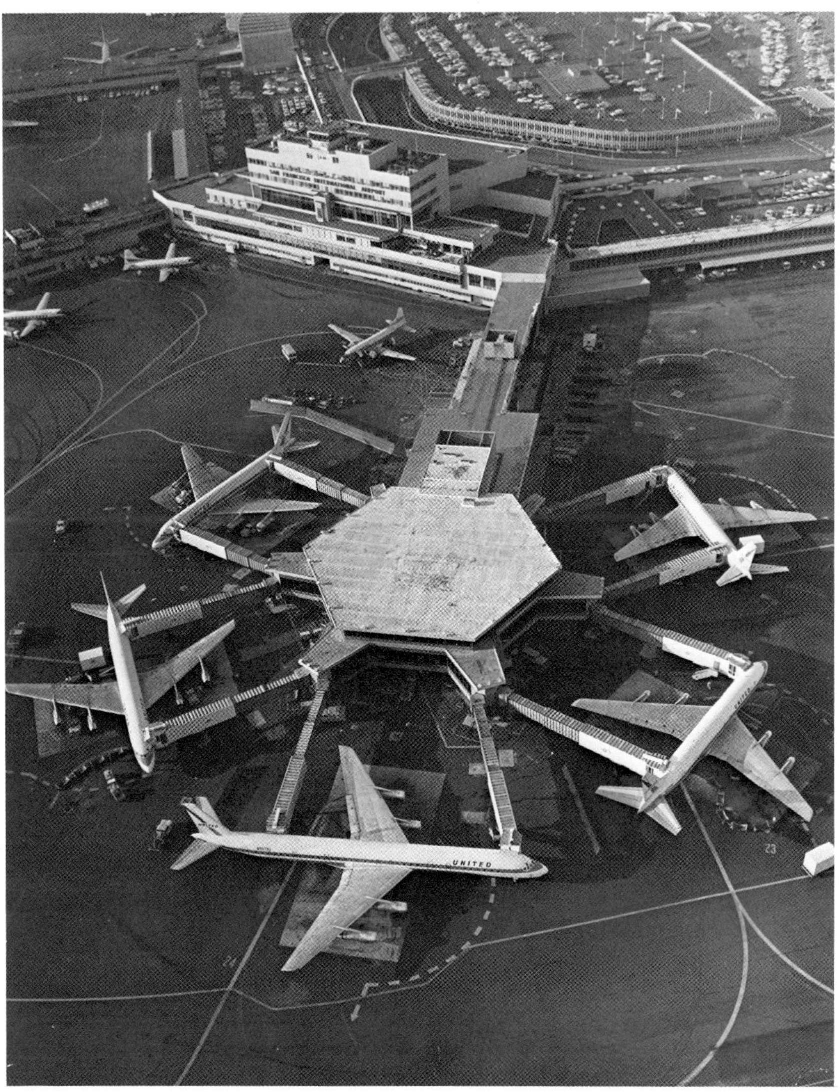

Typical United States airport scene of the 1960s and 1970s. Air view of the terminal building at San Francisco International Airport with United Air Lines' traffic pier in the foreground. The aircraft at the jetties are Douglas DC-8s with the DC-8-61 N8073U nearest the camera. Near the main building is a United Air Lines Convair CV-340.

AIRLINES OF THE UNITED STATES SINCE 1914

R. E. G. DAVIES

SMITHSONIAN INSTITUTION PRESS
WASHINGTON, D.C.

By the same author

A HISTORY OF THE WORLD'S AIRLINES

AIRLINES OF LATIN AMERICA SINCE 1919

Library of Congress Cataloging in Publication Data

Davies, R. E. G. (Ronald Edward George)
Airlines of the United States since 1914.

Reprint. Originally published: London: Putnam, 1972.
Bibliography: p. 578.
Includes index.
1. Air lines—United States—History.
I. Title.
TL726.2.D38 1982 387.7'0973 82-600203
ISBN 0-87474-381-8

Revised reprinting August 1982
Second reprinting March 1984
Published by the
Smithsonian Institution Press
with the permission of Putnam,
an imprint of the Bodley Head,
9 Bow Street, Covent Garden, London.

NOTES: Dates on maps, charts and tables appear in European form, as 10.12.29—10 December, 1929. Billions are U.S. billions, i.e., one billion equalling one thousand million. / Great care has been taken to ensure consistency in airline names and aircraft designations but this cannot be absolute. For example, Continental Airlines has itself used this form and Continental Air Lines.

Contents

List of Maps and Charts

List of Appendices

List of Tables

Foreword

by Secor D. Browne

Chairman, Civil Aeronautics Board

Alice and the Red Queen of *Through the Looking Glass* were obliged to run as fast as they could to stay in the same place. Many of us in air transport feel that this may be our principal activity. To the extent possible, however, it is useful to pause and look back over air transport history, and then look forward to speculate on our ultimate destinations.

Ron Davies has made an important contribution to such an appraisal. Not all of us will agree with his views of the past and predictions for the future, but I feel we will agree that he has made an extremely valuable addition to the literature of our industry.

Airlines of the United States since 1914 recounts the evolution of the United States as the leader in the advancement of commercial air transport. Circumstances may have accelerated developments in the United States and retarded developments abroad, but the fact remains that the United States has been, and so far remains, the world's leader. A competitive system of privately owned airlines has created patterns of public service, systems and company organization and techniques of aircraft design and supply which have established the world model.

This is not to say that progress has either been uninterrupted or totally satisfactory. Recurrent economic cycles have taken their tolls as reflected in varying responses to public needs, and in the effect on organizations and individuals. Many problems appear to be endemic, particularly the cycles of over- and under-capacity in terms of over-supply and under-supply of schedules and seats in both domestic and international services. Moreover, although the airplane seat and ton mile provide some of the best bargains in the world's economy, a balance between prices and costs, particularly labor costs, has rarely been achieved. Other costs, such as air traffic or highway access congestion and delay, airport, terminal and related facility charges and the economic burden of a tolerable environment for the community, all combine to aggravate the problem. As a result there is a continuing gap between the needs of the carriers for profits and the needs of the public for service at a low price.

The purely domestic problems of trunk and local services extend to the international arena where conflicting interests of politics and prestige are often added to public service and economic considerations. The difficulties of balancing the role of scheduled service against that of supplemental service are similarly bound up in factors often remote from either the public interest or economics.

The absence of any ideal solution is nowhere more evident than in the controversy over the proper role of regulation, and, indeed, whether there should be regulation at all. The old dictum says that if the Devil did not exist, the Church would have had to invent him. Similarly, if the regulator didn't exist, the airline industry would have had to invent him—and did in 1938. A current question is what would happen to the industry were it totally deregulated. One thesis is that there would be a rush by existing and new entrants to those routes thought to be profitable. Other routes would be abandoned. Price competition would be destructive. With the essential link between economics and safety there would be an inevitable major air disaster, possibly involving a prominent Member of Congress. Public outcry and congressional responses would lead to the re-establishment of regulation. Since this was the sequence of events in the mid-30s, why re-learn that lesson? This thesis has been challenged, but the lesson of history—so well treated in this book—cannot be totally ignored.

What lies ahead? The airlines are experiencing economic recovery in response to improvement of the U.S. and world economy, vigorous management efforts to match capacity to demands, and responsive regulation. If capacity can be held in check and labor and other costs brought under control, this recovery of airline fortunes should continue to the point where normal economic and population growth will again require expanded services and new types and increased numbers of aircraft. Emergence of another cycle in airline fortunes will obviously depend on how much restraint and wise judgment can be exercised by the industry and regulators, and how much political and economic security the world will see. This also is predicated on some compromise which will balance the required growth of the air transport system with preservation of an acceptable environment for communities and nations.

In the long run, as the author indicates, the outlook for commercial air transport is bright. Certainly the speed, safety, flexibility and economic advantages of air transport make it, as a system, superior to competitive modes for other than very short distances. Fixed guideways for passenger travel, other than urban and commuter services, inevitably call for disproportionate subsidy in terms of public benefits. The airways, if exploited efficiently in combination with aircraft and ground facilities truly representative of today's technology, form the backbone of the transport system of today and the future.

Washington, D.C.
12 January, 1972

SECOR D. BROWNE

Author's Preface to the Revised Reprinting

When the idea of reprinting *Airlines of the United States since 1914* was first discussed, the main issue to be resolved was whether to produce a book which was identical with the 1972 printing, or to attempt a second edition. An unaltered reprint would appear somewhat dated, but on the other hand, a new edition would require considerable work, time, and cost. A compromise solution therefore appeared desirable.

One major problem was that the United States airline industry had undergone a revolution. The Deregulation Act of 1978 swept in a new era, reflecting the most profound change in the control of the U.S. airline industry since the 1934 air mail scandal, which had precipitated the formation of the C.A.B. itself. The solution to making a historical commentary on this controversial issue has been attempted by the insertion of a small essay on the subject as an appendix (pages 675–78), which may serve as one historian's view of the onward course of history at a critical time.

Happily, most of the book needed few changes. Corrections are confined to a few dates and the provision of Allan Loughead's portrait on page 133. Where possible, however, improvements have been made to maps and diagrams, and to ensure clarity all the photographs have been reproduced from the originals.

Chapters dealing with the Local Service, Freight, and Charter companies have all been augmented. The list of Supplemental carriers on pages 627 and 628 has been updated, while the Commuter airlines have also been given their due share of attention, both in the appropriate chapter and with two additional tables (page 630).

These modest changes only touch upon the main events which have punctuated the ongoing course of airline history in the United States during the last decade. As a corollary to the deregulation process, the C.A.B. adopted a new system of airline categories on 2 October, 1980. All airlines grossing more than $1 billion per year were classified as Majors, and included all the former domestic trunk airlines, plus Pan American, Republic, and U.S. Air. Airlines earning between $75 million and $1 billion per year became Nationals, and included all the former regionals (other than Republic and U.S. Air, now Majors, and Air New England, which was too small), the former Intra-State airlines, and the larger Territorial, Supplemental and All-Freight carriers. All airlines earning less than $75 million per year were classified as Regionals, with a break point at $10 million separating the Large from the Medium.

The disappearance of two major airlines—National Airlines, by merger with Pan American, and the startling demise of Braniff Airways—have been noted in the essay on deregulation. But airline casualties have in fact been mercifully few during the past decade. The new freedom of entry provisions of the Deregulation Act have permitted, on the other hand, the foundation of many new airlines, mainly within the contiguous forty-eight states. Special mention should be made of Mid Pacific Air, which began intra-Hawaiian service, with 60-seat Nihon YS-11s, on 15 March, 1981, cutting fares by 50 percent.

The speculation about the supersonic services on page 572 deserves a short comment. For the record, British Airways and Air France opened Concorde service on 21 January, 1976, and Aeroflot began a short-lived Tupolev 144 passenger service on 1 November, 1977. British and French Concordes served Washington from 24 May, 1976, and New York from 22 November, 1977. The only U.S. airline ever to fly a supersonic airliner was Braniff, which began Dallas–Washington service on 13 January, 1979, with Concordes leased from British Airways and Air France. But the much publicized—and costly—service was terminated on 31 May, 1980, as the ailing airline had to trim its wings in a vain attempt to ward off bankruptcy.

Two air crashes during the past decade must be mentioned because of their spectacular circumstances and the enormous publicity and controversy they generated. On 25 May, 1979, an American Airlines DC-10 stalled and crashed on takeoff at Chicago's O'Hare Airport, killing 273 persons. One of the engines had literally fallen off, and the aircraft stalled in full view at the world's busiest airport. The National Transportation Safety Board apportioned the blame primarily to improper maintenance procedures, with other contributory causes such as design vulnerability and deficiencies in F.A.A. surveillance and reporting. The other spectacular crash occurred on 13 January 1982 when an Air Florida Boeing 737, having just taken off from the National Airport in a snowstorm, ploughed into the icebound Potomac River at Washington, D.C. The aircraft had been unable to maintain its climbing gradient because of the accumulation of ice on the wings. Only a few passengers survived. Both of these crashes, however, were isolated cases, fortunately uncharacteristic of an admirable safety record which has constantly been maintained by the U.S. airline industry.

In compiling this material I have received generous assistance from airline staff, particularly Anne Whyte of Pan American and Katie Childs of Republic. Blanche Womac of Douglas, the late Sam Brown and Mary Ransome at the C.A.B., and Marion Mistric at the A.T.A. have all traced elusive facts. Bob van der Linden had the soul-destroying job of collecting the photographs while John Stroud and Gordon Williams found pictures which had irritatingly disappeared from my files. To these people, and countless others, I am most grateful.

There seemed to be no reason to replace the original 1972 Foreword to this book. The basic ingredients of controversy are still with us, and Secor Browne's commentary is as relevant and pungent today as it was then.

R. E. G. Davies

The first scheduled air service. The St Petersburg-Tampa Airboat Line's Benoist Type XIV flying-boat on the rough plank slipway at St Petersburg just before the first flight to Tampa on 1 January, 1914.

CHAPTER ONE

The First Steps

St Petersburg—Tampa

On 17 December, 1913, exactly ten years after Orville and Wilbur Wright's now undisputed claim to have made the first power-driven, heavier-than-air, controlled flight, the city of St Petersburg, Florida, signed a contract with Thomas Benoist, aircraft manufacturer of St Louis, Missouri, for the operation of an airline. Two weeks previously, on 4 December, the company had been organized as the St Petersburg-Tampa Airboat Line by Paul E. Fansler, an electrical engineer, with the backing of city officials and businessmen. On 13 December, a contract was signed with the city of St Petersburg for a subsidy guarantee amounting to $50 per day during the month of January and $25 per day during February and March.

Much of the credit must go to Benoist. He had founded his company in St Louis in 1909 after making a fortune in the motorcar business, and his ambition was to demonstrate that aeroplanes were more than instruments of sport or machines of war; that they could be used as a practicable means of transport on a regular basis.

The conditions at St Petersburg were ideal for proving his point. The city was then a fast-growing community of about 8,000 people whose nearest retail and wholesale centre was Tampa, separated from it by Tampa Bay. To reach the local metropolis, the choice was a once-daily boat which took two hours, a 12-hr railway journey, or an arduous drive over dirt roads which took the greater part of a day. Benoist and Fansler had a captive market for their new product, air transport.

Benoist's aircraft selected for the task was the Type XIV flying-boat, 26 ft long, weighing 1,400 lb, and with a wing span of 36 ft. It was powered by a 75 hp Roberts six-cylinder engine driving a pusher propeller, flew at about 70 mph, and cost $4,150. The pilot was Tony Jannus, to whom the prospects of flying a regular schedule on the flimsy craft of plywood, spruce, and linen, was just as attractive as the racing and aerobatics which comprised the major proportion of aviation activity at that time.

Regular flights started promptly at 10 a.m. on New Year's Day, 1914, watched by most of the citizens of St Petersburg. The first passenger was ex-mayor A. C. Pheil, who paid $400 for the privilege. Subsequently passengers paid $5 for the single trip, and the same charge was made for 100 lb of freight. One interesting feature of this, the first regular airline tariff in history, was that an excess baggage charge of 5 cents per lb was made for passengers and baggage weighing more than 200 lb, a remarkable similarity with the rates charged 50 years later.

This first airline flight in the world took 23 min from the St Petersburg Yacht Basin to the mouth of the Hillsboro River at Tampa, a distance of 18 miles. With a following wind, the return journey took only 20 min, a feature of the service which repeated itself to the point where the local St Petersburg newspaper remarked on the way folks seemed anxious to get away from Tampa.

Settling down to fulfilling a regular timetable, with two round trips a day, the St Petersburg-Tampa Airboat Line was able to repay $360 of its

The Benoist Type XIV taxi-ing with flags flying from the interplane struts and Tony Jannus waving from the cockpit. (*National Air Museum, Smithsonian Institution*)

The Benoist Type XIV airborne on the world's first air route.

municipal subsidy in January and paid its own way in February and March. Late in January, passenger demand was such that a second, larger, flying-boat was put into service, flown by Tony Jannus' brother, Roger, who also undertook charter flights to local resorts. When the contract with the city expired on 31 March, 1914, the world's first airline had carried 1,204 passengers without mishap. Bad weather and mechanical breakdowns forced cancellations on only eight days. Repairs to both aircraft cost only $100.

Operations were continued during April, but the Mexican war scare, combined with the wane of the tourist season, led to a fall in business, and the service was terminated. As a postscript to this early airline adventure, three of the main participants died before the start of the next airline—Benoist was killed, ironically, in a tramcar accident in St Louis in 1917; Tony Jannus disappeared over the Black Sea while training Russian pilots

Left to right: Paul E. Fansler, organizer of the St Petersburg-Tampa Airboat Line; A. C. Pheil, the first passenger from St Petersburg to Tampa on 1 January, 1914; and Tony Jannus, the pilot of the world's first scheduled air service.

Tony Jannus in the cockpit of the Benoist Type XIV flying-boat.

at the end of World War 1; and his brother Roger was killed in an aeroplane crash on the Western Front.

Four Years of Inactivity

Although the United States was not directly concerned with World War 1 until 1917, the use of aircraft as instruments of war in Europe undoubtedly affected attitudes on the opposite side of the Atlantic. Attention was diverted from possible use of larger passenger-carrying aeroplanes to the more spectacular exploits of the fighters and reconnaissance types, confirming a widely-held belief that flying in heavier-than-air machines was a dangerous occupation, to be undertaken only by the expert or the adventurous, like mountaineering. The seal was set on this unfortunate public image when the United States entered the Great War and the best-known names in aviation became those of the ace pilots Eddie Rickenbacker and Reed Chambers.

When the war ended, Europe hastened to find work for a vast armada of aircraft whose military usefulness was finished. France and Britain, with that ideal proving ground for transport aeroplanes, the London—Paris cross-Channel route, founded airlines immediately, while Germany, denied the right to build any military aircraft whatever, concentrated on civil types as the means of preserving its aircraft industry. In the United States, on the other hand, the social and geographic conditions were unfavourable; there were few situations involving a water crossing, and the densest inter-city routes were already served by efficient railways, often providing excellent service under the stimulus of competition.

Another factor was the slowness of aircraft in the early 1920s. Cruising speeds were around 100 mph, with the result that average speeds, including stops, were only about 75 mph. This improvement over express trains like the *Twentieth Century Ltd* was not spectacular, and the prospect of a noisy ride in an open cockpit held little appeal compared with the luxury of the Pullman car.

There was one outlet for the aeroplane which, however, was quickly recognized: the carriage of air mail. Drawing possibly on lessons learned in Europe in the closing stages of the war, when urgent despatches were carried by air and Communications Squadrons organized by the Air Forces, the United States Government explored the possibility of setting up an air mail service as early as 1917. The outcome was so successful and had such a significant influence on the early progress of air transport in the United States that it is made the subject of the second chapter of this book. Operated by the U.S. Post Office, it constituted by far the major portion of civil aviation activity until 1927, when it ceased operations.

During this period, however, a few other enterprises entered the scene with some pioneering effort, not only for the carriage of mail, but also passengers. Pride of place should go to a company based in New York. Thomas Hart Kennedy, in his *Introduction to the Economics of Air Transportation*, published in 1924, records: 'Aircraft operated for profit on regular schedules, over advertised routes, in the United States has been confined to the Aeromarine Airways.' Though the statement was not strictly accurate, Aeromarine accounted for most of the private enterprise in air transport prior to the passing of the Kelly Air Mail Act in 1925.

Aeromarine

Many answered the call; few were chosen. Once the returning aviators, fresh from military adventures in Europe, had looked around and found their bearings, a number of enterprises associated with the general theme of starting an air service were announced in many parts of the U.S.A., mainly on the coast. Only a few of these, however, made actual flights with fare-paying passengers, and still less made any pretence at operating to a schedule. One was a company called Aero Ltd, which made a series of flights in August 1919 between New York and Atlantic City, using war-surplus HS-2 flying-boats, and, shortly afterwards, Florida West Indies Airways Inc operated some services in the Caribbean.

The stimulus in this latter area was the introduction by Congress of the Prohibition Act, which became effective on 30 June, 1919. The consumption of alcohol became a criminal offence in every bar or restaurant under the United States flag but did not apply to foreign territories such as Cuba or the Bahamas, which lay temptingly 100 miles offshore from Florida. Showing considerable élan and initiative, Aero Ltd promptly flew its aircraft south and is reported to have made 40 round trips from Miami to Nassau to satisfy the needs of thirsty Americans.

These tentative operations were quickly superseded by those of Aeromarine Airways Inc, founded as a subsidiary of the Aeromarine Plane and Motor Corporation of Keyport, New Jersey. Aeromarine was backed by Inglis M. Uppercu, formerly a New York motorcar distributor, who had built seaplanes for the Navy during the war. His pilots included Durston Richardson, and Ed Musick, who later became one of Pan American Airways' famous Clipper Commanders.

During the war, the United States armed services had developed a system of aircraft procurement in which the winner of a design competition sold not only his design but also the manufacturing rights. Thus, for example, Curtiss' original HS-2 coastal patrol flying-boat, sold to the Navy, was then built by other manufacturers, notably Boeing. When the war ended, the newly-formed Manufacturers Aircraft Association suggested to the Army and Navy that aircraft should be sold gradually, through private companies, under strict government supervision, to avoid glutting the market.

The idea was readily accepted and Aeromarine was one of the beneficiaries, converting HS-2s (which had cost the Navy $18,000 each) to six-passenger flying-boats, either with an open cockpit or with a transparent hood in the luxury model. These were sold to customers for $6,000 to

Aeromarine Airways' Curtiss Type 75 flying-boat *Santa Maria* used on New York—Atlantic City and U.S.—Cuba services in 1921. This type was a 14-seat conversion of the military F-5L. (*The Smithsonian Institution*)

$9,000 each, but, more important, were also employed by the airline subsidiary.

During the winter of 1920–21, Florida West Indies Airways (known later as Aeromarine West Indies Airways) began a successful experimental air mail service between Key West and Havana, having received a government Foreign Air Mail contract on 15 October, 1920. Aeromarine absorbed this operation, carrying passengers as a bonus, at $75 each. By this time the fleet had been augmented by some Curtiss F-5L flying-boats, big rugged dependable twin-engined biplanes, weighing seven tons fully loaded, and even when the payload was increased by Aeromarine's 14-seat conversion—called Type 75—had a cruising radius of four hours. Another carrier in this region was the America Trans Oceanic Company, which

Close-up of the Curtiss 75 *Santa Maria* showing bow entrance hatch and walkway above the forward cabin. (*National Air Museum, Smithsonian Institution*)

started service from Miami to the British island of South Bimini on 20 December, 1919, and operated one round trip daily for two full winter seasons, charging $25 return for the 50-mile flight.

Between 7 July and 11 September, 1921, an Aeromarine HS-2 made a special flight from New York to Chicago and back, via the Hudson River, Lake George, Lake Champlain, the St Lawrence River and four of the Great Lakes, to win the Glidden Trophy for setting up a world record flight for commercial flying-boats of over 7,000 miles. The average speed was 73·5 mph for an actual flying time of only 102 hr and there was not a single delay caused by any mechanical failure.

The flight gave Aeromarine such a boost that it was able to establish, at the end of September, the *High Ball Express* service from New York to Havana, via Atlantic City, Beaufort (South Carolina), Miami, and Key West. F-5Ls were used, fitted with eight seats in the forward cabin and four in the rear. The journey took two days, compared with four days by rail and boat.

Then on 1 November, 1921, two regular daily services were inaugurated, from Key West to Havana and from Miami to Nassau. The Havana trip took 1½–2 hr for the 105 miles, and cost $50 single, compared with $19 by steamer; the Nassau trip took 2½–3 hr for 185 miles, and cost $85 single ($150 round trip), compared with $25 by steamer. These services operated throughout the winter and terminated on 1 May the following year.

Aeromarine then instituted a commendable scheduling practice, neatly mitigating the effect of the highly seasonal nature of the Florida traffic. The fleet was flown north and, on 1 June, 1922, began a Detroit—Cleveland service, providing a short cut across Lake Erie to avoid the cir-

The Aeromarine West Indies Airways Curtiss 75s *Pinta* (nearest) and *Santa Maria*, used on the U.S. & Cuban Mail Service. This was the first international air mail service by a U.S. airline, and presumably the original FAM-1 Post Office contract. (*The Smithsonian Institution*)

cuitous surface journey via Toledo. *The Ninety Minute Line*, as it was called, maintained two round trips daily, taking $1\frac{1}{2}$ hr for the 95 miles, carrying passengers and baggage only, as Aeromarine had no mail contract for this route. The single fare was $25, compared with $9 by rail and $5 by steamer, both of which were much slower. The Cleveland—Detroit service ended on 1 October, when the fleet made its migration once again to the south.

During 1922 services were expanded and Aeromarine boasted three operating divisions: Southern: Key West—Havana, Miami—Nassau, Miami—Bimini, with special flights from New York to Havana; New York: New York—Atlantic City, New York—points in New England, New York aerial sightseeing; and Great Lakes: Cleveland—Detroit, sightseeing over Lake Erie and Lake St Clair, and special flights New York—Detroit, via Albany, Montreal, Buffalo, and Cleveland.

With this increased activity, however, Aeromarine appears to have over-reached itself, for in September 1923, after three years of regular

The Aeromarine Airways' Curtiss 75 *Ponce de Leon* in Cuban waters in 1921. Painted on the hull are the words Key West—Havana 75 minutes. (*The Smithsonian Institution*)

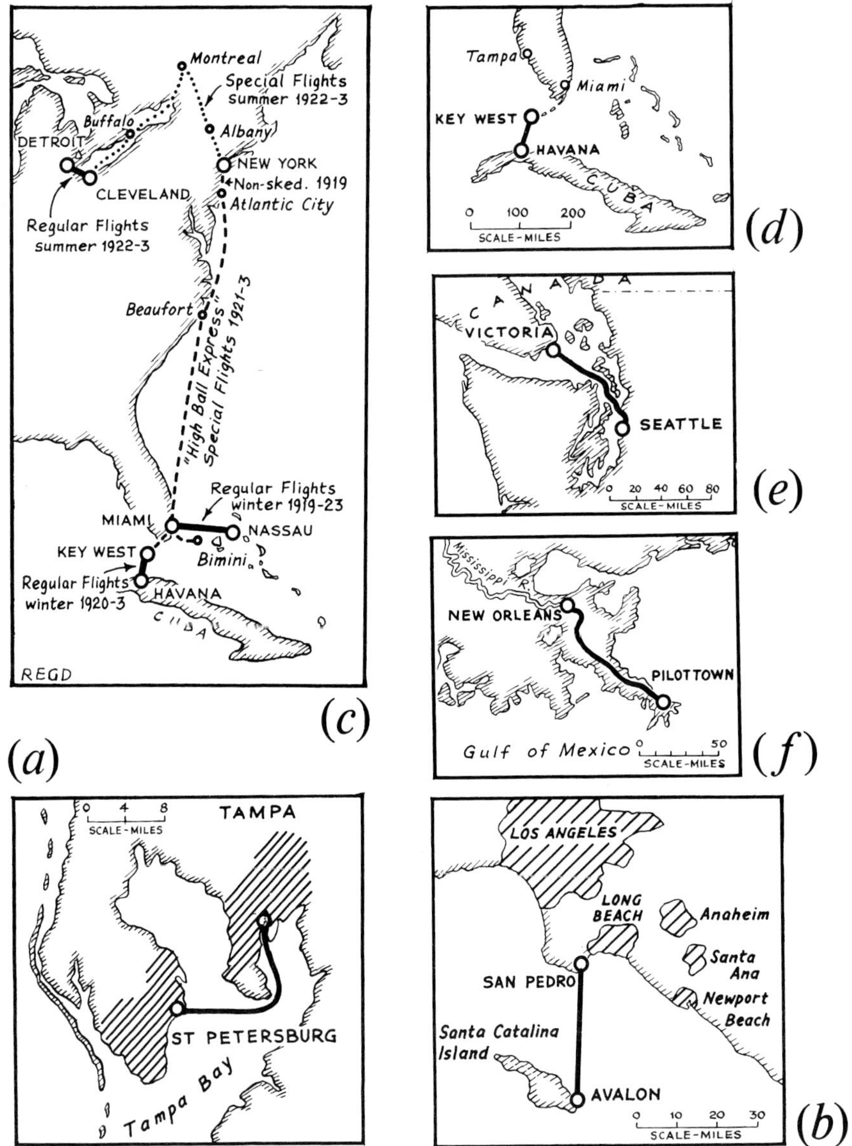

Fig. 1. This selection of maps illustrates the earliest air routes in the United States. (*a*): the St. Petersburg–Tampa Airboat Line, 1914—the world's first scheduled airline. (*b*): Chaplin Air Line, 1919—a passenger air route which is sustained to this day. (*c*): the various activities of Aeromarine Airways, which moved its operations seasonally between 1919 and 1923. (*d*): the first U.S. Post Office Foreign Air Mail Route, awarded to Florida West Indies Airways, 1920. (*e*): F.A.M. 2, Edward Hubbard, 1920. (f): F.A.M. 3, Merrill K. Riddick, 1923. All these operations are fully reviewed in the text of this chapter.

The route is boldly displayed on the hull of Aeromarine Airways' Curtiss 75 *Columbus*. (*The Smithsonian Institution*)

scheduled service, it ceased operations. In spite of carrying some 17,000 passengers on scheduled services, and probably as many on sightseeing trips, with a perfect safety record, the company could not pay its way. Early in 1924 it was reorganized, with new capital, changing its name to Aeromarine Airways Corporation; but there is no record of systematic airline service from then on.

The Foreign Air Mail contract, from Key West to Havana—which the U.S. Post Office presumably designated FAM-1 at the time—lapsed with the demise of Aeromarine.

Eddie Hubbard's Airline

Inglis Uppercu's company is given the credit in this book for operating the first post-war regular airline only after some considerable heart-searching on the part of the author. Aeromarine wins pride of place because of its greater frequency of operation, and the fact that it carried passengers over a network of routes. Judged on somewhat less demanding criteria, another operator, at the opposite side of the continent, can claim at least chronological parity, operating as it did a single route, for mail only, at a lower frequency, for a longer period than the eastern pioneer.

During the First World War Edward (Eddie) Hubbard had been an instructor to army pilots at Rockwell Field, San Diego, and in 1917 had become an experimental pilot for the Boeing company. On 3 March, 1919, he made a survey flight from Vancouver to Seattle, with sixty letters

On 3 March, 1919, Edward Hubbard (left) and William Boeing made a survey flight with mail, from Vancouver to Seattle, in a Boeing C-700. They are seen in front of the seaplane on arrival at Seattle. (*Boeing Airplane Company*)

and William E. Boeing as a passenger. The aircraft used was a C-700, a commercial version of an open cockpit floatplane trainer, fifty of which had been built by Boeing for the U.S. Navy. It had no tailplane (horizontal stabilizer), stability being obtained through a 50 per cent stagger of the wings and wing incidence combination.

After a series of trials in July 1920, Hubbard began a regular air mail service on 15 October of that year, from Seattle to Victoria, connecting

NC5270, the first Boeing B-1D (Boeing Model 6D), seen at Seattle after conversion to B-1E (Model 6E) standard. The wooden hull was covered with diagonal strips of spruce veneer and the wings were modified Boeing Model 40 units. This four-seat flying-boat is believed to have been used on the Seattle—Victoria mail service by Edward Hubbard. (*Gordon S. Williams*)

with the Japanese ship *Africa Maru*. The 84 miles were covered in 50 min by a Boeing B-1, the first commercial design of the Boeing Airplane Company. Operated as a private contract mail service under U.S. Post Office foreign mail appropriations, the main purpose was to gain a few extra hours for the mails by connecting with the first landfall made by the ship. The contract called for a maximum of twelve round trips per month, with maximum loads of 600 lb per trip. Between 25,000 and 50,000 lb of mail were flown annually by Eddie Hubbard's airline, or the Seattle-Victoria Air Mail Line, as it became known.

Hubbard was later to join with Boeing in more ambitious airline ventures when he became a director of Boeing Air Transport, but his original route was flown continuously under other names and in other hands until 30 June, 1937, completing almost 17 years of continuous operation.

The Gulf Coast Air Line

Although departing slightly from the strict chronology of first airline services, mention should be made at this point of another airline because of its basic similarity to Hubbard's operation. On 9 April, 1923, Merrill K. Riddick opened a route between New Orleans and Pilottown, at the very tip of the Mississippi Delta, a distance of 80 miles. Using HS-2Ls, the Gulf Coast Air Line Inc provided a mail link with the steamers leaving from, or arriving at, Pilottown on the routes to Cuba and the Caribbean islands, and to Central and South America.

Mails were carried under a foreign air mail appropriation, as on the Seattle—Victoria route, with the odd circumstance that there was no necessity to fly to foreign territory. Until the entry of Pan American Airways into the foreign air mail field, in 1927, Hubbard and Riddick were the only Post Office foreign mail contractors, under contracts FAM-2 and FAM-3, respectively.

The United States Army Model Airway

During the early 1920s, the Air Mail Service of the U.S. Post Office Department was the main contributor to airline progress in the United States (*See Chapter 2*). Indeed, there was only one other organization which operated on anything like a regular schedule over a distance of more than 100 miles. This was the Model Airway of the U.S. Army Air Service which, in the words of Capt St Clair Street, its Airway Control Officer, undertook to 'bear the brunt of the burden in the development of aeronautics in the United States until such time as the utility of aircraft for transportation has proven itself beyond doubt to the people of this country'.

Under the supervision of Capt Burdette S. Wright, the Model Airway

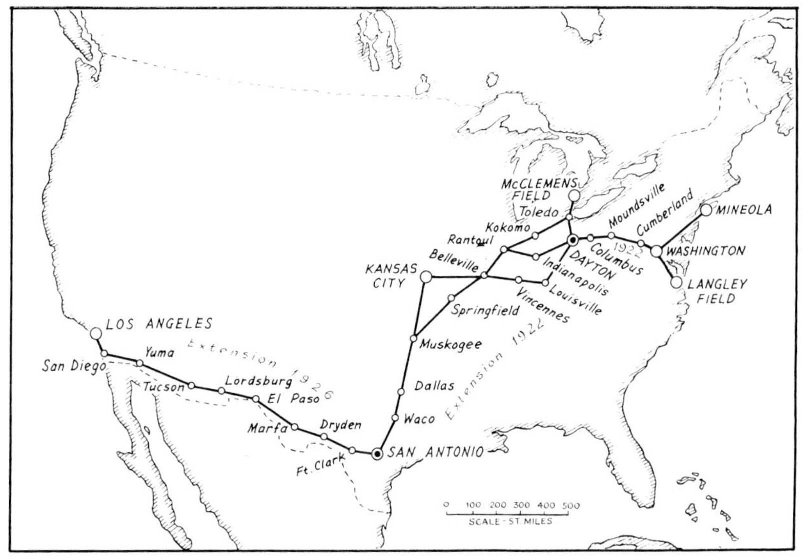

Fig. 2. U.S. Army Model Airway, 1922–1926.

began, on 19 June, 1922, a regular schedule of four services each way per week between Bolling Field, Anacostia, D.C., and McCook Field, Dayton, Ohio. The main objectives were to promote the development of aerodromes and air navigation facilities and, to this end, the route chosen was ideal as it included sections of contrasting terrain, from the rugged Allegheny Mountains to the flat plains of Ohio. Aircraft used were DH-4s—the same type as used by the U.S. Post Office—with the word 'AIRWAY' painted prominently on the underside of the lower wing.

On 4 December, 1922, a winter schedule began, on an extended route network stretching from Long Island, New York, to San Antonio, Texas. A cost accounting system was instituted with the object of assessing the basic economics of airline operation. A few passengers were carried, although these were restricted to military or government personnel, numbering two or three hundred each year. By 1926 the Model Airway reached Los Angeles, and continued to operate until the expansion of civil airlines, following the development of privately contracted mail routes.

Routes to Santa Catalina

Compared with the Post Office Mail, the Model Airway, Aeromarine, and the two contract foreign mail carriers, other airline operations during the first few post-war years were minute. One company deserves mention, however, possibly because the route it started has been operated more or less continuously ever since by an assortment of airlines ranging from trunk carriers to air taxi firms.

On 4 July, 1919, Syd Chaplin Airlines began services from San Pedro (in the port district of Los Angeles) on a 34-mile route to Avalon (the resort on the island of Santa Catalina), using one Curtiss MF flying-boat, which, incidentally, was shipped from the factory on Long Island by Railway Express. The company operated three round trips per day, exactly the same number as the total staff, and became known as Catalina Airlines.

Regular service ended on 15 September, after less than three months of operations, and although one of the pilots continued to make flights on demand, these too ended the following year.

At the end of 1920, Pacific Marine Airways was organized by Foster Curry, a vacation promoter from Yosemite. Operations began from Wilmington, opposite San Pedro, to Avalon, using two Curtiss HS-2Ls, until 29 June, 1928, when Western Air Express took over the company.

Other Early Airlines

Very few other companies qualify for inclusion in a list of airlines during this embryo phase in the development of air transport in the U.S.A. Until the existence of Ryan Airlines in 1925, none lasted more than a summer season or two, and made no significant contribution to progress.

During the summer of 1922 the Loening aircraft factory of New York sponsored the New York-Newport Air Service, using three Loening 23L

The Curtiss MF flying-boat used in 1919 to operate Syd Chaplin Airlines' San Pedro (Los Angeles)—Avalon (Santa Catalina) service. (*Gene's Photo & Rock Shop*)

One of the two Curtiss HS-2L flying-boats used on the Wilmington—Catalina service of Pacific Marine Airways. (*Western Airlines*)

pusher-engined Air Yacht flying-boats to carry socially and financially prominent people to the fashionable Rhode Island port. The Air Yachts carried four passengers per trip at a $30 single fare, which worked out at 20c per mile, enough to discourage mass travel. Shortly after beginning the second season, a crash at Newport led to the discontinuation of the line.

Serving a similar clientele, another enterprising venture was Balsam's Air Service, which provided a newspaper delivery service to Dixville Notch, New Hampshire, from a base at Garden City, Long Island, during the summer months. Three Curtiss Orioles flew the distance of 350 miles in about four hours, which compared very favourably with the 36-hr rail journey.

During the winter of 1923, the Curtiss Metropolitan Airplane Company carried newspapers from Miami to West Palm Beach, making room for the occasional passenger if space permitted.

None of these private concerns survived more than two summers*, and 1924 was a lean year for airline activity, for Aeromarine had closed down by this time. The reason for public apathy was, quite simply, that flying was regarded as somewhat hazardous, except, apparently, over short stretches of water, and there were few obvious locations for exploiting this medium. Where there were specially favourable economic situations, for example, service to resort areas for which passengers were prepared to pay a premium fare, some transient success was achieved. But the hard fact was that, for assured financial viability, normal airline operations were too costly without some form of subsidy, direct or indirect.

The outstanding example of a directly subsidized service was that promoted by the United States Post Office to speed up its long-distance mail deliveries. The contribution made by this historic organization to the initial development of air transport in the United States, indeed, in the world as a whole, is of such importance as to warrant a separate chapter.

*A summary of airlines operating from 1914 to 1924 is in Table 1, page 582.

CHAPTER TWO

The United States Air Mail Service

New York—Washington

The individual stories of the small airlines which survived precariously during the first few years after the Great War were colourful, almost romantic. They resulted from the efforts of determined promoters who sought to exploit the aeroplane as a transport vehicle in its own right. Sadly, their efforts were frustrated by the inadequacies of the material at their disposal. Few aircraft were reliable enough; operational facilities of such basic importance as good aerodromes were almost non-existent; the public had been nurtured on a diet of hair-raising stories of war exploits which aimed to emphasize the thrills involved in handling temperamental heavier-than-air machines. First-hand experience of these was gleaned from visiting barnstormers, pilots who offered a circus-like show of stunt-flying which served only to confirm the public's attitude of doubt. Not surprisingly, therefore, the little would-be airlines were unsuccessful in persuading enough people to pay enough money for a long enough period to support aircraft which, being the products of an infant industry, were hopelessly uneconomic. Indeed, the total output of all the small airlines which tried to operate without a subsidy of some kind was quite insignificant compared with the figures set up by the U.S. Air Mail Service.

In 1916, funds were made available for payment for the carriage of mail by aeroplane from the appropriation for Steamboat or Other Power Boat Service. Advertisements were issued inviting bids for a route in Massachusetts and several in Alaska; but none were taken up because at that time neither aircraft nor landing grounds were available, and the number of pilots in the entire U.S.A. was very small. However, the rapid development of aircraft manufacture and flying techniques stimulated by the war encouraged the Post Office to persist in its belief that an air mail service was a practical possibility.

Accordingly, when the Post Office received for the fiscal year ending 30 June, 1918, an appropriation of $100,000 for an experimental air service, it turned thought into action. Late in 1917 bids were requested from aircraft manufacturers for the construction of five mailplanes. Three bids were received, opened on 21 February, 1918, accepted, and delivery promised in 90 days. By modern standards, this would not seem to give cause for impatience, but the Post Office Department had the bit firmly between its teeth and eagerly took up a suggestion by Col E. A. Deeds (later to become one of the chief organizers of United Air Transport) that the Army might furnish aircraft on a temporary basis so as to advance the inauguration date. The offer was accepted and the events which followed epitomized the nature of air operations in the United States in 1918, reflecting the vision of the promoters, their zeal in setting praiseworthy targets, and the haphazard means at their disposal to achieve their goals.

Mail being transferred to an Army Curtiss JN-4H operating on the U.S. Aerial Mail Service. This type was one of the famous 'Jenny' series and the example illustrated bore serial number 38274. (*U.S. War Department*)

On 13 May, 1918, the Army officers who had been assigned to carry the mail were informed that their aeroplanes had arrived at Belmont Park, Long Island, ready for assembly. By the afternoon of the next day, two aircraft were actually completed and flown to Philadelphia, and one of them flew on to Washington on the 15th. At noon, President Woodrow Wilson came with members of his cabinet to the Polo Grounds to give the Postmaster General, Albert S. Burleson, his blessing at the inaugural ceremony.

Overcoming a slight delay caused by the absence of fuel in the tanks, the pilot took-off and followed railway tracks which he believed would lead him to New York—and was next heard of at a farm in southern Maryland. Fortunately for the official records, the service in the other direction was performed according to plan, which included a change of aircraft at Philadelphia. Lieuts Torrey Webb and J. C. Edgerton were the successful pilots, flying Curtiss JN-4Hs. The total elapsed time, New York—Washington, was 3 hr 20 min.

The standards of navigation when the Post Office Mail service opened on 15 May, 1918, were primitive in the extreme. Dr E. P. Warner recalls: 'On the third day of the service, the same pilot who had failed to find Philadelphia from Washington in his first attempt tried again. This time he was given careful directions by landmark to Baltimore, and instructions thereafter simply to keep Chesapeake Bay on his right; instructions which he followed with such sedulous attention to detail that he reached the northern end of the bay, followed the water around the end and down the eastern side, still keeping it always on his right, and landed in Cape

Among the Post Office's 1918 fleet were seven Standard JR-1B single-engined biplanes. All seven are seen in this photograph taken in August 1918. The three nearest aircraft bear numbers 1, 4 and 2 and the fifth from the front is No. 5. (*U.S. War Department*)

Charles on making the discovery that he was out of fuel and that the water now was not only on his right, but on his left and in front of him as well, and that only a narrow strip of land lay behind.'

In spite of early shortcomings such as this, however, the pilots learned quickly and the U.S. Aerial Mail Service, as it was designated officially, settled down to a fair record of punctuality and regularity, averaging 91 per cent completion of its scheduled flights during 1918. Initial public response was not exactly enthusiastic, however. The rate charged when the service started was 24c per ounce, including 10c special delivery, compared with 3c for ordinary deliveries and 10c for express; and the time saved compared with surface means was not substantial.

On 12 August, 1918, the Post Office took over the service, under the command of Capt Benjamin B. Lipsner, who had been concerned with running the mail service under Army direction and resigned his commission to take over. The Washington terminal was moved to College Park, in Maryland, and seven biplanes, built specially by the Standard Aircraft Corporation, were placed into service. Each could carry 300 lb of mail and cruise at 90 mph. On 15 July, 1918, the rate was reduced to 16c per ounce plus 6c for each additional ounce, including 10c special delivery charge; then, on 15 December, 1918, the rate was reduced to 6c per ounce, without special delivery, and eventually, on 18 July, 1919, to the standard rate of 2c. But the service did not prosper, mainly because of the inability of the Post Office to demonstrate a convincing case over a distance as short as 220 miles. A summary of operations and expenses is shown in Table 2 on page 583.

The New York—Philadelphia—Washington route served, however, as a training ground for a far more ambitious project, and by the time the service closed down, on 31 May, 1921, for reasons of economy, the trans-continental air mail was well into its stride.

The Transcontinental Air Mail

Bearing in mind that the U.S. Mail service started operations six months before the end of the Great War, it was something of an achievement for the Post Office Department to have obtained money for such outlandish experiments as the New York—Washington venture. Air mail appropriations for both 1918 and 1919 were only $100,000, but by the end of 1919 more than $700,000 had been spent, once the inhibitions of war-time priorities had been relaxed. Late in 1918 the Post Office took over a large number of war-surplus aircraft, including over 100 de Havilland DH-4B biplanes, built under licence from the British company, with the important modifications of fitting Liberty engines and reversing the relative positions of pilot's cockpit and fuel tank. With this substantial addition to its flying equipment, steps were taken to develop a transcontinental mail service.

Mail being loaded into one of the Post Office's large fleet of de Havilland DH-4Bs. The Ford mail van is worthy of study. (*United Air Lines*)

The first segment of the route to be opened was the Chicago—Cleveland leg, on 15 May, 1919. This enabled 16 hr to be saved on the New York—Chicago mails, either by trans-shipping the load off the westbound train early in the morning at Cleveland, or by catching up with the train on its eastbound journey. Less than two months later, on 1 July, 1919, the New York—Cleveland segment was opened, and through mail service from New York to Chicago began on 5 September. Meanwhile, at the far end of the projected route, services were opened from San Francisco to Sacramento, on 31 July.

The following year, the long extensions were made to connect the two extremities, Chicago—Omaha on 15 May, 1920—the Post Office likes to mark its anniversaries in fine style—and, finally, on 8 September, the first transcontinental link was forged, by inaugurating mail service over the difficult Rocky Mountain section of the route, via Cheyenne, Rawlins, and Rock Springs, Wyoming; Salt Lake City, Utah; and Elko and Reno, Nevada. The initial westbound trip averaged 80 mph and was flown without delays from any cause, mechanical, weather, or navigational. The aircraft carried 16,000 letters and saved 22 hours.

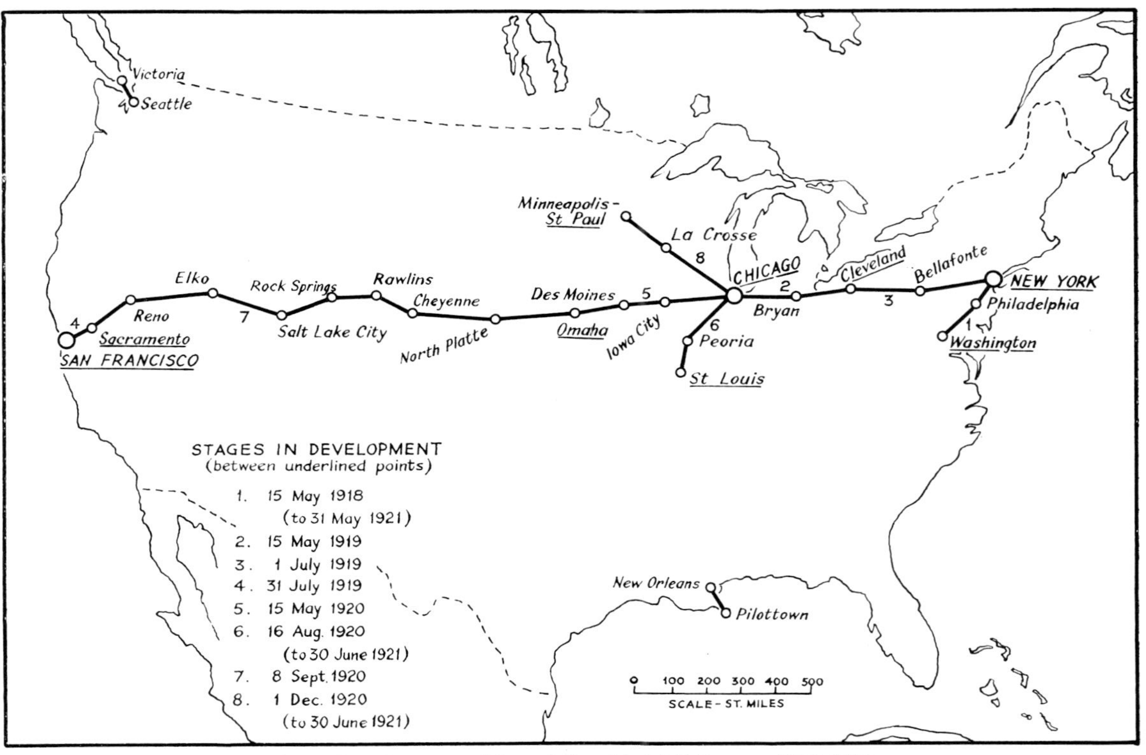

Fig. 3. Development of Post Office Air Mail Routes, 1918–1921.

One of the features, incidentally, of the American railway system was that no single company provided a coast-to-coast route, and transfers, normally at Chicago, involved different stations, companies and lines of responsibility. Thus the aerial mail service gave the Post Office the advantage of continuous surveillance, in addition to the saving of time.

During 1920 two branch routes were also opened, Chicago—St Louis on 16 August, and Chicago—Minneapolis on 1 December; but both were discontinued on 30 June, 1921, soon after, and for the same reasons as the New York—Washington route.

For the first few months of operating the transcontinental route, flights were made only in daylight hours, with aircraft shuttling back and forth over allocated sections of the route, and mail loads being transferred at interchange stations. Acutely conscious that the full time-saving advantage of the mailplane over the train had not yet been demonstrated—and conscious too of criticism and doubt as to whether the effort was worth the expenditure of public funds—the administration decided to risk putting on a show before its term of office expired on 4 March, 1921. Accordingly, on 22 February, an attempt was made to fly the route continuously without interruption for darkness.

Two of the U.S. Post Office's de Havilland DH-4s (before modification to DH-4B) at Omaha, Nebraska, in about 1920. (*United Air Lines*)

Four pilots set off, two from each of the coastal termini. Of the two who left New York, only one reached Chicago, where the weather was so bad that he, too, abandoned the trip. One of the two San Francisco aircraft crashed in Nevada, killing the pilot. The fourth flight made history. Frank Yeager took over the mail at Salt Lake City and flew through the night via Cheyenne to North Platte, handing it to Jack Knight, who took the load on to Omaha, where the aircraft to take over from him should have arrived from Chicago but was weatherbound there instead. Knight therefore flew on, helped by some bonfires to guide him across Iowa, and landed at Chicago early in the morning. Ernest Allison then had the comparatively easy task of delivering the transcontinental mails to New York, after a total elapsed time of 33 hr 20 min.

No. 253 was one of 135 de Havilland DH-4M2s built by Atlantic Aircraft Corporation (Fokker). This version had a gas-welded steel-tube fuselage and 110-gal main fuel tank. The example seen here was used by the Chicago–Omaha Division of the U.S. Post Office mail service. (*United Air Lines*)

This was the breakthrough. One completed flight out of four attempted does not sound like an outstanding success. But consider the circumstances: February was hardly the best time of the year for minimizing the ratio of night/day flying. Lighting was hastily improvised. The daytime route had itself been in operation for less than six months. Aircraft were still unreliable.

But the Post Office was working on the last of these problems. It had issued a specification in April 1919 for a twin-engined aeroplane capable of carrying 1,500 lb of mail at 90 mph. Such was the infancy of the American aircraft industry at the time when the Post Office was desperate that not a single company came up with an acceptable design. The Post Office thereupon tried a design of its own, taking the DH-4 and fitting it with two Hall-Scott engines on the struts between the wings plus additional vertical stabilizers. Then it bought eight all-metal Junkers-F 13s from Germany. These clean-lined monoplanes, able to carry up to five passengers with only a 200 hp engine, showed great promise; but unfortunately a series of accidents, some fatal, cut short this line of interest.

During the fiscal year 1921, several different types were tried, and the Post Office Department paid manufacturers $476,000 for new and modified aircraft. On 1 July, 1921, however, this practice was discontinued and the mail fleet was standardized, the type selected being the de Havilland DH-4B. A large number was obtained from the War and Navy Departments and put through the Post Office's own Air Mail Repair Depot at Chicago. Here, their fuselages were rebuilt, including metal mail containers providing increased mail stowage space; they were equipped with new undercarriages, with larger wheels; and the Liberty engines were improved to give more power and extra reliability.

Safety Standards

Reference has already been made to the casual, almost dare-devil approach to flying during the first post-war years. Faced, however, with the responsibility of flying regularly, rather than when all conditions were suitable or when it suited the pilot's convenience, the Post Office Air Mail pilots began to lose some of their near-suicidal tendencies. The Post Office administration was also unclear as to its comprehension of the dangers involved and on 25 July, 1919, the pilots were in revolt against their employers who were reported to have dismissed two flyers for refusing to take-off in fog.

Thus began the division of opinion between flying crew and airline administration which in varying degrees has lasted to this day. The fundamental problem, that of ultimate responsibility for the decision to fly, was the central issue then, in its most elementary form. When the matter was settled—within two days—the Post Office went a considerable way towards recognizing that a central office in New York or Chicago could hardly judge the weather conditions somewhere en route. But it did not go all the way to conceding the responsibility to the pilot, and delegated the right to the local field manager.

There was still much uncertainty about procedures affecting safety. Neither flying crew nor ground staff was irresponsible; but many lacked a full appreciation of the dangers involved. The fatality rate during 1919,

Jack Knight (*left*) was typical of the early pilots who forged the transcontinental mail route in the early 1920s. When the Post Office Department decided to attempt a day and night coast-to-coast demonstration in 1921, using DH-4s and pilots in relays, Knight took over at 10.44 p.m. at North Platte, Nebraska. His relief at Omaha had not arrived from Chicago so Knight flew on and landed at Chicago at 8.30 a.m. This vital night flight helped establish the practicability of the air mail. Col Paul Henderson (*right*) was Assistant Postmaster General during the development of the transcontinental air mail service. His main achievement was organizing a system of nation-spanning landing grounds and light beacons. He became general manager of National Air Transport and Transcontinental Air Transport, and in 1930 assisted Walter F. Brown in evolving legislation to amend the Air Mail Act of 1925 to provide incentives for passenger air services. (*United Air Lines*)

No. 299 was a specially modified Post Office de Havilland DH-4B with much increased mail capacity in a deepened fuselage. It also had modified-section wings built by the Aeromarine company. In 1922 this aircraft carried a load of 1,032 lb from New York to Washington. (*United Air Lines*)

the first full year of air mail operations, was almost nine deaths per million miles flown, a figure only slightly improved upon in 1920.

Some idea of the general level of aircraft reliability may be deduced from the fact that the average utilization in 1920 was about 75 hr per year, and that operating costs averaged $1.36 per aircraft mile.

When the Woodrow Wilson administration was swept out of office on 4 March, 1921, the Assistant Postmaster General, Otto Praeger, was replaced by Col E. H. O'Shaughnessy, one of whose first acts was to shut down the air mail service for three days, for a complete review and inspection. O'Shaughnessy was killed accidentally (by the collapse of a theatre roof) only a year after taking office, but he achieved much in that short time. In particular he gave the pilots a status which they had not hitherto enjoyed, having been regarded until then as adventurers without integrity. They were given the opportunity to advise on instrumentation and other detailed aircraft improvements arising as a direct result of their experience; and the allocation of pilots to individual aircraft gave a long-desired sense of pride in their equixment.

In 1921 the fatality rate was more than halved, and in 1922 was reduced to 0·57 deaths per million miles flown, a record which was not to be materially improved upon for ten years.

Col O'Shaughnessy was succeeded by Col Paul Henderson. Satisfied with his predecessor's achievements in improving air safety, Henderson set about the task of developing the technique of night flying.

The Lighted Airway

In the summer of 1922 the Post Office took over the night-flying system which had been developed by the Army during the previous year between Dayton and Columbus, Ohio, a distance of 80 miles, over easy terrain.

The Army method was to direct an intense and concentrated searchlight beam just above the horizon, and, in contrast with sporadic schemes tried in Europe at the time, to rotate it so that the pilot would see it at 10-sec intervals. Henderson's plan was to install beacons at every landing ground, regular or emergency, and to supplement these with other smaller beacons every three or four miles.

At the regular fields, a 36-inch, 500,000 candle-power revolving beacon was mounted on a 50-ft tower. It revolved three times per minute and could be seen well over 100 miles away on a clear night. At the emergency fields, an 18-inch beacon of 50,000 candle-power revolved six times a minute, and was visible for about 60 miles. Additionally, 36-inch beacons were located at the regular fields to floodlight the landing area to simulate daylight conditions as nearly as possible; white boundary lights and red obstacle lights were further refinements.

Where local electric current was not available, cell batteries were supplied for boundary lighting and small generators were installed at the foot of the lighting towers, each in charge of a caretaker.

At the small beacons every three miles along the airway, light was derived from acetylene gas. These flashed once per second, day and night, the cylinders of gas needing replenishment every six months.

During the first twelve months' work on the lighted airway, on the section between Chicago and Cheyenne, 289 flashing gas beacons were built; five terminal and 34 emergency landing fields were equipped with beacons, floodlights, and boundary markers; and 17 aircraft were specially equipped with luminous instruments, navigation lights, landing lights, and parachute flares. The basic principles of the latter installations have not changed to this day.

On completion of the programme on the key Chicago—Cheyenne section, in the summer of 1923, a regular transcontinental schedule involving night flying was tested for four days from 21 August. The best time was 26 hr 14 min eastbound and 29 hr 38 min westbound. Although funds ran out at the critical time, the four-day experiment was so successful that plans were put in hand immediately for regular, sustained night flying. On 1 July, 1924, an air mail postage rate was again established, on the basis of 8c per ounce for each of three defined sections of the route, or zones, Chicago—Cheyenne being the middle zone.

Regular night mail services began on 1 July, 1924, settling down to a definite schedule of 29 hr 15 min eastbound and 34 hr 20 min westbound. The Transcontinental Air Mail saved between two and three days over the trains. Pilots were changed six times en route, at Cleveland, Chicago, Omaha, Cheyenne, Salt Lake City, and Reno.

In 1924 the lighted airway was extended westwards to Rock Springs and eastwards to Cleveland. On 1 July, 1925, a New York—Chicago night service began, on a schedule of 8 hr 30 min eastbound and 9 hr 15 min westbound, thus saving a complete working day between the two biggest business centres in the United States.

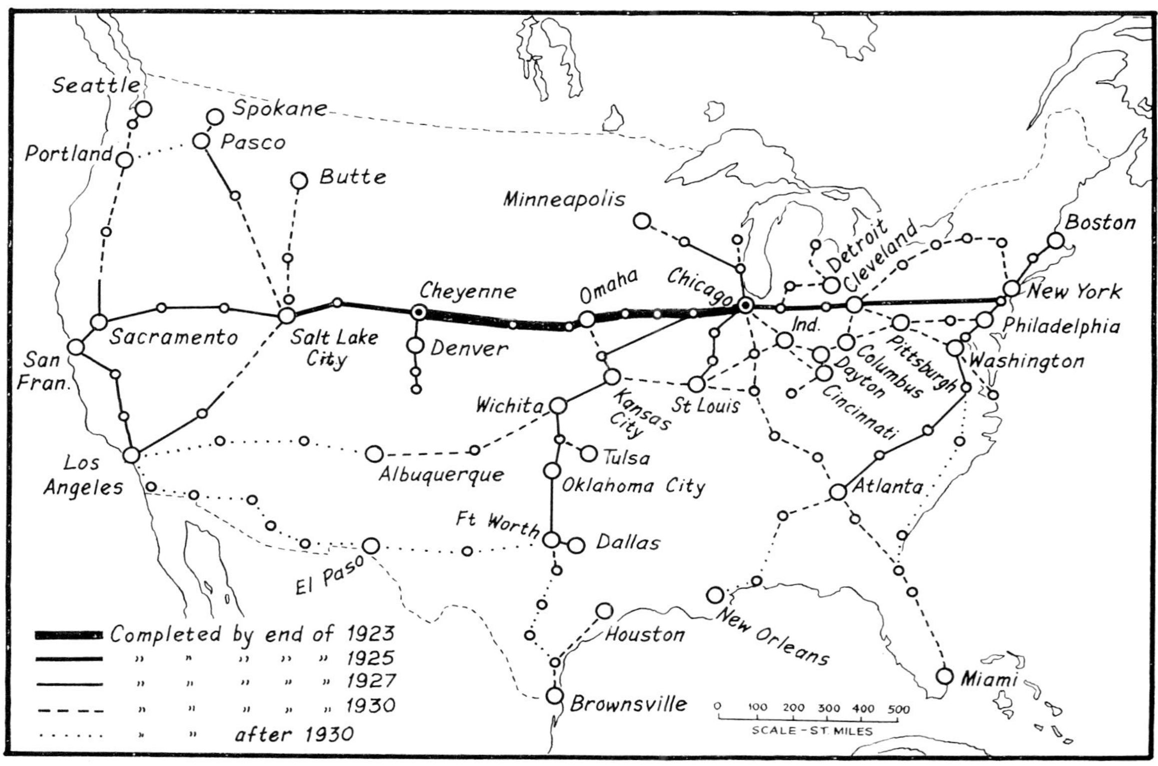

Fig. 4. Development of the Lighted Airways, from 1923.

Finally, by the end of 1925, the lighted airway system was completed to San Francisco, a distance of some 2,400 miles, at a cost of about $550,000. Dr Edward P. Warner described this achievement as the greatest of all American contributions to the technique of air transport operation. Considering the significant saving in journey time made possible by night flying this is probably no exaggeration, even measured against sophisticated developments introduced in recent years.

Equipment Improvements

In addition to the lighted airway, substantial improvements were made in other directions. As already mentioned, the fleet of Post Office aircraft was standardized in 1921 to 80 modified DH-4s, replacing a motley collection of seven Curtiss JN-4Hs, seven Standard JR-1Bs, 17 Curtiss R-4Ls, 40 DH-4s, 20 'Twin DH's, two Curtiss H-As, three Glenn Martin mailplanes, four Junkers JL 6s (F 13s) and one L.W.F. Type V.

By the end of 1925, however, the Post Office began to look for a mailplane capable of carrying greater loads than the DH-4—the business was showing signs of continued healthy increases. The Douglas company won the competition for a new aircraft, the Douglas M-4, forty of which were ordered at $14,0C0 each, deliveries starting in May 1926. The Post Office also acquired one M-1 and ten M-3s. In addition to carrying twice the load of the DH-4, the Douglas M-4 flew much faster—especially with a good tail wind. One trip from Chicago to New York was flown at an average speed of 167 mph, and the record was held by a Chicago—Cleveland flight, averaging 175 mph, on 30 January, 1927.

The Douglas mailplane also had longer range capability than the DH, making possible the elimination of several scheduled stops where the sole

The single example of the Douglas M-1, with wingtip-mounted landing light and U.S. Mail markings. Ten of the developed M-3 and 40 of the M-4 versions were operated by the Post Office. (*Post Office Department*)

purpose had been for refuelling. Douglas aircraft operated the heavy traffic route from Chicago to New York, and construction work on DH aircraft at the Post Office Repair Depot at Chicago was discontinued. Surplus de Havillands were scrapped or sold.

This Repair Depot, at Maywood, Chicago, was representative of the standard of aerodromes in use by the Post Office Air Mail. It had two runways, in L shape, one 2,500 ft, one 2,200 ft, and both 250 ft wide. These were 'centred one foot thick and rolled into clay with a ten-ton roller. The surrounding surfaces have been graded and levelled and the edges of the cinder runways feathered off. The entire field has been tile drained.' The hangars were 100 ft square, and the repair shop itself measured 100 ft by 300 ft.

A rare flying view of a Post Office DH-4. (*American Airlines*)

At the time of the introduction of the Douglas mailplanes, the Maywood Depot was coping with a fleet of 96 DH-4s, keeping 83 in flying condition, with 61 equipped for night flying. Aircraft entered the shops after 750 hr, or about 75,000 miles flying, for a complete overhaul, costing $3,000. Engines were removed after 100 hr service.

In 1926, the Post Office Air Mail appropriation was at its peak, $2,885,000. Of this, $1,180,000 went on wages and salaries, $200,000 on pilots' mileage pay, almost $300,000 on buildings and fields, $230,000 on fuel and oil, and $880,000 on miscellaneous supplies and services. For this expenditure, two and a quarter million miles were flown, at a regularity of 94 per cent, and 14 million air mail letters carried. 1926 was not atypical of the Post Office Air Mail in its finally developed form. Full statistics are shown in Table 3 on page 584.

The price in achieving this commendable record, in terms of human lives, was high. During the life span of the service, no less than 43 men were killed, of whom 34 were pilots. They had learned their trade the hard way, starting from the primitive technique of 'following Chesapeake Bay'. There was one individual whose idea of flying by dead reckoning was to look for his destination landing ground when he had smoked two cigars down to the butts. Pilots would descend murkily through dense fog, break out at 100 ft, to find themselves flying a parallel course between two murderous outcrops of the Alleghenies. One taxied his aircraft for 50 miles across the prairies, rather than take-off in the fog, while another delivered his mail load on a string of burros (small donkeys).

Perhaps the flying methods and attitudes are best illustrated by the following quotation from Ken McGregor's article, *Beam Dream*: 'Map reading was not required. There were no maps. I got from place to place with the help of three things. One was the seat of my pants. If it left that of the plane, when the visibility was at a minimum, I was in trouble and could even be upside down. Another was the ability to recognize every town, river, railroad, farm and, yes, outhouse along the route. The third? I had a few drops of homing pigeon in my veins.'

The End of the Air Mail

The Post Office had never intended to acquire an air mail service on a permanent basis. Had the original experiments of 1918 and 1919 failed—and they came perilously close to losing favour with those in control—the air mail, and with it the development of civil aviation as a whole in the U.S.A., would have been delayed for several years. If they succeeded, the intention was to hand them over to contract operators, partly because the air arm of the Post Office could easily become uncomfortably large, partly because there were substantial political undertones involved in a government department's taking on too much responsibility in a country passionately devoted to the creed of free enterprise.

As outlined in more detail in the next chapter, the Air Mail Act of 1925 and the Air Commerce Act of 1926 gave notice that the end of the Post Office Air Mail was near. On 15 November, 1926, bids were invited from private individuals to take over the transcontinental route, in two sections: San Francisco—Chicago and Chicago—New York. At the expiry date of 15 January, 1927, no satisfactory bid had been received for the latter route, but the longer section west of Chicago was awarded to William Boeing and Edward Hubbard on 29 January.

After new bidding, the important Chicago—New York section went to the newly-formed National Air Transport (NAT) on 8 March, 1927. By a prodigious manufacturing effort, Boeing started services on 1 July, and NAT on 1 September. New rates were set for the contract services: 10c per ounce up to 1,000 miles, 15c up to 1,500, and 20c over 1,500 miles. The last bag of mail flown by the United States Post Office in its own aircraft was carried from New York to Chicago on 31 August, 1927, by which time all Government air mail rates were at 10c per half ounce, regardless of distance.

On 1 July, on the same date that Boeing took over the Chicago—San Francisco route, the Post Office handed over to the Department of Commerce its most valuable asset, the Lighted Airway. The inventory, including the radio service, incorporated 17 fully-equipped stations, and 89 emer-

One of National Air Transport's Pitcairn PA-5 Mailwings. (*United Air Lines*)

gency landing grounds, of which 21 were automatically operated; 100 electric beacon lights in between emergency fields, of which 79 were automatically operated; and 405 gas rotating beacons. Arrangements were made to hand over aerodromes to municipal authorities, or to the Government in the case of Omaha and San Francisco where the aerodromes were on War Department property. By the end of the year, all the assets of the Post Office Air Mail were disposed of, with the exception of some stocks of equipment at Chicago.

During the 9½ years of its existence, the Post Office flew almost 15 million miles, completed 93 per cent of the trips scheduled and carried more than 300 million letters. As mentioned above, the cost was high, in more ways than one. $17 million were spent in Air Mail appropriations. There were 200 aeroplane crashes, and 43 people were killed and 37 seriously injured.

The return on this investment of money and lives was immeasurable. The accumulated experience in flying techniques, especially at night, and the ground organization of aerodromes and lighted airways, gave the first private operators a priceless asset. The aggregate effect was to give the United States a flying start in the field of commercial aviation, enabling it to overhaul Europe, in spite of the latter's eight-year head start, within two years of spectacular growth.

CHAPTER THREE

The First Regular Airlines

Foundations for an Industry

Although this is a book about U.S. airlines, an account must be given of the establishment of the regulatory framework against which an infant industry was nurtured. In the excitement of the tumultuous events in civil aviation progress which followed the passing of the Air Commerce Act of 1926, much of the preparatory work which led up to that important piece of legislation was forgotten. Yet the processes of law-making, dull and unromantic though they may have been when compared with the dashing exploits of Jack Knight and his colleagues, were just as fascinating in a different sense. For while the Post Office Mail Service was building up a record of achievement during the early 1920s, it was doing so in a legislative vacuum. As late as June 1925, a special report commissioned by Herbert Hoover, the Secretary of Commerce, had to record that 'all countries actively interested in civil aviation, except the United States, have laws regulating the use of aircraft and requiring the licensing of pilots'.

That the country which witnessed man's first powered flight should have lagged behind to such an extent was a paradox indeed.

The first attempt at Federal legislation of air traffic was made by Chief Justice S. E. Baldwin, of Connecticut, in 1911. His attempt to secure Congressional support for a simple matter of pilot and aircraft licensing failed; but as Governor of Connecticut he did manage to obtain the passage of the first State aeronautics law.

The National Advisory Committee for Aeronautics (NACA) was established on 3 March, 1913, as a rider to the Naval Appropriations Act. Its purpose was to 'direct the scientific study of the problems of flight, with a view to their practical solution'. Apart from this body (which quickly became recognized as an independent agency) the ensuing years were marked by public and official apathy to aviation as a business; while United States participation in war in 1917 steered aircraft development along fixed courses with limited objectives.

In 1919 President Wilson submitted to Congress a bill drafted by NACA that would have authorized the Department of Commerce to license pilots, inspect aircraft, and operate aerodromes; but no legislation emerged.

The idea was revived, however, under President Harding's administration in 1921, with NACA recommending a 'Department of Commerce' solution. At the same time, Congressman Julius Kahn proposed a bill on similar lines. When these attempts failed, the Secretary of Commerce, Hoover, took up the running, and set about building up a tide of opinion in favour of this kind of solution, seeking support from all associations connected with the aviation business, which appeared to be the only private enterprise actually soliciting government control.

During the same year, Senator James W. Wadsworth, Jr, of New York, introduced a 'Department of Commerce' bill, an effort which was to meet with partial success three years later.

In 1922, a joint conference was held in Washington by the committee of the Conference of Commissioners on Uniform State Laws and the committee of the American Bar Association. This was attended by representatives of the Government, aircraft manufacturers, and other interested parties, and agreement was reached on the main principle that Federal legislation was necessary. Meanwhile, the States passed the Uniform Aeronautics Act which, however, did not cover regulation, only matters of sovereignty and ownership, liability, and jurisdiction of torts and crimes. These States laws were actually far from uniform, although many provided for suspension whenever a Federal law was enacted. When the Air Commerce Act was passed, there were 26 different State laws governing flying.

The real issues were clouded during the immediate post-war period by the much-publicized crusade by Brig-Gen William L. 'Billy' Mitchell, of the U.S. Army Air Service. In 1919 he had promoted vigorously his theme of 'air power', and the creation of an all-powerful, all-embracing organization, controlling absolutely everything connected with aircraft and aviation, became for him an obsession. To demonstrate his case, he won a moral victory over the conservatively-minded Navy with the dramatic sinking of the derelict German warships in 1921, and Billy Mitchell's bombers became the darlings of the press. This led to his being sent by his superiors on a succession of overseas inspection tours until 1924, when he returned to resume his campaign against the Establishment.

He addressed the National Aeronautic Association in Dayton, Ohio, on the subject of a separate air force, and elaborated the theme in a series of articles in the popular *Saturday Evening Post* between 20 December, 1924, and 14 March, 1925. This coincided (or was it coincidence?) with an investigation by a Congressional Committee, headed by Representative Florian Lampert, a LaFollette Republican, of the operations of U.S. air services during 43 days of public hearings, ending on 2 March, 1925.

By this time, however, the bureaucratic wheels were beginning to turn. On 8 January, 1924, the U.S. Senate had actually passed a modified Wadsworth Bill for the creation of a Bureau of Civil Aeronautics. In the next session the Senate again passed the Bill but the House of Representatives supported a substitute Act, known as the Winslow Bill. Although the measure was reported too late for action, many of its provisions were incorporated in the Air Commerce Act of 1926.

The Kelly Act

The Contract Air Mail Act, passed on 2 February, 1925, was the first major legislative step towards the creation of an airline industry in the United States. Curiously, the main impetus came from the railways, which sought to curb the efforts made by the Post Office to carry its own mail. Their spokesman in Congress was Representative Clyde Kelly of Pennsylvania, whose advocacy for the cause led to the Act being named after him.

The bill provided for the transfer of air mail service from the Post Office to private operators, under a scheme of competitive bidding, for a period of four years. The first five contracts, for branch lines serving as feeders to the main Post Office transcontinental route, were let on 7 October, 1925, and, together with subsequent contracts, these are described more fully later in this chapter.

Hoover's Committee

Calvin Coolidge had been elected Vice-President under Harding in 1921; had assumed the Presidency when Harding died on 3 August, 1923; and was elected President of the 69th Congress, taking office on 4 March, 1925. A regular member of the Republican cabinet throughout this period was Herbert Hoover, Secretary of Commerce. Devoted to the cause of furthering civil aeronautics, Hoover appointed, in June 1925, a Joint Committee of Civil Aviation of the U.S. Department of Commerce and the American Engineering Council.

Chairman of the Committee was J. Walter Drake, Assistant Secretary of Commerce, and the list of committee members included such names as J. Parker van Zandt, Secretary of the U.S. Air Service; W. F. Durand, President of the American Society of Mechanical Engineers; Edward P. Warner, of the Massachusetts Institute of Technology; and C. T. Ludington, described in the report subsequently issued as 'aircraft operator'.

The American Engineering Council had already initiated some work in October 1924 and readily complied with Hoover's suggestion that they should join with the Department of Commerce. The result was a comprehensive survey of all aspects of commercial operations, covering problems of safety, traffic, regulation, legislation, equipment, personnel, insurance, and investment. In particular, it reviewed the progress made in other countries and contrasted this with the inertia in the U.S.A.

Whilst Hoover's Committee set about its work, the voice of Billy Mitchell was heard again. Following the loss of a naval flying-boat on 31 August and the tragic destruction of the airship *Shenandoah* on 3 September, Mitchell delivered a literary broadside to the press on 5 September which was even more wildly critical than before of the Army, the Navy, indeed the whole administration.

Not noted for any tendency to go out to meet trouble halfway, Calvin Coolidge was at last spurred to take effective action, briefed no doubt by the efficient Hoover.

The Morrow Board

Following the disciplining of Billy Mitchell in March 1925, Coolidge had alerted his financier friend Dwight Morrow that he might be asked to look into the question of aviation. Accordingly, on 13 September, Morrow read in his Sunday newspaper that he and eight others had been appointed members of an aircraft board. Next day he received from Coolidge a letter which began 'enclosed is a copy of a communication which you may have seen in the press . . .'

The Morrow Board was drawn from the Army, Navy, and bodies connected with aviation, plus politicians. Howard E. Coffin, president of the Hudson Motor Co and former President of the National Aeronautic Association, represented industry. Senator Hiram Bingham, of Connecticut, brought a wealth of flying and aviation experience. Representative James S. Parker, of New York, provided experience in transport legislative problems. Representative Carl M. Vinson, of Georgia, provided the Democrat view, whilst Dr William F. Durand, President of the American Society of Mechanical Engineers and member of NACA, unravelled technological problems. Durand was also on Hoover's Committee.

The Board heard testimony from 99 people between 21 September and 16 October; it consulted the lengthy Lampert Committee hearings, data from previous investigations, and the results of Hoover's Committee. Amongst those giving evidence was Billy Mitchell, who unfortunately failed to appreciate that this was a fact-finding body of men, and not a Congressional committee with its attendant opportunities for drama. Mitchell, in fact, failed to make his case.

The Morrow Board carried presidential weight. It was charged to recommend a national policy, in the full knowledge that this was likely to be accepted by the President and would be pressed upon Congress. The report was submitted to Coolidge on 30 November, and he worked the salient points into his Annual Message on 8 December. The report of the Lampert Committee, expected to take the initiative once again in support of an all-powerful Department of Air, was scooped by a week.

The report of the Morrow Board, fully supported by Coolidge and Hoover, rejected this solution but recommended that there should be separate civil and military national control. This was to take the form, on the civil side, of a Bureau of Aeronautics within the Department of Commerce.

The Air Commerce Act

The end of the road was in sight for the protagonists of 'air power'. Billy Mitchell's court martial sentenced him to five years' suspension and

Mitchell resigned. Representative Charles F. Curry, of California, who had been promoting various bills since 1919, and John M. Morin, of Pennsylvania, put in a last-ditch stand in Washington. Morin pleaded an excellent case and did not fall into the trap of proposing impracticable solutions. A man of few words, he met his match, however, in Coolidge, who, after being assured with conviction that the Morin Bill would get by every obstacle, is reported to have said, 'Well, it won't get by me. Good morning. I'm glad you called.'

Put into shape by Senator Hiram Bingham, of Connecticut, and Representatives Schuyler Merritt, also of Connecticut, and James S. Parker, of New York (Bingham and Parker had been members of the Morrow Board), the Air Commerce Act was signed by President Coolidge on 20 May, 1926. Following the Kelly Act of 1925 this was the next big step towards airline development in the U.S.A.

The Act instructed the Secretary of Commerce to designate and establish airways, to organize air navigation, arrange for research and development of such aids, license pilots and aircraft, and to investigate accidents.

On 3 June, an amendment to the Kelly Act of 2 February, 1925, reinforced the Bingham-Merritt-Parker Act in a practical fashion. The cumbersome method of paying the contractual carrier according to a percentage of the actual postage paid was replaced by a system of paying by weight. This turned out to be highly advantageous for the operators, who collected some $48 million between 1926 and 1931.

On 11 August, William P. McCracken, Jr, took office as the first Assistant Secretary of Commerce for Aeronautics. The first Air Commerce regulations came into force at midnight on 31 December, 1926.

Resumption of Airline Activity

In this chapter the narrative has recounted the legislative history through to the 1926 Air Commerce Act. Civil airline activity, however, had already gained some momentum by the time the Act was in force. As far as the early airlines were concerned, the Kelly Act was in fact of far greater significance, for it provided the source of the bread and butter. Certain companies did not even wait for the benefits of mail contracts and deserve special mention.

Curiously, the year 1924 had been a dead one for the airlines. Aeromarine had ceased operations. Only the ferry to Catalina Island was carrying regular passengers, and the Puget Sound and Mississippi Delta foreign mail contract companies still kept going. Indeed, the only event worth reporting in 1924 was the pioneering experimental mail service in Alaska, where a Fairbanks schoolteacher, Carl Ben Eielson, made a single round trip flight with mail from Fairbanks to McGrath on 21 February. Eielson had persuaded the Post Office Department to provide a DH-4 to demonstrate that there were means of transport available other than dog teams.

Jumping the Gun

The Kelly Air Mail Act was passed on 2 February, 1925, but the first five contracts were not awarded until 7 October of that year, with the result that no airline was carrying official mail until 1926. In 1925, however, two companies went ahead without the sponsorship of the Postmaster General.

On the West Coast, at San Diego, T. Claude Ryan was one of the many airminded engineers who had started a small aircraft factory. His stock-in-trade was converting second-hand aircraft with modifications of his own. The products were used for joy-rides and sightseeing trips typical of the period.

One of the much modified Standard biplanes used by Ryan Airlines on the Los Angeles—San Diego route when the service was opened in March 1925. Los Angeles-San Diego Air Line appears in capital letters on the side of the fuselage. (*Ryan*)

In 1924 Ryan acquired six war-surplus Standard biplanes, converting them from two-seat open cockpit trainers to five-seat cabin transports and fitting them with new 150 hp Hispano Suiza engines. Ryan Airlines opened a scheduled service between San Diego and Los Angeles on 1 March, 1925. This was the first regular passenger airline service to be operated wholly over the mainland of the United States, throughout the year. (Although Pacific Marine Airways had been operating from Wilmington to Catalina Island since 1922, there is considerable doubt whether this service ran except on demand for some periods during the year.)

The Los Angeles-San Diego Air Line, as Ryan's service was called, charged $17.50 single, $26.50 round trip for the $1\frac{1}{2}$-hr journey in the Standards. Cost of ground transport to the aerodrome was included, and Ryan reckoned to break even if he boarded one passenger per trip. The operation was so successful in its first year that he looked around for a larger aircraft to cope with the traffic, acquired the open cockpit Douglas Cloudster, which was Donald Douglas' first aeroplane, and converted it to carry eleven passengers in a closed cabin. During 1926, 5,600 people took the 120-mile flight but Ryan ceased operations in 1927, allowing the route to be taken over by other operators, while he concentrated on building aeroplanes—to good effect.

The second man to get under way with an airline venture without waiting

An early Ryan Airlines advertisement. It shows a different version of the Ryan-Standard biplane. (*Ryan*)

Ryan Airlines' Douglas Cloudster after it had been converted by Ryan to an eleven-seat cabin aircraft. (*Ryan*)

for the Kelly Act was Henry Ford, who was persuaded to take an interest in aviation by Harry Brooks, the son of one of his friends, aided and abetted by William B. Mayo, the Ford Motor Company's chief engineer, and Ford's son, Edsel. At the same time, William B. Stout, an aircraft engineer and designer, previously chief engineer of the aircraft division of the Packard Motor Co, was trying to find a backer to help him build an all-metal aircraft of his own design (though drawing heavily, let it be said, from European models, notably Junkers).

The interior of the Ryan Airlines Douglas Cloudster, showing main and forward four-seat cabin with a glimpse of the open cockpit. A very early example of an airline magazine rack is seen on the port bulkhead. (*Ryan*)

Stout found his backer in Henry Ford, who promptly put ideas into practice by starting a private daily express service between Detroit and Chicago, a distance of 260 miles, on 3 April, 1925. The Stout Metal Airplane Company was invited to move to a site at Dearborn, where $2,000,000 was invested in a new, modern airport, with two concrete runways, 2,600 ft and 2,800 ft in length, hangars, airship mooring mast, aircraft factory and the first airport hotel in the United States. On 31 July, the Ford Motor Company opened a second route, from Detroit to Cleveland, and on the same day purchased the stock and assets of the Stout company.

Maiden Dearborn IV, one of the corrugated Ford 2-ATs used by Ford Motor Company and Stout Air Services in the early days of the Contract Air Mail services.

Ford operated a number of single-engined Ford 2 ATs, the first all-metal civil aircraft in the United States. The company was among the successful bidders for two of the earliest contract mail routes for which bids were invited under the terms of the Kelly Act; and because it was already in operation, it was first off the mark, beginning official mail services on 15 February, 1926, having postponed the inaugural flight because of a $500,000 fire at the Dearborn plant.

The First Contract Mail Carriers

If 1924 had been a dead year for airline activity, and 1925 marked only by Ryan and Ford, 1926 was in pleasing contrast, witnessing as it did a flood of new companies, spurred into activity by the prospects of making profits out of mail contracts, as outlined in the Kelly Act. The first five contracts (CAM 1–5) were opened on 15 September and let on 7 October, 1925; others followed at intervals thereafter. Twelve companies began service between February 1926 and April 1927, and all except one were in full-scale operation before the end of 1926*. All were organized to provide feeder services to the main transcontinental route—still operated by the Post Office Department. With minor exceptions, all concentrated almost exclusively on flying the mails with aircraft designed for, or at least suitably converted for, the carriage of mail. Two of the twelve discontinued operations after a short period; the rest can trace their descendants to the major trunk airlines of today.

*See Table 4, page 585.

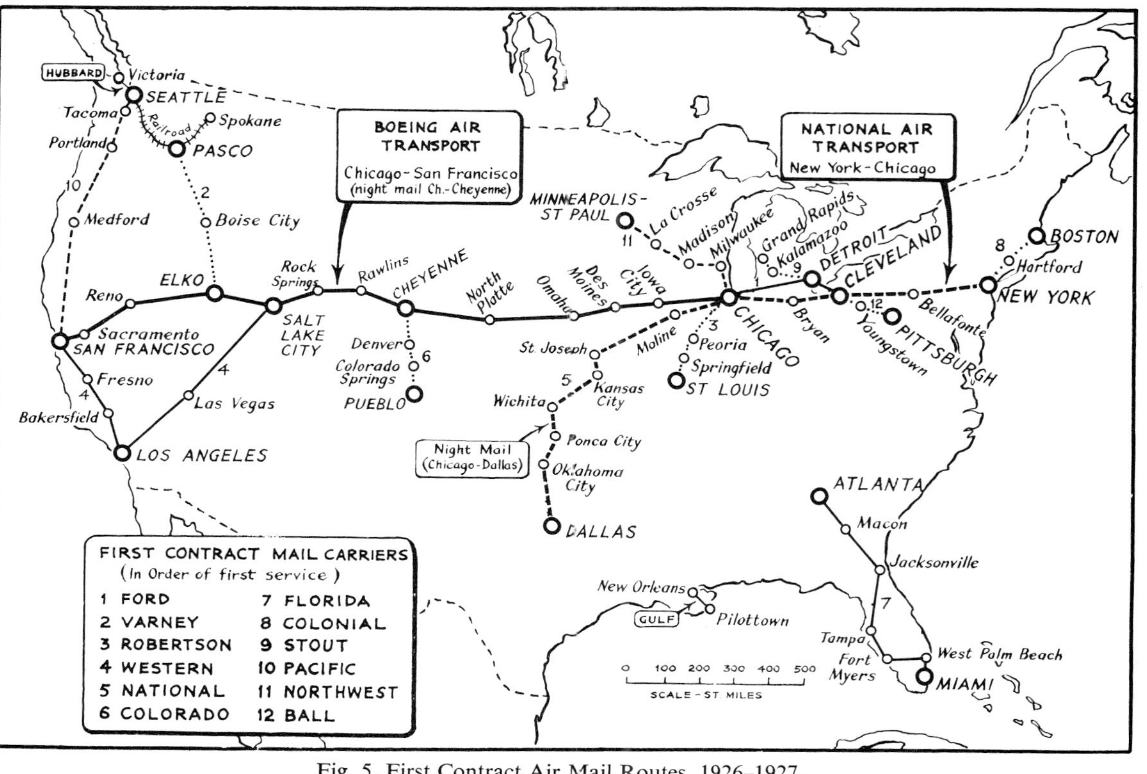

Fig. 5. First Contract Air Mail Routes, 1926–1927.

The twelve airlines are listed in Table 5, on page 586, which includes details of the route flown and the aircraft operated, and the part they played in extending the Post Office mail service to most of the major cities of the United States is illustrated in the map opposite.

There have been many arguments as to which airline can fairly lay claim to being first. In the table, no account is taken of the foundation date of the companies involved, for definitions become obscure and misleading. National Air Transport (NAT) was the first company founded specifically to operate as an airline, on 21 May, 1925 (closely followed by Western Air Express (WAE), on 13 July). But Colonial Air Transport could dispute this, pointing to a 1923 incorporation date. Robertson Aircraft Corporation traces its origin back to 1921—though not as an airline. And if this broader qualification is to be the criterion, then the Ford Motor Company was founded long before that; in which case, justice is done, for Ford was certainly the first to open service with official United States domestic air mail, carried under contract from the Post Office Department.

Almost every one of the twelve airlines possessed some special characteristic which distinguished it from its fellows. As they were to play such an important part in the subsequent history of airlines in the United States, their first steps are outlined below.

Western Enterprise

The wide, wild West beyond Denver appeared to hold out great promise for the development of air routes because of the distances involved, where the aeroplane could make good time over the surface competition. True to

Harris M. 'Pop' Hanshue (*left*) built up Western Air Express in the late 1920s to become a powerful influence during the pioneering years. Bitterly disappointed when the Postmaster General forced a merger with TAT to form TWA, Hanshue did not live to see the revival of WAE, which became Western Airlines. Vern C. Gorst (*right*) was an adventurous bus operator from Oregon who formed Pacific Air Transport in 1926, convinced of the practicability of air transport from Canada to Mexico. He sold his airline to William Boeing in 1928 and immediately formed another to start an air mail service to Alaska. After several unsuccessful ventures, Gorst returned to Oregon, where he died in 1953.

the tradition of the West, the men who pioneered the first mail lines were colourful characters, the kind who were prepared to take risks, and use unorthodox methods to promote their ideas if necessary.

Walter T. Varney was one of these. An ex-war pilot, he had dabbled in various aviation activities in the San Francisco area, including an air ferry service across the Bay. When the Post Office advertised for bids in 1925, Varney staked a claim for the route which he calculated no-one else would want: Elko, Nevada, to Pasco, Washington, via Boise, Idaho. He guessed rightly, but the venture was not so odd as it looked from the obscure place names. In fact, it linked the transcontinental mail route with the Northwest, via Pasco, a station on the Northern Pacific Railroad.

Varney Air Lines' inauguration on 6 April, 1926. In front of the Curtiss-powered Swallow biplane are *left to right*: Joe Taff and Franklin Rose, Varney pilots; Harold Bruntsch, friend of the Varney family; Mrs Walter Varney; Walter T. Varney; Thomas H. B. Varney; Leon Cuddeback, Varney's chief pilot; the Varney chauffeur; and an unidentified Post Office official. (*United Air Lines*)

Varney's bid of 8c per ounce was the only one, and the Post Office paid the standard rate, i.e. 80 per cent of the air mail postal revenues. On 6 April, 1926, Leon Cuddeback, the chief pilot, who had learned to fly at the Varney flying school, took-off from Pasco in a single-engined, (150 hp Curtiss K6) Swallow biplane, one of six purchased by Varney with the help of his father. Apparently, Cuddeback only just made it, for after returning from Elko on 8 April, the service was suspended until 6 June, pending delivery of more powerful engines, Wright J-4s, for the Swallows, and was actually resumed with the help of Vern Gorst, founder of Pacific Air Transport (PAT), who lent Varney three Ryan mailplanes.

The pilots earned $250 per month, with additional bonuses. When the Kelly Act was amended on 3 June, 1926, the ponderous system of counting

One of Varney Air Lines' New Swallow biplanes, in June 1926, after being fitted with a Wright J-4 Whirlwind air-cooled engine. The name Franklin Rose appears beneath the cockpit. (*United Air Lines*).

letters was replaced by a straight $3 per pound, which in practice was only slightly less than the original rate. Varney did well out of the Christmas mails, having designed a greetings card which weighed an ounce and persuaded the citizens of Boise and Pasco to buy them by the thousand.

Another resourceful figure was Harris M. 'Pop' Hanshue, a former racing driver and car dealer, who was appointed president of Western Air Express (WAE). This company was incorporated on 13 July, 1925, by Harry Chandler, of the Los Angeles *Times*, and James A. Talbot, of Richfield Oil, two of many Los Angeles citizens who had taken slight umbrage at the choice of San Francisco as the terminus of the transcontinental mail line. Awarded one of the first mail contracts, CAM 4, Western Air Express began service on 17 April, 1926, from Vail Field, Los Angeles, to Salt Lake City, via Las Vegas, with a fleet of six Douglas M-2 mailplanes. There were 20 employees. The same company, albeit under different names, has operated the route ever since, the longest continuous record in the United States.

On 23 May, 1926, Western Air Express began the first passenger service,

The entire Varney Air Lines fleet of six New Swallow biplanes lined-up at Boise, Idaho, in 1926. (*United Air Lines*)

Western Air Express' first four pilots and vice-president operations in front of a Douglas M-2 in 1926. *Left to right*: Fred W. Kelly, C. A. 'Jimmy' James, Alva R. DeGarmo, Maury Graham (pilots); and Major C. C. Moseley. (*Western Airlines*)

Harris M. 'Pop' Hanshue, first president of Western Air Express, hands over the first mail to Fred Kelly in a Douglas M-2 on 17 April, 1926, at Vail Field, Los Angeles. (*Western Airlines*)

A Douglas M-2 of Western Air Express over Vail Field, Los Angeles, in 1926.

charging $60 for the single flight from the Coast to Salt Lake, and 209 passengers were carried during 1926. This was an additional bonus over and above the mail payments which were earning $1,500 on a single flight which cost Western only $360 to fly.

Business was so good that Hanshue did not fight too hard in bidding for the route from Los Angeles to Seattle, CAM 8, which demanded expert flying, because of the need to traverse the Siskiyou Mountains on the California—Oregon border. This left the door open for Pacific Air Transport, organized on 8 January, 1926, by Vern C. Gorst, of North Bend, Oregon, and a successful bus operator in that area.

When Gorst heard about the Post Office mail contract which would compete with his buses, he decided to get into the business himself, and persuaded many of his fellow bus operators to sponsor a survey flight in a Ryan M-1, flown by Ryan himself, along the coast from San Francisco to Vancouver and back. He was awarded the contract on 27 January, 1926,

This red and silver Douglas M-4 of Western Air Express has been preserved. It is seen after reconditioning to represent an M-2.

This photograph is believed to have been taken at the inauguration of Pacific Air Transport's Los Angeles—Seattle service on 15 September, 1926. The pilot is Claude Ryan, and Vern C. Gorst, PAT's founder, is in the centre. The aircraft is a Ryan M-1. (*Ryan*)

A Pacific Air Transport Ryan M-1. This example, with wingtip-mounted landing light, appears to be an earlier version than the others illustrated. (*United Air Lines*)

A Pacific Air Transport Ryan M-1 at Angelus Mesa Field, Los Angeles, in 1926. (*Ryan*)

Pacific Air Transport's Fokker Universal C2696 at Seattle. (*United Air Lines*)

and immediately set about promoting his airline. Gorst was good at this. He raised $175,000, mostly from businessmen in the Northwest, partly by selling his own company stock. He hired pilots who had the joint qualifications of an ability to fly and a willingness to accept part of their wages in company stock. Some even brought along their own aircraft.

One reason why almost eight months passed before Pacific Air Transport started service was because careful preparations had to be made before venturing over the rugged territory between San Francisco and Seattle. PAT undertook a series of survey flights, installing makeshift lights and beacons and persuading the Standard Oil Company to paint the names of the towns on the roofs of its buildings. Gorst bought several miscellaneous aircraft and then standardized on the Ryan M-1 monoplane, ordering ten from Claude Ryan after the latter had demonstrated its reliability.

PAT launched its service from Los Angeles to Seattle on 15 September, 1926. Before the end of the winter, three pilots had crashed. Yet some hardy travellers were still willing to pay $132 for the doubtful privilege of being crammed in among the mail sacks for the 18½-hr flight. Unlike Western Air Express, however, Gorst did not make comfortable profits, as the

A Hispano-powered Ryan M-1 of Colorado Airways. This aircraft was used on the Cheyenne—Denver—Pueblo mail service. (*Ryan*)

mail loads were not so bulky. Seeking financial assistance from the Wells Fargo Bank, he met William A. Patterson, a man who was later to play a vital rôle in deciding the fortunes of Pacific.

Another pioneer of air mail services in difficult terrain was Anthony F. Joseph, who bid successfully for a branch line from the transcontinental route at Cheyenne, to connect up the Colorado cities of Denver, Colorado Springs, and Pueblo. Colorado Airways began services on 31 May, 1926, using a small fleet of Hispano Suiza engined Standard biplanes. These were replaced later by three Ryan M-1s. Joseph's original bid was for 80 per cent of the postage—the basis of calculation at first used, and abused—and this was later altered to a straight $3.00 per pound. By all accounts, Colorado Airways did not run too successfully, and on 10 December, 1927, Western Air Express was able to take over the route and air mail contract without having to purchase the rights or goodwill.

Swords into Ploughshares

Two of the early mail lines were started by ex-wartime airmen, whose love and enthusiasm for aeroplanes outlived their military adventures. One was Maj William B. Robertson, who was appalled at the wasteful destruction of perfectly serviceable aircraft and engines which occurred in the immediate post-war programme of scrapping redundant equipment. With the help of his brother Frank and H. H. Perkins, he therefore organized the Robertson Aircraft Corporation under the laws of the State of Missouri in February 1921 with a capital of $15,000. He then attended government surplus auctions and bid for aeroplane parts and engines, finding invariably that, because the only bidders against him were scrap metal dealers, he obtained the parts at a knock-down price. In this way the Robertson Aircraft Corporation built—or reassembled—more than 450 Standards, Curtiss JNs, and DH-4s. This turned out to be a very profitable business, and it was almost as a side-line that the Corporation bid for, and was granted, Post Office mail route CAM 2, from Chicago to St Louis. The aircraft normally used were DH-4s. One of the pilots was Charles A. Lindbergh. Regular contract mail flights began on 15 April, 1926, a date which, in a way, could be said to be the beginning of American Airlines.

In a different kind of way, two other ex-servicemen were starting another airline at about the same time. Reed Chambers and Eddie Rickenbacker were two war aces who, like the Robertsons, could not keep away from aeroplanes. Early in 1926 they organized the Florida Airways Corporation in New York and were granted CAM 10, the mail route from Atlanta to Miami, via Jacksonville, Tampa, Fort Myers and West Palm Beach. Florida Airways began a mail service on 1 April, with a Curtiss Lark, and carried passengers from 1 June onwards, after delivery of three Ford-Stout 2-ATs. Unlike Robertson, Florida Airways did not go on to play a part in the great merger programmes of the late 1920s, as it discontinued service after losing two of its three aircraft.

Scene before the departure of Colonial Air Transport's first New York—Boston mail service in 1926. The photograph, taken at Hasbrouck Heights (Teterboro), New Jersey, shows *left to right*; Leroy Thomson, H. I. Wells and Major T. O. Freeman, the airline's first three pilots, and Juan Trippe, general manager. The aircraft is a Fokker Universal.

Enter Big Business

Although Rickenbacker and Chambers were pilots, they had been shrewd enough to obtain backing from some fairly influential financiers, including Charles A. Stone and George Mixter, of Stone and Webster; banker Richard F. Hoyt; Anne Morgan; and Percy A. Rockefeller.

Another company started by New England financiers was Colonial Air Transport, whose founders included Governor John H. Trumbull of Connecticut, banker W. Irving Bullard of Boston and William A. Rockefeller.

Colonial was incorporated as early as 1923 but was inactive until it bid for the New York—Boston mail route, CAM 1. It faced rivalry from another aviation-minded group, Messrs C. V. Whitney, John Hambleton, and Juan Trippe, but merged their interests before obtaining the contract. Juan Trippe was appointed general manager. Mail and express service

Fokker Universal of Colonial Airways. This bears an early U.S. letter-series registration. (*Courtesy Peter M. Bowers*)

was started on 1 July, 1926, using Curtiss Larks, and passenger service began on 4 April, 1927. Unlike some of the early mail contractors who deigned to allow people on their aircraft without any regard for creature comforts, Colonial's fleet included two Fokker Universal and two three-engined Fokker F-VII passenger aircraft.

Early in 1927, also, Colonial was the unsuccessful bidder for the important New York—Chicago route, when the Post Office finally surrendered the transcontinental contract. The winner of that contest, National Air Transport, was a real pace-setter, already established on an existing mail route.

In 1924, Col Paul Henderson, former Assistant Postmaster General and 'father' of the night mail, had tried to interest Gen W. W. Atterbury, of the Pennsylvania Railroad, in commercial aviation and the idea of running an airline. Atterbury was not at that time won over. Then early in 1925, another figure entered the scene. His name was Clement Melville Keys.

A Canadian by birth and a graduate of Toronto University, Keys came to the United States and joined the editorial staff of the *Wall Street Journal* as a financial reporter. Studious, scholarly, and decisive, he mastered the intricacies of high finance and soon developed his own investment banking house. During the Great War, he became financial vice-president of the Curtiss Aeroplane and Motor Company, and when John N. Willys, who had bought into the company in 1916, returned to the motor industry at the end of the war, Keys was able to buy control of Curtiss for next to nothing.

Clement M. Keys (*left*) was a former *Wall Street Journal* financial editor who became deeply involved as a promoter of multi-million dollar aviation corporations which boomed around 1930. He controlled the Curtiss Aeroplane Company and, in 1925, formed North American Aviation, National Air Transport and Transcontinental Air Transport. Keys lost control of NAT to the United group in 1929, and saw his aviation empire crumble as quickly as it had grown to prominence. William B. Stout (*right*) was a pioneer of all-metal aircraft. He received backing, in 1925, from the Ford Motor Company to develop a line of transport aircraft which led to the Ford Tri-Motor in 1926, enabling airlines to carry passengers safely (in addition to mail) on some local routes around Detroit. He organized Stout Air Services when Ford became disenchanted with aviation, and sold out to NAT in 1929.

One of National Air Transport's original fleet of ten Curtiss Carrier Pigeons. (*United Air Lines*)

Keys is credited with the axiom 'ten per cent of aviation is in the air, ninety per cent on the ground'. It was in pursuit of this principle that in 1925 he formed North American Aviation for the express purpose of providing organization, finance, and inspiration for the development of a vast interwoven structure of airlines, manufacturers, insurance, and other aviation services, each nurturing the other.

Early in 1925, he approached Carl B. Fritsche, general manager of the Aircraft Development Corporation of Detroit, with the idea of launching an airline to link New York, Detroit, and Chicago. In complete contrast with the adventurous enterprise of the western pioneers and the ex-pilots, this was cold hard business, and it was big business. Keys proposed an initial capital of $2,000,000, which was ten times even that of Colonial Air Transport. Through his New York connections, he soon raised the New York share, half the total, whilst Fritsche raised $500,000 from Detroit. By chance, Henry Ford decided that his son Edsel should devote his full time to building cars; otherwise the Detroit contribution might have been $1,000,000 and the subsequent participation of Ford in airline history might have been very different.

Keys insisted that the remaining $500,000 should come from Chicago, but failed to raise it immediately from a city that depended for its wealth on the railway industry and activities such as food packing and distribution which were geared closely to railways. The money was eventually raised from the sons of some of the leading Chicago business men, and the resulting company, National Air Transport, was incorporated in the State of Delaware on 21 May, 1925. The Chairman was Howard E. Coffin, vice-president of the Hudson Motor Car Company of Detroit (and former member of the Morrow Board); Keys (whose shareholding was relatively small) was chairman of the executive committee; Fritsche was secretary; Jack Mitchell, son of the president of the Illinois Merchants Bank, was treasurer; and Col Paul Henderson resigned from his post of Second Assistant Postmaster General to become the general manager.

The total authorized capital of National Air Transport was fixed at an unprecedented $10,000,000.

On 7 November, 1925, NAT won the mail contract, CAM 3, for the important Chicago—Dallas route. This was more than just another feeder line to the transcontinental route, linking as it did the leading banking city of oil-rich Texas with the north, via the equally rich oil state of Oklahoma. NAT started service on 12 May, 1926, on a route Chicago—Moline—St Joseph—Kansas City—Wichita—Ponca City—Oklahoma City—Dallas. The fleet consisted of ten Curtiss Carrier Pigeons, built by one of Keys' companies.

Ford's reluctance to join forces with Keys may have been because he already had a foot in the airline door. As mentioned earlier in this chapter, the Ford Motor Company went into air transport shortly after the Kelly Act was passed, and indeed was the first to start Post Office contract operations, as its aircraft were already flying over the routes which became CAM 6 and 7, Detroit—Chicago and Detroit—Cleveland. Passengers were first carried in August 1926, and 657 were carried by the end of the first year. On 28 March, 1927, a private express service was begun from Detroit to Buffalo.

The Ford 5-AT-C NC8415 used by Stout Air Lines in 1929–30. The airline's Ford 4-AT-B NC7120 can be seen on the right.

Bill Stout, meanwhile, had founded Stout Air Services, winning the Post Office mail contract CAM 14, Detroit—Grand Rapids, on 31 July, 1926, and starting service two days later. Six weeks previously, on 11 June, Stout's old company, now Ford's, had demonstrated the first flight of the new Ford 4-AT Tri-Motor, and with this more commodious aircraft—the biggest civil aircraft in America to date—Stout was able to carry substantial numbers of passengers from the start—2 August, 1926—and adding a twice daily passenger service from Detroit to Cleveland on 1 September, 1927, avoiding the circuitous surface journey around the end of Lake Erie, via Toledo.

One of Northwest Airways' Stinson SB-1 Detroiter three-passenger biplanes.

The Smaller Businesses

If most of the colourful characters of the early contract airlines were to be found in the West, this did not mean that the Hanshues and the Varneys were blessed with a monopoly of the pioneering spirit. There were several examples of this in other parts of the United States.

Mail contract CAM 9, for instance, was awarded to Charles Dickenson, who began a service from Chicago to Minneapolis on 7 June, 1926, using Laird biplanes. This first service was short-lived, for, after a series of crashes, Dickenson ceased operating before the end of the second month of operations. The contract was taken over by Northwest Airways, incorporated on 1 August as a Michigan corporation by a group of Detroit and Twin Cities businessmen. On 1 October mail services began, at first

The silver and green Waco 9 biplane N2574 of Pennsylvania Air Lines. This was a sister aircraft of the *Miss McKeesport* used by Clifford Ball to open the Pittsburgh—Cleveland mail service in 1927.

with borrowed equipment, a Curtiss Oriole and a Thomas Morse biplane, pending the delivery of their first fleet, three Stinson Detroiters, aircraft capable of carrying three passengers at a speed of 85 mph.

Northwest Airways survives as Northwest Airlines Inc and has the unique distinction of a continuous record of service as a single company, without having participated in any completed merger or acquisition.

Another enterprising enthusiast, Clifford Ball, won the contract, CAM 11, for the difficult route from Pittsburgh to Cleveland, via Youngstown, and may be said to complete the list of the first round dozen private carriers who provided feeder services to the transcontinental Post Office route before that, too, was taken over. Ball started service on 21 April, 1927, under the name of the Skyline Transportation Company, although the company was always known as Clifford Ball's airline and he himself liked to refer to it as 'The Path of the Eagle'.

Ball started with two Waco 9 biplanes and did quite good business during 1927, carrying 19,600 lb of mail at $3.00 per lb.

Passenger Service Again

There was one more airline service during 1926 deserving of special mention. In connection with the Sesquicentennial—or 150th—anniversary of the signing of the Declaration of Independence, the Philadelphia Rapid Transit Service, or P.R.T. Line, was launched by prominent Philadelphia business men, including Thomas E. Mitten. The P.R.T. Line operated three times a day between the Philadelphia Navy Yard and Hoover Field, Washington, from 6 July to 30 November, 1926. Passengers paid $15 single, or $25 return, and during the five months of operation 3,695 people took the flight. Of 688 trips scheduled, only 75 were cancelled for any reason and there were no accidents. Reversing the normal practice, mail was carried as a fill-up load, under contracts CAM 13 (Philadelphia—Washington, until 9 October) and CAM 15 (Philadelphia—Norfolk, Va, 10 October–30 November).

The unregistered Fokker F.VIIa-3m *Wilbur* of Philadelphia Rapid Transit Service (P.R.T.) used in 1926. Beneath the crest on the fuselage are the words Under Mitten Management and below the cockpit U.S. Air Mail CAM13. (*Courtesy Peter M. Bowers*)

Most of the credit for this must go to the aircraft used, Fokker F.VIIa-3ms imported from the Netherlands, where they were already accepted as the latest successful version of a fine line of civil airliners. The operation was sustained largely through the technical competence of a Dutchman (also imported) formerly of KLM, the Netherlands national airline. His name was André Priester, and when the P.R.T. Line went into honourable retirement, he joined Anthony Fokker and Juan Trippe, who were interesting themselves in a new scheme to run an airline to South America.

The Philadelphia service ran at a financial loss but made an important contribution to the promotion of airmindedness in the United States. For although the transfer of contract mail carriage from the Post Office Department to civil operators was a step towards the spread of the commercial airline business, it did little to persuade the man in the street that flying in aeroplanes was any safer than before. Indeed, some of the early contract carriers did not distinguish themselves in this respect. But the P.R.T. Line demonstrated that an aeroplane passenger service could be both dependable and safe.

Although the achievement of the P.R.T. was solid enough, it failed to capture widespread attention—and indeed was almost lost from the record books, along with Aeromarine and some of the others. If the American public was to be jolted out of its apathy towards aviation in a big way, it needed a spectacular demonstration on a grandiose scale. But even the most ardent well-wishers could not have contrived an event which fitted this objective so perfectly as did the solo flight on 20–21 May, 1927, from Long Island, New York, to Le Bourget Airport, Paris, by Charles A. Lindbergh, a young pilot whose main apprenticeship had been flying mails for the Robertsons on CAM 2 from St Louis to Chicago.

Lindbergh was, in fact, the 79th individual to fly across the Atlantic but the first to do it alone; and the circumstances in which he did it were quite unique. First of all, the distance involved, some 3,650 miles, was set in advance by Raymond Orteig, the French owner of two New York hotels, who had offered a prize of $25,000 for the first nonstop flight between New York and Paris. Secondly, although having made a record transcontinental flight in his Ryan monoplane, *The Spirit of St. Louis*, on 10–12 May, Lindbergh was not the favourite against such opponents as Clarence Chamberlin, a pilot of repute, Commander Richard E. Byrd, of North Pole exploration fame, and René Fonck, the French ace. Thirdly, Lindbergh flew the course by the great circle route, precisely according to plan, without incident. By any standards it was an impressive performance.

The American public—and, for that matter, the world at large—were captivated by the romance of the achievement, the successful accomplishment of the near-impossible by a quiet, unassuming youth. It certainly opened the eyes of officialdom to the realities of what well-built aircraft could accomplish, properly handled. To the airlines, struggling for recognition, it gave a totally unexpected boost.

One of Boeing Air Transport's fleet of Boeing 40A biplanes built to operate CAM 18. In this picture it is seen flying with part of the forward cowling removed. (*Boeing Airplane Company*)

CHAPTER FOUR

Formation of the Big Four

Getting Under Way

A number of factors had combined to give air transport a new impetus in 1927. These were—to quote the most significant—the Kelly Act (2 February, 1925), the Air Commerce Act (20 May, 1926), the appearance of the first commercial aircraft able to carry a reasonable load of passengers, the Ford Tri-Motor (first flight, 1 June, 1926), and Lindbergh's flight (20–21 May, 1927). The Kelly Act provided some financial incentive to starting regular services; the Bingham-Merritt-Parker Bill gave the first airlines a legislative framework to work in and the promise of better navigational facilities, airports, and other services; Ford supplied a practical vehicle for people rather than mailsacks; and Lindbergh gave the public a lesson in what could be done if the wish to succeed was matched by ability, determination, and careful planning.

Suddenly, in the summer of 1927, the United States was caught in a wave of enthusiasm for aircraft and aviation which increased in momentum at an astonishing rate. Airline expansion accelerated so that the U.S.A., hitherto trailing behind some European nations and Canada in the traffic league tables, almost caught up the leaders in 1928 and raced past the field in 1929 (*Figure 6*).

During the next few years, scores of airline companies were established. Some were precariously founded on the proverbial wing and a prayer, and such was the intensity of the boom that many of these won through more by luck than judgement on the tide of a joyful seller's market. Others were set up with vast financial backing, to become pillars of the industrial world, interlocked by countless allied activities, and commanding enormous political as well as business influence. All the airlines, big or small, rich or poor, were characterized by a complete freedom of action, unfettered by regulations governing where or when or how they could operate routes, their only restrictions being fairly minimal ones governing safety and aircraft and pilot licensing. Any person who owned an aeroplane could start a service without asking anybody's permission other than that of the owners of the land he wished to use. It was a wonderful period of opportunity for private enterprise. (*See Tables 6 & 8, pages 588 and 593.*)

As the United States was a big country, there was enough room for everybody, or so it seemed. So tight was the shoestring on which some companies existed, however, that a minor accident or the illness of a key man was sometimes enough to suspend operations. Nevertheless very few of the infant airlines actually died. Many of the smaller fry, however,

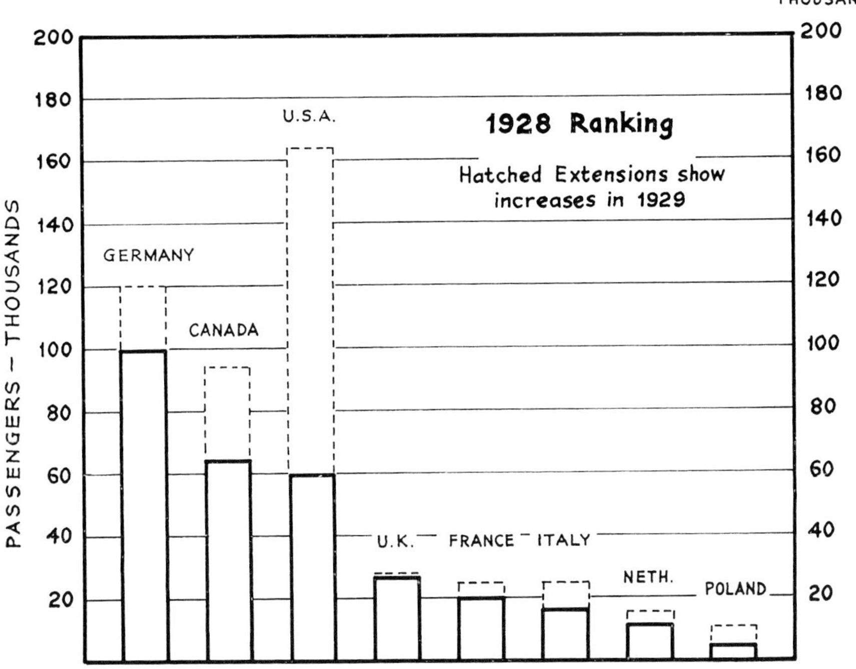

Fig. 6. World Air Traffic Ranking, 1928–1929.

were swallowed by the larger fish, and only the fittest survived. Some of the larger fought amongst themselves, made raids on rival territory, and for a while churned the aviation industrial waters into a maelstrom of intrigue. Eventually, after some three years of alarums and excursions, four giants emerged to dominate United States air transport; but the precise identity of the Big Four, as they were eventually called, did not become clear until the autumn of 1930. Indeed, but for a powerful demonstration of political power in controlling individual airline destinies there might well have been a Big Five.

As a prelude to the complex manoeuvres of the airline empire builders, and to set the seal on the young industry which had been sparked into life by Lindbergh, the Post Office Department surrendered the last of its mail routes to contract carriers, to launch the first coast-to-coast public air route.

The First Transcontinental Commercial Air Route

When, late in 1926, the Post Office Department advertised for bids on the coveted traditional transcontinental route, it split the route into two parts, east and west of Chicago, respectively. The restricted airline fraternity of that time assumed that the contracts would go to the most successful companies already in possession of mail contracts on the feeder routes. In fact, the latter were regarded partly as a contract mail-carrying apprenticeship, with a share of the coast-to-coast route as a graduation prize.

In this context, Western Air Express, with a good record of operating the reliable Douglas M-2 mailplanes across the mountainous country between Los Angeles and Salt Lake City, was favourite for the Chicago—San Francisco route; while National Air Transport, with its strong financial foundation, and a fleet of Curtiss mailplanes specially built for the job, was favourite for the Chicago—New York section. As it turned out, Western lost and National only won on a recount.

Harris Hanshue of Western Air Express did not bargain for a remarkable piece of co-operative joint enterprise by a shrewd group of airline-minded pioneers from Seattle. Eddie Hubbard, still flying the mails on the Seattle—Victoria foreign contract route, and a good friend of William Boeing who supplied his aircraft, heard of the Post Office call for bids on the San Francisco—Chicago route. He discussed the idea with Clair Egtvedt, designer-in-charge of the Boeing plant, and then approached Boeing himself for financial support. The result was that Egtvedt was given the job of designing a mailplane which also had room for two passengers as a bonus load, and Hubbard was given the job of establishing Boeing Air Transport, with Phil Johnson, Boeing's manager and chief salesman, as its first president.

Egtvedt set to work on the Boeing 40A; Hubbard went to Salt Lake City to organize the airline. The Mormon city was chosen because it had

The first of twenty-four Boeing Model 40A mailplanes built for Boeing Air Transport's San Francisco—Chicago service. The aircraft is seen at Seattle five days after its first flight on 20 May, 1927. (*Boeing Airplane Company*)

become the junction point between the Post Office transcontinental line and the two feeder routes to Seattle and Los Angeles, operated by Varney and Western respectively. William Boeing and Edward Hubbard were duly awarded the contract for the 1,918-mile Chicago—San Francisco route (CAM 18) at an unprecedented low bid of $2.88 per pound of mail for the whole journey, based on the calculation of $1.50 per pound for the first thousand miles, plus 15c per hundred miles thereafter. This beat by a substantial margin Western's bid of $4.25.

The low rate would have been impossible to achieve with the mail-carrying aircraft available at the time. There was little prospect of improvement as long as the customary Liberty engines were used, according to normal Post Office Department recommendations. Boeing therefore

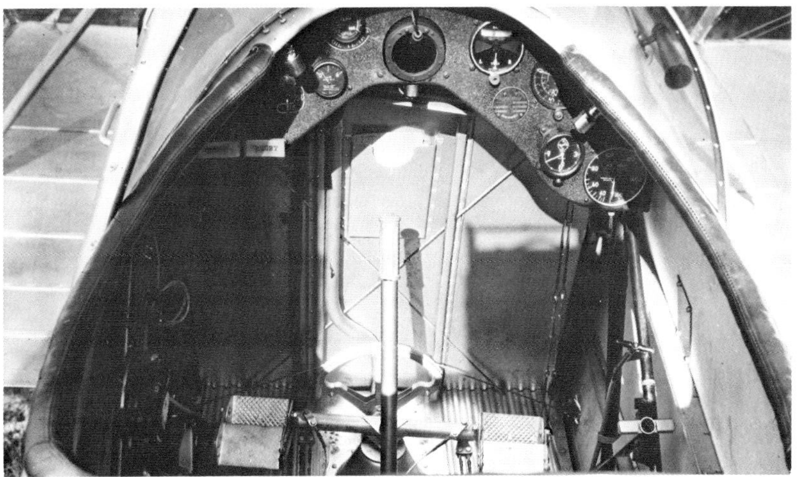

The pilot's cockpit in a Boeing Air Transport Boeing 40A.

A Boeing 40B-4 with 525 hp Pratt & Whitney Hornet engine and accommodation for four passengers. (*United Air Lines*)

approached Frederick D. Rentschler, formerly head of the Wright Aeronautical Corporation, then of Pratt & Whitney from Hartford, Connecticut. Rentschler and George Mead, the former chief engine designer of Wright, had developed the Pratt & Whitney Wasp radial air-cooled engine, which was chosen as the powerplant for the Boeing 40A.

The Chicago—San Francisco contract was awarded on 29 January, 1927, and services were scheduled to begin on 1 July. Only one aircraft was finished by 1 June, yet the whole fleet of twenty-four was ready for service and dispersed along the route by midnight on 30 June. To the astonishment of its critics and competitors, Boeing Air Transport made profits on the operation. During the first two years, the airline carried 1,300 tons of mail and 6,000 passengers. Though the accommodation was hardly luxurious, the two-passenger Model 40A was modified with Pratt & Whitney Hornet engines, as the Model 40B, and the service set up new records in reliability and regularity.

Boeing Air Transport's success was derived from two primary factors. The first was the ability to carry passengers to provide a bonus over and above the mail revenue; the second was the introduction of the air-cooled engines which, to quote Boeing himself, permitted the replacement of radiators and water with payload. The Chicago—San Francisco service accordingly settled down to a regular schedule of 20 hours.

The strongest bidder for the New York—Chicago section of the transcontinental air mail was National Air Transport, which, after all, had been formed by the Keys group for the express purpose of linking by air these two biggest industrial cities of the United States, along with Detroit, the automobile capital of the world. NAT's promoters were quite willing to share the cake if in so doing the rewards could be expected to be greater, and attempted to combine with Western Air Express in a joint bid for the entire transcontinental route. Harris Hanshue, however, sturdily independent, and suspecting eastern smartness, did not co-operate, possibly believing that, in his case, half a loaf (the Chicago—San Francisco section, which he felt sure of winning) was better than a part share of the whole. National then tried to combine with Colonial Air Transport, which also turned down the offer.

Bids for the New York—Chicago mail contract (CAM 17) closed on 8 March, 1927. Out of four contenders, NAT came third and Colonial Air Transport fourth. The lowest bid was from a certain Earle F. Stewart, who claimed to be able to carry the mails for 35c per pound, which the Post Office Department dismissed as frivolous. Second lowest came from North American Airways Inc (not North American Aviation), which underbid NAT's offer of $1.24 by one cent per pound. N.A. Airways was promoted by Charles A. Levine, a New York junk dealer who had come to prominence in the aviation field by sponsoring Clarence Chamberlin on his transatlantic flight. Levine proposed that NAT should buy a half interest in his company in exchange for the mail contract and 14 pilots from the Post Office Department, to whom he had promised jobs. Mainly on the grounds that this amounted to collusion, the Post Office threw out Levine's bid, and awarded it, on 2 April, to National Air Transport, which promptly hired the 14 pilots.

National Air Transport began service over the difficult Allegheny route between New York and Chicago on 1 September, 1927, using its Curtiss Carrier Pigeon mailplanes, already in service on the Chicago—Dallas mail route. These were quickly supplemented by 18 Douglas mailplanes, taken over from the Post Office Department, and eight Travel Airs. Unlike

Loading mail onto a National Air Transport Douglas M-2 at Hadley Airport, New Jersey. The pilot is Harry G. Smith.

Boeing, NAT regarded passengers as a nuisance rather than a boon, and travellers who wished to squeeze themselves in with the mail in the somewhat restricted space available had to plead for the privilege. NAT, in fact, increased the fare from $100 to $200 per trip to discourage them. Passengers were provided with flying suit and parachute, often asked to carry a sack of mail on their laps, and sometimes dumped at some point along the route to make way for the priority mail. In the first year of operations, only 168 passengers made the trip, most of them transfer connections from the comparative luxury of a Boeing 40A. All survived.

Three National Air Transport Douglas M-2s at Hadley Airport, New Jersey.

How the course of United States airline history might have changed, had the all-important transcontinental mail route awards gone differently, is difficult to speculate. Had NAT linked with Western Air Express there would probably have been no need for a TAT (Transcontinental Air Transport), from Keys' point of view. Had Western Air Express won the Chicago—San Francisco leg, there might never have been a United Air Lines. By taking a greater risk on its bid for New York—Chicago, Colonial Air Transport could have become a powerful force. Harris Hanshue and Western Air Express did not come out of the battle too well, all things considered; but this did not mean that WAE was a spent force.

The National Air Transport Douglas M-3 C1060 (c/n 624) after conversion to two-seater in February 1929. This aircraft is seen equipped with radio, underwing landing light and, on the fin, the American Railway Express sign.

National Air Transport's Douglas M-3 C7163 after being re-engined with a 525 hp Pratt & Whitney Hornet. The NAT fleet number 48 appears beneath the cockpit. On the right is an NAT Ford Tri-Motor.

One of National Air Transport's five-seat Travel Air Model 5000 cabin monoplanes. This example is C2907 with NAT fleet number 20. (*United Air Lines*)

Western Air Express red and silver Boeing 40B-4 NC843M at Los Angeles.

Growth of Western Air Express

Hanshue may have thought that he was out of luck with eastern financiers and politicians, but the dice rolled his way with eastern philanthropy, in the shape of the Daniel Guggenheim Fund for the Promotion of Aeronautics, formed on 18 January, 1926, with deeds of gift totalling $2,500,000 from the aviation-minded copper magnate of that name. Both interest and capital of the fund were to be used 'to promote aeronautical education

Mail being loaded onto a Western Air Express Boeing 95 while Charles N. 'Jimmie' James, one of the airline's first four pilots, climbs aboard complete with seat-type parachute. (*TWA*)

throughout the country, to assist in the extension of aeronautical science, and to further the development of commercial aircraft, particularly in its use as a regular means of transportation of both goods and people'.

Among the prizes and grants made by the Fund was a substantial financial contribution to Western Air Express. Because of its outstanding success flying the Los Angeles—Salt Lake City mail and passenger service, WAE was selected early in 1927 for the purpose of establishing a first-class passenger service between Los Angeles and San Francisco. A survey was made of air transport in Europe and manufacturers consulted on design criteria for a passenger airliner. After circulating general specifications to United States aircraft manufacturers, an order was placed with Anthony G. Fokker, of the newly-formed Atlantic Aircraft Corporation (subsequently the Fokker Aircraft Corporation) for three Fokker F-Xs.

The Western Air Express Fokker F-X NC5170 (c/n 1001) was the second example of this type built by Atlantic Aircraft Corporation. This picture was taken at Alhambra Airport, California, in about April 1930.

These aircraft represented a notable advance. With the typical Fokker high-wing monoplane design, and three of the new Pratt & Whitney Wasp radial engines, the F-Xs could achieve 150 mph, climb at 1,400 ft/min to 19,500 ft, and—what was remarkable at that time—could not only maintain height on one engine, but could climb to 7,000 ft on two. The maximum payload was twelve passengers plus 500 lb of cargo.

Passenger services opened between Los Angeles and San Francisco on 26 May, 1928, and continued to operate a three-hour daily service non-stop, serving luncheon en route. At the end of the first year's operations, more than 3,000 passengers had paid for tickets. WAE had maintained an on-time reliability of better than 99 per cent, the F-Xs had averaged 123 mph, and not one was even damaged. Part of this achievement was due to another outlet for the Guggenheim Fund, the investigation into the possibilities of a weather forecasting service, in co-operation with the U.S. Weather Bureau. This resulted in a reporting routine covering an airway extending 40 miles each side of the direct route, so that warnings could be given of approaching bad conditions, especially fog. Winds were

NC215M, seen at Alhambra, was one of the Fokker F-XA aircraft acquired by Western Air Express from other operators. This example had previously been used by West Coast Air Transport and Pacific Air Transport.

also studied and knowledge gained on the behaviour of the air at different altitudes, leading to recommendations on best cruising heights. Linked with this work also were some early experiments on the use of radio, and in this connection Herbert Hoover, Jr, joined WAE as a radio engineer. One of his tasks was to obtain from the Federal Radio Commission a licence to operate an aircraft radio station at Chicago, suggesting that Hanshue had ambitions well to the east of California.

In June 1928, WAE absorbed Pacific Marine Airways, the airline which had started a ferry service in 1923 from Wilmington, near Long Beach, to Avalon, on Catalina Island, with HS-2L flying-boats. There were indications of more ambitious plans when on 1 October, 1928, Hanshue and James Talbot created Western Air Express Inc, a $5,000,000 enterprise. Early in 1929 this company obtained control of the Fokker Aircraft Corporation and placed an order for five four-engined Fokker F-32s.

On 15 May, 1929, a daily passenger service was opened to Albuquerque, New Mexico, via Kingman and Holbrook, Arizona, and this line was

NC135H was one of the two Loening C-2H amphibians used by Western Air Express on its services to Avalon Harbor, Catalina Island, where it is seen in this photograph. (*Western Airlines*)

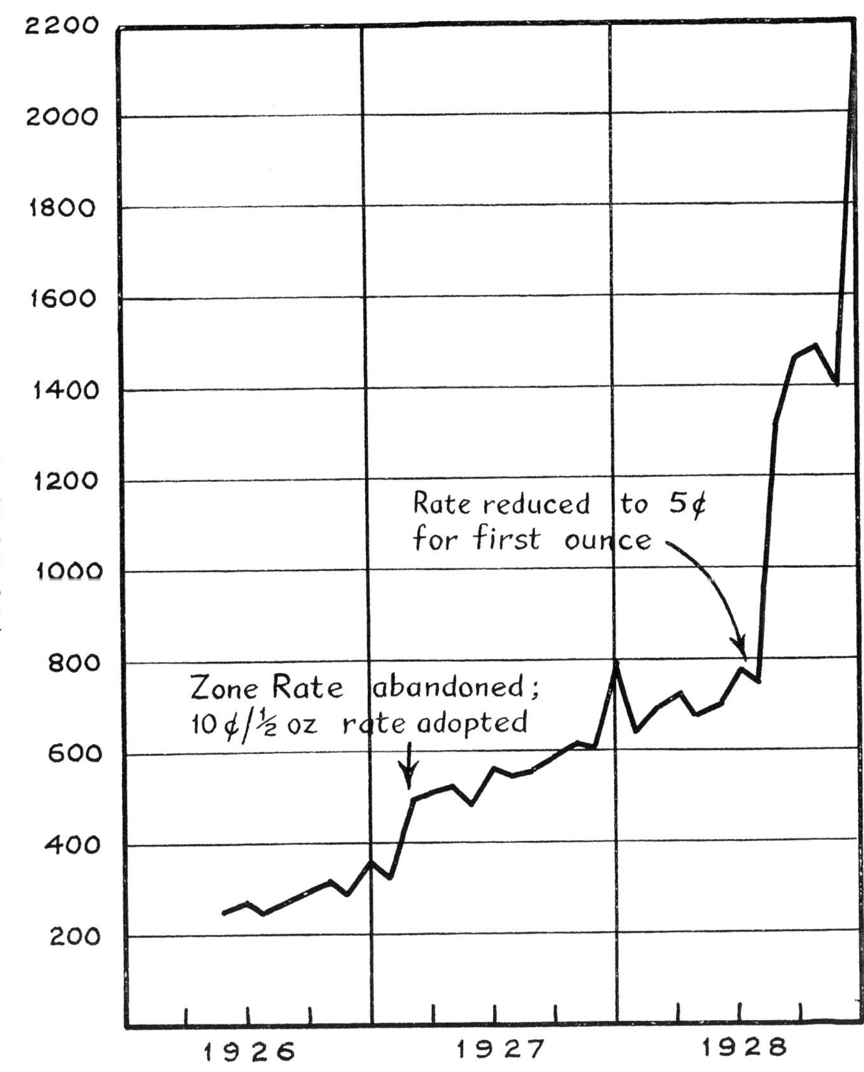

Fig. 7. Air Mail Growth: Western Air Express, Los Angeles—Salt Lake City, 1926–1928.

Meal service aboard a Western Air Express Fokker F-X. (*Western Airlines*)

extended to Kansas City, via Amarillo, Texas, on 1 June. The distance of 1,425 miles was covered in 13 hr, and there was no disguising the direction of Hanshue's ambitions. Additional local services were added in California, and the airline base was moved to the handsome new aerodrome at Alhambra, on 7 July.

Further consolidation of WAE's influence in the West was indicated by two more important airline acquisitions. West Coast Air Transport of Portland, Oregon, had begun passenger and express service between San Francisco and Seattle on 5 March, 1928, using a fleet of eight three-engined Bach Air Yachts. Later, after a successful year when almost 5,000 passengers were carried, it became a subsidiary of Union Air Lines of Sacramento, before WAE bought the line late in 1929.

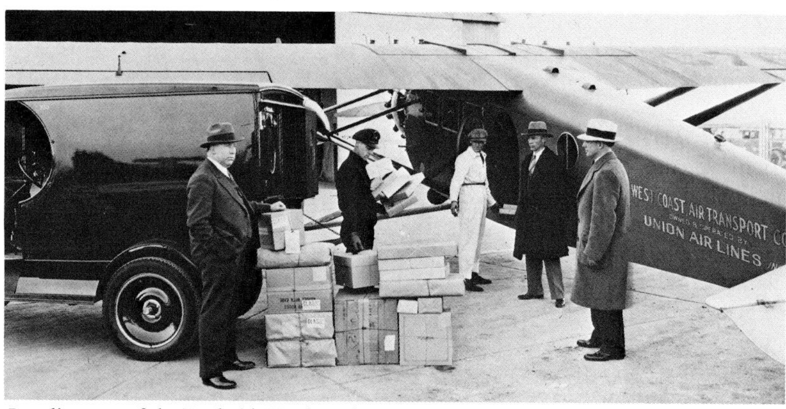

Loading one of the Bach Air Yachts of West Coast Air Transport Co which was owned and operated by Union Air Lines Inc. The aircraft is thought to have been of the 3-CT-2 or 3-CT-4 version but has not been positively identified. (*Western Airlines*)

Bach Air Yacht 3-CT-8 NC12297 of Union Air Lines. (*Gordon S. Williams*)

Another passenger-carrying specialist was Standard Airlines, formed on 3 February, 1926, as a subsidiary of the Aero Corporation of California, under the enterprising leadership of Lieut Jack Frye, together with Paul Richter and Walter A. Hamilton. Standard started regular services on 28 November, 1927, using Fokker F-VIIs, between Los Angeles and Tucson, via Phoenix (with an optional stop halfway across the desert, where there was a ladies' restroom). Frye arranged air-rail connections with the Texas and Pacific Railway and was able to offer a 70-hr transcontinental schedule on 4 February, 1929. Later he extended his route to El Paso, and by the autumn of that year, through arrangements with Southwest Air Fast Express (of which more later) and the New York Central Railroad, reduced the transcontinental time to 43 hr 40 min.

Hanshue bought Standard on 1 May, 1930, and could thus display on his timetables an imposing map of routes covering eleven western and southwestern states. On 2 May the El Paso route was extended to Dallas, but this success was short-lived, as Western Air Express became the unwilling partner to another ambitious airline in an historic shotgun marriage with Transcontinental Air Transport (TAT) imposed by the Postmaster General a few months later.

NC7888 *The Texan* was the only Fokker F-VIIa operated by Standard Airlines.

Boeing Air Transport's Boeing 80A NC227M being refuelled while passengers wait to go aboard. These aircraft were painted light grey with green and orange fuselage and tail trim and orange wings. (*Boeing Airplane Company*)

Formation of United

If Harris Hanshue was suspicious of easterners, Bill Boeing had no such inhibitions. His experience with Fred Rentschler had been a happy one, enabling a good aircraft designer to co-operate with a good engine designer to produce a money-making aeroplane, the Model 40A. Egtvedt was so enthusiastic about the Wasp engine that he set to work immediately on producing a three-engined Boeing, the Model 80, able to carry 14 passengers, going into service on the San Francisco—Chicago route late in 1928.

On 1 January, 1928, Boeing Air Transport acquired control of Vern Gorst's Pacific Air Transport, which not only provided a connection between the Boeing factory at Seattle and the transcontinental terminus at San Francisco, but also a market for Boeing aircraft—Pacific operated six four-passenger Boeing 40B-4s during 1928. On 17 December, 1928,

Boeing Air Transport's Boeing 80A NC227M. This view clearly shows the two upper wing fuel tanks. The cost of a Boeing 80A was $75,000. (*Boeing Airplane Company*)

One of the Boeing 40B-4s used by Pacific Air Transport on CAM 8 between Seattle and Los Angeles.

Pacific merged completely with Boeing Air Transport, as a sequel to the establishment, on 30 October, of the Boeing Airplane and Transport Corporation, a holding company for the Boeing Airplane Company, Boeing Air Transport, and Pacific Air Transport. Pacific continued to operate as a separate division of the parent company.

This was only the prelude to a much bigger merger. Rentschler suggested to Boeing that a partnership of Boeing Airplane Company and Pratt & Whitney would be a natural one. The deal was quickly agreed upon, and the resulting United Aircraft and Transport Corporation was formed on 1 February, 1929. Boeing had already bought out Chance Vought, a former racing driver who had built a successful line of Naval aircraft at Long Island City, New York. United promptly purchased the Hamilton Propeller Company and later added the Stearman Aircraft Company, of Wichita, and the Sikorsky Aviation Corporation, of College Point, Long Island. With a total capital of $146,000,000, this was a formidable company indeed. It needed to be, for there were jealous rivals coveting its preserves.

The Keys group was on the march. North American Aviation, Keys' $30,000,000 aviation financing company, had already bought into Varney

One of Pacific Air Transport's Boeing 40B-4s at Angelus Mesa Field near Los Angeles in June 1928. (*United Air Lines*)

Departure scene in 1928. The aircraft is one of Pacific Air Transport's four-passenger Boeing 40B-4s. (*United Air Lines*)

Air Lines—reaching towards Seattle—and was backing Maddux Air Lines, in an attempt to extend this California carrier's system up the west coast to the Boeing base. These were natural extensions, or branches, for Keys' other giant enterprise, Transcontinental Air Transport (TAT).

Whilst Keys attacked the West, United countered in the east. When Boeing Air Transport won the Chicago—San Francisco mail route, one of the losing bids was Bill Stout's. Stout had relinquished his mail contract on the Detroit—Grand Rapids route in 1926, and terminated freight and passenger service on 31 July, 1927. He established a twice daily freight and passenger service between Detroit and Cleveland on 1 November, 1927, and then inherited the two mail contract routes connecting Chicago with Cleveland, via Detroit, from the Ford Motor Company on 16–19 July, 1928, and also held the rights to extend to Buffalo. Paradoxically, the line became virtually an exclusive passenger carrier, as Stout voluntarily surrendered the mail contracts because of poor loads. One reason for this unusual bias was the possession of a fleet of Ford Tri-Motors, so popular with the public that 5,640 passengers were carried during 1928.

By purchasing Stout Air Services on 30 June, 1929, United Aircraft and Transport Corporation extended the Boeing system east to Cleveland, with the rights to reach the tip of New York State at Buffalo; so near, yet so far, with National Air Transport in charge of the mail contract to New York City.

National Air Transport had made impressive headway since winning the all-important Chicago—New York sector, managed as it was by Col Paul Henderson, with the Pennsylvania Railroad showing fatherly interest, and with an unlimited supply of Curtiss aircraft when needed from its

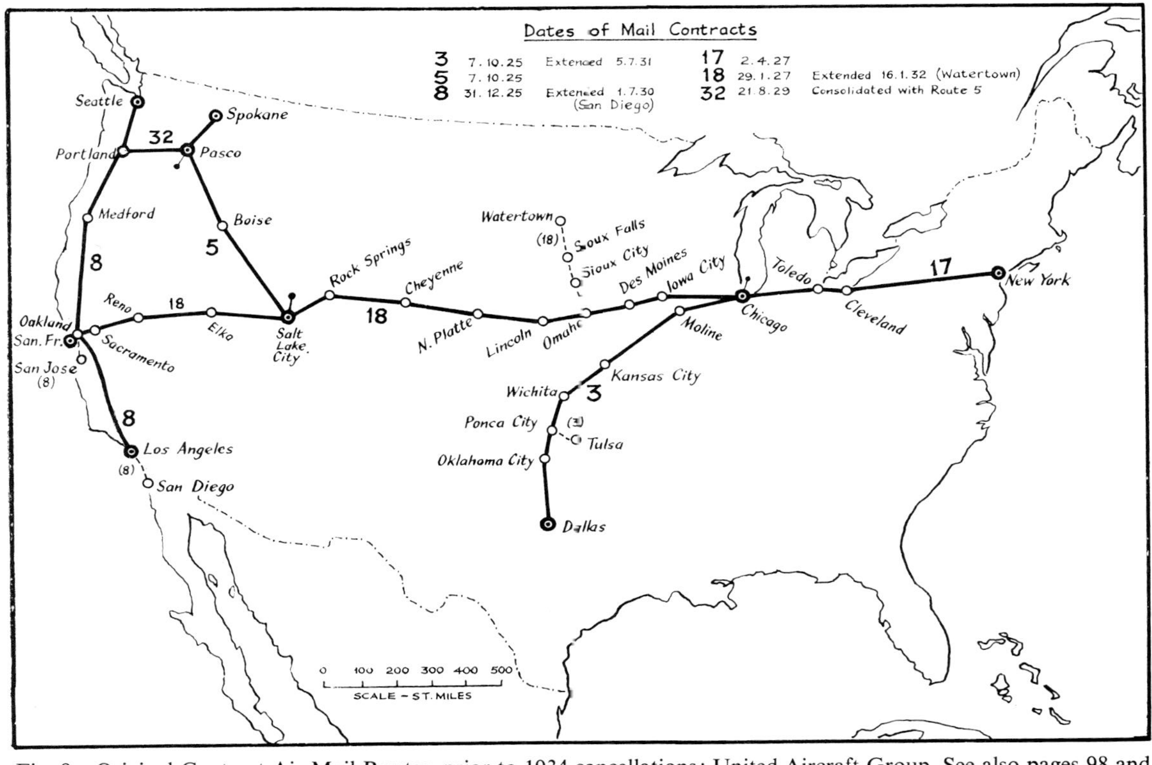

Fig. 8a. Original Contract Air Mail Routes, prior to 1934 cancellations: United Aircraft Group. See also pages 98 and 109.

One of the eight Curtiss Falcons added to National Air Transport's fleet at the end of 1928. (*United Air Lines*)

associated Keys company. On 1 February, 1928, a daily passenger service was opened from Chicago to Kansas City, using Travel Air 6000 single-engined aircraft, and a night mail service from Chicago to Dallas which saved a whole business day. Feeder services were opened from Detroit (connecting at Toledo) on 4 June, and Tulsa (at Ponca City). Yet, because of heavy mail commitments, passenger service was discontinued on 1 October. Another reason was probably that its associate, TAT, needed every passenger it could get for its combined transcontinental air-rail service which followed a route roughly parallelling NAT's. In 1928 eight Curtiss Falcons were added to the fleet, and at the end of the year the first Ford Tri-Motors were delivered, a convincing tribute to the passenger appeal of the 'Tin Goose' over other aircraft of the day.

Col Henderson had moved over to TAT but still effectively looked after NAT's fortunes and was finally won over to the cause of passenger service, even across the Alleghenies. He announced late in 1929 that NAT would be equipped with a fleet of new Curtiss Condor luxury airliners, and this was seen by United as a serious threat to operations east of Chicago.

A rare flying picture of one of NAT's Curtiss Falcons. This one is equipped with underwing landing light. (*United Air Lines*)

Towards the end of 1928 National Air Transport began taking delivery of a fleet of Ford Tri-Motors. The example illustrated is the Ford 5-AT-D NC436H (c/n 103) which was delivered in 1931 and used on the New York—Chicago route.

On 31 March, 1930, United Aircraft acquired one third of NAT's shares by an exchange of stock with the Chicago group who had been among Keys' original sponsors of NAT. Then began a battle of industrial giants for control of National. On 10 April, 70,000 more shares changed hands and at a stockholders' meeting Rentschler's representative withheld most of the vote in an attempt to prevent a quorum, which depended on a one-half outstanding share vote. Keys, however, had taken the precaution of changing the company's by-laws to reduce the quorum limitation to one third and had also issued 300,000 new shares to none other than North American Aviation Corporation, controlled (of course) by Keys.

Rentschler managed to counteract the latter move by having it declared illegal and, by buying up more shares on 17 April, was able to declare control of 57 per cent of the stock. After further corporate infighting, the officers and directors of United and NAT met on 23 April to draw up a truce. Keys was not present. Rentschler had won. United's purchase of NAT was formally completed on 7 May, 1930.

Ford 5-AT-D Tri-Motor NC436H bearing the markings of National Air Transport and United Air Lines. The NAT fleet number 98 appears on the rudder and fuselage. (*United Air Lines*)

Pacific Air Transport's Boeing 40B-4 NC10346 *Dana* at Seattle. In the hangar is a Boeing 247. (*Gordon S. Williams*)

Pacific Air Transport's Boeing 40B-4 *Whitney* after receiving United Air Lines' markings with a map of the U.S. on which was shown the United route system.

The prototype Boeing Model 95 C183E (c/n 1046), which first flew at the end of December 1928. It is seen in Boeing Air Transport markings with the American Railway Express badge on its nose.

Dual identity. This Boeing 95 used on the New York—Chicago route carries the names of National Air Transport and United Air Lines. NAT fleet number 103 appears beneath the cockpit.

The operations of Stout Air Services—specialists in passenger work—and National Air Transport—specialists in mail—were merged within the United organization shortly afterwards, NAT paying Stout $175,000 for goodwill, know-how, and debts. For some unaccountable reason, the Chicago—Detroit—Cleveland route was abandoned, a decision which United regretted for many years afterwards. Stout's Ford Tri-Motors were switched to the Chicago—New York route, providing at last a reasonable connection in tolerable comfort for the ever-increasing number of passengers discharged by Boeing Air Transport at Chicago.

United now set about the task of relieving Keys of any further respon-

The seventh Boeing 95, NC189E (c/n 1052), after receiving United Air Lines' markings. (*Gordon S. Williams*)

The original Stearman mailplane used by Varney Air Lines was the C2MB.

sibilities resulting from his purchase of shares in Varney Air Lines. Walter T. Varney had made some progress since the first risky steps with the Swallows. In 1927 the Elko terminus of the line was transferred to the busier Salt Lake City junction on the transcontinental mail route, and the following year the fleet was augmented by five Stearman Speedmails. On 23 September, 1929, the route was extended from Pasco to Seattle and Spokane. The line was in bad financial health, however, and when United dangled a $1,000,000 carrot in front of Varney early in 1930, it was only a matter of time—and an extra million extracted by Louis Mueller, Varney's attorney—before the company became a United subsidiary on 30 June, 1930. Boeing now had a more direct route between Chicago and the

At the time this photograph was taken the Stearman C3MB NC6499 (c/n 195) was being used by Varney Air Lines as an instrument flight trainer.

C9054 was one of the Stearman M-2 Speedmail fleet used by Varney Air Lines.

home factory at Seattle, a connection which had become more important now that the acquisition of National Air Transport had created the first genuine transcontinental passenger air route. With Chicago the hub of the fast-growing United States air network, and the transfer point moreover for most of the traffic on the United system, the head office of United Air Transport was transferred to the 'Windy City', and is still there.

Varney left and used his new wealth to start Varney Speed Lines in California. Mueller stayed on as chairman of the board of Varney Air Lines, which finally lost its identity on 30 September, 1933, when it was absorbed by Boeing Air Transport, by this time a division of United Air Lines.

This was the name by which United Air Transport's operating airlines had become known by the spring of 1931 and which was formally designated when, on 1 July, 1931, United Air Lines was organized as the 'World's Largest Air Transport System'.

The little-known Breese 5 monoplane built in 1926–7. Originally powered by a 200 hp Wright J-4 and later by a 220 hp J-5 engine, this Varney Air Lines' example (unregistered) is the only one known to have entered airline service.

Transcontinental Air Transport's Ford 5-AT-B Tri-Motor at an air-rail interchange point (either Waynoka or Clovis). The fourteen-passenger Aero Car trailer was used to transfer passengers and baggage between airports and railway stations. (*TWA*)

Formation of TAT

Transcontinental Air Transport (TAT) was formed on 16 May, 1928, as another colony in Keys' far-flung empire. It was backed by Keys' associated companies, the Curtiss Aeroplane and Motor Company, the Wright Aeronautical Corporation, and National Air Transport; the Pennsylvania Railroad; and a group of bankers and businessmen from St Louis, a city which has been a strategic point in the company's route network ever since. The total capital was $5,000,000. True to form, Keys himself, through North American Aviation, did not subscribe a large sum, but was president of the airline, with Paul Henderson, of NAT, as his vice-president.

The solid industrial backing was complemented by some solid judgement on the way to run an airline. A technical committee was formed, with wide powers of recommendation and advice to the board, and it was to be the policy of TAT that no decision involving technical or operational problems should be made without the blessing of the committee. The chairman of the committee was Col Charles Lindbergh, which was enough to give TAT the name by which it was popularly known, the *Lindbergh Line*.

In many ways the formation of TAT marked a definite step in the progress of civil aviation in the United States. In contrast to all the airlines which had been formed hitherto—with a few local exceptions—to carry mail, TAT was formed to carry passengers. It was curious that Keys, who had a perfectly good airline in NAT, should have completely failed to exploit the obvious passenger potential of the route from New York to Chicago, with the intervening major cities of Pittsburgh, Cleveland, and Detroit. Basically, the reason was a conviction, shared by Paul Henderson, that the aircraft of the day could not provide a reasonable standard of comfort, service, or safety over the uncharitable terrain of the Alleghenies. TAT on the other hand started life with a publicly known commitment to operate Ford Tri-Motors, with the built-in safety margin of three engines, and the intention from the outset was to traverse the mountainous parts of the transcontinental journey by train at night—a system commending itself to one of the chief sponsors, the 'Pennsy'.

TAT announced that the passenger capacity of the Fords would be reduced from 16 to 10 'so that tea and luncheon can be served aloft in an aerial dining car service'. All aircraft were equipped with kitchens.

Charles Lindbergh had also been a beneficiary of the Guggenheim Fund, having spent some weeks in seclusion on the Long Island estate of Harry F. Guggenheim, president of the Fund. There, Lindbergh wrote his book *We* and prepared himself for a personal promotional campaign almost unparalleled in industrial history. Time has hardly dimmed the memory of Lindbergh's spectacular achievement in flying across the Atlantic. But the effect he had on American airmindedness is almost forgotten. For, during the two or three years following his epic flight, he awakened the nation, almost single-handedly, to the enormous future possibilities of air transport.

Every flight which Lindbergh made was for a purpose, and that purpose was usually the furtherance of airline planning or technical improvement. He emerged from Long Island to carry out a Guggenheim-sponsored tour of the 48 States, visiting 82 cities in 260 flying hours. He covered more than 22,000 miles and was late only once. He followed this by flying nonstop from Washington to Mexico City on 13–14 December, 1927, and then to sixteen countries of Latin America before returning to St Louis on 13 February, 1928.

He then set about planning TAT's transcontinental route, disappearing from the public eye for several months. The route chosen was a courageous

Cheyenne Airport passenger terminal in about 1935. (*Western Airlines*)

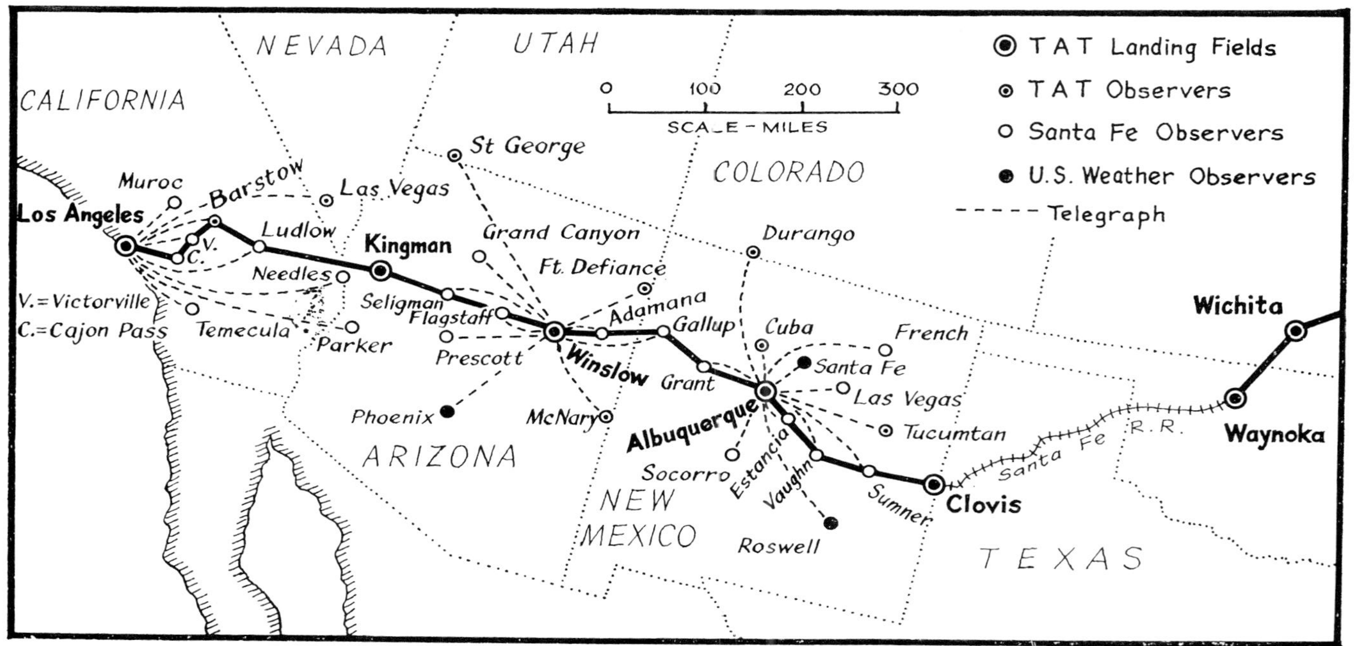

Fig. 9. TAT Weather and Navigational Organization (Western Section), 1929.

one, for it hardly touched the now firmly-established lighted airway which guided the Boeing mailplanes across the continent. Careful attention was given to the choice of terrain. The Alleghenies were unavoidable, but the course plotted across the Rocky Mountain system was far less arduous than United's route via Cheyenne. Good municipal aerodromes were chosen for the main stops, whilst other landing grounds were specially built at what were then comparatively remote communities en route. Corrugated iron structures typical of the aerodrome architecture of the day were spurned in favour of handsome, almost ostentatious, edifices. Altogether some $1,500,000 were estimated to have been spent on ground equipment.

The TAT weather bureau was a formidable item of infra-structure. It covered a 150-mile-wide band from coast to coast. Expert weather observers were stationed at strategic points. TAT supplied 14, the Pennsylvania Railroad 14, the Santa Fe Railroad 33, and the United States Weather Bureau nine. The lighting requirements exceeded those of the Department of Commerce. $3,000,000 was spent in 14 months, of which only $813,000 was on aircraft. (*See Figure 9.*)

Not that the choice of flying equipment was taken lightly: Lindbergh's committee weighed up the relative merits of six multi-engined aircraft, the Curtiss Condor, the Keystone Patrician, the Boeing 80A, a Sikorsky biplane, the Fokker F-X, and the Ford Tri-Motor. Only the last two were actually in quantity production, and Ford got the order, which was intended to be an interim step until the availability of the Curtiss Condor. The Ford Tri-Motor cost between $42,000 and $55,000 f.o.b. Dearborn and should have been good value for a flying machine which claimed to be 'more stable than a yacht, swifter than the wind, a new exultation, the thrill of an indescribable experience, complete, luxurious relaxation'.

A Ford 5-AT-C Tri-Motor at Port Columbus, the combined airport and Pennsylvania Railroad station interchange point for the transcontinental air-rail service. (*TWA*)

Maj Thomas G. Lamphier, Lindbergh's assistant in TAT, searched the country for pilots with adequate experience. He hired 38, of whom 17 still needed further training, according to the exacting standards set by the *Lindbergh Line*.

Between 20 June and 7 July, 1929, TAT carried 231 passengers on 'rehearsal' flights which totalled 50,000 miles of flying. 1,000 people applied for tickets on the first scheduled service which took place on 7 July, attended by as much ceremony as could be mustered. Promptly at 6.05 p.m. New York time, Charles Lindbergh pressed a button in Governor C. C. Young's office in Los Angeles. This flashed a light in Pennsylvania Station, New York, and the *Airway Limited* was on its way, while the band played *California, Here I Come*. The proceedings were broadcast over two radio stations in New York, one in Philadelphia, and one in Cincinnati.

Air view of Port Columbus airport terminal and railway station under construction during the first half of 1929. (*TWA*)

The train travelled through the night to Port Columbus, an elaborate air-rail interchange station seven miles east of Columbus, Ohio. It arrived at 7.55 next morning, where more than 5,000 people had braved the drizzle to watch the train-to-plane transfer. Two Ford Tri-Motors, NC9606 *City of Columbus* and the *City of Wichita* left Port Columbus at 8.15 a.m. and flew through the day to a point 4½ miles west of Waynoka, Oklahoma, arriving at 6.24 p.m. During the flight, via Indianapolis, St Louis, Kansas City, and Wichita, lunch was served on board between St Louis and Kansas City. Stops were precisely scheduled to the minute, as in railway practice, 15 min allowed for each.

The Atchison, Topeka & Santa Fe Railroad operated the night journey from Waynoka to Clovis, New Mexico, with breakfast in the Harvey

House restaurant. The final stage of the transcontinental journey was by Ford Tri-Motor again, via Albuquerque, Winslow, and Kingman, to the Grand Central Air Terminal at Glendale, Los Angeles. Passengers were offered free transport to San Francisco the next day either by train or by Maddux Air Lines.

The day after performing the button-pressing ceremony at Los Angeles, Lindbergh took the first eastbound Ford, NC9646 *City of Los Angeles*, out of Glendale Airport. This was before a crowd estimated at about 100,000, who were entertained by a preliminary display of ten training circuits and bumps as Lindbergh complied with the regulatory letter of the law.

The complete New York—Los Angeles air-rail journey took almost exactly 48 hr, and the total fare varied from a minimum of $337 to a maximum of $403 one way, depending on the standard of comfort on the

The covered walkway leading from the railway station to the airport terminal at Port Columbus. (*TWA*)

trains. The air portion of the ticket was $290. This worked out at about 16c per mile—about double the first-class rate after World War 2.

The arrangement with Maddux was necessary to provide competition with Western Air Express, which was offering service from California to the East, as far as Kansas City (*See page 88*) and which was popular in California, following the success of the Model Airline experiment promoted by the Guggenheim Fund.

Western Air Express' dominance had been rudely shattered when a Los Angeles car dealer named Jack L. Maddux became interested in the Ford Tri-Motor. After an effective demonstration of the aircraft's reliability, Maddux swung into action on 21 July, 1927, with a passenger service

Scene, on 8 July, 1929, before the departure of TAT's inaugural eastbound transcontinental flight. In front of the Ford Tri-Motor *City of Los Angeles* at Glendale Airport, Los Angeles, are Douglas Fairbanks, left; Mrs Anne Morrow Lindbergh, in dark dress; Miss Mary Pickford, with flowers; and Charles Lindbergh, in dark suit.

The Ford 5-AT-B NC9646 *City of Los Angeles* about to leave Los Angeles on the inaugural TAT transcontinental eastbound air-rail service. The pilot was Charles Lindbergh. (*TWA*)

Maddux Air Lines' Ford 4-AT-B 4532 (c/n 16), used on Los Angeles—San Francisco services. (*Courtesy Peter M. Bowers*)

from Los Angeles to San Diego and then a twice daily return service between Los Angeles and San Francisco, begun on 14 April, 1928. By the end of the year Maddux had carried 9,440 passengers, and was buying more Fords. Progress in 1929 was equally swift. On 10 February, a Los Angeles—Phoenix service was opened, together with other short-stage local flights in southern California. When TAT bought Maddux on 16 November, the latter had become the biggest operator of Ford Tri-Motors, with eight 4-ATs and seven 5-ATs, together with two Lockheed Vegas and two Travel Airs, and had carried 40,000 passengers during the year. By the beginning of 1930, the timetables showed the full schedules of TAT-Maddux Air Lines, and there the matter rested for a few uneasy months.

The passenger cabin of a Ford Tri-Motor.

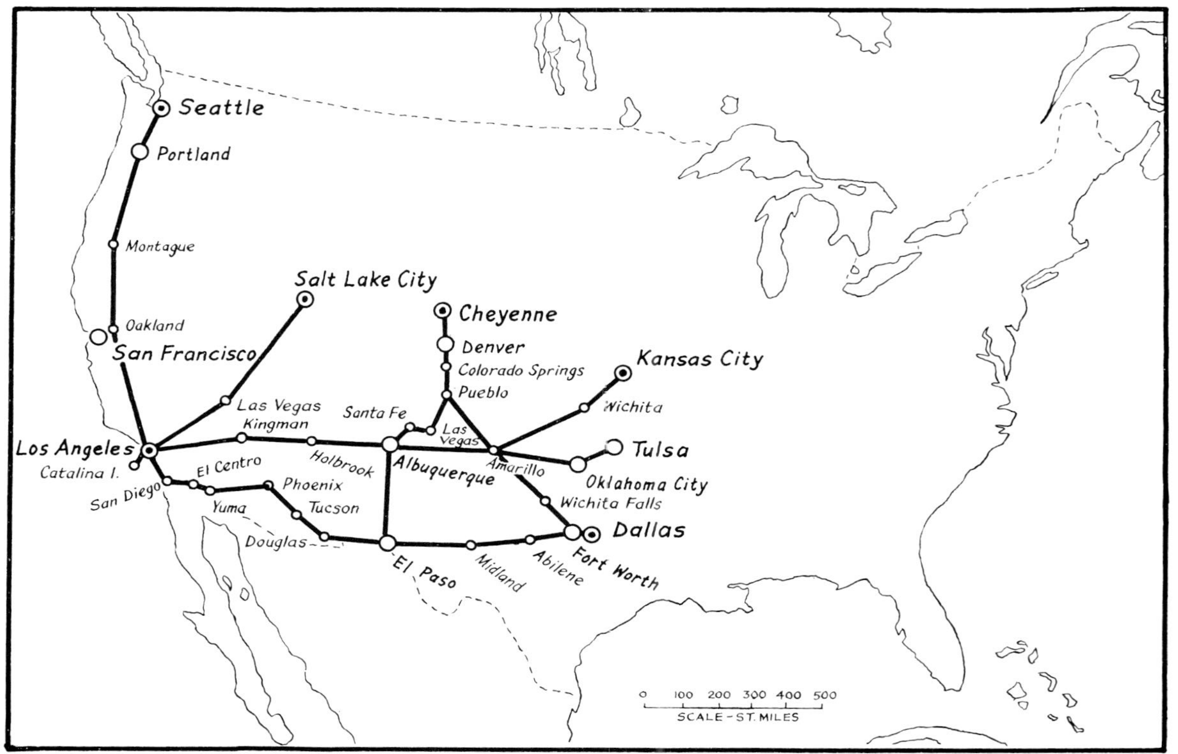

Fig. 10. Western Air Express Route Network, May 1930.

A Shotgun Marriage

This chapter deals primarily with the formation of what were to become known as the Big Four. Until October 1930 the complex process of mergers had not clarified and there were five big airlines, including Western Air Express, with two of the other four controlled by the same finance group. Then, dramatically, by a form of political pressure of the most blatant kind, the Five became Four. The fascinating story of the applied power of the Postmaster General who came into office with the Hoover regime in 1929 is the subject of subsequent chapters, but reference to his influence on other aspects of the history of United States air transport must be made from time to time; for Walter Folger Brown, the Postmaster General, played a vital part in shaping the destinies—even deciding the existence—of the giants of the airline industry. The development of air mail and air mail payments must also be chronicled in more detail elsewhere, and mention of it here is limited to the way in which it influenced the most important airline merger during the first quarter-century of United States airline history.

During 1928 and 1929, following the Lindbergh flight in 1927, the American industry and public became enthusiastic over aviation. Industry, mainly in the shape of financing companies, motorcar manufacturers and railways, entered the field; and the public was easily persuaded to part with its money. In fact, in the light-headed boom which immediately followed the Lindbergh hysteria, the Seaboard Air Line, a none-too-prosperous railway at that time, experienced a welcome demand for stock.

People wanted to get into the air, and the airlines, now springing up by the dozen, were eager to carry them. Unfortunately, many were to learn the hard way as few had bothered to do their arithmetic in order to establish the basic prerequisite of any successful business, namely that revenue should exceed expenditure. Certainly the public were willing to pay a reasonable rate. There were isolated cases of some people paying a most unreasonable rate—like $1,000 from Seattle to Salt Lake City—where there was a real seller's market. But the costs of operating aircraft at that time were high in relation to the revenue, and considerable reliance continued to be made on mail.

From Western Air Express' point of view, the contrast was dramatic. As long as it stuck to routes dependent on mail it was in the black (helped, admittedly, by the Guggenheim Foundation) and was able to announce at the end of 1928 that to date six regular quarterly dividends had been paid and that net earnings during the year were $700,000. This was the first time that an airline had paid a dividend to stockholders. In 1929, however, when it bought West Coast Air Transport, with no mail contract, and opened a completely new route, again without a mail contract, as far east as Kansas City, then its troubles began.

DIRECTORS
HARRIS M. HANSHUE, PRES.
MAJOR C. C. MOSELEY, VICE-PRES.
BYRON L. GRAVES, TREAS.
HARRY CHANDLER
WM. MAY GARLAND
G. E. NOLL
JAMES A. TALBOT

H. M. WRIGHT, SECRETARY

JAMES G. WOOLLEY, TRAFFIC MGR.

GENERAL OFFICES - LOS ANGELES
113 W. 9TH ST.
PHONE TRINITY 6754

LOS ANGELES AIRPORT - ANGELUS 1786
SALT LAKE AIRPORT - WASATCH 7023

WESTERN AIR EXPRESS

AIR MAIL — PASSENGERS

LOS ANGELES - SALT LAKE CITY

Los Angeles, Sept. 30, 1927

Stockholders,

WESTERN AIR EXPRESS, INC.,

Gentlemen:-

There is enclosed herewith a check in the amount of your partioipation in what is believed to be the first earned dividend ever distributed by a company engaged solely in transportation by airplane and entirely dependent for its revenue upon patronage of the service offered.

The distribution of this dividend will in no way affect the strong reserves being built up by your Board of Directors in furtherance of an expansion policy immediately impending, the prosecution of which should enhance the value of your investment.

Harris M. Hanshue
President

Harris M. Hanshue (*left*) and Walter Folger Brown seen by the starboard engine of a Western Air Express Fokker F-X.

WAE was not the only airline in this situation, and made strenuous efforts to compensate for passenger losses by mail payments. But by 1930, with an economic depression just beginning to make itself felt, there was little doubt that Harris Hanshue's honeymoon was over.

TAT never had a honeymoon. Its grandiose plans for ushering in a new era of passenger transport did not catch on, at least not in sufficient depth. In spite of the vast investment and the association with Lindbergh's name, TAT was losing money hand over fist, mainly because, once the novelty had worn off, there was little attraction in the 16c per mile fare structure. The air-rail system was obviously not the complete answer, and the pretentious rest rooms and ticket offices were emptying. TAT, in fact, lost $2,750,000 in the first eighteen months of operation.

Postmaster General Brown had a master plan for the nation's airways, especially the transcontinental system. This did not include the idea of allowing two airlines to operate competitively over the same route, each receiving mail payments. Consequently he insisted that, before awarding any mail contract for what was then known as the central route, there would have to be an amalgamation between Western Air Express and Transcontinental Air Transport. Possibly Brown thought that because North American Aviation had substantial holdings in both companies, it would be a natural merger, popular with both parties. He was mistaken.

Rightly or wrongly, Harris Hanshue believed that he could ride out the period of losses in his books, since he had a firm foundation of potentially lucrative mail routes. Additionally he mistrusted easterners and feared coming under the shadow of the North American Aviation group. His comments at the conference held by the Postmaster General are reported to have been unprintable; while later he made scathing remarks on the performance of the Condor, the pride of the Curtiss project department stating that to operate it across the Rockies would cost a lot of money because of 'what a hell of a long time it's going to take to tunnel through those goddam mountains'.

A third participant in the merger was Pittsburgh Aviation Industries Corporation (P.A.I.C.) founded by a group of Pittsburgh industrialists, including Frederick Crawford, C. Bedell Munro, George R. Hann, and a representative of the Mellon family. Their original intention was to put Pittsburgh on the aviation map as a rival to Cleveland and to operate a regular airline service across Pennsylvania, but they had been advised by the Department of Commerce that this was impracticable until lighted airways were completed.

Pittsburgh Airways' Travel Air Model 6000 C9840. (*United Air Lines*)

P.A.I.C. contented itself with fixed-base operations and gained some flying experience over the rugged territory east of Pittsburgh. Thus, when the Postmaster General called for bids on the central transcontinental mail route it considered that it held pioneering rights over the route. This was certainly a valid claim over TAT, which had never flown an aircraft east of Columbus, Ohio, and the point was conceded by Brown.

Unfortunately, another Pittsburgh company, Pittsburgh Airways, had actually started a sporadic service Pittsburgh—Philadelphia—New York, in December 1929, with two Travel Air J-6s, and it too claimed proprietary rights over the route. Furthermore, in August 1930, Pittsburgh Airways joined up with Ohio Air Transport, which claimed to have operated a route from Youngstown (near Pittsburgh) to Dayton, Ohio, and United States Airways, which had opened a route from Kansas City to Denver on 1 June, 1929, using seven-passenger Flamingo all-metal aircraft.

The three companies called themselves United Avigation, and although their ideas were too embryonic to be considered a serious and potentially viable operation, they constituted a threat to the smooth working of

Brown's master plan. Therefore, having also persuaded AVCO* (*See page 99*), which held some of the Western Air Express stock, to co-operate, the Postmaster General quickly put the heat on Hanshue, telling him that if he didn't merge with TAT there would be no mail contract for anyone.

So, after much preliminary sparring, and a 4·732 per cent minority participation from P.A.I.C., Western Air Express finally agreed to merge with Transcontinental Air Transport. The first step was to form the Eton Corporation under the laws of Delaware on 19 July, 1930. Five days later, the certificate of incorporation was amended, and with the transfer of certain assets and equipment formerly used by TAT and WAE, Transcontinental and Western Air Inc (TWA) was formed, with 1,000,000 authorized shares, of which 623,000 were issued.

P.A.I.C.'s minority interest was in exchange for a half-interest in the Pittsburgh-Butler Airport Inc.

The mail contract was awarded on 25 August, and the first all-air service from coast to coast under the new name of TWA was flown by a Ford Tri-Motor on 25 October, 1930, in 36 hr, with an overnight stop at Kansas City. On this date, the elaborate air-rail service was terminated.

One of Brown's conditions of a mail award was the ability to fly at night, plus six months experience to prove it. United Avigation did not measure up to this. Its bid—64 per cent of the maximum rate allowed—was ridiculously low (TWA's was 97½ per cent and it lost $1,000,000 in the first year of operations). Also United Avigation would not co-operate with anyone else, whereas P.A.I.C. would; but this did not stop them protesting to the Comptroller General, who was acting as a kind of watchdog on the Postmaster General to try to prevent him from indulging in too blatant a series of indiscretions.

Displaying an admirable grasp of the complex opportunities open for manipulation of routes, Walter Brown played a trump card. He split the United Avigation Group by awarding the mail contract over United States Airways' Kansas City—St Louis route to American Airways which promptly sublet it to the sitting tenant. The temptation of the mail contract (at maximum rate) was too much for United States Airways, who deserted the shaky three-way partnership with its eastern associates.

The stock of TWA was divided between TAT, WAE, and P.A.I.C. in the ratio 47½:47½:5, respectively. Harris Hanshue was made president of the new company but relinquished this in July 1931. R. W. Robbins, of P.A.I.C., took over the presidency in September. The job was no sinecure, for by this time the airline was losing money at the rate of $200,000 per month and one of its Fokker F-XAs had crashed at Bazaar, Kansas. The casualties included Knute Rockne, the Notre Dame football coach, and the aviation industry, TWA, and Fokker could have had no greater adverse publicity had the victim been the President of the United States himself.

* The Aviation Corporation.

The wreckage of the TWA Fokker F-XA NC999E in Kansas on 31 March, 1931. The famous Notre Dame football coach Knute Rockne was killed and the resultant publicity brought about the end of commercial operation by Fokker wooden-winged monoplanes in the United States. (*Western Airlines*)

Eastern Air Transport

One of the more important routes involved in what may be termed the second wave of mail contracts was the New York—Atlanta route (CAM 19). The successful bidder was Pitcairn Aviation Inc, organized in Philadelphia on 15 September, 1927, for the purpose of participating both in aircraft manufacture and airline operation. The contract was awarded on 28 February, 1928, and service began on 1 May, with a fleet of eight Pitcairn PA-5 Mailwing biplanes. The service was operated at night, following completion of the lighted airway, and stopped at important cities such as Philadelphia, Baltimore, and Washington, in addition to Richmond, Virginia, and points in the Carolinas. Pitcairn obtained the maximum rate of $3 per lb, which probably goes some way to explain why it made no attempt to offer passenger service.

On 1 December, 1928, Pitcairn took over the Atlanta—Miami route from Florida Airways which had pioneered the route in 1926 as CAM 10 but had allowed it to lapse. The new contract was redesignated CAM 25, and Pitcairn thus gained possession of a priceless asset: an air route between the densely-populated northeast and the Florida vacationland. Pitcairn increased its fleet to 16 Mailwings, and on 1 April, 1929, consolidated its position by opening a branch line to Tampa.

Early in 1929, Pitcairn decided to concentrate on the manufacturing side of the business, and sold the airline, complete with mail contracts and fleet, to none other than Clement Melville Keys, the indefatigable airline

One of the Pitcairn PA-5 Mailwings used by Pitcairn Aviation on CAM 19 between New York and Atlanta.

promoter, who then resold it, on 10 July, 1929, to North American Aviation, the same that had substantial shareholdings in TAT and NAT. The main shareholders were the Curtiss-Wright Corporation and, with Keys as chairman of Pitcairn, plans were made to change the company's allegiance in the matter of flying equipment.

Possibly as an immediate result of this, the name was changed on 17 January, 1930, to Eastern Air Transport Inc. In June the route was extended northward to Boston, and passenger service was started as far south as Richmond on 18 August. With the assistance of three Ford Tri-

Pitcairn PA-6 Super-Mailwing NC353E used by Pitcairn Aviation. This aircraft continued in service after the company name had been changed to Eastern Air Transport.

NC185H, seen in Transcontinental Air Transport markings, was the first of the Model 18 Curtiss Condors. It was built in July 1929 and passed to Eastern Air Transport.

Motors and a couple of Fokker F-Xs as interim types until the Curtiss aircraft were available, Eastern settled down to a programme of steady expansion. On 10 December, 1930, the first Curtiss Condors and Kingbirds were placed into service, with twelve and seven passenger seats respectively.

Although most of the glamour associated with airline empire-building during the early 1930s was concentrated on the transcontinental airlines and the overseas system of Pan American Airways, Eastern was also sitting on a goldmine in terms of passenger potential. Linking all the major

NC985V was one of Eastern Air Lines' Curtiss Condor CO fleet.

Eastern Air Transport's Curtiss Model T32 Condor NC12353 which was built early in 1931.

cities of the northeastern seaboard, where the climate was uncharitable for several months in the year, with the sunshine-laden resort areas of Florida, there was a natural market ready to be exploited. The airline therefore took some practical steps to retain its grip, consolidating a near-monopoly by acquiring, first, on 15 July, 1931, New York Airways from Pan American, to add Atlantic City to the network, and second, on 15 February, 1933, Ludington Air Lines Inc, a non-mail competitor on the New York—Washington route, and one which provided a considerable challenge until the Postmaster General stepped in. Throughout 1931 Condor service was expanded considerably, and on 7 January, 1933, with these aircraft, Eastern began a through service from New York to Miami in one day.

Enter General Motors

Throughout the development history of the three major airlines outlined above, the name North American Aviation has been prominent from time to time as a potent force. Inspired by Clement Keys, it represented the effort of the Curtiss-Wright Corporation to embrace the operating side of aviation in order to provide a guaranteed market for the products of its manufacturing groups. North American had controlled National Air Transport, founded TAT (which had acquired stock in Northwest Airways), purchased Pitcairn Aviation, subsequently Eastern Air Transport, and had invested in Maddux Air Lines and Varney Air Lines in the West.

Concurrently with this thrust for financial control of a considerable section of the entire United States airline industry, another industrial giant had made far more modest inroads. General Motors, the largest motorcar manufacturer in the world, came on to the airline scene on the rebound of the TAT–WAE shotgun marriage. Harris Hanshue and James

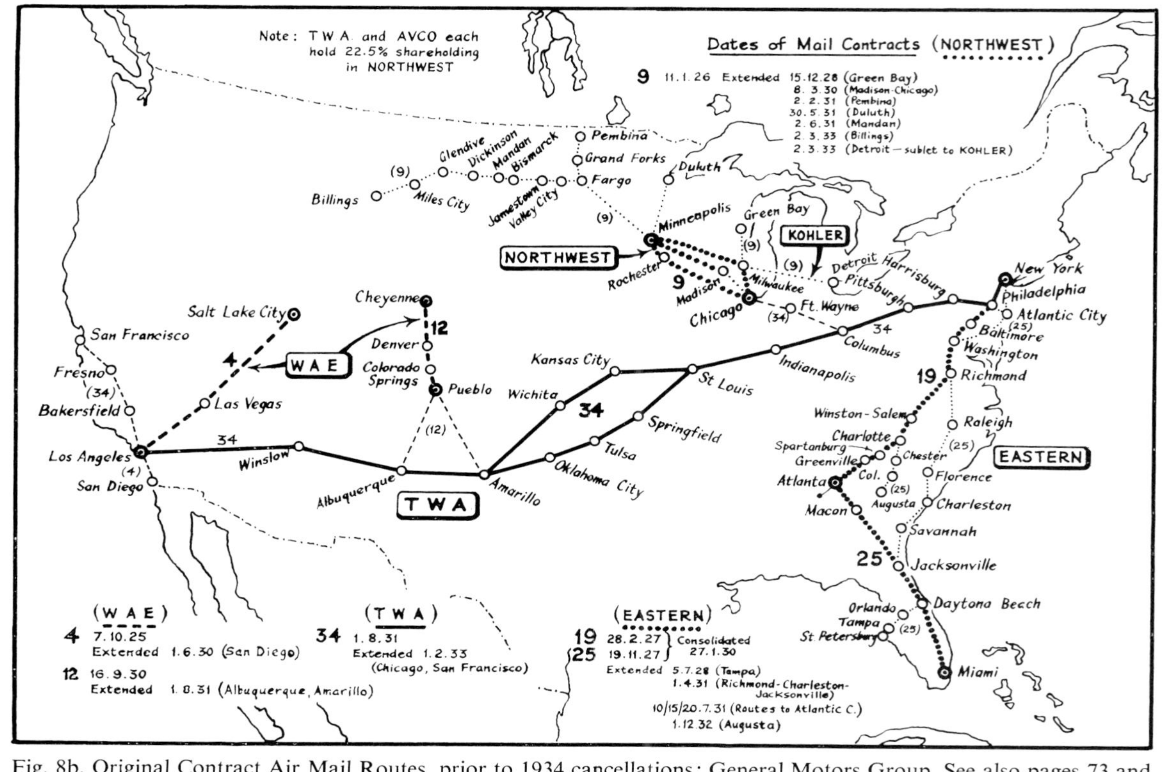

Fig. 8b. Original Contract Air Mail Routes, prior to 1934 cancellations: General Motors Group. See also pages 73 and 109

Talbot had resisted this merger because they had faith in the tremendous traffic potential of a coast-to-coast route terminating in Los Angeles, and had laid extravagant plans to obtain a lion's share of it. The formation of TWA left Western Air Express with a $47\frac{1}{2}$ per cent share in that airline —which proceeded to lose money at an astonishing rate—and, what was worse, decimated Western's own network, over the main part of which (through the acquisition of Maddux) their own subsidiary, TWA, was offering cut-throat competition with the parent company. In desperation, Western Air Express turned to General Motors for assistance. Through a newly-formed subsidiary, General Aviation Corporation, General Motors acquired effective control of Western Air Express, and with it control of the Fokker Aircraft Corporation which Hanshue and Talbot had bought in 1929. This transaction took place on 3 March, 1931, and cost General Motors a mere $90,000.

The Aviation Corporation

Many of these amalgamations and battles for power contained elements of romance and drama. But none was so fascinating as the story of the creation of American Airways. A late starter, in that the solid capital backing for an airline of national stature was not available until 1929, the rapidity with which the parent holding company engulfed one small company after another was astonishing. In fact, American quickly took its place as an equal amongst older established competitors, and had completed a coast-to-coast network by October 1930, albeit by an inconvenient route.

The inspiration which eventually led to the formation of American Airways may be said to have originated in Cincinnati. This was the home city of a fixed-base operator, the Embry-Riddle Company, started in 1925 by John Paul Riddle and T. Higbeen Embry with a capital of $10,000. In July 1927 the Post Office Department advertised the air mail contract (CAM 24) for the Cincinnati—Chicago route, and Embry-Riddle won it. Mail, express, and passenger service was started on 17 December, 1927, with three round trips per day, using Waco 10 biplanes.

An additional $90,000 was obtained from local businessmen, but this was insufficient to maintain an operation of the size demanded, and Embry-Riddle sought additional capital. One possible source was the Fairchild Aviation Corporation, as the Cincinnati partners were agents for Fairchild; but the Curtiss company began to make overtures, seeking an outlet for its products. Late in 1928, Sherman Fairchild learned of the Curtiss offer and suggested to the Fairchild board that, in order not to lose a good customer, they should step in quickly and invest in Embry-Riddle.

The Fairchild board went a little further than this, carried away possibly by the nationwide enthusiasm for aviation investment which was sweeping the financial world at this time. They agreed to organize a new subsidiary, with between $500,000 and $1,000,000, to finance not only Embry-Riddle, but also other transport operators, especially those with mail contracts.

This led to discussions between Fairchild and his banker friends, culminating in the formation of The Aviation Corporation (AVCO) on 3 March, 1929. The authorized capital was 10,000,000 shares, of which it was prepared to issue 2,000,000 at $20 per share. The issue was underwritten by Lehman Brothers and W. A. Harriman & Co at $17.50 per share, representing $35,000,000 paid into the company in cash. The AVCO board, consisting of 70 directors drawn from the higher echelons of American big business, proceeded forthwith to use the proceeds of the public sale to devour every airline or aviation interest which had so far escaped the clutches of Clement Keys, Fred Rentschler, or Harris Hanshue.

The first targets were themselves associations of several airlines, and by acquiring the Colonial Airways Corporation and the Universal Aviation Corporation between May and September 1929, AVCO had nine airlines under its belt within six months of setting up shop.

One of Colonial Western Airways' Pitcairn PA-5 Super-Mailwings which were used on the Mohawk Valley Cleveland—Albany route. (*American Airlines*)

Since beginning the New York—Boston mail and passenger service, Colonial Air Transport had acquired two sister airlines. On 17 December, 1927, Colonial Western Airways Inc began passenger, mail, and express service between Cleveland and Buffalo, via Erie, using Fairchild FC-2s. An extension to Albany was added on 1 June, 1928, via Rochester, Syracuse, Utica, and Schenectady. This Mohawk Valley mail route, CAM 20, also carried 850 passengers during its first year of operation.

Then on 6 March, 1928, Canadian Colonial Airways Inc was organized to operate Foreign Air Mail Route No. 1 (FAM-1) from New York to Montreal, via Albany, and services began to Canada on 1 October. Early in 1929, the three Colonial companies formed Colonial Airways Corpora-

Canadian Colonial Airways' Fairchild FC-2W2 NC8004 was used on FAM-1 between New York and Montreal. (*Smithsonian Institution*)

tion as a holding company, which also controlled Colonial flying schools, sales organizations, and other aviation interests; and it was this holding company which became part of the AVCO empire, in May 1929, by an exchange of stock.

Universal Aviation Corporation

Next on the list was the Universal Aviation Corporation which had been formed by a group of St Louis, Chicago, and Minneapolis investment bankers as Continental Airlines Corporation on 30 July, 1928, with a shareholding worth $2,300,000. The name was changed to Universal when the first service was opened, on 15 September, between Chicago and Cleveland, for passengers only. Universal owned five aircraft and employed only 25 staff, but this single route was eventually to form the lynch-pin in a coast-to-coast chain. In the $3\frac{1}{2}$ months to the end of 1928, 425 passengers were carried over the Chicago—Cleveland route.

On 31 December, Northern Air Lines and Robertson Aircraft Corporation were absorbed and the company became known as the Universal Air Lines System. Northern had started Chicago—Twin Cities passenger

A Fokker Super Universal of Universal Air Lines at St Louis at the end of 1929. (*H. B. Rueschenberg*)

service on 16 August, 1928, and although Universal's intention was to use Northern to extend beyond Minneapolis to the Dakotas, the idea was dropped. Furthermore the route to the Twin Cities was also surrendered as Northwest Airways was the favoured airline for Post Office mail contracts. Robertson, however, was immediately absorbed as an integral part of the Universal system. Not only was a mail contract involved (CAM 2) but the Chicago—St Louis route was another vital link in any possible east-west route system.

Robertson had made some headway since winning the mail contract in 1926. Early in 1928 an arrangement was made with the Illinois Central Railroad for ticket interchange, and passenger services began on 20 August, 1928. Universal bought the Robertsons out for $300,000. The latter joined up with C. M. Keys to form the Curtiss-Robertson Company, to build the Curtiss Robin. Retaining the corporate identity, the Robertson Aircraft Corporation was awarded the mail contract, CAM 28, for the St Louis—Kansas City—Omaha route, the first segment of which was a valuable westward extension to the Universal system.

The usual single-engined Pitcairn, Stearman, and Travel Air aircraft were used, and later a six-seat Fokker Super Universal and two Boeing 40B-4s were added. One ex-pilot recalls that he used to allow a passenger to sit in the right-hand seat, baggage on lap, and control column squeezed between them.

Universal next acquired Continental Airlines, originally organized in Ohio on 10 October, 1927, and which had started mail and passenger service on the Cleveland—Louisville route (CAM 16) on 1 August, 1928, using Travel Air 6000s, with an eastward extension to Akron on 15 November of that year. Next was Braniff Air Lines, formerly Paul R. Braniff Inc, organized in May 1928 by the brothers Paul and Tom Braniff, with backing from two Oklahoma oil companies, starting passenger service (no mail contract) on 20 June with four Stinson Detroiter aircraft. Last to enter the Universal fold was Central Airlines, another passenger line founded in 1928, operating between Tulsa and Wichita, with an extension to Kansas City from May 1929.

Airlines such as Braniff and Central had come in on the aviation boom in a rich area where fast passenger transport was at a premium. Tom Braniff, particularly, was highly successful at first, and carried 3,000 passengers by the end of the year on his *Tulsa-Oklahoma City Airline*, which was extended south to Dallas and Fort Worth on 11 February, 1929.

Both Braniff and Central—like many a promising airline of the day—found the operation of exclusive passenger services economically impossible without the supplement of a mail contract to provide a basic source of revenue. From Universal's point of view, a mail contract was of course welcome as part of the assets of one of its victims; but if the airline route network, however small, provided another link towards fulfilling its ambition to create a transcontinental route, this was sufficient incentive for the take-over.

Paul R. Braniff Inc's original Stinson SM-1 Detroiter was used on the *Tulsa-Oklahoma City Airline* in 1928. (*Braniff International Airways*)

Braniff's Travel Air 4000D 6239 *Daily Oklahoman* of 1929. Between the cockpits are the words Paul R. Braniff Pilot. (*The Smithsonian Institution*)

Braniff's Travel Air Model 6000 C6458. In the background is a Hamilton Metalplane.

Throughout most of 1929 Universal Aviation Corporation was in the process of welding a series of small airlines into a cohesive whole. Its ambition was to undertake an ambitious transcontinental air-rail scheme, on the lines of TAT (described more fully in the next chapter). The last acquisition was made in July 1929, when another tentacle of the octopus-like network reached out to northern Texas, when the Amarillo Airport Corporation closed down its route to Tulsa. Shortly afterwards, Universal itself was absorbed by the fast-moving Aviation Corporation.

Universal Air Lines System's prototype Fokker F-32. The aircraft crashed on take-off on its inaugural service flight and the airline cancelled its outstanding order for four.

The short, eventful, career of Universal was typical of the unpredictable and haphazard business methods employed during the wildest part of the aviation boom period. To quote a commentary made during the early 1930s: 'To figure out exactly how much cash or the equivalent of cash was paid into the Universal system, and remained in the various companies, is a puzzle which is almost impossible to solve. For example, Northern Air Lines Inc was organized in 1928, and except for ten shares of its stock issued for cash, totalling $1,000, 990 of its shares were issued to Northern Aeronautics Inc in return for the transfer of an account receivable from Universal Aviation Corporation, amounting to $72,000, which had been given in the first place by Universal to Northern Aeronautics in return for the assumption by the company of the obligation to repay certain advances totalling approximately $98,000 made to individuals, while Northern Aeronautics, in turn, issued its 5,000 shares of no par stock to

Loading mail onto a Stearman LT-1 at Wichita. The LT-1 was developed for Interstate Airlines. Three were operated and C8832 (c/n 2002), illustrated, is known to have passed to American Airways. (*American Airlines*)

Universal Aviation Corporation in exchange for stock of Universal Aviation Corporation and approximately 1,000 shares of stock of Mid-plane Sales and Transit Co. Who got what and who got paid?'

Some loose ends were neatly tied up in the St Louis—Chicago—Cincinnati triangle when the Aviation Corporation acquired Embry-Riddle—where the germ of the idea behind an amalgamated company was first born—and Interstate Airlines, which had been organized in June 1928 and began mail and passenger service on the CAM 30 route from Chicago to Atlanta on 1 December of that year. This important connection between the Great Lakes and the southeast had the added attraction to AVCO of linking Louisville, the terminus of Continental Airlines, with the Universal system hub at St Louis through two feeder lines from the north-south main route at Evansville. Interstate boasted a fleet of twelve aircraft, including seven Fairchilds and three Stearmans.

Fokker Super Universal NC8030 of St Tammany-Gulf Coast Airways. (*Courtesy Peter M. Bowers*)

Southern Air Transport

The final contribution to the pool which finally amalgamated to become American Airways was the Southern Air Transport System, of Fort Worth. This was another collection of airlines, rather like Universal, and added immensely to the area covered by the AVCO network, from Atlanta (the southern terminus of the former Interstate line) to El Paso, in the far west of Texas, and a seven-league stride towards the completion of a transcontinental route.

Originally, St Tammany-Gulf Coast Airways Inc had been incorporated in New Orleans with a capital of $85,000. It began passenger service on a route from New Orleans to Atlanta, via Mobile and Birmingham, on 20 August, 1927, adding mail service (CAM 23) using mainly Fokker equipment, on 1 May, 1928. In October 1928, Gulf Air Lines was organized by New Orleans interests with $225,000 additional capital as a holding company, and the St Tammany part of the name of the operating subsidiary

Texas Air Transport's Fokker Super Universal C8033.

was dropped. On 23 January, 1929, a mail service was opened to Houston, (CAM 29) and, shortly afterwards, the company merged with Texas Air Transport to form the Southern Air Transport System.

Texas Air Transport had been founded by Temple Bowen, a tough bus operator from Fort Worth, on 12 November, 1927. He started mail service from Galveston to Dallas (CAM 21) and passenger/mail service from Brownsville to Dallas (CAM 22) on 6 February, 1928, using a fleet of seven Pitcairn Mailwings. He expanded quickly in the spring of the following year, to San Antonio on 9 March, and El Paso on 16 March, with mail, adding passenger service within a few weeks.

The president of Southern Air Transport was A. P. Barrett, a Tennessee businessman and politician. Among the officers of the company was the vice-president and treasurer, C. R. Smith. Upon merging, the system was divided into three operating divisions, Texas Air Transport Inc and Gulf Air Lines Inc being Divisions 1 and 2 respectively, while all the passenger services were operated under the name of Texas Flying Service Inc. Stearman J-5s, Pitcairn Super-Mailwings, and Travel Airs were used for the mail runs; Fokker Super Universals, Travel Airs, and Curtiss Robins on passenger routes. Southern became part of the AVCO empire in January 1930, with Smith one of its more promising executives.

American Airways

The foregoing passages have chronicled the various companies which went into forming American Airways, on 25 January, 1930, as a means of tidying up the sprawling, interwoven structure of the airline operating companies controlled by AVCO. The authorized capital was 40,000 shares of preferred stock, at $100, and 10,000 shares of no par value common stock. Immediately prior to the merger, the Aviation Corporation owned 95 per cent of the Colonial Airways Corporation (three airlines), Southern Air Transport System (two airlines) and the Universal Aviation Corporation (six airlines); a substantial interest in

Embry-Riddle; and 100 per cent of Interstate, plus Alaskan Airways, which was an attempt by AVCO to get into the Alaskan Star Route mail contracts, competing with dog teams. Though theoretically possible to travel from Boston or New York all the way to El Paso by a combination of airlines operating under Aviation Corporation control, to do so in practice was a task reserved for the seekers of novelty. Still, it was a system of sorts, incorporating thousands of miles of routes, holding no·less than eleven mail contracts, and owning a substantial fleet of mail and passenger aircraft.

But the corporate structure was a mess. For example, the management and control of the operations of Colonial Air Transport, between Newark and Boston, was through Colonial Airways Corporation, while the control of Texas Air Transport was through Southern Air Transport. Both subsidiary companies, Southern Air Transport and Colonial Airways Corporation, had their own boards of directors, and although Aviation Corporation had substantial representation on each board, the membership of each board was by no means identical; and in exercising control through the boards of the subsidiary companies, consideration had to be given to the interests of the minority stockholders.

This U.S. Mail Pitcairn Mailwing bears on its fuselage the title Universal Division American Airways and also Robertson Aircraft Corp. A large landing light can be seen beneath the starboard lower wing. (*Courtesy Peter M. Bowers*)

Little wonder that Aviation Corporation sought to simplify such a situation. A proposal was made to all the subholding companies to sell to American Airways all stock in return for common stock of the latter, in proportion to the relative value of the assets of each of the former. The total was to be 10,000 shares, par value $1,000,000, of the preferred stock. The proposal was accepted by all companies involved, except Embry-Riddle Aviation Corporation. The reorganization was completed on 1 February, 1930, with 2,226 shares going to Colonial, 2,074 to Southern, 4,288 to Universal, and 1,025 to Aviation Corporation (Interstate, Alaskan, and Cuban Aviation Corporation). Embry-Riddle did not accept the 387 shares offered. The result was that all the operating subsidiaries came under direct control of American Airways, which, in turn, was controlled by its four stockholders, Aviation Corporation, Colonial Airways Corporation, Southern Air Transport, and Universal Aviation Corporation.

The Big Four

This chapter has dealt with a vital period in the history of the United States airline industry. By a complex mixture of industrial aggrandisement involving ruthless competition, substantial governmental influence amounting almost to control, and a great deal of native intelligence and vision, there emerged from an undisciplined rabble of airlines four major companies of substance. Almost thirty small airlines (some of which would rank only as air taxi operators in the 1970s) lost their identities to become (in order of the establishment of the corporate names by which they quickly became known) Eastern Air Transport (17 January, 1930), American Airways (25 January, 1930), TWA (25 October, 1930), and United Air Lines (1 July, 1931). This order of merit is, of course, purely academic, as the process was gradual—if the development of four great airlines in about two years, virtually from scratch, can be described as gradual. United, for example, was already operating as a unit long before it adopted its permanent name, while American was still operating as a disjointed collection of separate companies many months after the merger.

At the beginning of this chapter, reference was made to the existence of the Big Five, to include Western Air Express. The TWA shotgun marriage effectively killed the Californian airline's chances of marching with the mighty. Postmaster General Brown dealt Western a body blow from which it took years to recover. By any objective review, Talbot and Hanshue had a raw deal and every right to feel bitter. No airline had done more to pioneer aviation in a wholly sensible and constructive manner, and a review of the statistics shows that at the time of its eclipse it had far more experience, was carrying more passengers, and making more money than the airline to which it was forced to sell its birthright.

Such are the injustices of history. Leaving behind the ashes of defunct local airlines and parochial lost causes, the Big Four entered into competition for the biggest domestic air route of all, the transcontinental, with its promise of vast mail payments as the reward for efficient service.

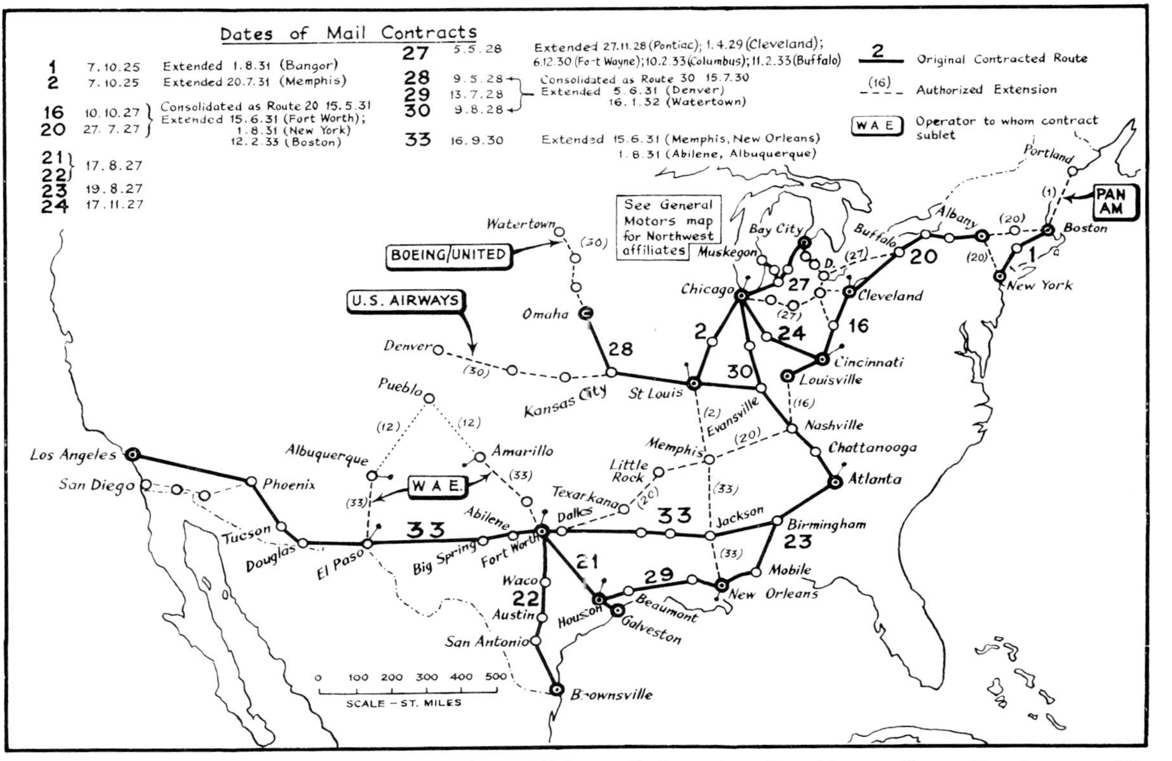

Fig. 8c. Original Contract Air Mail Routes, prior to 1934 cancellations: American Airways Group. See also pages 73 and 98.

Northwest Airways' Hamilton H-47 NC134E, seen in 1931. This picture is believed to have been taken at Valley City, North Dakota.

CHAPTER FIVE

Spanning the Continent

Walter Folger Brown

The former Secretary of Commerce under the Coolidge administration, Herbert Hoover, became President of the United States on 4 March, 1929. During his first year of office the world witnessed a dramatic statistical increase in air transport in the U.S.A. to the point where it overhauled acknowledged European pace-setters in the field (*See Figure 6*). Hoover was entitled to much of the credit for this accomplishment; for he it was who applied most of the pressure on President Coolidge to push through the Air Commerce Act.

Hoover had also observed that the early civil airlines lived or died on their relative success with mail contracts under the Kelly Act. From his point of view, therefore, the appointment of a staunch supporter and former assistant secretary in the Commerce Department to the key political post of Postmaster General did more than reward loyalty with high office;

it put into a position of great power a man who not only had some experience in transport affairs but was fired with the same ambition as Hoover's to weld the United States air transport industry into a cohesive and logical shape.

The man was Walter Folger Brown, a Toledo attorney. He immediately set about the task of examining the whole structure of air transport in the U.S.A. as a prerequisite to streamlining the air mail service. Methodical, thorough, and patient, Brown took many months digesting the facts. During his first year of office, he took no decisive step. But towards the end of 1929 there were straws in the wind. On 7 November he chose not to renew the first five mail contracts (CAM 1–5), electing instead to extend them for a period of six months. To those who could read between the lines, Brown was obviously not satisfied with the state of mail contracts under the Kelly Act.

He had cause for dissatisfaction. Of all the 32 mail contracts issued up to that date, only one combination offered a mail service over the transcontinental route, where the benefits of the faster service which the aeroplane offered could be most effective. There were others which covered distances of about 1,000 miles but these were few. In short, the air mail map was a patchwork quilt, looking decidedly threadbare in places.

Rail-Air

If the air mail network had its shortcomings, at least it was better than the passenger airline system—if such a disjointed collection of sporadic services could be called a system. Commercial aircraft were neither fast enough to offer substantial time savings over the railways, nor did they offer much comfort. Passengers could be forgiven for not leaping aboard aeroplanes in great numbers. There were, of course, exceptions. California, with its two large prosperous cities connected only by a meandering railway, was a natural happy hunting ground for prospective pioneer passenger airlines. (This is a case where history repeats itself—new airlines still continue to spring up.) Elsewhere, however, passenger lines did not flourish; for example, there was no passenger service south of Washington. North American Aviation, later Eastern Air Transport, did not introduce such facilities until 18 August, 1930.

One problem was a certain apprehension about flying by night. This was shared by operator and client, whether the Post Office Department or the paying passenger. At this time, the science of navigation by instruments and the use of radio was in its infancy in the United States, and the ability to fly during the hours of darkness rested entirely upon the dependence on the lighted airway, which was extended during the late 1920s to cover most of the main inter-city routes.

In the summer of 1929, a few airlines circumvented the dangers of night flying by organizing some ingenious schemes by which a route was divided into sections, with aircraft performing the daytime journey and the railways providing service at night. The most famous of these was the *Lindbergh Line* operated by Transcontinental Air Transport (TAT). This was a 48-hr service from New York to Los Angeles, using Ford 5-AT Tri-Motors in conjunction with the trains of the Pennsylvania and Santa Fe Railroads. As TAT was the founding airline of what was to become one of the Big Four of modern times, its formation and manner of business, including details of the route, have already been described.

Whilst TAT's was the most ambitious of the transcontinental air-rail services, starting on 7 July, 1929, the fastest and most luxurious combination across the United States, it was not the first*. Three weeks before TAT's inaugural flight, the Universal Aviation Corporation opened a 67-hr service from New York to Los Angeles on 14 June, 1929. The first part of the journey was performed in the *Southwestern Limited* of the New York Central Railroad as far as Cleveland. Universal's Fokker F-XAs then took over as far as Garden City, Kansas, via Chicago, St Louis, and Kansas City. The remainder of the journey was by the Atchison, Topeka, and Santa Fe Railroad, quite happy to serve more than one airline. On this inaugural journey, Mrs Mabel Walker Willebrandt, former Assistant Attorney General, and counsel for Universal, carried a quart bottle of Atlantic sea water to California.

Western Air Express may possibly dispute even Universal's claim as the first transcontinental air-rail service, for Harris Hanshue extended his airline's eastern route as far as Kansas City on 1 June, 1929, and the passenger had a fair selection of railways from which to choose his journey to New York. This combination suffered, however, from the rigid partition of the territory served by U.S. railways, with the traditional breaks at Chicago or St Louis. Thus, Universal's system had the merit of avoiding rail changes, except on interchange with aircraft; whilst TAT brought to a fine art the technique of making a virtue out of necessity, portraying the train-aircraft interchange at Port Columbus as a new step forward in transport progress.

On 4 August, 1929, a third transcontinental air-rail system came into use. Once again, the New York Central Railroad was involved, with passengers taking a 1.15 a.m. train to St Louis, where Southwest Air Fast Express (SAFE, of which more later) transferred them to Ford 5-ATs as far as Sweetwater, Texas. The Texas and Pacific Railway provided the overnight trip as far as El Paso, whence Jack Frye's Standard Airlines took over for the rest of the journey. The whole coast-to-coast adventure took about the same time as Universal's, assuming all systems running on time, and making connections.

For a time Western Air Express contemplated a hook-up with Universal, at the common point, Kansas City. A WAE/Universal link would have made possible an all-air service from Los Angeles to Cleveland, with only the New York Central's participation required to negotiate the diffi-

*The chronology of reduction in transcontinental air times is shown in Table 7, page 591.

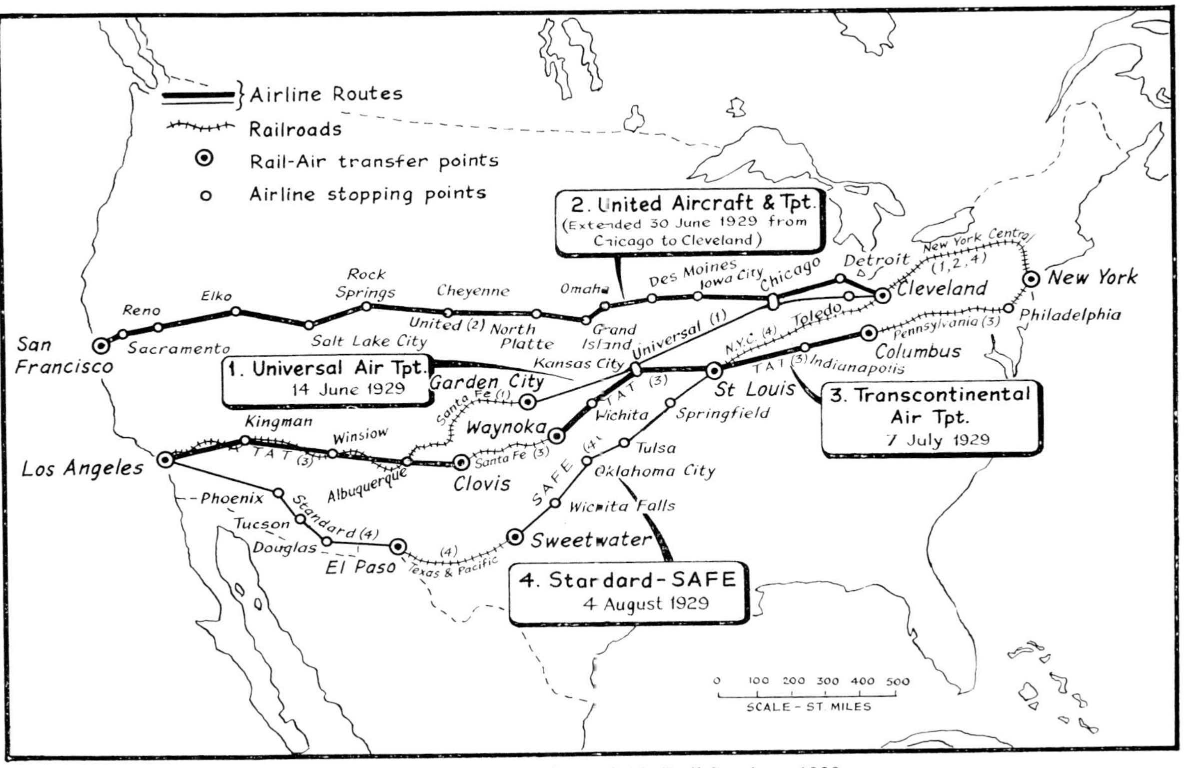

Fig. 11. Transcontinental Air-Rail Services, 1929.

cult terrain through New York State where, in any case, neither air company had much wish to fly without a mail contract.

Such an amalgamation of Californian and Midwestern interests was forestalled by the formation of American Airways on 25 January, 1930. This attempted to bring under one corporate organization the many aviation and assorted companies which the Aviation Corporation had taken under its wing—or ensnared in its web. In fact, whatever objectives may have been attained, the improvement of the route structure was hardly a blinding success; for although certain unprofitable lines were terminated—mainly because of the lack of a mail contract—those which were left could never be described as a viable system.

Theoretically, a passenger could travel from New York to El Paso by American Airways. But this involved, first of all, a trip due north up the Hudson as far as Albany (formerly a Canadian Colonial route); then along the Mohawk Valley to Cleveland (Colonial Western); on to Fort Worth (Universal); and finally to El Paso (Southern Air Transport). The Southern Pacific Railroad did the honours for the last part of the route to Los Angeles.

This was obviously unsatisfactory. It was far worse from the passenger's point of view than travelling coast-to-coast in the 1960s by a combination of Local Service airlines. To Walter F. Brown, with his eye mainly on the goal of creating a co-ordinated and comprehensive air mail route system, the whole industry appeared chaotic. After many months of gestation, his plans took shape. He conceived a method of air mail payment which, backed by suitable direction from himself in the matter of route networks, would achieve the dual purpose of improving air mail service and encouraging passenger travel. The first requirement was a change in the law regarding air mail payments.

The Watres Act

The Third Amendment to the Air Mail Act of 1925 (the Kelly Act) was approved by Congress on 29 April, 1930. It was sponsored by Senator Charles D. McNary, Republican, Oregon, and Representative Laurence H. Watres, Republican, Pennsylvania; and became known as the McNary-Watres, or plain Watres, Act. Its real architects, however, were Walter F. Brown and his second assistant, Warren Irving Glover, in charge of air mail. They were aided and abetted by three energetic lobbyists, William MacCracken, former Assistant Secretary of Commerce, now representing Western Air Express, Mabel Walker Willebrandt, representing Aviation Corporation, and Col Paul Henderson, former Second Assistant Postmaster General in charge of air mail, now representing—albeit reluctantly—National Air Transport, part of the United Air Lines group.

The main provisions of the Watres Act were as follows:

(a) Any air mail contractor with two years' operating experience could exchange his current contract for a ten-year route certificate, thus giving permanence to his contractual authority and stimulating long-term investment. Pioneer rights were to be recognized.

(b) The system of payment by weight of mail carried would be replaced by a system of payment by space offered. The maximum rate would be $1.25 per mile, to be paid whether or not the space was filled. This was aimed to reduce the potential revenue per flight from mail alone and eradicate anomalous situations whereby some carriers could earn four times more from mail payments than they could from passenger service.

(c) The Postmaster General could extend or consolidate routes 'when in his judgement the public interest will be promoted thereby'—in other words where such extensions appeared to improve the nation-wide system of mail routes.

In the original bill, there was a clause which would have given Brown even more dictatorial powers than he eventually received. This was to dispense with competitive bidding, leaving the selection of airline company entirely to the discretion—or whim—of the Postmaster General. But after a running battle with the Comptroller General, John McCarl, this clause was removed.

Virtually every clause in the Watres Act was worded in such a way as to exclude small airlines, thus favouring Brown's strongly and sincerely-held conviction that the salvation of the United States airline industry depended on its being concentrated in giant corporations. The definition of an air mail contractor with pioneer rights included the phrase '. . . lowest responsible bidder, who has owned and operated an air transportation service on a fixed daily schedule over a distance of not less than two hundred and fifty miles and for a period of not less than six months prior to the advertisement for bids'. This cut out the chances of many pioneer companies.

When the advertisements appeared, there was also a requirement that bidders should have flown at night for at least six months over a 250-mile route. This was not written into the Watres Act but Brown always claimed it as a justifiable measure on the grounds of safety. This again weighed heavily against the little men. In fact it ruled out one of the big men, TAT; but in the squabbling which accompanied the shotgun marriage of TAT and WAE, the illegality of the night-flying requirement does not appear to have been challenged.

Walter Brown also intended an extremely wide interpretation of the extension and consolidation clause. Given half a chance, he would turn a bare 250-mile route into a transcontinental system, if he considered such a step to be 'in the public interest'.

Armed with the Watres Act, therefore, the Postmaster General set about the task of re-drawing the United States airline map. Determined and dedicated, resolved to use the authority of his office to the utmost, he wasted no time, and literally within a fortnight of the passing of the Act, took the first fateful steps in a crusade which was to make airline history.

The 'Spoils Conferences'

Between 15 May and 9 June, 1930, Walter F. Brown held a series of meetings in his office in Washington. They were not secret; but the intention to hold them was given the minimum of publicity, and actual invitations to attend were given only to a chosen few. So quickly did the conferences fall upon the heels of the Watres Act that any ambitious operator aspiring to take advantage of the situation would have had to be an extremely keen follower of the aviation press and to have had an ear close to the ground in the corridors of the Post Office Department.

Thus, the men invited were those privileged to find favour, because they were the representatives of large corporations. Brown was convinced, quite sincerely, that the future of United States airlines rested on their being firmly based both in experience and capital resources. He had no time for small airlines with one or two 100-mile routes and purely local interests: '. . . we were not buying peanuts and pencils and pig iron; we were buying a service that was highly specialized and exceedingly hazardous, and there was no sense in taking the government's money and dishing it out to every little fellow that was flying around the map and was not going to do anything.'

An impartial inspection of the ranks of airlines operating at the time reveals that, by any criteria of economic or operational common sense, Brown was right. But the cold facts were that the privileged few invited to Brown's office represented United Aircraft, the Aviation Corporation, Western Air Express, TAT, Eastern Air Transport, and the Stout Line (by this time part of United), and that these companies obtained all but two of the twenty-two air mail contracts awarded under the provisions of the Watres Act.

In judging Brown's actions, one thing is clear: he was no monopolist. Indeed, in the major objective, the establishment of permanent transcontinental air services, both passenger and mail, the principle of competition was the key factor. The airline officials attending the conferences were few in number, and each knew fairly well that, barring unforeseen accidents, a rich prize was his for the asking. Yet the participants watched each other like hawks, and although deals were undoubtedly made, none took chances and no agreements were made under the 'Old Pals Act'. Moreover, everyone disliked the Postmaster General, whom they regarded as an immorally powerful agent of Washington bureaucracy.

Brown wanted two transcontinental routes, additional to the existing United Aircraft Boeing/NAT line from New York to San Francisco. He also insisted that they should each be operated by one company, and was not interested in an interchange arrangement, even by as few as two air-

Walter Folger Brown (*left*), Postmaster General during the Hoover Administration of 1929–33, was the architect of the major U.S. airline route networks which survive today. By ingenious manipulation of air mail contracts, using his almost-dictatorial authority, he rationalized an unco-ordinated system of dozens of small companies into the nucleus of the Domestic Trunk airlines. His single-minded policy involved some questionable activities which led to an inquiry, followed by the Air Mail Scandal investigations early in 1934. C. E. Woolman (*right*) began his career as an aerial crop-duster in the 1920s, and founded Delta Air Service in 1929. Until the 1950s, Delta's progress was no more than the industry's average, but a series of beneficial route awards, combined with good aircraft selection, created a quiet revolution. Delta is now threatening to augment the ranks of the Big Four.

lines. One was to be the 'central' route from New York to Los Angeles, via such cities as Pittsburgh and St Louis; the other was to be the 'southern' route from Atlanta to Los Angeles, via Dallas. Of these, the central route was quickly disposed of, albeit with some acrimony, by the device of forcing a merger between TAT and WAE to form TWA. In this case, Brown was responsible for sponsoring the creation of an airline that was to become one of the Big Four airlines of the United States, and as such has been dealt with in the preceding chapter.

The Southern Transcontinental

The case of the southern transcontinental route was far more complicated. First of all, Eastern Air Transport had a plan to associate with a small company called Delta Air Service, formed by C. E. Woolman, who had founded the world's first commercial crop-dusting company in 1925. Delta had started a service from Atlanta to Birmingham on 16 June, 1929, and extended this to Dallas, via Jackson, Mississippi, and other points in August of that year. Eastern planned to link up with Delta at a common point, Atlanta, and by use of the extension powers written into the Watres Act, to win the mail contract for at least a substantial part of the southern transcontinental route, subletting that part over which Delta had pioneer rights.

This plan was short-lived, however, as an important reservation was fed into the extension clause by the Comptroller General, John McCarl, who ruled that an extension must not be longer than the original route. This decision was taken and enforced on 24 July, 1930—in connection with an ambitious programme involving Northwest Airways—and put an end to any possibility of Eastern Air Transport becoming a transcontinental airline at that time. Delta was thus disqualified by the Postmaster General's night-flying provision, in spite of its fine record and pioneer rights, and forced to sell out to American Airways.

Bids were called for on the two additional transcontinental routes on 25 August, 1930. American, the newly formed airline of the Aviation Corporation, appeared to have the field to itself. Eastern had lost out under the extension clause, TAT and WAE were virtually forced into the central route, United was already in possession of a route, and Northwest was interested elsewhere. Everything looked nice and comfortable, except for one thing: the exasperating interference of Erle P. Halliburton, the owner of Southwest Air Fast Express (SAFE), known familiarly as SAFEway.

This airline began operations on 2 April, 1929, over a network of routes radiating from Tulsa, in the heart of the Oklahoma oil country. A fleet of nine Ford Tri-Motors (14-seater 5-ATs) carried passengers to Kansas City, St Louis, Fort Worth, and Dallas at about 6c per mile, or only about 50 per cent higher than rail fares. The service was popular because the extra fare was considered most reasonable by the affluent travellers in the oil country, the equipment was reliable, and both the climate and the terrain offered few hazards to flying. Nevertheless, Halliburton did not quite break even and needed only a mail contract of modest proportions to put him in the black.

In the summer of 1929, SAFEway had been one of the partners in a short-lived air-rail transcontinental scheme, but on 21 November, 1929, it went a step further. Under the provisions of the old Kelly Air Mail Act, Halliburton had applied to the Post Office Department for a transcontinental mail route, to be operated by SAFEway and its affiliate Southern Skylines. Encouraged by the high returns on his passenger business, he offered to carry the mail from New York to Los Angeles for $2.10 per pound, or less than one quarter of the going rate from Washington to Los Angeles by the most direct route, and slightly less than one third of the cheapest New York—Los Angeles tariff involving a change of aircraft and operator at Salt Lake City.

This did not fit in with Walter Brown's plans at all, and Halliburton got nowhere with the Post Office Department. But the Oklahoman had plenty of fight in him and began to thrash around in all directions—with conspicuous success. His first gambit was to enrol the support of William B. Mayo, of the Ford Motor Company, with whom he had some influence through being a good customer. Mayo was *persona grata* in Washington, and through him, Halliburton made a nuisance of himself.

Brown met his match in Halliburton on the night-flying clause included in the Post Office Department's advertisements for bids on the mail contracts. Halliburton read all the small print in the McNary-Watres Act and could not find a trace of a reference to night flying. From then on there was no holding him. He wrote to politicians, pointing out the illegality, threatened court action, suggested an investigation into the Post Office Department, and made it clear that he would involve the President of the United States if necessary.

On this point of controversy, there is much to be said in Brown's defence. As he later claimed, the original Air Mail Act empowered the Postmaster General to make such regulations as were necessary to carry out the provisions of the act. As the ability to fly at night was obviously desirable in the 1930 mail contracts, it was up to the Postmaster General to ensure that the successful bidder had the necessary qualifications. And six months' experience over a 250-mile route was demonstrably a reasonable proof. Still, the matter was never finally settled in a court of law, as another solution was found to the problem of what to do with Mr Halliburton.

To put no finer point on it, American Airways bought out Mr Halliburton for the sum of $1,400,000, which was roughly double the book value of the latter's assets. The way in which it was done provides a prime example of financial manipulation. It certainly provided some good ammunition for the investigators of Brown's activities when the Democratic Party swept into office in 1933.

American Airways was obviously not qualified to bid for the southern transcontinental route under the McNary-Watres Act, because it had only been founded for a few months, but fortunately the corporate identity of the original ancestors of that many-tentacled airline had been preserved. One of these was Robertson Aircraft Corporation, the original holder of CAM 2 from Chicago to St Louis. Robertson and SAFEway submitted a joint bid for the southern route under an agreement that if the contract were obtained, it would be sublet to a new company in which each would take an equal interest.

The joint bidders predictably received the contract, Atlanta—Los Angeles (CAM 33) on 15 October, 1930, and immediately sublet it to a new company, Southern Air Fast Express, subsequently Southern Transcontinental Airways Inc. The route was operated under this name until 30 June, 1931, when the subcontract was terminated and the original contract again sublet by Robertson direct to American Airways, which by now had come of age in Watres Act terms. In the meantime, American had purchased the one-half interest in Southern Transcontinental held by Southwest Air Fast Express, and Southern Transcontinental Airways was dissolved.

American got the money to pay off Halliburton from TWA. There was an agreement between the two airlines that, if each got the route it wanted, TWA would pay American $284,500 for 'an interest in the hangar and some property in Tulsa', plus $1,115,000 for 20,000 shares of Western Air Express held by American.

A great deal hinged on TWA's fortunes and in particular the disposal of the claims of United Avigation. Thus considerable pressure was exerted on the key figure of N. A. Letson, president of one of the component parts of United Avigation, United States Airways, which operated a passenger service from St Louis to Denver, via Kansas City.

Brown awarded a mail contract over the St Louis—Kansas City portion of this route to American on 15 July, 1930. American sublet it to United States Airways. United Avigation collapsed. TWA received its transcontinental award on 30 September, 1930, paid its $1,400,000 to American, who bought out SAFEway and Erle Halliburton.

At the same time, American Airways bought Standard Airlines from Western Air Express, which on 1 May had extended its route system as far east as Dallas, the inaugural service being flown by Jack Frye, the founder of Standard, in a Fokker F-X. So, by a remarkable series of quasi- and complete take-overs—Delta from Atlanta to Dallas, Standard from Dallas to Los Angeles, and SAFEway from nearly everywhere into oblivion—American was granted its coveted southern transcontinental route, CAM 33, on 16 September, 1930, and began service on 15 October.

Coast-to-Coast by American

Whether by accident or design the total number of mail contracts held at that time by American Airways was thirteen. Although superstition was probably not one of Postmaster General Brown's more obvious weaknesses, he nevertheless set about the task of reducing this number. By scrutiny of all the evidence, there are strong grounds for assuming that this was another gambit in the fascinating game of chess he was conducting with the Comptroller General, John McCarl. McCarl had ruled that extensions longer than the original route were illegal; but there was nothing wrong with the idea of consolidating two or more routes into one, provided they could readily be identified as a route in the sense that it went 'from somewhere to somewhere' (as Brown defined a route). By this

An American Airways Southern Division Fokker F-XA. (*Gordon S. Williams*)

This Pitcairn Super-Mailwing appears to be a PA-6 model. In the cockpit area it bears the legend American Airways Colonial Division and on the forward fuselage Colonial Western Airways Inc CAM 20. The registration is thought to be NC7856. (*American Airlines*)

means, involving a large measure of mathematical and geographical juggling, American Airways achieved a link from New York to Los Angeles, via Nashville and Dallas.

This desirable objective traced its origins in two modest contract air mail routes: CAM 16, Cleveland to Louisville, originally awarded to Continental Air Lines on 10 October, and CAM 20, Cleveland to Albany, originally awarded to Colonial Western Airways on 27 July, 1927. Route 16 was extended from Louisville to Nashville on 2 March, 1931, and then consolidated with Route 20, to form a new Route 20, from Albany to Nashville. Thus the original 463-mile Route 20 had more than doubled its length to 980 miles.

By two more extensions, Albany to New York on 15 June, 1931, and Nashville to Fort Worth on 1 August, 1931, this 980-mile route was almost doubled again, to 1,799 miles. Here it connected with the now well-established Route 33, the Southern Transcontinental, and the link from New York to California was complete.

Compared with American's former itinerary which had zig-zagged its way across the United States, the Nashville direct route was an improvement. Even so, the first part of the journey was somewhat laborious in practice, and American did not trouble to advertise it seriously. Although theoretically able to travel by air all the way, the passenger had to start northwards up the Hudson River route, much in the same way as in 1929 when Universal launched its air-rail service in conjunction with the New York Central Railroad. Thus American's transcontinental route in

1931 was still a train/plane service, using the Pennsylvania Railroad as far as Columbus, and involving an overnight stop at Fort Worth.

Another example of unorthodox lengthening of an original route—and grafting a substantial bough on to the trunk—was CAM 30. This was first let to Interstate Airlines on 9 August, 1928, and linked Chicago with Atlanta, via Evansville, whence a spur line went to St Louis. This spur was consolidated on 15 July, 1930, with CAM 28, St Louis to Omaha, via Kansas City. On 5 June, 1931, this route was once again extended, from Kansas City to Denver, a distance of 544 miles, which, for once, was no longer than the original route. American sublet this extension to United States Airways, perhaps as an operational convenience, perhaps for favours rendered.

Then on 16 January, 1932, in a kind of Solomon's judgement, Brown awarded American an extension from Omaha to Watertown. Hardly conforming to the principle of 'going somewhere'—Watertown was not exactly a metropolis of the Middle West—Brown was saved, however, from the embarrassing obligation to give a route to one of the smaller fry, of whom three were clamouring for a mail contract. Oddly, pressure was put upon the United group to operate it, under a subletting agreement with American. This was tough on United, which had remained studiously aloof from all Brown's machinations, contenting itself with three insignificant extensions, none of which was more than 120 miles long.

Errett Lobban Cord

Early in 1931, Century Air Lines Inc was founded by Errett Lobban Cord, who had risen from the ranks of motorcar salesmen to become the owner of the Auburn Motor Company. Possibly aiming to emulate Henry Ford, he tried his hand at running an airline, and at first met with some success. On 23 March, he established a passenger service between Chicago and St Louis and from Detroit to Cleveland, using a fleet of 14 Stinson aircraft, backed by 16 Auburn limousines for ground transport. Within a month he had signed an agreement with Tom Braniff, who was leading a crusade for independent airlines.

On 3 July, 1931, Century Pacific Lines Ltd, another Cord company, started a service from San Francisco to San Diego, via Oakland, Fresno, Bakersfield, and Los Angeles, again with Stinsons, and, more important, offering fares below railway rates. By the autumn of 1931, more than 55,000 passengers had been carried by this upstart airline. Extra stations were added in the Great Lakes area, making through service possible from St Louis to Cleveland, and an important extension in the west linked California with Phoenix.

This was cocking a snook at American with a vengeance. Cord was offering cut-price air transport to passengers and he followed this early in 1932 by offering cut-price mail carriage to the Post Office Department. Unfortunately, the Department of Commerce, responsible for navigation and safety, did not approve of the way in which Cord was able to operate so economically, which was by cutting salaries to the bone. In fact, he went too far, and had a strike on his hands in February 1932, when the newly-formed Air Line Pilots Association made its protest against being treated like cab-drivers.

Unable to win a mail contract, Cord offered his two airlines to the Aviation Corporation, which in April 1932 gladly exchanged 140,000 shares of American Airways stock for the assets. Cord became a director of AVCO.

At this time, the president of AVCO was Lamotte T. Cohu, who had taken office in March 1932 when Frederick G. Coburn was replaced. Coburn had begun to simplify the maze of routes and franchises which formed the sprawling American Airways network. Cohu was to pull back some of the countless millions of dollars spent on rationalizing and building the line, but no sooner had he taken office than Cord began to question the efficiency of American's top management. Appalled at what he considered to be pointless extravagance, he made an issue of an attempt by the AVCO directors to purchase some North American Aviation stock. This soon developed into a struggle for AVCO control. It was the biggest board-room battle since the Rentschler-Keys dogfight. On 15 March, 1933, Hoyt, Cohu, and other directors resigned. Cord emerged the victor, and appointed Maj Lester D. Seymour, formerly of United, to reorganize AVCO and American.

Transamerican Airlines' Fokker F-XA NC147H (c/n 1041). In the background is Pennsylvania Air Lines' Stinson SM-6000B NC10823. (*American Airlines*)

Thompson and Martz

Seymour's greatest accomplishment was to straighten the air route between New York and Chicago which, as late as the end of 1932, was so circuitous that it could hardly be taken seriously. The first step was to acquire Transamerican Airlines Corporation.

This had been founded as the Thompson Aeronautical Corporation early in 1928 and was the successful bidder for the route from Bay City, Michigan, to Chicago, CAM 27, on 5 May. Service began on 17 July, with a fleet consisting mainly of six Stinson Detroiters. On 1 April, 1929, a second route from Bay City to Cleveland, via Detroit, was opened, for overnight mail, and on 14 May a passenger service was introduced across

Stinson SM-1 of Thompson Aeronautical Corporation, with Packard diesel engine. (*Smithsonian Institution*)

Lake Erie, connecting the waterfronts of Detroit and Cleveland with frequent flights by Keystone-Loening amphibians. The 91 miles took 55 min and proved extremely popular. On 17 July passenger service was also added to the Michigan routes. From 26 June, 1930, Thompson experimented with Packard diesel-powered Stinson mailplanes and during the year added several more stops in northern Indiana. On 11 November an important 225-mile extension of the passenger service was made as far as Buffalo.

At the beginning of 1931 the airline-operating side of Thompson became a subsidiary of the parent company, under the name Transamerican Airlines Corporation. Identifying itself with the smaller independent element of the airline business, it operated in association with Braniff. When Century Airlines joined American, Transamerican took its place on the combined independent airline network in the Middle West.

The zenith of Thompson and Transamerican's enterprise came in March 1932, when the Corporation obtained a 75-year franchise from the Icelandic Government for landing concessions in that country. Whether or not the intention was to fly to Europe with the Keystone-Loening Air Yachts is not clear; what did happen was that on 15 April, 1932, Pan American Airways paid $5,000 to Transamerican for the option to develop the route and that in July of the same year the same company paid a further $55,000 for the complete landing rights in Iceland.

American Airways now stepped in and bought Thompson, including its mail contract. To conform with the law, this was sublet to American by Thompson Aeronautical Corporation which remained a paper company with an authorized capital at one cent a share, to save taxes.

This gave American a through route from Buffalo to Chicago. The other half of the New York—Chicago link-up was achieved by the take-over of Martz Airlines. This company had started as a division of the Frank Martz Coach Company, operating a service from Newark to Wilkes Barre —without a mail contract—using two Bellanca Airbuses and a Ford Tri-Motor. This was in September 1930 and an important extension to the route was made on 15 July, 1931, to Buffalo. American Airlines acquired Martz at the end of 1932. Because no mail contract was involved, the company was dissolved.

As TWA had been granted an extension of its main transcontinental route to give access to Chicago (via a branch line from Columbus) American had acted none too soon. With United Air Lines possessing pioneer rights, through its inheritance of NAT, the three major airline groups were now poised for a competitive battle over the New York—Chicago route, the most important city pair in the United States.

General Motors Again

The number of major airline groups in 1933 had, in fact, been reduced to three, each controlled by a holding company of considerable strength. United Air Lines continued as the airline subsidiary of United Aircraft; American Airways was that of Aviation Corporation; while TWA, Eastern Air Transport, and Western Air Express were all under the control of North American Aviation.

Originally an arm of the Curtiss-Keys industrial empire, North American changed hands in 1933 and its new owner, General Motors, acquired control without undue exertion on its own part.

The giant motorcar group had originally entered the airline field rather modestly in 1931, when it bought a substantial shareholding in Western Air Express. History was to repeat itself about two years later when, once again, through no aggressive promotion on its own account, General Motors was presented with the opportunity of expanding its airline holdings. Reacting against the Postmaster General's policy of creating rival airlines to the United empire (*See next chapter*) brokers acting on behalf of United Aircraft had quietly bought shares of Eastern Air Transport, i.e. North American Aviation, in exactly the same way as they had invaded National Air Transport. This time, however, Walter F. Brown put his foot down and United unloaded its Eastern shares to General Motors, on 28 February, 1933.

The Detroit company now began to take advantage of the widespread influence which it possessed through its control of North American. In addition to Eastern, Western Air Express (already controlled by General Motors) became a subsidiary, with Harris Hanshue as general manager. Shortly afterwards, on 1 June, 1933, East and West were linked when North American acquired majority control of TWA and all three General Motors' airlines appeared on the same map in the *Official Airline Guide*. Eddie Rickenbacker succeeded Hanshue as general manager of Eastern.

Northwest Airways employed at least nine Hamilton Metalplanes of the H-45 and H-47 type. The H-47 NC538E (c/n 63) is illustrated. (*Gordon S. Williams*)

Although Northwest Airways was almost certainly the biggest user of the Hamilton Metalplanes, some were employed by other carriers. The Hamilton Metalplane Model H-45 NC876H (*above*) is seen carrying the markings of Coastal Air Freight Inc. The same aircraft, possibly after modification to H-47 standard, is seen below with the badge of Condor Air Lines on its fuselage. (*Gordon S. Williams photographs*)

Although favouring the creation of massive units for development of transcontinental routes, the Postmaster General did not approve of ownership of more than one by the same company. North American therefore sold its interests in Northwest Airways, which it had acquired along with the purchase of TWA.

A Northern Transcontinental

During the late 1920s the area to the west and northwest of the Great Lakes did not offer a ready market for airline activity. Compared with the area served by the southern transcontinental route, the population to be served was neither as numerous nor as affluent. Nevertheless it had some potential, if only because the surface transport was not highly competitive, partly because of meandering routes caused by the difficult terrain.

The incumbent airline, Northwest Airways, holder of CAM 9, Chicago—Twin Cities, made the best of its resources. In July 1927 it tried its first passenger service, with Stinson Detroiters, but had to close down because of the severe winters experienced in Minnesota. Permanent service began, however, on 7 June, 1928, with Hamilton all-metal monoplanes being used from September. On 1 September Northwest established the first co-ordinated air-rail service in the United States, providing connections with three railways connecting with the West Coast (Great Northern, Northern Pacific, and Chicago, Milwaukee, & St Paul) and two connecting Chicago with the East (Pennsylvania, and Baltimore & Ohio). On 15 December a spur route was opened from Milwaukee to Green Bay, by which time Ford 5-AT Tri-Motors had been placed in service. Altogether it was a good year, with more than 6,000 passengers boarded.

Northwest Airways' Ford 5-AT-B Tri-Motor NC9676 (*left*) at Chicago Municipal Airport. In the centre is National Air Transport's Ford 5-AT-C NC426H and on the right a Pilgrim 100.

On 1 October, 1929, a new company—of the same name—was organized under Delaware law, and North American Aviation acquired a substantial interest, nominally through TAT. After the Watres Act, Northwest began to take advantage of the extension clauses, aspiring to reach the Canadian prairie capital, Winnipeg. This, however, became the test case on the definition of what constituted a reasonable extension, and the Comptroller General, John McCarl, ruled against it, as Minneapolis—Winnipeg was longer than the original route, Minneapolis—Chicago.

Northwest Airways used this Sikorsky S-38, NC303N (c/n 414-1), on services to Duluth in 1931. (*Northwest Orient Airlines*)

The route was extended therefore as far as the Canadian frontier, at Pembina, on 2 February, 1931, and other branch lines opened to Madison and Duluth, the latter served by a Sikorsky S-38 amphibian, as Duluth did not possess an airport. The Postmaster General and Col L. H. Brittin, head of Northwest, then worked out an ingenious plan for circumventing the extension clause. Brittin pointed out that some of his short feeder routes were unprofitable and that it would be to everyone's advantage to terminate them and transfer the lost mileage to westward extensions of the main Northwest trunk route. This was successfully accomplished and the line reached Mandan, N.D., on 2 June, 1931.

Early in 1933, the extension clause was invoked again, and on 3 March, Northwest added Billings, Montana, to its route westwards, and Milwaukee—Detroit at the eastern end, the latter being sublet to the Kohler Corporation. This was a piece of manipulation typical of Walter Brown. Although he frankly used every device to assist the formation and consolidation of large companies, he was fair-minded in his dealings with the smaller men, and always tried to ensure that they received a good price for routes and franchises conceded or surrendered. Thus, when E. L. Cord of American, having gained access throughout southern Michigan by buying Transamerican, then tried to steamroller Kohler into submission at a scrap price, Brown awarded the route to Northwest. Brittin did not particularly want the route, but it was preferable to letting the avaricious Cord into Milwaukee, and the subletting agreement was a neat compromise, acceptable to everyone except Cord.

Northwest Airways actually had to wait for almost another two years before completing its route to the West Coast, by which time the whole airline scene had undergone a revolution.

During 1930, another enterprise was offering air-rail service between Chicago and Seattle. Mamer Air Transport, of Spokane, had originally started a service to Portland, Oregon, on 15 April, 1929, without, however, the advantage of a mail contract. Mainly serving local points in the State of Washington, and including Ford Tri-Motors in its fleet, Mamer took a seven-league stride in the summer of 1930, when it came to an agreement with two railways. The Great Northern provided service between Seattle

Northwest Airways' Travel Air A-6000-A NC9933 (c/n 1084). The type was used between Minneapolis/St Paul and Chicago, Fargo and Bismarck in the early 1930s. (*Northwest Orient Airlines*)

and Spokane, the Chicago and Northwestern between Chicago and St Paul, whilst Mamer supplied an air link over the long segment between Spokane and St Paul. Although air operations were discontinued during the winter—the climate was not only frigid but there was no lighted airway—the service was improved in 1931 when Mamer extended to Seattle.

This line was doomed to failure, unhappily, by the lack of a mail contract, and although an attempt was made to maintain service during the summer of 1932, nothing more was heard of Mamer Air Transport after the winter of that year. Some agreement appears to have been made with Northwest, as Nick Mamer piloted the first service to Seattle by the St Paul based airline.

Waco 300 (JTO Special) NR42M (c/n 3001) used by Northwest Airlines. (*Gordon S. Williams*)

A Rational System

When Walter F. Brown left office following the Democratic landslide of November 1932, he left behind him thirty-four air mail routes comprising an integrated airway network of 27,000 miles. During the four years of his office, of which three were characterized by intensive and vigorous activity, he changed the airline map from a sporadic collection of mainly unconnected networks into a set of routes which 'went from somewhere to somewhere'. The fact that he achieved his ends by somewhat dubious means does not detract from the immensity of the task or the comprehensiveness of the result.

When Brown became Postmaster General, passengers were normally regarded by the airlines as a nuisance. Because of the system of mail payments, the major design objective of aircraft manufacturers was to produce load-carriers with little attention to creature comforts. The provisions of the McNary-Watres Act, master-minded by Brown, altered the mail payments system so as to encourage the manufacture of passenger aircraft. The mail pay was in effect a subsidy which changed the status of airlines from hand-to-mouth companies of uncertain stability into profitable organizations with security of tenure sufficient to justify capital investment, often on a large scale.

All these factors made it possible for the airline industry to set new and higher standards for its flying equipment. Brown's prime target of creating a competitive transcontinental system was completely successful, not only in its direct context, but in the trade-off effect on the manufacturing industry. As a direct result of Brown's mail contract policy (whatever its imperfections or malpractices) the United States aircraft manufacturers responded magnificently to produce the first generations of commercial airliners which quickly outstripped the best in Europe in technical standards and economic performance.

This aspect of the progress of U.S. air transport is elaborated more fully in a later chapter. It is sufficient here to relate the story of TWA's dramatic last flight before the effective cancellation of the air mail contracts on 19 February, 1934. At 10 p.m. the previous evening, a new aircraft, designed specially for TWA according to the airline's own specifications, took-off from the Union Air Terminal at Los Angeles. The pilot was Jack Frye, who only four years previously had been flying Fokker F-VIIs on his Standard Airlines route to El Paso. The co-pilot was Eddie Rickenbacker, who had entered the airline business flying single-engined Stouts with Florida Airways in 1926. He was now vice-president of Eastern Air Transport, a first cousin of TWA through the parent General Motors owned North American Aviation.

The aircraft was the Douglas DC-1 which set entirely new levels of design, performance, and economics, to usher in a new era of transport aircraft manufacture. Stopping only at Kansas City and Columbus, Frye and Rickenbacker touched down at Newark, New Jersey, more than

First of a great line. The sole Douglas DC-1, X223Y, seen on 1 July, 1933, the day on which it made its first flight. This was the aeroplane from which all the Douglas all-metal transports were developed. (*Douglas Aircraft Company*)

three hours ahead of schedule, in a new transcontinental record time of 13 hr 4 min.

This flight, made as a gesture of defiance in the face of impending legislative disaster, epitomized the success of Postmaster General Brown's determined work. Without the incentive of ruthless competition by powerful rivals, TWA would almost certainly not have ordered the Douglas monoplane. Without Brown's directives and intrigues, there would almost certainly have been no strong competition. TWA would in any case not have existed. The economic depression and the limited effectiveness of the slow aircraft of the previous generation would have forced its ancestor, TAT, into bankruptcy (though Western Air Express could perhaps have survived on its own). Above all, without the provisions for generous mail payments under the terms of the Watres Act, there would just not have been enough money around to carry the airlines over a difficult period.

Postmaster General Brown, in effect, created the necessary environment to stimulate the development of a new breed of aircraft. He went into office with a dream of an airline network to surpass the world. When he left office, this had been achieved, handsomely. More than this, the airlines were about to be equipped with aircraft which outflew the rest of the world's best; and the United States manufacturing industry has never faltered or looked back since.

A little-known American transport aeroplane was this Clark, or General Aviation, GA-43, NC13903, used by Western Air Express. The GA-43, bearing fleet number 25, is seen at Denver in the mid-1930s. In Europe Swissair used a GA-43, and SCADTA of Colombia also put one into service.

CHAPTER SIX

Survival of the Fittest

Vigorous Independence

While Postmaster General Brown's plans were designed to place the entire airline industry of the United States in the hands of three giant corporations, there were others who viewed this turn of events with something less than satisfaction. In the minds of some of the independent spirits, opposition took root in a number of ways: political—Democrat against Republican; West versus East (a rivalry to be found in other activities besides aviation); an instinctive dislike of large concerns; or just plain animosity towards Brown, who made no secret of his intentions to bend the law where possible as he proceeded to draw the new airline map. And his plan excluded the small men.

After the passing of the Watres Act, the formation of small airlines continued sporadically. In fact, their numbers increased considerably; but their chances of survival diminished as Brown strengthened his hold on all the important routes. Predictably, most of the small airlines came and went in bewildering succession, having survived precariously for a few months, perhaps for two or three seasons. A good hard winter was enough to polish off the majority; but some were made of sterner stuff, and put up a good fight.

Braniff and Bowen

The southern part of the Middle West of the United States, south of Omaha and down as far as Texas, was characterized by a rapidly-expanding economy, based largely on oil. This promoted the growth of a number of cities which, during the former railway construction period, had not been big enough in their own right to become large transport hubs. The new demand for travel, sparked off by the oil boom, was an incentive to ambitious airlines, which, moreover, found that climatic conditions in this area were good for flying. Thus, cities such as Tulsa, Fort Worth, Wichita, and Oklahoma City began to feature prominently on many airline maps.

With the passing of the Watres Act, some of the operators who had burned their fingers during the first mail contract period decided to try their luck again. One of these, Paul Braniff, together with his brother Tom, organized Braniff Airways on 3 November, 1930, to operate over exactly the same Oklahoman territory as the former Paul R. Braniff Inc had done before selling out to Universal Aviation Corporation.

The first scheduled flight, on 13 November, was between Tulsa and Wichita Falls, via Oklahoma City, using two six-passenger Lockheed

Thomas E. Braniff (*left*) began his civil aviation career in 1928 as a partner in the Tulsa—Oklahoma City airline, which was sold to the Universal Aviation Corporation the following year. Reorganizing Braniff Airways in 1930, he survived precariously without a mail contract during the Walter Brown period, and was finally rewarded for his tenacity in 1934 with the Dallas—Chicago mail contract. When he died in 1954, his airline's network stretched to Buenos Aires. Allan H. Lougheed (Lockheed) (*right*) built his first aeroplane in 1913. He began production in 1927 of the aerodynamically clean Vega cabin monoplane designed by John K. Northrop. This led to the successful high-speed Orion. Lockheed sold the company to Detroit Aircraft Corporation in 1929 which, however, was unable to survive. Lockheed died in 1969, when still a consultant to the revived company which Robert Gross and some associates bought for $40,000 in 1932.

Vegas. These aircraft were not as big as some of their contemporaries, such as Fokkers and Fords, but they were fast, and this was a great attraction for the travelling oilmen. On 5 December the route was extended northwards to Kansas City, and then on 25 February the following year to Chicago. Shortly afterwards, the authorized capital of the company was increased by $100,000, of which half was put up by a local businessman, Benjamin Clayton. A direct Tulsa—St Louis service started on 15 June.

Simultaneously, another kindred spirit was setting up shop just to the south of Braniff's area, and his history was an echo of that of the Oklahomans. Temple Bowen, the former bus operator who had sold Texas Air Transport to Southern Air Transport, opened another Lockheed Vega service from Fort Worth to Houston, via Dallas, on 1 October, 1930. This route, too, was quickly extended, so that by the end of the year, Oklahoma City and Tulsa were also served by Bowen Air Lines.

Early in 1931, mainly at Braniff's instigation, a number of the small companies formed the Independent Scheduled Air Transport Operators' Association. This organization did not necessarily believe that, being united, they would therefore conquer; but they fully appreciated that divided they would certainly fall, and consequently appointed an attorney, William I. Denning, to look after their interests in Washington, and in particular, the Post Office Department.

Other members of the Association included the Reed Airline, started by Sergeant Joe Reed, an ex-World War 1 Air Service mechanic who just loved aeroplanes. He began a service from Lawton to Wichita Falls and Oklahoma City on 1 September, 1931, with a six-passenger Travel Air. Initially successful, a second Travel Air and a six-seater Buhl Air Sedan sesquiplane were added to the fleet.

The artificial economic base on which the small airlines scratched an existence is illustrated by Joe Reed's experience. In spite of the absence of any kind of subsidy, the depressed demand because of the economic slump forced Reed's fares almost down to bus levels. His wife managed all the book work without pay; Joe flew one aircraft himself. The balance between death and survival of the Reed Airline was slender indeed.

Two other independent airlines existed to the north of the Braniff/Bowen sphere of direct influence. Rapid Air Transport (not to be confused with Rapid Air Lines, an earlier company formed to operate sight-seeing trips over the Black Hills) began a St Louis—Omaha route on 31 March, 1930, and Hanford's Tri-State Air Lines operated Lockheed Vegas between Sioux City and St Paul the following year. Both members of the Independent Operators' Association, they merged in December 1933 to become Hanford-Rapid Air Lines.

Further west, Wyoming Air Service was first organized on 9 May, 1930, and flew between Great Falls and Cheyenne. A scheduled Denver—Billings service began on 16 April, 1931, under the name Wyoming-Montana Air Service. This company was later to have a chequered career before finally becoming absorbed by Western Airlines.

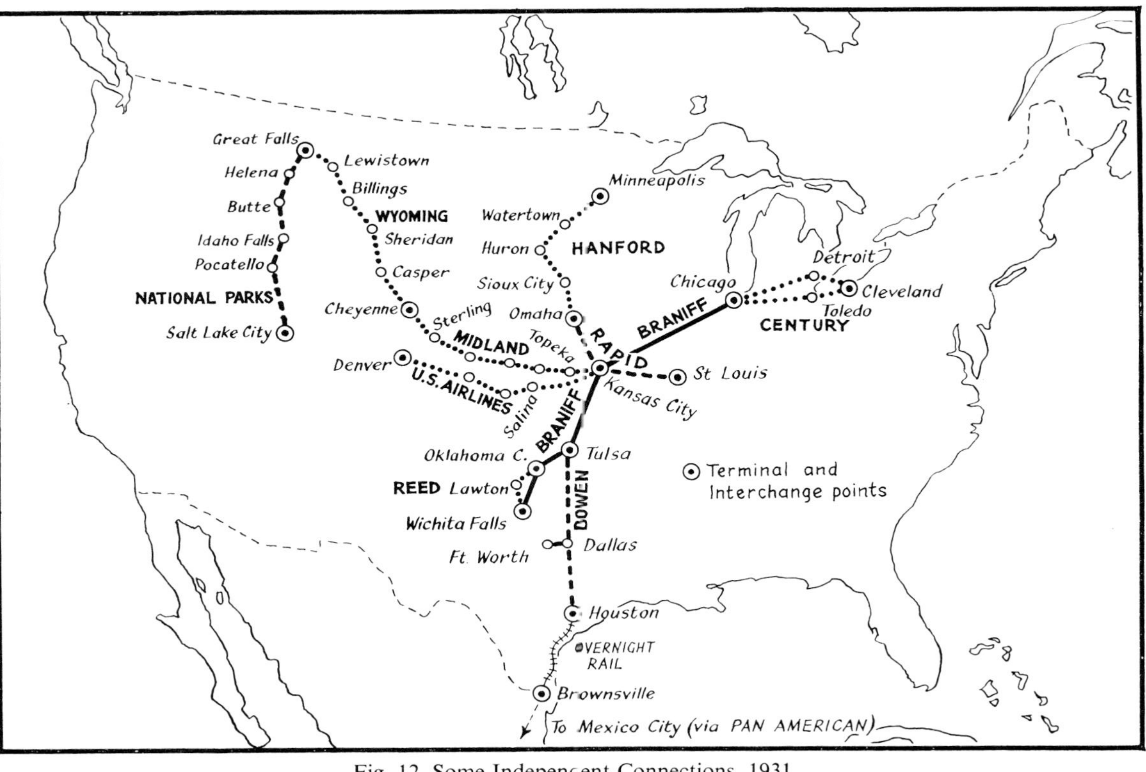

Fig. 12. Some Indepencent Connections, 1931.

Other companies which, at one time or another, were members of the Association, were United States Airways (concerned with the complicated dealings in the formation of TWA); Midland Air Express, yet another Lockheed Vega operator on a multi-stop route from Kansas City to Cheyenne; the Oklahoma-Texas Air Line, operating Ryans from Wichita Falls to Oklahoma City; Century Air Lines; and Transamerican Airlines Corporation.

In aggregate, the member companies of the Association were able to offer air service over quite a large area of the Middle West, as is shown on the map (*Figure 12*). But in practice, the system was ponderous, even if the equipment was the fastest then in service.

The Lockheed Vegas were certainly fast. They could provide a competitive advantage over the slower Fords or Fokkers. Temple Bowen, operating on the customary shoestring, was prepared to carry mail between Dallas and Louisville at 25c per mile, and, he firmly believed, still make a profit. He was therefore not over-enamoured with the news that Postmaster General Brown had awarded the mail contract at 53c to American Airways which acquired the route by one of Brown's suspicious-looking 'extensions'.

Bowen's indignation should perhaps have been tempered by the thought that he himself had sold Texas Air Transport to American Airways for $175,000, and was now using the money to provide stiff competition with the airline which had in effect financed him. These moral issues aside, Bowen was indignant when the Post Office Department franked letters 'Fly with the Air Mail' which, he charged, was free advertising by a Government department on behalf of American Airways. He retaliated by inscribing his aircraft with the message 'Fly Past the Air Mail' which, indeed, his speedy Vegas often had to do when the uncharitable American Airways refused to wait for Bowen connections. All in all, competition was a pretty cut-throat business down Texas way in the early 1930s.

Robertson and the Mississippi Valley Route

Another former Post Office mail contractor who sold his assets to one of the big airline groups and then set up in business again was Frank Robertson, in partnership with his brother, Maj William Robertson. Having sold the Robertson Aircraft Corporation to the Universal Aviation Corporation, the Robertsons set up the Curtiss-Robertson Company in St Louis to manufacture the Curtiss Robin, a small private aircraft. C. M. Keys, of the Curtiss group, held half the stock of the company, which fell by the wayside when the depression virtually wiped out civil flying.

The Robertsons then started the Robertson Airplane Service Company, opening a scheduled passenger service on 27 April, 1930, from St Louis to New Orleans, via Memphis, Greenwood, and Jackson, with a branch from Memphis to Hot Springs via Little Rock. Using single-engined Ryan

This Ryan Brougham Model B-5, NC738M, was one of a fleet operated by Robertson Airplane Service Company, but the title Robertson Air Lines appeared on the fuselage.

Broughams, the Robertsons hoped to stake a claim over what was virgin territory from the point of view of a mail contract.

Walter Brown, however, did not look kindly upon the Robertsons, whom he considered to have done very well already out of the Post Office, having sold their line and contracts to what was now American Airways for $300,000—not bad business for an original investment of $30,000. The manner in which Brown sought to prevent the Robertsons from undermining American's investment was ingenious. To impartial observers of the interpretation of the Watres Act, it was remarkable, to say the least. To the opponents of Brown's policy of favouring big business groups over the little guys, it was considered little short of criminal.

In a notorious decision on 15 June, 1931, Brown extended American's recently-won route from Atlanta to Los Angeles (CAM 33)—the SAFEway deal—at Jackson, Mississippi. One of two extensions went north to Memphis, the other south to New Orleans. Both were at right angles to the original route. In addition, he extended the Chicago—St Louis route (CAM 2) southwards to Memphis. All this happened on the same day that American's route CAM 20 was extended from Nashville to Fort Worth. Overnight, Brown had filled in a gaping void on the American Airways map, and at the same time deprived the Robertsons of a golden chance of breaking in on the Post Office mail contract money (*See Figure 13*).

Robertson Airplane Service Company did not help its own cause by procrastination in the matter of a possible merger with the Wedell-Williams Air Service Corporation of New Orleans. This had been founded in August 1929 by Jimmy Wedell, a racing pilot, and H. P. Williams, a wealthy lumberman. They started services between New Orleans and Fort Worth, via Baton Rouge, Alexandria, Shreveport, and Dallas, and also to Houston, on 30 November, 1929, plus an amphibian service to Grand Isle. There is some evidence that Wedell and Williams had some influence in Washington, and if they and the Robertsons had been able to combine their efforts, Brown might have given way. Together, they might well have qualified for a mail contract under the various clauses of the Watres Act, not to mention

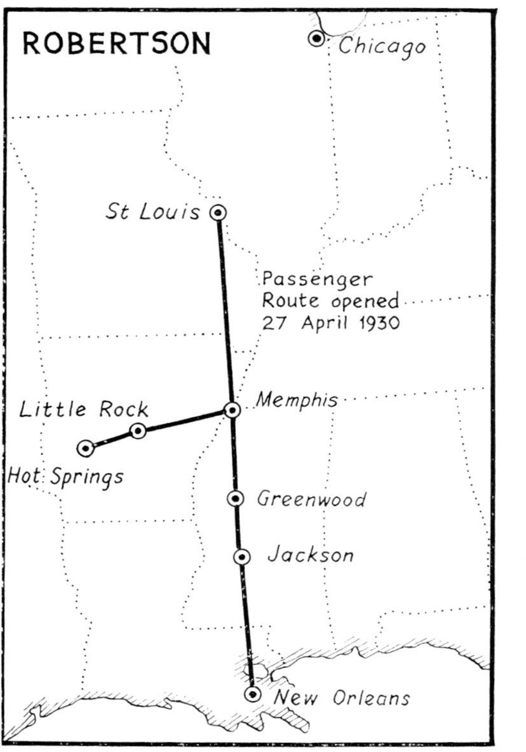

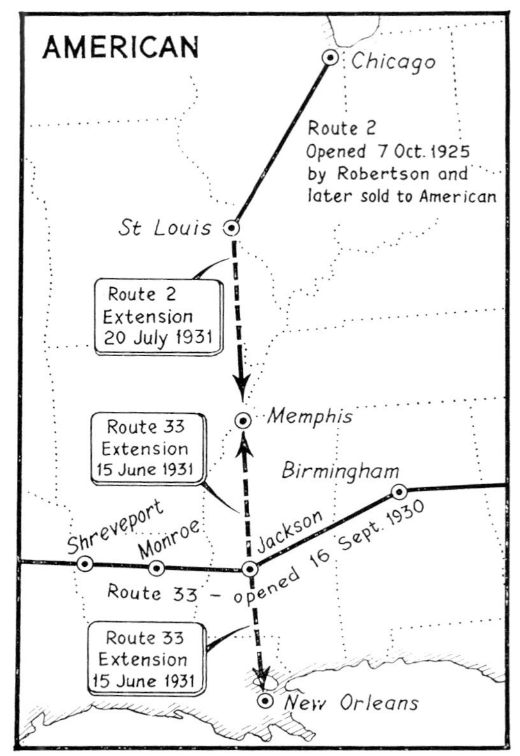

Fig. 13. Two Contenders for the Mississippi Valley Mail Route, 1931.

some unofficial interpretations of Brown's such as night flying and going from 'somewhere to somewhere'. The citizens of St Louis, New Orleans, Dallas, and Houston could no doubt have put up a good case that they were 'somewhere'.

The whole affair of the Mississippi route was, of course, to be dragged up at the later investigations; and it remains today as one of the most remarkable examples of how a regulation could be stretched to the limits of legal interpretation to satisfy the wishes of a single-minded politician.

Pickwick Airways operated this Bach Air Yacht 3-CT-8 NC8069 (c/n 11), which was powered by one 525 hp Pratt & Whitney Hornet and two 165 hp Wright J-6 engines.

Walter Varney Again

On 29 March, 1929, Pickwick Airways, founded by Charles F. Wren, entered the growing list of airlines in California with a thrice daily passenger service between Los Angeles and San Diego. This was a modest beginning to a rapid territorial expansion, for by July, Pickwick's three-engined Bach cabin monoplanes were flying to San Francisco; and in September a route was opened to Mexico City. By the end of the year single-engined Fairchilds and Ryan Broughams were added to the fleet

This Pickwick Latin American Airways Ryan Brougham Model B-5, NC314K (c/n 213), was photographed after the airline had extended its operations into Latin America. (*Ryan*)

and ambitious extensions to the route made as far as Guatemala City and San Salvador.

Whether or not Pickwick Airways cherished a vision of challenging Pan American Airways in Central America may never be known. Within six months of reaching San Salvador, the airline terminated all its services. This is not necessarily to Pickwick's discredit; airlines with far greater resources were to fall victims to Pan American, as will be recounted later.

Pickwick is mentioned at this point because it acted in effect as a prelude to the re-entry of the colourful Walter T. Varney into the field of airline operation. Varney had sold his original airline and route to United for $2,000,000 on 30 June, 1930—just about the time when Pickwick folded up.

This Mexican-registered Lockheed Orion bore the name Lineas Aereas Occidentales SA beneath the cabin windows and Varney Speed Lines Inc, in very small letters, on its fin. The words Correo Aereo de Mexico and the Mexican flag appeared on the engine cowling. Used on Varney's Mexican service in 1933.

By January 1932, Varney Air Service Ltd, was operating between San Francisco (Alameda) and Los Angeles, and with the acquisition of Lockheed equipment this became known as the Varney Speed Lanes Air Service. Later in the year Varney began negotiations with the Mexican Government for a long-term mail contract and, discontinuing the California service, a service was opened between Los Angeles and Mexico City, with Lockheed Orions, early in 1933. This was known variously as the Varney Speed Lanes System or Lineas Aereas Occidentales, according to taste.

Predictably, this venture did not get very far either. In February 1935 the Mexican Government withdrew its 20-year contract, after only nine months operation. Varney, however, was undeterred by this setback and concentrated on another string to his bow, the Southwest Division of Varney Speed Lanes (*See page* 197).

Pennsylvania Air Lines

One of the first dozen contract mail carriers of 1926 was Clifford Ball who, in fact, was the last to get under way, because of what was then

NR32K, a New Standard biplane used by Clifford Ball on the Cleveland—Pittsburgh route. This example appears to be a D-24. (*United Air Lines*)

difficult flying terrain in the Pittsburgh region. The original contract was awarded on 27 March, 1926, but Ball's service from Cleveland to Pittsburgh did not start until 21 April, 1927. Development was unspectacular, and no changes or extensions were made to the route, although Ball tried a large number of single-engined aircraft, including Ryans, Travel Airs, and Fairchilds, as well as his original Waco 9s and 10s.

In November 1930, the company was taken over by Pittsburgh Aviation Industries Corporation, who paid $137,000. P.A.I.C. was headed by Frederick Crawford, C. Bedell Munro, and George R. Hann, prominent Pittsburgh industrialists, and was the same organization which played a minor, yet vital, role in the reluctant merger of TAT and WAE.

P.A.I.C. changed the name of Ball's airline to Pennsylvania Air Lines, which by this time was operating passenger services to Washington. On 8 June, 1931, possibly as a reward for its co-operation in the TWA affair, the Postmaster General made one of his few awards to a small operator by extending mail service on route CAM 11 to the Federal Capital.

Pennsylvania Air Lines' Stinson SM-6000B NC10823 (c/n 5039) at Bettis Field, Pittsburgh, in 1930.

National Parks Airways' Fokker Super Universal C6769 (c/n 804) at Salt Lake City. (*Western Air Lines*)

National Parks Airways

One company which even Walter F. Brown could not touch was a comparatively small carrier from Salt Lake City, National Parks Airways, formed by Alfred Frank on 30 December, 1927. On 1 May, 1928, he began a passenger service to Pocatello, Idaho, and on 1 August extended the route to Great Falls, Montana, via Idaho Falls, Butte, and Helena, using three Fokker Super Universals and two Stearmans. Also on this date Frank obtained a mail contract for the route, designated CAM 26, one of the last to be awarded before the Hoover-Brown administration took office.

After the passing of the Watres Act, Frank sought to extend his mail route, quite modestly, to Missoula and Billings, in Montana. National Parks was obviously the pioneer operator in western Montana and there was some local indignation when the Postmaster General showed no inclination to award such an extension. Indignation rose to anger when, eventually, a route into Billings from the eastern approaches went to Northwest Airways, in a typical piece of Walter Brown manipulation. Brown won a short-term advantage, only to reap an unpalatable harvest

Stearman C3MB C6486 (c/n 172) operated by National Parks Airways on the Salt Lake City—Great Falls mail route. (*Western Airlines*)

later when some harsh words were uttered at a Congressional investigation. Yet once again, Brown had a point. In cold transport economic terms, there was more sense in connecting the northwest corner of the United States with the Great Lakes area through the agency of an airline based in Minneapolis than through one based in Salt Lake City. Nevertheless, the affair was unfortunate at the time and the Postmaster General would not have ruined his master plan by letting the contract go to National Parks.

Western Air Express Fights for its Life

Immediately prior to the absorption of most of Western Air Express' resources of strength and stamina in the TWA deal, Harris Hanshue, with Jack Frye as an associate, was able to claim with some justification that he had built up the greatest airline in the world, in terms of route mileage. Pride, they say, comes before a fall, but this may not be a fair appraisal of WAE's plight, nor would it judge Hanshue correctly. Exuberant and outspoken, perhaps; but Hanshue had a right to be proud of his achievement and to enjoy the satisfaction of watching the successful result of his early vision and enterprise.

Stearman 4-DM Junior Speedmail NC774H (c/n 4011) as operated by Western Air Express in 1930. This aircraft was later converted to a Model 4-E.

The years following the formation of TWA, however, were of continual struggle. The main objective was to keep Western Air Express alive as an autonomous unit. Otherwise California would have been excluded completely from any mail contracts and all services possibly taken over by easterners. Hanshue therefore held on grimly to the route and mail contract (CAM 4) which was the all-important Salt Lake City—Los Angeles link between the well-established United Air Lines transcontinental route and the booming population of Southern California. He also still retained another southern feeder off United, from Cheyenne to Pueblo, via Denver and Colorado Springs (CAM 12). Serving the main cities of the State of Colorado, which was to be without a through service direct to the East or the West for many years, this route was a surprisingly good revenue earner.

The Western Air Express Fokker F-14 NC129M (c/n 1404). Unlike most other Fokker transports this was a parasol monoplane. (*TWA*)

On the other side of the coin, however, Western had to surrender its coastal route to the northwest. The United group held the mail contract, and there was insufficient passenger traffic to permit a second competitive carrier breaking even without mail revenue. Western had obtained the route to Seattle through the purchase of West Coast Air Transport Corporation in 1929, but now had to sell it to Pacific Air Transport, a United subsidiary, on 16 March, 1931. The price paid was $250,000.

In April 1930, WAE became the first operator of the biggest land transport aircraft then in existence, the 32-seat Fokker F-32, a four-engined giant of its time. Built in traditional Fokker style as a scaled-up F-X, the four engines were mounted in tandem pairs on the main struts between the single high wing and the undercarriage. Western bought two of these aircraft, at a cost of $110,000 each. Although offering excellent standards in passenger comfort, this was to prove a bad investment, as the F-32 suffered from technical deficiencies, mainly from engine failures.

Just before the disposal of the West Coast route, WAE had turned in desperation to General Motors, which bought a controlling interest through its subsidiary, General Aviation Corporation. This was a good bargain for General Motors, who obtained some 30 per cent of the stock for $90,000.

Things then began to look a little brighter. On 1 August, 1931, the Postmaster General awarded two extensions to air mail route CAM 12, southwards from Pueblo. One branch was to Albuquerque, the other to Amarillo.

Western Air Express' four-engined 32-seat Fokker F-32 NC333N at Los Angeles with the airline's 24,000 sq ft hexagonal hangar on the left.

Another view of WAE's Fokker F-32 NC333N. (*TWA*)

At the same time, he awarded two 'extensions' to American's southern transcontinental route, CAM 33. One branched northwest from Fort Worth to Amarillo, the other north from El Paso to Albuquerque. Both these new American routes were then sublet to Western Air Express, which was able to offer through mail and passenger service from Cheyenne, on the United Air Lines transcontinental route, to Texas and the Mexican frontier.

Western had consolidated its position in the eastern Rocky Mountain region by setting up Mid-Continent Air Express, on 21 September, 1929. WAE supplied the capital while General Aviation Company, i.e. General Motors, supplied the aircraft, six-passenger Fokker Super Universals. The initial route was from Denver to El Paso, via Albuquerque, and in November 1929 a branch was opened from Pueblo eastwards to Kansas

Fokker Super Universals of Mid-Continent Air Express. (*Western Airlines*)

City, via Dodge City and Wichita. A Pueblo—Amarillo service started in May 1930 and Dallas was reached, via Wichita Falls, in August. Thus, when Western Air Express was granted its southern extensions to CAM 12, it was already the sitting tenant through Mid-Continent. Once the mail contract was secure, the subsidiary company became superfluous, and was fully absorbed in October 1931.

One of the Boeing 95 mailplanes of Western Air Express.

In the following year, Western Air Express disposed of its short flying-boat route from Wilmington to Catalina Island, selling it to the Wrigley family, who owned the island. This had the effect, among other things, of trimming the fleet to twelve Fokker Super Universals, four Boeing 40B-4s, and four Boeing 95s.

Early in 1933, Western became part of the North American Aviation empire, when General Motors took control of that aviation group. This amalgamation has already been described on pages 97 to 99. By this time, General Motors held 52 per cent of Western Air Express stock. It should have been well pleased with its investment. Almost 100,000 passengers had been carried since its first service, without passenger fatality or serious injury.

The Little Guys

The personalities already mentioned in this chapter, such as Tom Braniff, Temple Bowen, Frank Robertson, Walter Varney, and Al Frank, were the most prominent of the independently-minded airline pioneers whose love of aviation was too strong for them to stand by and watch the entire air network of the United States fall into the hands of Big Business. They were prominent in their time because they pioneered routes over wide areas; later they were in the public eye when their activities were paraded before the Congressional inquiry into Postmaster General Brown's machiavellianism; some of them reaped their reward when the United States air routes were redrawn in 1934.

The Temple Bowens and the Walter Varneys, however, were representative only of the piece of the independent iceberg which showed. The growing enthusiasm for air travel was sustained long after the publicity of the Lindbergh epic flight, and continued to flourish in spite of the advent of the greatest economic depression in United States history. Almost anyone with enough dollars to buy second-hand aircraft capable of carrying a few passengers could still attract business. Of course, attracting business was one thing; maintaining it was another; and making a profit without some sort of subsidy was normally impossible. The obvious form of subsidy was in mail payments. A less obvious one was when an operator was in the advantageous position of having a good seller's market, and thus able to charge a high fare to meet the high operating costs of uneconomic aircraft.

Such an operator was Nevada Airlines, which began services between Los Angeles and Reno, Nevada, and between Reno and Las Vegas, on 15 April, 1929. The fleet consisted of three Lockheed Vegas, and the chief pilot was Col Roscoe Turner, of air racing fame. Nevada Airlines cashed in on the marriage and divorce laws of the State of Nevada, which demanded a mere three days' notice for marriage and three months for divorce. The airline could cut down the travel time from 22 hr by train to 3 hr or less by air. Quite a gay dog while it lasted, Nevada Airlines ceased operations before completing a year's service, defeated by inexorable economic laws. The Vegas were fast, averaging 140 mph, but they could not make money except at high fares. There were just not enough short-notice demands to fill the aircraft.

If Nevada claimed to be the fastest airline, others claimed to be the busiest. Vern Gorst, formerly of Pacific Air Transport, began a service across Puget Sound, from Seattle to Bremerton with intermediate flag stops, on 15 June, 1929. Two Loening amphibians maintained eleven daily flights each way, every hour, on the hour*—still the cherished dream of every airline thirty years later. 15,000 passengers were carried by Gorst Air Transport in 1930 and the service remained popular until the mid-thirties.

Gorst was also a director of Air Ferries, which claimed to be 'the busiest air transport line in the world' operating a ferry service across San Francisco Bay, also with Loening amphibians. These kept up a regular schedule from San Francisco to Alameda, Oakland, and Vallejo, taking six minutes for the crossing and two minutes for the turnround. In 1930 Air Ferries carried 60,000 passengers, an impressive total, even allowing for the shortness of the journey. Like Gorst Air Transport, Air Ferries was still operating several years later, by which time Walter Varney had also become a director. It came to an abrupt end in 1936 when the San Francisco-Oakland Bay Bridge was opened.

Water crossings were natural potential air routes then, even as they are today. In the late 1920s, moreover, water and river craft were not as fast or as well appointed as now, and the speed of hydrofoils or hover-

* This phrase means hourly on the hour during the period of operation, not throughout the 24 hours.

Loening Air Yacht C2C, NC3728, of Gorst Air Transport.

This Eastman Sea Rover Model E-2, NC463M (c/n 7), was also used by Gorst Air Transport.

Loening Air Yacht C2C, NC64K, was operated on San Francisco cross-Bay services by Air Ferries, before the Bay Bridge was completed.

craft was unknown. Companies such as the air ferry services mentioned above were therefore to be found wherever a stretch of water divided two populated areas with some community of interest. Occasionally, a company would have ambitions beyond the immediate horizons across the bay. Alaska-Washington Airways, for example, started off on 15 April, 1929, with quite a flourish, with four separate—and separated—routes: Wenatchee—Pasco, Olympia—Seattle (both in the State of Washington), Ketchikan—Juneau—Sitka (Alaska), and, through its Canadian associate, Victoria—Vancouver—Nanaimo (British Columbia). Like all the ferry services, business was brisk; other routes were added, the fleet built up to ten Fairchild and Lockheed Vega floatplanes, and almost 12,000 passengers were carried in 1930. Its most ambitious project was a 1,060-mile service connecting Seattle with Juneau, Alaska, which began on a twice weekly basis on 1 June, 1930. This, however, could not be sustained, because of the lack of adequate weather reporting or radio aids, facilities which were absolutely essential in an area whose climate seems at times to consist of constant rain and storm. Nevertheless, this small airline deserves considerable credit for having been the first to try to provide an air link between the United States and what was then one of its overseas territories.

There was ample opportunity for enterprise in the coastal area between New York and Boston and along the island-studded coast of Maine. In August 1929, the Curtiss Flying Service operated amphibians from Boston to Hyannis, Martha's Vineyard, and Nantucket; and to Portland, Rockland, and Bar Harbor. (A sister company, the Curtiss Flying Service of the Middle West, had received a little-known mail contract (CAM 31) for a route from the Chicago Loop to the Municipal Airport at 63rd and Cicero (later known as Midway) using a nine-passenger Sikorsky and a five-passenger Ireland amphibian. The service operated during the summer of 1929.)

By 1931, Curtiss was operating a service from its own North Beach Airport (built on reclaimed land in Flushing Bay, Long Island), to Newark Airport and Floyd Bennett Field. Maj William Robertson also started the Metropolitan Air Ferry Service on 4 September, 1931. The timetables mentioned an hourly service, by Ford Tri-Motors at low rates. In fact, 'multi-colored transport planes' were used exclusively. (This was probably a misprint for 'multi-engined'.)

The Curtiss-Robertson services were the first examples in the world of an inter-airport link in the same city, foreshadowing the helicopter services twenty years later. New York had become a focal point for intensive air traffic and the need for a good airport within easy reach of downtown Manhattan was accentuated during the period of excess enthusiasm following the Lindbergh flight in 1927. The air-minded citizens of Newark, just across the Hudson River from New York, decided that the city needed a municipal airport. Independent surveys were carried out by Capt René Fonck, the French air ace who had been one of the disappointed con-

Colonial Western Airways' Ford 4-AT-B Tri-Motor NC7683 outside the first hangar at Newark Metropolitan Airport, New Jersey, in 1929. This Ford was destroyed in a crash at Newark just after take-off on 17 March, 1929, and all fourteen passengers were killed. It was described at the time as 'the worst accident in the history of heavier-than-air aeronautics' in the United States. (*Port of New York Authority*)

tenders for the Orteig prize. The 68-acre Newark Airport was completed in nine months on a piece of otherwise worthless marshland. It cost $1,750,000, including a 1,600-ft asphalt strip and a 120-ft square hangar. By 1930 Newark had become the busiest airport in the world and the terminus for all important long-distance flights, both for passengers and mail.

Another New York airline terminus was situated on the East River at the end of 42nd Street. From this point speedboats took passengers to North Beach—a marine terminal as well as a landplane base—to connect with those companies which offered flying-boat services. One of these was Coastal Airways, which flew six-passenger Fairchild 71 floatplanes up the Hudson River to Albany. The service began on 28 May, 1929, but ceased at the end of the year. Airvia Transportation Company also operated an over-sea New York—Boston service from 22 July of the same year, using Italian-designed Savoia Marchetti S.55 flying-boats based at North Beach. These were twin-hulled, tandem-motored, 14-passenger aircraft. Airvia charged $30 single, including luncheon en route. Beginning service in July 1929, it too was out of business by Christmas, after an unsuccessful attempt to merge with Coastal.

On 1 June, 1930, a subsidiary company of Pan American Airways, New York Airways, began service from North Beach to Atlantic City. Originally incorporated in the early days of Pan American, it used a Ford Tri-Motor, a Fokker F-X, and a Sikorsky S-38. The route was extended to Baltimore and Washington on 2 August, 1930, and sold to Eastern Air Transport on 15 July the following year.

Pan American had no sooner left North Beach than it formed an association with a company with its roots in New England. On 20 July the Boston and Maine and the Maine Central Railroads jointly organized Boston-Maine Airways Inc. For its first services, it engaged the services of Pan American Airways, which was interested in some preliminary survey work on the northeastern approaches of the U.S.A. with the long-term view of pioneering transatlantic flights. With Pan American providing management, equipment, and service, Boston-Maine Airways got off to a start on 1 August, 1931. Colonial Airways provided a link service from New York to Boston; Boston-Maine's route ran north to Portland, Rockland, and Bangor; whilst Pan American continued on to Calais, St John, and Halifax, Canada. These operations were discontinued in 1932.

The two railway companies resumed air operations on 11 August, 1933, as Boston-Maine Airways, operating two ten-passenger Stinsons from Boston to Bangor and Burlington. A feeder service through Vermont was added on 27 October, in an association with Central Vermont Airways, founded by the railway of that name in July 1933. The Burlington route was extended to Montreal on 20 March, 1934.

Boston-Maine/Central Vermont Airways' Stinson 6000 NC975W (c/n 5006).

And so the catalogue goes on, from the sublime to the ridiculous, from the modest to the pretentious. There was Continental Airways, which had a full page in the *Airline Guide* in 1930 to advertise connections from Chicago to almost every city east of the Alleghenies. Its Travel Air cabin monoplanes, however, carried passengers only as far as Port Columbus, the rail-air interchange station which the city of Columbus had built in 1929 for TAT. Continental passengers reached New York and all places south to Norfolk, Virginia, via the Pennsylvania, Chesapeake & Ohio, and Norfolk & Western railways. The airline did start an all-air service on 18 July, 1931, and added Lockheed Orions to the fleet by the end of the year, but that was the end of the road.

Scenic Airways had been one of the first purchasers of the Ford Tri-Motor, in June 1928, to operate sight-seeing flights around the Grand Canyon. In the summer of 1929 it was also performing a useful ferry service across the seven-mile wide Canyon, but thereafter its activities were intermittent.

Pride of place for impudence must go to Isthmian Airways. This company began service in the Panama Canal Zone in 1930, using Hamilton metal seaplanes. Cristobal to Balboa took 30 min, which Isthmian claimed to be the fastest transcontinental service in North America.

And so all the little guys in the airline business came and went, that is most of them. Occasionally, a happy circumstance permitted one to pick up a crumb from the Postmaster's table. One or two found a specialized niche. Some scraped through for a while. Tough characters like Braniff and Bowen simply wouldn't take 'no' for an answer, and were not averse to palming a few aces in an effort to trump Walter Brown's tricks. But the vast majority fluttered and died after a few brief months, to perish like moths in a candle flame. Eventually, however, one did more than kindle a flame; it detonated an explosion. And Walter Folger Brown's carefully constructed edifice came tumbling down.

Stinson Model U NC12192 of Columbia Airlines. (*Gordon S. Williams*)

CHAPTER SEVEN

Upheaval and a Fresh Start

The Ludington Line

The spark which set off the chain reaction resulting in the downfall of Walter Folger Brown was the Ludington Line, or, to use its corporate title, the New York, Philadelphia and Washington Airway Corporation. This was started by a group of Philadelphia financiers, headed by C. T. Ludington, ably assisted by Gene Vidal and Paul Collins. The first tentative steps were taken in August 1929, when the Washington-New York Air Line operated a few services with Lockheed Vegas. Additionally, Ludington was responsible for the Cape Cod Airway, linking Philadelphia with resort areas in New England, including Newport, Rhode Island, and Woods Hole, Massachusetts, using a Travel Air 6000 and a Fairchild 71.

With this limited experimental service as its store of experience, the Ludington Line launched forth on 1 September, 1930, on a route linking Newark, Camden (the airport for Philadelphia) and Washington. Using the Lockheed Vegas, plus Stinson Tri-motors and Consolidated Fleetsters, regular services were maintained at the coveted frequency of 'on the hour, every hour' from 8 a.m. to 5 p.m. Stations on the Pennsylvania Railroad were used for ticket-selling and passenger pick-up.

The public flocked to use this new service, operated for the first time between major population centres at a frequency comparable with railway schedules. 15,000 passengers were carried in the first three months and Ludington found time also to run a vacation service from Camden to Atlantic City during September and October, and to add a stop at Trenton on 24 November. Vidal and Collins were justified in their faith in passenger traffic as a generator of airline profits in their own right—a claim which had cost them their jobs with TAT when that airline ran into financial straits. In fact, after the first year of operation, the Ludington Line made a profit of $8,073, probably the first time that this had been achieved from airline passenger services alone.

Encouraged by this success Vidal attempted to obtain a mail contract, but was dismayed to discover that the Postmaster General favoured Eastern Air Transport, which won the contract in July 1931. Eastern's bid was 89c per mile, more than three times that of Ludington's 25c. Gradually the pressures of competition took effect. Eastern put 18-passenger Curtiss Condors on the route and as a subsidiary of North American Aviation could draw on substantial resources. Ludington maintained its servicc throughout 1932. On 23 January, 1933, it even began a thrice weekly service to Nashville, via Roanoke and other intermediate points; but this was the last fling. After carrying 124,000 passengers in two years, Eastern Air Transport bought the line on 15 February and quickly absorbed it into the main system. A few days later, on 28 February, 1933, General Motors purchased control of North American, largely at the instigation of Eddie Rickenbacker, who subsequently became vice-president under Thomas B. Doe.

Eastern was really bowling along by now. Responding to a growing public demand for quicker transport between the northeastern states and the vacation areas of Florida, a 13-hr through service was inaugurated between New York and Miami on 7 January, 1933, using the now much-improved Curtiss Condors, and eliminating the night stop at Jacksonville. This same equipment was used on regular, 10 trips per day, service between New York and Washington, starting on 1 July.

Fulton Lewis and Randolph Hearst

During the latter months of the Republican administration under Hoover, there had been an investigation of air mail contract awards when James A. Mead headed a committee to look into the conduct of the Post Office Department. But this was a half-hearted affair which gave Walter Brown a clean bill of health. When the Democrats took office in March 1933, however, scrutiny of the past record of the air mail began to probe more deeply.

This activity was undertaken not only by political interests but also by Fulton Lewis, an enthusiastic journalist of considerable ability who was then a young reporter of the Hearst press and a popular radio commentator in Washington. A friend of Lewis', William Briggs, who worked for Ludington, mentioned in conversation that his company had failed with its 25c bid for a mail contract. Shortly afterwards, Lewis chanced to see a Post Office Department notice announcing the 89c award to Eastern.

Scenting a possible story, in true American newspaper reporting tradition, Lewis began to search through the Post Office Department public records. His interest multiplied with each visit to the extent that he sought, and obtained, permission from William Randolph Hearst to devote his full time to his private investigation. This was the kind of story which made good copy for the front pages and the billboards, and Lewis turned over every proverbial stone to produce a comprehensive report. He interviewed airline and other officials all over the United States and unearthed enough evidence to engineer a nationwide scandal, the kind dear to Hearst's sensation-oriented heart.

In January 1932, Fulton Lewis sent his report direct to Hearst, at his San Simeon retreat in California. There, to Lewis' chagrin, it seemed to get stuck. Eventually, however, political pressure became too strong, and late in the summer of 1933, the report was delivered to the Black Committee.

The Black Committee

On 26 September, 1933, the Senate set up a Special Committee on Investigation of the Air Mail and Ocean Mail Contracts. The Chairman was Senator Hugo L. Black of Alabama, and the committee included two other Democrats, William H. King of Utah and Patrick A. McCarran of Nevada, and two Republicans, Wallace H. White of Maine and Warren R. Austin of Vermont. A. G. Patterson was appointed special investigator. The hearings began on 28 September, 1933.

Oddly enough, the original purpose of the committee was to look into ocean steamship mail contracts and the question of subsidy. The domestic and foreign air mail contracts were only dragged in because of political protests made on behalf of some of the aggrieved independent operators who considered they had had a raw deal from the Postmaster General when he was riding roughshod over the normal criteria by which justice should have been dispensed.

Walter Brown's tactics seemed habitually twisted. Yet ironically, in the critical case which was to prove his downfall he was following his consistent and wholly admirable principle of seeing that the small operators received a good price for routes surrendered through the loss of a mail contract. When E. L. Cord would not buy out Jack Kohler for a reasonable figure Brown had persuaded Northwest to do so, and then sublet the route back to Kohler. To sugar Northwest's pill, he also gave some liberal extensions westwards, much to the disgust of Al Frank, of National Parks Airways. Frank complained to Senator King, of the Black Committee, who was instrumental in adding the air mail to the subject matter for investigation.

Investigator Patterson heard about Fulton Lewis' report and, after personal intervention from Senator Black himself, Hearst finally gave permission for the material to be surrendered for perusal and inspection by the committee. In October 1933, Patterson alerted about 100 Interstate Commerce Commission (I.C.C.) investigators in a dozen cities, and at a predetermined time, they served warrants to seize innumerable documents from a number of key airline offices, all pertaining to the air mail contracts. In addition, Postmaster General Farley ordered a complete comb-out of Post Office files, under the direction of his solicitor, Karl Crowley.

During January 1934, President Roosevelt was informed of the course of the investigation and of the developing crisis. Everything depended on Crowley's analysis of the situation. He finished his report on 7 February and discussed the inevitable consequences with Farley. The next day, after an audience with the President, the Attorney General, Homer Cummings, was consulted, although this was a formality, as only Crowley had been sufficiently cognizant of the complexities of his own report to be in a position to pass judgement.

Cancellation of the Air Mail Contracts

President Roosevelt cancelled the Air Mail Contracts, and thus rendered null and void the provisions of the Kelly Air Mail Act and subsequent amendments, on 9 February, 1934, at 4 p.m. Authority was granted under postal laws granting the Postmaster General punitive powers when conspiracy was apparent. To quote the Attorney General's legal opinion: 'There can be no reasonable doubt that the arrangements, understandings and agreements out of which the route certificates subsequently grew (before 1934, and following the 'Spoils Conference') were highly irregular and interfered with the freedom of competition contemplated by the statutes.'

At the time of the cancellation the newspapers' greatest problem was to decide which exaggerated statement or comment to omit from the headlines. Certainly the opponents of the cancellation were widely reported. Charles Lindbergh, the nation's aviation hero, sent a telegram to the President, 'Your present action does not discriminate between innocence and guilt and places no premium on honest business. Your order of cancellation of all air mail contracts condemns the largest portion of our commercial aviation without just trial.' *Fortune* magazine summed up:

'The President of the U.S. put United Aircraft out of the air-mail business, at least temporarily. He also put Errett Lobban Cord (American Airways) out of it; and General Motors . . . and a half dozen small operators. He threw 800 men and women out of work and made 6,000 others fear for their jobs. He kicked askew the underpinnings of a $250,000,000 investment shared by 200,000 stockholders.'

Appalled though *Fortune* may have been, however, the act of cancellation at the time was not as universally unpopular as many later historians have indicated. In the furore which was to follow, during the dreadful episode of the temporary Army Mail Service, the mood of the times has often been forgotten. Also, some researches made previously into the affairs of the Post Office were forgotten. In March 1932, for example, a Congressional Committee had begun hearings on a bill directing the Postmaster General to revoke all the contracts awarded subsequent to 1930 without public advertisement. But a Republican Congress easily repelled this intrusion into Walter Brown's affairs. In February 1933, the Crane Committee had declared, 'Interlocking financial interests have in the past prevented the full, free, and independent development of aviation. They have resulted in the waste of public funds and run counter and do violence to the very purposes for which the subsidy has been provided.'

Another Subcommittee on Aeronautics revealed excess profits made by aviation companies on government orders. Aircraft companies were found to be involved with the activities of munitions companies in the export field, and this, too, was being looked into. Huge profits were revealed in aviation stock dealings. Thus, the public were not too vehement in their objections to Roosevelt's decision, which took effect on 19 February, 1934, ten days after the White House order.

The next day, an emergency having been created, the terms of the order were put into effect '. . . that the Postmaster General, Secretary of War, and Secretary of Commerce . . . co-operate to the end that necessary air mail service be afforded. It is further ordered and directed that the Secretary of War place at the disposal of the Postmaster General such airplanes, landing fields, pilots, and other employees and equipment of the Army of the United States needed or required for the transportation of mail during the present emergency over routes and schedules prescribed by the Postmaster General.'

Army Air Mail Service

On the very same day that the cancellation of the air mail contracts was announced, President Roosevelt summoned Gen Benjamin D. Foulois, Chief of the Army Air Corps, and asked him if the Army could carry the mail during an emergency. Having spent several weary years seeking recognition for a neglected arm of the United States defence services, Foulois eagerly accepted this golden opportunity to demonstrate that the Air Corps could put on a show. He could hardly have done otherwise. His many critics would have done precisely the same in his shoes.

What happened next is best related by Franklin D. Roosevelt himself: 'On 20 February, 1934, the Army Air Corps commenced this temporary assignment. It was realized that familiarity with the routes would have to be established, in order to maintain schedules; and the ten-day interval between my Executive Order and the date the Army actually began to fly the mail was devoted to the establishment of stations and equipment and the making of test flights. This was particularly essential because winter flying presents additional hazards.

'On 16 February, 1934, before the Army Air Corps began its assignment, two planes crashed. These accidents did not occur while mail was being carried, but while the pilots were flying over the routes to familiarize themselves with them. Minute and definite instructions were thereupon issued to all stations to pay particular attention to safeguarding lives, even if it were necessary to sacrifice efficiency in mail service, and detailed

One of the U.S. Army Air Corps aircraft used to fly the mail in 1934, with some of those involved in the operation. The aircraft appears to be a Douglas O-38B. (*Western Airlines*)

instructions were issued to endeavour to obtain the safest equipment and to provide the utmost precautions for flights.

'However, weather conditions were extremely bad throughout the country for flying; and the accidents continued to occur. On 10 March, 1934, I sent a letter to the Secretary of War, ordering temporary curtailment of the air-mail service by the Army. . . . On 19 March, the Army Air Corps resumed carrying the mail and continued successfully to maintain its schedules until 8 May, 1934. Its last scheduled flight was 1 June, 1934.

'In the meantime, I wrote to the Congressional committees in charge of the new air-mail legislation, requesting them to expedite the passage of it. Pending the adoption of new legislation, advertisements for bids were issued on 30 March, 1934, for the transportation of air mail by commercial air companies on the most essential mail routes.'

This unemotional statement of the facts hardly reflects the whole picture. The time given to the army pilots to survey and fly the routes to gain enough experience was patently inadequate. The rigidity of the conditions of military service and the regulations combined to prevent the

An Army Air Corps Douglas O-38E which was used to carry mail during the 1934 crisis. (*Western Airlines*)

An Army Boeing P-12E fighter which carried mail over AM Route 18 in 1934.

This U.S. Army Air Corps Keystone B-4A bears the inscription AM Route 4 on its fin and was presumably used over the Los Angeles—Salt Lake City sector of the transcontinental route when the Army flew the mail in 1934. (*Western Airlines*)

This Douglas B-7 was used in 1934 by the Army to fly mail over AM Route 4. (*Western Airlines*)

temporary enlistment of air mail pilots with years of experience on the mail routes—they could not be expected to take a pay cut equivalent to half salary. The net result was that 200 officers and 324 enlisted men manfully attempted to operate 16,000 miles of mail routes (these had been reduced from the 27,000 commercial route miles) with 148 combat aircraft and a few Martin B-10 heavy bombers.

This equipment was no better suited for the carriage of large volumes of mail than were the old de Havilland DH-4s of a previous era. As Roosevelt observed, the weather was atrocious. Not only was February a notoriously bad month for flying; but this particular February was one in which the meteorologists thumbed through their records to find precedents. Foulois' men were, naturally, anxious to prove their worth. Their zeal probably overcame in many cases their sense of discretion. Flights were attempted when natural caution should have dictated cancellations. Inevitably, there were accidents and casualties.

But Roosevelt did not perpetrate 'legalized murder' as Eddie Rickenbacker has described it; and army pilots did not 'begin dropping out of the sky like acorns' as so noted a historian as Henry Ladd Smith would have it. The cold facts are that, of the total of ten army pilots who died, only four lost their lives while carrying the mail.

The U.S. Army Air Corps Martin B-10 *State of Utah* was used on AM Route 18 during 1934. The photograph was taken on 9 May, 1934. (*Douglas Aircraft Co via Harry Gann*)

Nevertheless, with such inflammatory statements flying about the newspaper headlines, objective judgement was not in fashion. The same public which had been apathetic, if not sympathetic to the cancellation of the mail contracts, now suddenly became aroused, and the weight of public opinion forced Roosevelt to act, and to act quickly, to end one of the unhappiest episodes in the whole history of air transport.

Black Revelations

By the time the last Army Air Corps aircraft had made its final mail flight on 1 June, 1934, the Black Committee had completed its work, having worked through from 25 September, 1933, until 25 May, 1934. After filtering away the thick banks of emotional smoke which had all but suffocated the essential material, the statistical facts emerging from the investigation told a fascinating story of how the United States airline industry had been propped up by substantial public funds.

Except for some isolated freak cases, of little national importance, the viable airline network mileage, that is, the mileage which could pay its way, was synonymous with the mail routes and was distributed as follows:

Airline	*Contract-bid Mileage*	*Extension Mileage*
American Airways	7,752	4,156
North American Aviation (TWA, WAE, EAT)	5,616	2,516
United Air Lines	5,956	484
Northwest Airways	407	1,621
National Parks Airways	509	—
Pittsburgh Aviation Industries	140	195
Total	20,380	8,972

Of this grand total of 29,352 miles of mail routes, 4,573 miles were discontinued or suspended.

In the last three years of Postmaster General Walter Brown's overlordship, $56 million were paid to the airlines in mail payments. The Post Office received $18 million back in air mail revenue, leaving an excess cost of $38 million. If the Post Office handling charges are added to this figure, the total cost to the public in taxes was $46 million.

To perform the work, the airlines incurred expenditures of $20 million, and if a reasonable profit of 7½ per cent is allowed, the difference between cost and revenue shows a net profit to the airlines, over the three years 1931–1933, of $34 million.

These figures are set out in more detail in Table 9*, which is summarized from records of the Post Office Department, together with estimates made by Paul T. David. While some airlines may dispute the exact amounts involved, they are of the right order of magnitude. At the kindest of

* See p. 602.

interpretations, the conclusion is that the public paid something like $10 million per year from 1931 to 1933 for the carriage of its air mail.

The question is: was this service worth the expenditure from public funds? Looking back from the vantage point of today the question would appear almost irrelevant. The three years represented only the beginning of a vast expansion of the United States airline industry. The experience gained in operating aircraft, running airlines as big businesses, providing equipment of increasing quality to meet competitive demands, improving efficiency of maintaining the fleets: all these vital factors of airline management found coherent form during the Brown era. Thanks to the broad conception of Brown's policies, the United States airline industry acquired a stature which was soon to dwarf that of any other nation. To meet the requirements of the new airlines, the American aircraft and engine manufacturers responded with designs which rendered obsolete all previous types, either in the United States or elsewhere. Within a few years the full benefits of such progress were to make the airlines of the United States the envy of the world. For its part, the world beat a pathway to the doors of the American manufacturers, particularly Douglas, and the public got its money back a hundred times over in foreign earnings.

Brown reached many of his own self-imposed objectives. He removed the privilege of transcontinental monopoly mail rights held by United, which saw its percentage of total domestic mail payments drop from 66 per cent in 1928 to 34 per cent in 1933. The Aviation Corporation share rose from a mere 7 per cent in 1928 (by predecessor companies) to 27 per cent in 1933, while the various ancestors of the North American combine who could muster 21 per cent in 1928 saw this rise to 30 per cent in 1933. A fact which many of Brown's detractors forgot or ignored was that the total percentage of domestic mail obtained by the three big groups in 1933—the height of Brown's power—was 91·1 per cent, which was actually less than the 91·5 per cent obtained by the combined ancestor companies in 1929—before Brown's policies took effect. In spite of everything he did, therefore, the smaller companies, or independents, actually retained as much of the cake as they had ever had.

An interesting commentary on the situation is found in the comparative percentage figures after four years of subsequent Democratic administration, resolved to reverse the ills of the Republican regime. In 1938, when the Grandfather Rights were distributed, the descendants of the guilty airlines of 1934 still accounted for almost 73 per cent of the total air mail payments.

To return to the Black revelations: it was quite clear that the growth in passenger business had been heavily subsidized by the mail payments authorized by the Postmaster General, and distributed according to his dictates. At the time, in a land recovering from a colossal economic depression, little evidence was required to create a scapegoat. Unfortunately for Walter Brown, too much of his approach to the problem smacked of chicanery and deception; and the 'Spoils Conferences' appeared as acts of collusion on a grand scale. In fact, Brown was exonerated from such charges many years later, but at best the 'Spoils Conferences' were a first-degree blunder.

Individual stories of financial gain did nothing to enhance Brown's reputation—though he himself was not involved. The most spectacular was Frederick B. Rentschler and his $253 investment in United Aircraft. In 1929, during the Wall Street boom, this was valued at $29,575,000, a fairly good appreciation factor. Rentschler drew $800,000 in salary between 1929 and 1930, took a profit of $9 million out of his investment, and with bonuses, cleared $10·5 million. For the man whose vision founded Pratt & Whitney, which in 1967 was calculated to be providing the power-plants for 85 per cent of the world's airliner capacity, this may not seem excessive. Many men have made a great deal more from less laudable activities, and have been judged kindly. But in 1934 the many ordinary people in the U.S.A. who had lost fortunes, big and small, and who had been ruined by the Wall Street crash, thought that ten million per year out of the taxpayer's pocket—for this was the oversimplified conclusion drawn—was going too far.

A Fresh Start

President Roosevelt was a big enough man to recognize quickly that he had erred in his judgement of the air mail problem. Furthermore he wasted no time in trying to straighten things out. He tacitly admitted his mistake, and on 30 March, 1934, exactly one month after the Army Air Corps had started along its perilous road, the Post Office Department invited new bids for air mail contracts. The terms made it clear that these contracts were to be temporary, specifically three months from the date of first service, subject to two additional three-month extensions at the discretion of the Postmaster General.

This expedient decision saved the United States airline industry from degenerating from a state of disarray into one of complete chaos. During 1933, the airlines had managed to achieve some sort of financial stability, thanks to air mail payments, or, to call a spade a spade, air mail subsidy. In that year, Western Air Express made $230,000 profit, United Air Lines $175,000, and TWA $130,000. Eastern Air Transport lost $175,000 and American Airways $160,000. The Big Three (United, Aviation Corporation, General Motors) therefore were just profitable as a whole, to the tune of $200,000.

When the mail payments were so unceremoniously stopped, the effect on the airlines was quickly calculated to be disastrous. Monthly losses were variously assessed at $375,000 for American, $300,000 for United, and $250,000 each for TWA and EAT, figures which, coincidentally, worked out at approximately the value of the former mail payments.

Most of the airlines carried on with their passenger services, albeit on a much restricted route network. But the deep concern felt by all was perhaps epitomized in a notice sent to all his staff by Richard Robbins, president of TWA, which, in effect, suspended the whole airline from active duty.

With considerable relief on all sides, if with a certain amount of sheepish embarrassment on the one hand and an element of truculence on the other, forty-five airlines gathered in a room at the Post Office Department on 20 April, 1934, to watch Postmaster General James A. Farley open the bids. These had been set at a top limit of 45c per mile—somewhat lower than the average rate achieved during the last year under Brown—and the low level of some of the bids revealed that many operators had learned some lessons. This applied as much to the former Post Office favourites, whose bids were generally consistent with genuine costs of operation, as to the formerly belligerent independents, who now refrained from entering desperately uneconomic submissions.

On this eventful day, the pattern of the air transport routes was indelibly inscribed on the map of the United States. For although widely thought to be temporary, since that was the designation given to them by the Post Office Department, later legislation confirmed the awards made on 20 April (and others a week later) as permanent (*See Table 10*). The new map did not look fundamentally different from the old one, a feature which must have given some satisfaction to the ostracized and disgraced Walter Brown.

FEB 21 34 DISTRICT OFFICE PHILA. PA.

TRANSCONTINENTAL & WESTERN AIR, INC.
Municipal Airport,
Kansas City, Mo.

February 18, 1934

TO ALL T & W A PERSONNEL:

Effective February 28th, 1934, the entire personnel of T. & W.A. is furloughed. Between now and that date, the Management will work out plans which will involve the least possible hardship to the personnel and make arrangements for the continuation of its curtailed schedules.

Faithfully yours,
Richard W. Robbins
Richard W. Robbins
President.

Republican Achievements

The Air Mail scandal completely overshadowed every other aviation activity in the latter part of 1933 and early in 1934, a period when the nation devoted some time to reviewing the shortcomings of the late administration. Concentration on an identifiable scapegoat, Walter Brown, meant that substantial progress in many fields of aeronautics went unrecognized and unappreciated.

The establishment of an elaborate system of lighted airways which transformed night flying into normal operational practice, was a major achievement, resulting from elaborate and comprehensive planning, construction, and organization. From the lighting of the first Federal Beacon on 7 December, 1926, at Moline, Illinois, on the Chicago—Dallas route, steady progress was made so that by the end of Hoover's term, 18,100 miles of airways were illuminated by night. In 1932 the maintenance of the lighted airway cost $213 per mile, so that about $3,600,000 was being spent annually on this aspect of safety alone.

Feeling his way gingerly, the first head of the Aeronautics Branch of the Department of Commerce, William P. MacCracken, had laid the first foundations of an aviation administration on a budget of $550,000 for the first fiscal year, 1927. Much of the work was handled by existing branches of the Department the lighted airways came under the Lighthouse Service, for example, while air mapping was handled by the Coast and Geodetic Survey. MacCracken did, however, establish an Information Service, and most important, an Air Regulations Division.

This Division undertook the herculean task of licensing not only all aircraft and airmen flying at the time, but also of keeping up with the rapid expansion which the Branch itself was fostering. By 1932, thanks to Hoover's constant encouragement, the meagre half million dollars of 1927 had risen to more than ten million. The aviation community could afford to feel smug at Coolidge's comment about Hoover, 'That man has offered me unsolicited advice for six years, all of it bad.'

The scale of effort which the inspection of aircraft entailed was enormous. The average inspector was paid about $4,000, for which he worked about twelve hours a day, examining three to four aircraft during that time. By the spring of 1932, about 80 per cent of the nation's 10,000 aircraft had been licensed. They were required to be affixed with the letter N on the wings and rudder and additional letters included C for commercial and X for experimental.

Overworked inspectors could be excused occasional lapses, like the one who declared, 'I don't like that plane and I'll tell you why—I just don't like it'; while another so lost his self-control as to rip some wing fabric with his pocketknife and state, 'I don't think this is strong enough.'

Part of the Air Regulation Division, the Engineering Section, drew up rules covering the airworthiness of all new aircraft. The Branch published a *Handbook for Airplane Designers* in 1927 and got under way with the issue of nine approved-type certificates during that year, followed by 38 in 1928, after which came a deluge, severely testing the technical resources of the Aeronautics Branch.

Another source of grave concern was the unrestricted freedom of flying schools which had sprung up with the aviation age. The number grew from two in 1926 to 250 in 1929, and the administration put an end to certain cavalier practices by an Amendment to the Air Commerce Act, promoted by Senator Hiram Bingham, which made compulsory the inspection of flying schools. This regulation, together with others covering such matters as safe flying altitude and stunt flying, were typical of the unsung backroom work accomplished during the period of explosive expansion of the airlines, which were among the main beneficiaries of the new disciplines.

Air traffic control became a necessity as airports became busier, although this was not handled federally until the Roosevelt administration. Each city was normally responsible for control at its municipal airport, but progress was somewhat hesitant. At Chicago, for instance, three signalmen had the unenviable task of standing at the point of intersection of the main runways, giving signals to aircraft by the use of coloured flags.

An Accident Board was set up in the spring of 1928. This faced opposition on a variety of grounds, including a resentment against confidential reporting, while a formula of accident classification was painstakingly worked out. Manufacturers, operators, and pilots alike gradually came to accept, however, that all were potentially blameworthy, and eventually Clarence Young, the Director of Aeronautics who took over from MacCracken, had to make the first major decision to ground a commercial aircraft type, following the Fokker F-XA crash on 31 March, 1931.

By 1933, tremendous strides had been made in the quantity and quality of navigational equipment of all kinds, primarily in the field of radio. Two-way radio and teletype communications were in general use, and in addition a big step forward was made by the establishment of aural radio-range beacons, whose N and A beams were installed at 99 points by the end of Hoover's administration. Although problems of interference through multiple transmission or terrain peculiarities still persisted, instrument flying was coming into use, and 100 pilots had passed their instrument rating test by September 1932. Remote control of radio stations, including radio-range beacons, and teletyped weather maps were successfully introduced in 1932.

When the Democrats set about their housecleaning in 1934, therefore, the real and much-publicized air mail scandal was only one side of the Republican coin held up for inspection. The other side was an infrastructure which was to provide a sound base for development in the middle and later 1930s when a new breed of aircraft, designed to meet the challenges engineered by Walter Brown, were to demand even higher standards from the airline industry.

American Airlines' Cyclone-powered Douglas DC-3 NC17331 *Flagship Arkansas.* (*American Airlines*)

CHAPTER EIGHT

The DC-3 Era

Redrawing the Airline Map

On 20 and 27 April, 1934, Postmaster General Farley gathered the airlines together to try to salvage the pieces of the airline map which had been cast to the four winds with the cancellation of the air mail contracts on 19 February. The main conditions for attendance were that no company or person involved in the notorious 'Spoils Conferences' should be eligible for new route awards; and that (under new legislation to be enacted) all airline operations should be irrevocably separated from aircraft manufacturing. This spelt the end of holding companies such as the Aviation Corporation or the United Aircraft Corporation in their original all-embracing capacities. But it did not mean the finish or even a fall from prominence of the major units which dominated the airline industry.

Roosevelt's drastic action had forced all sides of the business to examine the situation in a cold rational manner. Emotional and political bias were cast aside in an effort to fashion an airline structure which would not only

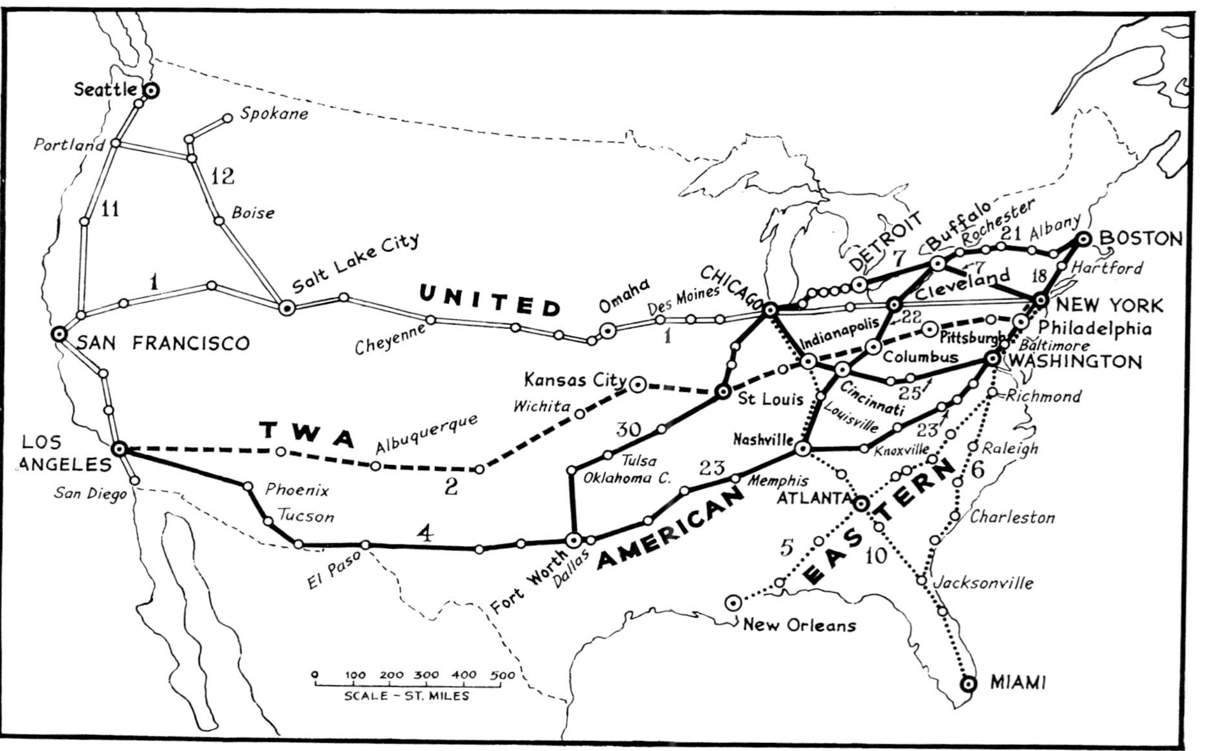

Fig. 14. Trunk Airline Mail Routes, 1934 (The Big Four).

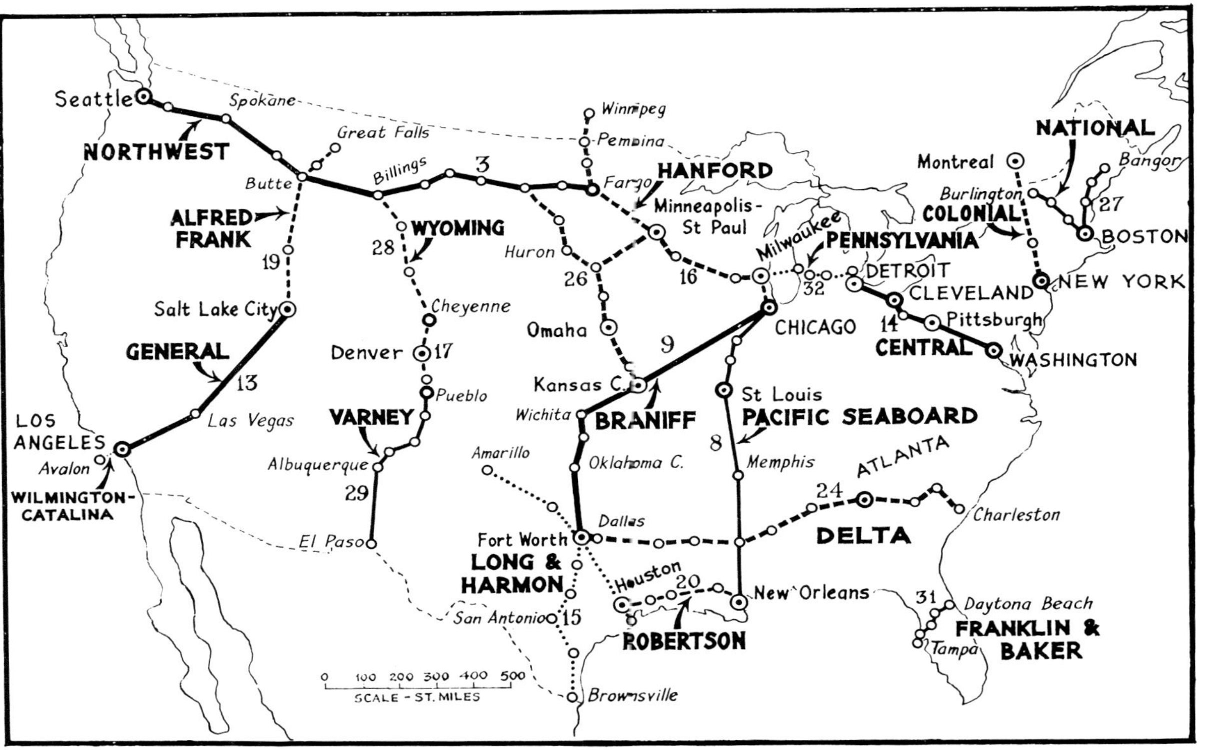

Fig. 15. Trunk Airline Mail Routes, 1934 (excluding the Big Four).

give credit to the operators who had pioneered the extensive route networks but would at the same time provide opportunities for new blood. Ironically, the net result of this policy was a list of carriers bearing a striking resemblance to those which had come in for so much criticism by the Black Committee.

By and large, common sense prevailed. Former airlines which had benefited from the 'Spoils Conferences' re-appeared in the thinnest of disguises. American Airways became American Airlines, Eastern Air Transport became Eastern Air Lines, and so on. Happily this did not precipitate a storm of self-righteous protest, and the change was accepted without demur. Roosevelt's action had revealed conclusively that only large companies, with substantial financial resources, and years of experience in all aspects of airline operations, could be given the responsibility of running the trunk airline industry of the United States.

By a strange combination of circumstances, one of the biggest tycoons of the Walter Brown era, E. L. Cord, president of American Airways, was qualified to attend the new contract meetings with the Postmaster General because he had never attended any of the 'Spoils Conferences', having risen to prominence just afterwards. By a possible error of judgement, Cord did not make extensive claims. Perhaps he thought that Farley's authority would be short-lived; or that the awards would be of very short duration. At any rate, Cord asked for, and obtained, a more direct transcontinental route than that of the old American Airways. Equally, TWA and United obtained transcontinental routes which were virtually untarnished from the palmy days of W. F. Brown. Other companies were allowed a legal entry into the business; but an analysis of the new airline map of the United States revealed that these were still small fry compared with the Big Four. But at least they had a foothold, however small; and no-one could point an accusing finger at the administration on the grounds of favouritism, political manoeuvre, or corruption. All in all, the stigma of shady practice was removed, and the airline world seemed a healthier place after 1934.

The effect on the public was succinctly described at the time in *Southwestern Aviation* which stated: 'There is at least one satisfied customer in the audience as the curtain drops on three months of painful readjustment of the Nation's air mail system. He is the patron of the service—the citizen who buys the air mail stamps. He emerges from the lifting fog and finds service to nineteen additional cities and to four States that had no air mail connections prior to annulment of the contracts. He discovers 28,548 miles of air mail routes as against 25,248 miles under the previous system. He sees four transcontinental routes spread out across the Nation instead of the three of Mr Brown's vintage. He understands that the cost of the service to the Government has been cut in half; and on July first, he can send a letter for six cents instead of eight, enabling him to send more letters "via Air Mail".'

The reduction in costs to the Post Office Department was significant.

In the Brown era the aircraft rate per mile was invariably 44c or thereabouts. In the Farley era the highest rates awarded were 39.50c and the average was considerably lower. Eastern, for example, came down to 19c on two of its main trunk routes; American received Newark—Fort Worth at 13c and Chicago—Fort Worth at an incredible 8c. Most of the newcomers to the air mail business, such as Long & Harmon, Pacific Seaboard, Hanford, and Franklin & Baker, managed to break in by submitting bids below 20c.

The majority of the awards went simply to the lowest bidders. In general these were composed either of former mail contractors who had turned over a new leaf or of established non-mail operators who had so long campaigned for a place in the sun. But there were exceptions. Although a spirit of good will and a wish to bury hatchets prevailed, the administration was anxious to emphasize that it would not automatically accept low bids without qualification. It rejected the low one by Kohler Aviation Corporation for the route from Detroit to Muskegon 'for the reason that it has an officer and a director in the person of Mr Richard W. Robbins, one who was an active participant in the 1930 conferences between air mail contractors and Post Office officials which resulted in the contractors, including Mr Robbins' company, being awarded illegal contracts.'

Fokker Super Universal NC9792 (c/n 840) of Northern Air Transport.

Northern Air Transport was refused the contract between Fargo, North Dakota, and Seattle because of inadequate equipment, illegal bid form, and absence of statement regarding financial responsibility. Syra Aviation Corporation's low bid of 29.5c per mile from Boston to Fort Worth was rejected because the Post Office Department 'found it advisable to rearrange the route from Fort Worth to the East in order to provide a shorter and more direct east–west route through the Southern section of the country to the Pacific Coast, and a more direct and quicker all-air passenger service from the East to Mexico via Brownsville, Texas'. At the second opening of bids, American Airlines won the contract at 13c.

The Ford Tri-Motor played an important part in establishing passenger air transport in the United States. *Top*: Model 5-AT-D NC439H *Puget* (c/n 106) was operated by Pacific Air Transport and United Air Lines. *Centre*: NC435H *Olympia*, seen at Seattle, was the Model 5-AT-D (c/n 102) operated by National Air Transport, Pacific Air Transport and United Air Lines. It passed to Johnson Flying Service and was flying until the 1960s. *Bottom*: NC 9655 *Glacier* was the 5-AT-D c/n 110 operated by PAT and UAL. It is seen with wing hold chutes lowered. (*Gordon S. Williams—two lower photographs*)

Whereas United lost its route to Dallas—Bowen Airlines hastened to take over the ground facilities there—TWA's loss was probably the most severe of all the big airlines. Although retaining the transcontinental route, it lost the important Columbus—Chicago—Oklahoma City cut-off, and the Los Angeles—San Francisco link. For the next five years, TWA operated 40 per cent of its system without the benefit of mail contracts.

The new pattern of air transport outlined by Postmaster General Farley is set out in Table 10* and on the maps on pages 168 and 169, which demonstrate how the old Big Four carriers retained their birthright. Also shown is the degree of infiltration achieved by the smaller airlines into the former preserves of the big companies. Many of these, however, lasted only a year or two, thus confirming to some extent W. F. Brown's expectations when he saw the sole hope of a stable industry in the existence of a few strong airlines. A summary of the airlines actually operating during the summer of 1934 is shown in Table 11, page 604.

Flirtation with Speed

The Ford Tri-Motor had enjoyed its period of glory when the Fokkers had fallen out of favour in 1930 and Henry Ford had lent his name and prestige towards popularizing passenger air travel. But there were signs of restless dissatisfaction by the leading brains in the aircraft manufacturing and designing world who were seeking greater refinements in their art. The first commercial airliner to expose the limitations of the Ford was the Lockheed Vega, designed by John K. Northrop, which entered service with International Airlines on 17 September, 1928. The

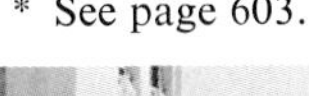
* See page 603.

The aircraft which highlighted the speed limitations of the Ford Tri-Motor was the Lockheed Vega. The Vega 5-C illustrated, NC624E (c/n 53), was the first of several operated by Transcontinental and Western Air and had earlier been used by Southwest Air Fast Express. It is seen at Grand Central Air Terminal, Glendale, California. (*Western Airlines*)

In 1931 Transcontinental and Western Air introduced the Northrop Alpha which incorporated the multi-cellular stressed-skin wing as used later on the DC-2 and DC-3. The example illustrated is NC942Y (c/n 6), an Alpha 3. Note the old WAE 'Indian Head' incorporated in the livery.

The Boeing Model 221 was the second Monomail. It had a retractable undercarriage and could carry six passengers and 750 lb of mail. Registered NC10225, this aircraft first flew in August 1930 and entered service with Boeing Air Transport. (*Boeing Airplane Company*)

The original Boeing Model 200 Monomail, NC725W, after conversion to eight-passenger Model 221A. It first flew on 6 May, 1930, and was the first all-metal streamlined transport aircraft, with unbraced fully-cantilever wing. Both Monomails finished their days with Inland Air Lines (*Gordon S. Williams*)

The Lockheed Orion was the first transport aircraft to exceed 200 mph. *Top*: NC231Y, one of several Orion 9-Ds operated by American Airways. *Centre*: NC13747 was an Orion 9-D2 of Northwest Airways. *Bottom*: NC975Y was an Orion 9-D freighter (c/n 172) owned by Air Express Corporation. Beneath the title Air Express Corporation were the words Fastest Service Coast to Coast. (*Gordon S. Williams*)

On 13–14 May, 1934, Jack Frye of TWA flew this Northrop Gamma 2D, NR13757 (c/n 8), from Los Angeles to Newark, New Jersey, in 11 hr 31 min with 440 lb of mail. (*Gordon S. Williams*)

construction of the first aircraft took only six months and cost only $17,500. Built of wood, and efficiently streamlined—in direct contrast with the Ford—it could carry six passengers at 135 mph. Although its carrying capacity was only half that of the Ford, the superior design wiped out the deficiency, and Edward P. Warner estimated that the operating cost per seat-mile of the two airliners was approximately the same.

The next year, 1930, witnessed the debut of two more six-seater aircraft. TWA introduced the Northrop Alpha, built by the designer of the Vega, and with performance improved through the use of engine cowling and wing fillets, although using the same Pratt & Whitney Wasp engines. United Air Lines experimented with the Boeing Model 200, which incorporated all-metal, stressed-skin construction in addition to the standards achieved by Northrop. Almost twice the weight of the Lockheed and Northrop designs, the Boeing Monomail, as it was called, was powered by a Pratt & Whitney Hornet engine, more powerful than the

This Northrop Gamma 2D, NX13758 (c/n 9), was used by TWA as an experimental overweather laboratory, under the direction of 'Tommy' Tomlinson. (*Gordon S. Williams*)

Wasp, but not enough to achieve comparable speeds. Nevertheless, a cruising speed of 135 mph (158 mph max) was reached, partly through the use of a retractable undercarriage. Its tailwheel and wheel-brakes marked the end of skids once and for all.

Only two Monomails were built, the second designated the Model 221. Both were modified to 221A standard and passed to Inland Air Lines (formerly Wyoming Air Service). One crashed and the other was withdrawn from service, an ignominious end for an aircraft type which played such a large part in revolutionizing civil aircraft design.

Lockheed met the challenge by producing an airliner, the Orion, which was the first in the world to exceed a speed of 200 mph. Introduced first

The wooden Lockheed Vega 5-C NC47M (c/n 99) of Air Express Corporation, which operated a fast transcontinental freight service in 1933–34. (*Gordon S. Williams*)

by Bowen Air Lines in May 1931 it was the first on which flaps were used to reduce landing speed and increase the angle of descent. Undoubtedly, the speed of this breed of aircraft captured the public imagination, and many airlines, especially those without strong manufacturing ties, turned to Lockheed. Braniff, Bowen, and Varney, particularly, were prominent in using the publicity value of the Orion's speed to struggle for survival against the giant corporations backing the Big Four.

TWA used the Northrop Gamma in 1932, which employed essentially the same aerodynamic improvements as the Orion's. In April 1932, a 24-hr transcontinental mail service was demonstrated, and some passengers were carried in the following November. Jack Frye flew across the continent in 11 hr 31 min on 13–14 May, 1934, in a Northrop Gamma.

D. W. 'Tommy' Tomlinson of TWA did a tremendous amount of research flying with the Gamma, especially at high speeds and high altitudes, a programme of meticulous pioneering work which was to reap high dividends in later years.

Lockheed, meanwhile, had established itself as builders of high-speed aircraft. On 19 March, 1933, the *New York Times* was able to report that

NC13211 (c/n 4), with fleet number 53, was one of seven red and silver Consolidated Fleetster Model 20-A parasol monoplanes which began to enter service with TWA late in 1932. (*Gordon S. Williams*)

Among the aircraft disposed of by American Airlines in 1934 were sixteen Pilgrim 100A and 100B single-engined monoplanes. (*American Airlines*)

American Airlines employed at least fourteen Vultee V-1 and V-1A eight-passenger single-engined monoplanes. The example illustrated is NC13767 (c/n 5). Introduced in 1934, the V-1s were the fastest commercial airliners of their day. (*American Airlines*)

One of American Airways' Stinson A three-engined strut-braced monoplanes—some were sold to ANA in Australia.

NC11722 was a Stearman 4-CM1 operated by American Airways, later American Airlines. It may have been one of the eight Stearmans disposed of in 1934. (*Gordon S. Williams*)

NC12354 (c/n 22) was one of a fleet of Curtiss T-32 Condors used by American Airways. This aircraft, the first sleeper-plane used in the United States, was lost in a fatal accident near Liberty, New York, in 1934. (*American Airlines*)

Air Express Inc was 'hitting perilously close to a 16–17-hr daily service coast-to-coast'. This all-express company used Lockheed Orions, specially converted to carry freight, and was created by Philip H. Philbin of Denver. It ranked, in spite of its brief span of existence, as one of the pioneers of air freight—lobsters to Los Angeles, flowers to New York.

With all the remarkable advances made in speed—the Orion of 1931 flew twice as fast as the Ford of 1926—progress in some respects had been slight. The Lockheeds, Northrops, and the Boeing 200 were all small aircraft and were thus unable to produce seat-mile cost improvements over the Ford Tri-Motors. Furthermore they were all single-engined aircraft and were thus regarded as more dangerous.

The Vultee V-1A, the most advanced of all the high-speed airliners of the early 1930s, symbolized the end of the single-engined era. In July 1934, American Airlines, getting under way once again under the new Post Office mail contracts over a much-improved network, set about rationalizing its fleet by advertising 51 miscellaneous aircraft for sale, including 23 Stinson Tri-motors, 16 Pilgrims, and eight Stearmans. It then introduced, on 9 September, the 235 mph Vultee, an eight-passenger metal aircraft which incorporated all the previous design refinements of its type, plus further improvements in machined finishing and additional soundproofing. American used the Vultee on routes from the Great Lakes to Texas, supplementing its transcontinental Condor sleeper service. But the small, high-speed civil airliner had become an expensive luxury, and was swept aside by a dramatic development which sought to marry the technical advances made by Northrop and Lockheed with the one ingredient necessary for success: operating economy.

The First Modern Airliner

Boeing's next airliner was the Model 247, the world's first civil aircraft to embrace those features of design which gave real economic advantage. In 1931, Boeing had built the B-9 bomber in a competition for the U.S. Army Air Force. Although unsuccessful, Boeing profited by its B-9 experience and built the B-247, based on the B-9. The design incorporated twin engines, with the latest NACA cowlings, and positioned further in front of the wing than had been the practice. The structure was rugged, but lacked wing flaps, and was quite small, able to carry only ten passengers. Boeing could have built a larger version, with two 700 hp Pratt & Whitney Hornet engines instead of the 525 hp Wasps, and must have regretted the decision in favour of the smaller type.

The Boeing 247 first flew on 8 February, 1933, and, such was the pace in the early 1930s, entered service on 30 March with United Air Lines. The original orders had been placed by Boeing Air Transport, National Air Transport, Pacific Air Transport, and Varney Air Lines, and the United Air Lines Group quickly built up its fleet just as the new Democratic government was preparing for the Black Committee investigations.

First of the clean twin-engined monoplane transports with retractable undercarriages—the prototype Boeing 247 which first flew on 8 February, 1933. (*Boeing Airplane Company*)

United had thirty 247s in service by the end of June. It had established a coast-to-coast record schedule of 19¾ hr on 1 June, 1933, beating TWA's 26¾-hr Ford Tri-Motor timing, begun on 5 November when the Kansas City stop was omitted—the Northrop service mentioned earlier was not established permanently.

By September, United was operating eleven round trips daily between New York and Chicago, of which ten were with the Boeing 247. Nine were routed with one stop at Cleveland, with a journey time of 4¾ hr. At this time United was the undisputed leader of the route, with American and TWA each operating only one flight each day.

One of the 247's shortcomings was poor performance at some of the high-altitude airports in the Rocky Mountains. The problem was solved

One of United Air Lines/Boeing Air Transport's first Boeing 247s. (*United Air Lines*)

As NR257Y, this Boeing 247D came third in the England-Australia race in October 1934. It is seen at Chicago in United Air Lines' service as NC13369, bearing on its fuselage a map of the air race route and the inscription 'This plane carried the Stars and Stripes across the finishing line in the world's greatest air race'. This Boeing has been preserved in the National Air Museum in Washington, D.C. (*United Air Lines*)

Boeing 247 NC13326 (c/n 1707) seen at Seattle after modification to Model 247D. It bears United Air Lines' 1940 livery and the name *City of San Diego*. This aircraft was used by several operators and was finally wrecked at Allegheny City Airport, Pa, in November 1942. (*Boeing Airplane Company*)

This Boeing 247D entered service with United Air Lines in 1934 and, after being leased to Western Air Express, was used by United for research until October 1945. It then had various owners in Mexico and was finally wrecked at Mexico City in May 1952. (*United Air Lines*)

by fitting variable-pitch propellers developed by one of United's associate manufacturing companies, Hamilton-Standard. These not only reduced normal take-off run by 20 per cent but increased rate of climb by 22 per cent, cruising speed by 5½ per cent, and raised the ceiling on one engine by between 2,000 and 4,000 ft. All 247s were modified to take the new propellers and were known as 247Ds. Seventy-five were built, of which 70 were for United Air Lines and three for DLH, the German airline. A few were still flying thirty years later and at least one remained airworthy in 1967.

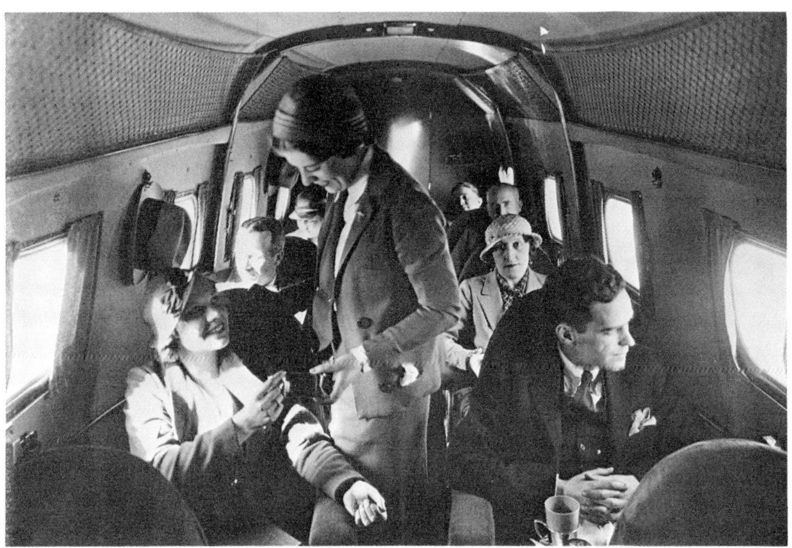

Cabin service aboard a Boeing 247. (*Western Airlines*)

Douglas Enters the Field

Any history of United States air transport must observe that the 1934 Air Mail cancellation scandal changed the course of events. Yet 1934 was noteworthy for another reason: it was the year of introduction of the world's first successful modern airliner, the Douglas DC-2.

United's original order for 60 Boeing 247s effectively tied up production for many months and at that time the interlocking relationships between manufacturer and airline were such that competitor airlines could find it difficult to obtain deliveries. Jack Frye, TWA's vice-president of operations, therefore decided to challenge United by trying to have a better airliner built by another manufacturer working to a TWA specification.

In a famous letter dated 2 August, 1932, Frye set out the TWA requirements for an all-metal, three-engined airliner, able to carry twelve passengers in hitherto unmatched comfort, at a cruising speed of 146 mph. The aircraft had to be fully equipped with the latest and best navigational

Jack Frye (*left*) began his career with Standard Airlines, and moved via Western Air Express to TWA. Working closely with Lindbergh, he wrote the famous 'Jack Frye letter' in which he outlined the original specification for a modern airliner. Of the five addressees, Douglas was successful with its DC-1 design. Later a close associate with Howard Hughes, with whom he made several spectacular flights and co-operated in drawing up the specification for the Constellation, Frye parted company with Hughes and TWA in 1947. Charles Lindbergh (*right*) was chief pilot of Robertson Airlines before making world headlines with his solo transatlantic nonstop flight in 1927. This dramatic achievement did much to popularize air transport in the U.S.A. and Lindbergh subsequently became technical adviser to both TAT and Pan American Airways, planning transcontinental and trans-ocean services, including Great Circle routes, via the Arctic to East Asia and to Europe. (*Culver Pictures Inc*, *right*)

aids, climb at 1,200 ft/min to a ceiling of 21,000 ft, and have a range of more than 1,000 miles, at a gross weight of 14,200 lb. Here was a formidable challenge, circulated through the medium of Frye's letter, to all the leading manufacturers, Curtiss-Wright, Ford, Martin, Consolidated, and Douglas.

What followed reads almost like a fairy story. Donald Douglas gathered together his team of engineers and designers, decided to enter the competition, and within five days two of his key men, Arthur Raymond and Harry Wetzel, were on a Santa Fe train bound for New York, where an appointment had been fixed with Frye, and with Richard Robbins, TWA's president, and technical adviser Charles Lindbergh. From Douglas, Raymond was assistant to James 'Dutch' Kindelberger and Wetzel was vice-president and general manager, and they represented a team which included Ed Burton, Fred Herman, Fred Stineman, George Strompl, and Ivar Shogran, all of whom were to become identified with the famous line of Douglas Commercial airliners whose fate rested on decisions to be made at the end of that train journey.

After three weeks wrangling, during which time Douglas successfully pleaded its case for two engines, Lindbergh made the toughest request: that the new aircraft should be able to take-off on one engine with full payload from any of TWA's aerodromes, and that it should be able to maintain level flight on one engine over the highest mountains along the route. Accepting this stringent demand, Douglas got the order. The contract was signed for the DC-1—Douglas Commercial Number One—on 20 September, 1932, at an agreed price of $125,000. TWA also signed an option on 60 additional aircraft at $58,000 each, excluding engines.

The DC-1 incorporated all the modern refinements of the Boeing 247 and added several more. Most important were the multi-cellular wing structure, developed by Northrop, and the clean aerodynamics developed under the supervision of Dr W. B. Oswald, of the California Institute of Technology. Severe was hardly the description for the competition for the engine. Both Pratt & Whitney and Wright occupied part of the Douglas erecting shop, with a white line drawn across the floor between them. During development, engines were often changed overnight, and intense secrecy was imposed by each engine manufacturer.

The sole example of the Douglas DC-1, the ancestor of all Douglas Commercial airliners.

The DC-1 made its first flight on 1 July, 1933, equipped with Wright 1820-F Cyclone engines. There was some consternation in the Douglas camp as the fuel appeared to cut off each time Carl Cover, the test pilot, attempted to climb; but this was soon put right by turning the carburettors back to front. Soundproofing of a high standard was installed under the supervision of Dr Stephen J. Zand, an acoustics expert, and the Douglas airliner was delivered to TWA, by now a highly satisfied customer, in December 1933. Tommy Tomlinson represented TWA and gave Douglas his cheque at a ceremony at Los Angeles Municipal Airport.

The total development cost of the DC-1, as estimated by Douglas, was $307,000. The first 25 aircraft which followed it off the production line resulted in a net loss of $266,000; but from then on, Douglas got out of the red, and stayed out for 34 years. After some haggling, TWA finally agreed to pay $1,625,000 for the initial order of the modified DC-1, to be known as the DC-2.

The DC-2

The first production DC-2 made its maiden flight on 11 May, 1934. This was less than three months after Jack Frye's famous DC-1 transcontinental flight and three days after the first commercial flights began again after the unfortunate interlude of the Army Air Mail Service. It went into

NC13786 was one of TWA's second batch of Douglas DC-2s. It was delivered in February 1935 and remained in TWA service until it crashed at Pittsburgh in April 1940.

scheduled service on TWA's Columbus—Pittsburgh—Newark route on 18 May, and a week later began flying from Newark to Chicago. Within a span of eight days, it broke the speed record from New York (Newark) to Chicago four times, and virtually chased the Boeings off the route, knocking half an hour off the 247's $5\frac{1}{2}$-hr flight time. On 1 August, 1934, TWA introduced the DC-2 on the transcontinental route, with an 18-hr schedule for the *Sky Chief* service, which left Newark at 4.00 p.m. and arrived in Los Angeles at 7.00 a.m., stopping only at Chicago (thus starting a New York—Chicago nonstop service), Kansas City, and Albuquerque. TWA retired its Ford Tri-Motors in September 1934.

United Air Lines reacted swiftly to the DC-2/TWA challenge by converting its entire fleet of 247s to 247Ds, with better engines and improved interiors. But there was nothing to be done about the obstructive wing spar which bisected the Boeing aircraft's cabin. TWA and Douglas had also increased the DC-2 seating to 14, compared with the DC-1's twelve and the Boeing's ten, and Boeing could not match the landing docility of the DC-2 with its specially developed flaps.

Except for United, the leading airlines queued up for the DC-2, and

TWA, having received its first twenty Douglas DC-2s by the end of August 1934, retired its remaining Ford Tri-Motors. The Ford 5-AT-CS shown, NC410H (c/n 69), was operated for a short period on twin floats from the Downtown Skyport in Manhattan on an experimental airport-to-downtown service. (*Gordon S. Williams*)

NC14274, American Airlines' first Douglas DC-2, seen at Chicago Municipal Airport in 1934. On the apron is an American Airlines Ford Tri-Motor—soon to be replaced by the DC-2s. (*American Airlines*)

TWA ordered six more. American Airlines put the Douglas airliner on New York—Chicago in December 1934, but did not use it on its transcontinental route which was longer than the routes of the other airlines operating coast-to-coast. It placed its faith in sleeper services to ease passenger discomfort and general fatigue, starting with the Curtiss Condor, specially fitted out with sleeping berths and with Dr Zand's soundproofing.

Eastern Air Lines took fourteen DC-2s and put them on the New York—Miami route, with stops at Washington, Charleston, and Jacksonville. This was the beginning of Eddie Rickenbacker's famous *Great Silver Fleet.*

Most of the other domestic airlines put DC-2s into service as quickly as possible. General Air Lines was one of the first, starting services on 8 May, 1934. Its aircraft were leased from Western Air Express, whom it

General Air Lines' first two Douglas DC-2s, NC13731 (nearest) and NC13732. They were delivered in August and September 1934 respectively. (*Western Airlines*)

Braniff Airways' Douglas DC-2 NC13716. This had been TWA's sixth DC-2 and it was sold to Braniff in July 1937 after three years in TWA service.

succeeded, hoping for legislation which might have permitted some link between manufacturer and airline. The Black-McKellar Act, however, ruled that this was out of the question, and the future of the Los Angeles—Salt Lake City airline looked precarious indeed. At the end of 1934, William A. Coulter, the eastern coal-mine owner, who had financed Pennsylvania-Central Airlines, tried to buy General Motors' shares in both Western Air Express and Eastern, but General Aviation (General Motors) forced a liquidation dividend as a condition of sale, almost wiping out the meagre assets. On 29 December, Coulter appointed Alvin P. Adams to set up an independent Western Air Express Corporation. General Air Lines and the old Western Air Express Inc were dissolved, and a link was formed with United Air Lines. WAE had to sell its four DC-2s to Eastern in order to make ends meet.

Panagra introduced the DC-2 on its west coast South American route on 17 September, 1934, when it completed a daylight flight from Cristobal, C.Z., to Lima in the same day for the first time. Other domestic users were Braniff and Northwest.

This Douglas DC-2, N4867V of Johnson Flying Service, was originally delivered to Pan American Airways in March 1935 as NC14296. It is known to have been in service as late as 1968. (*R. E. G. Davies*)

Significantly, there were many export orders for the DC-2. These were stimulated by the success of the KLM DC-2 entered for the England—Australia air race, between 20 and 24 October, 1934. All three major American builders of commercial transports were represented in the race, which was won by a specially-built de Havilland Comet racing aircraft. Much of the fame went, however, to the KLM Royal Dutch Airlines' DC-2 PH-AJU *Uiver*, commanded by K. D. Parmentier and J. J. Moll, flying from Mildenhall, England, to Melbourne, Australia, with three passengers, in 3 days 18 hr 17 min, coming second in the overall placing. The Boeing 247 came third. KLM ordered fourteen DC-2s and was followed by other European and Australian airlines. Douglas' place in the civil airliner field was assured.

A unique photograph of the first of all the Douglas DC-3 series. It is the DST (Douglas Sleeper Transport) X14988 (c/n 1494) seen in American Airlines' livery and without the dorsal fin. The upper berth windows can be seen. The aircraft was retained by Douglas for test flying and delivered to American Airlines on 11 July, 1936, as NC14988 *Flagship Texas.*

The Douglas Sleeper Transport and the DC-3

Following the cancellation of the mail contracts in February 1934, American Airlines Inc was formed on 11 April in order to qualify for new contracts expected to be authorized under the forthcoming Black-McKellar legislation. The company leased, and later purchased, the equipment of the old American Airways, and began operations on 5 May with the transcontinental Curtiss Condor sleeper service. On 13 May, C. R. Smith was appointed president, the company having recognized his organizational and managerial capability during his early career with Texas Air Transport and Southern Air Transport, two of American's ancestors. The Condors were also used to build up frequency on the New York—Chicago route to four round trips per day by September 1934, and the DC-2 was introduced in December, by which time American had been granted important route extensions from New York to both Washington and Boston.

On 31 December, to comply with the terms of the 1934 Air Mail Act, the Aviation Corporation distributed to stockholders all the stock of

American Airways and Canadian Colonial Airways. All the former routes of American Airways had been operated as sub-contracts to the original route certificate, with the exception of the New York—Montreal Canadian Colonial route. Actual distribution of stock began on 1 July, 1935.

Towards the end of 1934, C. R. Smith had discussed with his chief engineer, Bill Littlewood, the possibility of combining the roominess of the Curtiss Condor with the modernity and speed of the DC-2. The sequel to their discussion was a telephone call from Smith to Donald Douglas proposing that the DC-2 be stretched into a sleeper aircraft. Douglas was reluctant at first to interrupt a successful line, but was persuaded when Smith undertook to take twenty of the new type. American Airlines obtained the money from the Government's Reconstruction Finance Corporation, which loaned $4,500,000 to launch the new Douglas Sleeper Transport, or DST, as it became known. The initial contract was actually for ten DSTs, but after the roll-out and test flight, which occurred on the same day, 17 December, 1935, the order was increased and modified to eight DSTs and twelve DC-3s. This latter was the dayplane version of the DST, identical in geometry, but with 21 seats instead of the 14 berths in the sleeper model. The first DST was delivered to American Airlines on 8 June, 1936.

American Airlines introduced the DST as a dayplane on the New York—Chicago route on 25 June, 1936. The *American Eagle* and the *American Arrow* services, as they were called, set entirely new standards, with nonstop flights in both directions, thus surpassing TWA's DC-2 service of February 1935, which was nonstop in the eastbound direction only.

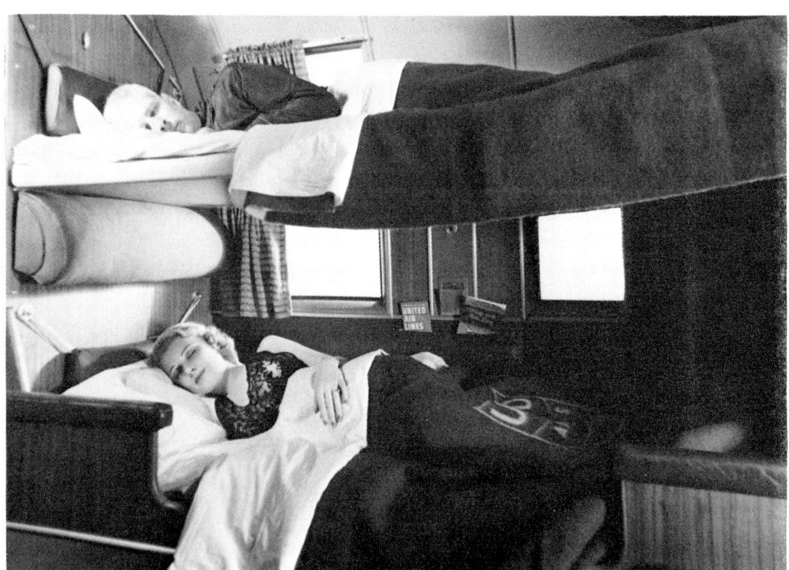

Sleeping berths in a United Air Lines Douglas DST.

On 18 August American took delivery of its first DC-3, the production of which was now increasing in momentum. The DC-3s released DSTs for the job they were designed for, and on 18 September, 1936, the *American Mercury* inaugurated a skysleeper service from coast to coast on a 16-hr eastbound and 17¾-hr westbound schedule. This was a through flight, eliminating the change of aircraft previously scheduled at Dallas where

On June 25th American Airlines inaugurated Non-Stop Flagship service, both ways, twice daily, between New York and Chicago. At christening ceremonies in each city the Flagships were acclaimed by socialites, prominent business men, public officials and Naval officers . . . who were curious to see this new Flagship of the air. The most heart-warming applause came from old-time air travelers on the inaugural flights who judged the Flagship to be everything claimed for it by officials of American Airlines and Douglas Aircraft.

FLAGSHIP FACTS WORTH REMEMBERING:

1. American Airlines' giant Flagships are the largest, fastest, land transport planes in America . . . Top speed, 220 m.p.h.; Cruising speed, 190 m.p.h.
2. Flagship interiors are most spacious, most luxurious . . . quietest.
3. The Flagship's NON-STOP cruising range is the longest of any land transport in the world: more than 2,000 miles.
4. There is no extra charge for NON-STOP Service in Flagships.

NON-STOP

THE AMERICAN EAGLE

EASTBOUND

Lv. Chicago . . . . . . 12:00 Noon (CST)
Ar. New York . . . . 4:55 P.M. (EST)

WESTBOUND

Lv. New York . . . . 12:00 Noon (EST)
Ar. Chicago . . . . . . 3.45 P.M. (CST)

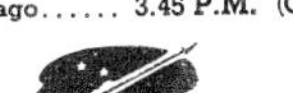

THE AMERICAN ARROW

EASTBOUND

Lv. Chicago . . . . 5:00 P.M. (CST)
Ar. New York . . . . . . 9:55 P.M. (EST)

WESTBOUND

Lv. New York . . . . . . 5:00 P.M. (EST)
Ar. Chicago . . . . 8:45 P.M. (CST)

Extract from American Airlines' timetable effective 15 July, 1936. This was almost certainly the first timetable to show schedules for a DC-3.

passengers boarded the Condors for the western section of the transcontinental journey. The *Mercury* later stopped only at Memphis, Dallas and Tucson on a 15 hr 50 min flight. The *Southerner*, its companion service, took four stops for a slightly longer schedule. By 1937, the full Douglas fleet was in commission, the eight DSTs on transcontinental routes, and the twelve DC-3s on New York—Chicago and New York—Boston.

Although termed a stretched version of the DC-2, the DC-3 was a vastly superior aircraft from a commercial standpoint. There was little difference in performance, as the extra power of the Wright 1820-G2 Cyclones or the Pratt & Whitney R-1830 Wasps (both were specified) barely compensated for the greater weight of the DC-3. The great advantage was in its superior economics. Good aerodynamics had provided for a 50 per cent increase in payload—21 instead of 14 seats—for only a 10 per cent increase in operating costs. The advent of the DC-3 marked the beginning of the end of profitless air transport operations and a real chance to escape from dependence on mail payments to make up the difference between operating costs and passenger revenue.

American Airlines' Douglas DST NC28325 *Flagship San Francisco*. (*American Airlines*)

The superiority of the DC-3 was not lost on the U.S. airline industry. Competition between companies, especially the three East Coast—California transcontinental lines, had always been keen; now it became intense. All hurried to obtain fleets of DC-3s from a manufacturer unattached to any individual airline through ancestral linkage. Although new legislation demanded that airlines and aircraft builders should be divorced, there were still many close associations, often preserved at a personal level. But gone was the system of the tied manufacturer, resulting in, for example, United always buying Boeings, TWA buying Fokkers, and American and Eastern buying Curtiss aircraft.

TWA became the second operator of the DST when it introduced sleeper equipment between New York and Los Angeles on 1 June, 1937, and from New York to Chicago on 18 June, with a 3 hr 55 min schedule. On 15 August, TWA also added the 21-seat dayplane during a period when it was benefiting from the award of new routes. The most important of these gave access to San Francisco by a branch (AM-37) from its trunk route at Winslow, Arizona, calling at Las Vegas, Nevada. A link with Chicago (AM-36) from Dayton, via Fort Wayne, also restored TWA's pre-1934 connection with that city.

United Air Lines managed to mitigate the competition of the DC-2 by modifying and smartening its Boeing 247s, and intensifying frequency. But the DC-3 outclassed the Boeing so emphatically that United purchased ten DSTs and five DC-3s, beginning service on the Los Angeles—San Francisco route on the first day of 1937. United operated eight DC-3 daily flights each way on this fast-growing Californian corridor, of which four were nonstop.

On the other side of the continent, competition on the busy New York—Chicago route had become a tense struggle. United countered American's growing challenge by starting a luxury DC-3 *Skylounge* service, with 14 swivel-seat chairs. The service began in February 1937 but was never a complete success, mainly because passengers were not keen to pay the $2.05 surcharge on the regular fare which United had to impose to compensate for the one-third reduction of seats.

In July 1937, one month after TWA and ten months after American, United became the last major transcontinental operator to introduce DST sleeper service between New York and California. Donald Douglas' misgivings about C. R. Smith's original order for the DST seemed now to be confirmed. Douglas is reported to have asked Arthur Raymond, 'Who the hell is going to buy a sleeper plane? Night flying is about as popular as silent movies.' And he was right. The big market for the Douglas airliner was concentrated on the 21-seat DC-3.

The complete dominance of the DC-3 in the United States before World War 2 has probably not been fully appreciated. A fleet analysis just after

United Air Lines' Twin Wasp powered Douglas DC-3 NC16072 *State of California*. (*United Air Lines*)

the Pearl Harbor incident, only 5½ years after the DC-3's inaugural service, shows that 80 per cent of the airliners on U.S. domestic scheduled services were DC-3s (*See Table 13**). Although it had its share of accidents, some fatal, another significant fact worth recording is that during a complete twelve months period in 1939–40, when DC-3s monopolized the scene, the airlines enjoyed a 100 per cent safety record.

What the story would have been had the U.S. airline industry taken the course prescribed for it by Walter F. Brown is an interesting speculation. All credit is due to him for recognizing the need to consolidate large operating units and to give them a guarantee of stable, subsidized activity. Regrettably, however, he condoned the airline-manufacturer relationship, and the perpetuation of this would probably have slowed down progress in the technical field. Fortunately for the progress of air transport, Douglas was a free agent.

* See page 608.

Consequences of the 1934 Air Mail Act

The sad experience of the Army Air Mail Service did generate much that was beneficial to the airlines. The Roosevelt administration was forced to attend to civil air matters in earnest. A succession of legislative acts and amendments, combined with the results of valuable work carried out by a Commission of Inquiry, culminated in the establishment of a Government Department with an exclusive mandate to control and foster the airline industry. The procedures which were eventually to be crystallized into the Civil Aeronautics Act of 1938 took four years to evolve, starting in 1934.

Senator H. L. Black, who had headed the inquiry into the 'Spoils Conferences', and Senator K. McKellar joined in sponsoring a new Bill which Congress passed on 12 June, 1934. This was the Air Mail Act of 1934, sometimes known as the Black-McKellar Act. It made far-reaching changes in the whole structure of U.S. air transport. Three Government bodies were to control its destiny, the Post Office, the Bureau of Commerce, and the Interstate Commerce Commission.

The Post Office awarded the mail contracts, for an initial period of one year, to be extended indefinitely if the contractor performed satisfactorily. The temporary contracts awarded immediately after the Army Air Mail fiasco were confirmed on a semi-permanent basis—to the distress of some who had assumed that a new round of bidding for permanent routes would take place.

The Interstate Commerce Commission was charged with the responsibility of fixing fair and reasonable rates, within the upper limit prescribed by the Act, which linked rates to aircraft miles, with a sliding scale of increases based on load. Rates were to be reviewed at least annually.

The Secretary of Commerce was to specify speed, load capacity, and safety features of equipment to be used on each air mail route, and to regulate hours and benefits of pilots and mechanics. Accounting practices of the carriers were to be monitored by the Post Office and Interstate Commerce Commission.

An important clause in the Act prohibited, after 31 December, 1934, any air mail contractor from holding an interest in any other aviation enterprise except landing grounds and appurtenances thereto. Equally, other aviation enterprises were denied the right to enter the airline business. No person who had entered into any unlawful combination to prevent air mail bidding (i.e. the 'Spoils Conferences') could be employed in a managerial capacity by an airline. And all contractors were obliged to furnish information on stockholdings of more than 5 per cent, a financial statement, and the original amount paid for corporation stock.

Finally, the President authorized the appointment of a commission of five members 'for the purpose of making an immediate study and survey and to report to Congress not later than February 1, 1935, its recommendations of a broad policy covering all phases of aviation and the relation of the United States thereto'.

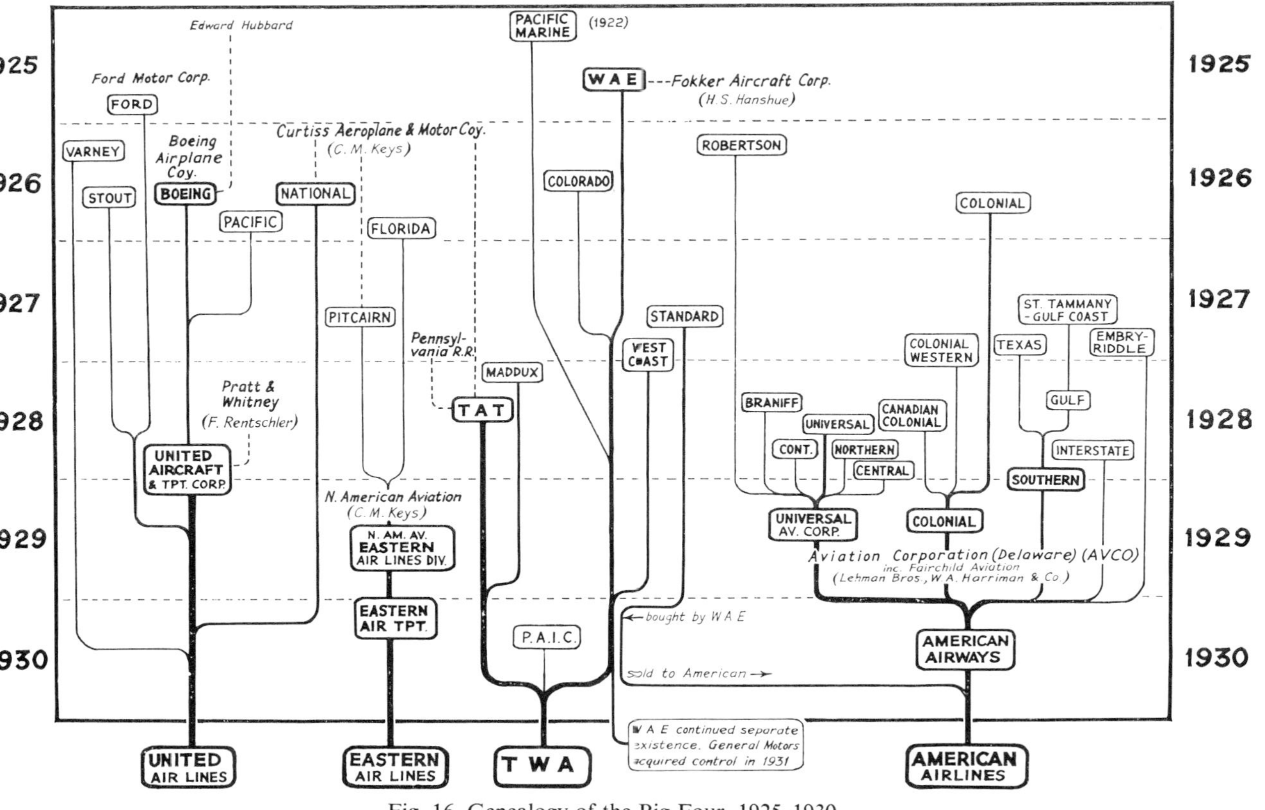

Fig. 16. Genealogy of the Big Four, 1925–1930.

The chief offenders of the W. F. Brown era hastened to mend their ways, but did not make too big a showing of repentance. As recounted above, American Airways became American Airlines on 11 April, 1934. Transcontinental & Western Air Inc organized TWA Inc, to give a corporate title to their well-known abbreviation, on 17 April, although TWA Inc owned no assets or flying equipment; later, on 27 December, both corporations were consolidated under their former name, presumably allowed by the administration once the spirit of the law was seen to be observed. The controlling interest of TWA passed from General Motors to John D. Hertz Sr, the Yellow Cab magnate, and Lehman Brothers, bankers. Western Air Express, after a defiant few months as General Air Lines, reverted to its old name (but not its vigorous independence) on 29 December. United Air Lines remained comparatively unscathed, merely divorcing itself from the United Aircraft empire.

A stout rearguard action was fought by one of the old giant holding companies, North American Aviation, which disposed of its interests in Western Air Express and TWA, and some manufacturing activity, retaining only General Aviation and Eastern Air Transport as two divisions, one manufacturing and one operating. After the reorganization of the industry in 1934, this was the only company retaining a joint interest in building and operating aircraft, and did so on the plea that, although ownership and interlocking relationships were taboo, the precise wording of the law did not preclude one company from carrying on both activities simultaneously. The old Eastern Air Transport became Eastern Air Lines, and Rickenbacker was named general manager. On 16 October, 1935, the last Pitcairn Mailwing was retired, and after a trial with Lockheed Electras in 1935 and 1936, Eastern settled down to the highly profitable operation of Douglas twin-engined airliners.

On 31 December, 1936, Eastern paid $160,000 for the Wedell-Williams Transport Corporation, which had taken over the New Orleans—Houston route from the Robertson Airplane Service. Then, on 22 April, 1938, North American Aviation finally conceded the principle of separate operating companies, and sold its holdings through a public stock offering. After an attempt by John Hertz, the entire stock was bought by Rickenbacker, with the help of some friends, for $3,500,000.

NC14958, a Lockheed Model 10B Electra of Eastern Air Lines.

NC14263, one of Northwest Airlines' fleet of Lockheed Model 10A Electras. *(Northwest Airlines)*

Northwest Airlines was incorporated on 16 April, 1934, to replace the former Northwest Airways, but was successful in winning only that portion of the northern transcontinental mail route from Fargo, N.D., westwards. This deficiency was remedied on 31 December of that year by purchasing, from Hanford's Tri-State Airlines, the Fargo—Chicago (and incidentally the Fargo—Winnipeg) routes. Northwest did not have DC-2s like most of the major operators of the day, preferring instead the new twelve-passenger, 190 mph, twin-engined Lockheed L.10 Electra, which went into service—the world's first by this type—on 11 August, 1934. Later, in September 1937, Northwest added the L.14 *Sky Zephyr*, with two extra seats, and 30 mph faster than its predecessor, and finally became a DC-3 operator in March 1939.

Many of today's airlines first got under way with the new deal for the airlines in 1934. In the southeast, particularly, there were significant events. Delta Air Corporation, unsuccessful in preserving its independence in the big business days of 1930, now re-emerged as the successful bidder for the Atlanta—Fort Worth and Atlanta—Charleston routes, the controlling interest being acquired by C. E. Faulk, a former Louisiana newspaper proprietor. Delta's first equipment was a modest fleet of second-hand Stinsons, but moved into the Lockheed Electra class in 1936.

In Florida, the National Airline System, under the direction of George Baker, opened its first service on 15 October, 1934, on a St Petersburg—Daytona Beach route, with a fleet of three Ryan monoplanes, adding Stinson Tri-motors the following year. Service was extended to Miami and the company became a corporation on 8 July, 1937. In September of that year, National joined the smaller airlines in purchasing Lockheed Electras, and can claim the odd distinction of being the only major airline in the U.S.A. never to have operated a Douglas twin-engined aircraft.

A new airline sprang up in the Rocky Mountain area. Walter T. Varney, who had already made sporadic sallies into the airline business, reappeared by forming the Southwest Division of Varney Speed Lanes (the other Division was in California) in co-operation with his former associate, Louis H. Mueller. Varney won the mail contract for the Pueblo—El

Paso route, via Santa Fe and Albuquerque, and began operations on 15 July, 1934, at first from Denver with passengers and freight only on the first leg, but curtailing it to the contract mail portion when the headquarters were moved to El Paso. On 17 December, 1934, the company was reorganized as Varney Air Transport Inc, with Mueller taking over control. Varney withdrew to continue his adventures in Mexico. Mueller's fleet was four nine-passenger Lockheed Vegas, and business was not exactly brisk during the first few weeks, averaging five passengers per week. In 1935, Robert Six acquired a substantial shareholding in the company, which made steady, if unspectacular progress.

The first modest expansion came on 14 May, 1937, when Varney Air Transport purchased the Denver—Pueblo air mail route from Wyoming Air Service, and replaced the Vegas with three Lockheed 12s. On 1 July Varney became Continental Air Lines Inc, which moved its headquarters back to Denver on 31 October. Wyoming Air Service also sold another section of its north-south route, from Denver to Cheyenne, to United Air Lines, the two sales totalling $243,000. In April 1938, Wyoming was reorganized as Inland Air Lines Inc.

An Inland Air Lines' Boeing 247D. (*Western Airlines*)

Operating in the same area of the northern Rocky Mountains, mainly in the State of Montana, National Parks Airways was taken over by Western Air Express on 1 August, 1937, as the California airline gradually began to try to expand its route network to something approaching its former coverage in the pre-1934 days.

One of the biggest new beneficiaries under the route awards was Braniff Airways, which was granted the important mail contract from Dallas to Chicago on 7 May, 1934, thus achieving a long-thwarted ambition. The route included the booming cities of Fort Worth, Oklahoma City, Kansas City, Tulsa and Wichita, among others. Mail flights began on 17 May and passenger service on 30 May, with Lockheed Vegas.

On 1 January, 1935, Braniff added the Dallas—Amarillo mail contract through the acquisition of Long and Harmon Airlines, which had been the successful bidder in 1934. In March 1936, the network was also ex-

Braniff Airways' metal fuselage Lockheed Vega DL-1 NC8495 (c/n 156) was used on services between Dallas and Chicago.

tended to Houston, Brownsville, and other Texas cities, when Bowen Airlines, another successful bidder, also withdrew. Bowen's crusading airline went down fighting—its last aircraft was the Vultee, the 'world's fastest equipment'—but even Texas was not big enough to sustain it as a viable concern.

Although losing the right to serve Tulsa, through a technicality (service began a day late, on 2 July, 1935, because of late delivery of aircraft) Braniff began to expand healthily, now that its shrewd acquisitions provided a sound network base, and on 12 June, 1937, the airline joined the ranks of its seniors by putting DC-2s into service on the Dallas—Brownsville route, following soon on the Chicago section.

Another fortunate contestant for mail contracts in 1934 was Pacific Seaboard Airlines, which switched its sphere of influence dramatically by winning the Mississippi Valley route from Chicago to New Orleans by the narrow margin of 1c per mile from the Robertson Airplane Service

This Stinson 6000B, NC11175 (c/n 5025), was the first type operated by Chicago & Southern Air Lines.

Company. Mail service began on 3 June, 1934, and passenger flights started two weeks later. The name of the company was changed to the more appropriate Chicago & Southern Air Lines, and its six-passenger Bellanca Pacemakers, which had opened service originally on a coastal stopping service from Los Angeles to San Francisco, were replaced by ten-passenger Lockheed Electras. Robertson did win one route, from New Orleans to Houston, but after a few months decided to withdraw from the airline business, and handed over to the Wedell-Williams company, which itself was absorbed by Eastern Air Lines in 1937.

A newcomer in the northeast was Central Airlines, which underbid Pennsylvania Airlines for the Washington—Pittsburgh—Detroit route. In June 1934 Pennsylvania Airlines acquired the Kohler Aviation Corporation, which became the Western Division of the parent unit, but incurred the displeasure of the Post Office because of non-observation of the 'Spoils Conferences' participation disqualification. Pennsylvania continued to operate passenger services, but after a bitter struggle the two companies agreed to a merger, to form Pennsylvania-Central Airlines (PCA) on 1 November, 1936.

The Civil Aeronautics Act of 1938

The Air Mail Act of 1934 authorized the President to appoint a commission of five members to recommend an outline for the future of civil aviation in the United States. Accordingly, on 11 July, the Federal Aviation Commission was appointed under the chairmanship of Clark Howell, editor-in-chief of the *Atlanta Constitution* and a member of the National Committee of 1932. The vice-chairman was Edward P. Warner, by that time a recognized authority on aeronautics. The Commission submitted its report to the President on 22 January, 1935. It recommended that air transport should be given the same status as other forms of transport, that the Post Office should be free to use any existing service, and that competition should be preserved and promoted. In particular, it also recommended the creation of an Air Commerce Commission, as a temporary measure to co-ordinate and control aspects of mail rate fixing, safety regulations, and operation of an airways system, until an overall transport agency could take over the entire responsibility. On 31 January Congressman Clarence Lea of California introduced a House bill to enact a law along these lines, but in forwarding the report to Congress, President Roosevelt in effect disagreed in principle, and said so. Furthermore, on 7 June, as an extension of the Emergency Railroad Transportation Act, the President recommended that 'air transportation should be brought into a proper relation to other forms of transportation by subjecting it to regulation by the same agency'. Warming to his theme, Roosevelt went as far as expressing the hope that the Interstate Commerce Commission should '. . . ultimately become a Federal Transportation Commission with comprehensive powers'.

Senator McCarran, who had been active in promoting air transport legislation during the passage of the Black-McKellar Act, tried to introduce a new bill on 10 June (replacing a previous bill he had initiated on 21 January) to put into effect the President's wishes, but during the hearings, a rift appeared between the Post Office and the Interstate Commerce Commission. After being rewritten, the bill failed to reach a vote on the floor of the Senate and died with the adjournment of the 74th Congress in 1936.

An amendment to the 1934 Act was sponsored by J. M. Mead, of the House Post Office Committee, and passed on 14 August, 1935. This was a further step towards giving the airlines self-sufficiency. It replaced the annual mail contracts with three-year contracts, thus encouraging the airlines to plan ahead and, more important, giving investors confidence in the industry. The amendment bill also authorized moderate increases to the route mileage (frozen at 25,000 miles under the 1934 Act) to prevent abuses under extension clauses.

If the administration appeared to be dragging its feet on airline affairs, this was not true of aviation generally. Important strides had been taken in 1934 in matters of safety. On 19 June an amendment to the 1926 Air Commerce Act gave extensive powers to the Secretary of Commerce regarding the investigation of accidents, including the issuing of a public statement in the case of those involving fatalities. On 1 October, revised safety requirements for airlines became effective, the most important being that for flying at night and over terrain not readily permitting emergency landings, multi-engined aircraft capable of flying with one engine inoperative were required. Also stricter regulations were brought into force concerning such criteria as minimum flight altitudes, weather minima, and landing and take-off procedures by using operations manuals approved by the Bureau of Air Commerce.

The Roosevelt administration was able to relieve the austerity imposed on the airlines when on 1 July, 1937, considerable funds were released to modernize the nation's airways system. A total of $7,000,000 was allocated, the most important project being the conversion of the airway broadcast and radio range network to a simultaneous system, and during the fiscal year 1938 contracts were let covering equipment at 165 stations.

Civil aviation was gaining momentum, and Roosevelt belatedly conceded the principle of separate responsibility by a specialist government department. The comprehensive plan fought for by McCarran was gaining support, although the Post Office and the Interstate Commerce Commission were not his most enthusiastic advocates. In the autumn of 1937, the President appointed an Interdepartmental Committee to review proposed legislation and soon, on 4 January, 1938, a bill was proposed which broadly met the separate requirements of the crusading Senator McCarran and Congressman Clarence Lea.

The Civil Aeronautics Act of 1938 was signed by President Roosevelt on 23 June, and most of its provisions, including permanent route certification, became effective on 22 August. The law created a new kind of Federal agency, designed to keep its functions as the agent of Congress distinct from those as the agent of the President. It created a Civil Aeronautics Authority (C.A.A.), consisting of five members, of whom no more than three could be members of the same political party. They were appointed for six years and were not allowed a financial interest in any aviation activity. Within the Authority was also created the office of Administrator to deal with executive and operational functions, as distinct from safety and economic regulation, and a three-member Air Safety Board was also set up. All nine members were appointed by the President, with the concurrence of the Senate. The Administrator could be removed by the President at will, the others only for cause.

The Authority was given regulatory powers applying to airline tariffs, air mail rates, and business practices, the last item applying to accounting, statistics, mergers, and competition. The Administrator gave his attention to civil airways, navigation facilities, and regulation of air traffic, including airports. The Air Safety Board took over investigation of accidents and recommendations for accident prevention.

From this time any airline wishing to operate a route, with or without mail contracts, had to obtain a route certificate from the C.A.A. (later the C.A.B.). The rights granted were not exclusive and competition was specifically included among the many factors to be considered. But the prospect of an open free market, in which all could participate under a benevolent and indulgent bureaucracy, was removed (if any still cherished the hope), and the next years saw the adoption of a system of strictly controlled competition.

In spite of initial uneasiness—there was a sudden series of accidents immediately the C.A.A. began its work—the new Act was responsible for a degree of stability and carefully stimulated growth which was to become a model for the world. Through manipulation of, for example, nonstop route awards, some of the dangers of monopoly or inequality of corporate strength were circumvented. After satisfying the C.A.A. with their qualifications, all existing airlines were granted permanent certificates for their networks, which became known as Grandfather Rights. Delta Air Corporation had the honour of receiving the first of 23 awards.

The five members of the Civil Aeronautics Authority were named by President Roosevelt on 7 July, 1938. The chairman was Edward J. Noble, a well-known industrialist, and the Administrator was Clinton M. Hester, a veteran public servant from Montana. One of the first acts of the new Authority was to announce, on 27 September, 1938, that the President had approved the construction of a new airport for Washington, only 3½ miles from the Post Office Building, and Washington National Airport was opened on 16 June, 1941.

On 23 March, 1939, the Authority recommended in its first comprehensive airport survey that the provision of an adequate system of airports serving the whole nation should be a matter of national concern and a proper object of Federal expenditure, including public works or work-relief funds. The total amount envisaged as appropriate to the task was $125,000,000, an indication that the C.A.A. did not intend the airlines or the airways to be regarded as modest claimants on the public purse.

On 1 May, 1939, the airways modernization programme was completed, resulting in a Federal Airways System covering 25,000 miles, and including 231 radio range stations, 100 u.h.f. cone-of-silence markers, and 21 fan markers.

Within the next two years, during which the airlines thrived under an Authority which gained respect for fairness and concern for the public interest, the President reorganized the whole structure. On 30 June, 1940, the five-man Authority was transferred to the Department of Commerce and renamed the Civil Aeronautics Board (C.A.B.). The Air Safety Board was abolished and its functions assigned to the C.A.B. The Administrator was also transferred to the Department of Commerce, retaining his original functions and adding certain safety-regulating duties, all as the Civil Aeronautics Administration. The C.A.A. continued to exist as a paper entity embracing the C.A.B. and the Administration. Donald H. Connolly, a Lieut-Col in the U.S. Army, was named as the first Administrator of Civil Aeronautics.

Beginning a New Era

During the period between 1934 and 1938, while the government cogitated over the problem of how to control the airlines, the companies themselves behaved quite well. The annual flood of transient enterprises dwindled to a mere trickle (*See Table 12, page 606*), in contrast to the prodigal days of the pre-1934 era (*See Table 8, page 593*). Very few airlines born in the late 1930s survived more than a season; those that did were promptly taken over by the trunk airlines.

Marquette Airlines was a typical case. Founded in January 1938 as Midwest Airlines (the name was changed almost immediately), it began service with Stinson Tri-motors on 20 April on a lucrative-looking mail route (AM-58) between St Louis and Detroit, via Cincinnati, Dayton and Toledo. This cut right across trunk airline territory, and not long afterwards the Marquette directors agreed to TWA buying the outstanding stock. TWA leased the route from 15 August, 1940, but the C.A.B. did not give its blessing to a complete acquisition until April 1941. The airline purchase was completed on 5 December, 1941, the 564-mile route costing TWA $350,000.

Up in the northeast corner of the U.S.A., the C.A.B. allowed the Boston & Maine and Maine Central railroads to retain control of the pre-1934 Boston-Maine Airways. This airline operated two Lockheed Electra routes to Montreal and to the fishing lakes of Maine, having acquired the rights for the whole area by buying National Airways on 1 March, 1937. On 19 November, 1940, the airline changed its name to Northeast Airlines,

Lockheed Model 10A Electra NC16056 (c/n 1070) is seen with the markings of Boston-Maine and Central Vermont Airways.

Interior of a Boston-Maine and Central Vermont Airways' Lockheed Electra. The seat pockets contain timetables of the airline and Maine Central Railroad.

Hanford Air Lines' Lockheed Model 10A Electra NC16050 *Sioux Chief* (c/n 1061).

a considerable simplification from its previous title which indicated all its ancestors.

Two other small companies began service in New England in 1937. The Airline Feeder System started on 4 October from Springfield to New York, via Hartford, New Haven and Bridgeport. Mayflower Airlines began two routes between Boston and Nantucket in July, followed by a route from Boston to Springfield on the day that the Airline Feeder System opened. These two airlines—no more than air taxi services by today's definitions—did not last long. A.F.S. ceased in October 1939 and Mayflower was purchased by Northeast on 5 January, 1945.

The pre-war history of the companies which had survived the 1934 crisis was comparatively uneventful. Hanford Tri-State Airlines, having dropped the Tri-State part of its name, came under new management on 1 July, 1936, when A. S. Hanford Sr relinquished control on the death of his son in an aeroplane accident. The name was then changed to Mid-Continent Airlines in August 1938, by which time the small route network through the corn country had been extended southwards to Tulsa via Kansas City. In similar modest vein, Chicago & Southern Airlines was able to open a branch line from Memphis to Houston on 1 March, 1941.

In April 1939 an important change of ownership took place in TWA, when Howard Hughes, heir to the Hughes Tool Company fortunes, and famous record-breaking pilot, became the principal stockholder. Only just over a year later, on 8 July, 1940, TWA took air transport another step forward by introducing the 33-passenger Boeing 307 Stratoliner on its transcontinental routes, cutting the shortest time to 13 hr 40 min, two hours less than the DC-3's.

The Model 307 represented a minor victory for Boeing over Douglas, and gave the Seattle company's civil division a little compensation for having to bow out in 1934 when the Douglas DC-2s took over the mainline transport routes of the United States airlines. Both Pan American and TWA had been parties in sponsoring a large four-engined Douglas airliner as early as 1936 but had decided to play safe and follow the progress of more than one manufacturer. Boeing had designed a supremely successful bomber, the B-17 Flying Fortress, and the Model 307 was a fairly straightforward development, employing the same four-engined layout, wing and tail. The fuselage was the most notable advance on airliner design practice for several years, being the first to be pressurized to keep the internal air pressure always at an acceptable level. The Boeing 307's main capability was to fly at 14,000 ft, a much higher altitude than that normally achieved by DC-3s. To gain this capability of flying 'above the weather' a pressure differential of 2½ lb/sq in was required. A by-product of this specification was that high octane fuel had to be developed to obtain higher supercharger pressure to maintain engine power.

TWA's pursuit of high-altitude flying was largely the result of many years of creative research into this unknown environment by Tommy Tomlinson. During 1935–1936 Tomlinson was estimated to have done more

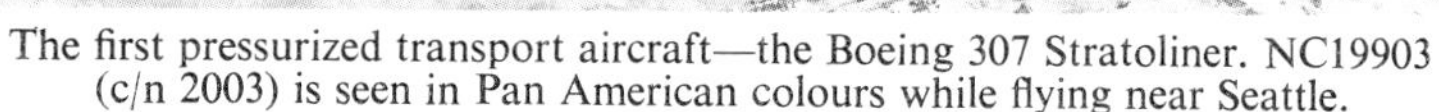

The first pressurized transport aircraft—the Boeing 307 Stratoliner. NC19903 (c/n 2003) is seen in Pan American colours while flying near Seattle.

flying at over 30,000 ft than all other pilots combined. His conclusion that 95 per cent of weather problems ended at 16,000 ft led directly to the Stratoliner design.

Unfortunately the Boeing 307's career was short-lived as a transcontinental record-breaker, for on 24 December, 1941, TWA's fleet was withdrawn from civil work and transferred to transatlantic wartime service. Only ten were built, including Pan American's, but they were reliable and rugged, and survived World War 2 to return to regular airline service for a few years. In fact, several were still flying in the early 1960s in remote airline communities in South America and Southeast Asia.

Douglas had actually begun a four-engined design in 1936, following joint discussions with the Big Four airlines and Pan American, all of which needed an airliner with much greater range and carrying capacity than the DC-3's. Under an agreement dated 23 March, 1936, each subscribed $100,000 towards the cost of developing the DC-4E, designed to carry a maximum payload of 11,000 lb, or 60 passengers, for more than 1,000 miles. The half million dollars from the airlines was only one sixth of the eventual development cost, which was inflated because of the considerable refinements in design, before its first flight on 7 June, 1938.

The most obvious outward feature was the nosewheel undercarriage. Although already used on smaller types, this was the first such venture with large airliners. Significantly, all subsequent types built in the U.S.A. followed this pattern. Powered controls also made their appearance on the DC-4E, and the use of slotted flaps permitted an increase in wing loading.

United Air Lines put in a token bid for the honour of being the first

U.S. airline to operate a modern four-engined landplane by ordering six DC-4Es in July 1939. (Pan American and other companies already had four-engined flying-boats, and Imperial Airways, KLM, Deutsche Lufthansa, Syndicato Condor and others outside the U.S.A. had four-engined landplanes.) On 1 June, 1939, the first Douglas DC-4E went into experimental service for a brief period, but this was short-lived. The specific aircraft involved was the prototype; United did not like it and sold it to Japan, where it subsequently crashed.

United Air Lines was also actively involved with one of the first big merger cases with which the new Civil Aeronautics Board had to deal. During the latter 1930s United and Western Air Express came close to a complete amalgamation. The Californian airline was struggling hard for survival and meeting its customary ill luck. After celebrating ten years of accident-free flying on 17 April, 1936, there were two crashes during the next two years. On 26 June, 1939, William Coulter and a group of stockholders tried to sell Western to United. The deal was recommended by the

The sole example of the Douglas DC-4E, which flew some experimental services for United Air Lines in June 1939.

C.A.B. Examiner, but was turned down by the Board itself. Some of the objectives of the merger were achieved when an interchange service was inaugurated from Los Angeles to New York on 1 September, but all ties between the two companies were severed on 11 March, 1941. On 17 April of that year, Western Air Express was renamed Western Airlines, by which time it boasted a fleet of seven DC-3s and five Boeing 247Ds, the latter inherited from United.

Another recipient of United's cast-off Boeing 247s was Pennsylvania-Central Airlines (PCA) which after the merger of 1936 steadily consolidated its position on a system of routes west of Washington, D.C. A new route to Buffalo, via Baltimore, Harrisburg, and Williamsport, was added to its Great Lakes network late in 1937, and service was extended to Chicago and Sault Ste Marie, at the southern and northern ends of Lake

Western Airlines' Douglas DC-3 NC18600.

Boeing 247 NC13348 (c/n 1730) was bought by Pennsylvania-Central Airlines from United Air Lines in January 1937. Markings were red. (*Gordon S. Williams*)

Pennsylvania-Central Airlines' Cyclone-powered Douglas DC-3 NC21787 *Capital Ship Milwaukee*. PCA later became Capital Airlines.

Michigan respectively, in 1939. PCA found itself linking a number of large cities of good traffic-generating potential. The Boeing aircraft were plainly inadequate, and DC-3s entered service in January 1940. The C.A.B. gave PCA further support on 30 January, 1941, by extending its network southwards from Pittsburgh to Knoxville and Birmingham.

Although in post-war years PCA was to become one of the world's leading passenger-carrying airlines, the DC-3 purchase and its timing illustrated the difference between the Big Four and the smaller domestic trunk carriers. For as PCA moved on to DC-3s, so the leaders of the industry were tackling the next stage of development. As outlined above, the Douglas company was combining four engines with further refinement of its well-tried design knowledge. Boeing was capitalizing on its bomber experience and TWA's prompting to make the first pressurized airliner. Behind the scenes, Howard Hughes, now the owner of TWA, added his vision to Lockheed's aerodynamic talents and high-speed aptitude to develop a new airliner which was to surpass the best of Douglas and Boeing.

These momentous technical advances occurred at about the same time that the establishment of the Civil Aeronautics Board stabilized the administration of the airlines on a rational basis. Although the onset of World War 2 was a great handicap to the speedy completion of many plans, these were the real foundation on which the massive United States airline industry was built. Since that time, the U.S. airlines' share of the world's total air transport productivity* has never fallen below fifty per cent.

* Excluding the U.S.S.R. and China.

Two men who played a major part in establishing Pan American Airways as one of the world's great airlines—Juan Trippe (*left*) and Charles Lindbergh.

CHAPTER NINE

Pan American goes South

Preliminary Sparring

One of the most publicized dates in the history of United States air transport is 28 October, 1927, which marked the beginning of Pan American Airways' regular scheduled service. Before the Fokker F-VII piloted by Hugh Wells took-off on this historic flight, however, a great deal of industrial manoeuvring had taken place, with three enterprising groups concerned with thc in-fighting.

The stake was high: the development of United States civil air transport throughout Latin America. Much depended on the élan and imagination of the participants, and there was no lack of these qualities in any of the three.

The first trans-Caribbean route was not promoted by a North American company. Strangely, Aeromarine had not expanded further south than Florida and the Bahamas, and it was left to the national airline of Colombia to make the first move to link the mainland of South America direct to Florida. In 1925 Dr Peter Paul von Bauer, managing director of Sociedad

Colombo-Alemana de Transportes Aereos (SCADTA), flew a delegation from Barranquilla to Key West, via Central America and Cuba, in two Dornier Wal flying-boats. These aeroplanes had been supplied by the ambitious Kondor Syndikat of Berlin. He went to Washington to negotiate landing rights in Florida and the Canal Zone but unfortunately arrived in the capital just when Billy Mitchell's campaign for Air Power was at its height. The idea of a German-sponsored airline—as indeed was the nature of SCADTA's backing—based only a few hours' flight from United States territory, and with the right to fly into it, was not popular. Von Bauer's request was denied by the State Department.

The next year a group of northerners began to show interest in the Caribbean. Juan Trippe, who had operated Long Island Airways briefly in 1923, persuaded bankers John A. Hambleton and Cornelius Vanderbilt Whitney to join him in bidding for the New York—Boston air mail contract. Losing out to Colonial Air Transport, they formed a temporary alignment with their rival but soon became frustrated at the reluctance of the New England company to extend its ambitions south of New York. Trippe and his friends thereupon went their own way, seeking more adventurous fields in the south. Joining Anthony Fokker, the Dutch aircraft designer and manufacturer, Trippe made a trial flight not only down to Florida but across to Havana, where the broad horizons of the potential airline market in Latin America lay spread out before him.

While Trippe was temporarily engaged with New England routes, another group was also casting an eye in the direction of the Caribbean. Eddie Rickenbacker and Reed Chambers had organized Florida Airways early in 1926 and operated for about nine months between Atlanta and Miami. Rickenbacker was backed by an impressive group of banking people, Percy A. Rockefeller, Charles Stone, Charles Hayden, George Mixter (vice-president, Stone and Webster), Richard F. Hoyt, and Anne Morgan. From the start a route to Havana had been an objective, but because Florida Airways had no good connection to the north, it lost money and went into bankruptcy. The backers did not completely lose interest in pioneering air services to the south, however, and although Rickenbacker went his own way, they kept their financial powder dry, pending a suitable opportunity to open fire.

Meanwhile, Dr von Bauer tried again and converted a young army officer, Capt J. K. Montgomery, to his cause. Von Bauer's interest waned when he realised that full U.S. support could only be achieved through a U.S.-controlled airline, and Montgomery was left to promote the idea of a trans-Caribbean air service. This he did with conspicuous success, interesting Richard D. Bevier, whose father-in-law was Lewis E. Pierson, a banker, and George Grant Mason. They began discussions with President Machado of Cuba, and on 8 March, 1927, Pan American Airways Inc was incorporated in New York City. The formalities were completed on 14 March, 1927, under the laws of the State of New York.

The next move was the formation of the Aviation Corporation of America by Trippe's group on 2 June, 1927. Articles of association were drawn up by Robert Thach, a lawyer and war ace friend of Trippe. The triumvirate of Trippe, Hambleton, and C. V. Whitney each put up $25,000, and invited friends to put in capital up to a total of $300,000. Having friends was one of Trippe's strong points, for the money was quickly subscribed by Grover Loening, W. Averill Harriman, William H. Vanderbilt, Edward O. McDonnell, Sherman M. Fairchild, John Hay Whitney, William A. Rockefeller and Seymour H. Knox. They engaged a Dutchman, André Priester, as their operations expert. Priester had come over with Fokker, and was one of Trippe's best investments, for he was later to become a key figure in establishing Pan American's record for safety and high engineering standards.

There were thus three separate financial groups determined to bid for the high stakes of Latin American air routes, with the important bonus of foreign air mail contracts in the offing. Preliminary discussions began between the three, although each continued to try to strengthen its own position. Trippe's group proposed to put its $300,000 into the newly-formed Pan American Airways, which was making progress in obtaining a mail contract to fly to Cuba. The Trippe investment was to represent 45 per cent of the capital of the new Pan American, while Montgomery's and Hoyt's (ex-Florida Airways) groups were to subscribe the remainder.

On 8 July, 1927, Trippe formed Southern Air Lines Inc, later to become New York Airways. On 16 July, Montgomery's group, Pan American, won the coveted mail contract for the Key West—Havana route. On 1 July, 1927, the Chambers–Hoyt group formed Southeastern Air Lines Inc, which was reincorporated in Delaware as Atlantic, Gulf and Caribbean Airways on 11 October. (*See Table 14, page 609*).

The Fairchild FC-2 *La Niña* which was used by Pan American to carry its first mail from Key West to Havana, on 19 October, 1927.

The First Service

To comply with the terms of the mail contract, and to save $25,000 deposited as a cash guarantee, Pan American was obliged to make a flight not later than 19 October, 1927. At that time, it possessed no aircraft, although a small fleet of two Fokker F-VIIs was due for delivery. The company saved both its reputation and its money by borrowing an aircraft which had arrived fortuitously in Florida en route to Santo Domingo. The aircraft, named *La Niña*, was a Fairchild FC-2 floatplane on a delivery flight to West Indian Aerial Express, a small airline which had just begun operations. Hastily chartered by Pan American, the pilot Cy Caldwell flew 30,000 letters in *La Niña* from Key West to Havana on 19 October, 1927. The mail had arrived from New York on the *Havana Special* of the Florida East Coast-Atlantic Coast Line railroads, and was contained in seven sacks, weighing 251 lb. The flight took 1 hr to cover the 90 miles, arriving at 9.25 a.m.

Nine days later, on 28 October, 1927, regular mail services began over the Key West—Havana route. The first regular flight carried 772 lb of mail, the Fokker F-VII *General Machado* setting off from Meacham Field at 8.25 a.m., piloted by Hugh Wells, with Ed Musick as navigator. This flight took 1 hr 20 min. It was also one of the Fokkers which opened the first passenger service on 16 January, 1928.

On 6 December, 1927, President Coolidge's message to Congress had recommended that a comprehensive system of air mail services should be established to South America. Coincidentally, the next day, Pan American took delivery of a Sikorsky S-36, which, however, was unsuccessful and was superseded by the improved S-38.

On 8 March, 1928, the Foreign Air Mail Act was passed by Congress, and on 30 March the Postmaster General advertised for bids on a wide-ranging network of mail routes throughout Latin America. The scene was set. The sparring ended. The in-fighting began.

The Aviation Corporation of the Americas

After some inconclusive meetings, in which there seemed little hope of the Pan American Airways group agreeing with Trippe's Aviation Corporation of America, the Atlantic, Gulf and Caribbean group (Hoyt, Stone, Rockefeller) found itself in a strategic position, able to act as a catalyst between the opposing elements. Hoyt laid down two basic principles: (a) no one party was to control; and (b) everything must be paid for in cash.

The three groups finally merged on 23 June, 1928, by forming the Aviation Corporation of the Americas—a subtle change of name of Trippe's company. Incorporated under the laws of the State of Delaware, 40 per cent of the stock was held each by Trippe's and Hoyt's groups, and 20 per cent by Pan American, Montgomery's group. On 27 June, the new holding company purchased the assets of the three former companies, together with subsidiaries. The capital was $500,000. Pan American Airways Inc, was set up as the operating subsidiary.

Juan Terry Trippe had held the trump card in the final round. Although the old Pan American Airways had the U.S. mail contract, Trippe had obtained monopoly landing rights in Cuba from President Machado himself. Montgomery could thus exercise its mail franchise only with the co-operation of the Aviation Corporation. Trippe never forgot the success of these tactics, and his subsequent long-term planning was to be characterized by this foresight in securing foreign footholds.

The new Pan American was awarded every foreign air mail route for which bids were invited. The company fitted exactly the concept of a U.S. chosen instrument for overseas air mail service. With one exception all contracts were let for ten years at the maximum rate, $2 per mile. Lower bids were meaningless without the security of foreign landing rights which Trippe shrewdly obtained.

The geographical scope and long-term significance of these contracts were of such importance that they are set out in full below:

Contract Number	*Route*	*Date Awarded*	*First Service Date*	*Weekly Round Trips*
FAM-4	Key West—Havana	29 May, 1928	29 May, 1928*	7
FAM-5	Miami—Cristobal, via Cuba and Central America (with extension to Paramaribo, via Venezuela)	13 July, 1928	4 Feb., 1929	1
FAM-6	Miami—San Juan, via Cuba, Santo Domingo (with extension to Port of Spain)	13 July, 1928	9 Jan., 1929	3
FAM-7	Miami—Nassau	24 Oct., 1928	2 Jan., 1929	3
FAM-8	Brownsville—Mexico City (with extension provisions)	16 Feb., 1929	10 Mar., 1929	7
FAM-9	Cristobal—Santiago, Chile (with extensions to Buenos Aires and Montevideo)	2 Mar., 1929	17 May, 1929	2
FAM-10	Paramaribo—Santos (with extension to Buenos Aires)	24 Sep., 1930	27 Nov., 1930	1

* Already operating U.S. terminus moved from Key West to Miami on 15 September, 1928. Pan American base moved on 29 October, 1928.

In awarding contracts involving the establishment of more than 13,000 miles of routes, the United States Government was consciously taking an aggressive step to counter the growing share of South American trade by European countries. In one sense, therefore, Pan American Airways was an instrument of U.S. foreign policy, as it was to provide the transport nervous system of a complete framework of economic expansion into Latin America.

In understanding the difference between Pan American's terms of reference and the preferential treatment which it appeared to enjoy in the decade following its first flight, it is important to recognize the principles laid down under Coolidge through his capable Secretary of Commerce, Herbert Hoover. The Congressional act governing the award of foreign contracts differed from its domestic counterpart in two important particulars. Contracts could be let, first, only to a company capable of operating on a scale and in a manner which would uphold the dignity of the United States in the eyes of its Latin-American neighbours; and second, that contracts could be let only to such interests that were *persona grata* to the Latin American governments. Thus diplomacy was integrated with commercial criteria.

The threat from Europe was serious, stemming mainly from French and German enterprise. In November 1927 the French airline Aéropostale had started a coastal service from Natal, in northeast Brazil, to Buenos Aires, and on 1 March, 1928, a mail service was opened between Toulouse and Buenos Aires, with a scheduled time of eight days, including five days on a fast destroyer between St Louis, Sénégal, and Natal. Aéropostale had set up subsidiaries in Argentina and Venezuela, and made no secret of its ambitions to circumnavigate South America with air routes.

The Germans were no less enterprising. In an effort to find outlets for its aircraft industry, which was forbidden to manufacture military aircraft under the terms of the Treaty of Versailles, Germany sponsored several airlines in South America, in Argentina, Bolivia, and particularly Brazil, which became the nucleus of the expansionist activities of the Kondor Syndikat of Berlin. Kondor demonstrated the practicability of air services in Brazil on 3 February, 1927, with the *Linha da Lagoa* from Pôrto Alegre to Rio Grande, while VARIG and Syndicato Condor were formed later in the same year, the latter as a subsidiary of the German national airline, Deutsche Luft Hansa. On 20 January, 1928, Condor was granted permission to establish a network of air services throughout Brazil, and with a firm German footing already established in Colombia (SCADTA) and Bolivia (LAB), the United States Government could be pardoned for its concern.

The Caribbean

Pan American's first objective was to encompass the Caribbean and to this end it obtained in January 1929 the services of Col Charles Lindbergh as technical adviser. While in no way underrating Lindbergh's capabilities in this rôle, his value to Pan American was more as an ambassador than as a technician. After his famous transatlantic flight, he had been invited by the President of Mexico and a number of Central American countries to make a goodwill tour. Setting off from Washington, D.C., on 13 December, 1927, he arrived back in St Louis exactly two months later, having in the meantime visited every country bordering on the Caribbean and the Gulf of Mexico.

NC9776 was one of Pan American Airways' Sikorsky S-38 twin-engined amphibians. (*Pan American World Airways*)

Lindbergh had demonstrated his faith in landplanes, believing that if a well-built aircraft could fly, it could also float. This view was at first shared by André Priester, who rejected Ford Tri-Motors because of their metal construction. The practical necessities of a Caribbean service, however, precluded the use of landplanes. Routes were either over water or across short stretches of land. Building harbours for flying-boats was relatively easy, and both climate and water conditions were favourable. In contrast, in most of the countries of the Antilles, West Indies, and Central America, landing grounds were mainly of the most primitive type—or non-existent. Accordingly Pan American decided to work the majority of its operations around the Caribbean with Sikorsky S-38 amphibians, which went into service on 31 October, 1928. This versatile little craft carried eight passengers, the same as the Fokker F-VII, and did all that was asked of it. Pan American, meanwhile, undertook a sustained programme of pioneering hard labour, preparing bases around the island chain of the Caribbean.

The provision of handling and landing facilities was assumed to be the responsibility of the operator, and there was no question of such work

Pan American Airways' Fokker F.VIIa-3m NC3314.

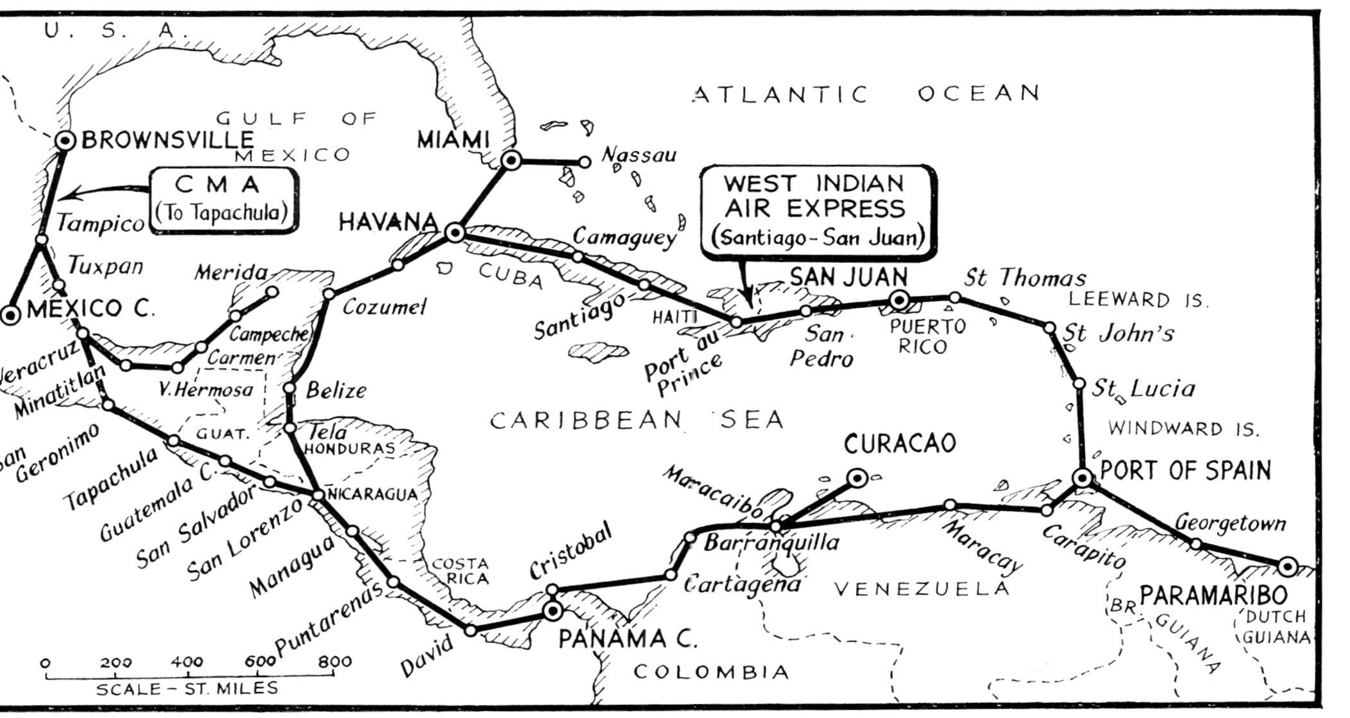

Fig. 17. Pan American's Caribbean Network, 1928–1930.

being done by the local municipality or state administration, whose meagre funds were required for more pressing local purposes. If the United States wished to operate air services, permission was forthcoming, but that was all that could be expected from the impoverished and often corrupt Central American governments of that era. Pan American's maximum mail payment of $2 per mile for loads up to 800 lb was therefore well spent. Certainly, the company and its officers did not waste a cent in those days, and fortunately its officers were rich men to whom Pan American was a vocation, not a means of earning their daily bread.

The map on page 217 and the table below show the rapid progress made in encircling the Caribbean. The service dates shown in the table are for mail only, though on the route to San Juan passengers were carried from the start. On other routes, passenger service followed quickly after the inaugural flights.

Contract Number	*Route*	*Segment Opened*	*Date*
FAM-4	Key West—Havana		19 October, 1927
	(transfer of U.S. terminus to Miami)		15 September, 1928
FAM-7	Miami—Nassau		2 January, 1929
FAM-6	Miami—Port of Spain	Miami—San Juan	9 January, 1929
		San Juan—Port of Spain	22 September, 1929
		—Paramaribo	23 September, 1929*
FAM-5	Miami—Paramaribo	Miami—Canal Zone	4 February, 1929
		Canal Zone—Curaçao	21 June, 1929
		Curaçao—Venezuela	May 1930
FAM-8	Brownsville—Canal Zone	Brownsville—Mexico C.	10 March, 1929
		Mexico City—Guatemala	2 September, 1929

* Transferred from FAM-5.

The development of the Caribbean network marked the beginning of Pan American's history of acquisition of other companies. West Indian Aerial Express which (possibly without board approval) had assisted Pan American to honour its first mail contract, was threatened with extinction immediately when the U.S. Foreign Air Mail Contracts were awarded entirely to that company. Based in Santo Domingo, West Indian had started services between Port-au-Prince, Haiti, and San Juan on 3 December, 1927, and had extended this route to Santiago de Cuba on 1 March, 1928. West Indian was backed by, among others, Sherman Fairchild and Graham Grosvenor, to the tune of $92,000, and operated several Fairchild FC-2s and a Keystone Pathfinder. Without the hidden subsidy of a U.S. mail contract, they were forced to sell out to Pan American on 15 December, 1928.

A more important acquisition was Compañía Mexicana de Aviación (CMA), founded in Mexico City on 20 August, 1924, by two U.S. citizens, W. L. Mallory and George L. Rihl, to carry payrolls on a charter basis throughout the oilfields near Tampico, using four 60 mph open-cockpit

This Whirlwind-powered Keystone Pathfinder was the flagship of West Indian Aerial Express of Santo Domingo. The airline was taken over by Pan American Airways.

Lincoln Standards. On 16 August, 1926, CMA signed a ten-year contract with the Mexican Department of Communications and Public Works which virtually secured preferential flying rights throughout Mexico. On 15 April, 1928, Fairchild 71s opened scheduled services from Mexico City to Tampico, and on 15 October a new route was opened to Merida, in the Yucatán Peninsula.

On 23 January, 1929, the Aviation Corporation bought the entire stock of CMA for the purpose of obtaining exclusive operating rights in Mexico.

One of the Lincoln Standard biplanes operated by Compañía Mexicana de Aviación, which became a Pan American subsidiary in January 1929.

All other competition was thereby effectively eliminated in that country. A fleet of Ford Tri-Motors was then purchased to replace the Fairchild 71s.

Pan American advanced quickly on all fronts. The move from Key West to Miami on 15 September, 1928, was an important step, for it provided better rail connections with the north, a direct air link through Pitcairn Aviation's mail route to New York, and, by doubling the mileage of the air route to Havana, earned more mail revenue at $2 per mile. The Sikorsky S-38s were also supplemented by larger Fokker three-engined landplanes, the F-Xs. Altogether, during the early days of expansion, Pan American operated, among other miscellaneous types, 38 S-38s, 28 Ford Tri-Motors, twelve Fokker F-Xs, three Fokker F-VIIs, and 31 small Fairchild types.

During the latter part of 1928 there was a considerable influx of new capital, from almost all available aviation sources, except the Boeing-Rentschler-United group. Stock was offered at $15 a share, and early subscribers were given perpetual warrants to buy two shares at the $15 price for each share held. The Boeing group changed its mind later and bought 50,000 shares at $57.50 per share.

Passenger service was inaugurated to San Juan when the new 36th Street Airport was opened at Hialeah, Miami, on 9 January, 1929. Passengers were first carried on the route to the Canal Zone on 22 May, 1929. The journey time on the 2,064-mile route was 56 hr, including two overnight stops, at Belize and Managua. Then on 2 December, 1930, after taking over a fleet of 14 Consolidated Commodore flying-boats from New York, Rio and Buenos Aires Line (NYRBA) (*See page 224*), a direct cut-off service was opened via Cienfuegos, Cuba, and Kingston, Jamaica. The mileage was cut to 1,385 and the time to 29 hr 15 min. The 600-mile Kingston—Cristobal stage was the longest operated at that time. It was to serve as a long-range flying laboratory, a proving ground for direction finding and navigational experiments. These were to pay handsome dividends when Pan American Airways spread more ambitious wings in the exciting years which were to follow.

The Fairchild 71 NC9726 was one of Pan American Airways' early fleet, used in Central America. (*Pan American World Airways*)

Pan American Airways' Mexican-registered Ford 5-AT-B X-ABCC (c/n 11) went to CMA. It is seen at Minatitlan.

PANAGRA

Considering the distances involved, Juan Trippe achieved his objectives in South America in an astonishingly short period of time. By July 1929 Pan American was offering service to Santiago, Chile, by the west coast route and by November 1930 had consolidated service to Buenos Aires by the east coast route. By the end of 1930 the route mileage of the Pan American system was 20,308, a spectacular increase from the 251 only two years previously.

Buenos Aires, the largest city in the Southern Hemisphere, was the main goal. The shortest route was along the west coast of South America and across the Andes by the most convenient pass. The east coast route on the other hand had the advantage of serving more important cities but was longer and more difficult to establish in terms of aerodromes and ground and sea facilities. Powerful interests resisted Pan American intrusion on both routes. Trippe's action in dealing with both problems was typical of his methods: precise, prompt, and effective. On the west an acceptable compromise was reached with the main commercial opponent; on the east the chief rival was absorbed ruthlessly, with tacit support from the Postmaster General.

Until the advent of air transport, the household word for long-distance travel down the west coast of South America was Grace. The W. R. Grace

Panagra's Ford 5-AT-D Tri-Motor NC433H *San Felipe* at Trujillo in Peru.

Fig. 18. Pan American and Panagra Network, 1930 (prior to Pan Am's acquisition of NYRBA).

company was engaged in many commercial enterprises, especially shipping, and did not look kindly upon Trippe's ambitions. A stalemate situation was reached in which, through the political influence of each, Grace blocked Trippe's path southward through Colombia, whilst Trippe blocked Grace's path northward through Panama. Trippe applied pressure by some smart work in Peru and Chile.

On 16 September, 1928, the Aviation Corporation of the Americas bought a half interest in Peruvian Airways. This local airline started in 1927 as a crop-dusting company, Huff-Daland Dusters, in which C. E. Woolman, of Delta, was a founder member. The company was renamed Peruvian Airways on incorporation on 4 September, 1928. Nine days later it made the first scheduled flight in Peru, from Lima to Talara, with a Fairchild monoplane. After Trippe's entry into the company, the line was expanded on 24 January, 1929, along the whole length of the Peruvian coastline, from Mollendo in the south, to the Ecuadorian port of Guayaquil in the north.

Not content with securing Peruvian rights, Trippe did the same in Chile, where, however, Chilean Airways was organized only as a paper company on 21 December, 1928. The Aviation Corporation acquired a half-interest on 31 December, but the airline never owned or operated an aircraft.

Faced with this kind of politico-economic opposition, the Grace shipping company found itself out-manoeuvred, and on 25 January, 1929, a compromise was reached by forming Pan American-Grace Airways Inc (PANAGRA), with Grace and Aviation Corporation of the Americas each contributing 50 per cent of the $1,000,000 stock. On 2 March, 1929, Panagra was awarded the mail contract from the Canal Zone—at $1.80 per mile to Santiago and Buenos Aires (FAM-9). In preparation, the fleet was augmented to total six Fairchild FC-2s.

In May the first direct air connection from the U.S.A. to Peru was accomplished. On 14 May a mailplane left Miami and took the Central American route to Cristobal, whence an S-38 of Pan American, on con-

The Panagra Ford 5-AT-C Tri-Motor NC8416 being loaded with cargo through a fuselage-top hatch.

A Loening Air Yacht of Panagra at Montevideo. Registered NC9717, this example is believed to have been the C2C version.

tract to Panagra, took the mail on to Talara. A Panagra Fairchild completed the journey to Mollendo on 19 May. The route was extended to Santiago on 21 July. In August, the first of three Ford Tri-Motors was assembled at Guayaquil, and through service to Buenos Aires was achieved on 8 October, and to Montevideo on 30 November, 1929.

On 1 January, 1930, two Sikorsky amphibians were acquired for the northern stages of the coastal route and on 16 January passenger service was opened from Cristobal to Arica, the most northerly city of Chile. On 26 April a new fast schedule was introduced, reducing the mail time from New York to Buenos Aires to 6½ days, and further reductions were made at the beginning of 1931, through the Commodore-operated cut-off route across the Caribbean. In the summer of 1932, new Eastern Air Transport schedules reduced the connection times at the U.S. end of the route. Passenger service was extended to Santiago on 15 August, 1931, and to Montevideo on 5 October.

NYRBA

Whilst Trippe settled for a half interest on the west coast, there was no compromise on the East. The formation in New York on 17 March, 1929, of the New York, Rio and Buenos Aires Line was a direct challenge to the Aviation Corporation of the Americas. The driving force—Trippe's opposite number—was Capt Ralph O'Neill, a former Boeing salesman in South America who saw clearly the enormous potential for air transport in that road-and-railway-starved continent. The chief financial backing came from James Rand, of the Remington-Rand Corporation, but he was supported by an impressive list of industrialists, including Reuben Fleet of the Consolidated Aircraft Corporation, F. C. Munson of the Munson Steamship Line, W. B. Mayo of the Ford Motor Company, J. E. Reynolds of International Founders, and Lewis Pierson of the Irving Trust Company. Pierson brought in his son-in-law Richard Bevier as vice-president, together with J. K. Montgomery. These three had founded the original Pan American Airways, before Trippe had outsmarted them on Cuban flying rights, and probably felt that NYRBA provided a good stick with which to beat their former tormentor.

In July, a proving flight was made to Buenos Aires, and the first NYRBA scheduled service opened on 21 August, 1929, from the Argentine capital to Montevideo, across the River Plate. On 1 September, the Buenos Aires—Santiago route was added, for both mail and passengers, with Ford Tri-Motors. The journey took 7 hr 15 min and was the first transcontinental

Fig. 19. New York, Rio and Buenos Aires Line (NYRBA), 1930.

air route in South America, beating Panagra by five weeks. Mail contracts were obtained from the Governments of Argentina, Chile, and Uruguay; by the end of the year the Fords were maintaining a twice weekly service across the Andes. On 22 November authorization was obtained from the Brazilian Government to operate within that country, and a week later a new route opened from Buenos Aires to Asunción, Paraguay. The former Assistant Secretary of Commerce for Aeronautics, William P. McCracken, Jr, became chairman of the Board.

NYRBA's big day was 18 February, 1930, when, the Consolidated Commodore having been christened in traditional style by Mrs Herbert Hoover, the first through service was started between Miami and Santiago, using the east-coast route via Brazil. These Commodores had been built specially for long ranges, a need resulting more from the shortage of adequate landing bases than from over-water crossings of great distance. They were elegant in appearance, able to carry 20 passengers in much greater comfort than hitherto, and presented a real challenge to Pan American Airways, now under Trippe's Aviation Corporation of the Americas banner.

The Consolidated Commodore NC660M *Cuba* (c/n 4) was one of the fleet operated in 1930 by NYRBA Line, and which passed to Pan American.

For this reason, NYRBA's progress began to meet opposition from every device which Pan American could bring to bear from its considerable commercial and political resources which were quickly being built up throughout South America. Not that Trippe broke unwritten commercial rules; but in this game there were few rules. Much rested on personalities. Perhaps Trippe was just a shade luckier than Ralph O'Neill in having the more persuasive negotiators. Perhaps Trippe defined his objectives more clearly. There seems little doubt, however, that he had more political influence in the U.S. Post Office Department, and this was the key factor.

When Pan American agents moved into NYRBA territory, certain problems seemed to arise for the latter. Some of the South American governments began to make life difficult for O'Neill; Argentina, for instance, demanded that mail should reach the U.S.A. in seven days rather than in the eight or nine which the Commodores required. O'Neill countered by positioning a Consolidated Fleetster to operate from Buenos Aires. After giving the Commodore twenty-four or more hours start, the

NC669M (c/n 14) was one of the fourteen Consolidated Commodores which Pan American acquired from NYRBA. (*Pan American World Airways*)

Fleetster caught it up at some point along the Brazilian coast. Pan American held the U.S. mail contracts as far as Paramaribo, Dutch Guiana, and NYRBA found its path blocked for mail and passenger traffic across the gap from Port of Spain, Trinidad, along the chain of islands to Miami.

Relations became quite strained, and deteriorated to the point of tension when the crew of a Pan American survey aircraft was refused help by NYRBA ground crews at Lake Montenegro, in northern Brazil. This had followed an instruction from NYRBA: 'Discontinue render any and all service to Pan American pilots taking effect immediately.' Physical violence of a serious nature was avoided when the proposed merger talks were made known.

NYRBA's cut-price mail rates were not cast in the W. F. Brown mould, and the Postmaster General made it quite clear that he would not award the U.S. mail contract for an east-coast route to Buenos Aires to any company other than Pan American. NYRBA's days were numbered; for

One of Pan American's Consolidated Commodores on the moving pontoon slipway at Dinner Key, Miami.

the irritations and impediments to the operation of a far-flung, precariously maintained, pioneering airline were becoming intolerable. On 19 August, 1930, James Rand agreed to sell out to Pan American for $2,000,000, which was about $3,000,000 less than the initial capital investment only a year and a half previously.

On 15 September, Aviation Corporation of the Americas formally acquired the assets of NYRBA, including the fleet of 14 Commodore flying-boats, and its subsidiary airline, NYRBA do Brasil, formed on 22 October, 1929. This airline was renamed Panair do Brasil on 17 October, 1930, and a new chapter began in the development of civil aviation in that vast country. Walter Brown awarded the east-coast mail route to Pan American at maximum rate, on 24 September, 1930, (FAM-10).

Filling the Gaps

The successful completion of the Panagra merger and the NYRBA purchase gave Pan American a grand circular route around South America. Trippe had won industrial battles with major U.S. companies; but winning individual battles did not necessarily win the war. He was still open to flanking attacks on all sides, and a few skirmishes still had to be fought to safeguard the route network.

Colombia presented an intriguing problem. Dr von Bauer, who had first thought of an air link direct to Miami, still controlled SCADTA. Colombia was rightly proud of the pioneering tradition of SCADTA, and the Government could be counted upon for support. Had von Bauer been firm, he could have stopped Pan American from flying down the west coast of Colombia, but common sense, diplomacy, and a little horse-trading combined to produce a compromise. Eventually, between 10 February, 1930, and 10 April, 1931, the Aviation Corporation of the Americas acquired no less than 84·4 per cent of SCADTA's stock, for $1,100,000. This was almost a secret agreement. Pan Am's controlling interest was not revealed, and von Bauer retained voting rights. But Pan Am got its through route down the west coast.

An interesting sidelight on Trippe's thoroughness is shown by his creation, on 15 November, 1927, of the Sociedad Anonima Colombo-Americano de Aviacion, a name so like SCADTA's as to border on the impertinent. But it was a constant reminder that Pan American was prepared to play rough if necessary; and the paper company was not dissolved until the day before SCADTA became AVIANCA on 8 June, 1940, and the German interests removed.

Another Colombian airline was organized on 24 August, 1931, by the airline pioneer, Gonzalo Mejia, and held a 15-year concession for a route from Medellin to Balboa, Canal Zone. Pan American acquired a 54 per cent interest on 13 April, 1932, and progressively increased this to full ownership by 1947. Rejoicing under the title of Uraba, Medellin, and Central Airways (UMCA), the immediate objective was merely local services connecting Medellin with the hinterland; but the long-term aim was to map out a route right through the heart of South America. This, however, was never realized.

The next step was to consolidate the position in Mexico. While Pan American had secured the route from the U.S. frontier along the Gulf of Mexico, a rival company was pioneering in central Mexico. The swashbuckling Theodore T. Hull had founded Corporacion de Aeronautica de Transportes (C.A.T.) in the spring of 1929, with American financial backing. He opened a route between Mexico City and Ciudad Juarez, using Ryan monoplanes, with a cross-route from Brownsville to the Pacific Coast port, Mazatlan. The airline lasted for a few hectic years, during which it formed a harsh training ground for many airline pioneers, including Gordon Barry, who later founded LAMSA in the same region when C.A.T. ceased to exist, and Lowell Yerex, who was to create a great airline, TACA, which became a household word throughout Central America. Wiley Post also flew for C.A.T.

Pan American took over C.A.T.'s main route on 26 February, 1932, by organizing Aerovias Centrales S.A. The Brownsville connection with the Pacific coast was dropped, but Pan American used Centrales to develop a west-coast route from Mexico City to the U.S. frontier at Nogales and Mexicali. Three Lockheed Orions were used on this exacting operation. In due course, the route was taken over by CMA—already a wholly owned Pan American subsidiary—on 18 December, 1935, while all the central routes were ceded to Gordon Barry, who established LAMSA.

The final hole which needed plugging was in Cuba. Here North American Aviation obtained a foothold by establishing Compania Nacional Cubana de Aviacion Curtiss S.A., on 8 October, 1929, and offered a minor threat to Pan American by operating 740 miles of domestic routes in Cuba. Pan American benefited from the decline of the Curtiss-Keys empire and bought the airline outright on 6 May, 1932, dropping the word Curtiss from the title in the process.

A Lockheed Orion operated in Mexico by Aerovias Centrales SA, one of Pan American's Mexican subsidiaries during the 1930s.

The Northrop Delta 1B, X-ABED (c/n 4), which was to have been operated by Aerovias Centrales SA, but blew up on its delivery flight.

Withall the loose ends tied up*, Trippe now had the freedom he needed. With mail contracts providing financial stability, a virtual monopoly position assured, he could develop equipment according to Pan American specifications, rather than having to buy what the manufacturers decided. The result was the establishment of a thoroughbred line of flying-boats which were to set ever higher standards and to identify the name Pan American with those standards throughout the airline world.

The First of the Clipper Boats

Although one of the major benefits from the take-over of NYRBA was the addition of 14 handsome Consolidated Commodore flying-boats, the twin-boom Sikorsky S-38s still had a part to play. Also, the basic design principles were developed to produce larger versions of the Sikorsky line.

On 20 December, 1929, Pan American placed orders for the large

*A summary of Pan American's acquisitions in the Caribbean during the period 1927-1932 is in Table 14, page 609.

The first of Pan American Airways' Clippers. NC752V *Southern Clipper* (c/n 2002) was one of three Sikorsky S-40s which entered service in November 1931. (*Pan American World Airways*)

Another view of the Sikorsky S-40 *Southern Clipper*. (*Gordon S. Williams*)

twin-boomed Sikorsky S-40, the first of a long series of four-engined flying-boats. This, the first to be christened *Clipper*, the subsequent trade mark of the airline, carried a crew of six and 40 passengers, or twice as many as the Commodore which they replaced. Weighing more than 34,000 lb (again, twice as much as the Commodores) they were easily the largest civil aircraft in service at that time.

The first S-40, under the command of Charles Lindbergh, took-off from Miami on 19 November, 1931, bound for the Canal Zone. Four days later, the arrival of a Commodore at Buenos Aires marked the first through passenger service along the east-coast route. Only three S-40s were built, however, for in 1932—during the depths of the U.S. economic depression—Pan American took the unprecedented step of sponsoring two even larger flying-boats. The first of these was the Sikorsky S-42, which marked a positive advance in performance and design. No previous aircraft in

Interior view of a Pan American Sikorsky S-40 Clipper.

One of the truly great commercial flying-boats—a Pan American Airways' Sikorsky S-42. (*Pan American World Airways*)

Pan American's fleet, landplane or flying-boat, had cruised much above a bare 100 mph. The S-42 weighed more than 20 tons, and carried 32 passengers over longer ranges at a higher speed and a greater standard of comfort than ever before.

For the first time airline publicists could use the word luxury with confidence to describe comfort standards; but the most significant of the S-42's achievements was its ability to carry its full load, plus ample supplementary baggage and freight, for a distance of 750 miles, whereas its predecessors were severely limited in payload for flights of more than about 250 miles.

The S-42 cost $242,000, including engines, propellers, instruments and radio equipment. Its wing loading was higher than that of any previous commercial aircraft, and was not exceeded by any other type until 1942, or eight years after its first scheduled service, on the Miami—Rio de Janeiro route, on 16 August, 1934. Other improvements included wing flaps, extensive flush riveting, engine synchronizing indicators (also on the S-40), propeller brakes, and automatic carburettors.

With the S-42s as flagships, Pan American flying-boats began to accumulate millions of miles of experience. Just as the Key West—Havana route had been a trial run for expansion into the Caribbean, and the Caribbean in turn a proving ground for the wider horizons of South America, this vast continent now became a new point of departure for even greater ambitions. When, a few years later, Juan Trippe was to break out of the North American continent, he paid tribute to the work of the men and machines which had conquered the civil air lanes of the South:

'The first long-distance, over-water route flown anywhere in the world was the 600-mile journey across the Caribbean from Kingston, Jamaica, to Barranquilla, Colombia. For five years Pan American has flown this route; it has been our laboratory of preparation for the service instituted today. There our technical staff has developed our ocean direction-finding and navigation apparatus, and there our flight captains and their crews have qualified for over-ocean service.'

Transition to Landplanes

1934 witnessed the introduction to Pan American's Western Division of the Douglas DC-2, the twin-engine low-wing monoplane capable of carrying 14 passengers at a cruising speed of 160 mph. Pan American was the second airline to acquire this modern aircraft, the development of which has been fully described in Chapter 8. These were followed by Lockheed L.10 Electras and Douglas DC-3s, during a period of Latin American expansion during the 1930s.

Pan American's Douglas DC-3 NC33609 (c/n 4100). (*Pan American World Airways*)

Rio de Janeiro's Santos Dumont Airport, with a Pan American Airways' Douglas DC-3, in the foreground, and Panair do Brasil's DC-2 PP-PAZ. (*Pan American World Airways*)

One of Pan American's Sikorsky S-43 Baby Clippers. The example seen taking-off is NC16927 (c/n 4316). (*Pan American World Airways*)

Also in 1934, after further negotiations with the Brazilian Government, arrangements were made under which domestic services within Brazil were developed by the Pan American subsidiary, Panair do Brasil, leaving the parent company to concentrate on long-distance international routes. Pan American continued to enjoy what were to become known as cabotage rights, that is, the right to carry traffic wholly within a foreign country, in this case Brazil.

Because of the size of the building programme necessary to bring all airports up to Electra or DC-2 standards, flying-boats continued to serve some coastal routes and to link many islands in the Caribbean. In 1936 Sikorsky S-43 Baby Clippers replaced Consolidated Commodores; while in a unique operation up the Amazon River, developed entirely by Panair do Brasil, Fairchild 91s (XA-942s) replaced Sikorsky S-38s.

At the end of 1934, Pan American's Latin American services used 103 land airports and 56 marine bases. Certainly the flying-boat services were not yet regarded as obsolete, for in April that year the new Dinner Key international air terminal marine base was commissioned at Miami. Constructed entirely at Pan American's expense at a cost of $300,000 for

Pan American's Fairchild 91 or XA-942 amphibian NC14744 (c/n 9402). Used on services in the Amazon River region of Brazil. (*Pan American World Airways*)

NC81V *Caribbean Clipper* (c/n 2001), one of Pan American's Sikorsky S-40s, at Dinner Key, Miami. The landing stage, on floating pontoons, is seen on the left of the picture. (*Pan American World Airways*)

the passenger station alone, this was for many years the outstanding air passenger terminal in the United States, embodying all Pan Am's experience.

Improving the Infrastructure

The success of a far-flung route network like Pan American's did not depend solely on a combination of good aircraft and astute diplomacy. The advantage of these two assets would have been nullified by poor management and administration; but it is to Pan American's credit that at no time did the technical development of its flying equipment outstrip the airline's ability to exploit to the full the progress made in providing increased speed, range, and comfort.

In the field of radio and meteorology, for instance, Pan American worked constantly to break new ground. In 1932 investigations were

The houseboat terminal at Pan American's Dinner Key base, Miami.

conducted to develop a loop-type direction finder aboard aircraft, incorporating an amplifier which could be used with a standard communications receiver. This was superseded by the ATM aircraft receiver which saved both weight and space. Constant improvements were also made in ground direction finders and work was put in hand to perfect the long-range high frequency Adcock equipment first used by Britain in World War 1. Eventually patented by Pan American in 1934, the equipment was used and tested in Latin America, but found its greatest usefulness when the airline pioneered trans-ocean flying. At the end of that year, Pan American and Panagra together operated 69 ground radio stations in Latin America.

In 1931 Pan American developed a tropical forecast technique to try to overcome the uncertainty of weather forecasts, using methods of air mass analysis. In 1932 a number of upper air meteorological stations were established and from their records the operations department was able to determine the best flight levels and courses, so as to take advantage of the most favourable winds.

The success of these developments, unspectacular though they were compared with the flying achievements, is proved by the statistical record: during the three years 1932–1934, the worst annual regularity record—the percentage of scheduled flights actually completed—was 99·46 per cent. During the depression years of the early 1930s, United States trade as a whole dropped dramatically; but Pan American increased its revenue from air mail postage in almost inverse proportion. In addition to mail, international air express service was inaugurated in 1930. To overcome the ponderous shipping regulations covering the documentation of cargo, Pan American undertook a complete revision of the system. The result

Pan American's second Dinner Key base at Miami, in 1932. All three of the airline's Sikorsky S-40s appear in the picture.

Express and mail being loaded onto Pan American's Sikorsky S-40 NC80V *American Clipper.*

was a simplified Pan American International Waybill, which after a short time was universally adopted throughout Latin America.

Also an arrangement was concluded in 1934 with the Railway Express Agency Inc to act as receiving offices throughout the United States for all shipments of air express to foreign destinations served by Pan American, and vice versa.

Route Development

A cursory glance at a map of Pan American's South American services in the 1930s reveals that the east-coast route to the major Brazilian cities of Rio de Janeiro and São Paulo involved flying a circuitous route around the northeast corner of the continent, adding perhaps a thousand miles to the direct route. Unfortunately at that time, on a straight-line path between, for example, Belem and Rio, there were no roads, no railways, and few rivers navigable throughout their length. Much of the area was covered solidly with almost impenetrable jungle, and there were few populated settlements.

Pan American staff made an overland survey of the area, however, in 1931, following with two aerial surveys in 1934 and 1935, but operating rights were not obtained until 1940. The need was urgent, not only for the direct economy of flying fewer miles, but also to offer better service to the public. The basic problem was one of travel fatigue. Passengers flying to Brazil or Argentina were faced with the prospect of a journey $2\frac{1}{2}$ times longer than any possible wholly within the U.S.A., not including the trip to the Dinner Key Terminal. Because the total traffic demand did not permit the economic operation of more than two or three trips a week, a stopover for rest at Paramaribo or Belem would often lead to several days delay. On the other hand, night operations were still hazardous because of inadequate weather reporting experience and facilities, but to install full night landing equipment along the route for twin-engined operations would have cost at least $9,500,000.

Pan American therefore joined in sponsoring long-range four-engined aircraft, capable of over-flying many of the time-wasting stops en route to the Southern Hemisphere. The types were the early DC-4, and the Boeing 307 Stratoliner, the first airliner able to cruise at altitudes which would clear most of the turbulence caused by cumulus cloud common in the tropics, a capability achieved by pressurizing the fuselage to maintain a constant equivalent altitude of 8,000 ft inside the cabin. The Boeing 307 had a normal maximum range exceeding 1,000 miles, could carry 33 passengers, and cruised at 185 mph.

Barreiras Airport, in the interior of Brazil, was a major feat of construction undertaken to provide a shorter route to Rio de Janeiro. It is seen in 1940 with Pan American's Douglas DC-3 NC59410 on the right. (*Pan American World Airways*)

The airport at Barreiras, approximately halfway between Belem and Rio de Janeiro, is a permanent memorial to Pan American's efforts to exploit improved aircraft performance with ground facilities of equal calibre. Constructed entirely by Pan American, all material had to be brought inland from Belem, first by rail to Joazerio, then by boat and raft up the San Francisco and Rio Grande rivers. Racing to beat the end of the rainy season when the water level of the rivers would fall too low, a raft capsized on a sandbar. The load, a vital tractor, was raised, disassembled, dried out, reloaded, and brought to Barreiras in time to assist the completion of the first temporary runway. This had to be abandoned because of terrain problems, undiscovered until final jungle clearance. A new site was selected on a plateau which was all but insurmountable, and supply trucks had to carry reduced loads because the approach road was overhung with cliffs.

In spite of these and other difficulties, Barreiras Airport was opened in September 1940, and Pan American opened an accelerated service to Rio de Janeiro, with a Boeing 307 as far as Belem, connecting with a one-stop Rio-bound DC-3.

Back to Cinderella Status

The firm foundations which Pan American laid for its South American network before 1930, and the efficient and thorough methods used to capitalize on the flying start, combined to transform the whole concept of travel throughout the continent. At first regarded with suspicion, if not open hostility, by governments justifiably apprehensive of a new kind of United States colonialism, Pan American gradually came to be recognized as a symbol, not of aggrandizement, but of progress. The air transport expertise which Pan American pilots, engineers, and administrators brought to Latin America contributed in no small measure to the social well-being of many millions of people.

Paradoxically, when these benefits began to be realized and appreciated, the spirit of adventure and romanticism which had characterized Pan American's early history was replaced by business routine, and the publicity which had formerly accompanied every step taken in the southward expansion was replaced by a comparative lack of interest.

Pan American's success in the south was never recognized fully in the U.S.A. by such criteria as regularity and punctuality of service over a long and exacting network, the maintenance of scores of landing strips and waterways in remote areas, a distinguished safety record in tough flying conditions, or, for example, construction projects such as Barreiras. All these fine achievements which helped to change the course of economic history in Latin America were submerged beneath the momentum of air transport history which Pan American was itself making elsewhere. If Pan American never received the contemporary recognition it deserved, it had only itself to blame. For, once the security of South American development seemed assured, Juan Trippe turned his attention towards far more ambitious endeavour.

China Clipper, one of Pan American's three Martin M-130s. (*Pan American World Airways*)

CHAPTER TEN

Ocean Conquest

Modest Beginnings

The year 1931 was largely a consolidation period for Pan American. In Latin America, the irritating opposition in Colombia was removed by purchasing control of SCADTA and forming UMCA. Organizationally, the somewhat clumsy title of the parent company, the Aviation Corporation of the Americas, was changed to Pan American Airways Corporation on 29 April. Rather confusingly, a new corporation was formed as a subsidiary, using the former parent company title, for special purposes in non-Latin American regions.

But the year brought Pan American's first tentative steps outside the Latin American area. A subsidiary, New York Airways, began services from North Beach Airfield, Long Island, to Atlantic City on 1 June, 1930, using a mixed fleet of aircraft, Ford Tri-Motor, Fokker F-X, and Sikorsky S-38. North Beach was the old Curtiss-Wright Field, built on reclaimed land in Flushing Bay, and which was eventually to become LaGuardia Airport in 1940. The route was extended to Washington, via Baltimore, on 2 August, 1930, but was sold to Eastern Air Transport on 15 July, 1931.

This was not, however, the end of Pan American's activities in New England. Hardly had New York Airways been disposed of when on 25 July a Pan American Fokker F-XA made a survey flight from Boston to Bangor, Maine, via Portland. Three days later, with characteristic thoroughness, a second survey flight was made, this time with a new Sikorsky S-41, an improved version of the S-38, in order to proceed further north into Canada. St John was reached on 29 July and Halifax the next day.

On 31 July, 1931, Boston-Maine Airways Inc opened a new mail route, FAM-12. The company was organized by the Boston and Maine, and Maine Central railroads, and Pan American did the flying under contract. This was wholly satisfactory for Pan Am, which not only gained valuable operating experience in unfamiliar northern latitudes, but also got paid for doing it. The Boston—Portland—Bangor sector was flown by the Fokker F-XA, the remaining sector by two S-41s, one of which was lost in Boston harbour. The service was short-lived, ending on 30 September.

While a route from New York to Halifax was remote from the main axes of the Pan American network, there was nothing illogical about the choice. Once Latin American domination was assured, Juan Trippe was free to turn to greater ambitions. He had dreamed of ocean conquest at a very early stage in the development of Pan American, even when the

Glenn H. Curtiss Airport (also known as North Beach Airport), Long Island. Built on the site of the Gala Amusement Park in 1929 and enlarged in 1932, this is now the 650-acre LaGuardia Airport which handles more than 12mn passengers a year. Compare with view on page 543.

The Ford 5-AT-C Tri-Motor NC411H used by New York Airways on New York—Atlantic City—Washington services in 1930–31. The aircraft, seen at Atlantic City, is thought to have been leased from the Ford Motor Company.

A Fokker F-XA of Boston-Maine Airways Inc and Pan American Airways Co. The small lettering on the fuselage reads Pan American Airways Co. Management Equipment and Airmail Service.

Sikorsky S-41s were used north of Bangor on FAM-12. The example illustrated is NC784Y (c/n 1105). (*Pan American World Airways*)

limited range of the flying-boats then available restricted nonstop operations to stages of no more than 250 miles. On 26 June, 1931, he gave notice of his serious and far-reaching intentions by issuing a letter to leading aircraft manufacturers, asking for 'a high-speed, multi-motored flying-boat having a cruising range of 2,500 miles against 30-mile headwinds, and providing accommodation for a crew of four, together with at least 300 pounds of air mail'. The link between this action and the opening of the route to Halifax seemed a clear pointer to the direction of Pan American's future route expansion.

Atlantic Preparations

Following the methods successfully established in Latin America, Trippe began by trying to promote a favourable political climate. As early as 1928 and 1929 a programme was prepared to investigate all possible air routes across the Atlantic, and preliminary conversations were held with representatives of Imperial Airways Ltd of London and of the Compagnie Générale Aéropostale of Paris.

One possible route was the mid-Atlantic, using Bermuda and the Azores as island stepping stones. On 1 July, 1930, both Pan American and Imperial Airways obtained permission from the Bermuda Government to operate a U.S.A. Bermuda service, but this lapsed in April 1932. Aéropostale, which had set a cracking pace in South America, acquired an exclusive landing concession in the Azores. Meetings held in New York late in 1930 were unfortunately frustrated by Aéropostale's own financial problems, culminating in the demise of the airline and, among other sequels, the cancellation of its Azores landing concession by the Portuguese Government.

When the dust had settled, Trippe, as usual, seemed to have got what he wanted: a joint enterprise, the Pan American-Imperial Airways company, was formed on 14 May, 1930, and an agreement permitting Pan American to use the Aéropostale landing concession in the Azores was concluded on 1 January, 1932. Nevertheless, the political hurdles across the Central Atlantic began to look formidable, especially after the collapse of Aéropostale and with the increasing pressure from Germany.

When also the further extension of the northeast coastal route via Halifax was prevented by difficulties in obtaining landing rights in Newfoundland, Pan American turned to yet another solution to the problem. In July 1932 it purchased from Transamerican Airlines (formerly Thompson Aeronautical Corporation and one of the predecessor companies of American Airlines) a 75-year Icelandic landing concession for $55,000 and obtained from Denmark the authority to study a possible airline route across Greenland (a Danish territory). The company also obtained the services of the distinguished Arctic explorer and scientist, Dr Vilhjalmur Stefansson, and participated in two exploratory expeditions to Greenland during 1932 and 1933, covering both east and west coasts.

These expeditions collected valuable scientific data on possible airport sites and weather conditions, in addition to improving the cartographical coverage of the whole area.

During 1933 the Lindbergh *Jelling* expedition to the Scandinavian countries via Greenland and Iceland began. Lindbergh flew a Lockheed Sirius, specially fitted with Pan American navigational equipment; the *Jelling* was a supply and base ship, commanded by Maj Logan, who had originally recommended Botwood as a site for a transatlantic airport in Newfoundland. Dr Stefansson prepared detailed reports of all aspects of the route from Labrador to Iceland. Altogether the expedition was prepared with typical Pan American efficiency.

During the summer of 1933, Lindbergh surveyed Greenland along the west coast to 70 deg N and along the east coast to 74 deg N, plus the whole of the southern tip, and the west coast of Iceland. He visited the Faröes, Shetlands, and western Norway, and flew to the Baltic, Leningrad, Moscow, and back through the Scandinavian countries, returning to the United States via Spain, Portugal, the Azores, and South America.

Lindbergh's final reports, made in 1934, covered all aspects of airports and harbours, meteorology, and terrain, and were supplemented by those from the *Jelling*. In essence, they concluded that the difficulties of an air service to Europe via northern latitudes had been greatly exaggerated; and that although strong winds and bad weather did occur, their frequency and severity was not as bad as had been commonly imagined.

Pan American, in letters to the Bureau of Air Commerce in January 1935, placed on record its wish to start a transatlantic air service. The various possible routes were enumerated, and the letters were acknowledged on 4 February, 1935. On 12 December, 1935, the State Department announced that understandings had been reached with several countries to facilitate transatlantic air transport; and the Director-General of Civil Aviation of Great Britain advised the Secretary of Commerce that he would approve Pan American's request for a permit, subject to the U.S. Government's approval of that airline. This was given in September 1936.

Compared with the new Dinner Key marine air terminal at Miami, there were no adequate civil seaplane bases in the northeast coastal region of the U.S.A. or in the Canadian Maritime Provinces. In 1933, therefore, Pan American acquired its own seaplane base at Port Washington, Long Island; and in the following year began negotiations with the City of Baltimore for the lease of a marine base to be constructed by that city.

Meanwhile attempts to clear the political path across the mid-Atlantic met frustrating delays. After Aéropostale's collapse, Pan American took several years to obtain a permit from Portugal for landing rights in the Azores, a privilege also granted to Imperial Airways. Furthermore, not wishing the transatlantic service to terminate at Lisbon, Pan American applied to the French Government on 16 December, 1935, for a 15-year permit to operate two services a week to points in France to be designated by the French Government.

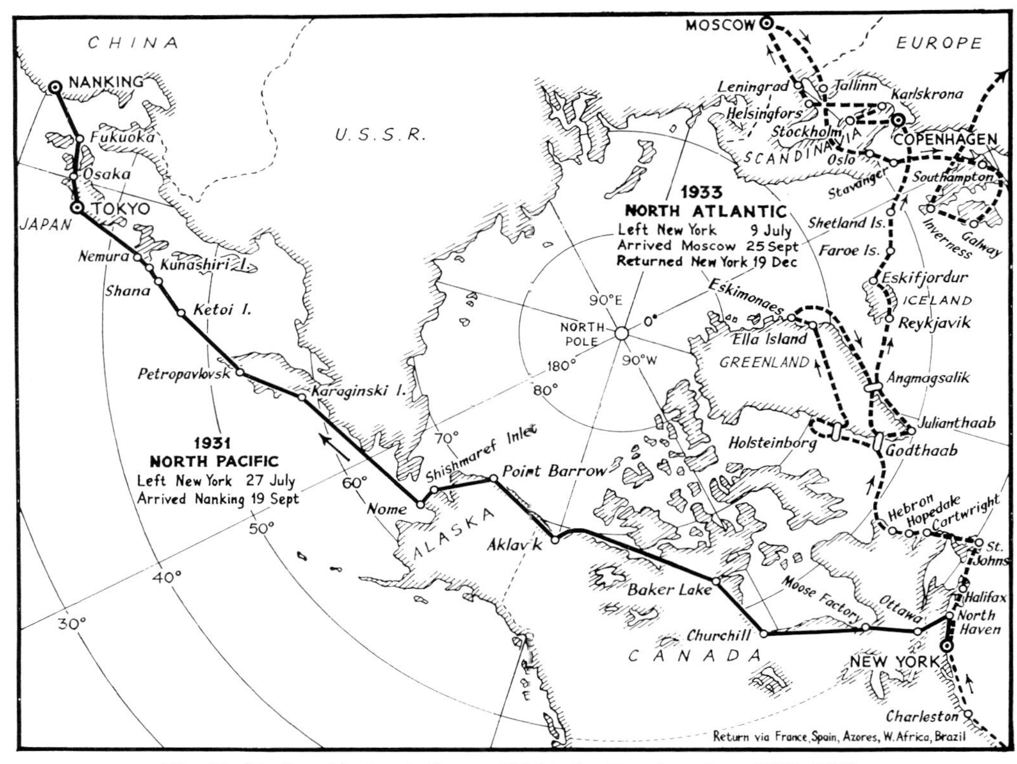

Fig. 20. Lindbergh's Arctic Survey Flights for Pan American, 1931–1933.

All these arrangements were so time-consuming, however, that Pan American made more aggressive moves to exploit the northern route via Greenland and Iceland. The original Icelandic concession obtained from Transamerican was to lapse if regular services were not started by 1936; and failure to obtain clearance from Newfoundland made this virtually certain. The key to the northern route appeared to be co-operation with the Danish Government, for at that time, both Greenland and Iceland were under Danish sovereignty. Pan American accordingly arranged for joint trial flying and observation programmes in Greenland during 1936 and 1937, with Danish participation.

The master plan at that time was for Pan American to inaugurate a service from Copenhagen to Reykjavik by the summer of 1936; then to operate local services in Iceland and some experimental flights from Iceland to Greenland; to extend the route westwards to North America by the summer of 1937; and to begin full scheduled services from Copenhagen to the U.S.A., via Iceland and Greenland, by July 1938.

In an attempt to encourage foreign aspirations Pan American forwarded in November 1936 a proposed agreement for a co-operative arrangement with Det Danske Luftfartselskab (DDL), the Danish national airline. Even more significant was a similar proposal to Det Norske Luftfartselskap (DNL), the Norwegian airline. This resulted in studies of possible amphibian operations by Sikorsky S-43s on a route from Stavanger to Reykjavik, via the Shetland and Faröe Islands. These proposals were quickly taken up in March 1936; and DNL ordered an S-43, to be delivered by 25 May, 1936. For its part, Pan American obtained permission to construct a radio station in Iceland, and this was actually established, staffed, and operated throughout 1936 and 1937.

A combination of manufacturing delays and political complications prevented the fulfilment of these plans. Sikorsky was unable to deliver the aircraft in time, and in any case, the anxiety to rush the project left inadequate time to prepare the operation. Norway ran into difficulties obtaining Icelandic landing rights, and Pan American's Icelandic concession lapsed. Although a law was passed authorizing an extension, Germany put pressure on the Icelandic Government to delay or cancel it. Altogether, these and other handicaps led Pan American reluctantly to abandon this intriguing avenue of approach to Europe.

Pan American was not the only airline to recognize the full importance of establishing a transatlantic air route by way of the Arctic. Germany had sent an expedition to Greenland in 1929, and Britain based one there in 1930 and 1931; while several other European countries were interested, not least those with territorial advantages such as Denmark and Norway —hence Pan American's determined attempts to come to terms with the Scandinavians.

Finally, however, the first discussions held between Pan American and Imperial Airways in 1928 at last bore fruit. The blockage in Newfoundland was removed, and on 22 February, 1937, the United Kingdom Director-

General of Civil Aviation authorized Pan American to conduct a civil air transport service into, through, and away from the United Kingdom, Newfoundland, and Bermuda, for a period of 15 years from 1 June, 1936, on a frequency of two round trips a week over routes terminating at an airport serving London. The United States granted reciprocal rights to Imperial Airways, and similar permits were obtained the same year from Eire, Canada, and Bermuda.

How much of the delaying process can be blamed on the British Government is a moot point. Indignant protagonists of the Pan American cause could rightly observe that the British opening of the door coincided with the setting in motion of their own plans to establish a transatlantic service. Yet these tactics were regarded as perfectly logical and fair by any European country skilled in the business of diplomatic bargaining which had been going on for centuries. In contrast with the countries of Latin America which had no aircraft industry to protect and whose national aspirations for international air routes could not be attained in the foreseeable future, European countries fought Trippe at his own level, with a watchful eye to their own interests.

Trippe came to terms with the new order. But the process took longer, and more concessions had to be made. As time went on, the whole world became involved in the spread of intercontinental air routes and the give and take of international bargaining became standard practice. What was regarded as obstructionist in the 1930s is now regarded as normal. And in other decades Pan American itself was to find itself in the position of trying to restrict the entry of competitors into its own territory.

Pacific Preparations

Although the conquest of the Atlantic Ocean was Trippe's main goal, work began on surveying possible routes to the Orient as early as 1931, during the period when Boston-Maine Airways was providing Pan American with its first taste of northern operations. In some respects the route across or round the Pacific Ocean could be regarded as easier; for although the essential 2,400-mile nonstop crossing from California to Hawaii was many hundreds of miles longer than the longest segment of an Atlantic stopping service, this was the lesser obstacle. Throughout Pan American's history of expansion, the big problems had been ones of international politics, and the route to the Orient was no exception.

In July 1931, Col and Mrs Lindbergh made a survey flight for Pan American from New York to China, by the Great Circle route, their course taking them through Nome, Alaska, the extreme northeast of Siberia, the Kurile Islands, and Japan. This was probably the first Arctic flight which was made for the specific purpose of mapping out an intercontinental highway, in contrast to previous flights which had been made for their own sake, more as an adventure. The aircraft was the Lockheed Sirius, equipped with the latest radio and navigational aids which Pan American could supply. Unfortunately the success of the flight could not be followed up, as the Soviet Union would not allow American aircraft to use bases in Siberia, a necessary prerequisite for the Great Circle route because of the limited range of the aircraft then available.

Once again, the refusal by the Russians was not unreasonable in the circumstances: at that time the United States did not recognize the Government of the Soviet Union. The decision, though negative, did clear the air. Pan American knew where it stood and consequently looked elsewhere for the solution to the Pacific Ocean crossing.

By the time the choice of route was changed, some of the necessary consolidation had already been completed for the Great Circle route. At the North American end, the new Aviation Corporation of the Americas changed its name to Pacific Alaska Airways Inc on 11 June, 1932. A few months later, this company purchased the entire assets of Alaskan Airways Inc and Pacific International Airways of Alaska Inc on 1 September and 15 October respectively. These two companies had together spent about $500,000 in pioneering air services in Alaska, and held 15 Star Route mail contracts between them, the only such contractors carrying the mail by air. After abandoning the scheme to fly to China by the Great Circle route, Pan American adopted a different policy with regard to its Alaskan commitments, and the subsequent story of the development of Pacific Alaska Airways is dealt with in Chapter 12.

At the Asiatic end of the route, another difficulty had to be resolved. Trippe's target was the great Chinese trading city and port of Shanghai. But under its international treaties, China was obliged to extend to other powers any commercial rights given to one of them. At this time, Japan and China were not on diplomatically friendly terms; in fact, after the so-called Manchurian Incident, there was open enmity between the two nations, which was to flare into war a few years later. A mutual solution to the problem of Pan American access was found. The company would establish its terminus at some part of the Chinese mainland controlled by a foreign power, for example Hongkong, and meanwhile would take steps to acquire an interest in a Chinese airline which would provide a connecting route to Shanghai.

This latter task was easily accomplished. Harold Bixby, an efficient organizer and administrator, was sent out on Pan American's behalf to secure Route No. 3, from Shanghai to Canton via Wenchow, Foochow, Amoy, and Swatow. This was vital because one of the Chinese airlines, Eurasia, was Sino-German and represented Luft Hansa's enterprise in the Orient much as the Kondor Syndicat represented it in South America. The other Chinese airline, on the other hand, was American-influenced and this quickly became Pan American-controlled.

Forty-five per cent of the stock of China National Aviation Corporation (CNAC) was held by China Airways Federal Inc, a subsidiary of Intercontinent Aviation Inc, which in turn was owned by North American Aviation Inc. CNAC was founded on 8 July, 1931, Pan American bought the 45 per cent on 31 March, 1933, and operations started on Route No. 3 on 7 July, 1933, using Douglas Dolphin amphibians.

By the end of 1934, Pan American's plans for conquering the Pacific Ocean were crystallized. Russian intransigence ruled out the northern Great Circle route but the Chinese manipulation had securely anchored the western end. The only alternative was to use the chain of islands across the mid-Pacific. Here at least there were no political problems. Hawaii, Midway Island, Wake Island, Guam, and the Philippines were U.S. territories. The problem was reduced to operational and technical aspects: finding aircraft with sufficient range, and establishing adequate bases en route.

Pan American's first Sikorsky S-42, NC822M (c/n 4200X), which entered service on the South American east coast route in August 1934.

The first step in long-range aircraft development was taken by refitting a Sikorsky S-42 as a long-range survey aircraft. It was stripped of passenger accommodation and then further modified to give it an endurance of 21½ hr and a range of just under 3,000 miles by devoting its entire useful load to crew weight and fuel capacity. Exhaustive tests were made to improve fuel consumption by the use of automatic carburettors, the careful study of indicated air speed as a guide, and the installation of totalizing fuel meters. On 23 March, 1935, a modified S-42 flew nonstop from Miami to the Virgin Islands and back, a distance of 2,500 miles. The aircraft was then ferried to Pan American's newly-formed Pacific Divisional headquarters at Alameda, in San Francisco Bay.

The problem of bases was tackled with zeal and determination and probably ranks as the most efficient single programme of preparatory work ever accomplished in starting a new air route. The necessary permits having been obtained from the Secretary of the Navy for the use of certain areas at Midway, Wake, and Guam, the *North Haven*, a 15,000-ton cargo ship, left Pier 22 at San Francisco on 27 March, 1935, with a remarkable load: two complete villages, five air bases, 250,000 gallons of fuel, 44 airline

The jetty at Pan American Airways' Wake Island base, with a Martin M-130 tied-up.

technicians, 74 construction staff, together with appropriate provisions, including motor launches, landing barges, electric generators, windmills, water storage equipment, and fuel tanks. During that summer, complete flying-boat bases were constructed and equipped at Midway, Wake and Guam, and the bases at Honolulu and Manila reinforced.

Building the base at Wake Island was a particularly tremendous achievement. Cargo had to be lightered to Wilkes Island, transferred to an improvised railway, lightered again across the lagoon to Peale Island, and thence to the building site. Clearing thousands of coral heads from the lagoon exhausted the supply of dynamite. No fresh water was available, wells produced only salt water, and the distillation plant taken on the *North Haven* was inadequate. The soil of Wake was unproductive. All these difficulties were overcome. A combination of meticulous planning and specialist expertise in many fields of activity enabled Pan American to finish its task of preparation in 55 days.

On 16 April, 1935, the S-42 made its first survey flight from Alameda to Honolulu, returning on the 22nd. On 12 June it took-off again to survey the Honolulu—Midway sector, and additional flights were made on 9 August and 5 October to survey the Midway—Wake and Wake—Guam sectors respectively. Such preparation was typical of Pan American's methods, and in this instance so much was at stake that nothing could be left to chance. On the same day that the S-42 arrived back at San Francisco on its final survey, Pan American was awarded the trans-Pacific mail contract (FAM-14) at $2 per mile.

The finishing touches were put to taking care of local apprehensions in Hawaii. On 20 June, 1935, Pan American entered into an agreement with the Matson Navigation Company and the Inter-Island Steam Navigation Company for co-operation in establishing a trans-Pacific air service. Pan

American was to furnish meteorological services to the Matson Line and to contract for transport of passenger baggage on Matson ships. Both shipping companies were given an option to purchase Pan American shares at $37 per share. These options were duly taken up on 27 March and 25 August respectively, when the market price was about 50 per cent higher. Meanwhile, authorization was granted by the Philippine Legislature on 17 October, 1935, to transport passengers, mail, and property to and from the United States for a period of 25 years.

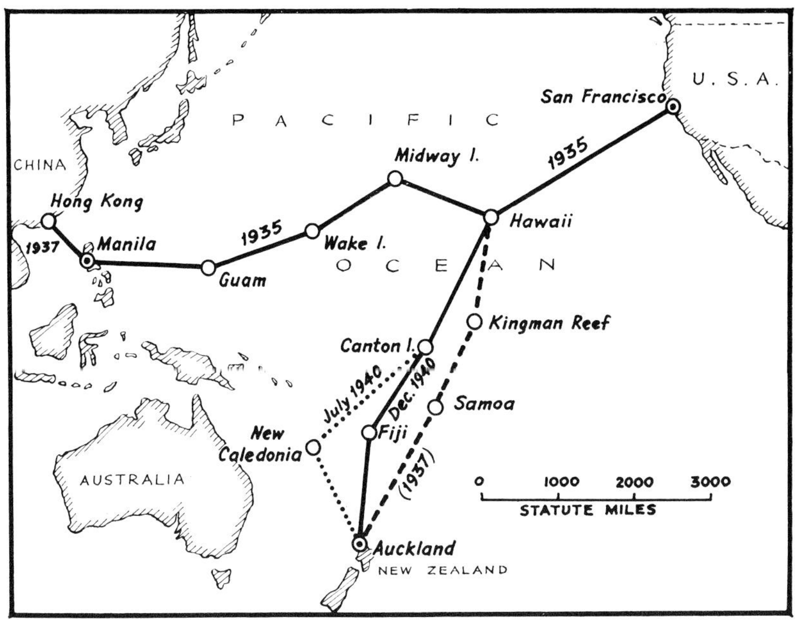

Fig. 21. Pan American's Pacific Routes, 1935–1940.

Pacific Conquest

When Pan American issued its specification for a long-range flying-boat in 1931, two bids were submitted, one of which was for the Sikorsky S-42, described above. The other was for the Martin M-130, substantially bigger, with a take-off gross weight of 52,000 lb (compared with 43,000 lb), a span of 130 ft (114), a length of 91 ft (69), a wing area of 2,170 sq ft (1,330), a speed of 130 mph (145), and a passenger capacity of 32. The M-130 cost $417,000 fully-equipped, compared with $242,000 for the S-42, and $78,000 for the Douglas DC-2, the biggest contemporary American landplane.

The Martin M-130 was a beautiful boat, incorporating all the new features of the Sikorsky S-42, and more, such as cooling gills, galley installation (incorporated in 1936), integral fuel tanks and a fuel transfer system. The first M-130, NC14716 *China Clipper*, was test flown over the Atlantic in October 1935 and ferried out to Alameda on 11 November.

Thus, when Capt Ed Musick and his crew inaugurated the first scheduled air mail flight across the Pacific Ocean on 22 November, 1935, the result was a foregone conclusion. Every stage was completed on schedule, and the *China Clipper* arrived at Manila 59 hr 48 min after taking-off from San Francisco Bay.

Pan American Airways' first Martin M-130, NC14716 *China Clipper*.

Capt Musick's crew was quite an assembly of talent. It included five transport pilots, three aeronautical engineers, three licensed radio officers, and two master mariners. 125,000 people witnessed the take-off from San Francisco; most of the population of Guam, and a substantial section of the population of Manila, welcomed the *Clipper* on its triumphant arrival. It carried 111,000 letters outward bound, arriving at Manila on 29 November; on the return flight 98,000 letters were carried, arriving in San Francisco on 6 December.

Development of the trans-Pacific route proceeded apace. Two more M-130s were delivered, the *Philippine Clipper* (NC14715) while the first flight was taking place, and NC14714 *Hawaiian Clipper** early in 1936. Cargo service was authorized in March 1936. An operating permit was obtained from the Director of Air Services in Hongkong effective from 17 September, 1936, and five-year mail contracts were obtained both from Hongkong and the Portuguese colony of Macao effective from 28 April, 1937. Britain was not too enthusiastic at first in allowing Pan American

* Later the name was changed to *Hawaii Clipper*.

NC14714 *Hawaiian Clipper*, Pan American's third Martin M-130.

into Hongkong; but the threat of Macao, on the Chinese mainland, possibly becoming the trans-Pacific air terminal changed its attitude.

In preparation for the inauguration of trans-Pacific passenger service, Pan American once again called the *North Haven* into service. On this occasion her cargo included solar water heaters, terrace furniture, bridge tables and beach umbrellas, plus a load of top soil from Guam for the artificial gardens of arid Wake and Midway. When the first passenger flight took-off from San Francisco on 21 October, 1936, the formerly uninhabited atolls were equipped with attractive hotels, lawned and landscaped, and with electricity and shower baths.

In November 1936, the CNAC Shanghai–Canton service was extended to Hongkong, to complete the Chinese link. Then on 7 January, 1937, the first of the improved S-42s, the S-42B, was delivered to the Pacific Division at Alameda. Slightly enlarged, more powerful, and with a higher payload, the new Sikorsky boat (NC16734) first made a survey flight to New Zealand and was then despatched to Manila, where it was named *Hong*

The Martin M-130 NC14715 *Philippine Clipper* at Midway.

Kong Clipper, and assigned to the rôle of flying once a week between Manila and Hongkong, connecting with the Martin M-130 service terminating at Manila, from May.

Prior to the Hongkong extension the three Martins were maintaining a once-weekly schedule, San Francisco—Manila, in a round-trip elapsed time of 13 days, including two days layover in Manila. However, with increased experience and as the initial teething troubles of the trans-Pacific operation were reduced, it became possible to reschedule the flights so that the entire round trip to Hongkong and back to San Francisco could be completed by the M-130s in 14 days. The S-42B operation, which was very expensive because of the long supply line for spares and the need to provide full staff for operations and maintenance for only one aircraft, could be eliminated.

Although the new schedule was successful in the early part of 1938, the *Hawaii Clipper* crashed between Manila and Guam in July, and the frequency of the trans-Pacific service unfortunately had to be reduced.

Across the South Pacific

On the same day that Pan American opened the trans-Pacific mail service, on 22 November, 1935, an agreement was also signed with the New Zealand Government for landing rights at Auckland. Studies had been conducted of trade and transport conditions in Australia and New Zealand as early as 1932, while during 1934 a private ship had made extensive marine and weather surveys of a possible route from Hawaii to Australasia. There were two possible routes, either via United States island possessions, Kingman Reef and Samoa, or via Canton Island and either Fiji or New Caledonia.

The first task of the Sikorsky S-42B on delivery was to make a survey flight of the route to New Zealand via Kingman Reef, where the steamer *North Wind* had been stationed as a supply ship. Departing from San Francisco on 17 March, 1937, Capt Musick arrived at Auckland on 29 March and returned to Honolulu on 30 April. The Martin 130s being fully occupied on the route to the Orient, and the delivery of the new fleet of Boeing 314s being delayed, Pan American decided to begin the service to New Zealand with the S-42B. This took place on 23 December, 1937, and completed a successful return flight via Kingman Reef. On its second scheduled flight, on 11 January, 1938, however, this aircraft was lost and Musick and his crew were killed at Pago Pago, Samoa, in a refuelling fire and the South Pacific service was temporarily suspended.

This was a major setback, but Pan American continued to seek a satisfactory route to Australasia. Once again political problems had to be overcome, in this case the right to land at Canton Island, the possession of which was disputed by Great Britain and the United States. Trippe appears to have bluffed his way into Canton Island. When the British cruiser *Essex* arrived to find out what some Americans were up to, they found a party of men digging guano for sale in New York, claiming immunity under an old law under which the U.S. Government could grant protection to any company engaged in such activity, provided the area was uninhabited. The outcome was that a condominium was set up, with both flags flying. The U.S. Department of Agriculture retained the property rights, and leased these to Pan American for a dollar. A licence was issued for the use of Canton Island on 31 March, 1938. This was followed by a French concession to establish a base at Noumea, New Caledonia, on 22 December, 1938.

The year 1938 was rather depressing for Pan American and especially for the great team of air crews, operational staff, technicians, and workpeople of all kinds who had created the trans-Pacific service. The route was losing money fast. The establishment of the bases on remote atolls and the continuous maintenance required to keep a regular schedule going over an exacting route was extremely expensive. Yet the mail rate was fixed at $2 per mile, the maximum under the Foreign Air Mail Act of 2 March, 1929.

Unlike the Latin American routes, there was little compensation from passenger revenue. Fine aircraft though they were, the Martin M-130s just did not have the necessary payload capacity to earn their keep over the route, particularly the critical 2,400-mile stretch from San Francisco to Honolulu where passenger loads sometimes had to be restricted to as few as two.

In addition, no sooner had the Hongkong service been started when the outbreak of war in the Far East depressed westbound travel. Finally there was the double tragedy of the S-42B loss and death of Capt Musick—an idol of the Pan Am staff—plus the crash of the M-130 *Hawaii Clipper*.

When the Civil Aeronautics Act was passed in 1938, therefore, Pan American took immediate steps to reduce the drain on its resources caused by the continued operation of the Pacific route. Members of the Civil Aeronautics Authority heard the case in February and March 1939, and after several months of cogitation—surprising though this may seem today—issued an order increasing the mail rate to $3.35 per mile, effective from 1 April, 1939.

From then on the Pacific operation improved. Survey flights were completed to Auckland via the new route (Canton Island and Noumea) in August and November 1939. Hearings were held before the Civil Aeronautics Board in October and, after strong support from the Navy and Post Office Departments, a route certificate was granted on 7 June, 1940. Oddly enough, serious question was raised as to whether this route was in fact required by the public convenience and necessity, the new criteria set out in the C.A.B. legislation.

The first air mail flight left San Francisco for Auckland on 12 July, 1940, the beginning of a regular fortnightly schedule with Boeing 314 equipment (*See page 257*). The first passenger flight left on 13 September the same year.

Growing tension in the Far East led to Pan American seeking a new terminal at the western end of the Pacific route. After appropriate representations a certificate was granted, on 29 April, 1941, to operate to Singapore and a fortnightly Boeing 314 service was opened on 2 May. Trans-Pacific service was maintained on a weekly frequency by the continuance of a Martin 130 service to Hongkong on the alternate fortnight.

On the South Pacific route, authorization was given on 16 October, 1941, for the inclusion of Suva, Fiji, as an intermediate point. Additional Boeing 314 deliveries permitted the establishment of a local service to Honolulu, beginning on 10 August. The growing emergency, however, curtailed all the Pacific operations just when ideal equipment for their operation was becoming available. A new Boeing 314A was sold to the United States Government for work in Africa, but two Sikorsky S-42Bs were transferred to Manila to provide connecting service to both Hongkong and Singapore.

Then on 7 December came the Japanese attack on Pearl Harbor. An S-42B, NC823M *Hong Kong Clipper*, was destroyed at Hongkong; all stations on the main Pacific route were destroyed by Japanese air attack; the South Pacific route was closed down, and the Pan American Pacific route system was abruptly reduced to the San Francisco—Honolulu sector.

The Bermuda Service

The political barriers with the United Kingdom having been resolved in 1937, the two nations quickly got to work to establish a service from New York (Port Washington) to Bermuda. On 25 May, 1937, Capt Harold E. Gray made the first survey flight with an S-42B, while the Imperial Airways Short C class flying-boat *Cavalier* simultaneously made the reciprocal flight. Three more surveys and an official inaugural flight were made during May and June, and the regular scheduled passenger service began on 18 June without incident. The once-weekly frequency was maintained, with Imperial Airways matching it with a reciprocal service. Pan American increased the S-42B service to twice weekly on 25 August, 1937. The *Bermuda Clipper* (NC16735) made its first flight from the new base at Baltimore on 17 November, 1937. Imperial's *Cavalier* was regrettably lost en route, due to icing, on 21 January, 1939, and Pan American continued to operate alone, supplementing the S-42B with one of the Boeing 314s during the spring of that year.

The Bermuda operation provided an excellent flying laboratory for the study of Atlantic weather and flight problems, and in particular for gaining experience of inflight icing conditions. De-icer boots and de-icing equipment for the propellers were fitted to the S-42s, the largest aircraft of its day so fitted. Pan American also experienced for the first time the use of foreign-owned maintenance facilities and radio stations on a reciprocal basis, a procedure which was put into action with complete success.

The Greatest Flying-Boat

Planning the transatlantic route clearly demanded the acquisition of additional flight equipment. The three Martin 130s were required to maintain the Pacific service. Although in their time these were the largest transport aircraft in the world, they were unsuitable for carrying large payloads across long ocean stretches, and the high headwinds anticipated on the North Atlantic route were an extra handicap. In 1935, therefore, Pan American engineers prepared specifications for aircraft larger than the Martin, and various manufacturers were invited to submit tenders.

Pan American Airways' Boeing 314 NC18603 *Yankee Clipper*. This aircraft opened the world's first transatlantic scheduled air mail service by heavier-than-air craft, on 20 May, 1939. (*Pan American World Airways*)

Boeing won the design competition and a contract was signed on 21 July, 1936, for six great flying-boats, the Boeing 314s. These incorporated all the lessons learned from Pacific operations, especially the study of low fuel consumption, control deck layout, fireproofing, and accessibility of engine nacelles for emergency repairs in flight. 100-octane fuel was first used in regular transport service in the 14-cylinder double-row Wright Cyclone engines of the Boeing 314s.

This magnificent aircraft outstripped all rivals in size, load-carrying ability, and performance. It weighed 82,500 lb, had almost twice the power of the Martin, and could carry 74 passengers on short hops, 30 to Hawaii, allowing for normal fuel reserves. Efficient and elegant, it was in a class of its own, and the finest civil passenger-carrying flying-boat ever built. Each one originally cost $550,000 (later increased to $696,000 for the Model 314A).

The first Boeing 314 was delivered to Pan American Airways at Astoria, Oregon, on 27 January, 1939, and was placed in service on the Pacific where an additional aircraft was needed to replace the *Hawaii Clipper*. As a matter of interest, the original delivery date specified in the contract was 21 December, 1937; even the best manufacturers were sometimes less than perfect then, as now.

The remaining aircraft were delivered at monthly intervals, the last on 16 June, 1939. Two were allocated to the Pacific, four to the Atlantic. Even after delivery, the Boeings developed the problems which so often seem to attend a new airliner, and both airframe and engine had to undergo modification. During the period of trans-Pacific operation when two Martin 130s and two Boeing 314s were in commission, the Boeings were not even able to perform their full share of the scheduled weekly trips to Hongkong, let alone perform additional service to Hawaii.

These disappointments were amply compensated, however, by the success of the North Atlantic Boeings. NC18603 arrived at the Baltimore base of Pan American on 24 February, 1939, and was christened *Yankee Clipper* by Mrs Franklin D. Roosevelt on 3 March at a flamboyant ceremony in New York attended by a large number of public dignitaries and high officials.

On 26 March the *Yankee Clipper* made a survey flight of the North Atlantic, by the southern route from Baltimore, outward via the Azores, Lisbon, Biscarosse, Marseilles, and Southampton to Foynes, Ireland, returning via Southampton, Azores, and Bermuda. There can be no greater tribute to the Boeing 314 than to state that Pan American Airways, with a history of cautious experiment and pre-service survey, started the world's first scheduled service across the North Atlantic after this single pre-inaugural flight.

After the Civil Aeronautics Authority had given Pan American a much-needed financial stimulant by raising the Pacific mail rates on 12 September, 1939, the airline lost no further time in adding to its fleet of Boeing 314s and ordered six more on 29 September. Using the experience gained in the early months of operations, both in the Pacific and the Atlantic, the new aircraft were much improved, and designated 314As. The take-off weight

Air view of Pan American's Marine Terminal at LaGuardia, with a Boeing 314 taxi-ing out for departure.

was increased from 82,500 lb to 84,000 lb., the fuel tankage was increased from 4,200 to 5,448 gallons, whilst oil capacity was decreased. The propellers were modified, resulting in better take-off performance. The contract called for delivery between 20 April, 1941, and 20 January, 1942. Because of the onset of World War 2, however, Pan American agreed to sell to the British Purchasing Commission three of the 314As and a contract to this effect was signed on 29 August, 1940, with the full approval of the United States Government. The aircraft were used extensively in maintaining the vital air link between the United Kingdom and the United States, via Africa, when virtually the whole of Europe was in enemy hands.

The Marine Terminal at LaGuardia, New York, in 1939, with the Boeing 314 NC18603 *Yankee Clipper* at the jetty.

The North Atlantic

When on 22 February, 1937, the British Government finally authorized Pan American to conduct air services across the North Atlantic to London on a reciprocal basis with Imperial Airways, the months which followed were ones of intense activity. Within three weeks, Pan American ordered, on 15 March, three Boeing S-307 four-engined land aircraft with pressurized cabins. The company believed that the use of landplanes would solve the problem of westbound crossings (against the prevailing headwinds) over the northern route during the winter, when freezing temperatures are encountered at normal flying heights. Most clouds over the North Atlantic during this season can be topped, however, at 20,000 ft—hence the need for a pressurized cabin.

While the S-307 did not have sufficient range to carry passengers economically across the ocean, and the intention was to use the aircraft mainly for Alaskan services, Pan American did want to use them for experimental flights across the North Atlantic, carrying mail and express only. The London terminal was to have been Croydon Airport, and the route from New York would have been via Montreal, Moncton, Hattie's Camp (later Gander), and either Shannon or Dublin.

In the spring of 1937 the Atlantic Division was established as an autonomous operating unit, and by June a staff of 113 had been assembled at Port Washington. In November the base was moved to Baltimore, after a series of North Atlantic survey flights with one of the Sikorsky S-42Bs (NC16736 *Clipper III*). These were typical of Pan American's methodical approach. The first departed from Port Washington on 25 June, 1937,

The Boeing 314 NC18604 *Atlantic Clipper* moored off Pan American's Marine Terminal at LaGuardia, New York.

to Shediac, New Brunswick. The second, on 27 June, reached Botwood, Newfoundland. The third left on 3 July, called at Shediac and Botwood, and proceeded to Southampton via Foynes. A fourth flight was made on the same route on 22 August, and a final transatlantic survey was made by the southern route, via Bermuda, Azores, Lisbon and Marseilles, to Southampton on 16 August.

Meanwhile, on the political side, the infrastructure of a commercial operation was being carefully planned. On 26 July, 1937, a conference was held in Dublin to review the results of experimental flights carried out up to that date. This was attended by Pan American and Imperial Airways and by officials of the United Kingdom and Irish Governments concerned with aviation, postal services, and meteorology. Agreement was reached on the use, for example, of common codes and other procedures proved to be successful by Pan American.

In February 1938 the Canadian Government invited Pan American and representatives of the British Air Ministry and the Irish Government to a conference which resulted in agreement of standardized weather and communications procedures. Further progress was achieved at a meeting in Dublin in March 1939; and out of the three conferences there emerged a permanent organization, known as the Transatlantic Air Service Safety Organization (TASSO) which was destined to play an important part in the future control of communications and weather service for international commercial aviation.

On 17 January, 1939, preliminary authority was granted by the French Government for operating rights in France and this was confirmed on 15 July. In February Portuguese authority was obtained for operations to Lisbon and the Azores. On 26 March, the newly-christened Boeing 314 *Yankee Clipper* made its maiden transatlantic flight.

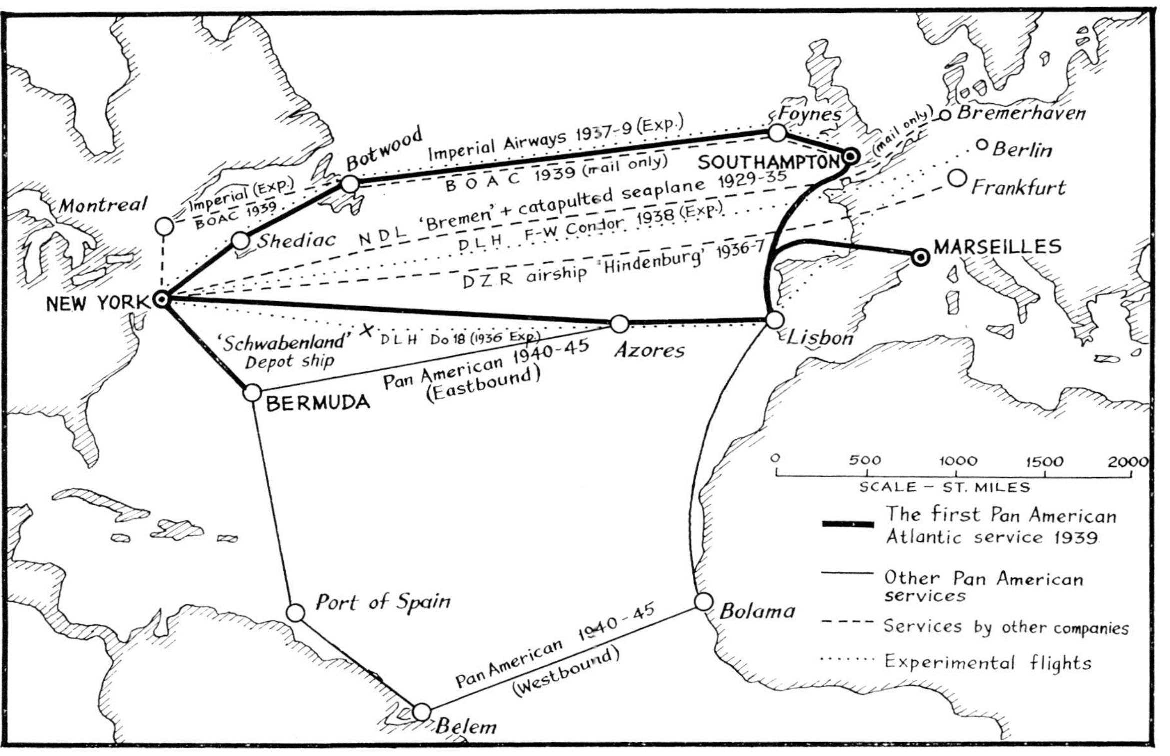

Fig. 22. Pioneer North Atlantic Services, 1929–1940.

The development of the incomparable Boeing flying-boat, together with the consummation of firm bilateral agreements, both with governments and airlines, put Pan American in an impregnable position competitively on the North Atlantic. British flying-boats lacked the load-carrying ability at the required ranges; the French were late off the mark; the Germans had demonstrated remarkable ingenuity with depot ships, catapult

TABLE 1 U. S. A.—CANADA—NEWFOUNDLAND—EIRE—ENGLAND

Eff. June 24, 1939

	Flight #100	Miles	Pan American Airways Co. (PAAA) (zz)		Flight #101	
Sat.	7:30	0	Lv. **Port Washington, N. Y., U.S.A.#★**....... EST	Ar.	14:00	Thu.
"	12:30	593	Ar. **Shediac, N. B., Canada#**............... 60 MT	Lv.	11:00	"
"	13:30		Lv. **Shediac, N. B., Canada#**................ "	Ar.	10:00	"
"	16:30	1067	Ar. **Botwood, Newfoundland#**............... NLT	Lv.	7:00	"
"	18:00		Lv. **Botwood, Newfoundland#**............... "	Ar.	5:30	"
Sun.	8:30	3061	Ar. **Foynes, Eire#**........................ 15 MT	Lv.	16:30	Wed.
"	9:30		Lv. **Foynes, Eire#**........................ "	Ar.	15:30	"
"	13:00	3411	Ar. **Southampton, England#★**.............. GCT	Lv.	14:00	"

#Mail only. No passengers carried until further notice. However, consult your nearest PAA office or Travel Agent for latest information.

TABLE 1A U. S. A.—AZORES—PORTUGAL—FRANCE

Eff. July 5, 1939

	Flight #120	Miles	Pan American Airways Co. (PAAA) (zz)		Flight #121	
Wed.	12:00	0	Lv. **Port Washington, N. Y., U.S.A.★**........ EST	Ar.	7:00	Tue.
Thu.	7:00	2375	Ar. **Horta, Azores**.......................... ALT	Lv.	14:00	Mon.
"	8:00		Lv. **Horta, Azores**.......................... "	Ar.	13:00	"
"	17:00	3432	Ar. **Lisbon, Portugal★**...................... GCT	Lv.	8:00	"
Fri.	7:00		Lv. **Lisbon, Portugal**........................ GCT	Ar.	16:00	Sun.
"	15:00	4251	Ar. **Marseilles (Marignane A'p't), France★**... "	Lv.	8:00	"

TABLE 1B (U. S. A.) BALTIMORE—NEW YORK—BERMUDA

	Flight #160	Miles	Pan American Airways Co. (PAAA) (x)		Flight #161	
We.,Sa.	9:00	0	Lv. **Baltimore, Md., U.S.A.■★**............. EST	Ar.	16:00	Th., Su
" "	10:30	186	Ar. **Pt. Washington, N. Y., U.S.A.■★**....... "	Lv.	14:30	" "
" "	11:00		Lv. **Pt. Washington, N. Y., U.S.A.**........... "	Ar.	14:00	" "
" "	17:00	956	Ar. **Darrell's Is., Ber.**...................... 60 MT	Lv.	9:30	" "
" "	17:15		Ar. **Hamilton, Ber. (launch)**.................. "	Lv.	9:10	" "

PASSENGER FARES (U. S. CY.)

(Subject to Official Passenger Tariff)

Between / And	Botwood, New-foundland	Foynes, Eire	Horta, Azores	Lisbon, Portugal	London, (South-ampton) England	Marseilles (Marig-nane Airp't) France	New York (Port Wash-ington) U. S. A.
Botwood, Nfl.........	—	$466.20	*	*	$505.80	*	$268.20
Foynes, Eire........	$259.00	—	*	*	108.00	*	606.60
Horta, Azores.......	*	*	—	$208.80	392.40	$370.80	428.40
Lisbon, Portugal.....	*	*	$116.00	—	199.80	176.40	556.20
London, (Southampton) England...	281.00	60.00	218.00	111.00	—	*	675.00
Marseilles, (Marignane Airp't) Fr.	*	*	206.00	98.00	*	—	675.00
New York (Port Washington), U. S. A....	149.00	337.00	238.00	309.00	375.00	375.00	—

Baltimore or New York (Port Washington) and Bermuda.... One Way **$70.00**—Round Trip **$120.00**

North Atlantic schedules and fares as they appeared for the first time in a Pan American Airways timetable, June 1939.

The first transatlantic passenger service by heavier-than-air craft. Passengers boarding the Boeing 314 *Dixie Clipper* at Port Washington, New York, on 28 June, 1939, for the Azores, Lisbon and Marseilles. (*Pan American World Airways*)

launching, and the ill-fated *Hindenburg* Zeppelin, but service with their fine Focke-Wulf Condor landplane, ready by 1938, was delayed through political difficulty. Although not involved directly in the European theatre of World War 2 until 1942, the U.S.A. was nevertheless viewing with suspicion what appeared to be growing imperialism of a particularly aggressive nature by the Nazis.

On 17 May, 1939, the Civil Aeronautics Authority granted a certificate for the North Atlantic route; the President gave his approval the next day. European terminals designated were Southampton and Marseilles, and the U.S. terminal New York, with Baltimore an alternative.

Comforted by the now proven superb performance of the Boeing 314s, the world's first transatlantic scheduled air mail service began on 20 May, 1939, with the Pan American *Yankee Clipper*, commanded by Capt A. E. Laporte. 1,804 lb of mail was carried on the southern route, Port Washington—Azores—Lisbon—Marseilles, in a scheduled time of 29 hr. The same aircraft, commanded by Capt Harold Gray, opened the northern mail route on 24 June. In this case an additional complement of 20 guests was carried to Southampton, via Shediac, Botwood, and Foynes.

On 28 June, the *Dixie Clipper*, commanded by Capt R. O. D. Sullivan, had the honour of opening the first transatlantic passenger service, by the southern route, with 22 passengers. The *Yankee Clipper* opened the northern service, with 17 passengers, on 8 July. The standard fare was $375 single, $675 return.

Pan American was able to bask in the glory of a great achievement for only a short while. The outbreak of World War 2 in Europe on 3 September, 1939, led to a curtailment of the southern and northern routes at Lisbon and Foynes respectively, both terminals being in neutral territory. But the imminent danger of hostilities extending many hundreds of miles from the actual scene of battle forced the abandonment of the northern route on 3 October.

TWA Boeing 307 and crew on war service.

CHAPTER ELEVEN

World War Two

Supporting the Allied Cause

If there were any Americans who imagined that the United States would be able to avoid involvement with Hitler's European war, they were brought abruptly down to earth when the Japanese launched their aerial attack on Pearl Harbor on 7 December, 1941. There were some, however, to whom the dramatic news was merely the confirmation of long-held fears. Among the foresighted were the airlines, through the perception of their agency, the Air Transport Association (ATA), under the vigorous presidency of Edgar S. Gorrell.

As early as January 1936, the ATA had proposed to the War Department a plan for mobilizing civil airlines at a time of emergency. Details were worked out mutually between the civil and military representatives, culminating in a revised plan completed on 1 November, 1937. Gorrell was meticulous in keeping this study up to date and in February 1941 consulted C. R. Smith, president of American Airlines, about its practicality. Smith appointed M. P. Stallter to crystallize Gorrell's recommendations into an exact programme whereby, at a given time, all the nation's airlines should cease operations and make their flying equipment available to the Services at a moment's notice.

Such orderly mobilization was obviously necessary; but immediately before Pearl Harbor there were many who never dreamed that such a course would ever be taken. Fortunately for the United States' future allies, already weakened by 28 months of war against a formidable enemy, a few airlines not only foresaw the need for action but, by the time the Japanese attacked Hawaii, were already solidly committed to supporting military effort in various ways.

In October 1940, for example, United Air Lines had begun contract training of military personnel at its Oakland Training Centre. By 1943 more than 5,000 aircraft mechanics had been trained for the Army, followed by more than 1,000 for the Navy. Fully alert to emergency needs, United gave instructions on 16 December, 1941, to all its staff to give absolute priority to Service personnel, or requests for official travel; an instruction which pre-dated the official directive by three days.

Pan American Airways became involved in war preparations on 2 November, 1940, when a subsidiary, the Pan American Airport Corporation, signed a contract with the U.S. Government for the construction of a number of airfields in the Caribbean area. This requirement resulted from an agreement signed by Cordell Hull, U.S. Secretary of State, and Lord Lothian, the British Ambassador, to exchange fifty obsolete destroyers for certain bases in British territory stretching from the Bahamas southward through the West Indies to British Guiana.

At about this time, Britain's dire need for aircraft was being supplemented from transatlantic sources. On 11 November, 1940, the first Atlantic Ferry operation was undertaken by the Canadian Pacific Railway Air Service Department, a trickle of supply which was later to become a flood from U.S. factories. British Overseas Airways Corporation (BOAC) began a Return Ferry Service between Montreal and Blackpool via Gander, with B-24 Liberators, on 4 May, 1941. On 29 May, 1941, Ferrying Command was organized as an independent unit of the U.S. Army Air Force. Commanded by Col (later General) Robin Olds, it began life with two officers, four men, and the world as its oyster. In four years, mostly under the leadership of Lieut-Gen Harold L. George, who took over from Olds on 1 April, 1942, the Command was to grow to the largest air transport system in the world, employing more than 200,000 men, and operating some 166,000 miles of routes.

The first objective was to ferry aircraft across the North Atlantic from Montreal, which was to be the reception point for aircraft flown direct from U.S. factories. Work was undertaken almost immediately to spread the load from Montreal by constructing new bases in Maine, at Presque Isle and Houlton, which were in the extreme northeast corner of the U.S.A. and 300 miles nearer Europe.

In June 1941, TWA came into the picture, by opening the Eagle Nest Flight Training Centre at Albuquerque, to train British airmen. Some administrative difficulties were encountered at first, pending permission from Naval authorities to use its reserve pilots as instructors; but these problems were resolved by July, and satisfactory terms of engagement were worked out between Col Olds, head of Ferrying Command, and Air Chief Marshal Sir Frederick W. Bowhill, in charge of the Royal Air Force Ferry Command. TWA's Eagle Nest Centre trained thousands of RAF personnel, who remember it with affection and respect.

Ferrying operations by the United States began on 21 June, 1941, when Atlantic Airways, a company owned jointly by Pan American and BOAC, began flying 20 aircraft to Africa, by the southern route via the Caribbean and the South Atlantic. Shortly afterwards, on 1 July, the Army Air Corps Ferrying Command made its first North Atlantic shuttle flight when Lieut-Col Caleb V. Haynes flew a Consolidated B-24 Liberator from Bolling Field, D.C., to Prestwick, Ayrshire, via Montreal and Gander. In this period, until 18 October, 22 flights were made by the 'Arnold Line', as the operation was dubbed after Gen Henry H. Arnold, the Commanding General of the Army Air Forces. It stopped flying only when conditions became so unacceptable for B-24s as to be almost suicidal.

On 31 August Haynes also began the first South Atlantic shuttle flight to the Middle East, flying Gen Brett to Cairo and arriving back at Bolling Field on 7 October. Simultaneously, arrangements were being made between the War Department and Pan American Airways to support British forces in the Mediterranean theatre. A contract was signed for Pan Am to set up a permanent and regular service to Cairo, using B-24 Liberators. The airline founded two subsidiaries, Pan American Airways - Africa Ltd, on 15 July, 1941, to provide route facilities and transport service for delivery of lend-lease cargo and the return of ferry pilots; and Pan American Air Ferries Inc, on 24 July, 1941, which undertook the ferrying of lend-lease aircraft to Khartoum.

Drawing on the considerable fund of experience in building airports and providing the complete infrastructure for an airline operation in barren territory, Pan American - Africa completed the work in 61 days. Airports at Dakar, Accra, Lagos, Kano, Maiduguri, El Geneina, El Fasher, and Khartoum were either built or substantially improved. If, a decade or so earlier, Pan American was judged to have received special favour in being designated the chosen instrument for development of foreign air routes, especially in South America, it now went a long way towards paying off its debt to the U.S. Government, for it and the British Forces in the Middle East benefited greatly from the high-speed momentum sustained by Pan Am on its trans-African route. The U.S. airline, in turn, paid tribute to the foresight of the British in surveying the route during the 1930s and actually beginning a trans-African scheduled service with de Havilland D.H.86s, using grass strips.

Pan American began scheduled services to Khartoum on 21 October, 1941, as envisaged in a Presidential directive on 3 October covering the delivery of lend-lease aircraft. Ferrying Command also began services from Bolling Field to Cairo on 14 November, and the route was extended to Basra a few weeks later.

The President's decree was far-reaching, empowering the Secretary of War to deliver aircraft 'to any territory subject to the jurisdiction of the United States; to any territory within the Western Hemisphere, the Netherlands East Indies and Australia on behalf of any country to which I shall have authorized the delivery of defense articles under the Lend-Lease Act'. Britain, traditionally self-reliant, took additional steps. Its Ministry of Aircraft Production, under Lord Beaverbrook, had established a ferrying organization, Atfero, in March 1941, and on 15 July this was formally transferred to RAF Ferry Command, under Air Chief Marshal Bowhill.

In the light of subsequent events, this was not a moment too soon. For a few months later, on 7 December, 1941, when the Japanese struck, Ferrying Command halted all shipments to its country's allies and held aircraft available for the U.S. Army and Navy, having completed 1,331 aircraft deliveries to United Kingdom authorities.

The Airlines Mobilized for War

When the Pacific war started, the first United States airline to get involved was obviously Pan American, as its operations spanned the area of hostilities. On 7 December, 1941, the day of the attack, *Anzac Clipper*, a Boeing 314 one hour off Pearl Harbor, was diverted to Hilo and returned to San Francisco. *Philippine Clipper*, an M-130, had just left Wake Island. It returned to pick up all Pan American staff and, although machine-gunned by the Japanese, succeeded in bringing them back safely to Honolulu. The Sikorsky S-42 *Hong Kong Clipper* was destroyed at its base in Hongkong.

Another Boeing 314, the *Pacific Clipper*, found itself stranded in Auckland, New Zealand. Under the command of Capt Robert Ford, this aircraft returned to New York on a long westbound flight, via Sydney, Surabaya, Trincomalee, Karachi, Bahrain, Khartoum, Leopoldville, Natal, and Port of Spain. The 31,500-mile flight was the first one made completely round the world by a commercial aircraft.

The same day, Western Airlines saw its aircraft requisitioned to fly desperately-needed ammunition to the West Coast of the U.S.A. A source of danger hitherto thought only to be theoretical now appeared very real and simultaneously came the realization of the ill-prepared state of coastal defence.

On 12 December, 1941, the Assistant Secretary for War and Gen Arnold directed Ferrying Command's Col Olds to call on the airlines for the transport of vital men and materials. The first agreement was made with Pan American, on the next day, to extend its African service to Teheran, with the further prospect of an extension to the Soviet Union. Additionally, the ferrying of aircraft to both Russia and China was contemplated. Pan

American was to contract for a service from the U.S. through to Singapore, via West Africa and India. Its first-line flying-boat fleet of eight Boeing 314s and two Martin M-130s was to be sold to the Government and operated on its behalf by Pan Am. This plan, however, never materialized because of the Japanese offensive in southeast Asia.

On 14 December American Airlines took part in a copybook exercise, when the War Department called the Air Transport Association and asked for the immediate and secret movement of special troops to a destination in South America. The plans so carefully—and far-sightedly—initiated by Edgar Gorrell were put into effect. American Airlines was selected for the job. Pilots in flight were ordered to land at the nearest airport and discharge passengers. The aircraft were then flown to a secret Army base and fifteen aircraft loads of troops were flown to Brazil.

TWA's Boeing 307 Stratoliner N19908 seen at Prestwick during its wartime transatlantic operations.

On 16 December, Col Olds began a series of discussions with TWA which culminated in signing a contract on 24 December providing for transport service anywhere in the world and for the sale of TWA's five Boeing 307 Stratoliners to the Government.

Other airlines overtaken by events were Pennsylvania-Central Airlines (PCA), two-thirds of whose fleet of *Capitaliners* were commandeered by the Army in December; Chicago & Southern Air Lines, which began a modification contract on 14 December to fly aircraft direct from the factory to the airline's base at Memphis; and Delta Air Lines, which suffered the same fate as PCA.

On 1 January, 1942, M. P. Stallter, the man selected by C. R. Smith on behalf of the ATA to draw up a master emergency plan for the airlines, was assigned to the office of Brig-Gen Donald H. Connolly, the Military Director of Civil Aviation. The United States was divided into five parts, each assigned to an airline: American in the east, Eastern in the southeast, Braniff in the southwest, Northwest in the northwest, and United on the West Coast. The basis of this plan was that aircraft could be assembled in strategic positions, both from the point of view of geography and of maintenance and refuelling resources.

At the end of February the War Department requisitioned 200 aircraft from the total fleet of 360, and Col Gorrell called the heads of airlines together to allocate these on a fair basis.

On 20 January, 1942, in ATA Bulletin No. 7, Gorrell outlined to the airlines their responsibilities and his desire that they work out procedures in co-operation with the Military Director of Civil Aviation. Both Gorrell and Connolly stressed that only as a last resort would the civil agencies, the C.A.B. and the C.A.A., be sidetracked. Nevertheless, whether voluntarily or compulsorily, future action by the airlines would be channelled along lines strictly laid down by the military authorities.

On Active Service

The first overseas flights made by a U.S. domestic airline on a regular schedule were by Northeast Airlines, which began carrying passengers and freight in the North Atlantic region on 13 February, 1942, a contract having been approved on 31 January. Earlier, on 11 January, Northeast had made a survey with a C-39 (military DC-3) flying from Presque Isle to Gander, via Moncton, Goose Bay, and Stephenville, to determine the practicality of scheduled service. This was the first expedition since Colonel Lindbergh's *Sirius* exploration in the early 1930s, and was made under the direction of Lieut Crocker Snow, who made important recommendations. Among these was the decision to replace the C-39 with the C-53 (a later version, with more powerful engines) which duly inaugurated the regular services. Inadequate though the C-39 may have been, operations could hardly have been easy with any aircraft on a route to Newfoundland, via Labrador, in the month of February, with navigational aids almost non-existent.

The route was extended northwards, on 5 April to Argentia, on 24 April to Narsarsuak (Bluie West 1), and later to Søndrestrømfjord (Bluie West 8). The difficulty of operating in this area is perhaps well illustrated by a description of the landing at Bluie West 1 by Capt (vice-president of NEA) Anderson quoted in Reginald M. Cleveland's book *Air Transport at War*: 'The shore line was reached in a heavy snowstorm which reduced visibility to less than a mile, and with winds later computed to be over sixty miles per hour on the surface. Extreme difficulty was encountered in locating the fjord which led to the airport, and it was found only by climbing through the overcast in unfamiliar mountain terrain, orienting on a radio range with countless multiple courses, simultaneously experiencing a 180-degree wind shift, and finally spiralling down 8,000 feet through a hole in the overcast over the airport.'

Northeast made its first flight to Iceland in May and to Stornoway, in the Outer Hebrides, on 3–4 July, again under the command of Capt Anderson. During 1942 the airline also carried troops within Iceland, in anticipation of enemy raids on that strategically situated country.

Northeast made a series of flights to the remote fastnesses of northern Quebec Province and the Northwest Territories of Canada, beginning on 1 November. Reaching northern Quebec, just south of Ungava Bay (Crystal 1) and Frobisher Bay, Baffin Island (Crystal 2) on that date, another route was pioneered on 21 November by a flight from Crystal 2 across northern Hudson Bay to Southampton Island and thence to Churchill, Manitoba. On 16 March, 1943, the first trip was made to a point in Baffin Island, just north of the Arctic Circle (Crystal 3). Finally, on 28 March, a round trip was completed to Arctic Bay, at the extreme north of Baffin Island, to remove weather station personnel requiring medical treatment, and to replenish supplies both there and at Fort Ross. Three trips were made in all, and a total of 2,300 lb of supplies was taken to these outposts of human settlement. 9,910 miles were flown in 13 days, over some of the most inhospitable, barren, and frigid land ever to witness the operation of a civil airliner.

Next in chronological order to start overseas scheduled services was Northwest Airlines, which began regular operations to Alaska on 29 March, 1942. The route was from Minneapolis/St Paul to Fairbanks, via Edmonton, Grand Prairie, Fort St John, Fort Nelson, Watson Lake, Whitehorse (all in Canada) and Northway and Big Delta, in Alaska.

This was the sequel to a contract signed between Northwest and Gen Olds on 26 February. Already possessing some experience in Alaskan flying—the airline had applied for a route under normal C.A.B. procedure on 3 February, 1941—the first flight was made from Fargo to Fairbanks on 2 March and the first official flight for Ferrying Command on 21 March.

As with the Northeast operation, there were tremendous problems of navigation because of the complete absence of equipment established on the ground. Flying was characterized by bitter cold, in which rubber hoses shattered like glass, and to breathe or to expose skin to the outside air was to invite permanent disability. Whereas Northeast had a special problem on its Crystal operations—the discovery that the Magnetic Pole had been wrongly mapped—Northwest's main difficulty was with the Northern Lights whose effect in interfering with radio communication was quite unpredictable.

Northwest came to be regarded as the leading Alaskan operator among several rivals. Scheduled services were maintained from Anchorage to Adak, and, once the direct Japanese threat of invasion was removed from the Aleutians, three daily round trips were flown between Minneapolis and Attu, far out at the end of the island chain, and only 2,000 miles from Tokyo. Later, another route was added from Seattle to Anchorage.

Northwest flew much vital material and supplies for building the Alaska Highway. It supplied a 24-bed hospital to Nome to replace one destroyed by fire, and ferried many aircraft to the U.S.S.R. by the route through Alaska and Siberia. Altogether, Northwest's wartime record was wholly admirable and few questioned the permanent establishment of routes to Alaska and the Orient when the War ended.

Western Airlines' Lockheed Model 18 Lodestar NC25638.

Another airline which mounted an Alaskan ferrying operation was Western Airlines. Left with only three DC-3s and a Lockheed Lodestar to perform its route schedules, the company flew one of the most difficult supply routes of World War 2, from Great Falls, Montana, to Fairbanks and Nome, Alaska, via Edmonton, Alberta. In spite of one of the worst winters in recorded history, when even the southernmost point of the route experienced temperatures of minus 40 deg, Western maintained a perfect safety record. In addition, it conducted a pilot training programme in Salt Lake City, turning in an impressive record of military support activity.

TWA's contract with Col Olds has already been mentioned. In meeting far-reaching demands, considerable store was set on the capability of the Boeing 307s which formed its front-line fleet. Backed by Tommy Tomlinson's many years of research at high altitudes, TWA knew more about 'flying above the weather' than any other airline in the world. Further investigation had shown that great strides could be made by taking advantage of strong wind currents and evolving the system of pressure pattern techniques which are commonplace today.

On 26 February, 1942, a Boeing 307 made a survey from Bolling Field to Cairo, as a prelude to regular transatlantic flights for what was to become the Air Transport Command. A military V.I.P. Boeing 307 service to Britain started on 18 April, 1942, and continued throughout the war. Altogether 5,000 trans-oceanic flights were made, 112,000 passengers were carried, and 20 million lb of important war cargo were flown during a three-year period. Three of the Boeing 307s were allocated to the North Atlantic and two to the Washington—Cairo service. During June 1942 one aircraft also operated a shuttle service between Natal, Brazil, and Accra, Gold Coast, over the South Atlantic.

Breaking the Pan American monopoly of carrying important passengers abroad, TWA had the privilege of carrying President Roosevelt on two overseas trips, in a Boeing 307 commanded by Capt Otis Bryan. Other crews flew Generals Marshall and Eisenhower, Admirals King, Tower, and Leahy, Generalissimo and Madame Chiang Kai-shek to Cairo, and Joseph P. Davies on his famous mission to Moscow.

After Northeast, Northwest, and TWA, came Eastern Air Lines, whose scheduled overseas service started on 1 May, 1942, from Miami to Trinidad. Two months earlier, emergency operations had begun in co-operation with Ferrying Command. Six DC-3s—withdrawn from *The Great Silver Fleet*—began military operations between Eastern's Miami base and Middletown, Pennsylvania, on a thrice daily frequency, and from Miami to San Antonio once a day. The first overwater survey was made on 14 April, from Miami to Trinidad, via Cuba and Borinquen Field, Puerto Rico.

The Trinidad service was increased to once daily on 18 May, a trial flight was made to Natal on 24 June, and scheduled services started to that strategically situated airport on the northeastern tip of Brazil on 1 July, 1942. The route was via Atkinson Field, British Guiana (by courtesy of Pan American's airport construction department), and Belem. Frequency was twice daily, later increased to four, and care had to be taken to avoid flying over the coastal part of French Guiana, which for a time was controlled by enemy forces. The traffic of vital men and materials on the outbound leg was balanced by loads of equally vital supplies on the inbound leg: mica, quartz crystals, crude rubber, together with returning crews from merchant ships sunk off the Brazilian coast by German convoy raiders.

On 1 September, Eastern Air Lines created its Military Transport Division (M.T.D.) based at Miami. A month later, this unit put into service the new Curtiss C-46 Commando, a big twin-engined landplane capable of carrying twice the payload of the DC-3. Eastern received the fifth aircraft off the production line and first put it to work on the Miami—Middletown route. Like most new civil transports, the C-46 had its share of teething troubles, and Eastern can take much of the credit for putting them right. The Miami base identified more than 300 faults, and recommended modifications, most of which were accepted by the manufacturer. The aircraft were grounded for two weeks while a serious hydraulic problem was solved, and then a C-46 made a proving flight to Natal on 8 February, 1943. Within a month, fifteen C-46s were in full scheduled service and by July were maintaining three round trips per day to Natal, supplementing a single DC-3 round trip.

In September night flights were started to Natal, using slip crews, taking advantage of new alternate landing fields and the increased range and speed of the C-46. At about this time also, Eastern established an excellent weather reporting system based on carefully timed and located reports by designated aircraft flying on its disciplined schedules.

The C-46's greatest achievement was to extend the Miami—Natal ser-

The Curtiss C-46 played a major part in United States wartime transport and many war-surplus C-46s passed to civil operators. N1386N, with red, white and blue livery, is seen in post-war service with Braniff International Airways as a cargo carrier.

vice across the Atlantic on 1 June, 1944. A base having been hewn out of the rocky outcrops of Ascension Island, 1,448 statute miles east of Natal, a route was maintained to Accra, itself 1,356 miles from Ascension. The C-46s were modified by fitting extra 250-gallon tanks. Navigation was made by dead reckoning and celestial observation at night.

This unique service continued for just over five months, until 10 November, 1944. Flights to Natal continued, however, until 15 October, 1945, when Eastern's Military Transport Division was disbanded.

United Air Lines joined the ranks of overseas military airline contractors on 15 May, 1942, when it began a service from Patterson Field, Fairfield, Ohio, to Anchorage, Alaska, via Chicago, Minneapolis, Fargo, Regina, Fort St John, Whitehorse, and Fairbanks, a distance of 3,489 miles.* A second United service to Alaska started on 27 June from Salt

* For this operation, Delta Air Lines provided a feeder route from Atlanta, where a modification programme was in hand, to Patterson Field, via Mobile and Memphis.

Pan American World Airways was also a Curtiss C-46 operator. N74170 is seen here with cargo conveyor in position. (*Pan American World Airways*)

Lake City via Edmonton. These were discontinued temporarily on 4 August, 1942, but resumed on a different route in January 1943, from Seattle to Anchorage, via Ketchikan, Juneau, Yakutat, and Cordova. All United flights to Alaska terminated on 15 November, 1944.

Consistent with its considerable resources, United undertook a second major task for the Air Transport Command on 23 September, 1942, when a trans-Pacific service was opened. The first route was from San Francisco to Brisbane, via Honolulu, Canton Island, Nadi (Fiji), and New Caledonia. The 7,350 miles were flown in 50 hr in new Douglas four-engined landplanes, the C-54 Skymasters, described by an astonished U.S. serviceman on one of the islands as the 'biggest damned thing he'd ever seen'. As the theatre of war moved northward with the combined U.S. and Australian defence of the South Pacific, so did United's operation, taking in such historic staging points as Tarawa, Guadalcanal, Port Moresby, and Nadzab, New Guinea.

When United's contracts were terminated on 31 March, 1945, almost 20,000 tons of men and materials had been transported 21 million miles, using 77 United crews. 1,700 trips were made across the Pacific, and 1,800 on the Alaska shuttle.

Mention has already been made of wartime transatlantic flights by Pan American (holder of exclusive route authority from the C.A.B. in peacetime), TWA, Northeast, and Eastern. To these established airlines was added another new carrier, early in 1942. Five years before, a shipping company, American Export Lines, had established American Export Airlines (AEA), with the intention of operating a transatlantic service to Europe. Only after a long struggle with Pan American was it awarded, on 10 February, 1942, a temporary C.A.B. certificate to operate to Lisbon. On 26 May services began from New York to Foynes, Ireland, using the new Sikorsky VS-44 flying-boats. During the winter, the 'boats took the easier southern route via Port of Spain, or Bermuda, and Bathurst (Gambia).

Pan American no doubt had its own private views on these incursions by all and sundry into areas and world routes which it had truly pioneered since the first twinkle in Juan Trippe's eye. But there was a war on and a job to be done. Pan Am's contribution was indeed enormous, for not only did it maintain its contract with the Army, as already outlined, but it also completed a cost-plus-fixed-fee contract with the U.S. Navy on 1 September, 1942. This was to reinforce Northwest and United in providing essential services to Alaska. Already operating civil routes in the area, its investment in radio aids, aerodromes, navigation aids, and staffing now paid handsome dividends. Without delay, ten services per week were started from Seattle to Fairbanks, via Juneau, five a week onward to Nome, and one a week to Bethel. On 25 September the first contract trip was made with an R4D-1—the Navy DC-3—from Seattle to Kodiak, and this was increased to a semi-scheduled operation as more aircraft were delivered. By April 1943 the Kodiak route was extended to Dutch Harbor and Adak, and eleven DC-3 aircraft were in service on Alaskan routes by the end of 1943.

On 22 March, 1944, Pan American made its first flight to Point Barrow, on the northern coast of Alaska, to support a survey being made of oil reserves in the area, and a charter service was started with Lockheed L.10 Electras in July. Meanwhile, considerable improvements had been made to the schedules to the Aleutians. On 21 April an accelerated service from Seattle to Adak, with a single stop at Anchorage, cut the 6,000-mile round trip to 36 hr, by the use of slip crews, replacing the 84-hr service including night stops.

Pan American's Alaskan contract ended on 31 July, 1944. During the War, the airline made 15,000 ocean crossings, including 3,800 across the Atlantic on behalf of the Air Transport Command, 3,000 trans-Pacific on behalf of the Naval Air Transport Service, apart from its Alaska work, African network, and services over the 'Hump' in China and Burma. Pan American carried President Roosevelt to the Casablanca Conference, and acted as flying host to Winston Churchill, Admirals King and Nimitz, and a host of other important people. In conjunction with BOAC and the Eastman Kodak company, it pioneered a system of microfilming of mail to save weight, known as the V-Mail or Airgraph system. Altogether, this record was impressive by any standards, and when the special efforts in South America—described later—are also taken into account, the conclusion must be that Pan American's contribution to the United States war effort was unmatched.

Of all the big U.S. domestic carriers, American Airlines' rôle was the most varied. Its exercise in moving troops to Brazil a week after the attack on Pearl Harbor has already been mentioned. In May 1942, it joined Northeast Airlines in an extensive operation flying servicemen to strategic points on a route connecting Maine with Labrador, South Baffin Island, Greenland and Iceland. Pausing in June to make nearly 200 trips from Edmonton to Alaska to support the emergency situation there, American began regular operations across the North Atlantic in October 1942 and joined in the South Atlantic service the following December. Early in 1943, American was flying through to India, and the next year was achieving 150 transatlantic trips a month.

Among the various missions assigned to American was a survey flight to Marrakesh, Morocco, by the northern route through Newfoundland, in April 1943; a special flight to Australia in June 1943; and more than 1,000 flights across the 'Hump' in July with C-87 Liberators, carrying five million lb of cargo. Altogether, American's overseas performance was nothing if not versatile for a certificated domestic airline.

But perhaps the greatest relative wartime achievement was that of Northeast Airlines. Until May 1941, Northeast did not even own a DC-3, nor venture beyond New England and Montreal; yet by 4 July, 1942, it had completed a flight to Scotland, and went on to underpin an entire wartime operation throughout the Arctic region.

A Matter of Organization

Frequent reference has been made to various official bodies which exercised overall control over individual companies through contractual arrangements. As several different titles were involved, some elaboration is appropriate, especially as such organizations as Ferrying Command (later to become Air Transport Command), the Naval Air Transport Service, and the South Pacific Combat Air Transport all operated fleets of aircraft in their own right.

The activities of Ferrying Command in supplying aid to the United States' allies have already been outlined. After Pearl Harbor, initial contracts were satisfactorily placed with selected airlines to meet priority needs. Some airline expertise was then injected into the Command on 14 April, 1942. C. R. Smith, president of American Airlines, was selected by Gen Arnold (Commanding General of the Army Air Forces) to become executive officer of Ferrying Command, holding the rank of Colonel. Under Smith, plans were crystallized to assign tasks to airlines in a logical manner, according to the location of maintenance bases.

At the same time, the Air Service Command was also making contracts with airlines to provide cargo services between its main depôts and sub-depôts, so as to free the equipment of the 50th Transport Wing for tactical operations, which were transferred to the Troop Carrier Command, established on 30 April, 1942. Air Service Command drew up separate contracts with five airlines for domestic cargo services: American, PCA, Eastern, Braniff, and United; and with four airlines for overseas work: United, Braniff, Eastern, and American.

There was so much friction between the two Commands that, in a memorandum dated 12 June, Gen Arnold noted some duplication of effort and responsibility. More important, L. Welch Pogue, chairman of the C.A.B., protested against unnecessarily heavy demands on airlines for that reason. Consistent with the urgency of the occasion, action was quickly taken. On 20 June, Gen Arnold ordered the unification of all air transport services within the Army, and created Air Transport Command (ATC). Its powers were all-embracing, covering aircraft ferrying, transport of men and materials, and control of operations and maintenance of air routes and airfields.

In addition to the stringent demands made upon flying operations, the airlines were no less active on the ground. Production of combat aircraft was already well under way to fulfil orders from the United Kingdom before the United States entered the war. By 1942, production had reached a high rate, but increasing complexity and rapid technical development of both airframe and systems began to outpace the ability of the factories to keep up to date with modification programmes. A plan was evolved, therefore, whereby aircraft were completed, and other companies, some of them airlines, were sub-contracted to make the necessary alterations.

In January 1942, United Air Lines was asked by the Army Air Forces Materiel Command to modify two Boeing B-17s for special photographic missions. The work was carried out at United's maintenance base at Cheyenne, and one of these aircraft was used for the first aerial reconnaissance of Japan.

In February 1942, seven more four-engined bombers arrived at Cheyenne, to be modified for Britain, with British kits, including such precision instruments as bomb-sights. On 1 March, seventeen more aircraft arrived, also for Britain, and hundreds more followed. In May, two big hangars were built and an entire new organization established. Production in this huge new facility started in September, including provision for night work under floodlighting. In all, United Air Lines modified 5,500 Boeing B-17 Flying Fortresses and in the process trained 5,000 technicians.

Northwest experienced a similar revolution in its engineering department. Early in 1942, a base was established at St Paul, to deal with extensive changes in North American B-25s for the Royal Air Force. A new hangar was completed on 7 December, 1942, which was able to cope with B-24 Liberators in addition to the B-25s. One of these aircraft was later to return from a bombing raid on Kiel with so many holes that parts of it looked like a skeleton, and was known as 'the most shot-up plane in the European theatre'.

In February 1943, Northwest also began the Airmen's Transition Training Programme for the ATC at Billings, Montana, specializing in training C-46 pilots.

Other airlines were brought into the aircraft manufacturing or flying school industries. Delta opened a modification centre at Atlanta in February 1942 and dealt with 1,000 aircraft. In February 1944, the entire department was drafted for emergency work, on 45 Boeing B-29 Super-Fortresses. Mid-Continent Airlines modified the B-25s for Gen Doolittle's raid on Tokyo in April 1942 and throughout that year undertook an extensive training programme. Pennsylvania-Central opened the Roanoke Naval Transitional Flying School on 21 December, 1943, and trained hundreds of student pilots. In brief, every available airline employee, whether in the air or on the ground, worked full time, and overtime, throughout the war.

Air Transport Command made a magnificent contribution to the war effort. Advised largely by airline personnel and with a fair proportion of ex-airline men in positions of responsibility, the ATC became in effect an enormous airline, with contracted carriers operating certain routes more or less autonomously but subject nevertheless to the overall control of the ATC.

The Pacific route was established within a few weeks of the attack on Pearl Harbor, and the first aircraft was delivered to Hawaii on 13 January, 1942. As already narrated, airlines were operating under contract over the Atlantic and to Alaska by April 1942, in which month also China

National Aviation Corporation (CNAC), a subsidiary of Pan American, began operations over the Burma–China 'Hump' with lend-lease aircraft, in co-operation with the 10th Air Force. On 16 April, too, the Consolidated Aircraft Corporation began regular trans-Pacific services from the factory at San Diego. This operation, which became known as the Consairway, was operated for much of the war like a regular airline.

Within a week of the consolidation which created Air Transport Command in June 1942, five Wings were commissioned, North Atlantic, Caribbean, Pacific, South Atlantic, and Africa-Middle East. By the end of the year, these were augmented by the Alaskan and India-China Wings, and the Africa-Middle East Wing was divided into two, North and Central African. On 17 November, 1942, the ATC opened a regular trans-Sahara route between Accra and Oran, using a fleet of six C-87 Liberators. On Christmas Day of that year, a C-54 made the first flight from Marrakesh to Prestwick, a prelude to regular operations in the following month.

In 1943 there was considerable expansion of activity on all fronts, including the new European Wing, started at the beginning of the year. On 31 July a Sydney—Townsville—Port Moresby service started; while by the end of the year operations on the life-line between India and China averaged a flight every eleven minutes.

As the war progressed, so the ATC grew from strength to strength. On 6 February, 1944, the first flight was made direct from New York to Calcutta. In the Pacific theatre, services were constantly improved to provide regular contact between forward areas and command bases, with routes radiating from Honolulu in all directions, and reaching out to almost every atoll able to sustain an airstrip. In Europe, shortly after the breakthrough in France, the ATC opened a London—Paris service on 2 September, 1944, a Casablanca—Algiers—Marseilles service on 11 September, and by October was operating direct from New York to Paris.

Complementing the Army Air Transport Command was the Naval Air Transport Service (NATS), created on 12 December, 1941, by Frank Knox, Secretary of the Navy, on the recommendation of Commander C. H. 'Dutch' Schildhauer, USNR. The first transport squadron was formed on 9 March, 1942, at Norfolk, Virginia, with a fleet of four R4D (DC-3) aircraft for Atlantic operations. Other squadrons were formed at Alameda, to cover the Pacific, and at Kansas City, to provide a link between naval and continental bases. Contracts were drawn up with Pan American and the newly-formed American Export Airlines, and a NATS VS-44 made the first trans-oceanic flight on 15 May, 1942. Under a reorganization in February 1943, Pan American's Atlantic Division came under NATS responsibility, as did the entire Atlantic service of AEA.

In April 1943, the Service received its first four-engined landplane, the Douglas R5D (the Army C-54 Skymaster, and later the civil DC-4) which was ultimately to become the backbone of the Naval civil aircraft fleet. A NATS R5D was equipped to carry 50 airborne troops, 24 hospital

U.S. Army Air Force Douglas C-54 Skymaster. Many Skymasters passed to civil operators after the war and 79 civil DC-4s were built to give a total of 1,245 including the original DC-4E. (*Douglas Aircraft Company*)

litters or a light tank, a truck or two scout cars or 155-mm howitzers. It could carry a total payload of seven tons over a distance of 500 miles or a much reduced load over a 2,500-mile stage.

Other aircraft commissioned were the four-engined Consolidated PB2Y-3 patrol bombers converted to transport service, the Martin PBM-3 Mariner, and the Martin Mars—flying-boats.

The last-named of this trio of flying-boats was a giant in its day. Weighing 148,000 lb against, for example, the Boeing 314's 84,000 lb, it dwarfed all other aircraft in service anywhere in the world. In November 1943 it made a nonstop flight from Patuxent, near Washington, to Natal, a distance of 4,250 miles, in 29 hr, with a payload of 50,500 lb. An even larger version saw post-war service with the Navy.

By this time further NATS squadrons had been formed, in San Diego, Seattle, Honolulu, Oakland, and Patuxent. Daily services were maintained

The Naval Air Transport Service Martin JRM Mars *Hawaii Mars* in company with the XPB2M twin-finned prototype. At top right is the starboard fin and rudder of the photographic Martin PBM Mariner.

from San Francisco to Pearl Harbor, Seattle to Adak, Miami to Rio de Janeiro, and a shuttle service from Pearl Harbor to Suva in Fiji.

In November 1943 a new Wing was created, the Naval Air Ferry Command, with three squadrons, based at New York, Columbus, and San Pedro. By the end of 1943, NATS was staffed by 8,000 men, was operating four transatlantic routes (to Reykjavik, to Foynes, to Lisbon, and across the South Atlantic), and was keeping pace with the advancing forces throughout the Pacific, mainly by routes radiating from Pearl Harbor, with Pan American supplying under contract the link from San Francisco.

During 1944, the NATS increased its activity at a fine pace. Early in the year, 22,500 priority passengers were being carried every month, an average of 1,200 miles each, plus more than eight million lb of cargo and mail. By the middle of the year, the Pan American contract to Alaska was terminated, and all Atlantic contracts ended. On 3 March, 1945, the NATS was established as a Fleet Command. Two new squadrons were commissioned, a trans-Pacific unit at Honolulu, and an Air Evacuation unit at Guam. On 21 August, some of the older squadrons were combined to form the Asiatic and Atlantic Wings of the new Command.

Thus, on VJ Day, the NATS was able to look back on a proud record of transport service throughout World War 2, performing the rôle of an overseas airline, second in stature only to the Air Transport Command of the Army Air Force. By the end of the war, 26,600 staff were operating a fleet of 429 aircraft, of which 159 were four-engined Douglas R5Ds. The only airline still under contract was Pan American, for the shuttle service from San Francisco to Honolulu.

To return once more to the Pacific theatre of war: during the height of the fighting in the islands of Micronesia, the changing fortunes, setbacks, and triumphs of the United States and Australian forces demanded complete flexibility of action on the part of the supply services, particularly those units engaged in air transport. Thus, in addition to the ATC and NATS, a number of *ad hoc* temporary organizations were sometimes set up to deal with a sudden threat. One of these deserves special mention.

On 23 August, 1942, a contingent of Marine Utility Squadron 253 took-off from San Diego in response to an S.O.S. for additional logistic support from beleaguered forces in Guadalcanal. Fifteen Douglas R4D-1s flew across the Pacific and were positioned in New Caledonia, from which outpost they proceeded to operate the 880-mile route to Guadalcanal as fast as aircraft could be loaded. Flying over water, unarmed against the danger of Japanese fighter attack, and navigating by dead reckoning without ground aids (except perhaps for the headlights of a jeep at night), more than 1,000 flights were completed between 1 September, 1942, and 1 February, 1943. Outward loads consisted mainly of petrol and ammunition; inward loads of sick and wounded, 18,000 in all.

The operation was given permanent recognition under the name of South Pacific Combat Air Transport (SCAT) and expanded considerably to the extent that 72 movements were recorded in one day.

The 'Hump'

The most concentrated air transport service during the whole of World War 2 was almost certainly the air ferry operations over the mountains from India to China between 1942 and 1945. This exhibition of strategic air power supplemented the ground supply route by the Burma Road, magnificently conceived but tortuously slow in action. The beginning of the 'Hump' operation, as it came to be known, was modest enough, a DC-3 flight officially by Air Transport Command, but by Pan American in practice, carrying fuel for Gen Doolittle's Mitchell bombers destined for Tokyo. This was in April 1942, but by the end of the year ATC was moving towards more concentrated action.

During this period considerable credit must go to China National Aviation Corporation (CNAC) for its pioneer work on the route, which was started during the Sino-Japanese War, long before the Japanese attack on Pearl Harbor. CNAC bore the brunt of the burden until April 1943, when reinforcements arrived from the U.S.A. The story of the delivery of these reinforcements is itself an epic narrative.

Responding to an urgent call for help, the Curtiss-Wright Corporation stepped up production of the C-46 Commando at Buffalo, and sent thirty of them to Homestead Field at Miami. Air Transport Command assembled 30 pilots, 15 from Northwest Airlines, ten from TWA, and five from its own ranks. Led by Lieut-Col William C. Goldsborough, all 30 aircraft arrived in Karachi by 21 April. This historic mass flight was routed via Borinquen Field (Puerto Rico), Port of Spain, Georgetown, Belem, Natal, Ascension Island, Accra, Kano, El Geneina, Khartoum, Asmara, Aden, and Salalah. After hasty training of further crew members recruited from units in India, the C-46s went to forward bases in Assam, and began scheduled services over the 'Hump' in May 1943.

Some staggering statistics have been assembled to illustrate the intensity of efforts over the Tezpur/Jorhat—Kunming shuttle service. In a single month's operations, the ATC recorded 5,000 flights; in January 1945, 44,000 tons were carried, or an average of almost 1,500 tons a day. On occasion, aircraft were taking-off at a rate of one every two minutes, or as soon as the runway was clear. This was achieved over terrain whose rugged grandeur dwarfed the Rocky Mountains, in weather at times worse than over the North Atlantic, and with the threat of Japanese fighter attack always imminent.

Although the largest aircraft used on the 'Hump' were some C-87 Liberators flown by the ubiquitous American Airlines for four months under contract starting in July 1943, pride of place on the roll of aircraft honour must go to the C-46. Almost forgotten—indeed despised—today, when in a succession of books all the plaudits have been bestowed on the DC-3, the C-46 had its hours of glory in the steaming jungles of Assam, the paddy-fields of China, and over the impossible and impassable crags of the cordillera of southeast Asia.

One C-46 was out of action for only four days in a whole month, for the essential 100-hr check—these were before progressive maintenance programmes. During each of the remaining 27 days, the aircraft averaged more than two round trips over the 'Hump'. Like many other C-46s, it probably wound up as a hulk at the end of a runway, or was cannibalized as war surplus, or was sold for a song, or even given away; a sad ending to the active life of a fine transport aircraft, whose full record of achievement has yet to be written and given full recognition.

Pan Am Secures a Flank

Although during its formative years of the early 1930s Pan American Airways and its associates became a leading force in the economy of Latin America, it did not enjoy a monopoly in this respect. Indeed, the continued progress and route development of German-owned or German-sponsored airlines became a significant factor in the extension of the economic penetration in that continent by the Third Reich. There can be little doubt also that this was closely tied to German political ambitions.

Germany's airline activity was centred around the powerful Kondor Syndicat, based in Brazil, fed and nurtured by Deutsche Luft Hansa (DLH), and an efficient tool of the German propaganda machine. Long-distance connections with Europe were provided by DLH, medium-haul and feeder routes in Brazil were provided by Syndicato Condor, the operating subsidiary of Kondor. Furthermore, in addition to promoting other airlines in Brazil by rendering invaluable technical assistance and providing aircraft on cheap terms, Kondor's influence spread to other countries in South America.

By 1941, airlines dependent upon German sponsorship, either in capital support, technical assistance, flying equipment, or crews—or a combination of all these—included Viação Aérea São Paulo (VASP) and Emprésa de Viação Aérea Rio Grandense (VARIG) in Brazil, Lloyd Aereo Boliviano (LAB) in Bolivia, Deutsche Lufthansa Sucursal en Peru, and Sociedad Ecuatoriana de Transportes Aereos (SEDTA) in Ecuador. A glance at the map shows how this straggling combination of companies could cause apprehension in the United States. With very little imagination, a route could be traced directly from Natal, on the northeast tip of Brazil, to the Panama Canal, a vital link in the communications structure between the Pacific and Atlantic, and of paramount importance to the defence of North America. U.S. forebodings were hardly mitigated by the knowledge that Condor was developing its route structure by building airfields in the upper reaches of the Amazon basin, even before a route was established to connect them with the coast; also that SEDTA applied to operate a route to the Galapagos Islands, a move that made no sense commercially but a great deal of sense strategically in relation to the Panama Canal.

Against this German air transport empire, the United States had Pan American, operating the trunk route to Buenos Aires via the east coast of

South America; its associate, Panagra, down the west coast; and control of SCADTA in Colombia. During the 1920s, SCADTA had been the main German airline influence in South America, but in 1931, when Pan American took over during Juan Trippe's triumphal march down the west coast, German enterprise sought other fields.

The original technical and flying staff of SCADTA remained, however, so that German influence in the Colombian national carrier was still significant. Nevertheless, direct contact with the Panama Canal Zone was prevented. On 24 August, 1931, Pan American, in co-operation with Colombian citizens, formed Uraba, Medellin and Central Airways (UMCA), to operate between Medellin and Panama. Thus SCADTA never did extend its route network to Panama, in spite of its proximity. Other changes were made, mainly in expanding the domestic network throughout Colombia. Another company, Servicio Aereo Colombiano (SACO) was absorbed and on 8 June, 1940, SCADTA was given a more national identity by renaming it Aérovias Nacionales de Colombia (AVIANCA). The stock of the new company was still mainly in the hands of Pan American, to the extent of 64 per cent, with the Colombian Government holding a substantial part of the remainder.

On 8 June, 1940, the German employees of SCADTA were dismissed. They hung on tenaciously to their Colombian foothold, however, and set up another airline, Aérovias Ramales Colombianas (ARCO), in the Llanos region of eastern Colombia. As the area was within a bomber's flight distance of Condor's bases in the Amazon region of Brazil, the Colombian authorities, under pressure from the U.S.A., took no chances. On 25 April, 1941, AVIANCA purchased ARCO, with one of the conditions of sale being that none of the former personnel would take part in the aviation business again.

South of Colombia, Panagra became the instrument for protecting American political interests by securing the air transport system. Panagra had started a local operation in Peru in December 1935 through a subsidiary, Aérovias Peruanas, but this was sold to Faucett, one of the oldest established airlines in the area, in April 1938, in exchange for a 20 per cent shareholding. Thus a neat balance was preserved between U.S. interests, providing the through service down the west coast, and Peruvian interests, both national and private, in operating the local services.

Deutsche Lufthansa Sucursal en Peru upset the equilibrium by entering the Peruvian arena in 1938. Its main route was between Lima, the Peruvian capital, and La Paz, the Bolivian capital and centre of the Bolivian network of LAB—also German-influenced—whose services linked up with those of the Brazilian Syndicato Condor at Corumba and Guajara Mirim. Using the trusty Junkers-Ju 52/3m as standard equipment, Lufthansa could theoretically book passengers direct from Berlin to Lima by a series of airline connections entirely under its control, and with the DLH service to Santiago, Chile, had two outlets to the Pacific Ocean. Now this may have been simply an enterprising piece of commercial opportunism on the part of the Germans; but the U.S. State Department took no chances.

Considerable pressure was brought to bear on the appropriate governments. In Peru DLH Sucursal's operating permit was withdrawn in February 1941 and the routes taken over by Panagra on 1 April. The Bolivian LAB was nationalized in May, a United States loan was negotiated, and Panagra took a 23 per cent interest as payment for a management contract. For the duration of World War 2, LAB was to all intents and purposes an affiliate of Panagra. In Ecuador, the U.S. airline tried to run its German competitor out of business by operating the superior Douglas DC-2 in direct competition with the Junkers-Ju 52/3ms of SEDTA. The Government cut off SEDTA's fuel supplies and finally requisitioned its aircraft in September 1941.

So, before the United States entered World War 2 in an active rôle, a possible area of vulnerability had been protected against a potential hostile air power. The pattern of possible attack can only be the subject of conjecture; but there can be little doubt that the threat was real. In June 1939, two four-engined Focke-Wulf Fw 200 Condor landplanes were delivered to the Brazilian Syndicato Condor. The 26-passenger aircraft was the world's first successful modern four-engined commercial land monoplane. It was a practical demonstration of German technical prowess —and therefore of considerable propaganda value—and it was also a forceful reminder to the U.S.A. that the world was getting smaller, that the Atlantic Ocean was no longer a comfortable barrier against foreign attack. The Fw 200, ancestor of the Condor bomber built for the Luftwaffe, could reach the Panama Canal from bases in South America, and the German airlines were obligingly surveying routes, preparing aerodromes, and acquiring operating experience.

When Germany started the war in September 1939, Syndicato Condor took over DLH's services in South America, and ominously began an intensive programme of expansion in the shoulder region of northeast Brazil, amounting to some 3,000 route miles. Some of its other activities then became highly suspect. Long detours were made between Rio de Janeiro and Buenos Aires, and the Brazilian Government believed that this was connected with the blockade-running strategy of German shipping. The Fw 200s were therefore grounded and only put back into service in May 1941 with Brazilian crews—the Condor crews having been German or Brazilians of recent German extraction. Final German ownership was severed in April 1942. Brazilians took over, and the name of the airline was changed to Cruzeiro do Sul on 21 November, 1942.

During World War 2, Pan American continued to expand its empire of subsidiaries and affiliates in Latin America. Turning its attention to the Caribbean area, it took a number of important steps to consolidate its dominant position there in the face of challenge from rivals and against the background of a widespread expansion of airline activity as a whole throughout the entire Latin American region.

Chief antagonist for airline supremacy in Central America was a New Zealander, Lowell Yerex, head of the TACA organization. Originally a charter operator, Yerex seized his opportunity to supply a very obvious need. Transport services in the area consisted of scattered stretches of narrow-gauge railway and occasional pieces of road built for a fruit or chicle plantation. TACA began its first scheduled service in Honduras in 1934 and Yerex proceeded to expand to the other Central American states, by establishing autonomous units in each and supplying a connecting link through a parent company based in El Salvador.

The main route of TACA El Salvador became the spinal column of an intricate system which, in spite of the unorthodox business methods prevailing at the time, worked well enough. TACA received little subsidy, but by practising straightforward economies, making full use of cheap labour and second-hand aircraft, the operation was a success. After trying many old aircraft types, the Ford Tri-Motor—cast off by the United States airlines—became TACA's standard equipment. The airline became an institution in Central America and its name drifted into the language as a household word.

TACA's success drew the attention of transport interests in the U.S., notably American Export Lines, the shipping company which was also taking more than a passing glance at the North Atlantic air route. A contract was drawn up on 1 October, 1940, for the purchase of TACA by American Export Airlines, the shipping company's operating subsidiary, but the C.A.B. turned down the application on 4 December, 1941, just a few days before the Japanese attack on Pearl Harbor.

Pan American, jealous of its position in one of its traditional stamping grounds, had already stepped in, modestly at first, to protect its interests. On 11 October, 1940, it founded Aérovias de Guatemala, beginning services on 7 November. By coincidence, gentle persuasion, or political string-pulling, or a mixture of all three, TACA's franchises in Guatemala were cancelled in January 1941.

During the early 1940s TACA actually made progress, despite Pan American's harassment. TACA El Salvador was granted permission to operate to Balboa, Panama Canal Zone, on 3 January, 1942, and later that year opened service to Havana. Under a temporary permit the route was extended to Miami in May 1943, and in 1944 TACA opened up in Mexico. Already loosely connected with the British West Indies—Yerex had founded British West Indian Airways (BWIA) in 1939—TACA was also expanding into the mainland of South America.

In 1943 various American investors began to take a hand in the affairs of this rising airline with its important franchises in strategically-placed Latin American states. On 27 January, 1943, the name was changed to Inter-American Airways, with a capital of $5,000,000, but on 26 November of the same year, reacting no doubt to public opinion, the company reverted to its old name, TACA Airways, with a capital of $10,000,000. Yerex now owned 54 per cent of the shares, with the rest American-owned by, among others, TWA and the Pennsylvania Railroad. In 1943 also, a TACA Airways Agency and a TACA Airlines Investment Corporation, both wholly-owned American subsidiaries, were established.

These manoeuvres, however, had little effect on the Pan American Establishment. Although TACA found footholds in most of the smaller states of Central America, its success in the larger countries in the area, such as Mexico, Colombia, and Venezuela, was limited. Pan American's dominance in these was solidly based and mostly of long standing (*See Table 14*). In 1943—protecting the outermost flank, perhaps—Trippe acquired a 45 per cent share in Bahamas Airways Ltd which had operated local services in the Bahamas since 1937. Pan Am's old ex-NYRBA Consolidated Commodores were put on these routes on 1 December, 1945.

Between 1943 and 1945 six more companies were affiliated to Pan American. Some of these appear to have been conceived in the same manner as the Guatemalan prototype: the joint establishment of a national airline, with strong Pan American financial interest, followed shortly afterwards by the withdrawal of franchises and consequent demise of the sitting tenant, TACA. There is little doubt, however, that the association with an airline of such substance and immense international prestige as Pan American was of immeasurable value to the entire airline industry in Central America and the Caribbean. The small companies in Central America are still in existence and flourishing, although Pan American interest has been reduced substantially. Details of these airlines are in Table 16 on page 639. Compared with these intricate manipulations, the situation in Mexico was more straightforward. Pan American controlled major airline affairs, as its subsidiary, Compañía Mexicana de Aviación (CMA), was by far the largest airline in that country, or indeed in the whole of Latin America until the late 1940s. Compared with most, its fleet was comparatively modern, with DC-3s opening a route to Havana in October 1942. A connection to the Guatemalan frontier, at Tapachula, and a second route to the United States border, at Nuevo Laredo, were opened in 1943. The capital shareholding was increased in December 1944, at which time Pan Am's share was 56 per cent.

Of CMA's dozen or so rivals—in aspiration if not in effectiveness—one showed promise, as it had obtained the permit to operate between Mexico City and Acapulco, a new resort on the Pacific coast, soon to become one of the most desirable vacation spots for U.S. travellers. Pan American bought a 40 per cent share in this up-and-coming airline, Aeronaves de Mexico, on 18 December, 1940, thus increasing its stake in the Mexican airline market.

Possibly this was with foreknowledge, or even clairvoyance, of opposition in Mexico from U.S. sources, namely United Air Lines, which was taking a good look at Lineas Aereas Mineras (LAMSA). This airline had been founded by Gordon A. Barry, an American citizen, on 27 August, 1934, first in a small way to serve a silver mine, then expanding into northern Mexico, where, in 1937, it took over the not inconsiderable route structure of Aerovias Centrales, the former Pan American subsidiary. Barry had wider ambitions, especially when granted a route to the U.S. frontier at Ciudad Juarez, the Mexican border city opposite El Paso. Unfortunately the resources of the company were inadequate to support routes of low traffic density until United came to the rescue with a loan of $250,000 on 6 October, 1942, which was then adjusted to take the form of a 75 per cent shareholding in LAMSA on 17 September, 1943. The C.A.B. authorization carried a provision that the route network should not be extended beyond the Mexican frontier. United naturally tried to make a direct connection through its domestic network, but the necessary route extensions south of Denver were never achieved. The name of LAMSA was changed to Lineas Aereas Mexicanas in October 1943.

There were other straws in the Mexican wind. After obtaining permission from the Mexican authorities on 25 October, 1940, American Airlines was awarded routes to Mexico City from Dallas and El Paso on 14 April, 1942. Significantly the C.A.B. turned down American's application at first, concluding that an adequate case had not been made by the normal criteria of public necessity and convenience; but President Roosevelt over-ruled the decision on the grounds of emergency wartime requirements. Services opened on 3 September, 1942.

Such a decision by the President was ominous. For if one airline could make out a case for a foreign route on emergency grounds, so could many more. But the onslaught on Pan American's backyard was to come after the war. In the case of Mexico, Braniff also obtained a route late in 1943, and like American, set up a Mexican subsidiary; but the route was not started until after the war, and in fact was revoked on 26 October, 1946.

Meanwhile, Domestic Business As Usual

Like knights of old, the airlines had sallied forth to serve their country when faced with a dire national emergency. Thanks to the initiative of the ATA president, Edgar Gorrell, they were able to cope with strenuous, even excessive demands for air transport in a wartime rôle overseas, at the same time retaining their independence and identity.

The burden of effort was not without compensation. Airline experience in operating transport aircraft and managing a complete logistic programme was invaluable to the requirements of military strategy, and the airline people found themselves almost in a position of privilege. They enjoyed priority treatment befitting serving officers, yet retained the freedom of civilian life, and were not subjected to many of the irritations of military discipline. The airline staff, especially the flying crews, were masters of their own fate to a greater degree than most serving officers, while carrying at least as much responsibility. The calls made on individual airlines for aircraft and service over routes quite foreign to their experience (and foreign in the literal sense) provided a challenge which would never

Another U.S. transport which saw considerable wartime service was the Lockheed Model 18 Lodestar which was first operated by Mid-Continent Airlines in March 1940. *Top*: United Air Lines' *City of Fresno*; *centre*: TWA's flight research laboratory NC33604; and *bottom*: N54549, post-war, in the red and yellow livery of Transocean Air Lines. (*United Air Lines, TWA and Gordon S. Williams*)

have come their way during peacetime. The time would come, after the battles, when the wider horizons, so unexpectedly explored during the war years, would in many cases find a permanent place in the airline world.

Operations like the Cannon Ball route to Calcutta, flying C-46s to Ascension Island, or C-47s to Baffin Land, and pioneering new routes in faraway places were, on the other hand, an exciting interlude to the mainstream routine of domestic airline work. The request to start a scheduled service to Adak, Espiritu Santo, or Narsarsuak, provided a challenge and inspired a spirit of adventure which the 9 a.m. to Boston or Chicago could never emulate. However, life had to go on within the U.S.A. and the airlines did well to maintain domestic business as usual during the war, a feat far less spectacular than overseas exploits, but which was in a different way no less onerous.

Equipped almost exclusively with Douglas twin-engined airliners, the total fleet available for normal civil schedules was reduced by military requisition to less than half the normal complement. Colonial Airlines, for example, retained only two of eight aircraft, and many other companies were desperately stretched. Offsetting the shortage of seats, fortunately, was the favourable marketing environment which ensured high load factors. Because of wartime tolerance of shortages, airlines were not pilloried for failing to provide perfect public service. Waiting for space available became a familiar routine while the system of priorities for government and military personnel, worked out in co-operation between the military commands and the ATA, led to many being turned out of their seats at the last moment before departure, to make way for a priority passenger.

The net result was a tremendous increase in aircraft productivity levels. The aircraft were worked harder, putting in more than ten hours a day of revenue flying instead of the seven or eight pre-war; and between 80 per cent and 90 per cent of the seats were sold, compared with the normal 60 per cent. Thus, in spite of smaller fleets, the average number of passenger-miles flown per day was approximately the same as before the war, and in fact, in 1944, 4,000,000 passengers were carried, just exceeding the 1941 figure.

All this was in addition to domestic military work. In March 1942, Pennsylvania-Central Airlines signed a contract to operate the first domestic scheduled military cargo service, between Washington and Chicago, and shortly afterwards Continental Airlines began a transcontinental cargo run between San Francisco and Harrisburg. The big airlines, of course, were active in this rôle, and American Airlines, turning swords into ploughshares, began a scheduled all-freight DC-3 service between Los Angeles and New York as part of its regular timetable on 1 August, 1944. Modified Liberators were later drafted into service for American.

During World War 2, the number of United States airlines remained virtually unchanged. Excluding the Wilmington-Catalina Airline, 16 companies were operating at the beginning of the war and 15 were still active at the end. The one which disappeared was Inland Air Lines, formerly Wyoming Air Service, 83 per cent of whose capital stock was purchased by Western Airlines on 7 October, 1943, a move formally approved by the C.A.B. on 23 May, 1944.

This resultant route amalgamation restored to a great extent some of the former status of Western Airlines, but only as a long-term investment, gambling somewhat on the attitude of the C.A.B. Building up the network from the one route left to it after the 1934 Mail Contracts fiasco was a painstaking process. Theoretically, Western now provided service from California to the Dakotas and Minneapolis; but only the adventurous or the foolhardy would have bought tickets to explore the meandering chain of stopping places in 1944.

In contrast, the airline structure of the United States as a whole gradually began to consolidate during World War 2. Formed only in 1938, the C.A.B. was still feeling its way, taking care not to repeat past errors of administration, and above all guarding against the pitfalls of condoning the two extremes of monopolistic routes or a free-for-all. The C.A.B., in fact, cut its teeth in the process of route awards during World War 2.

The most far-reaching decision concerned the matter of eastern terminal points of the transcontinental networks of American Airlines, TWA, and United Air Lines. By a quirk of fate, American Airlines had emerged from the 1934 scandal far stronger than before. Its so-called southern transcontinental route was directly competitive as an East Coast—California route, and enjoyed, moreover, the distinction of serving the important cities of Philadelphia, Washington, and Boston, as well as New York. This gave C. R. Smith's airline a definite advantage over TWA and United, which were permitted to serve only Philadelphia in addition to New York. On 10 May, 1943, the C.A.B. removed the anomaly by giving them rights into Washington, and on 12 June, 1944, to Boston. In the May decision, TWA was given access to San Francisco, traditionally a United preserve, and subsequently, on 13 August, the C.A.B. amended its order to include Western Airlines, which started service on the fast-growing Los Angeles—San Francisco route on 1 May, 1944.

The Washington award to United provided some competition to Pennsylvania-Central Airlines, whose main route from Chicago to the Capital had blossomed during the war from secondary to major trunk status. United began service on this route in September 1943, but PCA was compensated for this incursion by the award, on 16 December, 1944, of access to New York from Chicago, via Pittsburgh and Detroit.

On 12 June, 1944, American's control over the New York—Boston route ended when the C.A.B. authorized the entry of Eastern Air Lines and Northeast Airlines into this dense short-haul market. Another important monopoly had already disappeared on 19 February of that year when Eastern's comfortable position on the New York—Florida vacation market was broken by the award of a route between Jacksonville and New York to National Airlines, which already operated a network in Florida.

Other airlines benefited in minor ways from the C.A.B. policy of cautious expansion. Continental gained access to Kansas City and San Antonio; Delta to New Orleans; Chicago & Southern to Houston. Western's network was further strengthened by the award of a direct Los Angeles—Denver route on 11 November, 1944.

During this period of route development, the standard airliner was the DC-3. The only U.S. four-engined type of landplane in existence at the outbreak of war was the Boeing 307, in service with TWA, whose small fleet had to be surrendered for military service. The Douglas C-54 transport was developed during the war but did not see service, as the DC-4, until peacetime. A similar career awaited the Constellation, Lockheed's brilliant challenge to Douglas supremacy. Pressurized, to a more advanced stage than the pioneering Boeing 307, it was 80 mph faster than the unpressurized DC-4. Sponsored by TWA, now under the leadership of Howard Hughes, the C-69 or R7V-1, as the military and naval versions were called respectively, entered service during the last year of the war. It made its dramatic entry into the air transport world when Howard Hughes and Jack Frye made a spectacular nonstop flight from the Lockheed factory at Burbank, California, to Washington on 19 April, 1944, in just under seven hours.

Poised for Take-off

Thus, by all the important criteria the airline industry of the United States came out of World War 2 a great deal stronger than when it went in. Administrators had met innumerable challenges and solved endless problems more complex and testing than any they were likely to meet in peacetime. Pilots and crews equally had responded to tasks which in the normal course they would probably have refused to undertake. By so doing they had taken part in a search to evaluate the limits of tolerance and endurance, and the aspects of safety which stem from these factors.

Individual airlines emerged from the war with better route structures and flying equipment. The DC-3, mainstay of the airlines in the 1930s, was relegated to a secondary rôle, and four-engined aircraft were accepted as the minimum requirement for major routes. In addition to their obvious advantages as transport vehicles, offering superior comfort, speed, and reliability, they were even more profitable, and their range enabled the airlines to eliminate many unremunerative stops on long-distance routes. Air navigation had improved through the techniques developed by wartime bomber forces, while the invention of radar was immediately adopted by civil air traffic control organizations.

Altogether, World War 2 was tough for all concerned; but it taught many hard lessons, which had to be learned quickly and thoroughly. Military demands accelerated technical progress in many directions—although to assert that the war was responsible for the development of

United States four-engined airliners is quite wrong. These were already projected and designed before the war started, having been sponsored by a robust airline industry.

Airlines achieved, through conflict, a versatility and flexibility beyond the most optimistic predictions. The latter war years witnessed a frustration of abounding talent and material because of the restrictions on civilian travel during hostilities. When the restrictions were removed in 1945, the airlines were poised for a flying start into a new age of progress.

Pacific Alaska Airways' Fairchild 71 NC9709 on twin floats. (*Gordon S. Williams*)

CHAPTER TWELVE

Airlines in U.S. Territories

Pioneers in the North

The State of Alaska today possesses most of the characteristics of any of the contiguous 48 States in terms of living standards, amenities, and economic activity. Its industries are flourishing and it has become a sought-after resort area. Thanks to air transport, the several hundred miles of Canadian territory which separate it from the main part of the U.S.A. are no longer a barrier.

When the first aeroplanes flew, however, Alaska was a comparatively little-known Territory of the Union, regarded as geographically remote, and identified with vast regions of barren tundra of interest only to geologists. The Alaskan Gold Rush of the early part of the century had petered out, and its abundant mineral wealth of other kinds was virtually untapped. It had little industry and until 1924 the population had been on the decline.

The restoration of the upward population curve coincided with the first experimental air mail service from Fairbanks to McGrath (272 miles) on 21 February, 1924. On that day, Carl Ben Eielson flew a de Havilland DH-4 between these points to demonstrate the feasibility of the aeroplane as a means of transport in Alaska. In the same year, from Fairbanks, Noel Wien started his first operations as a charter pilot.

In 1928 Eielson organized Alaskan Airways, as an operating subsidiary of the Aviation Corporation, the financial holding unit which owned American Airways and was also sponsoring an airline in China. Alaskan Airways effectively combined the routes of three trail-blazing fixed-base companies which provided sporadic air services: Wien (Fairbanks—Nome, Kotzebue, and Point Barrow), Bennett and Rodebaugh (Fairbanks—McGrath), and Anchorage Air Transport (points northwest of Anchorage). In October 1929, Wien and his brothers incorporated Northern Air Transport, but on 9 November Eielson himself was unfortunately killed in an air accident.

One of Pacific Alaska Airways' Fairchild 71s. (*Gordon S. Williams*)

At this time air services in Alaska were pioneers in the truest sense. Aircraft such as Fairchild 71s, Stinson Juniors, Travel Air and Waco biplanes were coaxed into performing missions for which insurance cover was totally inappropriate. Single-engined performance was pitched against terrain and weather which today would be considered suicidal. Forced landings were common, sometimes occurring a hundred miles from the nearest habitation. Although the severity of the Alaskan climate has often been exaggerated, the winters at inland points, especially north of Fairbanks, are extremely frigid. To be stranded with a broken-down aeroplane in these conditions was to fight for survival. The men who started the first airways in Alaska, therefore, were tough, resilient characters, inventive, determined, uncompromising, a special breed who were prepared to take much greater risks, both commercial and personal, than most of their contemporaries.

The comparative isolation of the aviation community was interrupted

NC14975, a Travel Air monoplane of Woodley Airways. It is believed to have been an A-6000-A model.

in the summer of 1931, when Charles Lindbergh arrived at Nome to undertake a survey flight to the Far East on behalf of Pan American Airways. Accompanied by his wife, Lindbergh flew the Lockheed Sirius to Japan and China, via Soviet territory, to prove that a route to Tokyo and Shanghai was not only possible, but contained fewer hazards than was generally assumed. Early in 1932, Dr Vilhjalmur Stefansson completed a report for Pan American Airways called *Intercontinental Trans-Bering Airways*. This, together with Lindbergh's report, encouraged Pan American, but unfortunately the Soviet Government refused landing rights as it had not been granted recognition by the U.S.A.

Part of Pan American's master plan for a Great Circle route to Asia, however, was to consolidate its position in Alaska, an obviously strategic area; accordingly, on 11 June, 1932, Pacific Alaska Airways was formed as its wholly-owned subsidiary. On 1 September this company purchased Alaskan Airways from the Aviation Corporation, including its fleet of Fairchild 71s and other small types, and took over its 40 employees. On 15 October of the same year, Pacific Alaska also bought Pacific International Airways, a smaller charter operator from Anchorage using similar flying equipment.

With the two small airlines Pacific Alaska inherited a number of Star Route Contracts. These were let by the U.S. Post Office and were related

A Waco single-engined biplane of Woodley Airways.

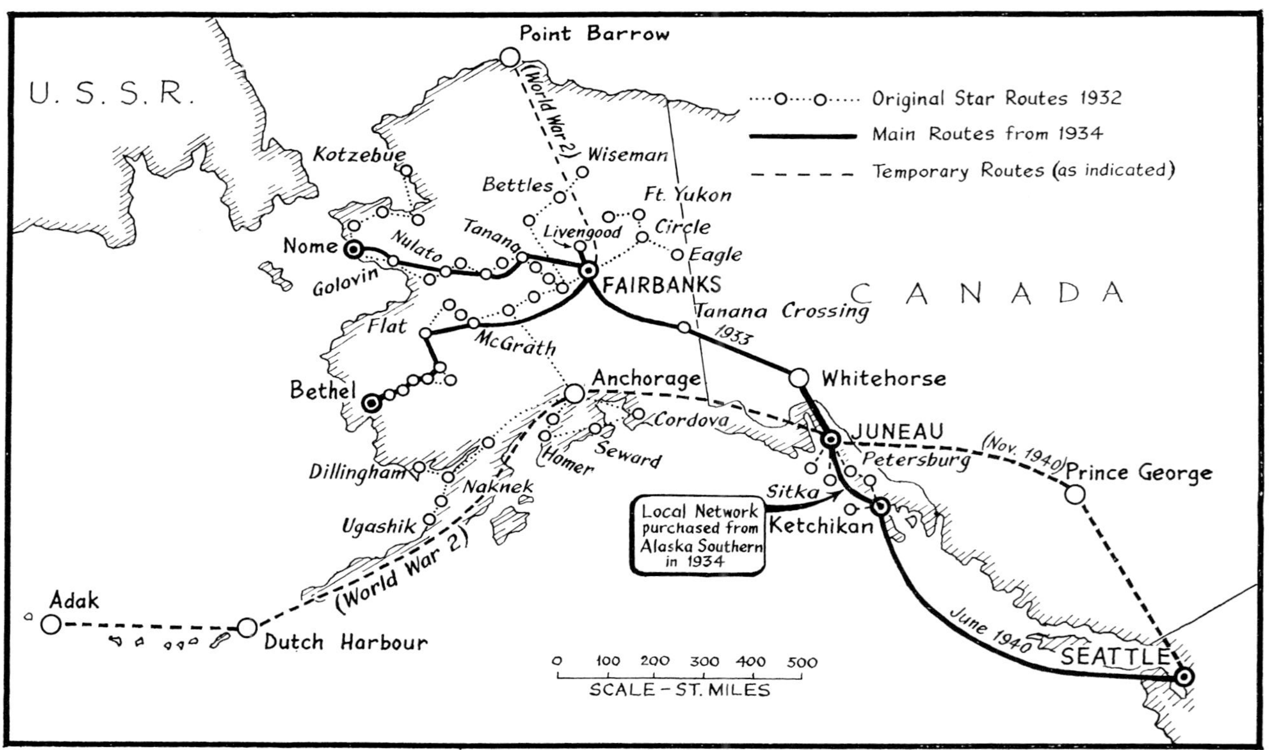

Fig. 23. Pacific Alaska Airways, 1932–1940.

Consolidated Fleetster 17-2C NC750V *Polaris* of Pacific International Airways, Anchorage. (*Gordon S. Williams*)

to special contract mail service by steamer, automotive equipment, or dog-team. Contract routes began at railway stations (much rarer than gold-dust) or at river landings. Each contract was for mail service between specific pairs of points, therefore a reasonably planned air route would have to include many separate Star Routes. Exasperatingly, at each terminus of a Star Route—i.e. at every stopping point of a multi-sector air route covering such service—the mail had to be unloaded, transported to the post office, checked, and taken back, all at the contractor's expense. Thus, when Alaskan or Pacific International bid for the Star contracts, some sectors were often underbid by the dog-teams. In fact, with one exception, all contracts assumed dog-teams as the basis for calculation of rates and service and were therefore confined to the winter season. In the summer, mail service reverted mainly to river transport.

In October 1932, Pacific Alaska improved its fleet by purchasing more Fairchild 71s, and the next year, three Consolidated Fleetsters, with which

Two of Pacific Alaska Airways' Consolidated Fleetsters on skis. The nearest aircraft is NC703Y. (*Pan American World Airways*)

the airline started the first mail service, on 3 September, 1933, between Fairbanks and the Alaskan capital, Juneau. The Fleetsters had an exciting career, for in March 1934 two of them were used to relieve the beleaguered Russian Chelyuskin Arctic Expedition which had been marooned on drifting ice floes after their ship had been crushed.

Late in 1933, the Star Route contracts came up for re-bidding for a four-year period, beginning 1 July, 1934. By this time, the deficiencies of the system had become apparent. The new contractual terms made possible a single bid, covering a whole route of several stages, thus opening the way for competitive bidding by airlines.

Specifically, to give an example, the number of mandatory landings on the Fairbanks—Nome route was reduced from 21 to 10, the cities of Fairbanks and Nome were designated as co-terminals in place of the tiny settlements of Nenana and Unalakleet, and the whole route was covered by one individual contract.

Pacific Alaska obtained this route, plus one from Fairbanks to Bethel, and the short Fairbanks—Livengood feeder. Routes to the north and east of Fairbanks went to Northern Air Transport which, later in 1936, adopted the name of Wien Alaska Airlines. To the southwest of Anchorage, the contracts went to Woodley Airways, founded by Arthur Woodley,

Wien Alaska Airlines' Boeing 247D NC13313 (c/n 1694). By October 1945 it had flown more than 16,000 hr. (*Gordon S. Williams*)

who began operations on 10 April, 1932, with a small fleet of six-seat Travel Air monoplanes.

By this time, small fixed-base operators were springing up everywhere in Alaska, where hitherto communication had been almost exclusively by water, either by coastal or river craft. At every port, cut off by land from its neighbouring ports, their aircraft offered speed and convenience to all comers, usually at exorbitant prices. Some companies took their name from the operating base, such as Cordova or Dillingham, others from the name of their founders, like Bob Reeve or Jim Dodson. They were in complete contrast to airlines such as Pan American and United. They operated on a financial shoe-string. The owner flew the aircraft, his wife kept the books. He sold tickets through friends and by the application of low cunning beat his rivals. His business ethics were born of the Klondike saloon and were hardly genteel. He would cheerfully risk his life and his assets (i.e. his aircraft) in a foolhardy gamble perhaps to make a quick

Cordova Air Service Bellanca CH-300 Pacemaker. (*Gordon S. Williams*)

dollar, perhaps to rescue a competitor in trouble. Such pioneering was quite unique. The men who contributed to the saga of Alaskan airline development belong to a distinguished company whose only parallel is to be found in the history of Canadian aviation, or of those in the remote fastnesses of northern Siberia.

The next stage in the progress of Pan American's subsidiary, Pacific Alaska Airways, was to consolidate the intermediate part of the route from Seattle to Alaska by purchasing Alaska Southern Airways on 13 November, 1934. This company had been founded in 1933 by Nick Bez, prominent in the fish canning industry of southeast Alaska, with a solitary Loening Commuter. Having made a handsome profit on fixed-base operations around the island communities south of Juneau, Bez started a fairly regular service between the Alaskan capital and Seattle, via Ketchikan, using two Lockheed Vegas. This was right across Pacific Alaska's path, and Pan American promptly hooked this particular fish before it could do much damage to the net.

Pacific Alaska Airways' Lockheed Vega 5-B floatplane NC336H (c/n 81) had previously been owned by Alaska-Washington Airlines and Alaska Southern Airways. (*Gordon S. Williams*)

Pacific Alaska then cleaned up its route structure. It withdrew from the feeder routes around Anchorage—this was when Arthur Woodley stepped in—and on 20 August, 1934, applied to the Canadian Government for permission to use Whitehorse as a staging post between Fairbanks and Juneau.

Altogether 1934 was an exciting year for air transport in Alaska, in addition to the new Star Route mail contracts, the Pan Am purchase of Alaska Southern, and the relief of the Chelyuskin Expedition. A fire almost destroyed the city of Nome, one of the former gold rush centres, and Pacific Alaska shipped what was then a substantial quantity of supplies to the stricken city, including heavy equipment, lumber and an emergency hospital.

Lockheed Vega 5-B floatplane of Alaska Southern Airways. (*Gordon S. Williams*)

One of its aircraft at this time was a single-engined Ford 8-AT, a rare member of the family of Fords, which Pacific Alaska tried out with wheels, floats, and skis. More important on a long-term basis, however, was the delivery of the first Lockheed L.10 Electra used to inaugurate a Juneau—Fairbanks passenger service on 2 April, 1935. This was the first regular service of Pacific Alaska on which exact times were quoted in the published timetables.

On 1 June, 1935, the Electra service was extended to Nome; a connection via the Kukoskwim River settlements was added in 1936, and on 1 November of that year, a Pilgrim 100-A was brought into service, an event which is believed to have initiated the use of the term 'Flying Boxcar'.

On 3 May, 1938, foreign air mail contracts were granted to Pacific Alaska Airways for the transport of air mail from Juneau to Fairbanks (FAM-15 and 16), the rate as far as Whitehorse in Canada at $1.55 per mile and thereonwards at $0.80. On 30 June, 1938, the Star Route contracts expired, so that the year may be regarded as a significant watershed in Alaskan air transport history. On 19 August, further notice was given of the start of a new era when the Northwest Division of Pan American Airways made the first of a series of ten round-trip survey flights from Seattle to Juneau, using a Sikorsky S-43 twin-engined flying-boat.

The Ford 8-AT-A NC8499 of Pacific Alaska Airways. In Alaskan service it was powered by a Wright Cyclone but had previously been fitted with a variety of engines including a liquid-cooled Hispano Suiza. The Ford 8-AT was a cargo carrier with about 3,500 lb payload. *Top*: As a landplane, with snow being cleared from the wing; *centre*: as a twin-float seaplane; and *bottom*: fitted with skis.

Pacific Alaska Airways' Lockheed Model 10C Electra NC14906 (c/n 1019). Although the dog team in this photograph is posed, this was a common means of surface transport in Alaska, and dog team connections were advertised in some airline timetables.

After some delay (because the survey demonstrated that twin-engined equipment was inadequate for a route with such a very high incidence of bad visibility) a four-engined Sikorsky S-42 opened the first mail service from Seattle to Juneau on 20 June, 1940, via Ketchikan. Passenger service began four days later. In November 1940, a DC-3 started a land route via Prince George, British Columbia, and in March 1941 Lockheed L.18 Lodestars were operating twice weekly Seattle—Juneau—Whitehorse—Fairbanks.

This marked the end of Pacific Alaska Airways as an autonomous unit; on 5 May, 1941, the Alaska Division of Pan American Airways took over its operations, together with those of Pan Am's Northwest Division. The new Division continued to operate to Nome (the Fairbanks—Bethel route had been conceded to a lower bidder, Star Air Lines, in 1938) and also acquired a naval contract to fly R4D-1s from Seattle to Kodiak via Anchorage. In March 1944, the Alaska Division became part of the merged Pacific-Alaska Division of Pan American.

Pacific Alaska Airways' Pilgrim 100-A NC742N, on skis. (*Pan American World Airways*)

NC33664 was one of Pacific Alaska Airways' Lockheed Model 18 Lodestars. (*Pan American World Airways*)

An Alaskan Airline Industry

After the end of World War 2 the many Alaskan carriers tried to put their fragmented house in order. The Star Air Service had emerged from some amalgamations in the early 1930s to be incorporated on 27 November, 1937, as Star Air Lines Inc. Having won some internal mail contracts in competition with Pacific Alaska in 1938, it obtained a C.A.B. operating certificate for most of them on 5 December, 1942. On 10 November, 1943, Star bought three more small airlines, one of which, Lavery Airways, held the important mail contract between Fairbanks and Anchorage, Alaska's two largest cities. On 6 June, 1944, the joint airline, now called Alaska Star Airlines, was renamed once again as Alaska Airlines. By 1945, Alaska was operating Douglas DC-3s, a great improvement on the Stinson Tri-motors of 1937, the single-engined Lockheeds of 1943, and the Lodestars of 1944.

Star Air Lines' Bellanca CH-300 Pacemaker NC259M (c/n 161). (*Gordon S. Williams*)

An Alaska Airlines Stinson SR-5E on skis. (*Gordon S. Williams*)

Down in the island chain of southeast Alaska, two companies had taken over where Nick Bez left off. Shell Simmons began Lockheed Vega operations from Juneau in April 1935 under the name of Alaska Air Transport and merged with Marine Airways on 27 May, 1939, to form Alaska Coastal Airlines. Another company was organized in Ketchikan in July 1936 by Bob Ellis, incorporated in January 1940 as Ellis Air Lines. On 27 May, 1939, a co-partnership agreement was drawn up between Alaska Coastal and Ellis, both of whom were awarded operating certificates by the C.A.B. on 5 December, 1942; and in May 1947 they gained approval from the C.A.B. for joint operation of the Juneau—Ketchikan route.

On 16 November, 1945, Ray Peterson, who had started fixed-base operations from Bethel in 1937, persuaded several small pioneer concerns to amalgamate under his presidency to form Northern Consolidated Airlines, an arrangement which received the approval of the C.A.B. on 1 December, 1947.

Alaska Air Transport's Bellanca CH-400 Skyrocket NC11E (c/n 608). (*Gordon S. Williams*)

Alaska Air Transport's Lockheed Vega 5-C NC47M (c/n 99). (*Gordon S. Williams*)

Marine Airways' Fairchild 71 NC119H on twin floats. (*Gordon S. Williams*)

Marine Airways' Bellanca CH-300 Pacemaker NC196N (c/n 181). (*Gordon S. Williams*)

Bob Reeve, who had led a chequered career around Valdez and in western Alaska, had acquired considerable experience on routes between Anchorage and Cold Bay during World War 2, and began irregular service to the Aleutians in April 1946. Reeve Airways was incorporated as an Alaskan company on 24 March, 1947, and obtained its certificate for an island-hopping route from Anchorage to Attu on 8 April, 1948. This was a distance of 1,783 miles (which goes some way to illustrate the size of Alaska) and Reeve's route network was unique in another sense, as he was permitted to serve the Pribilof Islands from any point on his scheduled route. Bob Reeve was probably the only airline operator in the world who owed the possession of an air route to the breeding habits of seals.

Thus, after the alarums and excursions of possible Japanese occupation during World War 2, Alaska emerged with eight local service airlines*. Each had an approximate, but often overlapping, geographical sphere of influence, and each was subsidized adequately by the C.A.B. to augment

*See Table 17, page 612.

Two aircraft used by Pollack Flying Service of Alaska. *Top*: Bellanca 31-42 Pacemaker NC16707 (c/n 254) and *bottom*: Stinson SR-6B Reliant NC15123. (*Gordon S. Williams*)

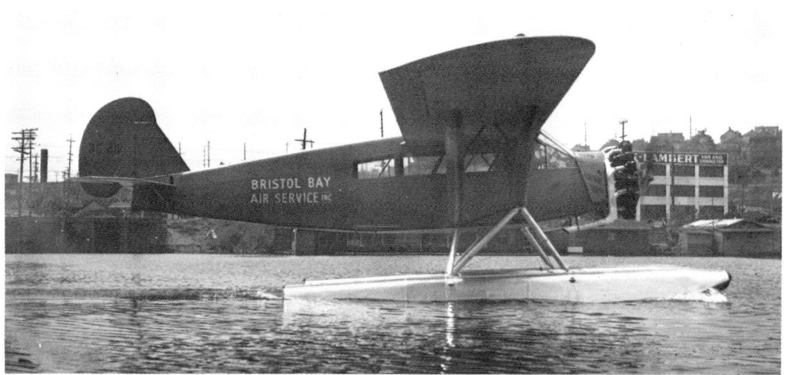

A Travel Air SA-6000-A operated by Bristol Bay Air Service. (*Gordon S. Williams*)

revenue rates which were already high, with passenger fares about twice the U.S. average. This high income level was necessary to cover the high expenditure. Everything in Alaska is expensive, mainly because almost all consumer and manufactured goods must be transported from the south; and the long, cold winter imposes additional cost burdens on an exacting maintenance and flying programme.

Post-war Development of Alaskan Trunks

The growing importance of Alaska, not only as a strategic point on the Great Circle route to the Far East, but in its own right as a potential State of the Union, with an expanding economy, led to the establishment of trunk airline services to complement the feeder routes of airlines like Wien, Northern Consolidated, Alaska Coastal, and Cordova.

The Pan American service from Seattle to Fairbanks and Nome was firmly established as an inheritance from Pacific Alaska which had done so much spade-work in the 1930s. To this was added a rival trunk service, operated by Northwest Airlines, as a continuation of—and undoubtedly as a reward for—excellent service rendered as an air service contractor in the defence of North America during World War 2. Northwest had built up a reputation second to none, surprising the Alaskan sourdoughs with its ability to cope with the severe climate; Northwest would no doubt maintain that conditions in Fairbanks are at least matched by those in Minneapolis or Bismarck in the depths of winter. At all events, it started a scheduled service in September 1946 from Seattle to Anchorage, added a cut-off service from Chicago to Anchorage via Edmonton in January 1947, and included Anchorage as a major staging point when it opened its Far East service on 15 July, 1947.

Then in 1950 the trunk service to Alaska took a fresh course when the C.A.B. decided that competition from an Alaska-based airline was justified. Arthur Woodley's company, Woodley Airways, had grown considerably in stature since its incorporation in January 1945. It was awarded an important route from Anchorage, Alaska's largest city, to Juneau, the capital, via Cordova and Yakutat, on 20 June, 1946. Boeing 247s were introduced; on 1 August, 1947, Woodley Airways became Pacific Northern Airlines (PNA); and on 29 September, 1950, the C.A.B. awarded PNA a Seattle—Anchorage trunk route.

Woodley Airways' Boeing 247 NC13310 (c/n 1691). This Boeing had previously been owned by National Air Transport, United Air Lines, Western Air Express, Wyoming Air Service, Inland Air Lines and the U.S. Army Air Force. It remained in operation until the winter of 1945–46.

When reviewing the award, President Truman decided that the authority should be extended to cover a Seattle—Fairbanks route for Alaska Airlines. Pacific Northern and Alaska both received the coveted awards on 24 May, 1951. Alaska started service with DC-4s on 17 August, in direct competition with Pan American; Pacific Northern, also with DC-4s, in October, against Northwest.

Alaska Airlines was at a disadvantage in relation to Pacific Northern because Fairbanks was only half the size of Anchorage, and generated traffic in about the same proportion. On the other hand, Alaska also had the direct Anchorage—Fairbanks route.

During the 1950s Alaska Airlines found itself constantly under fire from the C.A.B. On 25 March, 1953, a voting trust was established to prevent irregularities in accounts, and possible violation of the Civil Aeronautics Act. This trust was to be effective until 1 June, 1957, but the crisis was overcome and Charles F. Willis was elected president in May of that year. In August a permanent certificate was granted for the Fairbanks—Seattle route.

Willis believed in a little ambition and applied for a route to Irkutsk, U.S.S.R., early in 1958, as a prelude to the introduction of pressurized equipment, DC-6s, on 25 April, 1958. On 4 August Alaska Airlines inaugurated the *Golden Nugget* service, and a few days later, Willis and his friends bought 200,000 common stock shares from R. W. Marshall, who had hitherto held the company purse-strings.

Pacific Northern Airlines' Douglas DC-4 N3934C.

Pacific Northern Airlines' Douglas DC-3 N37465.

One of Pacific Northern Airlines' Lockheed Constellations.

Pacific Northern meanwhile had been making headway on the plum route from Anchorage. In 1953, service also began from Juneau to Seattle. The company sold 360,000 shares and obtained a $1,000,000 bank loan in order to finance an expansion programme based on the purchase of a fleet of Lockheed Constellations. These were introduced in 1954, and six were in service by the time PNA carried its millionth passenger in 1959.

The local Alaskan airlines kept to themselves, making improvements here and there to their fleets, and adding or exchanging routes in piecemeal fashion. Most of the small companies operated a variety of different aircraft types; in fact, Alaska became a veritable Pandora's Box, a collector's paradise. Northern Consolidated had Stinson Reliants, Cessna T-50s, Noorduyn Norsemen, PBY5As, a Republic Seabee, and (of course) DC-3s. Sigurd Wien had some of these, plus some Curtiss C-46s; in fact, as time went on, there was one of almost everything in the Wien hangar at Fairbanks. Shell Simmons of Alaska Coastal specialized in Grumman types. Mudhole Smith of Cordova had Stinsons and Pipers. Bob Reeve had a rare mixture of DC-3s, Sikorsky S-43s, Fairchild 71s, a Grumman Goose, and, of all things, a Boeing 80A.

Bob Reeve, founder of Reeve Airways (later Reeve Aleutian Airways) undertook incredible load carrying during the war with this Boeing 80A-1, NC224M. Painted yellow and known as *The Yellow Peril*, it had large double loading doors in the starboard side and carried loads of up to 11,000 lb—more than double its original payload. NC224M is seen here, without engines, at Anchorage in January 1958. On the left are the bows of a Reeve Sikorsky S-43. (*John Stroud*)

The majority of these aircraft were bought second-hand. Like the Local Service airlines, with whom they had much in common, the first new purchase was of the Fairchild-built Fokker F.27. On 31 October, 1958, Ray Peterson of Northern Consolidated took delivery of the first F-27B, a version developed specially for him by Fairchild, featuring a large freight door on the port side through which all kinds of unusual loads passed, including tractors, small trucks, and live whales. Sigurd Wien also bought F-27s, and in 1961 both he and Peterson also invested in the versatile little Pilatus Porter, a Swiss design, marketed by Fairchild, and adaptable to the small fields and low traffic levels characteristic of the bush services in Alaska.

By 1960, Northern Consolidated and Wien had emerged as the most influential of all the Alaskan local carriers, and on 1 October the C.A.B. authorized a wholesale redistribution of feeder routes in the area north and west of the Anchorage—Fairbanks line. Alaska Airlines, concentrating

Northern Consolidated Airlines' Fairchild F-27B N4903 *Carl Ben Eielson* (c/n 15).
(*Fairchild Aircraft*)

on the consolidation of trunk services, handed over several feeder routes, involving about three dozen stations, to Peterson and Wien, the former's south of the Yukon/Tanana Rivers, the latter's to the north. Sigurd Wien had a further and unexpected success on 12 December, 1963, when, having offered to purchase from Pan American the Fairbanks—Whitehorse—Juneau route, he cheerfully accepted a C.A.B. ruling that no payment should be involved in the transfer.

While the feeder airlines were adopting propeller-turbine types, the Alaskan trunk carriers were beginning to buy jets. On 30 August, 1961, Alaska introduced the Convair 880 on its *Golden Nugget* service on the Seattle—Fairbanks—Anchorage route. It was an immediate success,

Northern Consolidated Airlines' Fairchild F-27B N4903 with forward cargo door.
(*Fairchild Aircraft*)

Pacific Northern Airlines' Boeing 720 N720W. (*The Boeing Company*)

capturing 64 per cent of the market in the first year of operation. Pacific Northern started a Boeing 720 service from Seattle to Anchorage on 27 April, 1962, adding Ketchikan to the jet network two days later. At this time PNA also surrendered its local route from Anchorage to King Salmon to Northern Consolidated, marking another step in the rationalization of Alaskan feeder services.

Alaska was still having a little corporate difficulty but successfully resisted attempts to influence its affairs. On 23 March, 1964, the C.A.B. ruled that certain directors should not sit on the airline board because of admitted interlocking relationships with Raymond W. Marshall. A year later, on 29 March, 1965, Alaska Airlines lost its route authority from Seattle to Fairbanks, in favour of Pan American. In compensation, however, Alaska received a seven-year authorization for Seattle—Anchorage—Fairbanks, with a mandatory stop at Anchorage. Pacific Northern thus lost its monopoly on the route (Northwest's participation was mainly on through flights to Asia) but it too was compensated by the award of the Seattle—Ketchikan—Juneau route, exclusively, with Pan American withdrawing completely.

Both Alaska and Pacific Northern improved their equipment by ordering Boeing 727s and on 8 March, 1965, Alaska became the world's first civil operator of the large Lockheed Hercules Type 382, flown on a lease basis, and in May Alaska ordered two aircraft but had to cancel them.

Alaska Airlines' Boeing 727 *Golden Nugget Jet* N797AS. (*The Boeing Company*)

Tidying Up the Alaskan Airline Map

A wave of mergers swept through the Alaskan airline scene in 1967. In a few swift moves, a new stage of refinement took place which could well mark the foundation of a permanent establishment. The C.A.B. had long frowned upon the apparent contradiction of paying out subsidy to competing airlines—doubly irritating, as few Alaskan routes generated enough traffic for even one operator—and quickly approved amalgamations, once the parties had reached agreement and all the legal niceties were settled.

As the Alaskan airlines operated outside the territorial waters of the U.S.A. and questions of national defence and security had to be satisfied, White House approval for mergers had to be obtained. President Johnson duly granted this to Alaska Airlines and Cordova on 7 December, 1967, and to Alaska Airlines and Alaska Coastal in March 1968. Alaska Coastal had merged with Ellis Airlines on 1 April, 1962, so Alaska Airlines now controlled all local services in southeast Alaska, except the Juneau—Ketchikan—Seattle semi-trunk route of PNA. This latter airline had itself lost its identity by a merger with the U.S. trunk-route carrier, Western Airlines, completed on 1 October, 1967.

These mergers saw the passing from airline control of several colourful pioneers, notably Mudhole Smith of Cordova, Shell Simmons of Alaska Coastal, and Arthur Woodley of PNA. Up in the northwest of the State, however, the pioneers continued to rule the roost, even though they too agreed to merge. Wien Alaska Airlines changed its name to Wien Air Alaska in February 1966 and strayed from its normal sphere of interest by applying for trunk routes to Chicago and Seattle. This issue was not pressed, as on 15 March, 1967, it announced plans to merge with Northern Consolidated, receiving C.A.B. approval in February 1968. Thus two long-established friendly rivals at last joined hands, and seemed to have earned a dowry from the C.A.B. which recommended the award of an Anchorage—Fairbanks nonstop route, in competition with Alaska Airlines, on the grounds that the latter had not kept pace with market needs.

By 1968, therefore, the Alaskan airline picture had crystallized into a straightforward division of responsibility for feeder, or local airline services, on a geographical basis. Alaska Airlines was responsible for routes southeast of a line from Fairbanks to Anchorage; Wien Consolidated for routes to the northwest of that line. Both airlines shared in the line itself. Reeve Aleutian Airways continued on its independent way down the Aleutian chain, oblivious to all these machinations. By the merger of PNA and Western, passengers could, for the first time, travel direct to California by the same airline and the same aircraft, while Alaska Airlines survived as the sole Alaskan trunk specialist.

It was left to two little airlines to recapture the spirit of the old days of Alaskan pioneering. Western Alaska Airlines began local services from Dillingham on 13 March, 1959—recalling the activities of Dillingham Air Service in 1936—while Kodiak Airways started service to various points

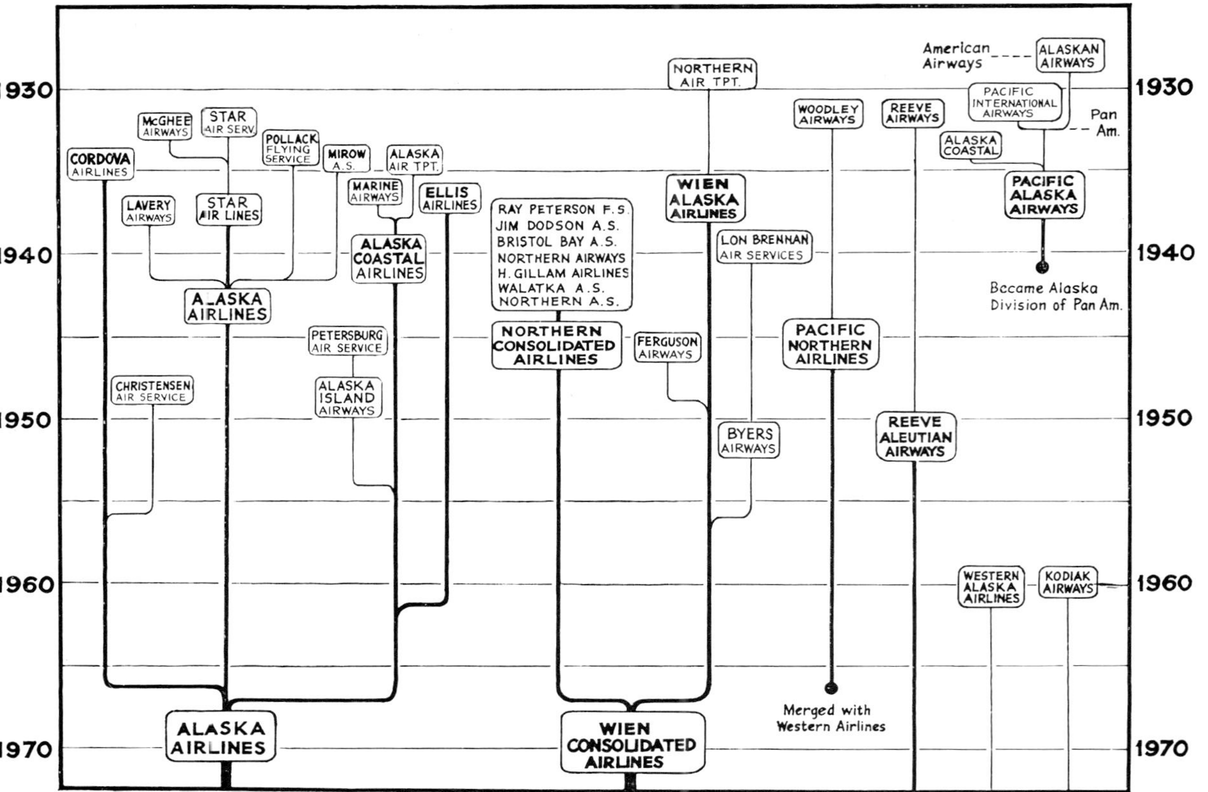

Fig. 24. Ancestry of Airlines in Alaska.

N461GB, one of Wien Consolidated Airlines' blue and yellow Boeing 737s.
(The Boeing Company)

on Kodiak Island, home of the biggest bears in the world, on 6 December, 1960. These two airlines merged on 1 April, 1973, to become Kodiak–Western Alaska Airlines.

Hawaii

The airlines of Alaska shared with certain other companies the distinction of having a special designation under C.A.B. carrier terminology. Though it had always taken an adamant stand against the moral injustice of colonialism, the United States had not been averse to a little quasi-colonialism in its own right when there appeared to be over-riding circumstances in favour of such a reactionary step. Consequently, over a period of about half a century, certain territories had come under the jurisdiction of Washington, mostly as the outcome of the Spanish-American War at the close of the nineteenth century. Thus the Philippines, Hawaii, Puerto Rico, Alaska, Samoa, and the Panama Canal Zone were neither states of the Union, nor were they foreign countries; and the C.A.B. could not classify their airlines either as Domestic or International Carriers, and created the term Territorial as a convenient expedient.

Not including the Alaskan pioneers, the oldest airline qualifying for this classification, and one which in its earliest years—before the creation of the C.A.B.—was grouped along with United States airlines as a whole, was Inter-Island Airways Ltd in Hawaii. This company was founded on 30 January, 1929, and was named after the Inter-Island Steam Navigation Company Ltd, which put up 76 per cent of the common stock. On 11 November of that year, Inter-Island began a scheduled passenger service with two eight-passenger Sikorsky S-38s, linking Honolulu with the outer islands of the Hawaii group, serving Maui, Hilo, and Kauai on a regular basis, and Molokai and Lanai on request.

Air mail contracts were obtained in 1934 and during the next few years the fleet was augmented by larger Sikorsky S-43 amphibians. On 16 June, 1939, the C.A.B. awarded a permanent certificate to this U.S. overseas

NC16934 was a Sikorsky S-43 operated in Hawaii by Inter-Island Airways, which later became Hawaiian Airlines. (*Gordon S. Williams*)

carrier, which subsequently changed its name to Hawaiian Airlines on 1 October, 1941. In that year three DC-3s were obtained and on 20 March, 1942, an inter-island freight service was started, fulfilling a genuine need for transporting perishable foods throughout the Hawaiian Islands. In 1944 TWA acquired a 20 per cent interest, but this was sold in 1948.

After the end of World War 2, Hawaiian lost its monopoly of air transport in Hawaii. On 9 June, 1946, Trans-Pacific Airlines (TPA) was incorporated under the laws of the Territory and non-scheduled services were started on 26 July. Progress to full scheduled airline status took almost exactly three years, and involved some protracted litigation. Common carrier status was denied to TPA on 9 September, 1947, by the U.S. District Court, which thought that the company's activities were not covered by the necessary legal documentation. Eventually, the C.A.B. authorized scheduled services on 29 November, 1948; the President gave his blessing on 17 February, 1949; and scheduled service began on 6 June of that year, to give Hawaii the benefits of competitive service.

Rolls-Royce Dart powered Convair CV-640 in Hawaiian Airlines' red and white livery.

In June 1951, TPA's certificate was amended to allow the carriage of mail at a rate calculated to yield an annual revenue of about $230,000 to supplement the passenger revenues which had failed to come up to expectations. Hawaiian Airlines was forced to follow TPA in asking for subsidy, a course which caused some bitterness as, before the entry of TPA on the scene, mail payments had been modest by comparison. Hawaiian's case for monopoly was based on substantiated financial evidence, but the C.A.B. observed that the amount paid to both Hawaiian companies was much less than that paid to many Local Service carriers, and the social value to the islanders was much greater.

TPA had originally claimed to be the 'poor man's airline' and made substantial inroads into Hawaiian's traffic until 1953 when the latter

Aloha Airlines' Vickers-Armstrongs V.745 Viscount N7416.

introduced Convair CV-340s as an improvement over the standard DC-3s. TPA, having received a renewal of its certificate late in 1954, replied by ordering propeller-turbine F-27s, and later improved its image by adopting the name Aloha Airlines as its official title on 11 February, 1959. The F-27 went into service in the summer of that year, and Aloha's share of the inter-island traffic went up from 30 per cent to 43 per cent.

Since that time the two airlines have operated almost identical route networks linking the Hawaiian Islands, competing strongly in terms of flying equipment. Aloha introduced Viscounts in June 1963 and Hawaiian Dart-engined Convairs on 23 December, 1965. Short-haul jets were added in the mid-1960s, BAC One-Elevens by Aloha in June 1966, and Douglas DC-9s by Hawaiian in March 1966. Aloha brought in Boeing 737s in March 1969 in an effort to remain fully competitive.

Competition was intense throughout the 1960s, but both airlines found increasing difficulty in matching mounting costs with adequate revenues. The C.A.B. had already experienced some embarrassment in dealing with the question of subsidy need. The news, in January 1970, of a proposed agreement between Hawaiian and Aloha to merge, came therefore as a relief. Hawaiian would own 51 per cent, and Aloha 49 per cent, of the joint airline. Hung Wo Ching, of Aloha, would be chairman, John Magoon, of Hawaiian, would be president.

Aloha Airlines' BAC One-Eleven 215 N11183 *Queen Kaahumanu*.

After endless sparring for position, however, Hawaiian abruptly terminated negotiations in April 1971, in a clouded atmosphere of mistrust. Hawaiian claimed excessive procrastination by Aloha; the latter charged Hawaiian with unfair scheduling practices aimed at weakening its bargaining position.

The Hawaiian Islands have presented intriguing problems to the administrators, for a number of reasons. When Hawaii became the 50th State of the Union on 21 August, 1959, its Public Utilities Commission claimed greater powers of jurisdiction over airlines operating wholly within the State. The matter was complicated by the fact that 40 per cent of the passengers carried by both Hawaiian and Aloha were and are residents of other States or countries; and that several of the routes fly over international waters by the legal definition of the term as recognized by the U.S.A.—three miles off shore.

The achievement of Statehood has in recent years given greater opportunity to many other smaller airlines which operated air taxi services between the Islands and which found only a narrow line of definition between some of their operations and those of a scheduled carrier. Since the mid-1960s these companies have swelled the growing list of so-called Third Level airlines, which are discussed in Chapter 18.

Hawaiian Airlines' Douglas DC-9-14 N902H.

Aloha Airlines' multi-coloured Boeing 737-291 N571GB *King Lunalilo*. (*The Boeing Company*)

Puerto Rico

In Puerto Rico, which still awaits Statehood, Caribbean-Atlantic Airlines (Caribair) was incorporated by Dionisio Trigo on 27 February, 1939, and on 1 June took over the operations of Powelson Air Service, which had started flights in October 1938 between San Juan, the capital, and Ponce, the second largest city. Later that year, using ten-passenger Stinson aircraft, a route was opened to the Virgin Islands, another United States possession in the Caribbean. A C.A.B. certificate for these routes was obtained on 23 July, 1942.

There was a steady improvement in flying equipment, first by lease of Lockheed L.18 Lodestars from National Airlines in April 1945, and then, a year later, by a fleet of three DC-3s. The network was expanded to include Ciudad Trujillo (Santo Domingo), Dominican Republic, on 27 December, 1948.

The C.A.B. renewed Caribair's certificate for five years from 13 November, 1952, and this was later extended indefinitely. Service opened to St Maarten, Netherlands West Indies, on 15 January, 1958, and this route was extended to Guadeloupe in 1961. By this time, Caribair had added Convair CV-340s to its fleet of DC-3s. To tackle the short runway at St Thomas, U.S. Virgin Islands, with its forbidding mountain crest ominously close to the climb path, the Convairs were fitted with JATO (Jet Assisted Take Off) rockets. In 1961 also, Trans-Caribbean Airways acquired a minority interest in Caribair, as a logical step in support of its New York—San Juan trunk service.

Caribair moved on technically from the DC-3 age by converting its Convair CV-340s to Rolls-Royce Dart-engined Convair 640s in December 1965, and by adding DC-9 jets in December 1967. It also moved away physically from the confines of Puerto Rico and the islands in the immediate vicinity by gaining C.A.B. authority for considerable route extensions throughout the West Indian chain of islands as far as Trinidad.

By 1968, however, Caribair's spirit in the Caribbean seemed to be on the wane. Trigo himself had lost his former zeal, unsuccessfully pleading for subsidy relief after paying his way for many years. Competition, including that from a lusty Third Level airline, Prinair, was increasing. The route structure needed strengthening, yet Caribair lost its case for a nonstop route from San Juan to Miami. The little airline, one of the most colourful of the U.S. Territorials, seemed ready for a take-over bid.

Eastern Air Lines' acquisition offer, made public on 27 October, 1970, therefore came as no surprise. Routes, properties, and the three DC-9s (not the CV-640s) would cost Eastern $10.4 million. On 21 May, 1971, the C.A.B. Examiner recommended a straightforward merger and a combined route structure, thus giving Eastern a valuable sphere of influence throughout the Caribbean.

Micronesia

After World War 2, on 4 July, 1946, the United States formally granted independence to the Philippines, but this by no means ended American influence in the western Pacific. A vast island-studded area of approximately the same size as the continental United States had formerly been administered by Japan under a League of Nations mandate. Consisting of the Marshall, Caroline, and Mariana Islands, some 2,000 in all, only 84 were actually inhabited and the total population numbered only 53,000. The United States took over the post-war administration of Micronesia, as the scattered islands became collectively known, with the U.S. Navy performing the rôle of caretakers.

Late in 1949 the U.S. Department of the Interior took over responsibility from the Navy and one of its first acts was to investigate the possibility of improving communications between the isolated islands. Transocean Air Lines, a United States non-scheduled and contract air carrier which had demonstrated considerable initiative in providing a variety of unusual services all over the world, was invited to participate in a survey, together with other air and sea carriers, naval personnel, and representatives of the C.A.B. When, early in 1951, bids were called for to undertake contracted air services throughout Micronesia, Transocean was the successful bidder, and began operations on a scheduled basis on 1 July, 1951.

The equipment used was a fleet of four PBY-5A amphibians supplied by the Navy. These were modified to carry ten passengers plus cargo. Transocean maintained the fleet, and provided crews, spares, and ground handling. With Guam as the main base, flights left on an infrequent but regular schedule to the outlying islands of Truk, Ponape, Majuro, Saipan, Yap, and Koror. The furthest point, Majuro, was almost 2,000 miles from Guam.

This Trust Territory operation was a social service in the true sense of the word, providing passenger service and supplying provisions for the islanders, who, incidentally, included the inhabitants of the famous Bikini atoll, evacuated because of the hydrogen bomb experiments. At this time, the Trust Territory was not open to tourists—although this restriction was academic, as only the most adventurous would have considered these remote and amenity-lacking spots in preference to the more obvious charms of Hawaii.

A Trust Territory Air Services Grumman Albatross. This company served the U.S.-administered islands of Micronesia, and was under the control of Pan American Airways from 1960 to 1968, as a subcontractor to the Department of the Interior.

After nine years of service to Micronesia, Transocean Air Lines, deeply entangled with all kinds of legal problems associated with the restrictions upon non-scheduled airlines, and frustrated in its attempt to become a second U.S. trans-Pacific carrier via Hawaii and Guam, finally terminated all operations and went bankrupt on 11 July, 1960. Faced with a social responsibility, the Department of the Interior asked Pan American, already serving Guam on its trans-Pacific service, to take over the Micronesia operation. Pan American used a mixed fleet of old Douglas DC-4s for the longer routes, where there were adequate aerodromes, and Grumman Albatross amphibians for the route to Ponape.

The whole question of air services linking the Trust Territory of the Pacific, both internally and externally, came up for review in the late 1960s. The Department of the Interior reviewed proposals from several airlines, including Pan American, Northwest, Hawaiian, and a new company, Air Micronesia, formed in 1967. Air Micronesia was owned jointly by Continental Airlines (31 per cent), Aloha Airlines (20 per cent), and the United Micronesia Development Association Inc (UMDA) (49 per cent). The last-named holds the option to purchase a further 2 per cent of stock from Continental within five years, thus giving it majority control, with subsequent right to acquire another 9 per cent.

The initial services of Air Micronesia were provided almost entirely by Continental Airlines, which, curiously, was the only United States Domestic Trunk airline without a single foreign route. However, its experience in flying across the Pacific Ocean was already considerable, as it supplemented its scheduled route system with an extensive contract operation for Military Airlift Command (MAC), employing eight Boeing 707-320Cs on a continuous transocean schedule, up to four or five daily services. Continental's Air Micronesia schedule began on 16 May, 1968, with a Boeing 727 linking all the main Micronesian islands with Okinawa in the west and Hawaii in the east. Under the new Trust Territory charter, Micronesia was now directly on line with trans-Pacific airline schedules, without the obligation to make all flight connections through Guam. Air Micronesia's contract also called for the construction of six hotels, one in each of the six districts of Micronesia, with, however, built-in safeguards against the worst excesses of commercial exploitation.

In 1971, Air Micronesia gained routes to Nauru and American Samoa, in a ruling on the Pacific Islands Local Service Investigation. Pan American was awarded the Hawaii—Samoa link. Continental Airlines, with a substantial interest in Air Micronesia, supplying the aircraft and technical support, can now claim to serve as a foreign point, at faraway Nauru, a tiny independent state in the western Pacific. Okinawa will become the second foreign point when it reverts to Japanese sovereignty in 1972.

Polynesia

Pan American's contraction in the west Pacific was contemporary with its ascendancy in the south Pacific. This involved the acquisition of an important transocean route which was pioneered at first by two foreign airlines: the New Zealand carrier, TEAL, and primarily the French TAI/Air France consortium. TAI began a DC-6B service to the Society Islands on 28 September, 1958, connecting from Noumea, New Caledonia, to Bora Bora, from which a local French airline, RAI, served the enchanting Tahiti with flying-boats.

The romantic island of Tahiti was by a substantial margin the greatest tourist attraction of the whole southern Pacific area, but access by air was complicated by the absence of a modern airport—hence the RAI flying-boat operation and the need to use Bora Bora. Anxious to attain a share of a potentially rich market, a United States company set about the task of opening an air service, using the most modern flying-boats available, a somewhat difficult undertaking, as flying-boats had all but become obsolete as long-distance aircraft.

South Pacific Airlines was founded in 1953 by the Robert Dollar Company as Dollar Airlines Ltd, with the objective of starting a direct route from Honolulu to Tahiti. It tried to solve the problem of flying-boat acquisition by purchasing an Australian company, Trans-Oceanic Airways, whose assets included two Short Solents, and subsequently buying an additional aircraft from the United Kingdom. This enterprising initiative was cruelly rewarded. At first operations were prevented by the staging of a series of hydrogen bomb tests at Christmas Island, strategically situated as a port of call half-way along South Pacific's route. Then United States airworthiness requirements led to extensive and costly modifications being made to the Solents, and, by the time these were complete, the French were planning to build a new airport on reclaimed land on the shores of Tahiti. South Pacific had no choice but to start again with landplanes.

Regular services were inaugurated from Honolulu to Bora Bora on 2 April, 1960, using Super Constellations obtained from TWA. The connection to Tahiti was made via the local service flying-boats of RAI, but these became unnecessary when the new airport was opened in Tahiti on 20 September, 1961. On 14 March, 1962, South Pacific added a service from Honolulu to Samoa, once every two weeks, but the airline had hardly begun to realize even the beginning of its full potential when the ground (or, rather, the water) was cut from under it by a decision of the C.A.B. on 28 January, 1963, to award the U.S. Mainland—Tahiti portion of a Pacific route case to Pan American Airways. This eliminated the vital link required by South Pacific to provide service directly from its main source of passenger traffic, the continental U.S.A.

While the C.A.B.'s decision was awaiting approval by President Kennedy, Pan American and South Pacific came to an arrangement on 18 September whereby Pan Am would lease South Pacific's route for 50 per cent of the operating profit for ten years, plus 10 per cent for another ten years. This agreement was made redundant, however, when on 12 November the C.A.B., with Presidential approval, finally authorized the direct Pan American service from California to Tahiti. Pan American took over the whole of South Pacific's operation in November 1964.

This C.A.B. decision caused controversy on the emotional grounds of a large powerful carrier apparently being aided in swallowing up a small competitor. Board member Minetti, particularly, disputed the majority decision in a sharply-worded dissent, pointing out that criticism of South Pacific's achieved performance was not strictly indicative of its future capability, given the right equipment, which it was prepared to buy, if it received authority for direct service. '. . . Pan American will become the gratuitous beneficiary of South Pacific's $2,000,000 investment, and will be able to cash in on all of the company's efforts and expenditures in developing the Tahiti market. In these circumstances, I regard it as unconscionable to deny South Pacific the mainland extension and to award Pan American entry into Tahiti.'

But the Board's decision was by majority vote, and Pan American duly became established as the U.S. carrier to Tahiti.

Little remains to be said about other U.S. airline activity in the south Pacific, which was confined to the brief appearance of Samoan Airlines which started services from Pago Pago, U.S. Samoa, to Apia, Western Samoa, on 14 July, 1959. This was suspended in October 1960 when it became evident that Polynesian Airlines, the Western Samoan airline, was able to provide sufficient service.

The Douglas DC-3 was still in widescale U.S. domestic service for several years after the war. This example was operated by Continental Air Lines.

CHAPTER THIRTEEN

Post-war Domestic Boom

Poised for Expansion

The permanent certificates for Grandfather Rights over a comprehensive nationwide route structure, conferred upon the airlines in 1938, created a stable environment in which the industry could develop as fast as the manufacturing industry could deliver the aircraft. Production of Douglas twin-engined airliners in large quantities throughout the 1930s had placed at the disposal of the airlines substantial fleets which could earn their own keep. These put the carriers on a sounder financial footing, reducing year by year their dependence on mail pay and subsidy. This process coincided with a continued growth of public airmindedness which was to surge upwards at an ever increasing rate towards the end of World War 2, when military travel requirements exceeded all previous demands.

During the war, the United States airlines made prodigious efforts on domestic routes, equipped almost exclusively with Douglas DC-3s. Utilization rates of more than ten hours revenue flying per day, combined with an artificially inflated average load factor of almost 90 per cent, were achieved in 1944. As traffic soared when the war ended, figures approaching these records were maintained with larger fleets of aircraft. Between 1943 and 1946 inclusive, a period of four years, the number of passengers carried by the domestic scheduled airlines increased four-fold, a rate of growth never exceeded before or since.

At the outbreak of World War 2 in Europe in 1939, the United States moved smoothly into world leadership in building the more powerful, longer-ranged, and faster successors to the twin-engined airliners of the 1930s. Germany, France, and Britain turned their full efforts towards fighter and bomber construction. Germany switched its Fw 200 Condor production entirely to military versions; Britain abandoned promising four-engined airliner designs from Shorts, Fairey and Miles; and France laid aside its plans for a four-engined development of the successful Bloch 220. The United States, on the other hand, as yet free from military commitments, proceeded with four-engined designs.

United Air Lines' experiment with the DC-4E in July 1939 was not a success, and TWA's bold venture into the realms of high-altitude flight with the Boeing 307 in July 1940 was curtailed by the outbreak of hostilities in December 1941. Boeing, in fact, suffered a diversion from promising civil airliner development when, like the European aircraft manufacturers, it had to concentrate on bomber production. But Boeing's rivals, the Douglas and Lockheed companies, went ahead to produce the first generations of thoroughbred lines of four-engined civil airliners.

The original DC-4—the ill-fated experimental version—had been sponsored by the Big Four domestic airlines and Pan American. Although United would have liked to have persevered with the DC-4E, it had to fall in line with its competitors, notably American Airlines, which favoured a smaller four-engined DC-4. Three of the Big Four (excluding TWA) and Pan Am ordered a total of 61 DC-4s on 26 January, 1940; but, although deliveries were originally scheduled for the spring of 1941, production delays, coupled with growing demands from the Army for the C-54 military version, led to the airlines and Douglas voluntarily terminating the contracts.

The DC-4 first flew on 14 February, 1942. Hope was renewed for a while that some DC-4s would be released in 1943, but the airlines had to abandon their plans until after the war, although United, for example, operated some under contract with the Army. C-54s and their Naval counterparts, the R5Ds, performed wonders in military service. Altogether 1,163 military models were manufactured, and no other four-engined transport was built in such large numbers. Douglas estimated that they made 79,642 ocean crossings during the war, and among their many and varied missions was transporting in an armada of 250 aircraft two divisions of troops from Okinawa to Tokyo, following Japan's surrender.

United re-ordered 15 DC-4s at $385,000 each on 11 September, 1944, but these were cancelled on 24 October, 1945, when the U.S. Government made available large numbers of surplus C-54s, at a price of $90,000 each. Western Airlines is believed to have been the first to operate a civil domestic airline service with a converted C-54, on 18 January, 1946, but was quickly followed by National and American, in February, and United, on 1 March, and by several others.

The notable exception among the sponsors of the DC-4 was TWA, which, under the leadership of Howard Hughes, backed the Lockheed Constellation series. First discussions were held with the manufacturer in June 1939, and TWA ordered nine aircraft in 1940. The Constellation made its first flight on 9 January, 1943, and, although C-54s were piling up the hours of service and experience, it made its mark on 19 April, 1944, when Hughes and the TWA president, Jack Frye, made their spectacular nonstop flight from Burbank, California, to Washington in 3 minutes less than 7 hours. The aircraft was immediately handed over to the Government for military use.

In his book *The World's Airliners*, Peter Brooks has described the Constellation as 'the secret weapon of American air transport'. The type was only ordered in small numbers, compared with the massive orders for Douglas transports, but its performance placed it in a new class. Partly because of its beautiful design, including an aerodynamically-tapered fuselage, it was about 70 mph faster than the DC-4, cruising at about 270 mph. Above all, it was pressurized, giving it high-altitude operating flexibility and passenger comfort, and it was larger, with 60 seats against the 44 seats of the unpressurized DC-4.

Brooks' metaphor refers to the fact that the DC-4 was regarded by European manufacturers as the competitive standard. He writes, 'As a result, British airliners built at the end of the war—particularly the so-called "interim" types—tended to be too modest in their designed capabilities and, in the event, fell even further short of foreign competition than they would have done in any case because of the penalties resulting from their hybrid origins. As soon as the war was over, the Constellation began to emerge as the world's most effective civil airliner and Douglas themselves were forced to develop the DC-4 into the much improved DC-6 to match the Constellation's capabilities.'

Britain, apparently, was not alone in being kept in ignorance. United Air Lines claimed that the Constellation's development was 'shrouded in mystery during the first several years, being kept a trade secret at the beginning and being taken over by the Army Air Forces and kept under military secrecy during the war. As late as October 1943 it was not being built.' United had reviewed a number of designs, including the Curtiss CW-20F (the military C-46), the Consolidated M-39 (the military B-24), the Constellation, and the DC-6, before ordering the DC-4.

United, like the other DC-4 sponsors, chose the DC-6, ordering 20 on 11 September, 1944, part of a total of 61 matching the original DC-4 order book, whose participants were given the opportunity of preserving their pre-war delivery positions. The contract was complicated by the

TWA's Douglas DC-4 N45341 seen while still bearing X certification. Later named *The Taj Mahal*, this may have been TWA's first DC-4.

fact that Douglas was not allowed to begin work on the DC-6 until wartime restrictions were eased, and clauses covering delivery involved definition of 'production notices'. After revision, the price of the standard model was fixed at $595,000. Deliveries were eventually scheduled from July 1946 onwards, United to receive the first aeroplane, American the second, and subsequent deliveries to be interspersed with others to Pan American, SILA (Sweden), the Provisional French Government, and ANA (Australia).

With the DC-6, Douglas demonstrated that it intended to meet the challenge of the Constellation, matching it in almost every performance respect, speed, range, and airfield capability. The cabin was fully pressurized, but it was narrower than that of the Constellation by about 14

TWA introduced Lockheed Constellations on the New York—Los Angeles route in March 1946. One of TWA's later L.749As, N6014C *Star of Delaware*, is seen off Manhattan. (*TWA*)

inches, making five-abreast seating layouts more cramped than in the Lockheed design.

The only other four-engined contender was the Republic Rainbow. This was a commercial adaptation of the XF-12, built experimentally for the Army Air Forces, to a 1943 specification for long range, high-speed reconnaissance, at very high altitudes. The XF-12 made its first flight on 4 February, 1946.

The Rainbow, with a design altitude of 40,000 ft, payload of 12,000 lb, and cruising speed of about 400 mph, held out great promise. Pan American and American Airlines placed provisional orders. But severe problems with the engines and controls caused the abandonment of the project.

With the Rainbow scratched, and Boeing left at the starting gate, the field was narrowed down to a straight race between Douglas and Lockheed.

Transcontinental Competition

The most competitive route over which to exploit these fine new post-war aircraft was the coast-to-coast route from the cities of the northeast (mainly New York, but also Boston, Philadelphia, and Washington) to California (San Francisco and Los Angeles). This 2,500-mile route offered passengers the maximum advantage compared with road or rail transport. At the same time, it offered the airlines the best chance of making profits, because the high potential revenue generated by the large terminal populations was combined with long stage lengths ideally suited to minimum operating costs. The prospect of lucrative business on a large scale led to a competitive battle between the three big airlines holding transcontinental rights, a battle which was always hard, often ruthless, sometimes vicious.

American, TWA and United inherited Grandfather Rights along the old routes which, ironically, the misguided Walter F. Brown, of Air Mail Scandal notoriety, had planned for them. American Airlines followed what was then known as the southern transcontinental route, via Nashville, Dallas, and El Paso, with an important alternative via Chicago and St Louis, both terminating at Los Angeles. (The true southern transcontinental route, as envisaged by Brown, actually came into existence in 1961.) Transcontinental & Western Air (TWA) held the route laid down by Lindbergh for TAT, via Pittsburgh, Columbus, St Louis, Kansas City, and Albuquerque. United Air Lines operated the traditional route pioneered by Boeing from New York to San Francisco, with the exception that Denver replaced Cheyenne as the main Rocky Mountains staging post from 1937 onwards, the right of entry having been purchased from Inland Air Lines. Also, a spur joined Salt Lake City with Portland, Oregon, over the Varney route of 1926.

All the great airliners developed during the 1940s were aimed primarily at offering ever more competitive service over this transcontinental route system. Until 1940 the standard aircraft had been the DC-3 which completed the 2,500-mile journey in times varying between 16 and 20 hr.

TWA's attempt to break clear of the limitations of the DC-3 by introducing the Boeing 307 Stratoliner cut the transcontinental travel time to 14½ hr. Withdrawn from service on 24 December, 1941, immediately after the United States entered World War 2, it re-entered the domestic scene on 1 April, 1945, but was soon outmoded by the new post-war types and retired from mainline service.

The DC-3 had a final fling, working out its last months of first-line service until the four-engined airliners arrived in quantity. For many years, in fact, the old Douglas airliner was quite indispensable, and several hundred of them kept the airlines going during the immediate post-war period. To take an example, United Air Lines had 77 DC-3s in service on 1 January, 1946, comprising its total fleet. Fifty-six of these were owned outright, 21 leased from the Department of Defense. Even in trunk-line service, the DC-3 was considered to be sufficiently useful as late as 1 August, 1949, when United purchased the 21 leased aircraft from the War Assets Administration for $290,000—about half the price of one DC-6.

On 1 March, 1946, after preliminary trial services, TWA put the Lockheed Constellation on the transcontinental route from New York to Los Angeles. Although United opened on the same day from New York to San Francisco with DC-4s, the contrast between the two standards of airline equipment was obvious. Apart from the superior comfort of the Constellation derived from its pressurization, it accomplished coast-to-coast schedules of about 11 hr, compared with the 13 or 14 of the DC-4. American Airlines started DC-4 services across the continent on 7 March, taking slightly longer than United because of its longer, southerly route.

Although delays in production postponed the date of entry into service, United and American were little more than a year late in providing pressurized transcontinental service. United opened a DC-6 ten-hour coast-

American Airlines began transcontinental Douglas DC-4 services on 7 March, 1946. The DC-4 illustrated is NC90423 *Flagship Washington*. (*American Airlines*)

American Airlines was first to operate the Douglas DC-6. Seen here before receiving a commercial certificate is N90704 *Flagship Oklahoma*. (*American Airlines*)

to-coast schedule on 27 April, 1947, stopping only at Lincoln, Nebraska. The DC-6s were fitted with 52 seats for daytime operations, or 24 sleeper-type seats for night use. American had been the first with the DC-6, on the New York—Chicago route, and added a transcontinental flight on 20 May. Westbound flights with the DC-6 took about 11 hr, eastbound flights about one hour less.

The ebb and flow of the fortunes of the competitive airlines and manufacturers at this time is a fascinating story. TWA lost its initial advantage with the Constellations when they were grounded by the C.A.B. from 12 July to 20 September, 1946, after accidents caused by the superchargers used in the pressurization system. When DC-6 services began, TWA met the challenge by scheduling a 10 hr 10 min eastbound flight by night, stopping only at Chicago, returning in 11 hr 40 min. Then United and American had their set-back when the DC-6 was grounded between 12 November, 1947, and 21 March, 1948. This followed an accident at Bryce Canyon, Utah, when 52 people were killed in a United DC-6, and an emergency landing at Gallup, N.M., by an American Airlines aircraft. The cause was traced to inflight fires resulting from a fuel leakage into the cabin heater system during fuel transfer procedures.

These incidents were a continuation of a dismal chain of events during 1947. Thirty-six domestic accidents, of which five proved fatal, marked it as the worst single year in air transport history. When 143 people were killed during a two-week period during the summer, President Truman appointed a Special Board of Inquiry on Air Safety, headed by C.A.B. chairman James M. Landis, and including leaders of all the main aviation agencies. The final report was inconclusive, for an analysis of all the crashes revealed no common cause. Some were traced to the malfunctioning of an aircraft system, some were judged to have been the direct result of lack of discipline on the part of the pilot, others were blamed on shortcomings in meteorological reporting or bad airway control. Generally, operators, manufacturers, government agencies, and the public all became aware that the new era of air transport carried added risks as well as benefits from improved technology.

The C.A.B. had made a number of important route awards in 1943 and 1944, all aimed to rationalize the nation's air routes on a sound, but not excessively competitive basis. Restrictions of access to main east and west coast termini by all three transcontinental carriers had been removed or eased. In the east United and TWA were able to serve Washington, in addition to American, and the same two airlines were also authorized to provide direct services to Boston. United began services westwards from Boston, via Hartford and Cleveland, in May 1945, while TWA simultaneously started a route via Albany, Binghamton, Williamsport, and Pittsburgh. American, holding the through rights from Boston via New York and Washington, did not introduce a by-pass route until June 1948, and even this was temporarily suspended until April 1949.

N37534 *Mainliner New York* was one of United Air Lines' fleet of Douglas DC-6s which went onto transcontinental services in April 1947. (*United Air Lines*)

United Air Lines had been unsuccessful in gaining a direct route to Los Angeles, the link between Denver and southern California having been granted to Western Airlines on 11 November, 1944. United had also been denied an application to merge with Western, but at last in 1947 a golden opportunity presented itself. As forecast in some of the testimony in the Denver—Los Angeles route award case of 1944, Western was faced with having to operate a difficult route over the Rocky Mountains and had to order special equipment for the task. The single long route, however, was insufficient to justify the operation of an economic fleet of DC-6s in the face of American's DC-6s and TWA's Constellations which, moreover, had the advantage of providing through service to Chicago and beyond. When Terrell C. Drinkwater assumed the presidency of Western on 1 January, 1947, he therefore sought a drastic solution to his company's growing crisis: to sell the Los Angeles—Denver route, plus the five DC-6 aircraft being purchased specifically to operate it.

On 7 March, 1947, Western and United filed a joint application to the C.A.B. for the route and equipment transfer. There were, as with nearly all route cases, opponents to the action, who charged that the whole affair was the result of the C.A.B.'s own errors in making the original award. The Board, however, recognized that to refuse the application would mean the death of Western Airlines, and accordingly approved the deal on 25 August, 1947, at an agreed price of $3,750,000, plus a further loan of $1,000,000.

The United/Western negotiations had removed the last obstacle in the way of persistent efforts to consolidate its routes west of Denver, and the C.A.B. had already granted this on 19 May, 1947, before the sale of Western's route. United started service on 17 July on a New York—Chicago—Los Angeles service, while TWA began a New York—Chicago—San Francisco service, and American paralleled United's service, also gaining access to San Francisco via Phoenix.

Comparatively unaffected by all these complex commercial manoeuvres, Northwest Airlines became a fourth transcontinental operator on 16 December, 1944, when the C.A.B. awarded an extension of its Great Lakes—Pacific Northwest system eastwards from Milwaukee to New York, via Detroit. Northwest began services coast-to-coast in June 1945, and a second arm to this northern route was added in March 1948, when Washington was served by way of Detroit, Cleveland, and Pittsburgh.

Northwest was not concerned with the traffic between the northeast and California, but the other three transcontinental carriers, United, American, and TWA, were locked in a battle for supremacy of service by equipment standards, as well as trading routes in the hearings at the Civil Aeronautics Board. The two Douglas operators, United and American, bene-

United Air Lines' blue, white and silver Douglas DC-6B N37558 *Mainliner Milwaukee*. (United Air Lines)

One of TWA's fleet of ten Lockheed L.1049A Super Constellations, flying over the Hudson. (*TWA*)

fited by further improvement of the successful DC-6. Discussions in 1949 with the freight operator, Slick Airways, led to the production of the DC-6A, essentially a DC-6 with slightly more powerful engines, a lengthened fuselage, special large doors and provisions for freight stowage. A slightly longer version, the DC-6B, proved to be the most successful of all the Douglas DC-4/DC-6/DC-7 series and gained the reputation of being the most economic airliner of its day. Its operating costs proved to be the lowest of any piston-engined transport, certainly lower than those of the DC-7 developments.

United Air Lines found the DC-6B far superior to the DC-6 across the Rocky Mountains and appreciated particularly the improved performance at high-altitude airports such as Denver and Cheyenne. Cautiously ordering only six at first, United nevertheless began the first DC-6B transcontinental service on 11 April, 1951, closely followed by American on 29 April.

TWA responded to this competition by introducing the L.1049 Super Constellation on 10 September, 1952. Lockheed had considered stretching its basic Constellation model in line with Douglas' policy, and Eastern Air Lines ordered ten of the new L.1049s in April 1950. Eighteen feet longer than its predecessor, the Super Constellation had 35 per cent more passenger capacity, 40 per cent more payload, and featured rectangular windows among other design refinements. Lockheed further developed the Super Constellation with a redesigned, stronger wing, and powered by the new 3,250 hp Wright Turbo-Cyclone compound engines. This allowed higher operating weights, and thus greater tankage for longer range, although the overall dimensions remained the same. TWA exploited the added range capability by introducing the first sustained nonstop transcontinental service when an L.1049C began the *Ambassador* service between Los Angeles and New York on 19 October, 1953. Although the

N303AA *Flagship Missouri* was one of the twenty-five Douglas DC-7s ordered by American Airlines in December 1951. (*American Airlines*)

westbound flights still called at Chicago, eastbound flights completed the coast-to-coast journey nonstop in less than 8 hr.

TWA's success with the Super Constellation prompted American Airlines to respond. In December 1951, it ordered 25 Douglas DC-7s, at a cost of $1,600,000 each. This further development of the DC-6 series featured higher-powered Wright R-3350 turbo-compound engines, giving it a cruising speed of 330 mph and coast-to-coast nonstop capability. It was 40 inches longer than the DC-6B, and carried 58 passengers. Four-bladed propellers superseded the three-blade units hitherto used on the Douglas types.

American put the DC-7 into direct competition with TWA on the New York—California route on 29 November, 1953, its *Mercury* service following only six weeks later than the Super Constellation *Ambassador*. Although at first the DC-7 was optimistically scheduled to make flights in both directions in less than 8 hr, the westbound timetable had to be amended to 8¼ hr because of the adverse prevailing winds. When the C.A.B. extended the regulations to permit crew duty of up to ten hours, American's pilots went on strike until some concessions had been made.

United Air Lines' Douglas DC-7 N6322C *Mainliner Philadelphia*, seen here after being renamed *Waipahu*.

United Air Lines was more cautious in ordering the DC-7, being apprehensive about the reliability and efficiency of the turbo-compound engines. This was a case, however, where passenger preference and consequent higher revenue potential from the nonstop service took precedence over the lower cost levels of the stopping service. A well-loaded nonstop DC-7 was more profitable than a poorly-loaded DC-6B, and United recognized in this instance that theoretical seat-mile costs was not the only economic criterion. It ordered 25 DC-7s on 25 June, 1952, and began putting them into service on 1 June, 1954.

As an interim measure, the possibility of transferring Boeing Stratocruisers* from the California—Hawaii service was considered by United,

Seen flying near Seattle is United Air Lines' Boeing Stratocruiser N31225 *Mainliner Stratocruiser Hawaii*. (*Boeing Airplane Company*)

but these went into mainland service only on the Los Angeles—Seattle route, on 1 December, 1953. A few months later, United sold its Stratocruiser fleet to BOAC, after a cost analysis showed them to be unsatisfactory for domestic routes.

TWA introduced an improved version of the Super Constellation, the L.1049G, on 1 April, 1955.

On 14 November, 1955, one of the most important decisions in the history of C.A.B. route awards was made in the Denver Service Case. The main result of this general extension of rights to transcontinental airlines was that TWA gained access to Denver and in exchange United could stop at Kansas City. American was given a direct route from Chicago to San Francisco, while Western could fly from Denver to San Francisco, and Continental from Chicago to Los Angeles. In effect all the main transcontinental airlines now competed on fairly equal terms in their choice of strategic stopping points. The new transcontinental route structure resulting from the Denver Case came into effect on 13 January, 1956.

* See page 379.

Coach Class Fares

During the early pre-war years of civil air transport in the U.S.A., several aspiring airlines attempted to win business by offering low fares. None survived such experiments, but many learned that operations could only be sustained by charging fares at fairly high rates per mile—between 8c and 10c.

The first airline to make a serious attempt to offer low fares on a practicable basis was United Air Lines, which established the first air coach service in the United States on 10 April, 1940. The route was from San Francisco to Los Angeles, via intermediate cities, and the fare between the terminal points was $13.90, at a rate of 3.5c per mile. The theory behind the *Sky Coach* service was that the ten-passenger Boeing 247s used were old, fully depreciated, and therefore cheaper to operate, at the same time offering lower standards of comfort, consistent with the low fares. The experiment ended on 23 April, 1942, when the armed forces absorbed a large part of United's fleet during World War 2.

After the war, the airlines were in no hurry to lower fares, finding themselves with a good seller's market. Pressure from the many enterprising non-scheduled operators, however, brought about a change of heart. United Air Lines admits 'the competition provided by non-scheduled operators, who offered minimum services at greatly reduced rates, forced several domestic trunk carriers to adopt similar reductions in rates and quality of service on certain flights'. The first scheduled airline to react was Capital Airlines, which started the first scheduled coach class service in the United States on 4 November, 1948, on the New York—Chicago route. Capital charged 4c per mile instead of the standard 6c, and justified its case before the C.A.B. by using high-density seating arrangements—60 in a DC-4—with a minimum of amenities in the way of cabin service. Also, the schedules were timed at off-peak hours, in an attempt to utilize equipment more efficiently.

Capital's action was soon copied by other scheduled airlines, who began to accept that, of all the stimulants to air travel, low fares was the most powerful. The C.A.B. was inundated with applications for coach tariffs under the same conditions as Capital's, and the burden was so great that it was compelled to issue a policy statement. Clearly apprehensive that uncontrolled general reduction of fares could defeat the airlines' objectives by getting out of balance with costs, the Board said, '. . . We would caution the carriers that the burden of proof for additional coach service is clearly on them. We do not propose to allow the indiscriminate extension of coach fares, nor do we intend to permit a general debasement of the existing passenger fare level.'

By the end of 1949, coach class air travel had reached major proportions on scheduled networks. On 27 December both American and TWA began coast-to-coast services with 60-seat DC-4s, at a single fare of $110. Within a few months, both airlines replaced the DC-4s with pressurized equipment, American with DC-6s and TWA with Constellations.

United continued to pursue its conservative line on the question of coach service. Early in 1950, and in spite of advice from his own planning group, president William Patterson was still cautious, stating that '. . . coach competition can become chaotic with a definite danger of perilously reducing the nation's entire fare structure'. However, he and United had to bow to the inevitable and started its first post-war coach service on 14 May, 1950, with a DC-4 service from Los Angeles to San Francisco. The fare was $9.95 one way, or about 3c per mile. Western Airlines, through its subsidiary, Western Airlines of California, added daylight service at the same fare on 1 June, 1950, and the two airlines engaged in a minor rate war down the Pacific Coast during the next few months.

At this time, the airlines voluntarily imposed all kinds of restrictions on coach class services, mainly to protect their own first class service and rate structure. Apart from the off-peak timing and lower on-board amenities, no discounts, no stopovers, and no refunds were allowed (and only 50 per cent on flights cancelled beyond the passenger's control). But the pressure of competition gradually eroded these restrictions. In September 1950, the C.A.B. issued another policy statement on coach fares, explaining that the objective of rate decisions should be to balance the ratio of fares inversely to the seating standards, so that the net revenue per flight should be approximately the same, whatever the fares charged.

Responding to this policy directive, United and Western set coach fares at 4·5c per mile on West Coast routes, and 3·5c within California, or $11.70 one way, a move which was also followed by California Central Airlines, an intra-state carrier operating under the jurisdiction of the California Public Utilities Commission.

United found, somewhat to its surprise, that its West Coast coach fares were a success, and became quite aggressive in its policy, introducing a New York—San Francisco coach tariff on 25 September, 1951, at $110 one way, exactly the same as American and TWA's New York—Los Angeles fare, although the latter distance was 100 miles shorter.

United's conversion to the principles of coach class travel came just as the full implications of a government recommendation were being considered by the C.A.B. In July 1951, the U.S. Senate Select Committee on Small Business had prepared a Report on the Role of Irregular Airlines in United States Air Transportation. This strongly criticised the Board's regulatory policy on non-scheduled airlines and its attitude towards low-price fares. The report concluded that public support for the low-fare non-scheduled operations had, in fact, proved conclusively that there was considerable demand for air transport which the scheduled airlines had neglected. The Board's attitude towards maintaining existing tariffs, the Senate Committee concluded, was of questionable merit.

The Civil Aeronautics Board responded to what it saw as a clear directive to change its policy. In November 1951 it denied the applications of four non-scheduled air carriers which wanted to open up transcontinental coach class operations. Then, on 6 December, it charged the scheduled airlines with expanding coach services on a much wider scale than hitherto, in particular by removing the restrictions on hours of flight, and abandoning the previously established minimum rate of 4·5c per mile.

Having fought for several years to uphold first class fare structures, and built up comprehensive analyses to oppose low fares, the airlines now vied with each other in their attempts to lower the transcontinental fares, both nonstop and via Chicago. These settled down to an agreed $99 coast-to-coast and $32 New York—Chicago, effective 9 January, 1952.

In acting as it did, the C.A.B. made a clear distinction between non-scheduled and scheduled operations. The large irregular carriers which had shown the initiative and enterprise to prove that the public would support low fares were, however, deprived of their birthright—or so they thought. The C.A.B interpreted the letter of the law and confined scheduled operations to the appropriate certificated carriers. But many saw in its action a denial of justice and poor reward for the spirit of enterprise which has traditionally been a cornerstone of the American society.

Throughout 1954 and 1955 coach class traffic grew swiftly. The network of coach routes expanded, while at the same time restrictions were gradually removed, until there was little difference between first class and coach class travel, except in the width of the seat and a gratuitous glass of champagne. As a result, coach class traffic and revenues grew as a percentage of the whole, until it equalled and then surpassed first class travel in importance.

Routes in the East

Though the battle for supremacy on the transcontinental route remained the chief competitive issue, rivalry was no less intense on some of the shorter routes, the majority of which were concentrated in the northeast section of the United States. In this, the most heavily populated area in North America, the greatest demand for airliner seats was on the routes connecting the largest cities. Analysis of origin-destination statistics shows that in this geographical region, traffic potential follows closely the well-known economic formula which relates traffic with terminal population and distance, with due allowance for per capita wealth and special community of interest factors.

New York—Chicago has always been the vital high-density air route of the United States, ever since operation of the DC-3 showed that profits were possible over the 740-mile stage distance, without mail subsidy. Other routes have produced higher passenger figures or greater seat-mile productivity, but New York—Chicago has been subjected to closest scrutiny by the participating airlines, each highly sensitive to the slightest penetration of their preserves by rival companies.

In the post-war period, American started the first DC-4 four-engined service on the route in February 1946. Moving quickly into top gear as the end of World War 2 brought the civil transports flooding back on to the airways, United followed with DC-4s in March. TWA then briefly led the way with pressurized Constellation service in April, but the grounding of these aircraft in July and a pilot strike in the late autumn curtailed this advantage.

A fourth competitor had been added to the New York—Chicago route on 16 December, 1944, when the C.A.B. authorized Pennsylvania-Central Airlines to operate via Pittsburgh and Detroit. PCA started service in July 1945 and was allowed to omit the Detroit stop in February 1948.

Pioneer of coach class service in November 1948 was Capital Airlines. The DC-4 illustrated, NX86557, bears the livery of Pennsylvania-Central Airlines but the legend *The Capital Airline* above the windows foreshadows the change of company name to Capital.

The company was renamed Capital Airlines on 21 April of the same year and, on 4 November, made airline history by starting the first sustained low-fare coach class service in the United States. Called the *Nighthawk*, it used DC-4s during the off-peak hours. The fare was $33.30 one way, or about two-thirds of the first class fare, and remained in force until competition from the large airlines brought a further reduction to $30.80 on 1 April, 1952.

During the next three years the whole area lying between New York and Chicago was the subject of a lengthy C.A.B. proceeding, the New York—Chicago Service Case, which embraced the consideration of airline service to all the major cities in between, notably Pittsburgh, Detroit, Cleveland, Toledo, and Akron. The Board issued its final opinion and order on 1 September, 1955, and granted virtually all of Capital's requests, at the same time turning down almost everyone else's. Capital emerged with nonstop authority between New York and Chicago, Detroit, Buffalo, Toledo, and Pittsburgh, the C.A.B. commenting in a statement of policy: '. . . While the Civil Aeronautics Act seeks the development of a sound national system, and not the advantage of an individual carrier as such, we find that this case is one where the strengthening of an individual carrier is required for the sound development of the national system of which it is a part. The selection of Capital will give that carrier an opportunity to round out its services and thereby strengthen its competitive position and to render more effective service in the area.'

Capital certainly did render effective service, having bought a fleet of Vickers Viscount propeller-turbine airliners from Great Britain, the full impact of which is discussed in a later chapter.

Another beneficiary from the New York—Chicago Service Case was Northwest Airlines, which obtained a direct Chicago—New York route—making five airlines competing nonstop—and TWA was allowed to serve Detroit as an intermediate point as an alternative to its traditional route via Pittsburgh.

Northwest Airlines was also a Douglas DC-6B operator. The red-tailed example seen here is N572.

The C.A.B. continued its policy of buttressing the position of the smaller trunk carriers against the Big Four by further awards in the Southwest—Northeast Service Case, decided on 21 November, 1955. Once again, Capital was among those favoured. Its routes from Washington south-westwards to Atlanta, as one terminus, and New Orleans, as another (extended from Knoxville in 1948), were consolidated into one route system, with the important bonus of a northwards extension to Philadelphia and New York.

The Board was wise to take some remedial steps against the wholesale dominance of the Big Four. Member Josh Lee had been concerned over the danger as early as 1946, and now said, '. . . if the domestic airlines settle down to a plateau of routine business dominated by a few large carriers whose policies set the pace, much of the competitive vigour will disappear. And again, judging from the pattern set in other fields of business, a mutual understanding will spring up between the big companies and they will resist progressive innovation and extras in service as the unnecessary dissipation of profits. The small carriers then being unable to do anything else, will follow suit and the public will be the loser.'

Two airlines had been forced to merge with others in the early 1950s.

Mid-Continent Airlines had made modest extensions from Tulsa southwards to New Orleans, in August 1945, and to Houston, in February 1946. St Louis was added on 23 January, 1948, but the company did not have the route strength or traffic density to enable it to progress beyond the status of a feeder airline, although officially designated a trunk. While most airlines were buying four-engined equipment in the immediate post-war period, Mid-Continent did not put DC-3s into service until December 1946, and introduced Convair CV-240s in 1950. Braniff International Airways' acquisition of Mid-Continent on 15 August, 1952, came as no surprise.

Of rather larger stature was Chicago & Southern Air Lines, holder of the north–south Mississippi River Valley route. Just before World War 2, the C.A.B. had given C & S a route to Houston, and immediately after the war, added a northeastward extension to Detroit, which the airline opened on 1 June, 1945. It thus covered a broad stretch of territory from the Great Lakes to the Gulf of Mexico. In June 1946, C & S DC-4s entered service, and, on 1 November of the same year, it became the first airline to put into effect a route awarded by President Truman in the momentous Latin American Case. This was from New Orleans to Havana, and in August 1948 a further penetration into the Caribbean saw C & S serving Caracas, Venezuela. Lockheed Constellations replaced DC-4s on the main domestic routes in October 1948, and on the international routes in December. Even though this latter network was extended to include San Juan on 10 January, 1953, the airline was unable to survive independently, and negotiated a merger with Delta Air Lines, completed on 1 May, 1953.

Delta Air Lines' third Douglas DC-7, N4873C, after the company's take over of Chicago & Southern Air Lines. (*Gordon S. Williams*)

In 1955, the C.A.B. weighed in with substantial route awards to Braniff and Delta, possibly to ensure that they, having absorbed two of the lesser fry, were not themselves engulfed. Both airlines were granted routes to Washington and New York in the Southwest—Northeast Case, Braniff starting service on 15 February, 1956, from Dallas to New York, via Memphis, Nashville, and Washington. Delta entered the same northeast market on 1 February, and also extended its network southwestwards to Houston.

Another much-travelled route during this period was New York—Boston. American Airlines held a monopoly on the service for many years,

Northeast Airlines began Boston—New York DC-3 services on 1 May, 1945. N19428, illustrated, was an aerodynamically-improved example with full undercarriage doors.

but this was ended on 12 June, 1944, when the C.A.B. allowed the entry of Eastern Air Lines and Northeast Airlines into this important market. Eastern began flights in November of that year, and Northeast started on 1 May, 1945, using DC-3s.

The Boston—New York route was big business compared with Northeast's former operations, and it made a brave showing, scheduling nine daily flights at first, increasing to sixteen return flights in November. American, however, regarded this route as one of its preserves and from April 1946 began twenty return flights daily, of which fifteen were nonstop. Northeast bought three DC-4s from PCA and introduced them on 15 May, 1946; but they were no match for American's strength, and the smaller company's fortunes declined. The interesting point about this example of intense competition is the importance placed on a route only 188 miles long, which by orthodox airline economic calculations is unattractive. But American's action was as aggressive in this case as on the 2,500-mile transcontinental route.

New York, the commercial capital of the United States and the hub of most of the high-density air routes, is only 350 miles from Montreal, the commercial capital of Canada. Although the route between these two important cities was one of the first to be operated for passengers on a regular basis, as early as 1928 by Canadian Colonial, it had been somewhat neglected during the 1930s. Eventually, in October 1939, the airline came under new ownership by a group of investors headed by Sigmund Janas, who put new life into the company, renamed Colonial Airlines on 1 May, 1942.

On 10 August, 1945, the company was awarded a route from Washington to Montreal and Ottawa, and in May 1946 one to Bermuda, scheduled flights beginning on 1 August, 1947. In spite of these concessions, however, Colonial, like its near neighbour, Northeast, had to struggle hard to remain in business. The network was not big enough to permit efficient integration of the fleet and deployment of effort.

For five years, a battle was joined between Eastern and National to gain control of Colonial. The first proposals by National failed because a block of non-voting stock was controlled by Eastern. After several reversals—

and contradictions—of government policy, during which President Eisenhower over-ruled an Eastern/Colonial merger proposal, and the C.A.B. issued a statement favouring a Colonial/National merger, Eastern emerged as victors. Colonial was taken over on 1 June, 1956, just after completing more than 25 years operations without a single passenger fatality.

The other main entry into Canadian territory was to Toronto, American Airlines having started a service on 24 June, 1941.

Since Eddie Rickenbacker took over Eastern Air Lines on 22 April, 1938, it had become by far the most important airline in the East. In 1939 services had started to San Antonio and Brownsville, on the Mexican frontier. In March 1940 Douglas DSTs were introduced on a sleeper service between New York and Houston. But the main effort was directed at providing more flights to Miami, quickly becoming America's leading winter vacation resort. By March 1941 Eastern was scheduling six daily services, the fastest in 8¼ hr, with two stops over the 1,100-mile route.

Eastern's comfortable monopoly position on the New York—Miami route was broken on 19 February, 1944, when National Airlines was awarded the Jacksonville—New York segment. The Florida-based airline had hitherto been confined to local operations almost entirely within the State of Florida, and was hardly ready for this substantial addition to its network. When the New York service was opened in October 1944, the aircraft allocated to the route were Lockheed L.18 Lodestars, National's flagships at the time, but obviously too small for the traffic on such an important route.

Nevertheless, encouraged by nonstop authorizations, National actually began to set the pace by introducing the four-engined DC-4s on a direct over-water route from Miami to New York on 14 February, 1946. Eastern followed shortly afterwards. In 1947 the competition had intensified to six nonstop National DC-6 services against a similar number with Eastern's Constellations. Then followed an almost disastrous interlude, from National's point of view. First, in November 1947, its first-line aircraft, the DC-6s, were grounded (as were all others of this type), and in February 1948 a pilots' strike began which continued until November, when the C.A.B. made it clear that the very existence of the airline was at stake.

The C.A.B.'s action in breaking Eastern's monopoly on the 'Gravy Run' from New York to Miami provided a significant case study illustrating the benefits of competition. It also remains as an example of judicious timing and use of the route-awarding authority invested in the Board. First of all, there had to be proof that the traffic was large enough to sustain two operators. Secondly, the new operator had some stake in the market served, and the choice of National, already serving Florida with local services, was therefore logical. Thirdly, as a by-product rather than a sole reason for its action, the C.A.B. probably saved National from extinction, for it might well have found itself struggling for survival after the exceptional post-war traffic had settled down to normal growth rates.

National became a rival to Eastern on another important route as a

National Airlines' Douglas DC-7B N6202B. Main markings were dark blue and red.

result of a C.A.B. order dated 19 February, 1948, when the Florida operator was given permission to serve the Washington—New York corridor, subject to certain restrictions. Meanwhile the popularity of Miami and other Florida resorts was enough to provide sufficient loads for concentrated effort on the main north—south route. Eastern introduced Super Constellations on 17 December, 1951, and added the L.1049C series of the successful Lockheed aeroplane late in 1953. National replied with DC-7 service on 15 December, 1953, and both airlines later used the developed version of this Douglas type, the DC-7B.

After twelve years of straight competition between the two rivals, the C.A.B. authorized a third, Northeast Airlines, in September 1956. Two of the ingredients justifying the choice were in evidence; Northeast had a substantial stake in the local traffic patterns at the northern end of the route, and New York—Miami was a natural extension southwards, albeit a dramatic revolution in the route structure. Also, the move gave Northeast a new lease of life and hope for the future, including the expectation of joining the ranks of non-subsidized airlines through being able to operate aircraft over stage distances long enough to reduce the system's average operating costs per seat-mile. Unfortunately, the third and probably the main ingredient appeared to be in short supply. This was the guarantee of sufficient traffic to permit the addition of a third carrier without damaging the fortunes of the two already operating. A spectacular traffic growth rate, showing signs of outstripping the ability of the existing airlines to provide the capacity, would have been ample justification. But Northeast discovered that there was insufficient Florida traffic left over by the veterans on the route in a traffic situation where the annual growth rate was slowing down. This was a good example to demonstrate that the public benefits of competition are normally achieved by the rival efforts of two, and no more than two, operators on the same route.

Eastern Air Lines also met strong competition on another of its main holiday routes, that from Chicago to Florida, which it held as a Grandfather Route through a connection at Jacksonville. Shortly after National made its challenge on the New York service, Delta Air Lines was granted entry into Miami from Chicago, after a series of route extensions which would have met with approval from Walter F. Brown in his heyday. Modest additions to Delta's original east–west route from Charleston to Dallas had been made in 1941, to Cincinnati and Savannah; and New Orleans was added in 1943. But all these were overshadowed in July 1945 by the award of a route southwards to Miami, with an extension of the Cincinnati service northwards to Chicago.

Delta opened this service, soon to be the main trunk route of the system, on 1 December, 1945, at a frequency of four daily flights, using DC-3s which made six en route stops. DC-4s began a nonstop service in November 1946, and there ensued a case-book chronology of competition through equipment standards. Eastern Air Lines added DC-4s to match Delta's in January 1947 and put Constellations on the route in June. Delta retaliated in December 1948 with DC-6s. Later, Eastern introduced Super Constellations, and Delta added DC-7s on 1 April, 1954. This was a good example of a comparatively small airline establishing itself in an important national travel market, transforming its route pattern within only a few years, and providing the spur of competition to one of the Big Four.

A developed Super Constellation, one of Eastern Air Lines' L.1049G type—N6235G.

The rate of Delta's expansion increased even further when new services to New York and Washington began on 1 February, 1956, and when, together with National Airlines, it was granted coast-to-coast route authority in the Southern Transcontinental Case on 11 March, 1961.

Western Sticks It Out

The only Domestic Trunk carrier based on the Pacific Coast, Western Airlines, was not so fortunate as Delta, National, and Capital, when it came to hand-outs from the C.A.B. Even when a good route was awarded (such as Los Angeles—Mexico City), political disagreement prevented its inauguration. Furthermore, internal dissension caused a number of strikes; and financial difficulties forced the sale of one of its best routes.

Faced throughout with stiff competition from United in most of its densest markets, Western did well to survive the first decade or so after World War 2.

Although the previous history of Western has been covered in earlier chapters, a brief recapitulation of the painstaking reconstruction of a once-great airline from the ashes of the 1934 route allocations and mail awards is perhaps appropriate at this point. Western started with only one route, from Los Angeles to Salt Lake City, via Las Vegas. It bought National Parks Airways in 1937 to extend the route to Montana. This formed its Grandfather Route network, but a group of stockholders almost sold this to United in 1939, and only the Civil Aeronautics Board's over-ruling of the Examiner's recommendation saved Western from extinction. 1943 saw the acquisition of Inland Air Lines, and a further extension was thus achieved eastwards from Great Falls, Montana, to Huron, S. Dakota, via Cheyenne and Rapid City. Theoretically, Western had a route from California to Huron, but it was so circuitous that no passenger could be expected to fly by Western between the two termini, and the points served were low traffic generators.

Gradually, the California airline began to rebuild, concentrating for a while on the corridor route between the two big population centres of the west, Los Angeles and San Francisco. Traditionally United Air Lines territory, this monopoly was broken during World War 2 when, first, TWA was authorized to compete in May 1943, and then Western in 1944. Beginning in May of that year, the latter was operating twelve return nonstop flights daily by September 1946.

On 20 March, 1945, the C.A.B. awarded to Western a nonstop route from Los Angeles to Denver, which the airline began in April 1946 with DC-4s, having claimed the first U.S. domestic service with that type on 18 January, 1946. When the award was made, United Air Lines had protested vigorously, and argued that, as a regional operator, Western would be too inexperienced to tackle such a route, with its stringent operating requirements over the Rocky Mountains. This was more than a case of a big company underestimating the capabilities of a small one; it was the result of a careful analysis of aircraft costs, and United's submission that a fleet of four DC-4s, expensively modified for this special route, was too small to be viable. And so it proved. Western ran into severe financial difficulties, and had to negotiate the sale of the precious Los Angeles—Denver route to United Air Lines.

Western was able to concentrate on its remaining routes, together with a new coastal extension northwards from San Francisco to Portland and Seattle, awarded on 19 May, 1947. The meandering route to Huron was also extended to Rochester, Minnesota, and, more important, to Minneapolis/St Paul. On 9 April, 1952, the C.A.B. gave its approval to the complete absorption of Inland Air Lines, which had hitherto been operated as a division of Western; then at the end of the same year, the Board approved the closing of the gap between Salt Lake City and Rapid City,

N93117, one of Western Airlines' red and white Douglas DC-6Bs.

thus permitting one-carrier direct service from Los Angeles to Minneapolis. Early in 1953, five DC-6Bs were put into service on the West Coast and California—Minnesota routes and Western introduced its famous *Champagne* flights in June 1954. On 14 November, 1955, in the historic Denver Case, a route from San Francisco to Denver, via Reno and Salt Lake City, was awarded, and Western built its fleet up to a respectable size.

During this period, Western's aspirations to become an international operator were continually frustrated. Although awarded a route from Los Angeles to Mexico City on 17 May, 1946, service was not started until 15 July, 1957, with DC-6Bs, following protracted negotiations with the Mexican Government. At the northern extremity of its straggling route in Montana, an extension just across the Canadian frontier to Lethbridge had been operated since March 1941, but although the C.A.B. extended this to Calgary and Edmonton in 1946, the Canadian Government did not give its permission until 30 April, 1950.

The only other Domestic Trunk airline in the west was Continental Airlines, headed by Robert F. Six, and based at Denver. During the first twenty years after its re-establishment in 1934, its activities were even more

Continental Airlines' Douglas DC-7B N8210H *City of Chicago*.

modest than those of Western. After World War 2, the first noteworthy event was the purchase of Pioneer Air Lines on 1 April, 1955, but this did little more than turn Continental into a large Local Service carrier in everything but official designation.

This image was abruptly changed when the Denver Case was announced on 14 November, 1955. Continental was awarded a Chicago—Los Angeles route, via Kansas City and Denver, and service was started on 28 April, 1957, using Douglas DC-7Bs. Simultaneously with this vital route award, Continental ordered propeller-turbine and jet aircraft in addition to the DC-7Bs, and completely transformed the shape of the airline within a few short years.

Interchange Services

In the rapidly expanding airline world of the post-war period, there were a number of situations in which both the carriers and the regulatory authority came to terms with reality and decided that some compromise would have to be made with the sacred principles of competition. There were certain markets where the absence of single-carrier service caused considerable inconvenience to the travelling public. On the other hand, the volume of traffic in these markets was not sufficient to justify competitive service, and also conflicted with the C.A.B. policy at the time on the airline route structures.

Accordingly, between 1948 and 1955, airlines paired off to meet special needs by setting up interchange agreements. These were analogous to railway practice under which a company could obtain access to off-route cities by obtaining permission to operate its trains over the tracks of another. The airlines met the case by an exchange of equipment, the two partners normally taking turns to operate aircraft for agreed periods over each other's sections of the interchange route.

Domestic interchange routes are summarized in Table 18 (*See page 613*), which shows how the majority of them became redundant when, at varying times, the C.A.B. reviewed complete travel markets and made extensive route awards parallel to the interchanges. The practice has also been copied in the international field.

The Second Line

When the trunk airlines turned to four-engined equipment in 1946 and began to dispense with refuelling stops on many of their longer routes, the DC-3s which the new aircraft replaced were relegated to more humble rôles. Local Service airlines had not yet been established as a class, and the Trunk operators still served hundreds of comparatively small cities. Under their coveted C.A.B. certificates, all these points had to receive service, unless specifically exempted by the Board. Although exemptions were sometimes granted, every one had to be argued separately, and wholesale suspension of trunkline service on many feeder routes was not

First U.S. operator of the Martin 2-0-2 was Northwest Airlines. Illustrated is NC93047.

to come into effect until the Local Service airlines had themselves been established for many years.

While in many cases the trunk carriers were glad to be relieved of unremunerative stations on their extensive route networks, preferring to concentrate on the major sources of passenger traffic at the big cities, some airlines valued their secondary networks as a traffic-generating asset, and took steps to retain them and to make them profitable. The replacement of the ageing DC-3 appeared to be an obvious objective in the search for greater efficiency.

Two manufacturers, Convair and Martin, developed aircraft specifically for the secondary airline rôle. Both had been prominent manufacturers of flying-boats, and now turned to landplanes in an attempt to share some of the post-war civil airliner business, heavily dominated by Douglas and Lockheed. Martin appeared to take the lead at first, its short-haul design, the Martin 2-0-2, making its first flight on 22 November, 1946, four months before that of the rival Convair CV-240. Substantial orders were placed, and Northwest Airlines became the first U.S. airline to operate a post-war twin-engined airliner, in November 1947. Unfortunately, the type suffered a setback when a structural deficiency in the wing was revealed by

TWA's first Martin 4-0-4, N40401 *Skyliner Baltimore*. (*TWA*)

an accident in 1948. All Martin 2-0-2s were withdrawn from service and returned only after considerable strengthening and re-engining. These were called 2-0-2As, and went into service with TWA on 1 September, 1950.

The Martin 2-0-2 was a great disappointment for its manufacturers. Not only did the large order book melt away, but United Air Lines and others which had ordered a later variant, the Martin 3-0-3, also withdrew their support.

Martin managed to salvage something from the ruins of a promising project by producing a pressurized and otherwise further improved version of the basic design, the Martin 4-0-4. TWA and Eastern together bought 100 of this type, starting service on 5 October, 1951, and in January 1952, respectively. Eastern, particularly, had good reason to be satisfied with its choice, retaining them in service on its secondary routes for ten years, after which they gained a new lease of life with some of the Local Service airlines.

Eastern Air Lines' first Martin 4-0-4, N440A. The falcon on the tail was red. EAL's *Silver Falcon* service began in January 1952. (*The Glenn Martin Company*)

The Convair CV-240 was sponsored by only one of the major Big Four, American Airlines, which originally ordered 100 (later reduced to 75) in 1945. United Air Lines had chosen the Martin 3-0-3, but even when this aircraft was unsuccessful following its first flight on 3 July, 1947, the company did not immediately join American in its choice. Indeed, a United study conducted in 1949 showed that, in spite of its apparent obsolescence, the trusty old DC-3 was actually operating at an average load factor of 54·6 per cent, more than three points higher than the pre-war peak in 1941.

American put the Convair CV-240, or the Convair-Liner as it became known, into service on 1 June, 1948, and it was an immediate success. It carried 40 passengers at a cruising speed of 235 mph and was a perfect running mate for the four-engined Douglases which formed American's first-line fleet. Western Airlines followed American on 1 September, 1948, and three other domestic trunk carriers, as well as Pan American, also became Convair-Liner operators.

United eventually had to depart from its loyalty to the DC-3, as the break-even load factor was rising to impossible heights, and the F.A.A.

NC94219 *Flagship Newark*, one of American Airlines' large fleet of Convair CV-240s, over Washington. (*American Airlines*)

Western Airlines' Convair CV-240 NC8403H, with ventral airstairs. (*Gordon S. Williams*)

One of Northeast Airlines' Convair CV-240s, N91237.

was also becoming restive about the safety standards, operating procedures, and weights of what was basically a 1933 design. On 20 February, 1951, therefore, United ordered 30 Convair CV-340s, a straightforward stretch of the CV-240. With up-rated engines, it could carry 44 passengers and could use more airports than the CV-240, notably United's key stations of Denver and Cheyenne, where aircraft habitually suffered from altitude problems. Braniff actually became the first Convair CV-340 operator, starting service on 1 November, 1952, with United following on 16 November. Subsequently other airlines swelled the growing number of Convair-Liner adherents.

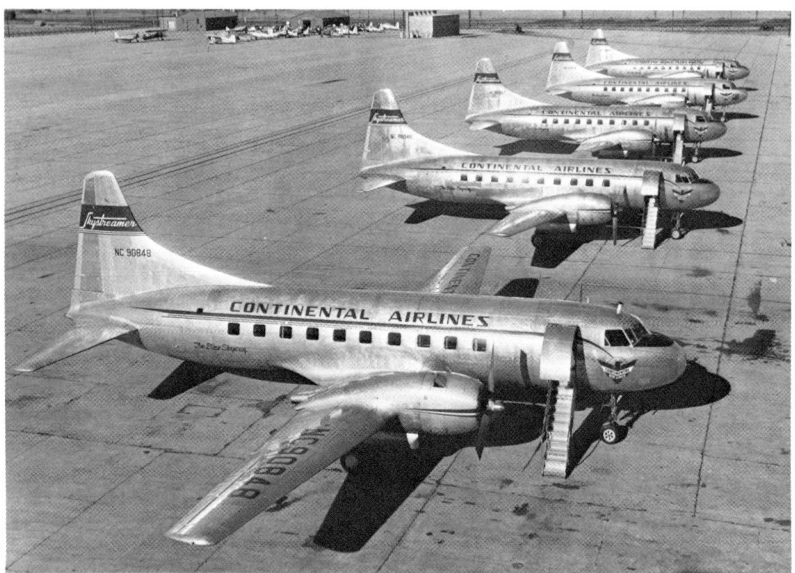

The fleet of five Convair-Liner CV-240s acquired by Continental Airlines in 1948. These aircraft have forward airstairs on the starboard side and each bears the title *The Blue Skyway* on the rear fuselage. *Skystreamer* appears on the fin stripe.

Further development of the basic type continued, and the Convair company did well to hold off a stiff foreign challenge. Although the promising British Airspeed Ambassador did not achieve worldwide success, the Vickers Viscount, thanks to its revolutionary powerplant, threatened to sweep the board. Convair produced the CV-440, or Metropolitan, whose improvement in load-carrying, performance, and passenger acceptance—it was noticeably quieter—was just enough to compete with the Viscount and continue to sell in the face of the new generation. Continental Airlines placed the Convair CV-440 into service on 1 April, 1956, but fewer U.S. airlines ordered the last of the line than did foreign flag carriers.

Vickers and the Viscount won much of the world's market for mainline short-haul airliners after British European Airways first put them into service in April 1953. Convair was reluctant to embark on an expensive

Braniff International Airways was the first airline in the world to operate the Convair CV-340, in November 1952. N3414 is seen in Braniff's red, white and blue livery. *(Gordon S. Williams)*

United Air Lines' Convair CV-340 with forward airstairs. The aircraft bears the name *Mainliner San Diego* but is believed to have been named *Fresno* at one period. *(United Air Lines)*

Convair CV-340 N4809C with Delta-C & S markings. *(Gordon S. Williams)*

Interior of a Continental Airlines Convair CV-340.

re-engining programme with propeller-turbine powerplants; and when it did, with Napier Elands in 1959, this turned out to be a costly failure. Paradoxically, after a further passage of time, the Convair fuselage was eventually married with propeller-turbines and was highly successful, the only example in modern times of a re-engined civil airliner achieving good sales in its own right.

Tighter Disciplines

Reference has already been made earlier in this chapter to President Truman's Special Board of Inquiry into Air Safety at the end of the disastrous year 1947. The Civil Aeronautics Authority, responsible for safety regulations of aircraft, navigation, and flying crews, came in for much criticism, in line with public instinct. Burdensome restrictions imposed by the Authority were condemned as unnecessary bureaucracy; but the C.A.A. got most of the blame when the crashes occurred.

The problem was serious. The war had inspired dramatic advances in technology, and the airlines found themselves in possession of flying equipment with far higher cruising speeds and in greater numbers than in pre-war days. Even more critical was the increased congestion at airports, coupled with faster approach speeds of the post-war airliners. To complicate further an already difficult matter of control, private flying began to expand in popularity at an unprecedented rate, adding to the saturation of air space.

The C.A.A. had little control of many aspects of flying behaviour which were a legacy from the pioneer years. The tradition of relying implicitly on the pilot's judgement died hard, and there was a natural reluctance on the part of flying crews to surrender their responsibilities to ground control, or to submit to what appeared to be unnecessary regulations imposed as an irritant by Washington officials who had no true knowledge of flying. Nevertheless, some of the causes of fatal crashes gave reason for alarm. In the early years after World War 2, there were cases of accidents when, for example, a crew member should have been wearing glasses, or he shut down the wrong engine, or let an aircraft run completely out of fuel, and there was one case of a pilot mistaking the lights of a slow-moving train for the runway lights.

An extreme example to illustrate the lack of co-operation between pilots and regulatory authority is one of a chartered DC-3 which took-off with ice and frost on the wings, with air temperature and dew point at 29 deg F, and overloaded by 1,500 lb. The pilot took-off in spite of the pleadings of two C.A.A. officials from the control tower and subsequently crashed. The C.A.A. men were powerless to refuse clearance when the pilot insisted on his rights within the existing regulations.

Gradually, regulations were tightened up. The C.A.A. imposed absolute minima of 200 ft altitude and ½-mile visibility for ILS (Instrument Landing System) approaches by scheduled airlines. The use of flight recorders was made mandatory, together with terrain indicators showing altitudes of 2,000 and 1,000 ft above the ground. Rules controlling visual flying procedures were changed, and continuous flying hours were restricted. Harsher penalties were imposed for breaches of discipline, and this provoked conflict with the Air Line Pilots' Association (ALPA).

The C.A.B. added to the problems of airline management by putting a firmer grip on reservations and booking procedures, and penalizing excesses of over-booking or infringements in selling tickets at illegal discount prices. At the nation's biggest traffic hub, New York, the Port of New York Authority closed down the Newark Airport on 11 February, 1952, following three crashes and 119 deaths, a drastic solution which, however, served to publicize the depth and magnitude of the increasing operational hazards stemming from technological complexity.

The authorities knew that in the areas around the busiest airports there was always a potential danger and did their best to eliminate unnecessary risk-taking. The airlines, for their part, accepted the growing list of restrictions at airports and in metropolitan zones as beneficial. As soon as one loophole in control was eliminated, however, other dangers arose. Evidence mounted to demonstrate that the air space above the United States was beginning to need even more stringent control.

Senator Mike Monroney described the air space situation by calling it 'almost as dangerous as a busy intersection at which the red lights were supervised by one agency and the green lights by another'. A more precise analogy in respect of some of the busier airlanes would have been to compare them with intersections with no lights, yet without speed limitation. Sooner or later, the laws of probability caught up with events and on 30 June, 1956, a United DC-7 and a TWA Super Constellation collided over Arizona, killing 128 people. No sooner had the C.A.A. established an airway in the offending area than on 31 January, 1957, a DC-7 and a Northrop F-89 jet fighter—both fortunately on test—collided. Tragically, some of the debris dropped in a school yard, killing two children, and only then did the C.A.A. demand that test flying should be carried out in sparsely populated and light air-traffic regions.

But still the toll of tragedy continued. Yet another DC-7 and an F-100 Air Force fighter collided near Las Vegas on 21 April, 1958. The report on the accident revealed almost unbelievably that the C.A.A. control tower at Las Vegas and the military Air Force base only six miles away were not in contact and maintained no co-ordination of flight data.

By this time there were almost 2,000 commercial airliners flying the nation's air routes (*See Table 19, page 614*). To relieve apprehension at the prospect of compounded technical problems when the new jet airliners arrived on the scene, comprehensive measures were taken to reconstruct the whole edifice of airway control, and most important, to co-ordinate civil and military aviation activities.

The F.A.A.

In 1955 a study group had examined possible improvements and, on the submission of a report on 10 May, 1957, under the direction of E. P. Curtis, the Airways Modernization Act of August 1957 (Public Law 133) established the Airways Modernization Board. Although the A.M.B. was short-lived, it was the beginning of a new era of sensible control of the nation's airspace. It identified separate zones for civil and military flying and, among other improvements, created three 40-mile wide transcontinental airways at between 17,000 and 22,000 ft altitude. On 23 August, 1958, the Federal Aviation Act (Public Law 726) went into effect, creating the Federal Aviation Agency (F.A.A.) and cancelling the Air Commerce Act of 1926, the Civil Aeronautics Act of 1938, and the Airways Modernization Act of 1957 all in one step. On 1 January, 1959, the F.A.A. absorbed the functions and personnel of the C.A.A. and the A.M.B., as well as some of the duties performed by the C.A.B. The C.A.B., however, continued to act as the independent agency responsible for the economic regulation of the airlines, as well as for determining the probable cause of aircraft accidents.

The first Chairman of the F.A.A. was Gen E. R. 'Pete' Quesada, the former chairman of the Airways Modernization Board, now superseded. He had served under President Eisenhower when the latter was in command of Allied Forces in Europe, and brought with him a formidable record of military achievement and reputation for organization. His stricter attitude towards civil air regulations was resented by some, but a weaker hand could have led to catastrophe if the United States had entered the jet age with an indecisive administration.

Quesada's main target for improvement was in flying skill and discipline. He instituted intensified training programmes, stricter inspections at more frequent intervals of flying ability, and stringent medical standards. These new rules were imposed on airline and private pilots alike, and the F.A.A. was especially concerned with the cavalier attitude shown by many private owners. Although this policy led to a running fight between Quesada and both ALPA and the Aircraft Owners and Pilots Association (AOPA), there was little opposition by ALPA to the introduction of airborne radar as a mandatory item of airliner equipment.

Barely twenty years after the issue of Grandfather Rights in 1938, the United States airline industry now stood poised for a new revolution, against which the transition from twin-engined to four-engined aircraft seemed trivial by comparison. The airlines themselves undertook enormous programmes of development and reorganization in preparation for the new jet airliners. Fortunately for them, the creation of the F.A.A., involving matters of safety, aircraft certification, pilot licensing, air navigation and air traffic control, coincided with the beginning of the jet age. The ability of the U.S. airline industry to take the jets in its stride is due in no small fashion to the foresight shown by Congress in strengthening and rationalizing the powers of government agencies responsible for the rules of the air.

Douglas DC-4s formed an important part of Pan American's post-war fleet. Illustrated is N88951 *Clipper Racer*. (*Pan American World Airways*)

CHAPTER FOURTEEN

Post-war International Boom

End of a Monopoly

Throughout the 'thirties, Pan American Airways held a complete monopoly over all U.S. international air routes. Under the visionary leadership of Juan Trippe, it had steamrollered its way through Latin America and had conquered the oceans. Trippe always found a ready solution to fit each problem. In his advance to Buenos Aires, the opposition was swept aside by astute political manipulation in obtaining traffic rights. At the same time Pan Am was protected by the Postmaster General's benevolent attitude towards the idea of a single American flag carrier. In pioneering flying over the oceans, first the Pacific, then the Atlantic, Pan American challenged the United States industry to produce the long-range equipment necessary for the task. It then applied the results of an assiduous programme of research and survey towards the goal of exploiting fully the capabilities of the winners of successive aircraft specifications. The airline had no active challengers until the end of the decade, but its record came under critical scrutiny from some Government quarters.

Postmaster General Brown had given Pan American a valuable quasi-subsidy by awarding generous mail payments for long-haul South American routes in 1929, and these were surprisingly perpetuated after the Air Mail Scandals of 1934. Continued high profits led the Civil Aeronautics Authority to investigate the airline's mail revenue, and the Postmaster General's annual report for 1940 disclosed that since 1929 the U.S. international flag airline had received more than $47,000,000 in mail payments, compared with $60,000,000 paid to all the other U.S. airlines combined. The latter, however, had flown more than eight times as many passenger-miles to achieve their total.

Pan American could—and did—defend its position by pointing out that no personal gain came from this high mail revenue, as the stockholders earned an average of only 2½ per cent in dividends, taken throughout the period. Furthermore, in ploughing back these earnings into development, the company had made the United States the undisputed leaders in long-distance international air transport. Its techniques in navigation, weather reporting, radio communications, ground handling, and maintenance were object lessons for the world to follow. Above all, the constant demands made on U.S. manufacturers had inspired them to produce flying-boats which were supreme in their class. Pan American had also played a leading part in the sponsorship of long-range landplanes which were to dominate the world's air routes after World War 2 and provide the United States with a priceless export market.

Nevertheless, during the debate over the mail payments, a number of issues were raised which undermined Pan American's position of supremacy. Few denied the value of its vision, courage, and ability. Neither did anyone doubt that the high prices spent on the best equipment were justified, although the unpredictable manner in which Trippe had appeared to change his favours indiscriminately between the aircraft manufacturers drew some criticism. But the debate brought into prominence the principle of competition, which was the guiding force behind all U.S. industrial and commercial thought. Thus, in the face of the first challenge by a U.S. carrier on a transocean route, Pan American found itself battling against inbred instinct as well as the facts of the case.

American Export Airlines

American Export Lines, a shipping company, had developed a successful freight and mail business to Europe. In November 1936 it started seriously to think about using aeroplanes for passenger services as a means of competing effectively with superior European ships. Preliminary studies showed such promise that in April 1937 American Export Airlines was incorporated, and application was made to the government for a transatlantic route, and in September 1938 a Consolidated PBY-5 flying-boat was ordered for survey purposes.

On 9 May, 1939, American Export Airlines applied to the newly-formed

C.A.B. for a certificate covering transatlantic routes to England and France, having shifted its ground slightly on its geographical objectives. In the summer of 1939 three transatlantic survey flights were completed by the PBY-5. In October the C.A.B. began its hearings but deferred a decision because of the outbreak of war in Europe. The airline continued its campaign, amending its application to include Lisbon and some Mediterranean points, and initiating in December a preliminary study with Vought-Sikorsky for three VS-44 Excalibur flying-boats.

American Export found many allies in various agencies who approved of the principle of competition. The Post Office moved away from the chosen instrument policy; the President was known to support competition; the Civil Aeronautics Act specifically provided for 'competition to the extent necessary to assure the sound development of an air transportation system properly adapted to the needs of foreign and domestic commerce'. Assertions that foreign airlines would compete effectively with Pan American were easily refuted by comparisons between U.S. and foreign civil transport aircraft. The European aircraft industry, particularly the British, were preoccupied with wartime demands. They were also obsessed with the idea of developing their Old World colonial routes as the prime consideration controlling aircraft range specifications. Even the U.S. Navy, hitherto a great friend of Pan American, felt that competition would do nothing but good.

NX41880, American Export Airlines' first Vought-Sikorsky VS-44 Excalibur flying-boat with U.S. flag on the bow. (*Sikorsky Aircraft*)

The long-term implications of the vital decision which the C.A.B. had to make were neatly summarized by Harlee Branch, a former Post Office official in charge of air mail and later a member of the Civil Aeronautics Authority: 'I feel that if this company (Amex) is thrown out with the resultant loss of somewhere between two and three million dollars, it will be a long time before another company will come in and invest . . . on the chance of being authorized to operate a service, and it will probably close the door to any additional service across the Atlantic.'

The President's proclamation of 4 November, 1939, declared Britain and France as a Combat Zone, and as Italy entered the war in June 1940, the only European air gateway was neutral Lisbon, hardly a major traffic hub. Arguments on the need for competition in the interests of 'public convenience and necessity' were therefore academic; but everyone con-

American Export Airlines' VS-44 NX41880 with the company's badge on fin and wingtip. (*Sikorsky Aircraft*)

cerned realized the importance of the fundamental issues. Fifteen months after American Export Airlines' application, and after 4,000 pages of testimony occupying 37 days of hearings, the Civil Aeronautics Board made one of the most important route decisions in its entire history. On 15 July, 1940, the President approved the verdict giving American Export a seven-year temporary authority to operate to Lisbon.

The Board took the opportunity of pointing out the important distinction between regulation and competition. Using the experience of the Interstate Commerce Commission as a precedent, it recalled that regulation had prevented abuse but had not encouraged development of the railways. The arrival of buses, airlines, and motor vehicles, however, stimulated the railways into improving their services.

Another fundamental issue was that of control by another common carrier. Section 408 of the Civil Aeronautics Act stated that 'it shall be unlawful . . . for any common carrier . . . to acquire control of any air carrier in any manner whatsoever'. In its decision in the American Export Case, the C.A.B. singled out the word 'acquire' as all-important, stating that this clause of the Act did not prevent another common carrier *starting* an airline.

Pan American Airways challenged this latter aspect of the case and carried it to the United States Court of Appeals, with the result that American Export Lines had to reorganize its corporate structure to create its airline as a separate company. This faced new financial problems and much depended on the award of a mail contract. The granting of American Export's modest request of $1,200,000 in mail pay from the Senate Appropriations Committee should have been a formality. The President, the C.A.B., the Post Office, the Departments of State, War, Justice, and Navy all approved of American Export Airlines. Pan American did not—and won the argument when the Committee turned down the mail contract.

The decisions to separate American Export Airlines from its parent, and to deprive it of mail pay, effectively dampened its challenge, but the injustice was exposed within a few years, strangely enough boomeranging back on Pan American. In any case, American Export was sufficiently encouraged to confirm its order for three VS-44s, and in the summer of 1941 took steps to establish an operating base at LaGuardia Field, New York. Then came the attack on Pearl Harbor, and, on 12 January, 1942, a contract was signed with the Naval Air Transport Service to operate a wartime transatlantic route.

Eventually, on 10 February, 1942, almost five years after its first application to the U.S. Government, American Export Airlines obtained a temporary certificate to fly from New York to Foynes, Ireland, and service was duly inaugurated, on a nonstop basis, with the VS-44s on 20 June. This was maintained throughout the war, in addition to its contract services for the Navy, which were terminated on 31 December, 1944. In January 1945, American Export started operations for the Air Transport Command to Casablanca, using Douglas C-54 transports on lease from the ATC.

Political Skirmishing

The exigencies of war cast aside delicate questions of national sovereignty applied to air routes, and carriers such as Pan American, American Export, and other internationally ambitious U.S. airlines could operate overseas mainly on a tide of good will. As World War 2 began to show signs of coming to an end, however, nations with an interest in civil aviation took steps to protect their interests when the flood of post-war services burst upon the intercontinental routes. Pan American's original transocean routes had been negotiated with individual nations, each special case being the subject of some hard bargaining. But these circumstances would not necessarily apply on a world-wide scale.

The biggest possible challenge to American supremacy would have come from a united British Commonwealth policy, in which Canada, Australia, New Zealand, South Africa, and India jointly could control the world's air routes by manipulation of landing rights. Lord Beaverbrook, charged with preparing the way for post-war British civil aviation, called a conference of the British Dominions in London in October 1943. Hastily prepared, the conference broke up after two days in secret session and could only be judged a failure. Out of the ashes of this Dominions Conference, however, emerged for the first time the definition of what were subsequently to be known as the Five Freedoms of the Air. These gave an international airline the right to:

1. Fly over a foreign territory.
2. Land for refuelling, repairs, or for non-commercial purposes.
3. Carry traffic from its home country to a foreign country.
4. Pick up traffic from a foreign country destined for the home country.
5. Pick up traffic from one foreign country and carry it to another foreign country.

There was another privilege, known as cabotage, which was the right of an airline to carry traffic from point to point wholly within one foreign country. This, however, was to be a rare situation in the post-war world and, in fact, less exploited than an additional Sixth Freedom, allowing an airline to achieve the coveted Fifth Freedom by an accident of geography. When its base was strategically situated en route between two traffic-generating points in different countries, a twenty-minute stop and change of flight number could combine the Third and Fourth Freedoms into one.

Conscious of its strength as the world's leading supplier of civil airliners and easily the world's biggest civil aviation power, the United States tended to adopt what was popularly known as the Open Skies policy. This was vigorously promoted by some politicians, notably Representative Clare Booth Luce who, in a speech in Congress on 9 February, 1943, advocated American dominance in the air, and took exception to what she suspected were British intentions to keep Pan American Airways from flying where Juan Trippe wanted it to when the war was over.

Mr L. Welch Pogue, the chairman of the Civil Aeronautics Board, took a more moderate view. In a notable speech at Minneapolis on 9 April, 1943, he said: 'It would be the height of naïveté to contend that the United States desires an *open sky* primarily to improve the welfare of mankind. By the same token it would be unfair to contend that the refusal of Great Britain or any other nation to conform to our views is necessarily reprehensible. Once again we are confronted with an attempt to rationalize an international problem on the notably fallacious and dangerous theory that since the *open sky* principle would conform to the requirements of the United States, it would be acceptable to the rest of the world—regardless of any political or economic incompatibilities that may exist.'

Having digested innumerable reports and recommendations on the subject of air commerce, President Roosevelt held an important meeting at the White House on 11 November, 1943, in which he stated his views on U.S. civil aviation policy, which were partly influenced by discussions with Britain's Prime Minister, Winston Churchill. The main points were that:

i. None of the Axis Powers should participate in airline activity.
ii. Every country should control its own domestic air routes.
iii. Although Pan American was entitled to a senior place among United States overseas carriers, it was not entitled to a monopoly.
iv. Each U.S. international carrier should have a designated sphere of operation.
v. The Government should not participate in airline ownership.
vi. Subsidies were justified where a route was needed for social or political reasons but could not pay its way commercially.
vii. There should be a free interchange of air and landing rights, except for routes wholly within the territory of another nation.
viii. There would have to be international discussion on the subject, preferably under the auspices of the United Nations.

With this clear lead, diplomatic wheels began to turn and discussions were started between the United States and Britain, and many other nations joined in formal and informal talks. Pressure mounted to a point where the British were prepared to hold an international conference in London, and faced with this attempt to steal a psychological march, Adolf Berle, Roosevelt's assistant and air adviser in the Department of Commerce, issued invitations to 54 nations to attend a civil aviation conference in Chicago.

Formation of ICAO

The Chicago Conference began its first session on 1 November, 1944, and lasted until 7 December. It was attended by the top men from all the leading civil air powers. The United States delegation, led by Berle, and the British party, led by Lord Swinton, became antagonists in a complicated exercise in transport economics, international law, and practical necessity. The U.S.A. found itself in a minority and was unable to press its Open Skies policy. The problem was that neither side had considered the arguments in sufficient depth. The U.S. was inclined to regard Europe as a single political entity when it came to exchanging traffic rights, and, by demanding access to all countries indiscriminately, laid itself open to the British and other requests that European airlines should be granted wider access to U.S. cities.

Ultimately, after much bickering, the Chicago Conference produced some limited agreement on the Freedoms of the Air, involving what was known as the Transit Agreement, covering the right to overfly and to alight for non-commercial purposes at airports in foreign countries. The Conference also produced several documents, the most important being the International Convention on Civil Aviation, which provided for the establishment of an International Civil Aviation Organization (ICAO).

A great deal of wrangling ensued on Capitol Hill when the documents signed by the United States delegates went up for ratification. Discussion revolved around the issue of whether the rights of foreign carriers should be decided by treaty or by executive agreement, that is, by the President signing international contracts without consent of the Senate, in the interests of speed, safety, or secrecy. This appeared to conflict with the Civil Aeronautics Act of 1938 which stated that foreign carriers should obtain a permit from the C.A.B. Eventually, the articulate L. Welch Pogue clarified the matter by distinguishing between the State Department, which gave permission to a foreign country to allow one of its operators to land in the United States, and the C.A.B., which prescribed standards of operation.

While all this was going on, another idea was being freely canvassed which, had it been successful, could have changed the course of United States international air transport. Senator McCarran was a great protagonist for a single chosen instrument and sponsored what he called

'The All-American Flag Line Bills' in the 78th and 79th Congresses. The idea was to form a co-operative venture in which every airline could purchase stock. Unfortunately, the industry regarded the whole scheme as a Trippe gambit, aimed at neutralizing the opposition. Only United Air Lines supported Pan American. The others organized the Airlines Committee For United States Air Policy, better known as the Seventeen Airlines Committee.

McCarran dismissed the policy of regulated competition as being ineffective, if not mythical, making a neat analogy with the railways, claiming that Southern Pacific and New York Central systems were by no means competitive merely because they operated in the same country. He was on weaker ground when upholding European airline history as an example of single flag lines superseding multiple carrier systems. William Burden, Assistant Secretary of Commerce, observed that Europe had hardly produced airlines, or aircraft, to match those of the United States, which had been the product of competition.

McCarran also tried to use shipping statistics to support his case but found that John E. Slater, executive vice-president of American Export Airlines, knew his shipping world well enough to counter the arguments effectively. The All-American Flag Line idea received its best support from William A. Patterson, president of United Air Lines, which at that time vied with American Airlines to rank as the biggest airline in the world.

To the surprise of many in the industry, Patterson declared in 1944 that 23 aircraft would be able to carry all the North Atlantic traffic in 1955, and to dilute this meagre potential between several carriers would be pointless. This conservatism was echoed by other learned reports, including one from Curtiss which took an even gloomier view. Juan Trippe himself was quite pessimistic, stating that for many years after the war a dozen aircraft would suffice.

Former Senator Josh Lee, a new member of the Civil Aeronautics Board, dismissed these assertions, throwing doubt upon the presumption to use past history as a basis for projecting the future of a new era. 'It would have been just as logical', he said, 'to have determined how many people crossed the American desert by stage coach, projected this figure, and announced that this is the number of passengers who may be expected to cross the United States by rail.' Gen Harold L. George, head of Air Transport Command, agreed. Having organized an operation to fly almost 3,000,000 passengers, the vast majority of whom had never moved very far from their own homes, he recognized the untapped potential of air transport and thought that the magnitude of over-ocean travel in the future would 'stagger the imagination'.

The debate went on, with the labour unions for the All-American Flag Line and the pilots against it. Finally, after weighing the evidence, the C.A.B. made its decision. On 14 June, 1944, it announced that it would receive applications for international route certificates from interested promoters. Senator Josiah Bailey, who chaired the Senate Committee on the All-American Flag Line proposal, tried delaying tactics, hoping to win by default, but his cause was now lost. On 7 February, members of the Committee announced that it favoured the principle of competition. And the C.A.B. settled down to the formidable task of allocating the world's air routes to the entire United States airline industry on a fair and equitable basis. A summary is contained in Table 20, page 616.

The North Atlantic Case

The C.A.B. designated five specific areas, three Pacific and two Atlantic, with the division point at Calcutta. The subsequent hearings were called the North, Central, and South Pacific; and the North and South Atlantic Cases. By far the most important was the North Atlantic.

Trippe's solution was simple: award the route to Pan American, which held the only permanent certificate. Alternatively, award a second route certificate to American Export Airlines—Trippe reluctantly conceded that the weight of official opinion was in favour of American Export's entry into the post-war scene.

The early days of New York International Airport. The passenger terminal and control tower seen in 1947. (*The Port of New York Authority*)

Ironically, the result of Pan American's own astute political bargaining now rebounded with full force. The C.A.B. agreed that American Export Airlines must divest itself of control by its shipping parent, but there was only one direction in which the orphan could turn for help—to another powerful airline; and there was nothing in the Act which denied the right of one airline to buy another, provided that the provisions of being 'fit, willing, and able' and serving the public interest were preserved. Thus, John Slater of American Export and Ralph Damon of American Airlines began to negotiate. It was a natural choice. United Air Lines had decided not to spread its wings internationally, and Transcontinental & Western (TWA), under the direction of Howard Hughes, believed that it had the resources, ability, and a good case, without the help of American Export.

After hearing other briefs from domestic airlines such as Pennsylvania-

Central and Northeast, the C.A.B. made its decision on 1 June, 1945, announcing that both American Export and TWA would be granted the right to join Pan American on the North Atlantic for a period of seven years. Answering protests from Pan Am, the C.A.B. summarized its case on two main issues, first that the principle of competition, already decided in the American Export case of 1940, should be upheld; second that the traditional division between domestic and international carriers, based on the wide differences between landplane and flying-boat operations, was no longer valid.

In general, American Export was authorized to serve the whole of northern Europe, north of the 50th parallel. The rest of Europe was divided between TWA and Pan Am. Both TWA and Pan Am were granted onward rights to India, the former by a generally southern route via Cairo to Bombay, the latter via Istanbul to Karachi and Calcutta. American Export and Pan Am had the right to fly to London, TWA to Paris.

Pan American, predictably, protested vigorously, mainly on the grounds that as the pioneer of services to Europe long before any other carrier had even thought of them it was entitled to a better distribution of the spoils. Accordingly, in July 1946, its certificate was amended slightly to add three more points, including Frankfurt.

American Export Airlines took immediate steps to exploit its new rights. On 1 June, 1945, the C.A.B. had approved a merger with American Airlines Inc (Transatlantic Division). In September six C-54 Skymasters (DC-4s) were delivered from the Surplus Property Board and the first survey flights made. On 24 October, 1945, American Export Airlines made the first commercial scheduled transatlantic flight by landplane, when a DC-4 flew from New York to Hurn Airport, near Bournemouth – London Airport was not quite ready to receive the new aircraft – in a record time of 14 hr 5 min. The Sikorsky VS-44s were retired.

On 10 November, 1945, American Export Airlines' name was changed to American Overseas Airlines Inc, and the merger was formally completed on 5 December. The service pattern was expanded to include Chicago, on 19 November, and Washington and Philadelphia four days later. By 26 December, AOA was scheduling daily transatlantic flights, of which five were from New York. In February 1946 weekly services began to Scandinavia and the Netherlands, and in May to Frankfurt and Berlin. In 1947 Iceland, Finland, and Scotland were added to the network, and AOA was able to announce its 15,000th Atlantic crossing on 3 September, 1947.

TWA gave due notice that its North Atlantic rivals could expect some stiff competition. Soon after American Export's first DC-4 service, a TWA L.049 Constellation made a proving flight to Paris, on 25 November, 1945. This was followed by a special flight for invited guests on 3 December, and regular New York—Paris services started on 5 February, 1946. The route was extended to Cairo on 1 April, and the Lisbon—Madrid route was opened on 1 May.

TWA began regular transatlantic Lockheed Constellation services in February 1946. This view shows the later L.749A, N6014C *Star of Delaware*. TWA markings were red. (*TWA*)

In one sense, TWA was in an even better position than American Airlines, for it could operate both its domestic and international services under the same name and without the restraints resulting from a separated corporate structure. Thus, on 3 May, 1946, a Constellation service was offered between Chicago and Cairo, via New York and European cities, without change of aircraft.

On 1 August, 1946, the C.A.B. awarded to TWA an extension of its route through southern Asia to Shanghai, where by connecting with Northwest Airlines' new route across the Pacific it could theoretically offer a round-the-world service to the travelling public.

On balance, however, 1946 was an unhappy year for TWA. Between 12 July and 20 September, 1946, the Constellations had to be grounded because of a leaking fuel system which caused some fires. The aircraft were hardly back in service before the pilots went on strike from 21 October to 15 November, 1946. In 1947, too, TWA had problems. After inaugurating a through passenger service to Bombay on 5 January and starting the U.S.A.'s first international all-cargo service, the *Shanghai Merchant*, to Cairo on 15 January, the airline was plagued with management changes at the highest level. Jack Frye, the veteran pilot who had been president of the airline since its formation, resigned, together with T. B. Wilson, the chairman, and Paul Richter, the executive vice-president.

At the end of the war there were signs that TWA was about to become involved in a world-wide chain of associated airlines, as a means of maintaining a comprehensive network in areas where it was restricted by the limitations of its international certificate. This policy was discontinued as an aggressive marketing programme, and survives only as isolated footholds in a few countries in the Middle East. TWA's overseas associates are summarized in Table 21, page 617.

Pan American actually introduced Constellations on the North Atlantic on 14 January, 1946, three weeks before TWA. American Overseas then became the third U.S. international Constellation operator on 23 June. A year later, Pan American exploited its route authority to the full by opening the world's first round-the-world service, using Constellations from New York eastwards to San Francisco, on 17 June, 1947. Strictly, of course, there was a missing link in the globe-encircling chain, but this was through Pan Am's inability at that time to fly across the U.S.A. with a revenue load. The limitation remained in effect for almost twenty years.

Pan American introduced Lockheed Constellations on North Atlantic services in January 1946. Seen here is the L.049 N88861 *Clipper Winged Arrow*. Pan Am markings for many years were very dark blue. (*Pan American World Airways*)

International Agreement and IATA

When the C.A.B. took its Atlantic decision on 1 June, 1945, this was made unilaterally in the sense that the Board had neither the authority over foreign landing rights nor of routes over foreign territory. True, the Chicago Conference had achieved some limited objective in this direction, but the whole framework of international civil air rights was as yet only loosely visualized. But the whole world recognized that the airline business was about to expand phenomenally and that international regulation was essential.

The first step was to form the International Air Transport Association (IATA)*, to be a voluntary organization whose main purpose would be to prevent airlines from practising unethical methods in rates and scheduling. In general the principle was to protect the weak from the strong, who might be tempted to try bullying methods, for example by flooding a route with excessive capacity to dilute a competitor's traffic, or by setting uneconomic rates on certain routes which could be cross-subsidized only by the larger airlines. On the other hand, the authority vested in IATA to control rates on a world-wide scale laid it open to charges of cartel methods,

* This was successor to the International Air Traffic Association founded in 1919.

and throughout its history the Association has had to watch carefully that its decisions could not be regarded as disreputable on this account.

Whatever the shortcomings, an organization of this kind was obviously necessary, and at a three-day conference held in Havana in April 1945, 41 airlines of 25 nations signed the original articles of association. Many more airlines quickly joined and soon most nations were represented. Headquarters were established at Montreal, close to PICAO, the provisional predecessor of ICAO, now getting under way.

Throughout the period immediately following the end of World War 2, there was undoubtedly a fear on the part of every nation that the United States would exert its powerful air transport strength to acquire world dominance. Only control or regulation of some kind could stop this happening. The world's civil air transport systems had broken down or suffered greatly during the hostilities. Most of Europe had been laid waste and re-establishment of an airline system was only one of many vast post-war reconstruction programmes. Aircraft manufacturers in Europe had turned their entire efforts towards producing fighter and bomber types, to the almost total exclusion of transports. On the Allied side this responsibility had been left to the United States, although there was no written agreement to this effect between Britain and the U.S., as is often alleged. Even before the war, the U.S. airline industry had sponsored civil airliners which were far ahead of Europe's best. Wartime orders for the C-54 and the military variants of the Constellation subsequently accelerated development at the very time when the British, French, German, and Italian industries had to put their designs aside.

When the war ended, the four-engined Douglas and Lockheed airliners were so in advance of possible European development that U.S. airlines could call the competitive tune and the best the European companies could do was to take their turn in placing orders for U.S. types until such time as their own battered aircraft industries were able to make up lost ground.

The Bermuda Agreement

Britain, potentially the biggest rival to the United States, was representative of Europe's attitude as a whole. Its support of the general objectives of the new IATA on fares and rates epitomised the apprehension common to almost every non-U.S. airline nation of a possible rate war. Pan American threw down the gauntlet on what it interpreted as restriction by an international cartel by announcing, late in 1945, that it would reduce the transatlantic one-way fare from $375 to $275. This brought the issue into the open and there followed a period during which the British and the Americans indulged in some unsavoury bargaining on frequency of service. On 30 November, 1945, Pan American gave way on fares and had to accept a half-share of an agreed ten frequencies a week which Britain considered was a reasonable post-war starting point.

Dissatisfaction with this arrangement, however, led to the two sides coming together in an attempt to work out a more permanent solution of the principles of rate-setting and frequency allocation. The United States and Great Britain met at Bermuda and signed a document on 11 February, 1946, which, with refinements, has since become a model for bilateral air agreements throughout the world.

The clauses of the Bermuda Agreement were, mainly, that:

1. Routes were mutually allocated by common consent on the basis of a fair exchange.
2. IATA would set rates, (a concession by the U.S.A.).
3. Fifth Freedom rights were exchanged, again on the basis of a fair exchange, (a concession by Britain).
4. Frequencies should be unlimited but subject to control by the two governments, to prevent abuse, (a concession by Britain).

Although Britain appears to have made major concessions, it did win the battle against unlimited competition which the United States airlines would undoubtedly have ruthlessly applied, given half a chance.

Examples of the exchange of routes were the British right to offer service from New York to Australia via San Francisco, and the U.S. right to offer service from London to certain points in Europe, such as Frankfurt and Rome. The British could use Hawaii, the U.S. gained access to Singapore. Later review revealed some loopholes and shortcomings, but the basic principles established at Bermuda were sound. Indeed, France lost no time in following Britain's example, and signed a Bermuda-type agreement on 27 March, 1946. Others followed, although some countries, notably Australia and India, were in no hurry.

After a little stonewalling by the remnants of the All-American Flag Line lobby, who crusaded for international co-operation by treaty rather than executive agreement, the Bermuda document was confirmed as a valid and legal contract by Attorney General Tom Clark on 18 June, 1946.

The Latin American Route Case

On 17 May, 1946, the C.A.B. announced its decision on the second major post-war international route allocation. While there was much to be said for Pan American's defence of its case on the North Atlantic, because of its pioneering rôle, Trippe's airline was on even stronger ground in the case of Latin America. This was Pan American's backyard. Throughout the 1930s an air transport empire had been carved out of the jungles and swamps by sustained and determined effort which had culminated in the establishment of an American airline whose name became a household word throughout the continent. Pan American had won a severe commercial battle against European rivals, and its success later became a priceless asset in time of war.

In spite of this apparent moral right as a sitting tenant, the Latin American Case resulted in an erosion of Pan American monopoly at least as great as on the North Atlantic. The C.A.B.'s original recommendations to the President were actually far more modest than the drastic measures which Harry Truman subsequently dealt out. He overruled the C.A.B. on four counts and, among other actions, awarded two routes to operators who had not even applied for them.

Pan American paid dearly for its failure to come to some amicable arrangement with Panagra, the jointly-owned enterprise formed in 1929 in association with the powerful W. R. Grace Shipping company. This shipping and trading company wanted to extend the Panagra route which terminated at Panama northwards to a U.S. gateway, such as Miami; but Pan Am would have none of it, believing that this would divert traffic from its own routes. The feud between the unhappy partners was well known throughout South America, and Truman believed that this was undermining U.S. prestige down the west coast of the continent.

The lucky beneficiary from the Panagra situation was Braniff Airways, which had been active in a small way by establishing a Mexican subsidiary, Aerovias Braniff, late in 1943. Services had started out of Mexico City on 4 April, 1945, connecting with Braniff's domestic system at Nuevo Laredo, and following with a Mexico City—Merida route on 1 July, 1945. Pan American regarded such activity in Mexico as sheer effrontery, having established and maintained Mexico's major airline, Compañía Mexicana de Aviación (CMA) since 1929.

President Truman, therefore, added insult to Pan American's injury by selecting Braniff for a through route from Houston to Buenos Aires, via Havana, Panama, Bogota, Quito, Lima, La Paz, and Asunción, with a branch to São Paulo and Rio de Janeiro. The intruder soon found itself in trouble. First the Mexican Government revoked Braniff's certificate on 26 October, 1946, leaving CMA, the Pan American subsidiary, in charge of trunkline affairs. Braniff then found that landing permits and operating rights were strangely difficult to obtain in the countries athwart its new international trunk route. However, in due course, Douglas DC-6s inaugurated the *El Conquistador* service from Houston to Lima on 4 June, 1948, when the company was renamed Braniff International Airways. On 8 February, service began to La Paz, Bolivia, the world's highest airport (14,000 ft above sea level) by employing a DC-3 on a connecting service from Lima. DC-4s, equipped with JATO (Jet Assisted Take Off) equipment, were introduced on 3 June. Rio de Janeiro was reached on 9 March, 1949, and Buenos Aires on 29 May, 1950, while Miami was designated a second Braniff gateway from the U.S. on 3 August, 1951.

If Braniff was the major threat to Pan American's supremacy, there were many other irritants. No less than seven companies gained access to the Caribbean and Mexican region. Colonial Airlines, for example, hitherto a comparatively small regional carrier in the northeast, was given a route to Bermuda not only from New York, but also from Washington; although the C.A.B. had originally refused the New York section, Truman was more generous.

Pan American did receive the valuable direct New York—San Juan route, later to become its densest segment, and Eastern Air Lines was given permission to fly from Miami to San Juan, which was never asked for. Chicago & Southern Air Lines won two routes southward from the co-terminals of Houston and New Orleans, one to San Juan via Havana, Port-au-Prince, and Santo Domingo, the other via Havana and Kingston to Curaçao and Caracas. Finally, National Airlines, one of the smallest domestic carriers, was granted access to Havana.

Mexican Problems

Reference has been made to the intrusion of Braniff Airways into Pan American's preserve in Mexico. The international airline posture of this country was a complex issue which was already the subject of dispute before the Latin American Case of 1946; and in fact was not solved satisfactorily until 1957.

During the C.A.B.'s consideration of the Case, there were already two U.S. sitting tenants of Mexican routes, apart from Braniff. American Airlines had obtained temporary permission from the Mexican Secretaria de Communicaciones y Obras Publicas (SCOP) on 25 October, 1940, to extend its New York—Dallas service to Mexico City, via San Antonio, Texas, and Monterrey, Mexico. C.A.B. permission was granted on 14 April, 1942, and service began on 3 September, 1942.

At the same time, Pan American Airways reinforced its position by supplementing the services operated by its Mexican subsidiary, CMA, with a route in its own name from Brownsville, Texas, to Tapachula, Mexico, on the Guatemalan frontier. Unlike the American permit, which was temporary, the Pan American authority was for 30 years.

A fourth U.S. airline gained a foothold in Mexico the following year, through acquisition of a local Mexican carrier. Believing that it could play a part in the development of civil aviation between the West Coast of the U.S.A. and Mexico, United Air Lines took a financial interest in Lineas Aereas Mineras S.A. (LAMSA) by loaning $250,000 to its owner, Gordon S. Barry, on 6 October, 1942. LAMSA's value to United lay in its route franchise, rather than in its corporate strength or volume of business. Originally founded by Barry to provide the only common carrier service to an important mine at Tayoltita, the company was habitually handicapped in sustaining operations, because of aircraft maintenance difficulties, shortage of spares, lack of airport facilities, and other attendant problems arising from trying to operate an under-capitalized airline.

When United became interested, LAMSA's main route was from Mexico City to Ciudad Juarez, via Torreon, where branch lines went to Mazatlan, on the Pacific Coast, and to Nuevo Laredo. United acquired complete control on 1 October, 1943, and changed the airline's name to Lineas

Among the aircraft operated by LAMSA was this white, green and red Boeing 247 XA-DIY *Estado de Chihuahua* (c/n 1693). This aircraft had previously served with Boeing Air Transport, United Air Lines, Western Air Express and the U.S. Army Air Force. It survived until February 1952. (*United Air Lines*)

Aereas Mexicanas S.A. In the furtherance of its plans to develop connection with its own network, United planned routes which would interconnect with LAMSA's at Nogales, Arizona. LAMSA obtained C.A.B. permission to reach Nogales, but United attempts to link up the nearest points on its U.S. network in California were never successful. Even after a further injection of United money into LAMSA, to the amount of $1,000,000 on 27 November, 1945, the Mexican subsidiary never fulfilled its promise, and eventually, on 22 July, 1952, United sold LAMSA to a group of Mexican investors for $1,230,000. The routes were absorbed by Aeronaves de Mexico; United withdrew its long-postponed application for a route to Nogales, and abandoned its ambitions in Mexico.

The reason for the failure of the United/LAMSA combination was the long and bitter wrangle between the United States and Mexican authorities over traffic rights and reciprocal services. When the C.A.B. made its Latin American decision on 17 May, 1946, the results in Mexico were largely academic, as no airline could put them into effect until a bilateral agreement was signed. Thus, Western Airlines and Eastern Air Lines, recipients of route awards from Los Angeles and New Orleans respectively, had to wait many years before starting services.

At the time, of course, Pan American officials were furious. Throughout the 1930s, Pan Am had had its own way in Mexico, and had done a wonderful job. By its support, CMA had become a model airline for Latin American countries to follow. It had begun a service to Los Angeles in September 1934, with Lockheed L.10 Electras, and had constantly improved its standard of flying equipment and passenger service, introducing DC-2s in 1937 and DC-3s in 1938. Before the Latin American Case was settled, CMA was planning to put into service three four-engined C-54s.

Now, suddenly, the Pan Am/CMA axis faced five potential competitors, Braniff, American, Western, Eastern, and United/LAMSA. The change from monopoly to competition could not have been more emphatic.

In retrospect, an objective analysis of the situation at the time suggests that the Mexican routes so heartily allocated by President Truman were symbolic of a revolution in the official Government attitude to Pan American. Hitherto Pan American had dictated affairs in the international airline field. After surviving the 1934 Air Mail scandals by a kind of special dispensation, it had become autocratic and tended to ride roughshod over opponents. Juan Trippe was a shrewd tactician who conducted his strategy in a gentlemanly way but never gave an inch, always took advantage of every opportunity, and was adept at contriving a few favourable situations himself in the furtherance of Pan American's interests. Finally, however, in the post-war Democratic administration of Harry Truman, the old order changed.

Henry Ladd Smith bluntly summarized the position in 1946: 'Pan American had fought most of the international aviation measures sponsored by such administration agencies as the C.A.B., State Department, and Commerce Department. It had done what it could to scuttle American Export Airlines as a competitor, even after the C.A.B. had designated Amex as a second international carrier. It had opposed administration doctrine and policy at Chicago and Bermuda. It backed such men as Senators Brewster, McCarran, and Bailey, who attacked the aviation course taken by the United States. It stood for monopoly against overwhelming support of competition. One of its vice-presidents . . . helped elect Mrs Clare Booth Luce to Congress, where she had become one of the administration's most publicized aviation critics.'

Pan American was unpopular with the Post Office Department, with almost all the domestic airlines, with the shipping world, and with the aircraft manufacturers. Foreign airlines resented its high-handed methods, and its action in rate-cutting had almost wrecked agreement between the U.S.A. and Great Britain. Altogether, Juan Trippe appeared to have crusaded too zealously on behalf of his airline.

At least, President Truman thought so, and with the Latin American Case, Pan American's monopolistic edifice in Latin America came tumbling down. This Case marked a watershed in the history of United States airlines, the end of an era when Pan American dwelt with the Gods and the beginning of one when it dwelt—albeit in a senior rôle—with lesser mortals.

Between 1945 and 1951 the Governments of the United States and Mexico held five series of conferences, all inconclusive, on the issue of reciprocal operating rights. The Mexicans were apprehensive about the possible domination of routes by U.S. carriers, an understandable attitude, bearing in mind the relative strength of Mexican airline resources at the time (not counting Pan American-controlled CMA). Finally, President Truman lost patience, and in 1952 withdrew his approval of the inoperative international certificates awarded by the C.A.B. in the 1946 Latin American Case.

When the Republicans took over in 1953, however, President Eisenhower reviewed the position and decided that this would be injurious to foreign relations and in a letter to the C.A.B. chairman, James R. Durfee, dated 8 March, 1957, ruled that '. . . on advice of the Attorney General, I am recognizing the validity of the certificates issued in 1946 and hereby approve them and determine that they stand unrevoked'.

The bilateral agreement between the United States and Mexico was signed on the same day and was to be effective from 5 June, 1957. Western Airlines was first off the mark, starting DC-6B service from Los Angeles to Mexico City on 15 July, 1957. Eastern Air Lines began a New York—New Orleans—Mexico City service on 23 July, with DC-7s, and added Washington as a co-terminal on 23 September. American Airlines added a nonstop route from Chicago to the Mexican capital by the end of the year.

Northwest Airlines' Douglas DC-4 N67067. (*Gordon S. Williams*)

Changes in the Pacific

A month after the historic Latin American Case was decided, the C.A.B. opened up the trans-Pacific route to a second airline. On 20 June, 1946, the C.A.B. awarded a Great Circle route to the Orient to Northwest Airlines, the President giving his approval on 1 August. As United was not interested in international routes, Northwest was the only possible alternative to Pan American. During World War 2 it had proved beyond doubt that it was fully qualified to cope with the severe climatic conditions of Alaska and the Aleutians. Traditionally serving the territory between the Great Lakes and the Pacific Northwest, the C.A.B. had given the airline an extension to New York in December 1944, thus making it a transcontinental carrier with access to the lucrative northeast market. Northwest made its first post-war scheduled flight to Anchorage on 1 September, 1946, and extended to Manila on 15 July, 1947.

Pan American could point with some justice to the pioneering efforts of the early 1930s, when Lindbergh had made his Great Circle flight to the Far East in the Sirius. This route to Tokyo was 650 miles shorter than the island-hopping route via Hawaii, and thus incurred lower end-to-end operating costs. On the other hand, the mid-Pacific route was more attractive from the passenger's viewpoint, in that the weather was normally better, and the stop at Hawaii was infinitely preferable to a stop at Cold Bay, or even Anchorage.

Pan American's pre-war route was confirmed and extended to reach Tokyo and Shanghai, points common to Northwest's new route system. There was reason to believe that in due course China and Japan would become a vast new market for air travel, based on normal demographic projections; and the route to Japan is still potentially one of the most lucrative of all U.S. international routes.

The portion of the trans-Pacific route between California and Hawaii was important enough for special consideration by the C.A.B., Hawaii being a United States territory, Presidential approval was not needed to confirm the Board's decision, made in July 1946, to award a route to United Air Lines. William Patterson of United had not shown much enthusiasm for foreign involvement, but accepted the offer of a route to Honolulu, quickly developing as a vacation resort mainly through the efforts of the Matson shipping line.

United's certificate was confined to San Francisco as a mainland gateway, service starting on 1 May, 1947. Los Angeles was not added as a co-terminal until 9 October, 1950. The delay of almost one year in beginning flights to the new destination was caused by late delivery of the Douglas DC-6. This was an improved version of the military C-54 which found itself eclipsed in performance by the Lockheed Constellation after the war. Subsequent grounding of DC-6s caused a brief suspension of United's Hawaii service from 11 November, 1947, but services were resumed soon afterwards with DC-4s leased from the Matson Navigation Company and Transocean Air Lines, both of which were unsuccessful in their bids to obtain scheduled air routes in the Pacific area.

In the reopening of hearings on the Hawaiian route, another carrier, Northwest Airlines, was granted access to Honolulu from Seattle and Portland on 29 July, 1948. Already operating to the Orient, the Hawaii route reinforced Northwest's status as a Pacific airline.

Consolation Prize

On 13 August, 1946, the C.A.B. reached its decision on the South Atlantic Route Case, and the President gave his approval three days later. Although the establishment of a route to Africa formed part of Pan American's long-term objective in constructing a worldwide network, the South Atlantic crossing was not exactly first priority. Furthermore, there was no serious opposition to Pan Am in this case, so the award represented a hollow victory. Both routes included in the award were anything but good generators of airline traffic. One crossed the Central Atlantic from New York via the Azores and reached Johannesburg, via Dakar, Monrovia, Accra, and Leopoldville. The other was a continuation of the direct San Juan service to Natal, on the northeast tip of Brazil, whence the route crossed the South Atlantic via Ascension Island, the strategically-situated speck of British territory developed as an air base during World War 2. Because of this fact, and reacting to pressure from the U.S. Government, the C.A.B.'s award reflected some concern for matters of national defence, as well as for its normal economic criteria.

Pan American could be forgiven for not sharing in the C.A.B.'s patriotic scruples. Of all the many routes awarded in the post-war share-out, only a few crumbs had gone its way off the Washington table. Bearing in mind its long history of pioneering in Latin America, and across the Pacific and Atlantic Oceans, the C.A.B. and President Truman appeared to reveal a mean streak when asked to recognize this work by giving permanent certificates and extensions. Pan American actually received little more than confirmation of route structures already carefully planned and built before the war. Much of the decline in fortunes could be blamed on a clash of political personalities, with the airline being rebuffed after exerting too much pressure, and the resultant awards were, at best disappointing, at worst insulting.

But the die was cast. Pan American had to learn to live with the new régime and with the new conditions of rivalry, both U.S. and foreign. Those who had grown up under Juan Trippe's leadership, however, were not surprised when he took forthright steps to protect his position and to resist the more ambitious attempts to usurp Pan American's traditional place of eminence as the chosen instrument of United States international policy.

Technical Leadership

If the newcomers to international routes wanted competition, Pan American was prepared to give it to them. At first, however, ways of avoiding this course of action were attempted, including a proposal to merge with TWA in 1947; but this was rejected by Howard Hughes.

Development of world routes immediately following World War 2 soon revealed patterns of traffic density with Pan American as a common denominator on the leading routes. Outstanding was the North Atlantic, where service frequency, both by United States carriers, and many other Canadian and European operators, grew to the magnitude of a shuttle operation.

For a while, the best airliner on the Atlantic route was the Lockheed L.749 (or L.049) Constellation. Elegant in appearance, superior to the Douglas DC-4 in pressurized comfort, all three U.S. airlines, Pan American, AOA and TWA at first forced the pace with the 'Connie', as it became affectionately known. Most of the leading foreign airlines were also forced to buy the Constellation, including the British flag-line, BOAC, whose resources had been so depleted by the war that it dared not risk waiting for a suitable home-built product.

First challenger to the Constellation came from the Boeing company, whose initial entry into the long-range civil airliner market had been the pre-war production of both the Boeing 314, the finest transport flying-boat ever built, and the Boeing 307 Stratoliner, so named because of its high cruising altitude for which a moderate degree of cabin pressurization was necessary. World War 2 effectively put a stop to development of these types, and Boeing became a specialist manufacturer of heavy four-engined bombers.

Pan American World Airways was the biggest user of Boeing Stratocruisers, with a total of twenty-nine. N1030V *Clipper Southern Cross* is seen here. (*Pan American World Airways*)

To support the B-29 and B-50 Superfortress bombers, Boeing developed the KC-97 tanker transport for the U.S. Air Force. In addition to building almost 900 military tankers, it produced 55 of a civil version, called the B.377 or, more familiarly, the Stratocruiser. The Stratocruiser looked as ponderous as the Constellation was graceful. It had a blunt nose and seemed to bore rather than cut its way through the air. Nevertheless, it was almost as fast as the Constellation, and, in fact, set up a number of point-to-point records. Most important, the passengers liked it, because its double-bubble double-deck fuselage arrangement allowed for a small lounge, or cocktail bar, to be fitted in the lower deck level. This was a great selling feature to passengers who liked to break the monotony of the long Atlantic crossing by a walk downstairs to the bar. Even today, veteran airline passengers reminisce about the Stratocruiser bar service much in the same way as the real old-timers recall the distant days of the promenade deck on the C-class flying-boats.

Pan American Airways ordered 20 Stratocruisers on 28 November, 1945, followed by American Overseas Airlines with an order for eight on 1 April, 1946. Pan Am was first into service, on 1 April, 1949, from San Francisco to Honolulu. New York—Bermuda followed on 15 April, then New York—London on 2 June, matched by AOA on 17 August, 1949. The only other airline to operate Stratocruisers on the North Atlantic was BOAC which, significantly, moved up into third place in the traffic ranking soon after starting service.

Other Stratocruiser airlines were United, using them on the Hawaii

American Overseas Airlines Boeing Stratocruiser N90941 *Flagship Great Britain* was renamed *Flagship Europe* and passed to Pan American as *Clipper America*. (*Boeing Airplane Company*)

run in January 1950, and Northwest Airlines, which followed suit. Both airlines were in competition with Pan American. President Truman had relented somewhat in his attitude to Pan Am for in the reopened Pacific Northwest—Hawaii Case in October 1948, the C.A.B.'s decision to give Northwest a monopoly was reversed. The Seattle airline later added Stratocruiser service on its long route to the Orient, on 28 April, 1952. Although the Stratocruiser suffered certain teething troubles, in company with every other major type of the period, its record of service was good enough to sustain it for many years, outliving other rivals. Its operating costs were slightly higher than those of the Constellation or the Douglas four-engined types, but its cocktail bar was so popular with the passengers that the airlines were loath to retire it.

Constellations nevertheless outnumbered Stratocruisers on the North Atlantic. TWA standardized its fleet on Constellations, and AOA also built up its strength in the early years with this type, introducing the *Irish Mercury* on 5 February, 1948, and the *Scottish Mercury* on 29 November of that year. TWA began an all-sleeper luxury service on 1 October, the *Paris Sky Chief* and the *New York Sky Chief*. These were the days when all the airlines were busy building a luxury image, and named services such as these, together with Pan Am's *President* and BOAC's *Monarch*, became familiar to regular transatlantic travellers.

During this period the air was undisturbed by controversial route awards on the scale of the 1945–1946 major Cases. Pan American had tidied up its network and undergone corporate reconstruction. In 1947, it restored service in the South Pacific and began flights to South Africa. But these were relatively minor developments, and even the technical competition on the North Atlantic was eclipsed in aviation news circles by speculation during the late 1940s about a possible merger between the two biggest passenger airlines on the route, Pan American and American Overseas Airlines.

The two airlines reached a tentative agreement to merge on 13 December, 1948. Four weeks previously John E. Slater had resigned as chairman of AOA. Negotiations dragged on for almost two years, until finally the C.A.B. rejected the formal merger application in May 1950. Whether or not President Truman had had a pang of conscience from his ruthless treatment of Pan American in the Latin American, North Atlantic, and North Pacific Cases will never be known. Certainly, he must have been reminded of Pan Am's fine record during World War 2, when, in 1946, he presented the Harmon Aviation Trophy to Juan Trippe, in recognition of the airline's contribution to the military success of the Allied powers 'at a time and in a manner that could not have been equalled by any other Allied agency'. Now, in an apparent complete change of

Northwest Airlines was among the few original Boeing Stratocruiser operators. The one illustrated is N74601 *Stratocruiser Manila*. (*Boeing Airplane Company*)

heart, he overruled the C.A.B. once again, this time in Pan American's favour, and on 25 September, 1950, authorized the merger with AOA.

The resultant reshuffle of route authority gave Pan American and TWA roughly equal opportunity to serve the main capitals of Europe, including all the main traffic-generating points, London, Paris, Frankfurt, and Rome. With its large fleet of Stratocruisers, Pan Am had the most commercially attractive equipment; on the other hand, TWA had the advantage of being able to integrate services between U.S. domestic and international routes. Pan American was conscious of this handicap, and constantly plied the C.A.B.—unsuccessfully—with requests for domestic authority. TWA, however, failed to exploit the full potential of through services to Europe from the many big cities on its route network within the U.S.A.

Almost like two adversaries displaying their strength before the battle, the PAA/AOA merger (which, incidentally, cost Pan American $17,450,000) had been preceded by two name changes. On 3 January, 1950, Pan American became Pan American World Airways Inc, after acquiring the assets of the Pan American Corporation; and on 17 May, 1950, Transcontinental & Western Air became Trans World Airlines Inc, neatly retaining the same initials, TWA.

For almost a decade throughout the 1950s competition in aircraft types on the North Atlantic route was intense. The introduction of a new stratum of Tourist Fares, internationally agreed by IATA, coincided with Pan American's first 82-seat DC-6B scheduled flight, to open the *Rainbow* service from New York to London on 1 May, 1952. This event, however, was overshadowed in the world's press by the epoch-making BOAC Comet 1 service from London to Johannesburg on the next day. History was later to record the initial success, beyond all expectations, of this the world's first jet airliner. Then came the tragic failure and de Havilland, builders of the Comet, paid the penalty of probing beyond the threshold of technical knowledge in high-altitude flying. But at that time, the effect of the Comet's flight was electric. The airline world beat a pathway to de Havilland's door, and Pan American ordered three Comet 3s on 20 October, 1952, the first time in history that a United States carrier had chosen a British airliner. The version of the Comet ordered by Pan Am was equipped with extra tankage to permit transatlantic capability, with stops, and was to be a prelude to further development. True to form, the U.S.

One of Pan American's 82-seat Douglas DC-6Bs, N6528C *Clipper Midnight Sun*. (*Pan American World Airways*)

airline set the pace, and BOAC did not order this series until February 1954. In the circumstances this was an unaccountable delay and, had history taken a different turn, would have allowed the American airline a clear lead in launching an Atlantic jet service.

A month after the beginning of the Tourist Fare era, which was to sustain the rapid growth of traffic between North America and Europe, the C.A.B. made permanent the route certificates originally issued on a seven-year basis in 1945. In 1953, TWA's Bombay route was extended to Ceylon. Two years later, in April 1955, a little more tidying up was applied to the

Pan American introduced Douglas DC-7Bs over the Atlantic in June 1955. The example shown is N777PA *Clipper Jupiter Rex*. (*Pan American World Airways*)

European termini, with TWA gaining access to Zürich, and Pan Am getting a route through Istanbul and Ankara.

Altogether, 1953–1955 saw Hughes' airline, with its all-Constellation fleet, make a bold effort to overhaul Pan American in the fight for passengers. On 19 October, 1953, TWA introduced the L.1049C Super Constellation, fitted with Wright turbo-compound engines developing 3,250 bhp, thus permitting considerable increases in take-off weight and payload compared with the standard versions. The airlines were now striving to attain nonstop capability between New York and the major traffic centres of Europe, particularly London and Paris. This objective supplemented the continued rivalry in schedule timing, with resultant demands on the manufacturers for improvements in cruising speed. On 15 November, 1954, Pan American introduced Stratocruisers with extra fuel tanks to achieve a nonstop eastbound crossing, and followed this with DC-7B service on 13 June, 1955. The DC-7B was fast, fitted as it was with the turbo-compound engines, but was less attractive to passengers than its predecessors. Like the stretched Super Constellation series, noise and vibration combined to neutralize much of the speed advantage as a marketing factor.

Pan American and TWA leap-frogged each other with introduction of nonstop services by new versions of their favourite airliners. TWA's L.1049G, the Super-G, began service on 1 November, 1955; the DC-7C, the Seven Seas, countered on 1 June, 1956. The DC-7C marked an important step

One of TWA's fleet of Lockheed L.1049G Super Constellations. (*TWA*)

forward, both in operational capability and resultant commercial success. Developed from the DC-7B in the short space of about a year, it featured an extra 10-ft wing span, increasing the wing area by 12 per cent—enabling weights and tankage to be increased—and simultaneously positioning the engines 5 ft further away from the fuselage, thus reducing noise and vibration.

The DC-7C was slightly slower than its immediate ancestors, but the range and comfort level were so attractive to the public that Pan American reaped an immediate benefit, pulling well ahead of its rivals on the North Atlantic route. Undoubtedly the nonstop capability was a great asset and competitive airlines fought hard to emulate Pan Am. Lockheed put an entirely new wing on the Super Constellation series to produce the ultimate aircraft of that famous line, the L.1649A Starliner. This had even more range than the DC-7C, and TWA started nonstop New York—London and New York—Paris services on 1 June, 1957.

One of Northwest Orient Airlines' Lockheed L.1049G Super Constellations. (*Northwest Airlines*)

While the North Atlantic route was the proving ground for new airliners, because it was by far the most competitive, there were other areas where U.S. airlines sought continuously to improve their schedules and standards by introducing new types. On the Pacific route to the Far East, Northwest Orient Airlines started L.1049G flights from Seattle to Tokyo on 1 July, 1955. Although this airline was the first to put the Super G into service, it remained loyal to the Douglas company and was among the first to exploit the range capability of the DC-7C, which supplemented Lockheed equipment from 28 April, 1957, onwards. On 2 August of that year, Northwest also had the satisfaction of receiving a permanent certificate for the Great Circle route to Tokyo, a status which was also granted to a short-cut route from New York, via Edmonton, Canada, making the connection with the Seattle—Tokyo route at Anchorage. Northwest enjoyed a monopoly on this route until 1969, when at last Pan American was allowed to compete.

Braniff International Airways maintained steady, if unspectacular service to Latin America with its DC-6s, and inaugurated through-plane service to New York and Washington on 18 August, 1955, by an interline agreement with Eastern Air Lines at Miami. Pan American had started a DC-6 through service from Los Angeles to Rio de Janeiro on 1 Novem-

N5900 was Braniff International Airways' first Douglas DC-7C.

ber, 1954, but was hampered in competing with Braniff in the South American west coast market by continued disagreements with its partner in Pan American-Grace (Panagra). Braniff added Bogota, Colombia, to its network in 1956, after the signing of a U.S.-Colombia bilateral agreement. DC-6 *El Conquistador* service started to the Colombian capital on 15 May, 1957, and DC-7Cs were introduced on the *El Dorado* service on the next day.

Perhaps the zenith of piston engined airliner achievements in long range ocean crossing was reached in the pioneering of Polar Routes. The first Great Circle service via the Arctic (the term Polar was not geographically correct when applied to Europe—California services) was inaugurated on 15–16 November, 1954, by the Scandinavian airline, SAS. The route from Copenhagen to Los Angeles was via Søndrestrømfjord (formerly the wartime Bluie West 8) and Winnipeg, and was as near to the Great Circle line as practicable. The DC-6Bs used were not unduly stretched in range; nor, surprisingly, was the weather a serious hazard; the main problem was navigation, for which a special system had to be developed because of the difficulties of flying in the vicinity of the Magnetic Pole. The time saved on this route was considerable: the journey lasted about 20 hr compared with the 30 hr via New York.

N731PA *Clipper Bald Eagle* was one of Pan American's Douglas DC-7Cs which made regular nonstop North Atlantic services possible. (*Pan American World Airways*)

TWA's nonstop North Atlantic aeroplane was the Lockheed L.1649A Starliner, introduced in June 1957. (*TWA*)

Canadian Pacific Airlines (CPA) joined SAS on the Great Circle route to the West Coast on 3–4 June, 1955, also with DC-6Bs; but U.S. airlines did not enter this market until 1957, when, however, the long-range aircraft then available made possible the elimination of some of the tedious stops in the remote parts of northern Canada. Pan American started DC-7C service on 11 September, 1957, and TWA followed with L.1649As on 2 October.

Twilight of an Era

The Comet 1 adventure was a gallant bid which failed to wrest airline supremacy from the United States because of the catastrophic crashes near Elba and Stromboli in 1954. But, failure though it was, the Comet heralded a new era in civil aviation. De Havilland had proved that jet propulsion was feasible and had pursued a course towards full demonstration of the possibilities of jet airliners in the face of considerable criticism and doubt. Most of the apprehension revolved around the known high fuel consumption of jet engines, but this was offset by the relatively low cost of turbine fuel, the enormous increase in block speeds, and an improvement in engine reliability which exceeded the most optimistic predictions.

Such overwhelming evidence was forthcoming, even with the experience of the short-lived Comet 1. But the grounding of Comets after the accidents gave the last generations of the piston-engined families a new lease of life, which saw them through until the jet age was ushered in permanently, late in 1958. In the intervening years between 1954, when the Comet 1s were taken out of service, and 4 October, 1958, when the Comet 4s of BOAC beat Pan American into jet service on the North Atlantic route by a short head, the Douglas DC-7Cs and Lockheed Super Constellations of various series hung on grimly. Airlines gambled precariously with future cash flow problems as they ordered additional aircraft, knowing that these would probably be obsolescent before their depreciation lives were fully run. Yet aircraft had to be ordered, to keep up with the inexorable traffic growth on world routes.

There were several indications of the impending demise of the piston-engined fleets. On 15 September, 1956, the Russian airline, Aeroflot, put into commission the Tupolev Tu-104 airliner on the Moscow—Irkutsk route, cutting the journey time from 20 hr to just over seven. This was the world's first sustained jet air service, and, within two years, the air map of Russia had completely changed and much of the country was linked by jet air services.

In the same year as the Tu-104's debut, BOAC should have started services across the Atlantic with the propeller-turbine powered Bristol Britannia. This airliner's development history was marred by production delays, following its maiden flight on 16 August, 1952. Moreover, just before the planned entry into service, there were some frustrating setbacks because of unusual icing problems in the Bristol Proteus engines. The transocean version of this basically fine aircraft did not therefore go on to the London—New York route until 19 December, 1957, the first time a British-built aircraft had flown regularly on the world's Number 1 long-distance route. Three days later, the Israeli airline, El Al, also put Britannias on the Atlantic route, and advertised with the slogan, 'No Goose, No Gander', a reference to the two much-used diversion airfields at Goose Bay, Labrador, and Gander, Newfoundland.

The Britannia had its few years of glory, quickly replacing piston-engined types on BOAC's network. On 10 March, 1957, the New York service was extended to San Francisco (with DC-7Cs), the first time that Britain had shown an airline flag in California. Negotiations proceeded to extend BOAC's route on across the Pacific, but the inauguration of a British round-the-world service was delayed until 22 August, 1959, because of sustained objections by Northwest Airlines through the C.A.B. Northwest still remembered the continual refusal of Britain to surrender traffic rights at Hongkong, and the incident recalled the problems of the Chicago Conference and the Bermuda Agreement some 14 years previously.

A glance at the individual airline traffic curves on the North Atlantic route reveals that the Britannia had a competitive effect which was perhaps not fully appreciated at the time, as the airlines were preoccupied with preparations for the jets. BOAC made impressive gains during 1958, almost entirely at the expense of Pan American and TWA. But the coming of the jet era revealed how completely Pan American had come to terms with the principles of competition. On 13 October, 1955, the airline world reverberated with the news that the U.S. flag airline had ordered 20 Boeing 707s and 25 Douglas DC-8s, to establish a commanding lead over all rival aspirants.

Passengers boarding a Challenger Airlines' Douglas DC-3 *Sunliner*. This airline was acquired by Monarch Air Lines in 1949.

CHAPTER FIFTEEN

The Second Level

Establishment of Feeder Services

During the late 1930s the continued success and growth of the established airlines served to increase the popularity of flying among all sections of the population. The people of America, in fact, were becoming airminded—a new word coined to express the realization of the practicality of air transport—and this airmindedness spread not only among businessmen, diplomats, and the affluent, but also into the lower echelons of commercial, public and domestic life.

Small communities with populations counted in a few thousands, rather than tens or hundreds of thousands, began to consider themselves worthy of air service, and began to agitate for such service in various ways. The movement was naturally stronger in areas of the U.S.A. where surface transport was poor, or distances great, and where, therefore, the aeroplane could demonstrate an obvious time-saving advantage over the train or the car. This process was not new, of course. Exactly the same motives had prompted the establishment of the pioneer airlines of the late 1920s. But these companies, or their descendants, were developing quickly to a point where their approach to the business was acquiring a new emphasis: of offering better service over established routes, seeking increased nonstop route authority, and gaining footholds in the most lucrative markets in the areas which they served.

A new stratum of airline was needed to continue the development of service to the smaller communities which sought their place on the airline map; a second level of carrier which could specialize in the shorter, sparser traffic routes between minor cities, and which could provide feeder or branch lines to the main trunk routes of the certificated domestic trunk airlines.

The first of these new airlines was Essair, of Houston, Texas, which in January 1939 was authorized to begin an experimental passenger and express service to Amarillo, via Abilene. In July, however, plans were suspended because of an appeal to the C.A.B. by Braniff Airways, which considered Essair's operations to be an intrusion into its geographical sphere of influence.

On 5 November, 1943, however, in a decision which was to have far-reaching consequences, the Board selected Essair to operate the service, expressing the opinion that such a company was better adapted than the trunk carriers to serve local needs. By this decision, the idea was crystallized that air transport had become big enough to support different levels of service. In the more modest levels of airline enterprise such as linking two small western cowboy settlements, a large airline could not be expected to divert much of its skills and energy, preoccupied as it would invariably be with competitive rivalry and standards of service on main routes like New York—Chicago, or coast-to-coast.

Implementing the 1943 decision into regulation, the C.A.B. established a new classification of Feeder Airline on 11 July, 1944, and Essair eventually started services, with full official blessing, on 1 August, 1945, over its original route from Houston to Abilene, using a fleet of three 12-seat Lockheed L.10 Electras. On 17 June, 1946, Essair changed its name to Pioneer Air Lines.

This regulatory process had occurred during the closing stages of World War 2, and the green light given to Pioneer coincided with the start of the air transport explosion of the immediate post-war years. Most of the route expansion authorized by the C.A.B.—which, of course, exercised the supreme authority—was aimed at providing air service to every citizen of the United States. This impressive objective was inspired partly by the knowledge that, towards the end of the war, factories were building thousands of fine transport aircraft by mass-production methods. These would be able to provide reliable service, when made available as war surplus. The politicians, for their part, found that promotion and agitation for local air services was a popular cause, and would-be feeder airlines found ready support from senators and congressmen in their areas.

During the first four years after World War 2, about 200 new cities appeared on the airline map of the United States. About half were authorized as additional stops on established air routes of the trunk lines; the rest were new points on new routes served by new feeder airlines. By 1950, the number of cities grew to 600.

By the end of 1946, four more small companies had begun operations, in addition to Pioneer. Three of these, Empire Air Lines (Boise, Idaho), Monarch Air Lines (Denver, Colorado) and West Coast Airlines (Seattle, Washington) were from western states and owed their existence to the outcome of the Rocky Mountain States Air Service and West Coast Cases. Two of the first three to start services in 1947 were also west of the Mississippi.

Arizona Airways of Phoenix operated this strangely painted Douglas DC-3. The airline merged with Monarch Air Lines and later became Frontier Airlines.

The full list of these feeder airlines is contained in Table 22*, which covers the early development of the 26 which operated, or aspired to operate, under the new C.A.B. authority. Many of the companies were able to draw experience as fixed-base operators; some, like Turner Airlines, appear to have been inspired by the enthusiasm of an individual; all were characterized by a rugged individuality and determination which has enabled the feederline industry to survive as an entity in the face of many handicaps and much competition.

One major bone of contention has been the Federal subsidy paid to the feeder airlines. By the early 1960s this was to build up to aggregate sums of as much as $60 to $70 million, and although representing a comparatively small proportion of the nation's total budget, this was by no means a negligible sum in the eyes of politicians who were opposed to the idea of subsidy as a political principle. Thus, as the feeder airlines began to find their feet and became an accepted section of airline industry, they

*See page 619.

One of Monarch Air Lines' Douglas DC-3s. Monarch was one of the ancestor companies of the present-day Frontier Airlines.

and the C.A.B. were to come under increasing pressure to reduce the subsidy requirements.

Because of their dependence for many years upon the trusty Douglas DC-3, the feeder airlines came to be identified largely with that aircraft. Many of the early companies, however, started life with smaller types. Pioneer Air Lines and Wisconsin Central (later North Central Airlines), for example, launched their operations with the twin-engined Lockheed L.10A; Robinson Airlines (later Mohawk Airlines) had Fairchild 24s; Empire Air Lines had Boeing 247Ds; while others had small Beech and Cessna types.

The C.A.B., however, soon insisted on a minimum standard of equipment: basically, that all aircraft should be twin-engined. Two operators, Mid-West Airlines and E. W. Wiggins Airways, ceased operations because of their inability to put twins into service. One, Parks Air Transport, never got under way for the same reason. Others substituted superior types as quickly as possible.

The C.A.B. was able to enforce this requirement because the first operating certificates were issued only on a temporary basis; and if the airlines could not demonstrate sufficient technical ability or corporate strength

Like most local service carriers, West Coast Airlines made considerable use of Douglas DC-3s. This one is at its home base at Boeing Field, Seattle. (*West Coast Airlines*)

An early local service scene. Two Beech 18s, NC80217 *Air Chief Gayuqa* and NC80210 *Air Chief Niagara*, of Robinson Airlines, at Ithaca Municipal Airport. This company changed its name to Mohawk Airlines in August 1952.

by the time the renewal of the certificate was due, they forfeited the franchise. Fortunately such severe discipline was seldom necessary. The sheep having been effectively separated from the goats, the thirteen surviving airlines, universally equipped with DC-3s, were given permanent certificates on 19 May, 1955, and entered into a period of stability which was to last more than a decade.

One of the earliest feeder airlines, Southwest Airways, operated in the populous and affluent State of California, where air transport has been a thriving business since the pioneer days. The new carrier therefore had to devise additional incentives to compete in a thriving air travel market. Over a network of small cities, new passenger-handling methods were introduced to cut turn-round time to a minimum, thus obtaining more efficient operational use of the aircraft. For transit stops Southwest featured built-in air stairs, and kept one of the DC-3's two engines running, and the average stopping time was thus reduced to two minutes. Much of the paper-work involved in issuing tickets was eliminated by employing travelling pursers, but in spite of the advantages of such methods, Southwest never developed or exploited the system. Many years later the idea

Southwest Airways Douglas DC-3 N63106 at San Francisco. (*John Stroud*)

was taken up and refined by other airlines, culminating in the highly successful New York—Boston Eastern Air Line's Shuttle.

Another innovator was All American Aviation, later to become a Local Service carrier and renamed Allegheny Airlines. This company was originally founded on 5 March, 1937, to perform a highly specialized rôle, an experimental air mail pick-up service which incorporated devices for dropping and picking up the mail in flight. By this means 58 small communities in Pennsylvania, Delaware, Maryland, West Virginia and Ohio received air mail service from 13 September, 1938. Single-engined Stinson Reliants were used for this experiment, which showed enough promise for All American to bid successfully for Air Mail Routes 1001 and 1002,

All American Aviation, later Allegheny Airlines, operated a mail pick-up service with Stinson Reliants. The pick-up illustrated was at the 25th air mail anniversary commemoration at Washington National Airport. (*CAA*)

radiating from Pittsburgh. The trial period ended on 13 May, 1940, a permanent mail certificate was received from the C.A.B. on 21 July and scheduled operations under that authority began on 12 August.

This unorthodox mail service continued for many years and terminated only in June 1949, by which time All American Airlines had begun passenger services under a C.A.B. feeder certificate.

Outgrowing the DC-3

When President Eisenhower authorized the issue of permanent certificates on 19 May, 1955, the feeder airlines, now designated Local Service carriers, received a welcome injection of confidence. The stimulus of official recognition encouraged many of the airlines to look critically at their faithful

In 1952 Pioneer Air Lines bought nine Martin 2-0-2s from Northwest Airlines. N93055 *Kit Carson* is seen here. (*Gordon S. Williams*)

DC-3s and ask themselves whether they still held enough passenger appeal to maintain their image in a highly competitive airline society.

Two airlines had, in fact, already done so, in 1952. Living up to the spirit of its name, Pioneer Air Lines had bought nine 36-passenger Martin 2-0-2s in June 1952 from Northwest Airlines, having sold its fleet of eleven DC-3s to the United States Air Force at a profit of $841,000. This was used to offset losses on mail subsidies, but the C.A.B. took the view that Pioneer's action had been irregular, and possibly inconsistent with the regulations governing subsidy which was public money. Pioneer was unable to demonstrate that the Martins could be operated in such a way as to reduce subsidy. Under C.A.B. pressure, therefore, it reverted to DC-3 operation in March 1953. Two years later, the airline lost its identity in a merger with Continental Airlines on 1 April, 1955.

Southwest Airways also started service with four Martin 2-0-2s on 26 April, 1953. A case was made for improving equipment standards over new routes in northern California recently transferred from United Air Lines. Mail rates were set, on 22 May, 1953, at DC-3 levels, and Southwest continued to operate the Martins. Later, on 30 November, 1959, Pacific

Southwest Airways began operating Martin 2-0-2s, in April 1953. N93060, illustrated, was originally an NWA aircraft and had also worked for Transocean and Japan Air Lines. (*Gordon S. Williams*)

Air Lines (as Southwest had become) exchanged its fleet of non-pressurized 2-0-2s for a fleet of eight pressurized Martin 4-0-4s.

Permanent certification cast new light on Local Service operational requirements, and the formula under which mail subsidies were paid out by the C.A.B. was changed. Hitherto, industry and Board alike had come to regard the DC-3 as the standard against which all calculations were based, but recognition was now given to the growing needs of some airlines which, without the benefit of more modern aircraft, would face decreasing popularity with the public, declining passenger loads and higher subsidy demands as the inevitable sequel.

Two of the airlines most affected by competition in equipment were Allegheny Airlines (formerly All American) and Mohawk Airlines (formerly Robinson Airlines), both of which operated in an area of dense population and served many big cities. They were faced with a dual problem of having to cope with ever-increasing traffic demands which threatened to outstrip the capacity of the DC-3, at the same time having to provide connecting services at busy airports like LaGuardia and Washington National, where the Local Service airline DC-3 image suffered by comparison with the new equipment operated by the big trunk airlines.

Like other local service airlines which began with small aircraft, All American became a DC-3 operator. (*LeRoy W. Clark*)

Martin 2-0-2s entered service with Allegheny in 1955, but Mohawk went one better by starting Convair CV-240 flights on 1 July. With a fleet of four, purchased from the Chinese airline CAT, this was the first pressurized service by a Local Service airline. Mohawk's permanent certificate, incidentally, had incorporated extensions to Boston, when the routes of E. W. Wiggins Airways were taken over, and marked the beginning of a rapid traffic expansion for the Utica-based airline which in March 1956 purchased a further seven CV-240s from Swissair.

In the previous year, Mohawk had distinguished itself by becoming the first—and only—Local Service carrier to operate scheduled helicopter flights with a service from Newark Airport to Jennie Grossinger Field, in the Catskill Mountains. This operation lasted from 7 June until the end of

September, when it was discontinued because city-centre heliports were unavailable and the full benefits of the helicopter could not be achieved.

Mohawk, Allegheny and Pacific were the only airlines to supplement DC-3s during the first three years following the granting of permanent local service route certificates. Others could discern a genuine need for a bigger aircraft—the newer ones averaged about 40 seats against the DC-3's average of about 25—but the main problem was how to operate the replacement types as economically as their apparently ageless predecessor. Bought cheaply as war-surplus equipment, or from a second- or third-hand source, the DC-3 was economical to operate when load factors were low, invariably the case among the Local Service carriers. The nature of

One of Frontier Airlines' fleet of Douglas DC-3s—N64421. (*Charlie Wunder*)

feeder operations is that primarily the routes serve cities of small population and therefore of low traffic generative capability. Additionally one route serves many points, leading to complications in booking procedures; much of the traffic is directional and liable to seasonal variation. All these factors combine to depress average loads. The airlines began to discover that bigger and better aircraft were not necessarily the answer to the problem. A community which, for example, habitually generated ten passengers per day on the feeder service to the nearest big city tended to continue to generate ten per day when the newer type appeared—although there were some exceptional cases which produced better results and gave encouragement to airlines with a specially favourable traffic situation.

Airline economists began to discuss the merits of low aircraft-mile costs as opposed to low seat-mile costs, which had for so long been the sole criterion of airliner economic efficiency. An important objective became the minimum cost of flying an aircraft from one place to another, in safety, full or empty. Seat-mile costs were meaningless if the seats were not occupied. So, during the late 1950s, sporadic studies were made of what became known as the 'DC-3 Replacement', a specification which was little understood in all its implications in spite of wide circulation.

Southern Airways was also a DC-3 operator. N65SA is seen at Atlanta.

A very special Douglas DC-3, North Central Airlines' N21728. This aircraft was the 2,144th DC-3 and flew more than 50,000 hr with Eastern Air Lines before being sold to North Central in July 1952. N21728 was withdrawn from passenger service on 26 April, 1965, and modified for special duties. Modifications included provision of large panoramic windows. This aircraft has flown more than 84,000 hr and was presented by Douglas with a plaque stating 'This aircraft N21728 has flown more hours than any other plane in the history of aviation'. (*North Central Airlines*)

Ozark Air Lines' green and white Douglas DC-3 N2816D at St Louis. This aircraft, (c/n 1946), had been delivered to Swissair in June 1937 as HB-IRI. In Ozark service it had undercarriage doors and airstairs were fitted to the passenger door which was on the starboard side—a feature of early production DC-3s.

One of the difficulties was that the DC-3 achieved its economic levels with a remarkably good airfield performance. Sluggish though it may have appeared in the air, compared with the Convair twins and the four-engined types, the DC-3 was in a class of its own in the world of 3,000-ft runways, at altitudes up to 8,000 ft and in temperatures up to 120 deg F, conditions which were all too common in the networks of operators like Frontier Airlines, West Coast Airlines, and Bonanza Air Lines.

One airline, Lake Central, went so far as to study the possibility of putting the DC-3 back into production, with improvements, but was shocked to find out how much a new DC-3 would cost. The DC-3s may have been old and worn, but their first cost was so low that shortcomings in design of both airframe and engine were more than compensated for. In short, nothing could match the DC-3 for Local Service.

West Coast Airlines was the world's first operator of the Fokker Friendship. This example, N2702 (c/n 5), was a licence-built Fairchild F-27 and is seen leaving Seattle. *(Gordon S. Williams)*

Local Service Propeller-turbine Aircraft

In 1958, 201 out of the 229 aircraft in service with the thirteen Local Service airlines were DC-3s. The search for the elusive DC-3 replacement was beginning to look hopeless. Then the Dutch company, Fokker, dormant for many years as a civil aircraft constructor, suddenly re-entered the airliner business with a high-wing 36/40-seater aircraft, powered by two Rolls-Royce Dart propeller-turbines. The Friendship, as it was called, made its first flight on 24 November, 1955, but strangely enough the first of the type to enter airline service anywhere in the world was one built under licence by the American Fairchild company, and known in the United States as the F-27.

Propeller-turbines were not new to American experience, although all the development of this type of propulsion had been pioneered in the United Kingdom. The British lead had been so great that the first successful propeller-turbine airliner, the Vickers Viscount, made a spectacular entry into the U.S. market when, in 1955, Capital Airlines put them into service and built up an order book of 75 aircraft, an example which was followed more modestly by other U.S. carriers.

The first Local Service airline to operate the F-27 was West Coast Airlines, which began service on 27 September, 1958. Others followed in quick succession: Piedmont on 14 November, Bonanza on 29 March, 1959, Pacific in April, and Ozark on 27 September. Bonanza quickly disposed of all its DC-3s and claimed, on 1 November, 1960, to be the 'First All-Jet Airline in the World', a claim which appears to have been somewhat exaggerated.

Fairchild must have been encouraged by a Government decision, in September 1957, to guarantee up to 90 per cent of private loans up to $5,000,000 for any individual carrier purchasing new equipment. This was a partial acknowledgement of the difficulty in replacing the DC-3 and also an exposure of the shaky financial structure of most Local Service airlines, which had started life operating second-hand aircraft and were doomed to continue on those lines unless given new hope based on revised capital resources.

In spite of this encouragement, the expected orders for the F-27 did not materialize, beyond the five airlines mentioned. Once again, the carriers found that the additional aircraft-mile costs of the propeller-turbine powered type—attractive though the aircraft was to passengers—were not offset by sufficiently increased passenger revenue. The C.A.B. in fact instituted a close scrutiny of F-27 operations, and West Coast Airlines, in particular, was hard pressed to produce an overwhelming case to prove the economic superiority—and hence lower subsidy requirement—of the F-27 over the DC-3.

Theoretically, the larger F-27 might have been able to produce economies by offering fewer frequencies than the smaller DC-3 to carry the same amount of traffic. But on the sparse routes which characterized such a large proportion of Local Service operations, frequencies were already at an almost irreducible minimum. The F-27 was therefore often called upon to fly the same mileage as the DC-3, at a higher cost, yet could not generate sufficient extra passengers to produce a corresponding increase in revenue. This was a repetition of the experience of those companies which had prematurely bought Martins and Convairs a few years previously.

All the airlines which chose not to have the F-27 decided thereupon to buy Convairs or Martins. The Convairs were most popular, although Piedmont Airlines and Southern Airways elected to take the Martins. One by one, the Local Service airlines departed from the concept of a one-type operation. Piedmont was the last to capitulate, when Martin 4-0-4s entered service early in 1962.

Southern Airways re-equipped with Martin 4-0-4s. N141S was an ex-Eastern Air Lines aircraft.

Among the Convair customers was Allegheny, already boasting a history of bold experiment in the pre-war and wartime air mail pick-up service. In October 1959 it introduced a new kind of service and shortly afterwards a new kind of airliner. The service broke new ground by eliminating the need to book seats in advance. The customer went to the airport on the chance that there would be spare seats on the flight he wanted. He bought a ticket, wrote his name on it and had it time-stamped. These passengers were allowed on the aircraft in order of the time-stamp. The initial service of this unique non-reservation system was the *Penn Commuter* on the Philadelphia—Pittsburgh route. Load factors were considerably increased. Only about 5 per cent of the passengers were refused a seat and the successful ones received a 36 per cent discount below the normal fare.

In February 1960 Allegheny ordered five Convair CV-540s from the Napier Engine Company, of England. These aircraft were standard CV-340s, modified to take Napier Eland propeller-turbines in place of the normal Pratt & Whitney piston engines. Services were started to New

Allegheny Airlines' highly-decorated Convair CV-540 N440EL with Napier Eland propeller-turbines. It is seen at Washington National Airport. (*Del Ankers*)

England in April 1960 and the no-reservation commuter services extended to these routes in the summer.

Allegheny, of course, was challenging one of the Big Four, TWA, on the *Penn Commuter* route, and the larger airline matched the feeder in fare and capacity. Both airlines raised the fare from $11.82 to $13.65 on 1 October, 1961, and a C.A.B. investigation resulted in a further increase to $15 on 27 November. In March 1962 the fare was augmented by a 10 per cent tax, and Allegheny received a body-blow when Napier abruptly cancelled the Eland engine programme, although one Eland-Convair was used for a time. Two good ideas to improve service to the public were thus defeated by a combination of industrial circumstances and fare manipulation partly enforced by the C.A.B.

After the first demands for Fairchild F-27s there was a lull in propeller-turbine orders. Airlines discovered that the older Convairs and Martins were just as popular as the F-27s, though lacking the passenger appeal of the high wing which was one of the Fokker design's best features. Efforts were made to make the cabins more attractive; but the time came when the contrast between Local Service piston-engined aircraft and trunk airline jets forced the airlines to think seriously about further re-equipment.

The Local Service operators appear to have postponed decisions to augment their propeller-turbine fleets for a few years, in the hope that some ideal answer could be found to meet their peculiar and stringent requirements for a perfect feeder airliner which could match the economy of the Convairs and F-27s with the field performance of the DC-3s, and at the the same time offer a substantial improvement in comfort to the passenger.

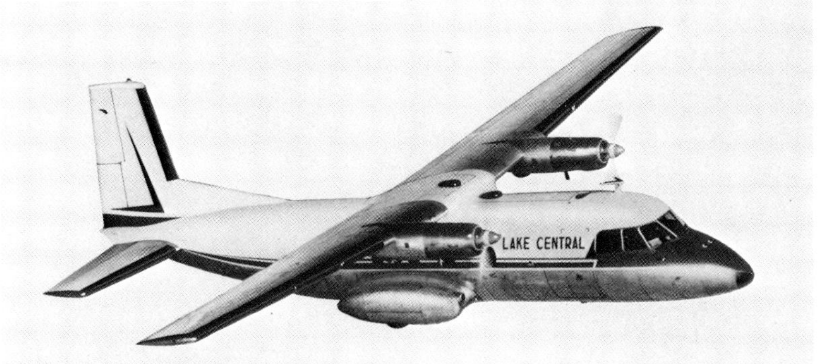

Lake Central Airlines' original Nord 262 livery is seen here on the prototype aircraft F-WKVR. Markings were red and blue. (*Nord-Aviation*)

Some hope was entertained for a small low-cost short-haul airliner which became the subject of considerable and exhaustive study, partly stimulated by a design competition sponsored by the F.A.A. and the Association of Local Transport Airlines (ALTA). This was won by the Nord 262, a 28-seat French aircraft with twin Turbomeca Astazou propeller-turbines, a combination which came closest to fitting the need, al-

One of Lake Central Airlines' Nord 262s, N26202, in the purple and gold Allegheny livery after the latter company had taken over Lake Central. The legend on the fin is *Claudette d'Allegheny*. (*Allegheny Airlines*)

though none of the competitors reached the ideal standards required. The aircraft was vigorously promoted, and Lake Central Airlines bought eight on 16 March, 1964. It started scheduled services on 31 October, 1965, but they were never a great success. In fact, on 12 August, 1966, the Nords were grounded for five months, following two inflight engine failures.

The deficiency of the Nord 262 was that it offered neither sufficient extra seats, nor improvement in performance and passenger appeal, to demonstrate a convincing superiority over other available types. One aircraft project which did appear to possess all these qualities was canvassed between 1962 and 1966. This was the de Havilland 126 (later the Hawker Siddeley 136), a twin-jet feederliner design, with 40 seats, jet appeal, and DC-3 field performance. Although well received by many airlines which saw great promise in the basic idea, the British company squandered an unprecedented opportunity to launch a new airliner type at just the right time, and did not proceed with a most promising project. Other companies also explored the idea, but were defeated by inflating costs and the understandable impatience of the airlines.

Faced with the realization that the prospects of a practicable jet replacement for the age-old DC-3 were growing dim, the Local Service industry finally gave up the search. For their immediate needs they turned to more propeller-turbine powered aircraft to meet their growing capacity demands; in the longer term, they turned to larger jets, and in so doing precipitated a realignment of policy, both from within the industry and from the C.A.B.

The new lease of life given to the propeller-turbine aircraft took two courses. First was a detailed reassessment of the possibility of re-engining the Convair twin-engined aircraft. Two engine manufacturers, Allison (a Division of General Motors) and Rolls-Royce, promoted the idea of matching the proved reliability of the Convair airframe, apparently as indestructible as that of the DC-3, with the reliability of propeller-turbines, in which the Rolls-Royce Dart, particularly, had excelled in service with Viscounts and F-27s.

Frontier Airlines' choice of turbine-powered aircraft was the Allison-powered Convair CV-580. (*Frontier Airlines*)

Lake Central Airlines' Convair CV-580 N73118. Close examination of the original photograph suggests that the markings have been painted on this picture.

North Central Airlines also adopted the Allison-powered Convair CV-580 but the aircraft shown is the piston-engined Convair CV-340 N90854 before being re-engined.

Trans-Texas Airways converted this Convair CV-240, N94239, to Rolls-Royce Dart powered CV-600 configuration.

First off the mark was Frontier Airlines, which put into service on 1 June, 1964, the CV-580, as the Allison 501 powered version of the Convair twin came to be known. This engine, also fitted to the Lockheed L.188 Electra, was more powerful than the Dart and ideal for the airfields on Frontier's mountain route system. Other airlines favouring the CV-580 were Allegheny (first service 1 June, 1965), North Central (1 April, 1967), and Lake Central (6 September, 1966).

Trans-Texas Airways elected to do its own conversions of Convairs with Rolls-Royce Darts, putting the CV-600, as it was called, into service on 1 March, 1966. Trans-Texas was beaten into second place by Central Airlines, which received its first CV-600 in time to begin services at the end of 1965.

The second course which some airlines took was to buy newer models of the Fairchild-built F-27. Allegheny started services with the strengthened F-27J on 1 December, 1966, and then Fairchild Hiller launched the FH-227, a version with a lengthened fuselage, allowing two extra rows of seats. As with the first F-27 there was a spate of orders, but, once again, the initial rush was not sustained. Mohawk introduced the FH-227 on 1 July, 1966, Ozark Airlines followed on 19 December, and Piedmont early in 1967.

N4216, Ozark Air Lines' second Fairchild Hiller FH-227B.

This last airline decided, however, that the stretched F-27 was still not big enough to keep pace with its sustained traffic growth, and on 16 August, 1967, signed, amid some surprise, a letter of intent for ten Japanese-built Nihon YS-11A 60-seaters, powered, like the FH-227, with Rolls-Royce Dart 10 propeller-turbines. Confirming the order, Piedmont started YS-11 service on 19 May, 1969.

One of Piedmont Airlines' fleet of Japanese YS-11s. This aircraft bears the name *Pee Dee Pacemaker* and the Japanese pre-delivery registration JA8746.

As a matter of interest, Southern Airways, alone among the Local Service airlines, never operated a propeller-turbine airliner, a distinction which it is probably proud to share with Pan American and TWA.

By the summer of 1968, almost 200 new twin-engined propeller-turbine aircraft (i.e. not including earlier F-27s) were sold to Local Service airlines. Many of these were new aircraft—a far cry from the days when old second-hand equipment was the rule. About 130 were re-engined Convair-Liners, representing the only time in modern history when a good airliner has been equally successful after conversion. This surge of orders, following a purchasing lull, probably indicates a lost market for the feeder jet, the ideal specification for which seems to have been as elusive as the DC-3 replacements.

Effect of C.A.B. Route Policy

Once the Local Service airlines gained the official recognition vested in the permanent authority granted in 1955, they began to expand their route systems. The C.A.B. acted cautiously at first, carefully avoiding the danger of arranging the supply of even more seats over sparse routes where there was little prospect of substantial traffic growth.

Some of the early awards were alternative routes of the early networks first pioneered by the Locals, and extended modestly during the early 1950s. Gradually the scattered collections of routes began to consolidate into recognizable patterns. Airlines reached out to larger cities, over longer distances. In 1955, for instance, Piedmont gained access to Washington; in 1956, Mohawk was granted routes to Detroit and Erie; in 1957, North Central claimed Omaha, Ozark started a route to Minneapolis, and Bonanza and Southwest both reached Las Vegas. In that same year, two other route awards had a special significance: North Central was granted a non-stop authority from Chicago to Duluth, a distance of more than 400 miles, while Mohawk entered the busy New York—Syracuse market in direct competition with American Airlines. Such a distance, and such a densely-travelled commuter route, was anything but typical of the kind originally conceived for Local Service.

During the next three years great strides were made to fill in some of the blank areas on the U.S. Local Service airline map. The C.A.B. initiated wide-ranging investigations, each affecting more than one airline. Thus in 1958, the Seven States Area Case provided considerable extensions to the route networks of Frontier, Central, North Central, and Ozark; in 1959 Frontier again benefited, this time from the Montana Service Case; in 1960 Central added 14 more cities in the Kansas City—Oklahoma Case; and North Central and Lake Central made similar gains in the Great Lakes Local Service Case. In the same period, West Coast and Pacific (formerly Southwest) gained important extensions up the Pacific Coast, and Trans-Texas Airways almost doubled its route mileage.

By this time the economic problems of Local Service operations were becoming evident. Making profits over stages of less than 100 miles, often with less than ten passengers per flight, was impossible, even using fully-depreciated DC-3s. Achieving high average loads was handicapped by the necessity to serve many small cities, sometimes as many as seven on one route. Few stations in rural areas could be depended upon to supply more than one or two customers. The expansion of the Local Service networks

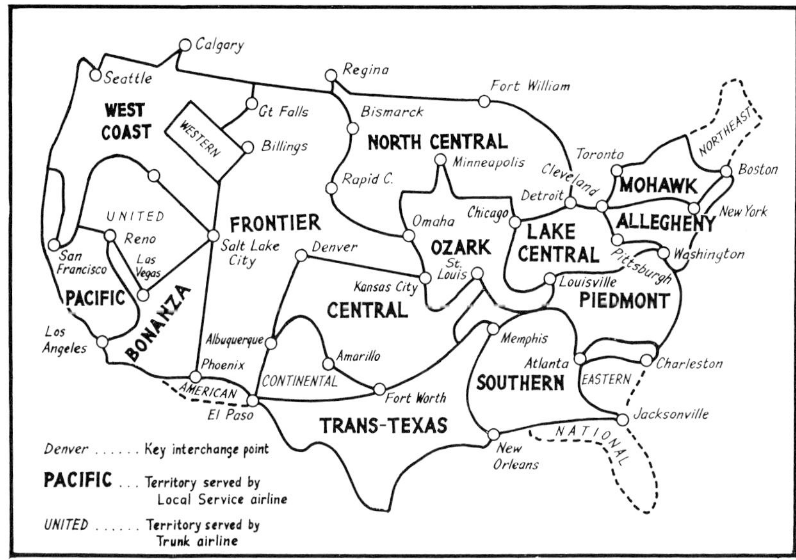

Fig. 25. Local Service Airlines—Territories Served during the Early 1960s.

Mohawk Airlines' Martin 4-0-4 N460M *Air Chief Delaware*, acquired from Eastern Air Lines.

throughout the U.S.A. during the late 1950s only aggravated the situation.

In 1959, therefore, the C.A.B. instigated a new policy, under the self-explanatory title of Use It or Lose It. Letters were sent to the Mayors of every city which received local airline service but failed to generate more than five passengers a day, or 1,800 per year. The policy involved the cancellation of route certificate and termination of service to such cities unless a substantial improvement was made to take them over this minimum level, or unless there were special circumstances, such as geographical isolation and poor surface transport facilities.

The small communities affected had often received support, verbal and documented, from its political representatives in Washington. These now had to moderate their enthusiasm for universal airline service to all and sundry, faced as they were with the embarrassment of having to authorize annual increases in subsidy for the Local Service airlines.

Use It or Lose It was a qualified success in challenging those who paid lip service to a facile theory, and persuaded those who cherished a vision of an ideal transport world to come to terms with economic realities. Some of the small cities found ways of generating more traffic, others failed to make the grade and were dropped off the airline map. The resultant cost savings helped to keep down the subsidy bill.

During the early 1960s the pattern of C.A.B. awards underwent a subtle change. Development of routes to cities which had never received air service was no longer a burning issue. Efforts were directed more towards improving existing services by route awards designed also to help the Locals to reduce expenditures, after the payment of agreed subsidy.

The period coincided with a transition time for the trunk airlines which were hurriedly buying jet aircraft to replace piston-engined equipment. First types in the latter category to be declared redundant were the twin-engined Convair-Liners and Martin 4-0-4s, and the Trunks found many interested bidders amongst the Locals. An understanding was reached between many companies in which the Local airlines took over a package of routes and aircraft from the Trunks, where the transfer was mutually suitable to both parties. The process might well have taken place sooner, for the increased performance of first-line civil airliners had long since created an anachronism: airlines like TWA or American competed ruthlessly on nonstop coast-to-coast routes, yet at the same time provided service over a number of multi-stop stages averaging 100 miles or so. Handing these over to the Locals made economic sense to both parties.

In 1961, Central took over routes from American and Braniff; Mohawk took some from Eastern. During the next few years, Continental, TWA, and Delta also diluted their networks, with Bonanza, Frontier, Piedmont, Allegheny, and Mohawk as the main beneficiaries.

Piedmont's authority to extend southward as far as Atlanta strengthened its ability to provide true feeder service from points in Carolina through the Atlanta hub, and the adverse effect on trunk airline service in the area was negligible, because the main purpose of the Trunks (Eastern and Delta) was to link major cities. Piedmont, in this case, linked a large city with some smaller ones. Perhaps this trend would have been wholly satisfactory, had it not been for one or two special cases setting precedents which, if followed up enthusiastically, could have laid the foundations for a fundamental change in the character of Local Service.

Early in 1962, the C.A.B. awarded to Bonanza nonstop rights on the route from Los Angeles to Las Vegas. This had previously been a Western Airlines preserve, with TWA and United participating on a restricted basis. This was not a case of a feeder airline entering a feeder market. Los Angeles—Las Vegas was a dense route, thanks to the booming popularity of the gambling and entertainment desert city, and ranked among the busiest markets in the U.S.A.

By 1964, Trans-Texas was flying nonstop between Dallas and Houston, and Mohawk added New York—Albany to the other busy commuter routes already on the network, New York—Utica and New York—Syracuse. Mohawk sensed the growing momentum and took steps to cope with the rapidly increasing demands made upon it in the face of stiff competition from American Airlines; to the astonishment of many who still looked upon the Locals mainly as depositories for second-hand aircraft, it bought a fleet of new jet airliners.

Local Service Jets

Under the presidency of Robert Peach, Mohawk Airlines had become firmly established on a number of commuter routes radiating north and northwest from New York. With a clientèle of critical businessmen who dismissed even a relatively young Convair-Liner as a 'coffeegrinder', the Mohawk image needed a stimulant. Promotions like the DC-3 *Gas Light Service*, with décor and personal attention modelled on a bygone era,

A late attempt to popularize the Douglas DC-3. Mohawk Airlines' *Gas Light Service* DC-3 N409D with special interior and exterior décor including a gas street lamp painted on the fin and rudder.

were of limited success. This novelty lasted from September 1960 until June 1962, when Mohawk disposed of its last DC-3s. To keep ahead of the competition, some innovation of a more permanent nature was necessary. The obvious answer was jet propulsion; the problem was the short average stage distance, coupled with some short runways, two factors which meant that the standard jets used by the trunk airlines would be hopelessly uneconomic.

On 26 July, 1962, Mohawk Airlines ordered four 69-seat British BAC One-Elevens. This was a twin-engined design, somewhat like the French Caravelle, pioneer of rear-mounted engines. The One-Eleven's engines were Rolls-Royce Spey turbofans which, combined with a lower operating speed than the transcontinental jets, enabled the BAC One-Eleven to offer low operating costs even over distances down to about 100 miles. Nevertheless, small though the aircraft was, its seating was still approaching twice the number in the Convair-Liners. The question was: could the passenger appeal of the jet stimulate the already booming traffic on Mohawk's routes, to the extent that load factors could be maintained at a high enough level to avoid increased subsidy?

Mohawk Airlines' first BAC One-Eleven 204 N2111J *New York*.

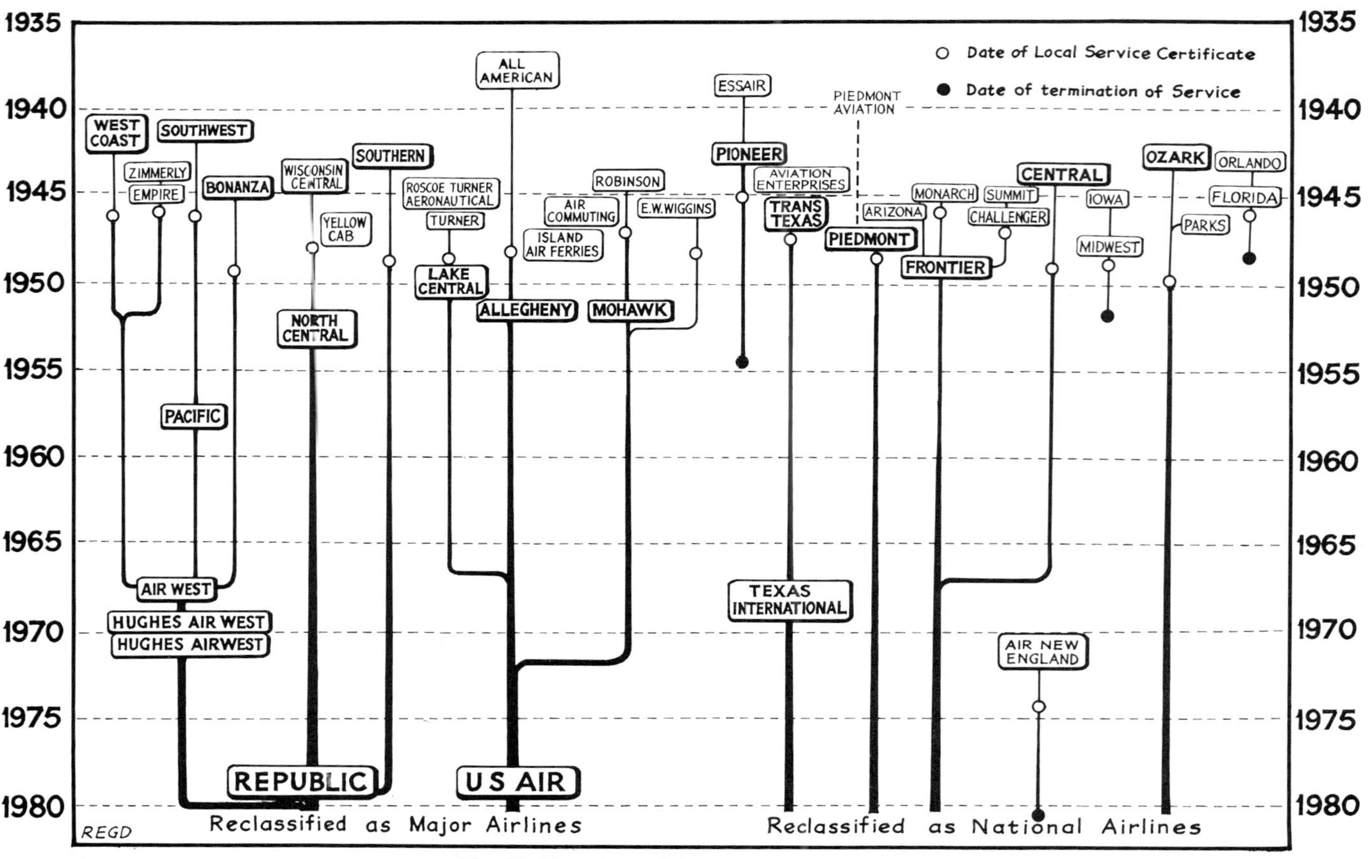

Fig. 26. Genealogy of Local Service Airlines.

The C.A.B. had its doubts and commented on Mohawk's action, genuinely believing that the airline had made an error of judgement, that it could not hope to improve its average loads of about 20 passengers per flight to the 30–35 necessary for the BAC One-Eleven to break even. The C.A.B. was probably also conscious that Mohawk was setting a dangerous precedent. For many fellow feeder carriers could well wish to join the ranks of jet airlines, but with a weaker economic case than Mohawk's. Robert Peach stuck to his guns, and the C.A.B. had to modify its objections, at the same time having to take a few knocks from the British press, which interpreted the whole affair as a piece of disguised protectionism.

Really, the C.A.B. had itself to blame for the turn of events. When awarding to Mohawk a route such as New York—Syracuse, it must have known that the airline could not operate cheek by jowl with American Airlines without top-grade aircraft. One of the well-understood principles in granting route authority was the assurance that the operator was adequately equipped. This resulted in a slightly vicious circle—an airline would purchase new aircraft as a pre-requisite to qualifying for an award. The C.A.B. would then find itself under pressure if its refusal of an application led to the cancellation of an aircraft order worth several million dollars.

But the deed was done. Mohawk was setting a tremendous pace. On 28 April, 1963, it claimed to be the first U.S. airline to serve all four New York airports when service began to White Plains, in Westchester County. Later the same year it began flights to Toronto. On 8 April, 1964, the C.A.B. approved a substantial route transfer agreement between TWA, on the one hand, and Allegheny and Mohawk on the other, covering through flights between Pittsburgh and Boston. Then, in October, Mohawk cleaned up its fleet by an agreement with Ozark in which a number of Martin 4-0-4s were consigned to the St Louis operator in exchange for some Convair-Liners. In January 1965, it ordered 18 Fairchild Hiller FH-227s.

The BAC One-Eleven went into service on Mohawk's main commuter routes on 15 July, 1965, and during the next year fully established itself as a successful airliner for this type of operation. On 1 July, 1966, the FH-227 joined in on some of the sparser routes in upstate New York, and put Mohawk on something of a pedestal among Local Service airlines. In fact, for some time, the Utica carrier had insisted on calling itself a Regional airline, a term which began to find favour among many of its colleagues.

Mohawk's jet order started a fashion. Within four years every one of the thirteen Locals ordered jets, mostly Douglas DC-9s, similar to but slightly larger than the BAC One-Eleven. Other airlines chose the three-engined Boeing 727, or the twin-engined 737 which retained the larger fuselage cross-section of the Boeing jet family but reverted to the former custom of wing-mounted engines.

The first DC-9 operator was Bonanza, which breathed sighs of relief on

1 March, 1966, when the appeal of the jet began to recoup some lost traffic on the Las Vegas routes. Bonanza, incidentally, caused further consternation in British circles by first signing a letter of intent for the One-Eleven and subsequently cancelling this in favour of the DC-9.

Ozark DC-9 service began on 8 July, Allegheny on 1 September, West Coast on 26 September, and Trans-Texas on 30 October, 1966. Southern on 15 June, and North Central on 8 September, 1967, completed the Douglas jet roll-call. Against these, Frontier, on 30 September, Pacific on 7 July, 1966, and Piedmont on 15 March, 1967, made up the Boeing 727 contingent. These 727s, in the main, were lent to the airlines by Boeing, pending the delivery of the 737s, which were experiencing some delay through design problems. Piedmont put the Boeing 737 into service on 1 July, 1969, and marked the end of an era by retiring its Martin 4-0-4s on 15 February, 1970. Lake Central and Central were the subject of merger negotiations which reached fruition before jet services began.

At about this time, the Local Service airlines, largely through their agency ALTA, intensified their campaign to obtain bigger and better routes from the C.A.B. Lengthy testimony was prepared and submitted which demonstrated that Local Service participation in the top 100 airline city pairs routes of the U.S.A. was meagre, and furthermore that the majority of these 100 were relatively short stages and therefore eminently suitable for economic operation by the compact jets now on order. Surprisingly, this campaign found favour with some sections of the C.A.B., partly because the potential profits from these routes—the Locals asked for no subsidy to operate them—could help the companies towards self-sufficiency. The policy would achieve the twin goals of reducing subsidy and permitting a reasonable return on investment, a principle always advocated by the C.A.B. in its rate-fixing policy.

Strangely, the industry often chose to forget the original concept of Local Service, which was to provide airline travel to every possible citizen of the United States, as a social amenity, and, within reason, that this should be done as a charge on the Federal budget. Certainly, the C.A.B. was faced with mounting opposition on the score of subsidy, and was under constant pressure to reduce it year by year. Feeder routes are by nature uneconomic, so that there was little prospect of their ever becoming self-sufficient. Thus the admixture of potentially lucrative routes appeared to be a workable solution. Unfortunately, once the local airlines were given the opportunity to participate in the higher strata of the U.S. airline route structure, their appetite was sharpened. Having tasted cake, they had little use for bread.

One of the Locals, in fact, was already growing rapidly. Frontier Airlines, serving the whole of the Rocky Mountain area, already had a network stretching from Canada to Mexico when in March 1962 the Goldfield Corporation of San Francisco bought the airline from L. B. Maytag. In a curious switch, Maytag took over National Airlines, a Trunk, while Lew Dymond, of National, came to Denver to become president of

Ozark Air Lines' Douglas DC-9-15 N970Z.

Pacific Air Lines' Boeing 727-193 N2979G in red, white and blue livery. The aircraft passed to Air West and was later leased to Braniff. (*The Boeing Company*)

Piedmont Airlines chose the Boeing 737-201 as its standard jet equipment. The airline's first Boeing was N734N seen here. Markings are dark blue with red lettering. (*The Boeing Company*)

The biggest aircraft to enter local service operation—the Boeing 727-291 of Frontier Airlines. Passengers are seen boarding N7278F via the ventral airstairs.

Frontier. He immediately began to plan further expansion and development. He took over some of Continental's routes and signed a contract for the conversion of his fleet of Convair CV-340s to Allison propeller-turbine power. On 11 August he ordered five Boeing 727s, a remarkable gesture in view of the current Frontier operating results, which showed low average passenger loads. In this sense, Dymond's decision on the Boeing trijet was a greater risk than Peach's BAC One-Eleven venture. Frontier's route density, serving as it did a sparsely populated area, with few big cities, was vastly different from Mohawk's commuter belt.

Frontier did have an advantage, however, in operating many longer stages, making possible more economic operations. Under the C.A.B. subsidy formula, the airline was well compensated for serving many small points—a large number only just scraped through the Use It or Lose It test. The Convair CV-580s turned out to be very successful, and Dymond began to bombard Washington with route applications. With Boeing 727s on order he could claim to be able to fly nonstop between almost any two cities within his territory, and he conducted a vigorous campaign to extend the Frontier network from Seattle to Houston and New Orleans in the Pacific Northwest—Southwest Case. On 3 June, 1966, however, the C.A.B. turned down Frontier's 'bid to join the ranks of unsubsidized airlines' on the grounds that traffic density was too low to sustain competing carriers.

But Lew Dymond had the bit between his teeth, and during the next two years his campaign for new routes, nonstop authority, and general expansion of activity reached a crescendo. Frontier's ambitions extended to almost every state in the U.S.A., and apart from extensive nonstop routes between key cities in the Rockies and Prairies, many of which were granted by a long-suffering C.A.B., the ultimate in Local Service airline applications came on 1 November, 1967, when Frontier filed for a coast-to-coast route from California to New York and Washington. So far, this ambition has not been realized, and the C.A.B. has indicated that route strengthening does have limits.

Having given the nod to the airlines on the issue of participating in trunk, or inter-city routes, the C.A.B. proceeded to match its words with deeds. On 23 December, 1966, North Central was the first to file for nonstop authority under the new policy: Omaha—Minneapolis and Milwaukee—Detroit followed by requests to serve Toronto, Kansas City, and Denver. By this time, Ozark had extended its Chicago—Sioux City route (awarded in 1965) to Denver; Piedmont was granted access to New York; Southern obtained several nonstop routes from rapidly-growing Huntsville; West Coast received the all clear on Spokane—Seattle; while Trans-Texas became an international carrier with rights into Mexico.

In 1967, Mohawk and Allegheny were relieved of many restrictions on their operating authority between most of the larger cities of the northeast; Ozark was permitted to fly nonstop from St Louis to Milwaukee; West Coast at last entered the Seattle—Portland market; and Frontier was awarded nonstop authority from Denver to Kansas City and Denver to St Louis. This last route was 570 miles long; it linked a city of more than

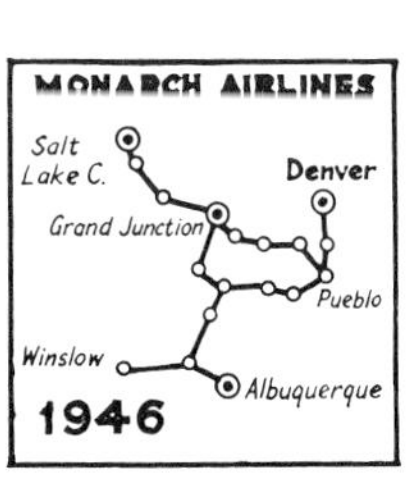

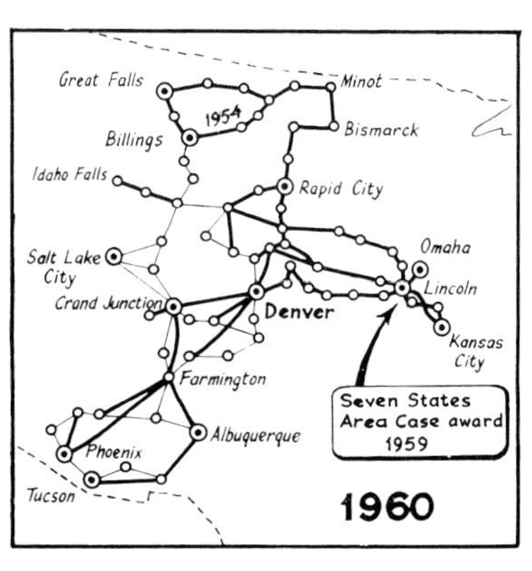

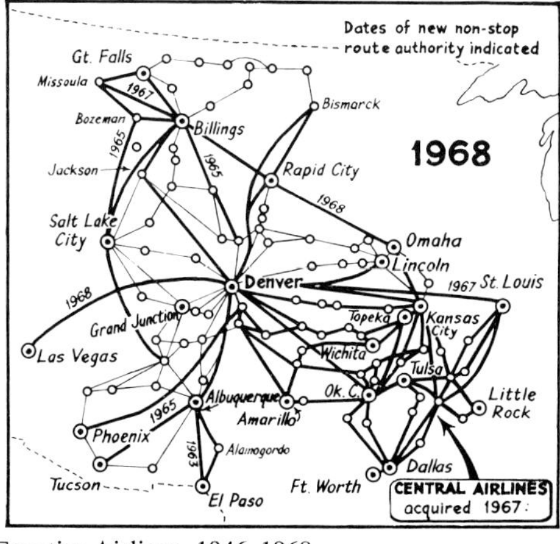

Fig. 27. Growth of Frontier Airlines, 1946–1968.

500,000 people with one of upwards of 2,000,000. Little wonder that the term Local Service was falling out of fashion.

More generous route awards flowed from the C.A.B. Ozark reached New York, with a direct route from Peoria, on 27 April, 1969, and North Central matched this from Milwaukee on 8 September, 1970. Following Ozark's access to Denver in 1966, Trans-Texas, on 1 March, 1969, and North Central, on 15 June of that year, augmented the Colorado capital's position as a Local Service connecting point.

When Trans-Texas, proudly renamed Texas International Airlines in 1968, opened a through service from Houston to Los Angeles, via Albuquerque, on 15 January, 1970, it became theoretically possible to cross the nation by using a combination of only two Local Service airlines. A change in terminology to something more appropriate than 'Local' seemed to be overdue.

Interior of a North Central Airlines' 100-seat Douglas DC-9-31. Alternating seats are blue and gold.

Locals into Regionals

The Local Service campaign for route strengthening was conducted with considerable finesse and determination through the early 1960s. It derived support and inspiration from a number of favourable factors. First was the sustained traffic growth of healthy proportions, averaging about 17 per cent per year during the period. This was reflected in higher passenger loads, permitting aircraft such as the DC-9s to appear economically viable, especially if the growth was projected on an orthodox historical trend line. Second was the continuing decrease in subsidy demands. Freedom from subsidy was still a long way off, but improvements were constantly made each year. Administratively, the airlines were better organized, operated more efficiently, and were financially far more viable than in the late 1950s. No longer were they dependent for their equipment on the second-hand aircraft trade. They had become good risks and could raise equity or loan capital for almost any purchasing programme. This did not end at aircraft alone. Large sums were spent on such items as new hangars, new headquarters buildings, and computerized reservations systems.

Eventually, however, the flowing tide began to ebb. In their eagerness to join the jet operators, some of the airlines invested in aircraft whose productivity was much greater than the superseded types. Success depended on the high traffic growth being continued for many years. Also, the size of the BAC One-Elevens, DC-9s, and Boeing 727s (about 80 seats) demanded average loads of about 35–40 to break even. This was possible on many routes; one or two airlines such as Bonanza, with its Los Angeles—Las Vegas run, possessed them even before the C.A.B.'s new liberalization policy. But a fleet of, say, five DC-9s needed many such routes for profitable operations, and there was a practical limit to how many dense routes could be passed on to an individual Local, or Regional airline.

Another factor was the degree of penetration into the new markets which the Locals could expect to achieve over the Trunks. In some cases, this could be expected to be substantial, if only because of the average American's love of choice, and especially if the quality of service offered by the previous sitting tenant had not been outstanding. But there were other cases where the trunkline service had not been so bad as to produce a wholesale swing of customer preference. Also—and this was a notable change of trend—the trunk airlines were beginning to think twice before condoning the growing intrusion into their traditional markets.

Gone were the days when a trunk airline was glad to dispose of a route because it was too short, or did not fit neatly into the network pattern, or tied up uneconomically an extra aircraft type. There were precious few of such routes left, and the Locals were now getting, in the Trunks' view, over-ambitious. The 'Friendly Skies of United'—to quote the promotional theme of that airline—were anything but amicable when faced with the loss of profitable routes. In another situation Eastern Air Lines discussed with Southern Airways the possibility of the transfer of a package of small routes in Florida and Georgia. A few years earlier, the deal would probably have gone through; but now Eastern realized that it could operate

Southern Airways' first Douglas DC-9-15, N91S.

Pacific Southwest Airlines' Douglas DC-4 N30068 at San Francisco in March 1957. This airline, perhaps more than any other, handicapped the development of Southwest Airways, later Pacific Air Lines. (*John Stroud*)

these routes at no great loss, thanks to the introduction of smaller jets, the DC-9s. Pacific Air Lines received tough competition, not from a Trunk, but from an enterprising intra-state Californian carrier, Pacific Southwest Airlines (PSA), which virtually forced the Local airline off several important routes including San Jose—Los Angeles. Lew Dymond found that TWA did not take kindly to his entry into the Denver—Kansas City/St Louis markets, and showed its pique by trebling its competitive jet schedules. When Trans-Texas announced its intention to intensify its Dallas—Houston nonstop service, Harding Lawrence, president of Braniff, was understood to be positively discouraging.

So the Locals' honeymoon was over. They had fought and won their battle to obtain enlarged route networks. Now, in 1968, they had to engage in a new, and tougher battle: to hold on to the new franchises and to operate them profitably in the face of trunkline competition, meeting at the same time their other commitments as Local Service carriers in the C.A.B. subsidy book.

A glance at the statistics, both traffic and financial, of the thirteen Local Service airlines in 1966 reveals that some were lagging behind the industry leaders by quite a large margin, so large that they were vulnerable to possible take-over bids. First to succumb was Central Airlines, from Fort Worth. On 15 September, 1966, it applied to the C.A.B. for permission to merge with Ozark, but this was withdrawn because of lender objections. But shortly afterwards, on 4 May, 1967, it agreed to merge with Frontier, a move which quickly passed through the necessary stages in Washington, and the merger became effective on 1 October of the same year, with Frontier the surviving carrier. The decision relieved the C.A.B. of the difficult problem of trying to find a way of strengthening Central's route network into a viable shape, an almost impossible task in a geographical area which allowed little room for competitive manoeuvre.

Next airline to discuss mergers was Pacific, which reached an agreement with West Coast in June 1967. This revived a former action of May 1964 when Nick Bez, of West Coast, tried to buy a controlling interest in Pacific, but was forced to withdraw because of questionable methods. Pacific was really in severe trouble, for C.A.B. nonstop route awards were not sufficient to stop the incursions of PSA. In a last desperate effort to achieve public recognition, Pacific actually launched a 'sweaty palms' parody of a safety campaign on 30 April, 1967, issuing passengers with survival kits and security blankets and announcing a safe landing with a 'Well, folks, we made it again.' Although reaching the columns of the *New York Times*, this kind of publicity did Pacific no good at all, and an enlarged merger proposal in August 1967 to amalgamate three airlines, Pacific, West Coast, and Bonanza, was greeted with relief. A new airline, Air West, received President Johnson's approval (necessary because of foreign routes) on 9 April, 1968.

The chief shareholder, Nick Bez, sold control to Howard Hughes, restlessly seeking airline involvement after surrendering TWA. Following a series of court wrangles, Hughes took over on 21 July, 1969, and began changing its image of an ailing airline, which was renamed Hughes Air West in July 1970.

The third airline to appear as a candidate for take-over was Lake Central Airlines, which never really recovered from its unfortunate experience with the Nord 262, on which it had placed so much faith (with, incidentally, encouragement from the C.A.B.). In April 1967, L. Thomas Ferguson of Allegheny was appointed president, and most of the Lake Central executives resigned. The merger with Allegheny was approved by shareholders and C.A.B. alike on 14 March, 1968.

Thus, after fifteen years of stability during which time the thirteen Local Service airlines came to be regarded almost as a permanent fixture, their numbers were suddenly reduced to nine. Two of them, Air West

Air West's Douglas DC-9-31 N9335. The airline was formed by the merger of Pacific Air Lines, Bonanza Air Lines and West Coast Airlines and has since been renamed Hughes Air West.

and Frontier, together covered an area almost half of the U.S.A. In a highly competitive environment, the ambition to grow and expand turned into a struggle for survival. Only the fittest could fight off a severe setback as the finances and operations were too delicately balanced to give the airlines complete immunity against injury, however temporary.

By 1968, the Local Service airlines were referring to themselves as Regionals, although this term, while apt, was not then recognized by the C.A.B. By the mid-1960s, the Scheduled Air Taxis (appropriately dubbed Third Level for a while, and later, more stylishly, Commuter) began to penetrate former Local Service preserves. These airlines multiplied prolifically and often repeated the development patterns of the early Locals (see Chapter 18, pages 466–94).

Allegheny Airlines, the largest Local Service passenger carrier, agreed to merge with Mohawk Airlines, the third largest, on 12 April, 1972, having received C.A.B. approval five days earlier. This created a "Very Large Regional." Otherwise, during the next few years, the Regional airlines were relatively stable—no more amalgamations and just one new entrant: Air New England—the result of a merger, in October 1970, of several scheduled air taxi companies—which received its Local Service certificate on 15 October, 1974, but abruptly ceased to exist on 31 October, 1981.

Allegheny renamed itself U.S. Air on 30 October, 1979. This ambitious title epitomized a new age for the Regionals. They spread their wings into areas previously undreamed of. Frontier came close to achieving its cherished coast-to-coast route; while Ozark, Texas International, and Piedmont had to redraw their route maps almost every month.

The other concurrent dramatic development was the merger of North Central and Southern on 1 July, 1979, to become Republic Airlines, which then bought Hughes Airwest on 1 October, 1980. Thus, with a rapidity that would have been impossible before deregulation, two new trunk airlines had been born.

In October 1980, the C.A.B. recognized the inevitable. Effective on 1 January, 1981 all U.S. scheduled passenger airlines were redesignated either Majors, Nationals, or Regionals, based on a qualifying level of $1 billion annual revenue for the Majors, and $75 million for the Nationals. This decision was a direct consequence of the epoch-making legislation, under the Carter Administration: the Airline Deregulation Act of 1978.

Republic and U.S. Air were elevated to Major status, and the other surviving Local Service airlines fell into the new National group, which was augmented by the former Supplementals (pages 447–65), Intra-State airlines (pages 548–54), and All-Freight airlines (pages 421–46).

The Regional airlines were subdivided into Large ($10–$75 million annual revenue) and Medium (less than $10 million. Air Wisconsin, one of the more vigorous of the newer generation of Commuter airlines, was already—and correctly—calling itself a Large Regional.

CHAPTER SIXTEEN

All-Freight Airlines

Prelude to a New Industry

The business of transporting air cargo as we know it today is a comparatively recent development. The first U.S. airlines specializing in the carriage of heavy freight, or cargo, instead of passengers or mail, were not founded until after World War 2. Experiment and research into such activity, however, began much earlier, in fact, almost at the birth of scheduled air transport.

One of the predecessor companies of United Air Lines, National Air Transport, was actually created for the purpose of carrying air express—that is parcels as distinct from letters. As early as 14 November, 1926,

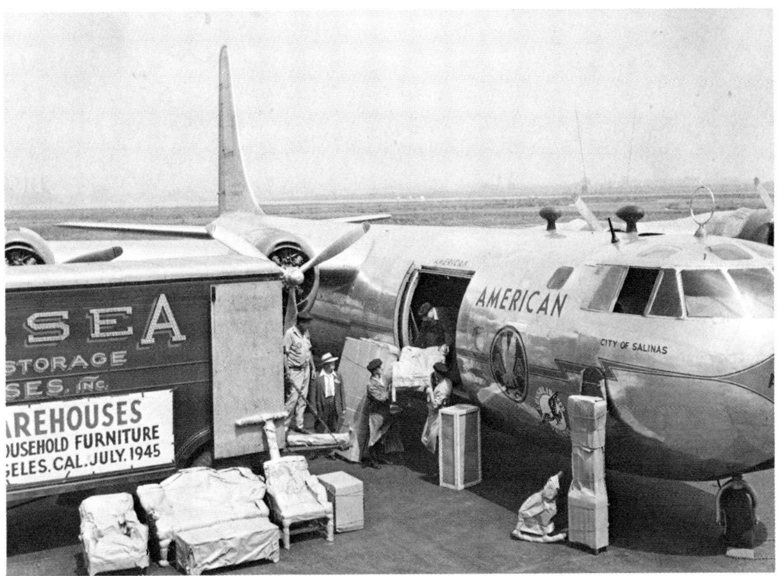

For a short period just after the war American Airlines undertook experimental cargo operations with the Consolidated Model 39 NX30039 *City of Salinas* which was a one-off civil development of the B-24 Liberator. It is seen at Los Angeles in July 1945.

the airline was incorporated with the participation of the American Railway Express Company. Two air express contracts were signed with that organization to carry small packages by air between Chicago and Dallas and between Chicago and New York. Although delays in obtaining the mail contracts necessary to launch the airline prevented these contracts being taken up, new ones were agreed to and the first air express service in the United States took-off from Hadley Field en route for Chicago on 1 September, 1927.

On the same date, Boeing Air Transport, Colonial Air Transport, and Western Air Express also signed up with American Railway Express; Pacific Air Transport came in on 10 April, 1928, and Varney Air Lines on 30 January, 1930. The American Railway Express Company became the Railway Express Agency (R.E.A.) on 1 March, 1929. The basis for the contracts was that, after deduction of out-of-pocket expenses for overheads by R.E.A., 75 per cent of the revenue should go to the airline, 25 per cent to the Agency. In the summer of 1932 the percentage share was changed to $87\frac{1}{2}:12\frac{1}{2}$.

A unique feature of the Ford Tri-Motor was the retractable wing compartments. Mail is seen being loaded into the lowered starboard compartment of a National Air Transport aircraft in 1930. (*United Air Lines*)

Four of the members of the R.E.A. air express system were divisions of the United Air Lines Group and these accounted for most of its turnover, estimated at more than 92 per cent in May 1934 when the airline industry was reorganized after the cancellation of the air mail contracts. Air express, however, was then still a minor factor in airline revenues, totalling only 3·68 per cent. Because of the low rates, express earned only one tenth of the total mail revenue, although generating one third of the ton-miles.

In the summer of 1932, American Airways, TWA, and certain smaller lines formed General Air Express as a rival to R.E.A., but on 31 December, 1935, a new uniform contract was signed after the two groups agreed to merge. After 1 February, 1936, all the airlines operated a single nationwide air express system.

Following the passing of the Civil Aeronautics Act of 1938, the airlines sought to clarify the legal position of their agreements with the Railway Express Agency in relation to air transport. After much discussion and negotiation, certain straightforward provisions recommended by the

Loading parcels into the nose hold of a Boeing 247 from a Railway Express Agency van at Los Angeles in about 1933. The words United Air Lines on the nose of the Boeing are on a sticker which was presumably applied for this posed photograph. (*United Air Lines*)

C.A.B. were agreed to, and the Board determined, on 2 March, 1943, that '. . . we see nothing which would justify us, in the light of existing conditions, in finding that they are adverse to the public interest or in violation of the Act, and therefore they should be approved'.

Fulfilling its rôle as a rate-fixing authority, the C.A.B. set an air express rate equivalent to $0.80 per ton-mile in 1938. This was reduced to $0.70 on 15 July, 1943, and to $0.614 on 1 January, 1946.

Air Cargo Inc and the First Freight Services

The airline industry began to develop an interest in air freight towards the end of 1940. Arising from certain misgivings over the net yields from its air express business, the Air Transport Association of America (ATA) initiated the formation of Air Express Inc on 25 June, 1940. This was a research organization in which the Big Four airlines (United, American, Eastern, and TWA) participated, and which led directly to the formation of Air Cargo Inc on 14 March, 1941. The other scheduled domestic airlines joined later, on 31 December, 1942, and All American Airways completed the membership on 30 September, 1944.

United Air Lines appears to have been concerned with air freight on its own account concurrently with ATA's activities. United's records show that the management consultant firm of Booz, Fry, Allen & Hamilton was retained in November 1940 to prepare a study of air freight. A two-volume report was submitted to United on 7 March, 1941, tabulating the

Loading mail onto a United Air Lines Douglas DC-4 in the early post-war period. (*United Air Lines*)

views of 583 executives in 121 industries. Meanwhile, on 23 December, 1940, United began what was probably the first all-cargo service in U.S. airline history. The *United Air Line News* reported the event: 'Inaugurated on December 23 in time to accommodate heavy pre-Christmas business, the flight leaves New York daily at 11.30 p.m. with arrival in Chicago at 3.40 a.m. After the first month of operation, C. P. Graddick, director of United Air Lines' air mail-express-freight department, described the innovation as a decided success. United's move in establishing an all-cargo trip, supplementing its combination passenger-cargo schedules between New York and Chicago, was based on the showing of steadily increasing loads partially attributable to the National Defense Program. The cargo flights are made by United's regular day Mainliners in which passenger space is utilized for mail and express, thereby permitting loads of up to 5,000 lb.'

The New York—Chicago freight service, actually an all-express aircraft-load experiment, was routed via Cleveland and operated in the westbound direction only. It ended on 31 May, 1941.

United commissioned another freight survey from the same consultants, who submitted a report on interviews with 604 executives in 70 industries of the West Coast on 4 August, 1941. After America came into the war other freight services were attempted, the first from New York to Salt Lake City between 1 November, 1942, and 31 May, 1943. This was superseded on 16 October, 1943, by a New York—San Francisco service, using three DC-3s returned from military use.

Air Cargo Inc, the Big Four's cargo research unit, opened an office in New York and began to function on 15 December, 1941. Fifty people were employed and others seconded from the airlines. During the next three years 35 market research studies were completed, together with 18 other reports on such subjects as aircraft requirements, ground transport problems, and tariffs. These were confidential to the airlines and never published. As the war drew to its close, the need for prompt action, rather than continued research, led to the winding up of Air Cargo Inc on 29 November, 1944.

By this time, American Airlines had filed with the C.A.B. the first schedule of rates for air cargo as distinct from air express, and began a regular transcontinental DC-3 cargo service on 15 October, 1944. United's coast-to-coast service was expanded and Los Angeles became a co-terminal with San Francisco on 15 April, 1945. TWA added a parallel freight route on 1 July, 1945, and United, whose experimental freight operation in 1940–41 had been wholly in association with the Railway Express Agency, issued its own tariffs on 1 February, 1946.

The Rate War

United operated three daily round trips from New York to California, using DC-3 Cargoliners, at a standard rate of 26·5c per ton-mile. Although this was considerably lower than the equivalent express ton-mile rate, any illusions that such a level would promote stability in the air freight business were quickly dispelled by the entry into the field by a new breed of entrepreneur airlines, led by ex-World War 2 pilots. Participating mainly in the passenger business on an irregular basis, there were a few who believed passionately in the future of air freight.

The scheduled airlines did not share the popular view that these carriers were enterprising innovators. Many years later the battered survivors of the Air Freight Case won recognition and respectability by admittance to the Air Transport Association. In 1945, however, they were regarded by established companies as a gang of unprincipled opportunists, and ruthless steps were taken to eliminate them.

Globe Freight Airline Inc and U.S. Airlines Inc were the first of the aspiring new freight carriers to seek official recognition by filing applications for certificates of public convenience and necessity to the C.A.B. late in 1945 in the Boston—New York—Atlanta—New Orleans Case. Others joined in, including Slick Airways and The Flying Tiger Line, which presented its three-pound document to the Board in October 1946.

The scheduled airlines met the challenge of the unscheduled freight lines in two ways. The first was through a series of petitions and counter-petitions with the Board, and the second was by a blatant rate war. Both led to some forthright language. American Airlines described the freight airlines as 'eager for a certificate, unconcerned with mounting losses and the unsoundness of carrying traffic at less-than-cost rates, threatening to carve the heart out of American's freight business and then presenting it to the Board as a basis for their certification as a common carrier'. Robert Prescott, of Flying Tiger, countered, 'I think it would be good to point out to the Board the amount of freight business American had when we started the business. Also, how do they tie up the statement that we are unconcerned with mounting losses when we are trying to get the rates up? Who has led to this rate cutting and who is the obvious ringleader of the present fiasco?'

Prescott was on good ground statistically. Although precise figures are unavailable for the early post-war period of cargo operations, because so much was non-scheduled and badly recorded, 30 million freight ton-miles were estimated for 1946, compared with less than 15 million for 1945. Slick Airways calculated that its 11·2 million freight ton-miles achieved during its first year of operations in 1946 was almost ten times the total of *all* the certificated airlines in the previous year.

Against these figures, the claims of the established airlines to have pioneered the air freight business sounded a little hollow. Admirable though the research of Air Cargo Inc may have been, this was all paper work and of little value to the general public if the airlines did not put into effect the recommendations of its own researchers. Slick, Flying Tiger, California Eastern and the rest of the new breed believed in action, not words, and went ahead on an intuitive basis. American and United and company met the threat by matching its words—in the C.A.B. Air Freight Case crossfire—by action, namely by instituting a devastating rate war.

During 1947 the rates of the non-scheduled carriers gradually dropped from between 22c and 20c per ton-mile to about 15c. The scheduled carriers ruthlessly cut their rates, United to 14c, American to a low of

Loading cargo into the Speedpak of an Eastern Air Lines' Lockheed Constellation. The Speedpak was an aerodynamically clean under-fuselage attachment. (*Eastern Air Lines*)

11c. Although such levels were hopelessly uneconomic, they were able to cross-subsidize freight losses with profits from passengers and mail. At this time they were also receiving substantial Federal mail subsidies over and above the payments for the service, and American actually applied for higher mail rates during the period when it was offering freight capacity at 11c per mile.

No quarter was asked or given between the two sides. The C.A.B., to whom both appealed as an impartial umpire, reviewed the situation at what has been described as a glacial pace. Under Economic Regulation 292.5, of 5 May, 1947, the C.A.B. did however grant to the all-cargo carriers authority to conduct common carrier services on a regularly scheduled basis, pending final Board decision on the Air Freight Case. Temporary certificates were granted to 14 all-cargo carriers but, because of high casualties in the Rate War, only six were still operating by the end of 1948. These were: The Flying Tiger Line, Riddle Airlines, Slick Airways, U.S. Airlines, Willis Air Service, and Seaboard & Western Airlines (*See Table 23, page 625*).

Shortly after the granting of scheduled authority, the leading freight airlines, Flying Tiger, Slick, and California Eastern, filed tariffs which were 12–39 per cent below those of the certificated carriers. Also, numerous variations on the basic tariffs involving special discounts for commodities, deferred delivery, and terminal assembly, were submitted.

Eventually, after many of the ambitious independent freight airlines had gone bankrupt, the C.A.B. issued its tentative decision on 21 April, 1948, subsequently amended to its Minimum Rate Order of 1 July, 1948. The basic rate was fixed at 16c per ton-mile for the first 1,000 miles, and 13c thereafter. Though modified by rates for special cases, routes, and commodities, this rate remained substantially in force until, effective from 21 September, 1953, following a petition from Slick Airways, the level was raised to 20c for the first 1,000 miles, and 16·25c thereafter.

The First Scheduled Cargo Airlines

The Air Freight Case dragged on another year until 24 April, 1949, when the C.A.B. finally announced its decision. It awarded experimental five-year scheduled all-freight certificates, effective from 12 August, 1949, to four all-cargo airlines: Slick, Flying Tiger, U.S. Airlines, and Airnews. The last-named was a strange selection, bewildering in its apparent irrelevance to the main issues involved. The airline was newly-formed and operated two DC-3s between Corpus Christi and San Antonio; but by 12 October, 1951, it had abandoned its certificate. Another of the four, a non-scheduled freight carrier, U.S. Airlines, had survived the Rate War of 1945–1947 by the shrewd decision to contract out of it. It resumed non-scheduled operations only after the Minimum Rate Order of 21 April, 1948, but in spite of its 1949 certificate, had to suspend scheduled operations in June 1951, after heavy losses. U.S. Airlines continued its precarious existence spasmodically on the New York—Miami freight route and on Air Force contracts; but, after a series of crashes in 1952 and two more bankruptcy proceedings, the C.A.B. finally withdrew its scheduled authority on 27 April, 1955.

Slick Airways

Outstanding among the airlines certificated in 1949 was Slick Airways, founded by Earl F. Slick in January 1946. Slick had begun operations as a contract carrier of air freight on 4 March of that year and had rapidly built up a substantial business by operating a fleet of ten Curtiss C-46E aircraft purchased from the Reconstruction Finance Corporation. For the first few years, success followed success, and the airline held its place as the nation's foremost freight carrier. It benefited from every progressive step made by the C.A.B., and with selection as one of the scheduled freight carriers in 1949, a profitable future seemed assured.

On 16 April, 1951, Slick became the world's first operator of the Douglas DC-6A, a version of the famous four-engined line of commercial aircraft specially designed for freight operations. Its sister passenger aircraft, the DC-6B, had entered service with United Air Lines only five days previously, so that Slick's promotion of a new aircraft type in an all-freight rôle marked an important advance in the relative stature of the cargo airlines. Unfortunately for Slick—and, for that matter, all the

The Douglas DC-6A N37590 *Cargoliner New York* was one of five delivered to United Air Lines in 1956. (*United Air Lines*)

freight airlines—the scheduled passenger airlines were also beginning to concentrate on freight development. American Airlines, particularly, ordered a fleet of ten DC-6As, and made no secret of its belated intention to go after the market.

American, in fact, had filed an objection with the C.A.B. in 1949, almost before the ink was dry on the first four certificates (which incidentally were the first to be granted since the Grandfather Rights of 1938). After the certificated carriers applied for judicial review, the Circuit Court of Appeals in Washington, D.C., unanimously upheld the C.A.B.'s decision in a notable judgement on 27 September, 1951.

By straightforward methods of promotion, however, and taking full advantage of an extensive combined route system and network of city and airport facilities, the scheduled airlines achieved their cherished objective of putting the freight airlines on the defensive. At this time, Slick was the largest all-cargo commercial operator, while Flying Tiger supplemented its commercial revenue by lucrative military contracts. By normal criteria, each should have been able to survive; but concentrated competition, particularly by American Airlines, revealed the sensitivity of air freight economics. The hard fact was that low freight rates could only be sustained by either high load factors or cross-subsidy from other sources of revenue. The excess of freight capacity provided by the aggressive passenger airlines (contrasting with their apathy during the halcyon days of seat shortage immediately after World War 2) bit into the all-cargo carriers' load factors. Flying Tiger was able to hold out because of its diversified operations; but Slick was forced to enter into merger negotiations in an effort to survive.

On 26 March, 1953, the two airlines agreed to merge, gaining approval from their respective stockholders on 6 August. Predictably, the passenger carriers protested on the grounds of the creation of a monopoly, but on 7 January, 1954, the C.A.B. approved the merger, subject to amicable settlement of labour problems involving seniority and integration of personnel. With Flying Tiger and Slick occupying adjacent hangars at Burbank, the stage seemed set for the start of a new era. Bob Prescott of Flying Tiger, Tom Grace of Slick, and the staff of the two airlines began to prepare for joint operations.

Tragically, in addition to the opposition of the passenger airlines, difficulties arose from other directions. First, the C.A.B.'s own lawyers objected; secondly, labour problems became acute. The Board delayed issuing the new certificate covering the amalgamated network, while the two airlines tried to meet the severe termination clauses in the labour agreements. The liability on the two companies would have been enormous, following as it did upon a decline in business in 1954 with the end of the Korean airlift, and consequent layoff of staff. Reluctantly, the merger proposals were dropped on 20 September, 1954, and, almost in despair, Prescott threatened to close down his airline's scheduled activities on the next day, a threat which, fortunately, was only a passing fancy.

Slick Airways' N90806, illustrated, was the first Douglas DC-6A. Markings were blue and white. Airfreight Route No 101 appears in small letters on the base of the fin.

Failure of the two major freight airlines to achieve an eminently sensible merger was a great blow to morale in that industry. Traditionally the underdogs, along with the other non-scheduled airlines, Slick and Flying Tiger, had been forced to fight their way up every step of the ladder. Even after the Minimum Rate legislation of 1948 and the route certification of 1949, the freight lines operated at best on an uneasy knife-edge of viability. Outstanding successes in real commercial terms were still elusive, and the vast potential of air freight traffic, continually predicted by theorists, never seemed to be realizable in practice. Thus, Slick went through difficult times following its abortive merger attempt. After a constant struggle to make ends meet on its scheduled freight services, it abruptly abandoned all scheduled commitments on 24 February, 1958.

D. W. Rentzel, Slick's chairman and a former C.A.B. member, had this to say: 'The regulatory situation in this industry has been and is such that continuation of operations is not warranted. The C.A.B. has been preoccupied with the problems of airlines which are entitled to subsidy. It has not had a similar interest in carriers such as Slick whose operations are supported by private capital and are not underwritten by the government. From the very beginning, its relationship with Slick has been that of court and applicant.'

Rentzel also commented bitterly on the lack of co-ordination with Defense Departments which had quantities of cargo piling up in its warehouses while Slick's DC-6As 'were sitting doing nothing.'

Although Slick had been admitted to the Air Transport Association in March 1956, the senior members of that body showed little comradely sentiment. American Airlines demanded that, because Slick had not gone through the customary mandatory procedures before terminating service, it should be deprived of its scheduled operating certificate immediately, rather than on the 1 January, 1959, date stipulated by the C.A.B. The latter took a more tolerant view, and gave Slick another chance.

Retaining its contract operations, the airline managed to turn the corner financially, buying in the process in July 1960 the Illinois Shade Cloth Company for $6,350,000, as a means of diversifying its activities and possibly as an insurance against future failure in air transport. Simultaneously it ordered six Lockheed GL 207 Super Hercules freight aircraft, a dramatic gesture which, however, never materialized into an operational fleet. Instead, Slick ordered six Canadair CL-44 propeller-turbine powered freighters on 16 October, 1959, following Flying Tiger's lead a few months previously. This unique aircraft, with its swing-tail for open-end loading, made its first revenue flight for Slick on a military contract flight from San Francisco to Manila on 11 February, 1962. This was a prelude to the reinstatement of scheduled commercial service on its transcontinental Route 101 on 1 October, 1962.

History repeated itself, however, and the airline's fortunes once more declined until on 27 August, 1965, the C.A.B. again authorized suspension of scheduled services. On 1 July, 1966, the assets being used in its military operations were transferred to Airlift International, which also acquired Route 101 on 22 July, 1968. Slick became a financial holding company, called the Slick Corporation, augmenting its Illinois Shade business with the Drew Chemical Company (purchased on 19 February, 1968) and a Pulverising Machinery plant. Thus after being a pioneer in its field, and for long a champion of the air-freight cause, Slick's airline interests were reduced to a minority stockholding in Airlift, whose influence had formerly been insignificant.

The Flying Tiger Line

If the story of Slick was one of disappointing failure following years of pioneer development, the story of The Flying Tiger Line was by contrast one of complete success. Enduring no less hardship and surviving as many vicissitudes in the hard world of air freight, Flying Tiger emerged eventually to become the world's greatest freight airline. This position of eminence was reached by a combination of the cavalier spirit of its founders, a measure of shrewd judgement as the airline matured, and a fair slice of luck in making some vital decisions at just the right time.

The Flying Tiger Line was founded as the National Skyway Freight Corporation on 25 June, 1945, by Robert Prescott, a former 'Hump' flyer in China with Gen Chennault's 'Flying Tigers', as the C-46 pilots were affectionately called in the Far Eastern theatre of World War 2. Backed by Sam Mosher of the Signal Oil Company, the N.S.F.C.—the name was selected in an attempt to acquire respectability—bought 14 Budd RB-1 Conestogas for $401,000. The $90,000 down payment required

NC45356 was one of the stainless steel Budd Conestogas used by the National Skyway Freight Corporation, later The Flying Tiger Line. The rear loading door can be seen in the down position. (*Flying Tiger Line*)

by the War Surplus authorities was raised partly by Prescott's former associates of the American Volunteer Group (AVG) who flew with him on the 'Hump'.

The Budd Conestoga was a strange craft. Built by a railway rolling stock manufacturer specializing in stainless steel construction, it invited comment from its pilots and operators ranging from amused astonishment to exasperated contempt. Its design was novel, to say the least. Nothing like it had been produced from the orthodox drawing offices of Douglas or Boeing. Its structure also was new, using stainless steel, wafer thin, for the surface skinning. But it did have a redeeming feature: its nosewheel undercarriage gave it a level floor while being loaded or unloaded, and the access through the large ventral door was better than that of the Douglas C-47 or Curtiss C-46. Unfortunately its flying characteristics were poor and sorely tried the patience of the crews.

The first Conestoga revenue-earning flight was in July 1945, when the N.S.F.C. flew a load of grapes from California to Georgia. On 21 August the carrier began cautiously to fly coast-to-coast, learning by experience, such as a crash on the third day of operations. At the end of the year, Mosher and Prescott raised $2,500,000 from a firm of Wall Street brokers to see them through the lean months as they scratched around for enough business to keep their aircraft busy. Although Prescott applied to the C.A.B. for common carrier authority on 6 August, 1946, disaster loomed ahead unless his fortunes changed.

The turning point came late in 1946 when Prescott bid successfully for a military contract with Air Transport Command. N.S.F.C. undertook operation of 28 flights per week across the Pacific, supporting U.S. bases in east Asia, at a rate of 53c per route mile. Beginning on 1 January, 1947, the line made $500,000 profit in the first six months and was cushioned against the more severe blows of the Rate War during the immediate post-war period. Although the profit margin was high by the standards of the day, the ATC still found itself saving $125,000 per month and extended the contract to 20 November.

Prescott's men would probably have found some way of doing the job with the Conestogas, if pressed, but the N.S.F.C. contract consisted of providing full crews plus operational and maintenance facilities for 32 Douglas C-54s supplied by the ATC. The company moved to Burbank and in February 1947, responding to popular pressure, its name was changed officially to The Flying Tiger Line Inc. With the military contract safe in his pocket, Prescott may have felt that the image of 'Hump' flying techniques no longer inhibited his market potential.

During the period of this important military contract, Slick Airways gained ascendancy over Flying Tiger in the commercial field. This was undoubtedly a short-term advantage, but later history was to show that Flying Tiger's experience in diversification was to see it through many a crisis; whereas Slick's specialization was eventually to lead to its downfall.

During the next few years, the history of The Flying Tiger Line was almost synonymous with the history of the progress of air freighting. The quaint Budd Conestogas had given way to Douglas C-47s in March 1947 and were supplemented by four-engined C-54s by the end of that year. In 1950, 25 Curtiss C-46s were acquired on lease from the U.S. Air Force,

A Flying Tiger Line Douglas DC-4, NC91071, with Californian mountain background. (*The Star News, Pasadena*)

A rare photograph of one of The Flying Tiger Line's Douglas C-47s, introduced in March 1947. (*Flying Tiger Line*)

A Flying Tiger Line Curtiss C-46, with both airscrews feathered, flies on the power of its JATO (Jet Assisted Take Off) unit. (*Flying Tiger Line*)

an almost clairvoyant deal which put Flying Tiger in a strong position during the Korean airlift which followed shortly afterwards.

The Flying Tiger Line weathered some rough economic storms during 1953—the year of the abortive merger with Slick—by buying aircraft and selling at a profit. One of these transactions involved the first two DC-6As from Douglas, whose positions on the production line Prescott sold for $1,100,000.

Emerging from the crisis of 1954, The Flying Tiger Line inaugurated an overnight DC-6A transcontinental service on 13 February, 1955. Shortly afterwards, on 2 May, the C.A.B. granted an exemption to participate in the experimental 3c air mail scheme, in which mail was carried on a space-available basis. Other carriers had done so for two years, but the freight carriers had been excluded when a C.A.B. member had reversed his vote. Insignificant in terms of revenue to Flying Tiger, the mail rate decision was nevertheless valuable as an indication of the growing stature of the all-cargo carriers, which were beginning to be treated as equals with the established passenger lines.

Encouraged by solid signs of growing prosperity, Flying Tiger ordered ten Lockheed L.1049H Super Constellation freighters in September 1955, and planned to dispose of all other aircraft in a rationalization plan. In the same year, the company entered the group charter business when the C.A.B. ruled that the 'right of first refusal' enjoyed by the passenger airlines was no longer necessary. Flying Tiger immediately booked 50 round trips to Europe at $250 less than the IATA fare. On 12 March, 1956, Flying Tiger's certificate was renewed for an additional five years.

A further step towards fleet modernization was taken in May 1959 with an order for ten Canadair CL-44D swing-tail propeller-turbine freighters. This aircraft, basically a stretched version of the Bristol Britannia, had four Rolls-Royce Tyne engines, and could carry a load of 65,000 lb of freight from coast to coast. The Flying Tiger Line described the aircraft as 'the first and presently the only uncompromised all-cargo aircraft essential to the development of the air-freight business'. Most important of all, it was calculated to have a 40 per cent operating cost advantage over the Super Constellations.

At the time of the CL-44D order, Prescott was engaged in another rate war, this time with the descendants of the very airlines which had once been his allies during the conflict with the big passenger airlines during the late 1940s. When the major trunk carriers moved into the jet age, they disposed of scores of old (and sometimes not so old) piston-engined equipment. Many of these perfectly sound aircraft were sold to the non-scheduled airlines for service under military contracts, in competition for which they cut their prices to the bone.

One of the Flying Tiger Line's fleet of Lockheed L.1049H Super Constellations. (*Watson Photos*)

The Flying Tiger Line refused to bid at prices below cost, but lost these contracts. The non-scheduled airlines, on the other hand, got the business, but often went bankrupt through miscalculation of costs. Both parties suffered, and Flying Tiger in fact lost money during 1959 and 1960.

Common sense began to prevail in Washington. On 1 October, 1960, the C.A.B. laid down minimum rates for military charters, and on 1 July, 1961, the Military Air Transport Service negotiated three-year contracts, giving preference to those companies with modern, turbine-engined, convertible aircraft. This description fitted the CL-44D perfectly, and on 16 July, 1961, Flying Tiger made its first trans-Pacific flight from Travis Air Force Base, near San Francisco, to the Far East.

The airline did not neglect other commercial lines of development. In 1962 it took steps to integrate its services with other forms of transport, so as to offer a more efficient door-to-door service. It became the first airline to join the Pacific Steamship Conference, and began an air-truck programme, *Skyroad*, covering 1,500 cities. The following year, Flying Tiger entered into joint rail-air freight service with the New York Central Railroad.

A Flying Tiger Line Boeing 707-320C, N322F, in modified red and blue livery. (*Flying Tiger Line*)

In August 1964, the C.A.B. revised the rules governing blocked space in cargo aircraft. Under this scheme, the shipper guaranteed to pay for a minimum amount of contracted space, while the airline guaranteed the space, which was then charged at discounted rates. Predictably, the passenger carriers objected and could hardly have been mollified by the next important decision of the C.A.B. which followed a month later. This was an amendment to Part 207 of the Economic Regulations, placing restrictions on the volume of off-route charter business which certificated scheduled passenger carriers could perform—a meagre two per cent of their total scheduled mileage.

The charter restriction became effective on 1 January, 1965. To celebrate the event, The Flying Tiger Line added two more CL-44Ds to its fleet, leased two Boeing 707-349C jets, and moved its operating base from Burbank to a fine new one at Los Angeles International Airport. The next year was equally satisfactory. On 2 March, 1966, the U.S. Court of Appeals

Interior of a Boeing 707-320C cargo aircraft with a cargo pallet being rolled into position. (*The Boeing Company*)

condoned the blocked space decision, and this was further upheld by the U.S. Supreme Court in October. By this time, Flying Tiger had ordered ten Douglas DC-8-63F jet freighters at a cost of $105,000,000.

In 1966, just 21 years after the founding of the airline, Flying Tiger could talk in monetary terms of this magnitude, having reached a stage when an operating profit was more than $20,000,000 for the year. This was a far cry from the days when Prescott and his friends put up $90,000 to buy the Budd Conestogas and wondered where they could find enough cargo to fill them.

Process of Attrition

When Flying Tiger entered the jet age it had only one real competitor in the domestic scheduled freight airline field, Airlift International Inc, the new name of Riddle Airlines Inc, one of the smaller struggling companies of the early post-war days. In May 1945 Riddle was incorporated under Florida State laws as an extension of a wartime operation in which the J. P. Riddle company flew a series of regular flights to Brazil for American transport instructors at a technical aviation school.

The airline began a specialized service for passengers and freight from New York to Puerto Rico but had to discontinue passenger service in August 1947 under C.A.B. regulations. Early in 1951, Riddle received a temporary certificate to operate scheduled freight services to Puerto Rico. This was greatly expanded when, on 27 April, 1955, the C.A.B. Examiner recommended a seven-year domestic certificate covering routes to Florida from New York, Boston, Detroit, and Chicago. Scheduled domestic freight service started on 20 January, 1956.

An American Air Export & Import Company (AAXICO) Douglas C-47 with passengers embarking, at Miami in November 1945. AAXICO was one of the earliest post-war non-scheduled operators. (*Miami Daily News*)

AAXICO Curtiss C-46F N1825M. (*Gordon S. Williams*)

Riddle's new authority was the outcome of the C.A.B.'s North—South Air Freight Renewal Case, in which U.S. Airlines lost its temporary certificate and ceased operations. Taking its place (although not taking over the identical route), a new company, American Air Export & Import Company, formerly an Irregular Carrier, inaugurated scheduled freight services from New York to Atlanta on 15 November, 1956. The name of the company was changed to AAXICO Airlines Inc on 31 December. With a fleet of C-46s, the airline spread its activities into all kinds of air freight business and in due course relinquished its scheduled services on 1 July, 1959. In fact, AAXICO decided that common carriage of any kind was too hazardous economically and withdrew from this also on 30 June,

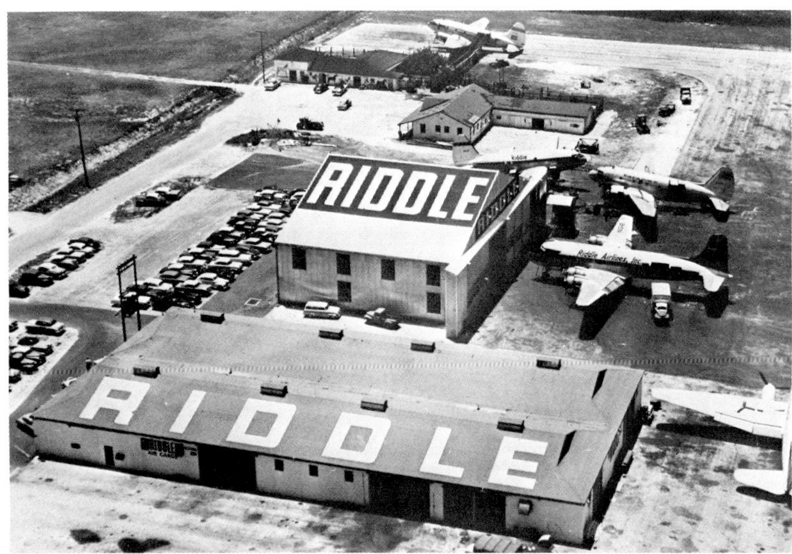

Riddle Airlines' headquarters at Miami. Executive offices and cargo warehouse are in the foreground with the maintenance hangar beyond. Three Riddle Curtiss C-46s and a Douglas DC-4 can be seen, all with different colour schemes. In the background is a Cubana C-46.

1960. From this time onward, the company became one of the military Logair specialists, for which it employed at one period a fleet of 23 C-46s. Its freight certificate was terminated on 9 October, 1962, and eventually Howard Korth, AAXICO's founder, completed a merger with Saturn Airways, a Supplemental Carrier, on 1 November, 1965.

To return to Riddle: as with all the other all-freight airlines, it went through hard times during the late 1950s, but managed to build up a fleet of 34 C-46s and two DC-4s by 1958. It obtained renewal of the New York—San Juan cargo route and acquired a complete new management which,

An Armstrong Whitworth Argosy freighter in Riddle Airlines livery. *(Sir W. G. Armstrong Whitworth Aircraft Ltd)*

among other innovations, ordered four Armstrong Whitworth Argosies from England on 20 February, 1959, as a move towards modernizing its fleet. These aircraft had much to commend them in this worthy objective. They were designed specially—almost cunningly—for the carriage of freight, including vehicles, which could be driven on or off on ramps, taking advantage of the low-slung fuselage, and front- and back-end loading. This was possible through the use of twin-boom supports for the tail structure, thus isolating the fuselage, and various other refinements were incorporated to assist easy loading. The power was supplied by four Rolls-Royce Dart propeller-turbines.

Riddle's purchase of the Argosies coincided unhappily with the loss of a Logair contract, which was, however, renewed on 1 July, 1960. The Argosy order was then reconfirmed and increased. The first one went into service in December 1960 and by the summer of the following year was reported to be setting records for service reliability. Although Riddle's certificate was renewed indefinitely in January 1962, the scheduled services continued to lose money and, with C.A.B. approval, the airline suspended all scheduled services on 30 June, 1962. The Argosies were returned to the manufacturer.

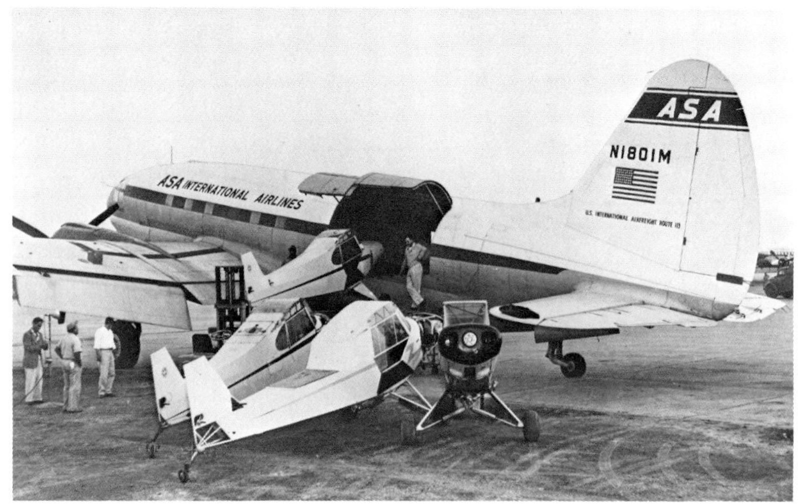

Light aircraft being loaded into an ASA International Airlines' Curtiss C-46. On the fin are the words U.S. International Airfreight Route 113. (*Moss Photo Service*)

Another sweeping reorganization of the management took place, with J. B. Franklin and J. H. Carmichael, formerly of Capital Airlines, taking over. The service pattern was gradually resumed with Douglas DC-7CFs on the Puerto Rico route in October 1962, and a daily Miami—New York C-46 service by 3 December, 1962. Riddle's fortunes then took a turn for the better. On 14 March, 1963, a $3·7 million loan was announced. With this substantial addition to its finances, two DC-8F jet freighters were leased from the Douglas company, which also agreed to defer payments on Riddle's DC-7Cs.

At this time, Riddle hoped to acquire an extension to its system by achieving a merger with Aerovias Sud Americana (ASA). This freight airline was founded in the summer of 1947 by a group of former U.S. Airlines employees, was certificated as a Large Irregular Carrier, and made its first flight from St Petersburg to Havana with a C-46 load of Willys Jeeps on 17 October, 1947. After building up a large trade in jeeps, tobacco, and flowers, ASA received a C.A.B. scheduled international freight certificate in August 1952 to operate to Bogota via intermediate points in Central America. In December 1959 this authority was extended to further points, and on 18 September, 1961, the C.A.B. Examiner recommended a merger with Riddle. The Board, however, deferred a decision, the case was prolonged, and ASA eventually filed a petition for bankruptcy on 12 May, 1965.

By the time the merger case was dismissed on 18 November, 1963, Riddle Airlines was concerned with other important developments. On 29 November of that year it changed its name to Airlift International Inc at a stormy stockholders meeting in which charges and counter-charges were exchanged between the floor and the platform.

Airlift International had taken on a new lease of life, however. On 30 March, 1966, it agreed to buy the assets and route certificate of the Slick Corporation, formerly Slick Airways, a deal which was promptly approved by the C.A.B. on 30 June. Airlift took over Slick's M.A.C. operations the next day. In September it declared an unprecedented profit of $3 million, which against $729,000 the previous year, and a substantial loss in almost all the previous years, was little short of miraculous.

In 1967, Airlift indulged in the luxury of ordering aircraft the like of which it could only have dreamed about four years previously: stretched DC-8s, Lockheed L-100s, sundry Boeings, and it even placed a deposit

Examples of Airlift International's smartly painted white, red and blue jet fleet. *Top*: Boeing 707-320C N525EJ; *centre*: Boeing 727-172C N732AL; and *bottom*: Douglas DC-8-63CF N6161A. (*The Boeing Company and Douglas Aircraft Company*)

One of Airlift International's swing-tail Canadair CL-44D-4s, seen loading air freight from a special loading platform.

for a U.S. supersonic transport. Hopes were revived of a renewed attempt to acquire the routes of the former ASA, so as to expand into South America.

On 20 May, 1968, Airlift consolidated its position when the Certificate of Public Convenience and Necessity for Route 101 was transferred from the Slick Corporation, effective from 22 July, 1968. The C.A.B. seemed determined that one of the last surviving air freight carriers could not complain that it had received less than a fair share of the all-cargo routes available. Furthermore, it ensured that The Flying Tiger Line should not be left with a monopolistic situation in a booming air freight market which was well able to support two transcontinental specialists.

International All-Cargo

If the establishment of domestic scheduled air freight services was a long struggle, the risks involved in international service were just as formidable. Mention has already been made of freight routes serving the Caribbean area, but these were unsuccessful, possibly because the traffic was too thinly spread for efficient and economic operation by the all-freight aircraft available. Most of these routes, to such destinations as Guatemala, Havana, and Panama, did not tap a potential single market which could form the foundation of a single trunk route.

On long-distance intercontinental routes, the problem of operating all-freight services profitably was different. On the world's leading transocean route, the North Atlantic, the frequency of service and aggregate capacity offered by a large number of competing flag carriers were so high that the freight shipper had a wide choice; and the rates were controlled by IATA so that an all-cargo carrier could exert little leverage through offering lower tariffs.

Because of these adverse factors only one carrier ever became established as an all-cargo operator on a transocean route: Seaboard & Western Airlines, which was organized on 16 September, 1946, as a North Atlantic all-cargo airline.

The first flight to Europe was made on 10 May, 1947, with a C-54, to Luxembourg, the small independent Duchy which was developing as a trading and communications centre through its leniency in bilateral agreements and foreign operating rights. Seaboard received a Letter of Registration as an Irregular Carrier on 8 July, 1947, but was sufficiently encouraged by early traffic results to apply for permission to carry transatlantic air cargo on a demand basis—a special situation implying something more than non-scheduled operations but falling short of completely regular services.

In December 1951, following sustained growth of business partly through contracts with the International Relief Organization (I.R.O.), the fleet of five C-54s was increased to twelve and consideration given to supplementing this by a more modern type. A $3,000,000 six-month military contract awarded in September 1954, and subsequently renewed, gave the airline sufficient corporate strength and stature to apply for permanent scheduled certification. This was recommended by the Civil Aeronautics Board and President Eisenhower gave his approval for a route from major northeast cities to Europe, effective from 16 August, 1955.

Seaboard & Western Airlines' Lockheed L.1049H Super Constellation N6501C *American Airtrader*. Outboard fins and rudders, underside of the nose and the engine cowlings were red.

Seaboard's scheduled freight service to Europe was inaugurated on 10 April, 1956, using a C-54, but shortly afterwards, the company took delivery of its first Lockheed L.1049H, the freighter version of the Super Constellation series. Transatlantic frequency rose to a daily service on 1 September, 1957, and further military contracts increased the scale of effort to the point where more aircraft were needed to meet the capacity demand. This resulted in an order for five Canadair CL-44s late in 1959.

Unfortunately, financial stability did not match steadily growing traffic, and Seaboard plunged into a desperate period of its life. In each of the three years, 1959 to 1961 inclusive, there was a net loss of well over $4,000,000. Under the leadership of Richard M. Jackson, the newly-elected president, however, courageous steps were taken, including a complete refinancing of the company and a drastic reorganization of the management. Seaboard survived precariously, managed to introduce its first CL-44s in August 1961, overcame some exasperating introductory problems with that aircraft, and made its first annual profit for six years in 1962.

Seaboard World Airlines' swing-tail Canadair CL-44 N229SW at Montreal.

Since that time, Seaboard World Airlines, as it was renamed on 26 April, 1961, has never looked back. By 1964, seven CL-44s formed the backbone of the operating fleet, with the L.1049Hs in retirement. Seaboard had sought many ways of strengthening its revenue base during its crisis years, and one of these ideas proved a permanent success. This was the Blocked Space agreement with European carriers, under which these airlines booked a set proportion of the space on Seaboard's aircraft on its daily round-trip schedules. Such an agreement with Lufthansa assisted substantially towards the transition to Seaboard's profitable operations in 1962, and the scheme was extended to Swissair in 1963. Interline co-operation was further expanded on 30 September, 1963, when a CL-44 was leased to BOAC for two years.

In June 1964, Seaboard World Airlines joined the ranks of the big jet freighter airlines by putting into service a Douglas DC-8F, leased from the manufacturer on a 20-year basis. An agreement was signed with Trans Caribbean Airways to make the DC-8F available for weekend passenger operations from New York to San Juan and Aruba, a neat method of

Seaboard World Airlines' Boeing 707-320C N7322C. Colour scheme is black and gold with white fuselage top. (*The Boeing Company*)

supplementing the primarily mid-week pattern of air freight demands on the North Atlantic.

The Giant Still Sleeps

The early enthusiasm of individualists like Robert Prescott and Earl Slick was based on the conviction that there was a tremendous future for air freight. As aircraft became bigger and more economic to operate, leading to a steady average decline in freight tariffs—albeit with some disturbing fluctuations during the formative period immediately after World War 2—many other airline people joined the pioneers in their confidence.

Learned professors began to write theses on the subject, scheduled airlines decided that freight revenue was worth promoting, manufacturers designed freighter versions of their standard passenger types. Statistics began to support the belief that air cargo was indeed on the threshold of immense growth. Hardly a year passed without renewed declaration of faith in air cargo by airlines, manufacturers, government agencies, and consultants. This was an oft-repeated theme during the first twenty years following the end of World War 2; yet signs of the awakening of the Sleeping Giant—as the air freight enthusiasts called their industry—were strangely elusive.

On the contrary, there was much discouragement and the faithful had to survive many setbacks. Whilst there were isolated examples of dramatic success, air freight as a whole continued to occupy a disappointingly low percentage of total air traffic. More significantly, would-be freight airlines died off like flies. Those that survived did so often by a combination of luck and government support (through military airlift contracts) and every all-freight airline surviving today has been through more crises than all the trunk passenger airlines put together.

The cold fact is that air freight growth rates have barely exceeded those of passenger traffic. During some periods growth was sustained only at crippling economic penalties, and the high costs involved in promoting growth often exceeded the extra revenue accrued. The development pattern of civil airliners also worked against all-freight airlines. As commercial transport aircraft grew in size, the capacity available for freight over and above that required for the passenger accommodation also grew as a percentage of the whole, both in payload weight and volume. Consequently, passenger airlines were continually able to offer a higher proportion of their capacity to the needs of the growing freight market. The trend has been constant, from the twin-engined to the four-engined piston generations, through to the developing families of jet aircraft.

Possibly as a parallel sequel, the market for specialized cargo aircraft has been restricted and none has reached sales figures calculated to encourage further innovation. Various attempts have been made to produce flying box-cars, with ingenious features calculated to reduce the cost of handling air freight. Straight-in nose loading was augmented by the addition of tail-end loading in the case of the AW.650 Argosy; yet this interesting design never sold extensively, mainly because its medium-range capabilities incurred operating cost levels only marginally below freight revenue rates. The swing-tail Canadair CL-44 too was a boldly-conceived design but only a handful of airlines, mostly all-cargo, ever bought them.

The prospects for a reversal of these trends are not bright. Only one of the original all-cargo scheduled airlines was still operating under the U.S. flag in 1982. Airlift had ceased to exist, and two of the great survivors had amalgamated when Flying Tigers, by now a multi-industry corporation, merged with Seaboard World Airlines on 1 October, 1980. Flying Tigers is a rare exception, pursuing a specialized field with little threat from potential newcomers. The market is limited, and the equipment is specialized: McDonnell Douglas DC-8-63Fs, with a 50-ton payload, are now augmented by Boeing 747Fs able to carry an incredible 125 tons across the world's oceans.

Meanwhile a new group of airlines has emerged, led by the innovative Federal Express. This company, founded by Fred Smith, recognized the need for accelerated package air mail during a technical age when, paradoxically, coast-to-coast post office air mail was often taking longer than surface mail during the 1920s. Federal Express started operations on 17 April, 1973, guaranteeing overnight delivery service to any part of the U.S.A. With a large clearing warehouse at Memphis, Tennessee, processing incoming and outgoing loads in all directions, the fleet of Federal Express rocketed from a few Dassault Falcon 20s in 1973 to an astonishing 76 aircraft in 1982, including 39 Boeing 727s and 4 McDonnell Douglas DC-10s.

Fred Smith, who was first obliged to start his airline as a scheduled air taxi operation to circumvent restrictive legislation, was a leading campaigner in bringing about the Deregulation of Air Cargo in November 1977, which, among other advantages, permitted the integrated use of thousands of delivery vans. Such has been the success of this remarkable airline that others have rushed to imitate it. Air express, the package service that had almost died a natural death in the 1930s, is now showing signs of a great revival, while Flying Tigers is now the only all-cargo airline left in the U.S.A. The wheel has turned full circle.

Lockheed L.049-51 Constellation N74192 of California Hawaiian Airlines, one of the early post-war non-scheduled carriers. This aircraft, c/n 1980, was built as a U.S. Air Force C-69 and passed to BOAC as G-AHEN *Baltimore*. After an accident it was rebuilt with parts of the sixth Constellation (c/n 1966) and became N74192. It was later sold to El Al as 4X-AKD. (*Gordon S. Williams*)

CHAPTER SEVENTEEN

The Charter Airlines

An Uncertain Start

No section of the airline industry has led a more chequered life than those companies variously known as Non-scheduled (or Nonsked), Irregular, Charter, or Supplemental Carriers. While all U.S. airlines have traditionally been competitors within their assigned sphere of operations, the charter airlines have not only competed with each other, but have also, as a group, had to fight continuously for survival against the powerful scheduled carriers.

Their visible opponents have been the larger airlines, which tended in the past to regard the non-scheduled industry as an infection which could become dangerous if not cauterized. Invisibly, the charter airlines have suffered from a widespread lack of understanding of their true rôle in the aviation world. There were times when the conduct of some of the charter companies appeared to be falling well below the standards of behaviour expected of responsible transport agencies; and the reputation of the whole was blackened by the actions of the minority.

To its credit, the Civil Aeronautics Board has acted fairly throughout the complicated history of the Nonskeds, keeping in mind always that it was charged not only with regulating civil air transport, but also with promoting it.

On 18 October, 1938, non-scheduled airlines were exempted from having to obtain Certificates of Public Convenience and Necessity and of certain other provisions of the Civil Aeronautics Act. The exemption was made in order to provide an opportunity to study the character of the various classes of non-scheduled operations, and to determine the extent of regulation necessary for each type of service.

Such caution on the part of the C.A.B. was understandable. At that time, the airlines involved were small, operating light aircraft in usually specialized rôles from fixed bases. Their resources were extremely limited and the opportunity for acquiring load-carrying transport aircraft was remote.

A dramatic change, however, occurred after World War 2. In the immediate post-war period, at the end of 1945 and early in 1946, many small companies were able to purchase, usually for a nominal sum, quantities of C-47 and C-46 equipment. A C-47 could be purchased for $25,000, at a rate of $4,000 per year. Vast quantities of war-surplus aircraft were available. At Ontario, California, for example, 2,000 aircraft were lined up, waiting for disposal.

The addition of just one C-47 could double or quadruple the load capacity of a typical fixed-base operator and this stimulated interest in seeking new outlets for business. Also, the cessation of hostilities released thousands of aircrew, many of whom wished to continue their flying activities, and the prospect of aerial tramping seemed to contain the necessary ingredient of adventure. In 1945, the C.A.B. estimated that 2,730 'airlines' were founded, with 5,500 aircraft. No operating certificate was needed for contract services.

A legion of ex-pilots, among others, founded their own companies, some of which have weathered the industrial and political storms to survive to this day. These were the exceptions. Most were doomed to failure from the start. Good military pilots, fighter or bomber, do not necessarily adapt themselves to civilian conditions. The early non-scheduled airline promoters could not always reconcile their spirit of enterprise with the many regulations for navigation, safety, and maintenance. Many were unable to cope with the administrative necessities and the Nonskeds, as they quickly became known, acquired an unfortunate reputation for unreliability and even sharp practice. Those whose true pioneer spirit was combined with a dedication to providing good public service were damned by association with the unscrupulous.

The Large Irregular Carriers

On 17 May, 1946, the Civil Aeronautics Board made an initial attempt to curb the worst excesses. It modified the 1938 exemption regulations so as to require from the carriers a Letter of Registration from the Board as a condition of operating large aircraft. They were authorized to engage in interstate and overseas air transport of persons and property (and foreign air transport of property only) between any two points, on an infrequent and irregular basis.

A Large Irregular Carrier was defined as one which operated a single aircraft of more than 10,000 lb gross take-off weight, or three or more aircraft of more than 6,000 lb whose aggregate weight was more than 25,000 lb. Letters of Registration were issued to a number of non-scheduled operators, qualifying them as Large Irregular Carriers. As a definition of an airline category, this was a brave attempt by the C.A.B. Though by normal standards the term 'large' was questionable, few argued with the term 'irregular'. In fact many of their activities continued as before to be highly irregular. But at least they were distinguished from the 1,500 or so Small Irregular Carriers, which were little more than air taxi operators.

Things got somewhat out of hand, the C.A.B. possibly misjudging the Irregulars' ingenuity and determination, and on 6 August, 1948, the Board announced that it would issue no more Letters of Registration beyond the 142 listed at that time. In December 1948, the C.A.B. tried to make the further distinction between Scheduled and Irregular by ruling that all non-scheduled operations should be limited to eight to twelve flights per month between the same two points.

On 20 May, 1949, the regulations were tightened slightly by terminating the blanket exemption in favour of individual exemption, authority for which each carrier had to plead its own case. However, any company operating on 19 June, 1949, was authorized to continue until its Letter of Registration was revoked or cancelled.

On 25 May, 1950, the C.A.B. issued its opinion and order in the investigation of Large Irregular Carriers. Henceforth it would deny applications from companies which had operated a quasi-scheduled service, but would grant exemptions to those which had maintained truly irregular operations. Carriers which had not operated during the preceding year lost their certificates.

In spite of many shortcomings the boisterous and irreverent young non-scheduled airline industry began to provide evidence that it could make a significant contribution to airline progress. In particular it proved its worth at times of national crisis. During the Berlin Airlift between July 1948 and August 1949, the Large Irregular Carriers moved 25 per cent of the passengers and 57 per cent of the cargo tonnage. Later, during the Korean War of the early 1950s, they flew 50 per cent of the total commercial airlift.

J. W. Bailey, of Overseas National Airways, has aptly summed up the directions in which the embryo industry sought new outlets for the use of the civil transport aeroplane:

1. Pioneering low fares, thus stimulating the air travel market as a whole.
2. Developing air cargo on a large scale.
3. Conceiving the idea of group travel.
4. Providing a military air transport reserve on a contractual basis.

In September 1951, the Civil Aeronautics Board made a bold attempt to clarify the whole status and scope of non-scheduled operations by instituting the Large Irregular Air Carrier Investigation. This was to last more than ten years, during which there were to be many pitched battles involving the carriers, government agencies, the public, and the judiciary.

On an interim basis the non-scheduled airlines were allowed to carry individually-ticketed passengers, but the difficulty of organizing flights, and a lack of communication with the general public combined to prevent healthy growth. The Nonskeds were hardly encouraged by the entrenched certificated route carriers which looked upon them as usurpers of a birthright. Furthermore, as a symptom of frustration and desperation, many of the more enterprising Irregulars resorted to methods which, though ingenious, were treading dangerously on the borders of legality.

North American Airlines

In November 1945 another airline joined the countless number of companies starting public service during the light-headed period following World War 2. Rejoicing under the name of Fireball Air Express, it was founded by Stan Weiss and Col Charles Sherman, and before very long was operating DC-3s from coast to coast on a route from Long Beach to New York, via Kansas City and Chicago. Within a year it had changed its name to a more decorous Standard Air Lines, under which title it held a C.A.B. Certificate of Registration as a Large Irregular Carrier.

One of its competitors was Viking Air Lines, started by Ross Hart and Jack Lewin. Based at Burbank, it too held a certificate from the C.A.B. After two years, however, the post-war air travel boom slowed down and both Standard and Viking pulled in their horns. Viking survived as a cargo operator under the name Oxnard Air Freight.

In January 1950, after a series of strategic conferences by the promoters of the two airlines, the North American Airlines Agency was formed. In addition to combining the operations of the two carriers, the Agency also acquired control of other Large Irregular Carriers (all holding C.A.B. Certificates), notably Twentieth Century Airlines, Trans-National Airlines, Trans-American Airways, and Hemisphere Air Transport. With a combined fleet of fourteen DC-3s, the transcontinental operation was resumed (with an extra stop at Albuquerque), charging a fare of $99 single, and $160 return.

The essential feature of the operation was that, by combining the aggregate point-to-point route authority conferred by the C.A.B. in its decision of December 1948—a limitation of eight to twelve flights per month per carrier—the North American Airlines (NAA) group was able to offer a regular and frequent service, which, by astute scheduling, could be maintained without breaking the strict letter of the law.

Part of North American's success was due to 'cutting out the frills', that is, the luxury amenities which were so heavily promoted by the route

North American Airlines' Douglas DC-6B N6120C. (*Harry Gann*)

carriers, and by so doing, reduce costs. The group also operated at high load factors—around 85 per cent—but passengers did not complain too much at being told to wait until next day, when the alternative was to pay the normal scheduled airline transcontinental one-way fare of $110 night coach or $159 first class. But it was untrue, as was sometimes hinted, that safety standards were in any way compromised. Indeed, throughout the history of litigation which was to follow, no criticism was ever levelled at North American on the grounds of maintenance or operating procedures, or of safety standards.

The service was popular with the general public, if not with the route carriers, and in 1951 North American supplemented the old DC-3s with DC-4s which, though unpressurized, could offer 'four-engined safety' still beloved by airline propagandists, and, more important, could give the company extra seating capacity to cope with the rising demand.

By 1953, North American was boldly applying to the C.A.B. for new routes, alongside the established carriers. For example, in the famous Denver Case, it proposed a Chicago—Kansas City—Denver—Los Angeles service at a flat 3c per mile, plus $2 per ticket, thus substantially undercutting the competition. The C.A.B. took a dim view of the *enfant terrible* and found North American to be 'unfit, unwilling, and unable' to perform the services, because of 'knowing and wilful violations of the Board's Economic Regulations'.

Unabashed, North American continued to prosper with its cheap fares policy, and continued to apply for new routes when the opportunity occurred. As for the violations, it steadily maintained that the C.A.B. had set the rules, and that, although the group had devised a scheme for stretching the provisions of the regulations, there was no evasion or breakage of the written letter of the regulation itself.

In 1954, North American reported that it had carried 194,000 passengers over 329 million passenger-miles. This latter figure was in excess of that of any of the three smallest U.S. Domestic Trunk airlines, so that this quasi-irregular operation was beginning to reach considerable proportions and was no longer a negligible activity in the field of air transport generally.

North American had enough confidence to acquire some new long-range DC-6Bs from Douglas.

Starting on 5 April, 1955, the company made five trips from Travis Air Force Base to Tokyo, using DC-4s, which was some grudging recognition of its existence. To emphasize its continued competitiveness, on 1 May, 1955, it began nonstop transcontinental service, using 100-seat DC-6Bs, charging $88 one way.

On 1 July, 1955, the C.A.B. revoked NAA's various certificates because of 'serious and wilful violations' of its economic regulations and ordered it to cease its 'unlawful operations' effectively from 1 September. National Airlines' R. A. Fitzgerald expressed the opinion of the scheduled industry by describing NAA as 'professional violators'. Violators or not, North American had certainly started something. On 16 September, all the transcontinental route carriers introduced a special excursion round-trip fare at $160 which, however, was valid for only 30 days and available only on certain flights. Then, on 15 November, 1955, the C.A.B. took a major step in clarifying its own mind by creating a new class of Supplemental Air Carriers.

Deciding that to attack was a good means of defence, North American made the next move, on 15 November, by asking the C.A.B. for a three-year exemption, effective on 1 April, 1956, to operate low-cost transatlantic coach services, proposing two round-trip daily services at fares of $125 New York—Shannon, or $140 New York—London, i.e. 43 per cent below the current tourist fares. NAA quoted its success in the U.S.A., pleading that, although its operating authority was revoked, an appeal was pending before the courts. Meanwhile it was continuing to operate, until a decision was made.

It had every incentive to press on until all hope was lost. In 1955, NAA carried 272,000 passengers, 40 per cent more than in 1954, making a profit of $1,000,000 on $15,000,000 revenue. It noted that nearly all its clientèle were first-time air travellers, and that it was stealing traffic from the bus lines and railways, not from the airlines. This was sound reasoning, but the C.A.B. did not at that time consider it to be relevant, although it appeared to be the main case being launched against NAA.

In January 1956, the C.A.B. turned down NAA's application, on the grounds that the issues were too complicated to be decided by the exemption process. It also stated that 'a very serious question remains unresolved' as to NAA's qualifications, in view of the fact that the airline 'had been found guilty of violations and its operating authority revoked'. North American maintained that it had done nothing illegal but that the C.A.B. had been 'hypnotised by its own science'. In February 1956, at the hearing of the House Commerce Transportation Sub-Committee, the chairman, Oren Harris (D. Arkansas) said 'I am impressed by your objectives, but not with your methods' and the point of legality was again obscured on 12 March when the C.A.B. used the phrase 'calculated conspiracy' in its charges against NAA.

By this time, North American appears to have taken the view that its problems with Government agencies were so involved that there was nothing to be lost by intensifying the battle. On 30 April it applied for exemption to operate to Luxembourg, cutting North Atlantic fares by 50 per cent. This move invoked the wrath of the State Department, as well as the C.A.B., for conducting unilateral negotiations with a foreign power.

Another of North American's problems was its name. As one way of making life difficult, some of the trunk route carriers, notably American Airlines, charged that the use of North American should not be allowed; NAA changed its name to Trans American Airlines, and the U.S. Court of Appeals upheld the use of the word 'American'.

The sands were running out for North American against massive opposition from the entire certificated industry, backed at this time by the Civil Aeronautics Board. On 11 June, 1956, the airline made a substantial concession by amending its exemption application, still pending, with an offer to discontinue the proposed service if the C.A.B. found that any competitor was injured thereby. It also agreed to charge 'such rates as the Board found proper'. This put the Board in a delicate position. To quote Stan Weiss: 'How could they say we should charge more when we were making money on what we were doing?'

In spite of everything, the C.A.B. rejected the application in July 1956, and although North American's lawyers used every device of legal procrastination, its filibuster eventually collapsed. After repeated stays of execution, the C.A.B. authorization finally ran out on 19 January, 1957. This was confirmed by the Supreme Court of the United States on 23 April.

North American, by then Trans American, leased its seven DC-6Bs to Eastern Air Lines. It was the last of the Nonskeds to do substantial passenger business for a decade. But its impact on the course of air transport in the U.S.A. was considerable. Stan Weiss and his cohorts forced the authorities to review the basic purposes for which the C.A.B. regulations were drafted; and his influence on fares is indelibly cast on rate structures which still survived into the 1970s. That his contribution was significant is proved by the knowledge that, although North American and the $99 fare lasted only five years, no-one who was connected with the industry at the time has ever forgotten it; and many believe to this day that the company was never given full credit for its achievement in pioneering low fares that a new stratum of the public could afford.

Irregular to Supplemental

During the bitter exchanges of the North American case, the C.A.B. decided on the public interest issues which were involved in the Large Irregular Air Carrier Investigation originally started in 1951. The Board concluded, on 15 November, 1955, that they were performing a useful service to the public and that their authority should be enlarged. Henceforth they should be known as the Supplemental Air Carriers, a term which, in the Board's view, more correctly described their function in air transport. In addition to unlimited charter business, they could conduct, on an interim basis, regularly scheduled individual services up to a maximum of ten one-way flights per month between any two points in the U.S.A. (later extended to foreign points). The Board did not at that time attempt to decide individual applicants' qualifications.

Upon judicial review in 1956, the Court of Appeals in the District of Columbia found that the Board's action was defective, but stayed its decision on the question of certification.

The First Inclusive Tours

An area which many of the Large Irregular Carriers viewed as a happy hunting ground for non-scheduled revenue traffic was the Caribbean, especially the U.S. territories of Puerto Rico and the Virgin Islands, where the problem of foreign bilateral agreements did not arise. One of the companies, Resort Airlines, of Southern Pines, N. Carolina, was the pioneer of the Inclusive Tour Charter (ITC).

In September 1945 Resort was incorporated by Clinton Davidson to develop inclusive air tours. These combined a round-trip flight, connecting ground transport and hotel accommodation into an integrated holiday tour. At first, operations were confined to New York State, to popular resorts such as Saranac and Lake Placid, but Resort soon sought wider fields to exploit the idea. Early in 1949, the C.A.B. denied an application for domestic and international authority, but President Truman overrode the decision, and in June of that year Resort was awarded its certificate as a Certificated Cruise Carrier to operate inclusive tours between New York, Washington, Chicago, and Miami to Canada and the Caribbean.

In 1950 Resort attempted a substantial expansion of its capital structure by selling additional stock to Fiduciary Management Inc, and obtaining an $800,000 bank loan. It also acquired the majority of the assets of an Irregular Carrier, Nationwide Air Transport Service. For a while, non-scheduled operations continued to provide the majority of business, but the main objective was to exploit the new and unique certificate. In October 1953 it augmented its fleet of Curtiss C-46s by purchasing three DC-4s from National Airlines. Typical of Resort's operations was the programme of 'Caribbean Flying Houseparties', between 19 December, 1953, and 15 April, 1954. Enterprisingly attempting to develop winter traffic, the DC-4 cruises lasted between two and four weeks. A single itinerary would leave New York, call at Washington or Philadelphia, and visit Nassau, the Virgin Islands, Puerto Rico, Haiti, and Miami, at an inclusive fare of $575. An extension period at, say, Haiti, would cost $105, and could be fitted in by dropping off the passengers and picking them up again on the next round trip.

This commendable first experiment with inclusive air tours on a large scale was unsuccessful, and Resort discontinued operations in September 1955. In 1956 the airline resumed non-scheduled operations under a Logair Defense Contract, and ordered two Lockheed L.1049Hs for the purpose. In February 1957 the C.A.B. renewed Resort's tour certificate for five years but ruled against a permanent certification. The new authority was broadened to permit service via intermediate points to anywhere in Canada and the Caribbean, and including Mexico, and Resort had to reinstate services within one year. Setting an important precedent, it was also required to serve a minimum of three intermediate points on each tour. Stopovers at Miami were to be limited to no more than one third of the total duration of a tour on which Miami might be included.

Resort regarded these restrictions as unnecessarily crippling and in June 1957 told the C.A.B. that, unless they were modified, it would have to abandon its certificate. Specifically, it requested a minimum of two intermediate stops instead of three, and that the Miami stop should be up to one third of the length of the tour, or seven days, whichever was the greater.

The issue involved in this case was an intriguing variation of traffic diversion. Resort was offering to the public not only a package tour, but effectively—since the tariffs were pitched on the low side—was also in a position to offer low fares over the scheduled routes of Eastern Air Lines and Pan American Airways to Florida and the Caribbean.

Eventually, after sporadic operation between 27 June and 24 September, 1959, the C.A.B. granted Resort permission to suspend scheduled services in December. On 1 July, 1960, non-scheduled operations were also discontinued after the loss of the Logair contract to World Airways on 15 June. By judicious sales and equipment leasing, however, the airline did not follow the familiar path of bankruptcy in such circumstances, and closed its books with about $3 million in the bank.

Supplemental to Scheduled

Running a somewhat parallel course contemporarily with Resort was another airline whose goal was the Caribbean. Trans Caribbean Airways was organized as a non-scheduled airline on 18 May, 1945, by Roy Chalk, and started operations on an exploratory basis in December of that year, using two DC-3s. $250,000 of additional capital was raised the following year, to purchase DC-4s, the first of which went into service to Puerto Rico in August 1946.

Trans Caribbean participated steadily in this market and in 1949–1950 was an active applicant in the Additional Service to Puerto Rico Case before the C.A.B. The main objective in this Case was to decide whether Pan American Airways' monopoly should be perpetuated, and, if not, which carrier should provide competitive service. The outcome was the choice of Eastern Air Lines, which was judged to be capable of providing

N8789R, Trans Caribbean Airways' first Boeing 727 (c/n 20143).
(*The Boeing Company*)

adequate competition in terms of equipment, in contrast with Trans Caribbean, whose unpressurized DC-4s were regarded as inferior.

Undaunted, Trans Caribbean began to purchase DC-6s and in September 1953 applied once again to the C.A.B. for authority to operate scheduled services to Puerto Rico. This was unsuccessful, but, on 15 June, 1956, bi-weekly flights began under the 1955 Supplemental authorization, at a $45 fare. Although the scheduled airlines had long protested that this level of fare structure was uneconomic and damaging, Pan American began a third class tariff on 21 June, 1956, at a $52.50 fare, 20 per cent less than the tourist rate. Eastern Air Lines followed suit.

Trans Caribbean Airways' sustained campaign for lower fares gained its just reward when, in February 1957, the C.A.B. Examiner recommended the airline for a scheduled certificate on the New York—San Juan route, noting that Pan Am and Eastern had not properly developed the route or provided for the peak traffic demand. Trans Caribbean announced in August that its fleet of three DC-6As would be converted to a 102-seat layout in order to cater for the specific needs of the route. On 15 November, its certificate was approved by the President for a five-year trial period. Described by the C.A.B. as an historic decision, this was the first case of a Supplemental or Irregular Carrier being reclassified as Scheduled. Trans Caribbean began scheduled services between New York and San Juan on 8 March, 1958.

The First Supplemental Airlines

On 29 January, 1959, the C.A.B. issued interstate certificates to 23 Supplemental airlines which it found to be qualified. Two more certificates were subsequently issued, making a total of 25. Also in 1959 the Transatlantic Charter Investigation was opened, and the Board decided to issue similar certificates for overseas and foreign routes; but the President withheld his approval.

On 7 April, 1960, the Board's action was again found to be legally defective on a technicality, namely that Section 401 (e) of the Civil Aeronautics Act contained an unqualified requirement for specification of terminal and intermediate points in a certificate and an explicit direction that no certificates should restrict the right of a carrier to add or change schedules or equipment.

The Board then presented the matter to Congress for legal clarification on 24 June, 1960, and, three days later, Senator Monroney's proposal for a temporary solution to the problem was adopted. This had the effect of validating existing certificates for 20 months, and the Supplementals were able to breathe again.

TRANSOCEAN
AIR LINES
SUPPLEMENTAL
Trans-Pacific
Service
APRIL - MAY - JUNE
1957

Part of the front cover of possibly the first published schedule of a Supplemental Airline.

Gradually a picture was emerging of the non-scheduled airlines as a group of respectable companies, rather than a band of outlaws; but the way to success was still far from clear. As if to confirm the impression of lack of responsibility, there were two serious fatal crashes in 1961, resulting in 160 deaths. Most of the Supplementals, however, operated to the highest safety standards and (possibly aware that infringements would receive maximum adverse publicity) strictly observed all F.A.A. operating, navigational, and maintenance procedures. But all suffered when one carrier met with misfortune, and, to meet an obvious need for co-operation, the Supplementals formed the National Air Carrier Association (NACA) in January 1962 as its own lobbying and public relations organization.

On 10 July, 1962, Congress enacted Public Law 87-528. This was a red letter day in the history of the Supplementals. The net effect was to confine the future rôle to charter work, but to terminate their participation in individually ticketed services. Supplemental air transport was defined as 'charter trips . . . to supplement the scheduled service . . .' which the trunkline carriers were authorized to provide. However, the scope of the term 'charter' was left undefined.

New Supplemental certificates were to be issued by the C.A.B. which was authorized to 'designate only the geographical area or areas between which service may be rendered'. On 30 September, 1962, the basic legislation was passed and with this tighter authority the Board set out to weed out the weaker carriers. By this time some of the stronger ones were easy

N375WA is one of World Airways' red and white Boeing 707-373Cs.
(*The Boeing Company*)

to recognize. World Airways, for example, had ordered three Boeing 707-320Cs in May 1962. This was not only the first jet order by a Supplemental, it was the first order for this long-range series of the 707. Almost simultaneously with the enacting of Public Law 87-528, Trans International Airlines (TIA) put into service its first DC-8. A remarkable transition from a total of 225 piston-engined aircraft to jet fleets had begun.

Interim certificates were issued to 15 Supplemental carriers (*See Table 24**). All were granted unlimited cargo and passenger charter authority for interstate (domestic) services; Department of Defense contracts for persons and property; and overseas cargo charters. Most carriers were granted civil passenger charter authority for overseas air transport, partly for use as backhauls in conjunction with military operations. A few were granted inter-territorial cargo and/or passenger charter rights; and several gained interim authority to perform foreign air transport.

One of the C.A.B.'s problems was that, although the Supplemental carriers had much in common, others differed from their companions as

*See page 627.

Saturn Airways' Douglas DC-6A N1281.

chalk from cheese. Zantop Air Transport, for example, was a specialist in transporting components between the Detroit car factories and satellite production lines or suppliers scattered throughout the U.S.A. The C.A.B. granted special exemption to Zantop for this specialist service on 9 May, 1962. Vance Airways, on the other hand, was interested in air taxi work, and the C.A.B. obliged with an exemption order on 19 December, 1962.

On the broader issues, the subject of ITC, lying dormant since Resort's demise, came up again in 1963 but the Supplementals lost the first round when in October 1963 the Board refused to authorize this type of passenger travel because such authorization would divert traffic from Pan American and TWA. As if to demonstrate its impartiality, however, the C.A.B. quickly favoured the Supplementals again when, on 24 February, 1964, under the Transatlantic Charter Investigation, five-year certificates were issued, effective from 18 April, 1964, to Capitol Airways and Saturn Airways.

Shortly afterwards, on 1 May, 1964, the Department of Defense announced that for the 1966 fiscal year, contracts would be granted only to carriers deriving 30 per cent of their revenue from commercial sources. This decision led directly to an airline merger in the Supplemental field. AAXICO Airlines, a prominent and almost exclusively military contractor,

Overseas National Airways' Lockheed L.188A Electra cargo aircraft N282F *Resolute*. Tail and fuselage markings are dark blue.

found itself ineligible to bid for Logair work, for example, under the new ruling. Negotiations resulted in the C.A.B. approving a merger with Saturn, effective 1 November, 1965, thus giving the joint airline the flexibility needed. Although the majority of stock was held by former AAXICO officers, the surviving airline was called Saturn.

At this time also, one of the former leading Supplementals, Overseas National Airways (ONA) came back into the picture. Founded by George Tompkins in June 1950, it had become by 1960 'the biggest and most respected Nonsked airline in the business' and claimed to fly more international passenger-miles than any other U.S. carrier except Pan American. Pride came before a fall. In that year, ONA swept the board in military contract bidding by undercutting all the others. These were the cut-throat days when a non-scheduled airline stood to lose out both ways. Either it bid a fair rate, calculated to cover costs of a sound operation, and lost the contract; or it bid low, won the contract, and lost heavily in the process. Late in 1960 the C.A.B. set minimum rates, but by this time ONA's fate was settled. It went bankrupt on 29 October, 1963, ceasing operations. But it was not disgraced and did not lose its certificate and, thanks to the efforts of Steedman Hinckley, was revived following refinancing from various banking interests, operations being resumed on 4 October, 1965.

In the old days, financing meant finding enough capital to buy a couple of second-hand piston-engined aircraft passed on from a scheduled carrier after seven or eight years' life. ONA's financing, however, was to the tune of $26,000,000 and the major portion of this was allocated to the purchase of new Douglas DC-8s. The status of the industry had, in fact, undergone a considerable change since 1962, and a vicious economic circle had been transformed into a benevolent one. Supplemental airlines were gaining support from the financial world, enabling them to purchase economic equipment, which made profits, increased earnings, and attracted more capital.

To quote the C.A.B. Examiner, the Supplementals had in fact 'earned their niche as an established part of the domestic air transportation system' by flying passengers and cargo. He also paid tribute to their 'substantial and valuable rôle' in providing services for the Department of Defense. Most significantly, he contended that, in the field of foreign charters, the record showed that these had been neglected by the scheduled airlines, to the detriment of the United States' position in international traffic shares.

This was in August 1965. The Examiner's recommendation was accepted almost in full by the Board and the President. On 14 March, 1966, to fire the opening shot pursuant to the Supplemental Air Service Proceeding, permanent interstate (domestic) authority was granted to ten Supplemental carriers. These were to the airlines listed in Table 24, less United States Overseas Airlines (USOA) which, after a spasmodic existence, had ceased operations on 30 November, 1964; AAXICO which had merged with Saturn; ONA; Standard; and Vance. The last three were later included, following the Examiner's recommendation on 15 December, 1966.

One of Overseas National Airways' Douglas DC-8-55s.

One of Standard Airways' leased Douglas DC-9-15s.

A Standard Airways' Boeing 707-138B, bought from Qantas.

These interstate certificates covered Inclusive Tour Charters (ITC), as well as other group and full-plane charters, and were for an indefinite period for the carriage of persons and property. Most important, Hawaii was no longer termed a territory but was a State in its own right and a tremendous vacation attraction. The same C.A.B. Order also granted Worldwide Military Charters, and the Department of Defense amended its 30 per cent commercial ruling to an objective of 40 per cent.

Adding salt to the scheduled airline wound, on 5 April, 1966, under the Reopened Transatlantic Charter Investigation, the C.A.B. issued certificates for the carriage of persons and personal baggage only, *including ITC authority*. These were effective from 26 November, 1966, to 18 April, 1969. Thus, rights for this very important sector of the passenger travel market were issued to TIA, World Airways, ONA and American Flyers Airline Corporation. The certificates for Capitol and Saturn were reissued to include ITC.

American Airlines, representing the scheduled industry, sought judicial review of the domestic decision, but the U.S. Court of Appeals for the District of Columbia held that the C.A.B. indeed had the right to grant interstate authority for inclusive tours.

Taking heart perhaps from this judgement, the C.A.B. took further action in what must have appeared to the scheduled airlines as a further rush of blood to the head, but which seemed sweet reason itself to the Supplementals. On 30 September, 1966, the President gave his approval to a wide-ranging international authority. Five-year certificates for persons and property, including ITC, were granted to eleven carriers, effective 26 November, 1966. Destinations varied but in addition to the Atlantic, already covered by the April decision, the Pacific, Latin America, and Canada now came within the scope of Supplemental civil air transport. Geographical areas were granted according to each carrier's experience. Some, such as World and TIA, found themselves with the world as their oyster; others received trans-border rights into Canada and Mexico only. All were granted the right to bid for military charters on a world-wide basis.

Coming of Age

The growth of the Supplemental Carriers since the signing of Public Law 87-528 in 1962 has been phenomenal. Revenues totalling $82 million in that year almost doubled by 1966—helped by a late spurt with the build-up of the Vietnam airlift from August 1965—and then doubled again by 1968. With both the Department of Defense and the Civil Aeronautics Board conscious of the danger of over-specializing, particularly on military contracts, the commercial content of the revenue earned rose steadily from a fifth in 1962 to almost a half in 1968.

Some airlines have emerged as leaders of their industry. World Airways, bought by Edward J. Daly in 1950, leapt forward when it won a Logair

Trans International Airlines' second Boeing 727-171C, N1728T. This aircraft was frequently used on TIA's service from Oakland to Hawaii. (*The Boeing Company*)

transcontinental contract on 15 June, 1960, and has led the Supplementals in earnings, both military and commercial, ever since. It has world-wide authority for charters and ITC, operates a substantial fleet of jet aircraft. Recalling the objectives of North American Airlines in the 1950s Daly applied unsuccessfully on 26 April, 1967, to the C.A.B. to operate a $79 transcontinental thrift fare scheduled service.

Trans International Airlines also made substantial progress in the later years. Its founder, Kirk Kerkorian, placed his faith in the Douglas DC-8 (as did most of the leading Supplementals) and went from strength to strength, especially in the commercial business. Other commercial leaders were Capitol, which added the word International to its corporate title on 22 March, 1967; ONA, staging a remarkable comeback after its fall from grace in 1963; and Universal Airlines, formerly Zantop, which, however, still depended on specialized air freighting for most of its revenue.

World, TIA, Capitol, and Saturn, a big military contractor, each made profits exceeding $2 million in 1967. Many of the Supplementals' former critics have been astonished at such financial success. How could these airlines charge such low fares and yet make so much money while operating basically the same equipment—and therefore incurring the same operating costs—as their scheduled rivals? The answer lies in a combination of factors.

Capitol International Airways' 250-seat Douglas DC-8-63CF Jet Trader, N4907C used mainly on transatlantic charter services.

First, the Supplementals' operating costs are in fact slightly lower because their annual aircraft utilization is higher, thus spreading the depreciation charge more thinly. One or two carriers have reached a figure of 15 hr per day in some years, and 12 hr per day is common. They can achieve these rates because, in general, they are able to schedule aircraft to their own plans, without regard to fixed travelling habits. The scheduled carrier on the other hand has to tailor his timetables to the passengers' demands.

Secondly, the charter operator's overheads are substantially lower than those of a scheduled airline. Costly booking and promotional procedures are performed mainly by the tour agencies which supply most of the commercial business; and, of course, the military contracts need no promotion. The costs of running an airline route network are negligible, because the charter airlines really have no network; they have only to maintain branch offices in a few key cities at home and abroad. In contrast, even a Local Service airline has to incur heavy costs in scores of city and airport offices, apart from maintenance and passenger handling facilities.

Finally, and most important, the charter company operates at a very high load factor, sometimes higher than 95 per cent, compared with the 50–60 per cent average bracket of the scheduled levels. In fact, the airline does not think so much in terms of load factor as in terms of charges for a complete aircraft load. The responsibility of filling the aircraft rests with the booking agent who charters the aircraft.

This is the formula on which the Supplementals have built a highly successful business and achieved a complete transition from the primitive conditions before the jets and before their legal position in society had been defined.

The Last Fences

Although the power of the C.A.B. to award domestic ITC authority to the Supplementals was upheld by the U.S. Court of Appeals for the District of Columbia, a different court, the U.S. Court of Appeals for the Second Circuit, decided in July 1967 that the C.A.B. had no such power for international routes.

On 27 May, 1968, continuing judicial consideration of World Airways Inc *et al v*. Pan American Airways, the matter was reviewed by the Supreme Court, which reached an inconclusive 4:4 tied vote, effectively confirming the lower court's decision. As this also threw into doubt the legality of the domestic ruling, prompt steps were taken in both Houses of Congress by legislators concerned for the future of the industry. On 9 July, 1968, Senators Mike Monroney and Warren Magnusen succeeded in gaining Senate support, and on 2 August Harley O. Staggers gained the Representative agreement. The two bills differed only in minor details and a joint wording was presented to the President who signed the Supplemental Air

Carriers irrevocably into the Inclusive Tour Charter business on 26 September, 1968.

And so another chapter was completed in the continuous process of fare reduction. International traffic growth has been sustained in the past by progressive lowering of passenger tariffs, with the introduction of tourist rates in 1952 and economy rates in 1958 as major landmarks. The year 1968 may be marked in the future as the third great year of significance in stimulating growth from fare reduction.

In a different sense it marked a triumph for the Supplemental Carriers, when the non-scheduled Davids overcame the might of the scheduled Goliaths. But having obtained a right to live, there was no guarantee that life would be easy. The Supplementals would continue to be challenged continually by the scheduled carriers.

However, most of the original thirteen carriers settled down to a steady existence. The leaders such as World, TIA, ONA, Universal, Saturn, and Capitol, developed extensive business in contracts of all kinds, including affinity tour groups and inclusive tours. Some were not so successful. Standard Airways and Purdue Aeronautics suspended operations on 24 September, 1969, and 1 May, 1971, respectively. Universal took over American Flyers on 4 June, 1971, and Vance International changed ownership on 3 November, 1970, to become McCulloch International Airlines, of Long Beach.

During the 1970s, there was much activity affecting the Supplemental airlines. There was a further attrition in numbers. Modern Air transferred its operations to West Berlin in 1972 before ceasing operation altogether in 1975. Universal, Overseas National, and McCulloch also went out of business, while on 30 November, 1976, Saturn was acquired by TIA, which changed its name to Transamerica Corporation in 1979. By 1980, only three passenger carriers (World, Transamerica, and Capitol) and four cargo carriers (Zantop, Southern, Evergreen, and Rich International) remained. These are briefly summarized in Table 24 (pages 627–29).

On the positive side, the hardy survivors enjoyed growing freedom. Indeed, they broke down successive fences standing in the way of sensible charter airline regulation. Undoubtedly, the progressive removal of charter restrictions was a contributory factor to the deregulation process, particularly the OTC, which removed the ponderous three-stop requirement, and the ABC, which removed the mandatory ground packages. (See pages 675–78.)

With the Public Charter regulations, adopted by the Board on 14 August, 1978, and confirmed by the Congress in the Deregulation Act of 1978, the National Air Carrier Association (NACA), which has faithfully acted as a promotional and lobbying organization for the charter airlines since 1962, can feel justifiably content that it has served to uphold one of the main tenets of a democratic society: that by public demand, bad laws are ultimately replaced by good ones.

A typical third level scene in 1967. The aircraft is a Piper Cherokee, of Pilgrim Airlines, at New London, Connecticut. (*R. E. G. Davies*)

CHAPTER EIGHTEEN

The Third Level

The First of the Many

In the first pioneering years of air transport in the United States there was no problem in placing airlines into categories to denote relative size, responsibility, or type of route network. They were all simply airlines, and they were all small. After the Air Commerce Act of 1926, and the subsequent manipulations of the Postmaster General in drawing the airline map, some larger companies emerged, to become the nuclei of what were later to develop as the Big Four Domestic Trunk airlines. Then the suspension of air mail contracts in 1934 and the introduction of new legislation marked a dividing point in airline history. Large numbers of small companies, which had operated precariously in the face of politically motivated suppression, disappeared entirely. The post-1934 survivors received Grandfather Routes from the Civil Aeronautics Board in 1938, and with one or two minor exceptions, emerged from World War 2 to become the Domestic Trunk airlines.

Throughout the whole period, small airlines had been formed from time to time, some existing for several years, but most of them terminating operations after a few months. By 1940, when the Civil Aeronautics Board was settling down to the task of regulating the airline industry, all the small companies had disappeared, with one exception, Wilmington-Catalina Airline Ltd. Although it operated only one 21-mile route, the C.A.B. was not at that time able to distinguish between different categories of airline, and accordingly included the diminutive carrier in its list of Grandfather Route awards.

Wilmington-Catalina was the determined heir to one of the oldest air routes in the U.S.A., from Wilmington, a suburb of the city of Los Angeles, to Avalon, the resort on Santa Catalina Island, 20 miles offshore from California. First operated by Syd Chaplin in 1919, the service was continued by Pacific Marine Airways in 1920, until this company was bought by Western Air Express in 1928. When WAE's contract to serve the island ended in May 1931, Philip K. Wrigley, owner of Santa Catalina, organized Wilmington-Catalina Airline. Using Douglas Dolphin amphibians to replace the old Loenings, this airline began service on 6 June, 1931.

Wilmington-Catalina Airline's Douglas Dolphin NC14204 taking-off. (*Courtesy Peter M. Bowers*)

When granted its C.A.B. Certificate on 13 October, 1939, Wilmington-Catalina was easily the smallest U.S. airline, and possibly qualified for the doubtful honour of being the smallest airline in the world. It was certainly in a different class from the others, its tiny route being removed by many orders of magnitude from the networks of even the smaller airlines of the day, such as Continental or Boston-Maine. Nevertheless, this was no transient operation, and the owners had no intention of allowing it to die. In a sense, the air route was one segment of a larger operation, that of providing entertainment in the attractive setting of Santa Catalina Island and the little port of Avalon. The absolute fare—as opposed to the rate per mile—was low enough to be subject to manipulation. In 1937, for example, it was $5.00 one way, which should have been enough to sustain the operating costs of the amphibians.

In August 1940 work began on a 3,400 ft runway at Avalon, in preparation for larger landplanes, and the company was renamed Catalina Air Transport, a title by which it had been known familiarly since the early 1930s. On 22 July, 1941, the route certificate was amended, designating Los Angeles as a terminal, and adding Wilmington and Long Beach as intermediate points. Two Lockheed Lodestars which had been ordered, however, never went into service, but were sent to the United Kingdom under the Lend-Lease programme of World War 2. Finally, on 3 September, 1942, services ended under wartime regulations, and the Dolphins were turned over to the U.S. Army Air Corps. During its eleven years of existence, the Wilmington-Catalina Airline carried 300,000 passengers on 44,000 trips.

When the war ended, United Air Lines decided to take over the Catalina Island route. This involved an agreement with the Santa Catalina Island Company, owned by the Wrigley family, controlling all the activities on the island; an agreement with Catalina Air Transport, a wholly-owned subsidiary of the Island Company; and the transfer of the C.A.B. Grandfather Rights certificate. This last was accomplished on 3 June, 1946, and United began DC-3 services on 1 July, serving the airport at Avalon from Burbank, Los Angeles, and Long Beach.

This must have been quite satisfactory to the C.A.B., relieving it of the responsibility of controlling a quaint survival of a pioneering age. Yet there was little doubt that the route to Catalina served a public need, and would continue to do so, although under the normal criteria governing fare structures, no airline could hope to make a profit over such a short-stage distance. On the other hand, the possibility of subsidy was out of the question as under no stretch of the imagination would a ferry service to a resort area be considered as a social amenity and thus qualify for federal support.

United's attempt to incorporate the 21-mile route into its nationwide system did not meet with complete success, although 400,000 passengers were carried in eight years, an improvement over Wilmington-Catalina's record. The big airline's decision to withdraw from the route (the last service was on 30 September, 1954) was based on an economic analysis showing that this kind of service required individual and special treatment, which an established scheduled airline was unable to provide. United complained of 'the peculiar nature of the Catalina traffic, which was subject to a severe directional and seasonal unbalance and involved such a short distance, made the maintenance of high load factors and high equipment utilization an impossibility'.

Immediately after World War 2, two other small companies had offered semi-scheduled ferry services to Catalina Island. Although these two, Pacific Marine and Amphibian Air Transport, lasted only a few months, being handicapped by United's competition, the modest corporate structure necessary to maintain such an operation appeared to be feasible, given a monopoly of the route. Accordingly, the Catalina Island Company sought such a company to replace United, under the terms laid down by the C.A.B. for the latter's withdrawal, and on 27 August, 1953, Avalon Air Transport began operations to the Island from Long Beach, using a Grumman Goose amphibian.

On 1 July, 1955, permission was given by the U.S. Post Office to carry mail under a Star Route contract, and the airline settled down to steady operation. In 1957 it acquired a 47-passenger Sikorsky VS-44 four-engined flying-boat (a survivor from American Overseas Airlines) to supplement the growing fleet of eight Goose amphibians. By 1963, when the company's name was changed to Catalina Air Lines Inc, the annual traffic totalled 80,000 passengers. The service became an accepted part of Southern Californian life, and the statistics appeared faithfully in the C.A.B.'s publications, though few employees of that agency knew how, or why, they ever came to be included.

Helicopter Experiments

United Air Lines correctly identified one of the major problems of a route such as Avalon's: the extremely short distance. Operating costs of conventional airliners soar as stage distance is reduced, and the cost per seat-mile below 50 miles reaches almost astronomical heights, out of all proportion to normally accepted fares on a mileage basis. There were, however, some situations where unorthodox tariff structures could be imposed because of the high level of convenience offered. For example, there were obvious compensations in increased efficiency by reaching closer to city centres than was possible when using major airports which demanded large slices of open land and were seldom within five miles of the downtown areas.

One ready solution to this problem seemed to be the use of helicopters, which aircraft designers and technicians have always regarded as a promising subject for research. Their development for use in airline operations appeared encouraging at first, for there were large cities in the U.S.A. where small patches of concrete could be found in the city centres, suitable only for helicopters. The operational and service advantages were obvious: no other vehicle could, for example, offer a 12-min service from the centre of Manhattan to the passenger ramp at New York International Airport.

But the helicopter came out only partly on the credit side. There were many disadvantages which curtailed unlimited expansion of helicopter routes. The shortcomings could be summarized as: (1) mechanical complexity, leading to unacceptably low aircraft utilization and increased costs; (2) fundamentally poor economics because of small size, slow block speed, and less efficient use of engine power in providing forward flight; and (3) noise. As time went on, another big question mark hung over helicopter operations: safety, for any accidents invariably occurred in

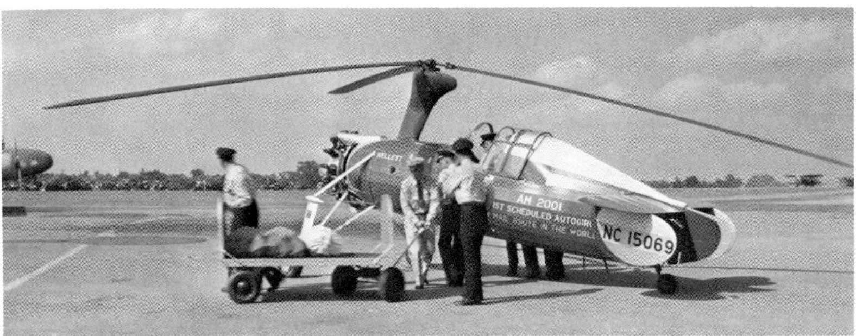

The Kellett KD-1B autogyro used by Eastern Air Lines on an experimental mail service between the post office in Philadelphia and Camden Airport, New Jersey, in July 1939. The autogyro, NC15069, bears the legend 'AM2001 First Scheduled Autogiro Air Mail Route in the World.'

densely-populated urban areas and thus received maximum publicity, although fortunately such incidents were few in number and involved relatively few casualties.

The world's first scheduled service using a rotary-winged aircraft was flown by Eastern Air Lines, which began experimental operations on 6 July, 1939, at Philadelphia. Mail was flown in a Kellett KD-1B autogyro from the roof of the Philadelphia Post Office to Camden Airport, and the service lasted about a year.

After World War 2, United Air Lines was the second airline to conduct experiments with rotary-wing aircraft, and on 19 July, 1946, applied to the C.A.B. for permission to operate five routes between Midway Airport, Chicago, and 32 suburban communities, at first with air mail, but with the intention of carrying passengers if the experiments were successful. A Sikorsky S-51 was delivered in May 1947 and a number of demonstration flights made in the Chicago area; but a study of operating costs was not encouraging, and the company withdrew its interest and sold the S-51.

When United entered the scene, the United States Post Office had already selected the city of Los Angeles as a test location for experimental air mail operations by helicopter. On 11 May, 1944, Los Angeles Airways (LAA) was incorporated by a group of Los Angeles businessmen; on 22 May, 1947, the C.A.B. awarded a temporary three-year certificate for local mail services; and on 1 October, LAA began the world's first regularly scheduled helicopter mail service, using Sikorsky S-51s. The route net-

United Air Lines Sikorsky S-51 intended for operation in the Chicago area in 1947. It is seen above the United Air Lines Douglas DC-4 N86577 *Mainliner Connecticut River*. (*United Air Lines*)

work consisted of four spokes radiating from Los Angeles International Airport, one to the downtown Post Office, and the others via circular routes to the San Fernando Valley, San Bernardino, and Newport Beach, the further point on each loop being about 50–60 miles from the international airport hub. Considerable route extensions were made to serve more points in the Los Angeles area, and the C.A.B. extended LAA's certificate in July 1951, at the same time authorizing the carriage of passengers.

On 20 August, 1949, Los Angeles Airways was joined by a second helicopter operator, Helicopter Air Services (HAS) of Chicago, which inherited United Air Lines' ambitions in that city. Shuttle services started between Midway Airport and the Chicago Post Office, using a fleet of six Bell 47Ds, cutting the journey time to nine minutes. HAS had been selected by the C.A.B. out of seven companies to operate local mail routes, and was authorized to serve 54 local post offices within a 50-mile radius of Midway Airport. By the end of 1949, three circular routes were in operation.

New York was the third city to receive helicopter service. In December 1951 the C.A.B. awarded a certificate to New York Airways to carry mail between the three airports serving the metropolitan area, Idlewild (later John F. Kennedy International), LaGuardia, and Newark. A few suburban routes were added later. The equipment used was the Sikorsky S-55, a larger version of the S-51.

When New York Airways started service, on 15 October, 1952, the United States then had three companies forming a distinct airline category, which, because of the type of equipment used, were designated the Helicopter Carriers. Their operations were characterized by their environment—operations within, rather than between, urban conurbations; their revenue source—exclusively mail; and their high dependence on subsidy, which in

Los Angeles Airways Sikorsky S-55 N414A taking-off from Long Beach.

Chicago Helicopter Airways Sikorsky S-58 N865.

the early years amounted to between two-thirds and three-quarters of the total revenues. In a sense, the Helicopter Carriers could be regarded as feeder services to the trunk lines, but they were serving a completely different market than that of the Local Service Carriers which theoretically performed the same function. The Post Offices of Los Angeles, Chicago, and New York certainly benefited from the improved convenience; but a high price had to be paid for the refinement, and this was paid from federal funds.

Passenger Helicopters

Some relief was sought by expanding the mail services to include the carriage of passengers, a course of progress which was interestingly analagous to the way air transport developed in the United States in the early 1920s. New York Airways was first, beginning inter-airport passenger services on 8 July, 1952. Although the last of three companies to start mail services, New York Airways had used S-55s, also suitable for passenger work. In addition to linking the airports, passenger services were also started to New Brunswick, Princeton, and Trenton, in New Jersey, and on 5 December, 1956, the first link was made with downtown Manhattan, by use of a heliport at West 30th Street on the Hudson shore close to the business section of the city.

National Airlines and Mohawk Airlines also attempted to start S-55 passenger services in 1954, National with local routes around Miami on 1 February, and Mohawk from Newark to the Catskill Mountains on 7 June. But both were short-lived.

Los Angeles Airways and Helicopter Air Services also acquired S-55s and began passenger services on 22 November, 1954, and 12 November,

1956, respectively. HAS had changed its name to Chicago Helicopter Airways (CHA) on 20 August, 1956, coinciding with its revised C.A.B. authority to link the new O'Hare International Airport with any point within 60 miles. During the many months while the major airlines completed the transfer from Midway to O'Hare, the demand for quick transport was substantial, and CHA doubled its traffic twice in successive years. For the 12-min flight between the airports it charged $6.00, but this was actually less than the average taxi fare for an hour's ride. Passenger services were also extended to the Chicago business quarter, by the use of Meigs Field, on the Michigan Lakefront. High frequency was maintained, at a minimum of hourly intervals on a triangular route, and in June 1957, CHA supplemented the seven-seat S-55s with larger twelve-seat S-58s.

The S-58 was essentially a scaled-up S-55, with a larger four-blade rotor replacing the three-blade rotor of the older type. It offered the passenger a significant improvement in accommodation, vibration, and noise level. Nevertheless, CHA sought further advances in its equipment standards by ordering, on 15 June, 1959, three Sikorsky S-61 twin-engined transport helicopters. Unfortunately, the early success of the airline changed to a decline as the major airlines completed their operational transfer to O'Hare Airport, and the once-busy Midway, formerly the world's top-ranking passenger airport, became deserted. Also a new high-speed freeway road system provided fast surface access to O'Hare, and CHA experienced the double disappointment of having to suspend mail services in December 1961 and deferring its S-61 order on 2 January, 1962.

Meanwhile better single-engined transport helicopters continued to be introduced into service with the other two U.S. Helicopter Carriers. New

A Sikorsky S-61L of Chicago Helicopter Airways.

View from 100 ft of a New York Airways Vertol 44B helicopter landing at the New York Downtown Heliport near Wall Street, in February 1961. (*The Port of New York Authority*)

York Airways deserted Sikorsky in favour of the Vertol (formerly Piasecki) company, which had successfully pursued the tandem twin-rotor principle with various designs for the U.S. Air Force. Eventually, a development of the series, the Vertol 44B, went into scheduled service with NYA on 21 April, 1958. It was the first transport helicopter to have its cabin arranged like that of a conventional airliner, accommodating 15 passengers, mainly two-abreast, on the starboard side of the cabin, with the aisle and baggage space on the left.

While Vertol concentrated on twin-rotor developments, Sikorsky explored another course, that of achieving amphibious capability, without incurring serious weight or drag penalties. The ability to fly over water safely was doubly advantageous. Many big cities, such as New York, San Francisco, and those along the Great Lakes, included large expanses of water within the city boundaries, some coming close to the business centres. Amphibious helicopters could thus make easier approaches to heliports located in densely built-up districts. Also, by flying as much as possible over water, the nuisance from the noise of the engines and rotors was much reduced.

Sikorsky developed the S-62 to this amphibious specification. Basically an S-55 re-engined with a General Electric T-58 gas-turbine, it first went into service with Los Angeles Airways on 21 December, 1960. Such was its success that it was directly responsible for the birth of a new helicopter airline, San Francisco & Oakland Helicopter Airlines (SFO), founded on

San Francisco & Oakland Helicopter Airlines' Sikorsky S-62 N978.

6 January, 1961. With two S-62s leased from Sikorsky, SFO began services in the San Francisco Bay area on 1 June, 1961, serving the San Francisco and Oakland Airports, and the downtown areas of San Francisco, Oakland, and Berkeley. By the end of 1962, almost 100 flights were being scheduled each day, and in February 1963, SFO purchased three S-62s for $1,000,000. A striking initial feature of the San Francisco helicopter operation was its independence of subsidy, and, because of this demonstrated viability, it received in November 1963 from the C.A.B. the first permanent C.A.B. certificate to be awarded to any helicopter carrier.

Los Angeles Airways took another step forward on 1 March, 1962, when it inaugurated the world's first multi-engined, turbine-powered, transport helicopter service, using the new Sikorsky S-61L. It could carry up to 28 passengers (although 22–25 was normal) at a cruising speed of 135 mph, and thus resembled the size and performance of the DC-3 when that aircraft

One of Los Angeles Airways' Sikorsky S-61L helicopters, N300Y, seen over Los Angeles. (*Sikorsky Aircraft*)

had made its debut a quarter of a century earlier. Peter Brooks describes the S-61 as the first truly practical transport helicopter in airline service, because it offered the prospect of all-weather operation, together with economic characteristics sufficiently favourable to reduce substantially the commercial subsidies.

The Vertol company, by now owned by Boeing, competed strongly with Sikorsky, and in fact achieved the first flight by the prototype Vertol 107 twin-turbine, twin-rotor design in April 1958, whereas the S-61's parent design lagged almost a year behind. New York Airways bought ten Vertol 107s at a total price of $4,350,000, on 12 January, 1960, but later amended the order to five. The first scheduled service took place on 1 July, 1962, by which time inter-airport helicopter flights in the New York area were being scheduled at half-hour intervals.

A New York Airways Vertol 107 landing at New York's West 30th Street Heliport in November 1960. (*The Port of New York Authority*)

Decline of Helicopter Service

The delay in Vertol 107 service was partly due to manufacturing problems, but New York Airways' reduction in its order was not entirely a reflection of sluggish traffic growth. The company faced continuous criticism by the C.A.B. on the subject of alleged excessive costs and increasing subsidy need. Although NYA's management confidently predicted gradual reduction of subsidy to zero by 1963, the annual results supported the opposite conclusion. Public concern mounted and in 1961 Congress voted to put a ceiling of $6,000,000 on the subsidy payments to the three certificated helicopter airlines. New York Airways suspended services to Bridgeport, Connecticut, and to the 30th Street Heliport, retaining, however, the service to Wall Street.

Subsidy expressed as a percentage of total helicopter revenues showed a decline, but this failed to impress Congress, which began to take a tougher line. In December 1964, the amount for the fiscal year ending June 1965 was abruptly cut to $4,300,000, and then formally terminated on 11 April, 1965. There was some temporary relief, but Chicago Helicopter Airways could not exist without help, and ceased operations on 31 December, 1965.

This Sikorsky S-61N, N307Y, bearing New York Airways and TWA markings, was used on services to the New York World's Fair in 1964. (*Sikorsky Aircraft*)

New York Airways had been the main spendthrift of subsidy, but was fortunate in having influential friends who were prepared to compensate for the removal of federal support. Pan American Airways had already assisted by buying two extra Vertol 107s (for $850,000 each) in January 1964, and leasing them to NYA for use at the New York World's Fair. United Aircraft Corporation, Sikorsky's parent company, also came to the rescue and supplied three S-61Ns for the same purpose, service starting on 27 April, 1964, to the rooftop of the Port of New York Authority Building at the Fair.

On 3 March, 1965, just before the cancellation of subsidy, demonstration flights had started from J. F. Kennedy International Airport to the top of the Pan American Building in the heart of New York City. These were so encouraging that scheduled service began on 21 December of that year. In passenger convenience, this probably represented the quickest, if not the most economical, customer service ever offered by an airline. Check-in time at the Pan Am Building was only 45 min before the departure of a Pan Am flight at J.F.K. Seventeen daily flights each took only seven minutes. The fare was $7.00 one-way, $10 round-trip.

This arrangement met the first requirement of the C.A.B.'s time-honoured 'public convenience and necessity' clause. The Board was relieved of the burden of proving the second requirement, necessity, because two airlines were prepared to underwrite New York Airways. On 25 June, 1965, it granted exemptions to Pan American Airways and TWA for financial participation in NYA. Those airlines acquired 24·4 per cent and 15·6 per cent stockholdings respectively. Pan American received direct service to its prestigious building in Manhattan; TWA to the passenger ramps at Kennedy, LaGuardia, and Newark Airports.

Los Angeles Airways also averted the danger of closure by a similar deal with Trunk airlines. In December 1965—when CHA retired—the

A New York Airways Vertol 107 above the landing pad on the roof of the Pan Am Building in Manhattan.

C.A.B. Examiner recommended that American Airlines and United Air Lines be allowed to acquire control of LAA through equal shares of a $3,200,000 loan agreement.

San Francisco & Oakland Helicopter Airlines was more soundly based financially, but also accepted help from American Airlines on 14 July, 1965, moving its base at San Francisco International Airport to American's concourse. By this time, SFO was operating the improved version of the S-61, the amphibious S-61N.

After twelve years of passenger operations, therefore, the Helicopter Carriers had been given a good chance to prove the efficiency of rotor-driven aircraft, but had failed to make their case. When the subsidy was withdrawn, they had to seek other artificial support. There was no great wave of protest from the American public as a whole, and very few sympathizers from the airline world itself, except from the interested sponsors like Pan American, United, TWA, and American.

Senator T. H. Kuchel, the Californian Republican, wrote to the C.A.B. Chairman in April 1965 (when the subsidy was cut off) suggesting that

Los Angeles Airways should be re-classified as a Local Service airline, and thus qualify for subsidy and a share of the $60,000,000 which was allocated annually to those carriers. But nothing came of this. Possibly the C.A.B. did not regard the type of service provided by LAA as a true social amenity, benefiting as it did only a minority of privileged citizens who wished to save a little time on the congested freeway system in the vast Southern Californian metropolis.

The Board had held serious doubts about helicopters for several years. On 17 May, 1960, simultaneously with the renewal of New York Airways' certificate for seven years, it affirmed that the type of equipment offered by helicopter operators need not be confined to rotary-winged aircraft in the true sense of the word. This was interpreted as permitting the use of VTOL (Vertical Take-off and Landing), STOL (Short Take-Off and Landing), and other direct-lift aircraft.

Later, in June 1965, the C.A.B. granted to SFO an exemption to operate air-cushion vehicles (ACVs), following the arrival from England of the first Saunders-Roe SR.N5 Hovercraft. These 'Jet Skimmers', as they were dubbed, began a trial demonstration programme on 10 August, 1965.

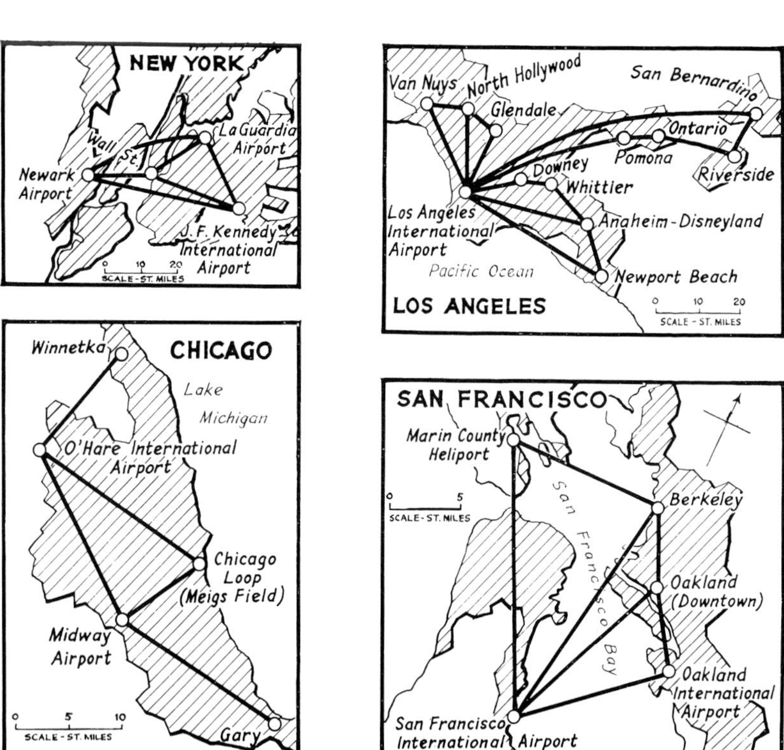

Fig. 28. U.S. Scheduled Helicopter Networks, 1965.

This, however, did not seem to be a satisfactory substitute for helicopters and a few more years were to pass before the next promising solution appeared. This was the introduction of STOL aircraft late in 1968 by Los Angeles Airways and New York Airways, following emphatic proof by certain operators that STOL operations were practicable in the same environment as helicopters.

In July 1971, after Los Angeles Airways had failed to erase the memory of an accident which had caused the temporary grounding of its S-61s, Golden West Airlines, the Third Level Twin Otter operator of Southern California, started negotiations to purchase the helicopter carrier.

Golden West was typical of the small airlines which had invaded the U.S. airline scene unofficially, unannounced, and unsubsidized. They had made their impact on the public by providing service where it was most needed in special traffic situations. They were unofficial in the sense that they were only required to submit to C.A.B. regulation when using aircraft weighing more than 12,500 lb. Variously known as Scheduled Air Taxi, Commuter, or Third Level airlines, their sudden rise to prominence has been one of the airline phenomena of modern times.

Scheduled Air Taxi

By the time Avalon Air Transport took over the route to Santa Catalina Island on 27 August, 1953, to maintain service on the oldest of all the air ferry routes in the U.S.A., a few other operations of a similar nature had sprung up. Some of these were almost identical in concept: they provided regular flights across a short stretch of water to communities which did not merit service by a Trunk, or even a Local Service airline. The initiative to open the service usually depended on individual local enthusiasm, in contrast with the wider corporate interests of a trunk or regional operator.

Most members of this new family of little airlines were already in the aviation business in one way or another. Typically, a fixed-based company would be offering, among other activities, an air taxi service from a central point to almost anywhere within reasonable range. The charges would be negotiable, which is to say, they would be as high as the market would bear; and full advantage would be taken of emergency situations. Sometimes, however, an air taxi company would find it worth-while to offer a reasonable fare to a popular destination in order to create and sustain traffic. As such traffic grew, it would often develop into definite patterns, with several people making up a small aircraft load quite regularly at the same time each day. The air taxi operator would thus find himself operating a schedule, and printing a modest timetable for the convenience of his clientèle.

This is how the Catalina services began; and an almost exact parallel was to be found on Lake Erie, where the group of islands lying offshore from Port Clinton, Ohio, provided holiday spots for yachtsmen and fishermen. In 1932, Milton Hersberger began flying a Standard biplane to the islands (or onto the ice during the winter). The islanders welcomed his service. He obtained a contract to carry mail and began a regular daily service. In 1935 he bought a Ford Tri-Motor, the first of three, and continued to operate until, in 1953, Ralph Dietrick bought the line, including the Tri-Motors, for $95,000. Dietrick had operated a similar service to the islands from neighbouring Sandusky, and merged his Sky Tours (formed in 1947) with Hersberger's Air Tours to form Island Airlines. With a route network of six points and a total route mileage of 25 miles, this was indeed an airline in miniature.

A similar operation was launched as the Provincetown-Boston Airline by John van Arsdale on 30 November, 1949, after some preliminary air taxi flights in the Cape Cod area of Massachusetts by the Cape Cod Flying Service. The distance from Boston to Provincetown, on the tip of the serpentine Cape Cod peninsula, was 45 miles across Cape Cod Bay, and by an odd quirk of Washington bureaucracy, van Arsdale ran into some certification problems because he flew beyond the three-mile limit and was theoretically an international operator. Common sense prevailed, however, and he settled down to profitable business. He supplemented his Cessna T-50s with Lockheed L.10s, and on 1 January, 1960, opened a subsidiary company in Florida, Naples Airlines, flying from Naples to Fort Myers and Marco Island. Here again was an interesting case of history repeating itself, for van Arsdale was doing what Inglis Uppercu had done in the early 1920s: move his fleet southward to the sun when winter weather discouraged travel in bleak New England.

Representing a different kind of operation was Reading Aviation Service, of Reading, Pennsylvania. Founded by Alfred Bertolet, a fixed-base operator and equipment agency of long standing, Reading exploited an inadequacy of the scheduled carriers by offering a good air taxi service between Reading and nearby Allentown, to Newark, serving New York. By August 1947 this had developed into a scheduled service and Reading was the first to engage exclusively in a commuter market.

An entirely unique situation, ready-made for a specialist operator, was the need for regular air services between the atomic research station of Los Alamos, New Mexico, and the nearest city, Albuquerque. In 1948, Clark Carr began regular flights over the sixty-mile route, under the name of Carco Air Service, and by 1960 was scheduling seven round trips a day with Beech Twin Bonanzas.

Still another type of opportunity was seized by E. Ross Miller and W. C. Brookmeyer when they started TAG Airlines (formerly Taxi Air Group) in July 1957. It operated one route, between Cleveland and Detroit, and thrived lustily, in spite of competition from five trunk and local service carriers which, moreover, charged less than $10.00 one way against TAG's $14, and used large modern aircraft against the little airline's ten-seat de Havilland Doves. The key to this paradox lay in the substantially more convenient service offered by TAG. It used the Lakefront Airport at Cleveland and the City Airport in Detroit, both only 10 minutes from the downtown business centres, whereas United and Lake Central used the municipal airports of both cities, each about an hour's journey from the city centre. Also, TAG offered frequent service 'On the Hour, Every Hour' against the mixed assortment of times offered by the other carriers, which also lacked the personal touch in identifying themselves closely with the Cleveland—Detroit passenger market. By 1963 TAG was carrying about 35,000 passengers per year. Unfortunately, services ended abruptly after a tragic crash into Lake Erie in January 1970.

The Third Level Explosion

Encouraged by the success of these little companies which continued to succeed when many had expected them to fail, others began to join the ranks. By 1962 there were approximately a dozen small scheduled air taxi operators scattered widely throughout the United States. At this time also, the term Third Level began to come into use. The Texas journalist, Ed Pickering, first used the expression in a prophetic series of articles in the U.S. magazine *Flight*, starting in August 1961. In the summer of 1962, the C.A.B. used the term when rejecting the application of Hi-Plains Airways to provide subsidized services in the prairie country on the evidence that there was no pressing public need and that any subsidy would probably duplicate that already being paid to Local Service, or second level, airlines.

The Third Level airlines operated under a special set of rules which were given formal shape when the F.A.A. was formed on 23 August, 1958. Under Part 298 of the C.A.B. Economic Regulations, air taxi operators were granted exemption to operate scheduled services, provided they did not use aircraft heavier than 12,500 lb auw. This ruling, originally made in 1952, was extended indefinitely in 1965. The operators had to comply with Part 3 F.A.A. regulations (F.A.A. Part 135) for safety and navigation, instead of the full Part 4 transport category (F.A.A. Part 21). Thus a scheduled air taxi, or Third Level carrier, could fly under VFR rules with only one pilot, who needed only a commercial rating (not air transport), and could use a single-engined aircraft. As time went on, certain airlines applied to the C.A.B. for permission to use aircraft in excess of the 12,500 lb limit, and where a genuine case could be made, and there was no valid objection from scheduled airlines, the Board usually granted such exemptions.

The reason for the choice of 12,500 lb seems shrouded in mystery, the most popular theory being that it was 'half a DC-3'.

By 1964 the F.A.A. began to keep records of these scheduled air taxi operators, in the absence of the C.A.B. which exerted no jurisdiction unless they used larger aircraft. Listing only those which were approved for IFR operations, the F.A.A. observed the remarkable growth in numbers, from twelve on 1 January, 1964, to 52 in the next year, and more than 200 by the end of 1968. This rate of expansion has been a phenomenon unparalleled in modern air transport history, all the more remarkable because there has never been any subsidy paid from Federal or State funds, nor

A Chatham Aviation Cessna 185 at LaGuardia Airport, N.Y., in 1967, when operating on the Metro Air Service. (*R. E. G. Davies*)

has there been any encouragement, direct or implied, from governmental agencies. All the airlines have been created spontaneously in response to a natural and real public demand. Defying many cherished laws of orthodox airline economics, the Third Level has displayed a powerful urge to survive, and the attrition rate has been lower than many experts predicted*.

One reason for this surprising viability is that the Third Level passenger pays far more per mile than on a Local Service or Trunk line, the rates seldom falling below 10c per mile, and often exceeding 20c. This offsets the higher operating costs at short ranges, and the passenger does not notice excessive pricing because the absolute amount is very small. An example of this desirable seller's market situation is Chatham Aviation, which charges $10 for the short trip from Morristown, New Jersey, to the New York airports on Long Island. The passenger is not concerned that the rate is 36c per mile; he is more interested in avoiding the tortuous surface journey across the heavily built-up metropolitan area of New York.

Third Level Relations with Other Airlines

When the F.A.A. began to collect data on the Third Level airlines, the services began to fall naturally into readily identifiable categories. These were:

(a) Suburban—within a large metropolitan area.

(b) Satellite-Hub—between a small city and a city airport with major airline service.

(c) Linear—between two or more remote communities, inadequately served by air transport.

(d) Special Geographic Situation—saving inconvenience by surface means, for example, across water.

(e) Special Social Situation—supplying a special need, for example, to a resort area.

Even at this lowly stratum of the airline hierarchy, there were differences between the great and the small. Some of the older-established companies

*All Third Level airlines founded before 1968 are listed chronologically in order of first scheduled service date in Table 25, page 631.

were beginning to be recognized as airlines of substance. Others continued a diminutive existence, content to serve an isolated and unique requirement. TAG Airlines, for example, was known to everyone in Cleveland. At the other extreme, Travel-Air-Service Inc, of Block Island (off the eastern end of Long Island), plied its 20-mile route to Westerly, Rhode Island, offering among its services to the public the carriage of dry cleaning, medicine prescriptions, and goods unobtainable on Block Island.

The certificated route carriers, trunk and local, began to take a closer look at these carriers; not that they posed a threat, but they were demonstrating effectively that some airline problems could best be solved by a set of rules alien to the C.A.B. book. To give the Board its due, it realised that regulations could be self-defeating if applied too rigidly, and its Local Service Use It or Lose It programme was a good example of the application of common sense. The Local Service airlines co-operated well with the C.A.B.'s attempt to eliminate services of such low passenger-generating capability that they became hopelessly uneconomic. The qualification standard agreed was an average of five passengers a day, and there were some routes where much of the allocated federal subsidy was being drained away.

In August 1966, West Coast Airlines came to a temporary agreement with one of the Third Level carriers, Eugene Aviation Service, to operate an isolated segment from Eugene to Roseburg, using Piper Aztecs, under contract. After a year, West Coast took over the service itself, using Piper Navajos, which it named Miniliners. This was the first example of a Local Service carrier learning a new technique of operating a low-density service by taking an example from the Third Level.

Another case was the Allegheny Airlines contract with Henson Aviation, of Hagerstown, Maryland. Starting on 15 November, 1967, Allegheny suspended its once-daily F-27 service between Hagerstown and Washington and contracted with Henson (then operating the Hagerstown Commuter over the same route) to provide four daily flights with Beech 80 Queen Airs. The service was called the Allegheny Commuter Lines, and was completely integrated with that airline's facilities in reservations, interline bookings, gate service, etc. Using Baltimore Friendship Airport as the Washington terminal, it was an immediate success. Allegheny guaranteed Henson against losses, but this was unnecessary. Additional traffic was created in a hitherto stagnant market, and $58,000 of subsidy was eliminated. Beech 99s were introduced on 1 July, 1968.

Allegheny expanded its Allegheny Commuter Service to other routes. Under similar contracts, Pocono Airlines operated Queen Airs from Hazelton, Pa., to Newark; and Vercoa Air Service started scheduled service from Danville, Ill., to Chicago, both services beginning in 1968; and more followed.

The idea caught on. During 1968, various agreements were made between Local Service and Third Level airlines. Some of these were cases of making a virtue out of necessity, caused by the withdrawal from service of the DC-3, the only aircraft which could operate into the modest airports of some small cities on the local networks. Frontier Airlines joined with Combs Airways in Montana on a route from Billings to Williston; and had agreements with Apache Airlines and the delightfully named Sedalia-Marshall-Boonville Stage Lines. Mohawk provided ticketing and ground services for Northern Airways on routes in some of the remoter parts of New England and upper New York State. North Central withdrew service from Mankato, Minn., in favour of Fleet Airlines.

Trunk airlines, too, appreciated the useful contribution to air travel which the air taxi companies provided and valued the additional interline service which they could generate. United Air Lines particularly encouraged the use of air taxis and co-operated fully with the National Air Taxi Conference, the industry agency for the group. United actually set up a small department to handle and promote interline business with air taxi operators and published a small directory of about 200 such companies.

In September 1965, American Airlines promoted the Metro Air Service to co-ordinate with its mainline services at the three New York airports. Five suburban Third Level services in the New York metropolitan area contributed to the scheme: Air Taxi Company (Red Bank, N.J.), Princeton Aviation Corporation (Princeton, N.J.), Chatham Aviation (Morristown, N.J.), Mac-Aire Aviation Corporation (Ronkonkoma, L.I., N.Y.), and Mid-Hudson Airlines (Poughkeepsie, N.Y.). American benefited by the traffic gained through direct passenger convenience offered; the Third Level carriers gained by the use of American's gate facilities at the major airports. It was a mutually advantageous scheme.

TWA had its own service connecting suburbs across Long Island Sound with its international terminal at John F. Kennedy Airport. Its chosen Third Level carrier was Piper Twinair, operating from Bridgeport from 1 May, 1966. In effect, this provided the city of Bridgeport with one-stop service to 29 cities in the United States and Europe. Late in 1967, TWA

A Beech 99 Airliner of Pennsylvania Commuter Airlines. (*Beech Aircraft Corporation*)

also provided gate facilities at Los Angeles International Airport for Cable Commuter Airlines, serving several satellite cities within the Los Angeles urban sprawl.

In 1968, Eastern Air Lines concluded a contract with Pennsylvania Commuter Airlines, of Lancaster, Pa., and Northeast Airlines made arrangements with Down East Airlines, of Rockland, Maine, and Cape & Islands Flight Service, of Hyannis, Mass. Later, in 1969, after detailed analysis of its entire route system, and the financial problems of operating ultra-short routes, Northeast took further steps to rationalize the airline structure in New England by seeking permission to transfer a further package of routes to Third Level (and Local Service) airlines.

Thus, all segments of the industry appear to have taken the excellent advice of George Haddaway, publisher of *Flight* magazine: 'The Third Level must realise it can not long exist by paralleling existing routes and schedules of the established lines. By the same token the established airlines would be wise to take the newcomers to their bosom as potential feeders or suppliers of business—not as competitors.'

Post Office Mail Contracts

Throughout the formative years of air transport in the United States, the Post Office was identified in one way or another as the sponsor of much important development. The Post Office Air Mail of the early 1920s was one of the great achievements of the pioneer days and received world-wide respect. Though marred by misguided behaviour on the part of the Postmaster General of the early 1930s, his sponsorship gave the airlines the support they needed in the embryo airline period, and was directly responsible for the early establishment of soundly-based companies which stood the test of time.

As passenger business expanded through the years subsequent to the reorganization of the airlines in 1934, the carriage of mail gradually declined in importance as the source of revenue. Then, after World War 2, when the railways experienced their catastrophic decline in passenger business, to become almost exclusively freight-carriers, the Post Office found that air mail, the standard method of carriage on all long-distances, now became necessary on much shorter routes. Unfortunately, airline schedules were geared to passenger demand, normally a daytime activity, which seldom fitted postal demand, ideally requiring transport during the night.

As early as 1961 Project Horizon, the Federal analysis of industry objectives, recommended that the air taxi industry be considered for carrying mail. At that time, the only employment of air taxis involved a limited number of Star Routes serving isolated communities. These contracts were awarded on an emergency basis and were not subject to C.A.B. authorization.

The C.A.B. subsequently amended its regulations to permit the carriage of mail by light aircraft, and encouraged the development of services and agreements with the Post Office Department, which first invited proposals from the Third Level operators in 1966. By the end of 1967, the Air Taxi Mail Programme had shown enough improvement to encourage further expansion of the system of linking by air taxi sectional centres serving as consolidation points for as many as 70 small post offices.

The Beech 18, employed by third level airlines, was already well established in the 1930s. This one, owned by Command Airways, was at Poughkeepsie, N.Y., in 1967. (*R. E. G. Davies*)

The 1967 programme involved the expenditure of almost $8,000,000 for about 130 routes operated by 36 airlines. Biggest operator was the ubiquitous Sedalia-Marshall-Boonville Stage Line, which had contracts for 28 mail routes. Typical rates were between 25c and 35c per mile, although some contracts were based on a poundage rate. All were negotiable and open to tender, and the rate depended mainly on the type of equipment used, normally the Beech 18, although other types were acceptable. One unique example of the Post Office preference for a scheduled air taxi mail service was the contract with Buker Airways, of North Springfield, Vermont. This was let at no less than 78c per mile for a Boston—New York—Pittsburgh—Cincinnati overnight service, using a Learjet Model 24. Such equipment was rarely employed, however, provided that the required distance could be flown conveniently for Post Office purposes during the hours of night.

Encouraged by the C.A.B., which waived its normal procedural rules so as to expedite the establishment of an efficient mail service with the minimum of delay, the Post Office Air Taxi Mail Programme went from strength to strength, and is already accepted as a permanent feature of the nation's mail service. Authority has been granted for an extension of air taxi mail contracts until 30 June, 1974.

Third Level Equipment

The first Third Level airlines (before they were even identified by such a term) operated a variety of different types of light aircraft, a large proportion of which were bought second-hand, or of even longer ancestry. Some enterprising companies made a virtue out of necessity, as did Island Airlines in making a tourist attraction of its veteran Ford Tri-Motors. Others improved their aircraft, as did Provincetown-Boston in re-engining its Lockheed 10s with higher rated power to achieve almost STOL performance. For many years, during the adolescent stage until about 1966, the most popular types were the Beech 18 and the de Havilland Dove, supplemented by various Cessna and Piper executive and private aircraft. A few airlines obtained special exemption from the C.A.B. to operate larger aircraft such as the F-27 or DC-3, but most observed the 12,500 lb limitation, preferring the unshackled freedom of flexibility in routes and schedules, without Washington control.

By 1967, many leading Third Level carriers had crystallized their ideas on the ideal airliner. High speed and long range were not essential, but good airfield performance and reliability were priority requirements. The winner of the unofficial design competition would have to concentrate on building an aircraft with the maximum load-carrying ability within the 12,500 lb auw limitation.

The de Havilland Aircraft Company of Canada won. Developed from a long pedigree of sturdy bush designs such as the Beaver, Otter, and Caribou, the DHC-6 Twin Otter turned out to be a real winner. Although described by one airline president as 'something the Wright Brothers forgot to finish', the alleged ugly duckling appeared to most of the other presidents in quite

A Cable Commuter Airlines' de Havilland Canada Twin Otter. This aircraft added a new dimension to urban transport in the Greater Los Angeles area. (*William Murphy*)

a different light. The most beautiful thing about the Twin Otter was its direct operating cost, which proved to be about half that of the Twin Beech's 6c per seat-mile. For the first time, this 18-seat turbine-powered aircraft, with an impressive take-off performance of barely more than 1,000 feet, made it possible to operate profitably without resorting to exorbitant fares.

An Executive Airlines' Beech 99 Airliner, serving many small communities in New England.

Other manufacturers took note of the rapid growth of the Third Level, and took steps to exploit the new market. Some, like Beech, Aero Commander, Piper, and Cessna, were aided by having many of the carriers as regional agents for their products. Thus, Beech found a ready market for the Beech 99, a good-looking 15-seater with higher speed but longer take-off distance than the Twin Otter's. Foreign manufacturers also quickly recognized the need. From Britain came the sleek and speedy Handley Page 137 Jetstream and other homely but efficient craft such as the Britten-Norman BN-2 Islander and the Short SC-7 Skyvan; while from Germany came the Dornier Skyservant, rather similar in concept to the Twin Otter, and the Hansa Jet Commuter.

Thus, the Third Level industry had revolutionized its equipment inventory in the space of a few short years. From a total fleet of less than 100 aircraft in 1964, almost 1,000 were in operation by 1968, of which only 19 per cent were single-engined, and almost 300 were turbine-powered.

Is History Repeating Itself?

The Third Level airline industry found its first opportunities for expansion on a wide scale when such aircraft as the Twin Otter and the Beech 99 began to present a reasonably modern image to the public, which hitherto had reserved judgement on what it regarded as an extension of general aviation. During 1967 and 1968, the rapid expansion mushroomed, and by December 1968 a passenger could travel from Seattle to Miami entirely by Third Level carriers, given sufficient time to make the changes.

A map of the Third Level routes became an elaborate affair, with concentration at the major hubs of New York, Chicago, Los Angeles, Dallas, Boston, and Seattle requiring special insets to make an adequate presentation. Although the density of lines on the map of Florida, for example, was entirely logical because that area was poorly served by Local Service, the Third Level impudently challenged all and sundry wherever the slightest opportunity arose.

The combined Third Level map in 1968 showed a remarkable similarity to that of the Local Service map some twenty years earlier. The great difference was that there were ten times as many small airlines in 1968 to echo the pioneer efforts of the Empires, Challengers, and Wisconsin Centrals of the earlier period. Gone, too, was the image of struggling companies, dependent on second-hand cast-off equipment for its operations, and Federal subsidy for its survival. The new airline breed boasted new equipment and did not ask for a penny of subsidy. The new aircraft were, of course, far more efficient than their predecessors. Had the early Local Service airlines possessed aircraft like the Twin Otter, airline history in the United States might have taken a different course. But at the time, the industry was not able to produce such a vehicle. Also, the Local Service airlines were conceived as a social need, a visionary idea on the part of idealists who perceived air service as a means of drawing the many threads of life in the United States more closely together—and well they succeeded. The Third Level, on the other hand, had no such aspirations. Self-reliant, enterprising, ruggedly independent, it charged the highest fares the market would bear—and was continually amazed to discover how much the public could endure in that respect, provided the service was efficient and convenient.

The Third Level carriers were beginning to seek mergers by 1968. Apart from the Metro Air Service, a loose association linked through a common sponsor, a few companies got together in other areas. Six airlines serving Seattle with scheduled taxi and ferry services operated in consortium as Puget Sound Airlines. In May 1968, Suburban Air Taxi (formerly Air Taxi) of Red Bank, New Jersey, merged with Reading Aviation to become Suburban Air Lines. The resultant network was 2,000 miles long, or as big as that of several of the Locals in 1956, while its fleet and annual turnover was as great as the smallest Local in the early 1950s. Two small carriers operating an identical route from Dallas to Killeen (serving Fort Bragg) decided to join, while in California the many Third Level operators were exploring the possibilities of amalgamation.

However necessary for financial viability, mergers were not a prerequisite for growth. Several Third Level companies thrived by aggressive marketing programmes. Two will suffice to illustrate both the high potential and the high risk.

On 1 November, 1967, Cable Commuter Airlines, founded by Roger Cable and Bill Myers, began service between Los Angeles International Airport and outlying communities at Palmdale, Inyokern, and Ontario. The response, especially from Ontario, was overwhelming. Passengers travelling by the main route carriers preferred to fly direct to the boarding satellite at the airport rather than drive along congested freeways and tackle the car-parking problems, while an $8.00 fare was cheap enough to discourage analysis of the rate per mile. Cable expanded rapidly during 1968, starting service to Orange County on 1 June and to Ventura a month later. More than 100,000 passengers were carried in its first year of scheduled service. By March 1969, however, a series of negotiations between several Third Level airlines in Southern California resulted in an important merger, the full significance of which is best illustrated by the map (*Figure 29*) of the rapid-fire ancestry of Golden West Airlines.

The second example is of route network expansion, rather than of route density. Sun Airlines, of St Louis, began services on 3 April, 1967, over a local network wholly within the State of Missouri, using Beech 18s. On 1 November, Sun startled even the more confident Third Level protagonists by introducing a Learjet on a tight schedule and adopting the slogan of 'The 33 minute Airline'—30 minutes in the air, 3 on the ground. The president, George Caleshu, put the attitude of his colleagues succinctly: 'We cater for the businessman. I don't care whether Aunt Jane flies or not', and referring to the competition: 'We look for holes in the schedules and try to plug them.'

By the end of 1968, Sun Airlines was displaying a map showing routes operating from Kansas City to Miami, via St Louis, Memphis, Nashville, Birmingham, New Orleans, and Jacksonville, although through tickets were not available between all points on the map. Nevertheless, the network was as large as that of a typical Local Service airline in 1950, and larger than that of many a trunk airline in 1940. Sun Airlines' demise in 1969 was unfortunately even faster than its growth.

At this stage, expansion is likely to be somewhat restrained by the various restrictive regulations under which the Third Level operates, particularly the 12,500 lb auw rule. When ground-rules for scheduled air taxi flights were first conceived, the aircraft in general use were six- to eight-seaters and were normally used in good weather. The F.A.A. never intended that one pilot should fly 20 passengers on minimum instrumentation, without radar, and without filing a flight plan. Faced with applications for operation of executive jet types, the C.A.B. has restricted passenger loads on these to twelve. As yet there is no clear-cut route policy. In one case, the C.A.B. gave a route (New York—New London) to a Third Level airline (Pilgrim Airlines) in preference to a Local (Allegheny Airlines). In another case, a Third Level (Empire State Airlines) had to suspend operations when a Local (Mohawk Airlines) was allowed to return to a route (Ithaca—Elmira—Washington) after several years of absence.

The Local Service legislation established two decades previously quite definitely aimed at providing service to small communities, as a social service, sponsored by the U.S. Government. This creditable objective has almost been forgotten as the once modest Local Service airlines set their sights on more adventurous and competitive horizons. Already the largest

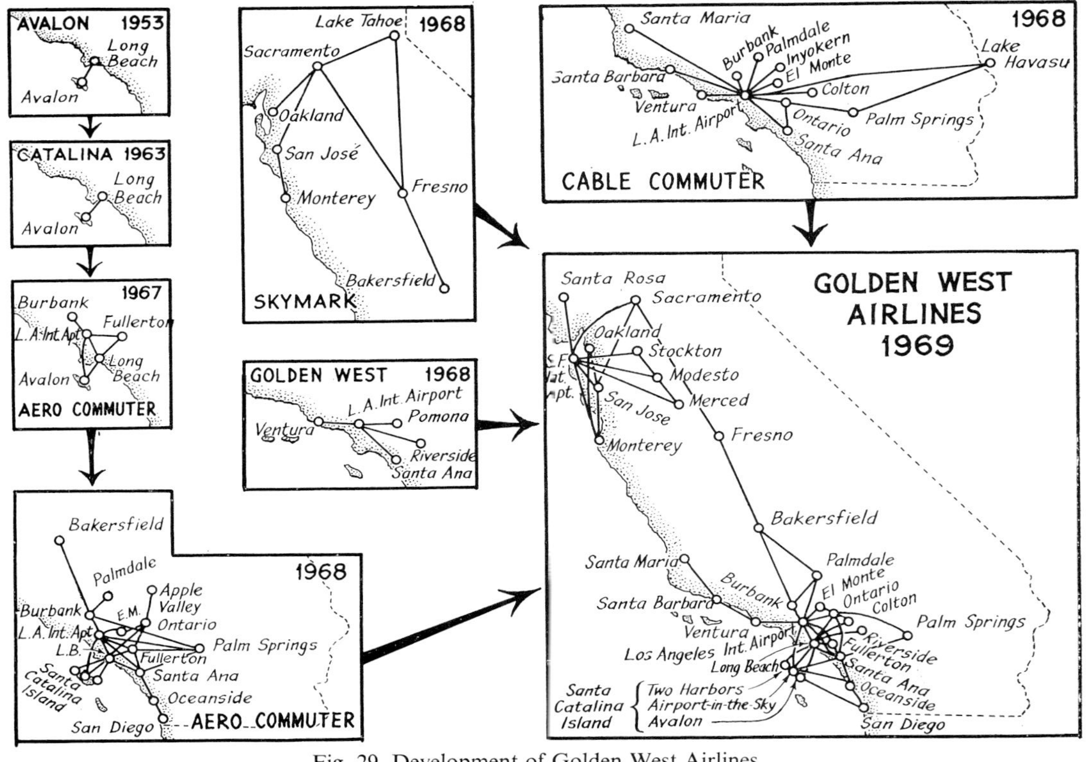

Fig. 29. Development of Golden West Airlines.

Locals carry as many passengers annually as the smallest Trunk, and the term Regional may soon be accepted *de facto* if not *de jure*. In exploiting this change in the basic structure of the industry, the self-created Third Level reached a point in 1969 when it was actually pleading for some kind of control from Washington.

The C.A.B. reacted by creating a new category of scheduled air carrier. Third Level airlines which provided at least five round trips per week between two or more points would be designated as Commuter Air Carriers. Meanwhile all the 3,500 air taxi operators, of whom the Commuters represented the elite, were required to register with the C.A.B. before 1 July, 1969.

The regulations governing the Commuters were uncomplicated and basic, concerning mainly guarantees of insurance, provision of quarterly statistical reports, and the filing of rates and schedules. Indeed, the next decade witnessed the appearance (and often prompt disappearance) of hundreds of small airlines which, to qualify for C.A.B. recognition, were required to operate "at least five round trips per week between two or more points." Those that qualified as Commuters were required to report regularly their operations and statistics, just like the Trunks and Regionals.

The twelve pioneers listed by the F.A.A. in 1964 were truly the apostles of a new airline religion. By 1968, 240 airlines were registered with the F.A.A. as Scheduled Air Taxi operators. This number was reduced to 138 in 1969, with the advent of C.A.B. designation and regulation. After stabilizing during the next few years, there was a moderate increase after 1972, when the C.A.B. relaxed the 12,500 lb auw aircraft limitation, permitting the Commuters to operate aircraft with 30 seats or to carry a payload of up to 7,500 lb. The number of airlines averaged about 180 during the mid-1970s. Then, with the advent of deregulation in 1978, when many regional airlines were permitted to terminate service to scores of small communities, there was another surge. By 1981, 270 Commuter airlines were estimated to be operating in the 48 contiguous states alone.

The aircraft fleet numbers remained relatively constant during the 1970s, from an average of 750 in the earlier years, rising to more than 1,000 by 1976. Of these, about 65 percent were multi-engined piston types, and about 25 percent were turbine-engined, with up to 40 jets included in the fleet count.

As always in a competitive environment, the best tend to rise to the top. The leaders of the industry are listed on page 630. A few of the original twelve apostles managed to survive the hazards of an unforgiving environment, including the indomitable John van Arsdale, whose Provincetown–Boston Airline is still in the top ten, and who entered the record books in March 1982 when one of his Douglas DC-3s reached 85,000 flying hours, an all-time high point for any commercial, and probably any other, aircraft. The record was previously held by a DC-3 of North Central Airlines (see page 397, centre photograph).

N7403, fleet unit 322, was one of Capital Airlines' fleet of sixty Vickers-Armstrongs 745 Viscounts, the first turbine-powered aircraft operated by a U.S. airline, entering service in July 1955.

CHAPTER NINETEEN

Propeller-turbine Interlude

Solidity of an Airline Hierarchy

During the eventful years of the post-war boom in domestic air transport in the United States, one characteristic of the airline structure remained constant: the distinction between the Big Four and the other Domestic Trunk airlines. The differences resulted from the basic route structure, inheritance of the Grandfather Rights allocated by the Civil Aeronautics Board in 1938. The Big Four, namely United Air Lines, American Airlines, and TWA, holding transcontinental authority, plus Eastern Air Lines, which blanketed the eastern third of the U.S.A., accounted for more than half of the seat-mile productivity of the entire U.S. industry, and maintained that proportion steadily year by year. These four major carriers became indispensible components of the U.S. transport industry and recognized as a national asset. Other airlines struggled to maintain a regional sphere of influence, and usually languished precariously on an inadequate route and capital structure. Many ceased operations and were absorbed in a cannibalistic process. Those few which survived were resigned to accepting their destiny as an underprivileged class.

From time to time, some airlines made effective expressions of protest against the Establishment. There were occasional forays into the bastions of tariff structures. Pennsylvania-Central Airlines (later Capital Airlines), for example, introduced a new low-fare service, the first coach fare, in 1948. This was highly successful, but Capital's advantage was short-lived as the other airlines promptly adopted the same principle. A later challenge by the Large Irregular carriers, notably the North American Airlines group, met with combined opposition from the Big Four. They were forced to cease operations after a bitter legal battle in which the C.A.B., under pressure from the entire industry and strong political persuasion, ruled against the continuance of a cheap transcontinental fare.

The Board, however, did appreciate that, unless something was done to preserve the smaller carriers from complete economic dominance by their senior competitors, they would all disappear. The airline structure of the United States in 1950 would then look almost identical to that mapped out by W. F. Brown twenty years earlier, a course of action which had led to political disgrace for its architect. The C.A.B. therefore saved some airlines from extinction by discreet route awards, although these did little injury to the Big Four. Gradual evolution did not constitute a serious challenge. Brazen revolution was required to provide a real threat.

In fact, the course for either evolution or revolution was a tough one for any would-be dissenter. Drastic changes in route structure were ruled out by a general acceptance by the industry, government, and public that, whilst the existing system might not be perfect, to tamper with it too much would set a dangerous precedent for continuous change which would eventually lead to chaos. Another possibility, that of a new challenge through differential pricing structure, was ruled out by the C.A.B.'s conservative policy on fares, which condoned a gradual transition, but could not authorize any carrier to maintain a fare structure which would give it a permanent advantage over its competitors.

There was one important method by which an operator could steal a march on its rivals: by introducing vastly superior standards of passenger service. This could be achieved by improving the methods of passenger handling, either in the cities or at the airports; or by providing better comfort during the flight, either by an inspired approach to interior seating layout or design; or by buying a fleet of aircraft whose superiority over the competition was clear-cut. Of all these, the last was the most effective, as a visionary decision could steal an advantage which could take many months, possibly several years, to match. But heavy investment was involved with replacement of a big enough portion of the fleet to exert sufficient competitive leverage. And this entailed a heavy risk which most of the smaller airlines, however desperate to capture a larger share of the market, were reluctant to take.

Capital Airlines and the Viscount

During the mid-1950s, one of the smaller carriers, Capital Airlines, made a brave attempt to gain promotion from the category of Other Trunks to Big Four. It chose what was at the time virtually the only way open to achieve this end, the introduction of a new commercial aircraft in large numbers quickly enough to set entirely new standards of passenger service. The new aircraft had to demonstrate a clear superiority over all comers, which in the age of modern post-war commercial aircraft implied the adoption of new technology. Capital's risk therefore was compounded in that it was dependent on the success of a completely new departure in commercial aircraft design. On the other hand, like most big risks, the potential rewards were great, and there was little that the C.A.B. or the Big Four could do to diminish them under the U.S. regulatory system.

The whole basis of Capital's revolutionary effort was to put into service a large fleet of British-built Vickers Viscount airliners. The Viscount was a four-engined landplane, approximately the same size as the Convair-Liner, but with one very important difference: its four engines were the new Rolls-Royce Dart propeller-turbines, a form of propulsion never used before on a commercial airliner. The propeller-turbine principle was one method of using the newly-developed power of jet engines, channelling most of the available thrust to drive turbines which were shaft-connected to propellers of the conventional kind. As with the pure-jet airliner, the early pioneering was carried out entirely by Britain and it was there that Capital cast its eyes as it sought the opportunity to expand.

The Viscount was developed from designs and specifications originally conceived by the Brabazon Committee, set up by the British Government in 1943 to make recommendations for the post-war development of civil transport aircraft. The British Ministry of Supply, at first responsible for buying aircraft on behalf of the nationalized airline corporations, ordered two Vickers VC-2 Viceroy prototypes in December 1946. A 32-seat Viscount 630, powered by the Dart engines specified by the Ministry on 27 August, 1947, went into experimental service with British European Airways (BEA) for a few weeks from 29 July, 1950, in the first major stage of a mutually profitable co-operative effort between manufacturer and operator. As a result of this collaboration, the production Viscount 700 series was made bigger, with 40–47 seats, and BEA ordered twenty, convinced that the claims made for the aircraft's operational superiority were justified.

BEA inaugurated the world's first propeller-turbine airliner service on the London—Cyprus route on 18 April, 1953. It was an immediate success, effectively demonstrating its competitive impact by increasing BEA's market shares on every route on which it made an appearance. This led to intense interest from airlines all over the world, and many companies visited BEA to study the Viscount's progress. In the latter part of 1953, Capital Airlines joined the queue.

After the usual negotiations, Capital ordered three aircraft at the end of May 1954, a pilot order which was a forerunner to a further 37 in August and another 20 in November. This was a momentous event in the history of British aircraft exports, indeed of British exports as a whole. For the first time since the days of the DH-4 in the United States Post Office Mail Service of the early 1920s—and even these were built in the U.S.A.—British aircraft were to fly the airways of America. The influx of 60 foreign-built aircraft into the United States was unprecedented, but fully justified. Trans-Canada Air Lines had paved the way for technical acceptance to North American standards by insisting on numerous modifications before opening its Viscount service on 1 April, 1955. The revolutionary power unit was the key to the Viscount's success in North America, and Capital made as much of the engine in its publicity campaign as it did of the aircraft.

The first Viscount was delivered to Capital on 16 June, 1955, and services opened on the Washington—Chicago route on 26 July, 1955, at a frequency of three a day, of which two were nonstop. As Viscounts were delivered there followed a general intensification of services throughout the densely populated area around the New York—Chicago axis and on routes to New Orleans. Everywhere the Viscount flew, Capital increased its market share. This in itself was an innovation, for, under the competitive system evolved by the C.A.B., a pattern was unfolding which was becoming fundamental to the U.S. domestic trunk industry: that the main airline on any route—inevitably one of the Big Four—always set the pace in the provision of new equipment.

There had been minor examples of one of the lesser companies making the running on an isolated route or two. Capital, however, ranking fifth among United States domestic carriers in terms of passengers carried, and sixth in passenger-miles, immediately began to influence the competitive momentum in the entire northeastern quadrant of the U.S.A., in the most congested pattern of air routes in the world. By mid-1957 three-quarters of Capital's seat-miles were flown by Viscounts. By 1958 there were sixteen daily Viscount services New York—Chicago (ten nonstop), fifteen New York—Detroit, ten New York—Pittsburgh, and ten Washington—Chicago, to cite the densest routes. The traffic curves showed a startling upsurge, and there was little doubt that Capital had found a winner as far as the fare-paying public was concerned. But, tragically, pride came before a fall.

In its eagerness to exploit fully the competitive advantage of the Viscount, Capital took delivery of 46 aircraft during 1956, in addition to the eight in service at the end of the previous year. On 24 July it ordered fifteen more, bringing the total to 75, and on the same date ordered 14 de Havilland Comets, stressing the low noise levels which would be imposed upon urban communities, resulting from the jet aircraft's rapid rate of climb.

Unfortunately, to quote J. H. Carmichael, Capital's president, the 'financial results for the year 1956 were disappointing'. In June 1957 the new orders for both Viscount and Comet were cancelled. Some observers suspected that all was not well with the Viscount; but Capital's results showed that the aircraft had been remarkably dependable, especially the engines, and the achieved cost figures were lower than had been computed when arriving at the purchase decision. The truth was that Capital had over-extended itself in the matter of depreciation expenses. Its agreement with Vickers-Armstrongs, the manufacturers of the Viscount, involved equipment purchase notes to be repaid in monthly instalments over a period of five years with the privilege of prepayment without penalty. But in fact Capital fell behind in its regular repayments to Vickers, who then applied pressure by threatening to foreclose.

In company with other airlines, Capital succeeded in obtaining a rise in general fare levels on 24 January, 1958, but this was fairly modest, amounting to 4 per cent plus $1 per ticket. On the same day, the airline began negotiations for nine Convair CV-880s, with the help of General Dynamics, builders of the 880; and asked for $12·2 million subsidy, spread over two years.

The federal support became necessary because C.A.B. action was too little and too late to strengthen Capital's route structure adequately. Even after introducing many nonstop flights over its basic route pattern, the average passenger journey length in 1957 had improved only to 383 miles, which was little better than half the industry average. Relief eventually came in the shape of substantial route extensions in March 1958, in the Great Lakes—Southeast Service Case, and Capital joyfully added points in Florida to its network.

From this time on, when in normal circumstances any airline would have been able to improve its fortunes, Capital ran into a series of misfortunes. In May 1958 a Viscount was involved in an inflight collision resulting in some fatalities; there was a strike in October; and then on 2 May, 1959, there were two crashes on the same day, one Viscount being struck by lightning, and a Constellation catching fire. This was hardly good for Capital's public image at a time when the Big Four were hitting back with new jet services plus propeller-turbine Electras. American's introduction of the Lockheed Electra on the New York—Chicago route on 23 January, 1959, was a severe competitive blow.

On 23 December Capital arranged with Pan American for the lease of seven Douglas DC-6Bs (later increased to eleven) in a desperate effort to provide extra capacity at low cost. When these went into daycoach service to Florida on 7 February, 1960, there had been another Viscount accident and it became obvious that, with Vickers growing apprehensive, Capital was in serious financial trouble. In May a group of shareholders met to attempt to overthrow the Board of Directors, following a $5 million loss in the first quarter of 1960. In June, Vickers granted a further extension of foreclosure—for the third time—and a plan was submitted for the repayment of the $33 million debt. But it was too late. At the end of July plans were announced for the purchase of Capital by United Air Lines and an application was promptly filed with the C.A.B. with the full agreement of the shareholders of both airlines.

In the biggest merger in the history of the U.S. Domestic Trunk industry, United Air Lines absorbed Capital Airlines on 1 June, 1961, becoming in the process the largest airline in the western world, measured in passenger-miles, passengers, or almost any unit of comparison. At the date of the takeover, United served 116 cities with a fleet of 267 aircraft.

There were many criticisms of Capital's handling of the crisis; but few fully appreciated the full extent of the problems, particularly the continued preponderance of short-haul routes. Although the C.A.B.'s award of routes to Florida was followed in May 1959 with one from Chicago to the Twin Cities, breaking Northwest's monopoly, these acted only as a palliative, not as a cure. Capital was not only starved of good revenue-producing routes (even the routes to Miami had to be operated at fiercely competitive fares) but it was over-burdened with a large number which were strictly local service by definition.

Many blamed the Viscount for Capital's downfall. This was not consistent with an objective review of the facts. Far from leading Capital to failure, the Viscounts kept the company abreast of, and even ahead of, competitors, over a crippling short-haul route structure, during a period of difficulty experienced throughout the industry. The heart of the trouble was excessive rate of purchasing, inability to service the debt, inadequate action by the C.A.B., and a run of bad luck with accidents. Although United rationalized the composition of its combined fleet after the take-over, the Viscounts were retained. Significantly, they remained in service for almost a full decade afterwards, suggesting that Capital's original choice of equipment for efficient short-haul routes had been wise.

Although the Viscount was clearly superior to its piston-engined competitors, being faster, quieter, comparatively vibration-free, and more economical to operate, the United States airline industry as a whole did not order the British aircraft in large quantities in the traditional manner appropriate to an outstandingly successful type. With a world-wide order book to fulfil, Vickers was in no position to offer quick delivery, and conse-

Continental Airlines operated a fleet of Vickers-Armstrongs 810 Viscounts.

The third U.S. operator of the propeller-turbine Viscount was Northeast Airlines. N6590C was a V.798 originally intended for Capital Airlines.

quently the Big Four turned to other solutions to their short-haul problems. Some traffic analysts believed that the Viscount was not large enough, and set up design criteria for a larger type. Others soldiered on with what they had, concluding that the Viscount's superiority was nevertheless not damaging them over their shorter segments, most of which were not competitive. There were mutterings in Britain that the U.S.A. had, as it were, put the shutters up to prevent the mass invasion of a foreign aircraft. This may well have been true, but there was little that could be done about it, and if the U.S. chose to protect its own, this was exactly what other countries had done in similar situations.

Vickers did manage to pull off another important Viscount order, again to one of the smaller domestic trunk carriers, Continental Airlines. Robert Six, president of Continental, began discussions with the manufacturer towards the end of 1955, soon after Capital had demonstrated effectively the Viscount's superiority. Continental was able to take advantage of improved technology, mainly in engine development, and order 15 of the Series 810. This was similar to BEA's Series 802, longer than the standard Series 701, allowing about 15 extra seats. The American aircraft had even higher-powered engines than BEA's, permitting a cruising speed of 350 mph, against the 305–315 mph of the earlier series. Continental put the Viscount into service on 14 February, 1958, at first on its Chicago—Kansas City—Los Angeles route, until the big jets made their appearance in 1959, when the Viscounts were transferred to the more important secondary routes. Unlike United, Continental did not retain its propeller-turbine fleet any longer than necessary and sold it to the British company, Channel Airways, in November 1965.

The only other U.S. Domestic Trunk to operate Viscounts was Northeast Airlines, yet another of the smaller companies making a bold attempt to match its stronger competitors by introducing outstandingly better equipment. Northeast had at first explored the propeller-turbine field by ordering five Bristol Britannias, but subsequently lost enthusiasm and transferred its allegiance to Viscounts in July 1958. Nine Viscounts were placed in service on the denser commuter markets and to Florida a few months later, and, although later eclipsed by the entry of the jets, they gave Northeast its first opportunity to break away from its old image as a pedestrian operator of New England local routes. Initial traffic gains in the Boston—New York—Washington commuter markets were substantial. On the New York—Boston market alone, Northeast's market share improved from 8 to 35 per cent.

Success for this Viscount operator was short-lived, for reasons that had little to do with equipment standards. On 30 April, 1961, Eastern Air Lines began its famous Shuttle Service, with its unique dual feature of no reservations and guaranteed seats. This innovation, even with piston-engined equipment, was so attractive to the regular business travellers on the high-frequency routes from New York to Boston and Washington that the Viscount's smoother, quieter, vibration-free ride was neglected by a public which kept a sane perspective of the fundamental requirements of a good transport system. Plagued by financial worries also, with mounting losses—the award of a temporary certificate to Florida had not been a cure-all—Northeast negotiated in July 1963 with both Vickers and General Dynamics for the return of Viscounts and Convair CV-880s respectively. Ironically, in spite of all the handicaps, the Viscount load factor during the first half of 1963 exceeded 60 per cent.

The Electra

Although the Big Four airlines did not join Capital in ordering the Viscount, they certainly did not ignore the threat, having taken a lively interest in what was going on in Europe, particularly BEA's outstanding success with the propeller-turbine airliner. By the time Capital had ordered Viscounts, the leading U.S. airlines were, like BEA, exploring the possibility of a successor to the pioneer type. American Airlines outlined a specification

N6101A *Flagship New York* was the first of American Airlines' fleet of 35 Lockheed L.188 Electras, which entered service in January 1959. (*American Airlines*)

N5525, one of forty Lockheed L.188 Electras operated by Eastern Air Lines. The fuselage stripes were two shades of blue. (*Eastern Air Lines*)

for a larger short-haul airliner for use on dense inter-city routes and this eventually crystallized into an order for 35 L.188 Electras from Lockheed on 10 June, 1955. Eastern Air Lines more than matched this by ordering 40 on 27 September.

The Electra was of conventional design, like the Viscount, but substantially bigger, with seating for about 86 passengers in typical coach-class layout. Its four Allison 501 engines gave the aircraft excellent field performance for its size, together with good operating economics. During the year following the initial American order, several major airlines ordered Electras, in spite of the imminence of jets, believing that the latter would be ideal for long-haul routes, but possibly difficult to operate profitably on short-haul sectors.

Lockheed quickly established a lead over the BEA-sponsored Vickers counterpart, the V.950 Vanguard, which was not ordered until 20 July, 1956. The Electra made its first flight on 6 December, 1957, well ahead of the Vanguard's on 22 April, 1959, and the Burbank company kept up the pace by delivering the first production aircraft to American Airlines on 5 December, 1958, just one day less than a year after first flight. American was plagued by a pilots' strike which began on 19 December and lasted more than three weeks and thus allowed Eastern Air Lines to become the world's first Electra operator on 12 January, 1959, with services between New York and Miami, adding propeller-turbine service to Puerto Rico on 22 February.

American was glad to have the extra capacity and speed on the New York—Chicago route from 23 January (two days before it began transcontinental jet services) and on New York—Detroit on 21 February. Capital's Viscounts had been a thorn in American's side for too long, and now the big airline reacted strongly. In contrast with Capital, to whom a route such as New York—Chicago was the major source of revenue, American regarded it as only one of many. Furthermore, it could draw on greater resources and thus take greater risks than its smaller rival. The Electras, therefore, with higher seating capacity and greater speed, immediately regained the competitive initiative for American, even though at times

N5001K, the first of National Airlines' fifteen propeller-turbine powered Lockheed Electras.

American's service frequency was in excess of the apparent traffic demand.

Electra service in the United States was further augmented during 1959 by National Airlines (New York—Miami on 26 April); Braniff (San Antonio—Dallas—New York on 15 June); Western (Los Angeles—Seattle on 1 August); and Northwest (New York—Milwaukee—Minneapolis on 1 September).

Lockheed's production was at a rate consistent with the normal quota of a major West Coast manufacturer, about eight per month. By the end of 1959 about 100 Electras were building up many thousands of propeller-turbine hours on U.S. domestic trunk routes. It appeared to be the ideal airliner for service on dense routes of short-medium stage lengths, where the 600 mph speeds of the jets could not be turned to good account because

This red and white Lockheed Electra, N7143C, was one of twelve operated by Western Airlines.

of the irreducible time in the terminal manoeuvres, both in the air and on the ground.

The Electra's rapid progress from conception to full airline service had been in remarkable contrast to that of another four-engined propeller-turbine airliner, the Bristol Britannia, which took $4\frac{1}{2}$ years between its first flight on 16 August, 1952, and its first service with BOAC on long-haul international routes on 1 February, 1957. The Britannia's main troubles had been with icing in its unusually-shaped engine intakes; but otherwise it was built like the proverbial battleship. The Electra, on the other hand, soon revealed some embarrassing defects during its first year of service.

When an American Airlines Electra crashed only a week after the first service, this was generally regarded as no more than an isolated incident by an industry which is forced to accept with equanimity a certain percentage of accidents involving fatalities, as an inherent risk resulting from the

N130US was one of Northwest Airlines' eighteen Lockheed Electras.

impossibility of attaining absolute perfection in human or mechanical behaviour. Soon, however, two more crashes occurred, one by a Braniff Electra at Waco, Texas, on 28 September, and another by a Northwest aircraft in Indiana on 17 March, 1960. There was no satisfactory explanation, and, with evidence that the aircraft broke up in flight, the F.A.A. ordered an immediate investigation.

This happened towards the end of Quesada's tenure as head of the F.A.A., and he took a line which required much courage and conviction. There was considerable pressure to ground the Electras, but after inspecting 52 aircraft, the decision was made only to curtail severely the operational limits on speed and altitude. On 25 March, 1960, the cruising speed was reduced from the original 400 mph to 316, and then to 295. This allowed reduced services to continue, mitigating the loss of revenue, meanwhile allowing an intensive study by Lockheed of the basic cause. After a full inquiry the Electra was found to be structurally defective in the wing and engine installation, and a full modification programme was undertaken by the manufacturer. This was estimated to have cost Lockheed about $25 million, whose ready acceptance of the burden was a tribute both to the integrity of the American industry and the strict surveillance exercised by the licensing authority in protecting the public interest.

Lockheed had marked up some important foreign sales, notably in Australia, New Zealand, and the Netherlands, but the crashes effectively dampened subsequent airline demand for the Electra. In fact, some of the existing orders were in jeopardy: Northwest, for example, withheld acceptance of eight of its order for 18 because 'Lockheed had not met contract specifications as to speed and performance factors'.

On 31 December, 1960, the F.A.A. removed its speed restrictions, satisfied that Lockheed had dealt with the root cause of the trouble, and after rigorous inspection, the aircraft returned to service from 24 February, 1961, onwards as Electra IIs. Overshadowed by the success of the jets, leading to the development of short-haul jets, they continued to do a workhorse job and as time went by even became popular among some passengers who preferred the particular seating layout offered by certain airlines. In the fullness of time, towards the latter 1960s, most Electras were demoted from trunk-line service and, following a familiar process, underwent a complete re-engineering to reappear as rugged freighters for some of the Supplemental Carriers.

Purpose Fulfilled

In the United States, the propeller-turbine principle took pride of place for barely three years. Capital's Viscounts went into service on 26 July, 1955, and the first pure-jets were commissioned in October 1958, with the full flood coming in 1959 and 1960. The timing was critical for Capital as (the financial crisis apart) the new generation was ushered in before the Viscount fleet was fully amortized. There had been uncertainty too among public relations staff as to the liberties they could take with words. Turboprop or turbine lacked impact in the psychology of the advertising and publicity world. Most airlines compromised with propjet, which was a little snappier, and one or two brazen companies threw semantic caution to the wind and called the Electra a jet. A precedent for such cavalier treatment of words had, of course, been set by TWA whose L.1649A Super Constellations, complete with throbbing turbo-compounded piston engines, were called Jetstreams—and the chances were that many a passenger still thinks to this day that his first jet flight was on that aircraft.

Many of the great airlines never bought a propeller-turbine airliner, notably Pan American and United, the biggest international and domestic operators respectively. TWA and Delta also missed out the propeller-turbine generation, and there is little evidence to suggest that any of these airlines suffered irrevocable damage thereby. The propeller-turbine types shone brightly for a brief period in airline history, and then faded. Yet they had their place and came very close to greatness.The Viscount turned British European Airways from a good airline into a great one, respected throughout Europe. The Britannia set the other British state airline, BOAC, on the road to success on the North Atlantic, beginning a sharp upward traffic trend which the Comet later augmented. Capital gave the Big Four the fright of their lives on the trunk routes from New York and Washington to the Great Lakes. But all the brave efforts came to nought in the end. The main commodity which the airlines had to sell was speed, and the propeller-turbine could not deliver an improvement over piston-engined equipment of sufficient magnitude, whatever the attraction of the quiet, smooth ride, or the claims of economic superiority. The next generation had speed, the glamour of dispensing with propellers, plus the unqualified magic word, beloved of Madison Avenue, *jet*.

Armed with the greatest single advance in technology in aviation history, the airlines of the United States set about the task of coming to terms with the engineers and scientists, and undertook a revolution in operational techniques to usher in a new dimension in air travel.

The first U.S. designed turbojet transport to enter service was the Boeing 707-121. N707PA of Pan American World Airways was the second production aircraft and one of several to carry the name *Clipper America*. (*Boeing Airplane Company*)

CHAPTER TWENTY

The Jet Age

The Magnificent False Start

Propeller-turbine airliners led the field for only a short time, and their superiority over the best piston-engined types did not compel universal acceptance in the United States, although the Viscount (because of its earlier introduction) was supreme for a few years for short-to-medium-haul work within Europe. The long-haul Britannia had a short-lived success on the North Atlantic before being displaced first by the Comet 4 and then by the Boeing 707 on BOAC's intercontinental routes. Although certificated by the U.S. authorities, the Britannia never went into service with a United States airline, Northeast cancelling and preliminary discussions with TWA coming to nothing. The truth was that the development of the propeller-turbine aircraft overlapped that of the jet. In fact the Comet 1 preceded the Viscount into service by almost a year, and, had it not been for the suspension of Comet 1 services, the use of propeller-turbines would have been even more restricted.

The idea of a jet airliner was born in Britain at the end of World War 2, and the original de Havilland design was for a fast transatlantic mail carrier with accommodation for only six passengers. After substantial modification the D.H. Type 106 was ordered in 1946 by the Ministry of Supply, which also ordered eight for BOAC. The prototype first flew on 27 July, 1949, and the thirty-six seat Comet 1 went into service on the London—Johannesburg route on 2 May, 1952.

A dream had become reality. Once thought to be an extravagant risk, the Comet was an astonishing success. Within a few months the startling timesaving achieved by its 500 mph speed, and the trouble-free regularity with which schedules were maintained, so impressed the world's airlines that they sought to emulate BOAC. From the manufacturer's point of view the most important order was for three long-range Series 3s, intended for use across the Atlantic, from Pan American World Airways, on 20 October, 1952.

This was regarded as a pilot order for a much larger one to follow, provided the aircraft met all its guaranteed performance criteria. In the event, the prospect of a British-built airliner in service with the United States flag carrier was short-lived; for disaster overcame and almost overwhelmed de Havilland.

When a Comet inexplicably disintegrated shortly after taking-off from Rome on 10 January, 1954, its reliability record had hitherto been so good that, after a careful examination of BOAC's and other aircraft, services were resumed on 23 March, with many convinced that sabotage had been the cause. On 8 April, however, another occurrence near Stromboli appeared to repeat so exactly the pattern of the earlier tragedy that a full Government Court of Inquiry was set up to establish the cause of the double disaster. Based on a reconstruction of the salvaged parts of the first Comet, the Court concluded that the Comet's cabin had burst as a result of metal fatigue under the stress of repeated pressurization cycles. It also concluded that no-one was to blame. The aircraft had been made in accordance with all the principles of aircraft engineering and with the knowledge of metal fatigue then accepted. Until this time no civil airliner had cruised at 40,000 ft altitude and water-tank testing of the pressure cabin had never been a requirement.

To describe the Comet 1 story as a failure would not be just, for it achieved a great deal. The operational record, in fact, though marred by accident, opened up a vista of the vast possibilities of commercial jet flight. The four airlines which operated the Comet 1 provided enough evidence to show that what had been a pipe dream in 1943 was a practical proposition in 1953. As the first of its line the Comet 1 was not a profit-maker by ordinary airline standards. But wherever it flew, passengers demanded to travel by no other way, and the prospects which lay before full-scale jet operations seemed to be unlimited.

Pan American Airways and the Jet Age

Although the Comet 1 was responsible for sparking off world interest in 500 mph air travel, the advent of jets was a step which would in any case have been taken in due course. Engine designers, aerodynamicists, stressmen, and all the many skilled tradesmen in the aircraft industry, had to find outlets for their inventive genius. One of these outlets, pursued by almost a dozen companies throughout the world, was the development of jet airliners.

There were three main reasons why the jet age swept in as early as it did. The first was the channelling of a surfeit of wartime aeronautical talent into civil projects. The second was the courage of manufacturers in risking millions of pounds, dollars, or francs, in ventures which by any standards were colossal risks, even when subsidized. The third reason was Pan American World Airways.

On 13 October, 1955, Pan Am ordered twenty Boeing 707 and twenty-five Douglas DC-8 airliners. To the airline world, the threat of American dominance immediately raised its head once more, echoing the apprehension which had been felt in 1946 at the Chicago Conference and the battle against an Open Skies policy. For the Boeing 707 prototype, already flying, was a 600 mph airliner, with almost twice the capacity of any current aircraft, and with an early prospect of transatlantic range capability. Its productivity measured in seat-miles or ton-miles was about four or five times that of the largest Douglas or Lockheed piston-engined airliner, and the commercial implications of this enormous stride were such that there followed an undignified rush to the West Coast of the United States, home base of all the big airframe manufacturers.

One senior airline executive was frank enough to admit: 'We ordered the Big Jets as quickly as we could; then asked our engineers and economists to prove that we had made the right decision.' If there had ever been any doubt as to Pan American's supremacy, the reaction of the world's airlines to its epoch-making order for forty-five jet aircraft in 1955 dispelled such doubts once and for all.

The Boeing Type 367-80, the Dash Eighty as Boeing people call it with affection, made its first flight on 15 July, 1954, five years after the Comet's. It was developed from the B-47 bomber and incorporated the same design principles, such as engine installation in pods suspended from the wings. As with many innovations, this arrangement was regarded by orthodox designers with suspicion at the time but subsequently became accepted as the best solution. Boeing gambled on the Air Force having to specify a fast tanker to refuel the B-47 and B-52 bombers in flight. The gamble came

Pan American World Airways was first to order the big jets, with twenty Boeing 707s and twenty-five Douglas DC-8s. The DC-8-33 N802PA *Jet Clipper Cathay* at Kennedy International Airport, New York. (*The Port of New York Authority*)

off; the Air Force ordered a production batch of tankers in March 1955; Boeing immediately offered the 707 to the airlines.

The Pan American jet order leaned towards Douglas in its preference. This was partly because of the solid Douglas reputation, but also because the DC-8's fuselage was slightly wider, giving a definite advantage in passenger preference. Boeing was forced to change its fuselage, and the two aircraft finished up remarkably similar in general appearance. The Boeing's wings had a slightly greater angle of sweep, 35 deg against 30 deg, and could be recognized by the preference for many small windows. In performance there was little to choose. The Boeing outsold the Douglas design mainly because of a two-year lead, and lower price. But in the early years, in spite of massive sales penetration into all the major airline markets of the world, both companies lost money on the programmes. Douglas wrote off $300 million in development costs up the end of 1960; Boeing was slightly better off, because of partial commonality with the military tanker, with which much of the development costs could be shared.

The Boeing 707-120, with four Pratt & Whitney JT3C-6 jet engines, first flew on 20 December, 1957. With a production and technical efficiency which was at that time unmatched anywhere in the world in peacetime, the Seattle manufacturer delivered the first service airliner to Pan American to permit its inaugural transatlantic jet flight on 26 October, 1958, only three weeks after BOAC's first Comet 4 service. De Havilland, thanks to an agonizing reappraisal of its jet construction policy and programme, followed by a vigorous effort to restore lost ground, had managed to deliver Comets to BOAC in time to give the British airline the honour of starting the first transatlantic jet service. But Pan American provided more jet capacity and enjoyed thereafter a period of unchallenged leadership on the busy North Atlantic route. TWA, meanwhile, went into decline, for its L.1649As were no match for Boeing 707s or Comets, and for a few years BOAC actually went into second place after Pan Am in the passenger numbers ranking of Atlantic air carriers.

By this time, incidentally, the Russian airline, Aeroflot, had projected itself straight from the piston-engined era into jets by introducing the Tupolev Tu-104 on to many mainline domestic services in the U.S.S.R. Developed from the Tu-16 bomber, it made its first flight on 15 July, 1954, went into service on the Moscow—Irkutsk route on 15 September, 1956, and has been in continuous service ever since. The Russians were the first to start sustained jet airline services.

To return to Pan Am: Juan Trippe and his planning team had recognized the importance of nonstop capability between New York and the main capitals of Europe. Soon after the original order for JT3-powered Boeing 707-120s had been placed, negotiations began for a longer-range version, to be powered by more advanced JT4A-5 engines, also built by Pratt & Whitney. This truly intercontinental airliner, the 707-320, went into service with Pan American on 26 August, 1959, only seven months after its first flight, and before any other company except BOAC had been able to start an Atlantic jet service.

The other United States transatlantic airline, TWA, elected to delay inauguration of its jet services until the longer-range Boeing was available, and concentrated on a rapid intensification of its domestic jet network. TWA Boeing 707-331s began the New York—London—Frankfurt jet route on 23 November, 1959, a precious year later than its rivals, surrendering a competitive advantage which took several years to regain.

In the initial stages of the Big Jet age, Boeing did all the front running—which made a gratifying change from having to play second, or third, fiddle to other companies. In the past, Boeing had just missed greatness in two major stages in the advance of commercial design, the first modern twin-engined piston airliner and its four-engined development. In both cases, the Boeing aircraft, the Model 247 and the 307 Stratoliner, had been eclipsed by the DC-2/3 and the DC-4/L.049 respectively, even though the

N715PA *Clipper Liberty Bell* was the second of Pan American's Boeing 707-321 Intercontinentals with true transatlantic range. (*Boeing Airplane Company*)

TWA also selected the Boeing 707 with initial fleets of -131 and -331 aircraft. The aircraft illustrated is a later B model with Pratt & Whitney turbofans. (*TWA*)

Seattle company had been the main innovator. With the big jets, however, Boeing did not allow the initiative to pass from its hands, and relentlessly pressed home its lead by a powerful marketing campaign, wresting many big airlines away from their traditional sources of supply.

To put no finer point on the situation, as one English observer remarked, 'Boeing saw Douglas off in a big way', and for the first time since 1934, leadership passed out of the hands of the company which habitually supplied at least two-thirds of the world's civil airliners.

Douglas, in fact, had to follow the Boeing lead in manufacturing a large-capacity, long-haul jet airliner, abandoning all thoughts of possible propeller-turbine developments. The DC-8-10 was originally conceived for transcontinental routes, but other versions were developed almost simultaneously, with different engines but with the same airframe. Pan American's version was the DC-8-30, with Pratt & Whitney JT4A-5 engines, which went into service on 27 March, 1960, eleven days after KLM, one of Douglas' ever-faithful customers, inaugurated its transatlanic jet service.

Domestic Jets

To the American travelling public, the term jet conveyed an image of progress and sophistication that transcended practical considerations of timesaving, noise or vibration. Every domestic airline tried desperately to replace its piston-engined fleets without delay. By an ingenious piece of interline co-operation, National Airlines was the first to operate a big jet within the United States. It leased aircraft from Pan American and began Boeing 707 service between New York and Miami on 10 December, 1958. This was most convenient for both companies, as Pan Am's traffic trough coincided with National's peak, so that the maximum utilization was extracted from the aircraft. The Boeing 707-120 had 111 seats and did the journey in 2 hr 15 min.

The arrangement with Pan American had been preceded by an agreement signed on 9 September not only for the reciprocal lease but also for an exchange of stock, plus the acquisition by Pan Am of additional National shares. The result of the arrangement, if consummated, would have made

Eastern Air Lines' first jet transports were Douglas DC-8s. N8609, illustrated, was a DC-8-21. (*Eastern Air Lines*)

Pan Am the largest stockholder in National (25 per cent) and National the largest in Pan Am (6 per cent). The C.A.B. decided, however, that such interlocking interests would set too dangerous a precedent and on 15 July, 1960, ordered both airlines to divest themselves of each other's stock.

The Boeing lease did at least allow National to prepare for service with its own jets—DC-8s on 18 February, 1960—without being outflown by Eastern.

American Airlines was the first to begin domestic jet service in the U.S.A. using its own aircraft, starting the transcontinental route from New York to Los Angeles on 25 January, 1959. The inaugural date of jet service by United States domestic trunk airlines is shown, by airline, in Table 27. American's coast-to-coast flights were a tremendous competitive challenge, following in the long tradition of rivalry between the major transcontinental airlines. Temporarily at a disadvantage, TWA took a gamble by begin-

American Airlines was the first carrier to operate U.S. domestic jet services with its own aircraft, on 25 January, 1959, initially with Boeing 707-123s. N7526A, illustrated, was a 707-123B—the first with turbofans. (*Boeing Airplane Company*)

ning service on 20 March, 1959, although only one Boeing 707 had been delivered. The single aircraft saw TWA through what would otherwise have been a disastrous month in terms of revenue loss.

United Air Lines was less fortunate. It had pinned its hopes on Douglas, whose experience in building civil airliners in large numbers was unparalleled, whereas Boeing had been comparatively dormant in the civil field for many years. As already remarked, Douglas decided to build a civil jet only when Boeing forced its hand, and the DC-8-10 made its first flight on 30 May, 1958, just five months before the Boeing 707 entered service with Pan American. United eventually started service on the same day as Delta Air Lines, on 18 September, 1959, by which time almost eight precious months had elapsed, with American holding the jet advantage, with traffic and financial statistics to prove it.

The third of the big U.S. jet airliners was developed by Convair, of San Diego. The CV-600, or Skylark or Golden Arrow, was originally conceived as a direct competitor to the Boeing 707 and the DC-8, before these types were modified to provide nonstop transatlantic range. The Skylark's main claim was that it was conceived to be significantly faster than its rivals. Originally sponsored by TWA, still strongly influenced by Howard

The third type of U.S. big jet transport was the Convair CV-880. The example shown, N8483H, was one of six leased to Northeast Airlines by TWA. (*Lenscraft Photos Inc*)

Hughes' leadership, late in 1955, initial orders were placed by TWA and Delta Air Lines in June 1956 and the aircraft, redesignated CV-880, made its first flight on 27 January, 1959, entering service with Delta on 15 May, 1960. The sponsoring airline and biggest name on the Convair order book, TWA, then ran into financial complications. It tried to divest itself of control by its major stockholder, Hughes, to whom the airline was indebted for the supply of aircraft through an unusual leasing arrangement with the Hughes Tool Company, which bought the airline's fleet on its behalf. As a consequence of legal delays, TWA did not begin Convair 880 service until 12 January, 1961.

American Airlines became intrigued by claims for the Convair 880's greater speed, and in August 1958 ordered 25, with an option on a further 25 (it was still called the CV-600 at that time). American's plan was to operate the Convair as a first-class express service, outstripping the Boeings

Developed to meet American Airlines' requirements was the Convair CV-990. It entered service as the CV-990A in March 1962 and N5605, illustrated, was one of 20 built for the airline. (*American Airlines*)

and Douglases, and it had great ambitions for cutting time on the nonstop transcontinental route.

Unfortunately, these high hopes were dashed when the Convair CV-990, as the American Airlines version was called, failed to meet its guaranteed performance, and the first of the series was not delivered until January 1961, and even then certain modifications remained to be done. American finally put the CV-990 into service on the New York—Chicago route on 18 March, 1962.

Much harm had been done to the whole programme by this time, and leading airlines not only stopped buying the product, but even cancelled orders or refused to accept delivery. Some aircraft remained unsold, the total sales were most disappointing, and modification of the entire production line was prohibitively costly. Convair sustained a heavy financial loss, the heaviest in the history of the aircraft manufacturing industry, one estimate putting the figure at about $425 million.

Modern Air Transport's Convair CV-990 N5615 *Polar Byrd I* was an ex-American Airlines' aircraft and it made the first round-the-world flight over both polar regions. This picture was taken at McMurdo Sound, Antarctica.

Ironically, the company had been responsible for one of the most widely quoted market forecasts of airline traffic. But there was obviously a bad misjudgement, for even had the CV-880/990 been successful technically and economically, break-even figures would still have been extremely difficult to achieve. Boeing had set the pace in the Big Jet race, with Douglas determined not to allow its traditional leadership to falter, and only a supreme blunder on the part of one of these companies could have given a third contestant a chance. And with the great industrial strength and integrity of these two formidable competitors, Convair never really had a chance, once the initial challenge had faded.

The Short-Haul Jet

The public became accustomed in the early 1960s to fast jet airline services over all long-haul routes, and over what could broadly be termed medium-haul routes such as New York—Chicago. Competition became intense over the transcontinental route, and important inter-city routes such as New York—Miami, Chicago—Seattle, or Los Angeles—Houston. Internationally, jet fleets were introduced at breakneck—and break-bank balance—speed. The North Atlantic route became almost a jet shuttle service in the summer season, and Pan American inaugurated its round-the-world jet service on 10 October, 1959, having just introduced jets on the Pacific on 5 September. (Several more years were to pass before Pan Am was permitted to forge the final vital link across the U.S.A.)

Once the public's appetite had been whetted by the speed, comfort, and outstanding reliability of the new jet airliners, the operators began to sense the pressure to extend such service to all their route systems, including the shorter range segments. Ways and means were found to extend the scope of the jets far beyond the limits originally planned. The passengers quickly adapted themselves to the new standards, accepted all the publicity for the jets at face value, and tended to make disparaging remarks about the 'old coffee-grinders'. They did not understand nor did they care about the theory of short-haul aircraft economics which held that the high fuel consumption of jet engines could be offset only by high block speeds and high annual utilization, neither of which could be achieved on short stages.

But the economic theorists overlooked two main considerations. First, lower seat-mile costs of propeller-driven aircraft were ineffective if the majority of the seats remained vacant (because the public stubbornly insisted on filling the more costly jets, when a choice was offered). Second, other factors came to light which were not foreseen when the first-generation jets were being developed. The reliability of jet engines improved to unforeseen levels, many times better than that of their piston counterparts. The lack of vibration had a beneficial effect on airframe reliability, and consequent lower maintenance costs, and the fuel itself was cheap—the jets

The first foreign jet transport to be adopted by a United States carrier was the French Sud-Aviation SE.210 Caravelle. The first units of United Air Lines fleet of twenty Caravelle VIRs entered service in July 1961, and they flew more than 117 million miles and carried more than 10 million passengers before being withdrawn in October 1970.

could operate perfectly on kerosene at half the cost per gallon of high-octane petrol. In short, the airline economists underestimated the capabilities of aircraft and engine designers, who continued to produce more and more efficient combinations of power, speed, payload, and field performance, with the result that the jets became intrinsically more economic to operate than the piston-engined types.

The first aircraft manufacturer to capitalize on the new realization of jet operating economy for short and medium ranges was the French company, Sud-Est Aviation (later Sud-Aviation) of Toulouse, which in 1951 put in hand the construction of the SE.210 twin-engined airliner, soon named the Caravelle. Drawing on the experience of other firms—using the nose and engines of the Comet 2 for example—Sud-Est designers took the unprecedented step of putting the engines at the rear of the fuselage. There were many advantages in this. The wing was left clear of major protuberances, vastly improving its aerodynamic efficiency. The powerplants were easily accessible for maintenance, and almost inaudible from inside the cabin. The engine position was viewed with extreme scepticism even after the Caravelle made its first flight on 27 May, 1955. Air France's order for 12, in November of that year, was regarded as an exhibition of patriotism, but the Caravelle continued to demonstrate its excellent capabilities and further orders began to come in, mainly from European countries.

In the United States, the Caravelle's story was strikingly similar to the Viscount's. In both cases the combination of passenger appeal and economy over certain ranges made them the competitive pace-setters. Just as Capital's order for the Viscount marked a procurement watershed in 1954, so did the order for 20 Caravelles by United Air Lines in 1960. In one respect, the French success was even greater; for whereas Vickers sold to a medium-sized U.S. Domestic Trunk airline, Sud's contract was with one of the Big Four, an achievement never before accomplished by a foreign manufacturer. United began Caravelle services on the New York—Chicago route on 14 July, 1961. As with the Viscount, the Caravelle gave excellent service, but did not succeed in making further penetration into the U.S. market, even with the assistance of the Douglas company as distributing agents, mainly because the United States industry was itself taking a long look at the short-haul jet market.

Britain had reacted to the threat of French Caravelle competition in Europe by putting into service, on 1 April, 1960, a short-haul version of the de Havilland Comet. Regarded at first as a case of turning necessity into a virtue, the Comet 4Bs of BEA turned out to be surprisingly successful, and operational experience suggested that genuine short-haul jet aircraft were practicable. By this time, BEA was already committed to its more permanent short-haul jet solution by ordering, on 12 August, 1959, 24 de Havilland Trident three-engined airliners. The Caravelle's rear-engined layout was adopted for the Trident, with the addition of a third engine in the tail section of the fuselage.

At this time, the Boeing company was known to be studying various designs for a short-haul jet. Its answer to a requirement for a medium-sized jet had been a shortened version of the 707, called the 720. This was first ordered by United Air Lines, and marked that airline's return to the Boeing fold after selecting Douglas in the initial jet buying spree. United put the Boeing 720 on the Chicago—Denver—Los Angeles route on 5 July, 1960, with American joining in on 31 July over the same route.

Although the Boeing 720 did not sell in such vast numbers as the parent 707, it was nevertheless an important development for the Boeing company,

First operator of the Boeing 720 was United Air Lines which introduced the type on 5 July, 1960. (*Boeing Airplane Company*)

Eastern Air Lines bought fifteen Boeing 720s. N8701E was the first of this fleet. (*Boeing Airplane Company*)

which adopted the policy of offering several variations of the same basic type, according to individual requirement, either transatlantic or trans-continental, nonstop or by stages. Hitherto, a manufacturer had usually found it uneconomic to build two or more aircraft types simultaneously, but Boeing's idea of creating an airliner family met with success.

Although its rivals alleged that the commonality of parts claimed by Boeing was largely illusory, it was an effective sales weapon, and in the early 1960s Boeing stepped into the forefront of civil airliner manufacturers, supplanting Douglas in the pre-eminent position it had held since 1934.

Acceptance of the family-of-airliners concept by the airline industry encouraged Boeing to make a further step by launching a three-engined short/medium-haul type, the Boeing 727, towards the end of 1960. The 727 bore a remarkable resemblance to the British Trident, against which Boeing marketing men had many a battle in the initial stages. The Trident might have achieved greater sales—and severely restricted those of the 727—but for an incredible decision on the part of BEA to withhold its order for Tridents until de Havilland compromised the design by reducing the

Western Airlines acquired a large fleet of Boeing 720Bs with Pratt & Whitney turbofan power. N93141 is seen at Los Angeles International Airport with two of the airline's Lockheed Electras in the background. (*L.A. Airport Photography*)

Initial orders for the Boeing 727 included one from Eastern Air Lines for forty. EAL's 727-25 N8128N is seen on a test flight near Seattle. (*The Boeing Company*)

TWA's first Boeing 727-31, N850TW, is seen here on the Boeing factory aerodrome at Renton. (*The Boeing Company*)

Braniff International Airways acquired a large fleet of Boeing 727s. The pale blue 727-27C N7272 is illustrated. (*The Boeing Company*)

passenger capacity. The Trident lost about a year of precious development time plus a narrow margin of operating cost advantage. Boeing was just the company to exploit the situation.

Thus, although the Trident first flew on 9 January, 1962, exactly thirteen months before the Boeing 727, the latter aircraft went into airline service first, with Eastern Air Lines on the Philadelphia—Washington—Miami route, on 1 February, 1964. United followed on 6 February (San Francisco —Denver), American on 12 April (New York—Chicago), and TWA on 1 June (Indianapolis—New York). The 727 had achieved the rare distinction of entering scheduled service with all the Big Four within a period of four months. It went on to sell in large numbers to every one of the Domestic Trunks, except Delta and Western, and also to Pan American, to some of the Local Service, and to many foreign carriers.

Britain had been the innovator in the case of the trijet, and took the initiative also in proceeding further with a new generation of twin-jets to succeed the Caravelle. First discussions with operators had begun as early as 1956 by the former Hunting company with its H.107, and this gradually evolved into the British Aircraft Corporation's BAC One-Eleven, following a reorganization of the British industry. Construction started in 1961 when British United Airways placed a pilot order, but the BAC sales team, remembering the lessons of the Viscount, lost no time in promoting the product in the U.S.A.

A major success for the British Aircraft Corporation was the sale of thirty BAC One-Eleven 401s to American Airlines. (*American Airlines*)

An aggressive sales campaign reaped its just reward. On 19 October, 1961, Braniff Airways ordered six BAC One-Elevens (later increased to 14); on 26 July, 1962, Mohawk Airlines, the largest of the Local Service carriers, joined Braniff in its choice; and, to emulate the Caravelle's achievement in selling to one of the Big Four, American Airlines signed up in July 1963 for 15, later increased to 30. Braniff started service with BAC One-Elevens on some of its secondary routes of medium passenger density on 25 April, 1965, Mohawk on its leading routes into New York on 15 July, 1965, and American on 6 March, 1966. One interesting facet of American's service was that it placed its new equipment in direct competition with Mohawk, also using One-Elevens. A situation in which one of the Big Four was forced to match the equipment of a Local Service carrier was far removed from the original concept of carrier classification and separation as defined and conceived by the C.A.B. in the 1940s.

The British Aircraft Corporation might well have made a considerable penetration into the United States civil airliner market had not Douglas picked up the signal that short-haul jet operations were practicable and that the shape and magnitude of the passenger demand/range curve indicated that there was room for another manufacturer. Having fulfilled a two-year contract to market the Caravelle in the Americas—an unsuccessful venture for both parties—the Santa Monica company revived an old project and launched the DC-9 from its expanding Long Beach factory, receiving an initial order from Delta Air Lines in April 1964.

N8961, one of Continental Airlines' gold-finned *Golden Jet* Douglas DC-9s.

The first of the line, the Series 10, differed in only minor respects from the BAC One-Eleven, but was slightly larger, had Pratt & Whitney JT8D turbofans instead of Rolls-Royce Speys, and carried the Douglas name, still respected among all short-haul operators to whom the DC-3 had become a legend. Whereas Boeing had sought to make a special feature of the commonality of parts between the 727 and the other Boeing jets, Douglas emphasized its preoccupation with design aspects aimed to reduce maintenance costs to an absolute minimum, at levels never previously achieved by any other airliner.

At first there were doubts as to Douglas' judgement in introducing another short-haul aircraft when two types, the Boeing 727 and the BAC One-Eleven, were already selling healthily in the United States. But in fact, the DC-9 met with even greater success than the One-Eleven, which it so closely resembled. Two of the Big Four ordered large numbers, TWA in July 1964, and Eastern in February 1965, while Continental, Northeast, and many of the Local Service airlines swelled the order book to a point where Douglas became embarrassed with its inability to match production rates with orders.

The rapid re-entry into short-haul airliner manufacture by the Douglas company, with substantially enlarged production facilities at Long Beach,

United Air Lines was the first U.S. carrier to order the Boeing 737. The first series 200 aircraft, N9001U, is seen taking-off on its first flight, at Seattle. (*The Boeing Company*)

was epitomized by the timetable of the first aircraft to enter service, by Delta Air Lines. The order was placed in April 1963, first flight was on 25 February, 1965, the F.A.A. certificate was obtained on 23 November, and Delta was able to add DC-9 flights to its published schedule on 8 December of the same year.

Both Douglas and Boeing lost no time in developing the breed of short/medium-haul airliners in the classic tradition of taking advantage of engine and other technical improvements. Douglas came close to making the DC-9-10 (the first series) redundant when it added 15 ft to the fuselage, allowing up to 115 coach-class seats, and found to its intense satisfaction that the operating costs of this DC-9-30 were only slightly higher than those of the -10. Making its first flight on 1 August, 1966, the DC-9-30 entered service on the Eastern Air Lines Shuttle Service (which Eastern claimed was the chief design criterion) on 1 February, 1967.

Boeing tackled the difficult problem of competing with Douglas and BAC for the short-haul markets by producing an aircraft which was, over-simplified, a twin-engined version of the 727. The Boeing 737 at first held high promise of achieving performance and economy standards far superior to its rivals; but the early hopes were not entirely fulfilled. The first version, in fact, the 737-100, met with comparative apathy in the market-place, following its sponsorship by the German national airline, Lufthansa, in February 1965. About a year after the first flight, United Air Lines became the first U.S. operator of the 'Fat Albert', as its critics irreverently dubbed it. But United's aircraft was the -200, the stretched version, and turned out to be a useful aircraft over so-called DC-9-type stages.

Although the success of producing a stretched version of a curtailed fuselage was a qualified one, there was little doubt about the development of the basic 727 in the other direction—a straight stretch of the trijet configuration. Twenty feet longer than the -100, the 727-200 could carry 178 passengers (as many as the 707-320C) over short and medium stages, and was an admirable solution to the problem of high-density routes such as the California Corridor. Northeast Airlines was the first operator, on 14 December, 1967.

The Boeing 727-200 has provided substantial evidence that it will take its place in aviation history as one of the great airliners. Although lacking the range of its predecessor, the 727-100, its economic performance was best over the bracket of distances which, within the United States, contributed most of the traffic volume. Its high capacity ensured maximum revenues, and its place as the last of a thoroughbred line meant that its operating costs were low. Consequently, the airlines fortunate enough to participate in dense, medium-haul route networks found the 727-200 a good profit-maker.

Three major U.S. airline customers for the stretched Model 200 version of the Boeing 727 were American Airlines, National Airlines and Continental Airlines. *Top*: N8609 Model 223 with American Airlines' sober red and blue livery which was only modified in 1970; *centre*: National Airlines' Model 235 N4744 with orange and red sun markings; and *bottom*: Continental Airlines' Model 224 N88701 with red, gold and black livery. (*The Boeing Company*)

Big Jet Development

By developing the Big Jet airliner, the world's major aircraft manufacturers had embarked on a course of technological development which generated a tremendous momentum. The airlines introduced their first jet fleets only just in time to precede the next innovation: turbofan, or bypass jet powerplants.

The Rolls-Royce engine company was the first to provide turbofan engines for a major airliner, when its Conways were fitted to a number of Boeing 707s and DC-8s, notably those of BOAC, Lufthansa, Air-India, VARIG, El Al, and Trans-Canada Air Lines. The Conway had rather more power than the contemporary Pratt & Whitney J-57s and J-75s, and and although the Rolls engine was not developed further after the early 1960s, because of basic design limitations, the lesson was clear—the turbofan concept offered an exciting new horizon for the engine designers.

The first Big Jets had been criticised for a number of reasons. Although the weight of adverse comment had not been sufficient to alter or curtail jet operations, it had nevertheless been enough to cause concern. One big shortcoming was the noise level, especially on take-off, when all engines were on full power, often augmented by even noisier water injection techniques. This had led to protests from several communities, and some airports, notably Washington National, had to delay the introduction of jets for many years. Noise suppression devices became almost a mandatory modification. The other major problem was the long runways needed at airports. Typically, a DC-8 would require runways of about 9,000 ft—or almost two miles—for take-off, compared with the 7,000 ft or so for the DC-7C. The Boeing 707-120 needed even more concrete, leading to caustic references to 'the lead sled' and the 'skilled thrill' as the seconds ticked by on what seemed to be a dangerously long take-off distance.

The further development of turbofan engines beyond the standard of the Conway changed this state of affairs. The additional power which the bypass design was able to add was beneficial in several ways and overcame some of the faults of older jets. Performance was improved by a substantial margin, not only in airfield capability but also in range, because the fan engines had a much lower specific fuel consumption than their predecessors. As an additional bonus, the fans were also quieter. Altogether they produced a quiet revolution which, though less spectacular than when the first jets displaced the piston-engined aircraft, was more effective in terms of progress from almost everyone's point of view. The airlines were happy, because they could fly further, more economically. The airport authorities were happy, because there appeared at last to be a halt to the continual demand for further extensions to already-extended runways. Most of all, the general public appeared to be satisfied, if not completely happy, now that the noisy jets had actually stopped getting noisier.

The aircraft manufacturers proceeded to take full advantage from every pound of extra thrust which the engine designers offered. Boeing was able

Braniff International Airways' first Boeing 707s were the unique short-fuselage high-power Model 227s for operation from high elevation airports in South America. (*Boeing Airplane Company*)

to prevent its family of airliners from becoming too unmanageable, as it no longer had to produce special versions for such airlines as Braniff International with its unique problem of high altitude airports in South America. Braniff's first Boeing 707-220 series was ten feet shorter than the standard -120, but no other airline had this version.

Boeing had already taken the opportunity of stretching the fuselage of the basic -120 by about eight feet as soon as extra power became available with the Pratt & Whitney JT4A-9 straight jets. With 12 ft added to the wing span, the Boeing 707-320 quickly made its mark as the Intercontinental Boeing, with greater range, capacity and profitability than before. Now, the advent of even greater power from the JT3D-3 turbofan—or bypass—enabled Boeing to add the suffix 'B' to all its versions. The 707-120B showed an astonishing 2,850 ft improvement in take-off distance; while the 707-320B was able to operate nonstop flights well in excess of 4,000 miles, including such routes as New York—Rome, or Seattle—Tokyo.

Douglas provided an interesting contrast in airframe manufacturing policy with respect to the use of engine development. Whereas Boeing sold several distinct model sizes for different airline requirements, Douglas retained the same basic airframe for all its models, from the DC-8-10 to the DC-8-50. The -10 was judged to be ideal for United States domestic operations, and in fact was ordered by United in preference to the Boeing 707, in spite of the later delivery which this entailed. The -20 was a higher-powered version, with Pratt & Whitney JT4A-3 engines replacing the JT3C-6s of the first model. The DC-8-30 was the intercontinental version, with JT4A-3 turbofans, matching the performance of the Boeing 707-320B. The -40 was the Conway-powered version, while the -50 had JT3D-3s, with 18,000 lb of thrust.

Douglas' decision to stay with the same fuselage length was possible because the original DC-8 design was longer than the Boeing 707, and, in fact, the Intercontinental Boeing 707-320B—the biggest of the series—was

Final development of the Boeing 707 was the turbofan-powered -320B (passenger) and -320C (cargo) aircraft. One of Pan American World Airways' 707-321C cargo aircraft is seen with pallets being loaded through the large forward door. (*Pan American World Airways*)

only $2\frac{1}{2}$ ft longer than the first DC-8. In developing its longer-range versions of the DC-8, Douglas merely added three more feet to the wing span, added more fuel tankage, and stressed the whole airframe and wings for higher weights.

Boeing and Douglas continued to develop their Big Jets in line with engine development until there came a time when airframe design criteria limited the amount the fuselage could be extended. In the case of the Boeing 707 the practicable limit was reached with the -320 series. Any further stretch would have resulted in the tail scraping the ground when the aircraft rotated on take-off. The 707's greater wing-sweep angle also imposed insuperable problems in terms of cost. Whether by accident or visionary design, Douglas was far less restricted and found, to its extreme satisfaction, that an extension of no less than 37 feet was possible on the basic DC-8 fuselage.

The remarkable DC-8-61 made its first flight on 14 March, 1966, and went into service with United Air Lines on 24 February, 1967. The unprecedented addition to the cabin capacity made it possible to increase the seating from a theoretical 174 in all-economy layout to 252, although

This view of N45090, National Airlines' first Douglas DC-8-61 emphasizes its great length—187·4 ft.

this maximum was used only by Supplemental airlines on charter flights. Nevertheless, the almost 40 per cent increment applied to all seating arrangements, and as this was achieved at an estimated cost increase of only about 5 per cent, the DC-8 airlines hastened to take advantage of this windfall. Many an airline executive has been heard to use phrases of the 'printing your own money' type.

Douglas went on to produce other versions of the -60 Series. The DC-8-62 had a shorter fuselage—only six feet longer than the standard DC-8's, but had enormous range, approaching 6,000 miles, and was capable of linking almost all the major populated areas of the world without a refuelling stop. Finally, the DC-8-63 combined the best qualities of both the -61 and -62, offering the full 37-ft stretch, together with about 5,000 miles range, and was especially adaptable for cargo work.

N8073U, one of United Air Lines' 198-seat Douglas DC-8-61s. (*United Air Lines*)

A Dream Come True

In the pioneering days of civil aviation, when the early Fokkers, Junkers, Handley Pages and Fords were plying their uncertain way along the world's early airlanes, a fashionable subject for ridicule was the prospect of carrying hundreds of people in heavier-than-air flying machines. Airships were thought to be a good long-term prospect, and strangely these were seldom the subject of humour. But cartoons illustrating large aircraft, with many rows of passengers, eating sumptuous meals in complete comfort, without parachutes, flying goggles or other necessities, were regarded with an indulgent smile, because no-one really believed that this was more than the result of an over-vivid imagination. If a cartoonist really wanted to insert a touch of the ludicrous, all he had to do was to indicate that the passengers were enjoying a motion picture while in flight.

As with many of the predictions of Jules Verne, fact has overtaken fantasy. The commercial airliner has become so much a part of modern life that its appearance or sound does not excite the slightest interest, though its noise is causing some concern. In the U.S.A. particularly, the air services of the nation have become an indispensable part of the daily routine. Probably the major contribution to this state of affairs has been the jet engine and its later developments.

For it was the Jet Age, with its dramatic improvement in all-round efficiency, which gained the full, unqualified acceptance of the travelling public. The fast, reliable, vibration-free travel, at reasonable fares, coupled with sound organization and service by the operating airlines, were demonstrably superior on nearly all counts compared with the competing media. Until the advent of the jets, there was still a good case for rail travel, based on amenities and comfort, which compensated the passenger for the longer journey time. But the jets not only eliminated the time differential on all but the shortest rail trips; the spacious cabins, high-class meal service, improved safety standards, punctuality, and reliability, all combined to set the seal, once and for all, on air travel as the only satisfactory means in the United States*.

The history of civil aviation and airliners could perhaps be over-simplified by dividing it into three eras. First there was the era during which an aeroplane—almost any aeroplane, it did not matter what type—was the subject of awe. Then came the intriguing period when development proliferated to such an extent that different types of aircraft were recognized by quite a large section of the public. Today, with most of the apprehensions of the new dimension of travel cast aside, the word jet has become synonymous with commercial aeroplane and few know, or care, which type is used by the airline. That all types have roughly the same characteristics and offer the same standards is generally accepted.

The airlines themselves tacitly accept this. There has been a subtle change in emphasis in promotion, publicity, and advertising. Seldom do the companies vie with each other in claims to have the biggest, or the fastest, or the prettiest jet. The accent is on refinements in comfort standards and amenities. All airlines serve good meals at appropriate times on flights whose journey time is long enough to justify them. Some carriers deliberately offer less than the maximum number of seats allowed by F.A.A. regula-

*At the beginning of the new age of the Wide-bodied jets, 2,159 out of the 2,628 aircraft in U.S. airline service were jet powered. (*See Table 26, page 646*)

Tourist/economy class cabin of a Northwest Airlines Boeing 707-320B. (*The Boeing Company*)

Tourist/economy class seating in one of the long-bodied Series 60 Douglas DC-8s.

tions in order to provide wider, or more widely spaced seats. Other carriers have introduced individual stereophonic music and films.

In short, the modern Big Jet airliner has reached a plateau of performance. The airlines are faced with the problem of using all their ingenuity to make the best use of this supremely efficient vehicle. One outstanding example has been the ability of the non-scheduled airlines to offer fares at remarkably low rates.

All the route carriers have striven to improve load factors and utilization of both aircraft and crew, in an effort to bring costs down. At the same time, revenue yields have to be maintained. As air transport in the United States moves towards its Jubilee, the struggle to sustain traffic growth at profitable levels, without the injection of continual improvements in airliner performance, will be the airlines' greatest challenge.

W. F. Patterson (*left*) was originally an accountant who looked after the affairs of Pacific Air Transport, one of the ancestors of United Air Transport. Patterson became general manager of United in 1931, was president from 1933 to 1963, and chairman until his retirement in 1966. Eddie Rickenbacker (*right*) started his flying career as a fighter pilot in World War 1. After early sparring for an influential position in the airline business, he eventually joined the General Motors organization, in charge of the Eastern Air Transport Division, which became Eastern Air Lines. He bought control in 1937, built up *The Great Silver Fleet* of DC-3s, and continued to maintain Eastern's stature after World War 2. Rickenbacker retired in 1963.

CHAPTER TWENTY-ONE

Twilight of the Gods

End of a Dynasty

When the Big Jets ushered in a new era for the airline industry, there were five Captains of Industry still firmly in command of the five biggest airlines of the western world. With one exception, all had been totally dedicated to air transport since it first took root in the U.S.A. True pioneers, they had become totally absorbed by their chosen careers, and such was their success and power that most of their rival companies had cause to consider the term total absorption in a different sense.

William ('Bill') Patterson, Cyrus ('C.R.') Smith, Edward V. ('Cap'n Eddie') Rickenbacker, Juan Trippe, and Howard Hughes were giants among a band of intuitive executives who counted few pygmies in their numbers. By a series of steps taken without falter and seldom along the wrong course, they led their companies to supreme heights in their own country and were regarded with something approaching awe by their foreign counterparts. They have left a legacy to their respective airlines which the passing of years will never diminish.

Their lifetimes' work is recorded in this book. For more than a third of a century, Bill Patterson was identified with United Air Lines, which came under his presidency in 1934. C. R. Smith guided American Airlines' fortunes over the same period of time. Juan Trippe headed Pan American from its very inception in 1927 for more than 40 years. Eddie Rickenbacker picked up the ailing Eastern Air Lines in 1938 and, almost single-handed, made it one of the biggest of the Four without the benefit of either a transcontinental or a transoceanic route. Howard Hughes came to TWA in 1939 when it was already great, and made it greater.

Cyrus R. Smith (*left*) established an early reputation for good management when vice-president and treasurer of Southern Air Transport (one of American Airlines' ancestors) in 1929. In a distinguished career as president of American, including responsibility for organizing wartime aviation, 'C.R.' built his airline up to a point where it vied with United for U.S. domestic leadership. He retired in 1968 after leading American Airlines for 34 years. Juan T. Trippe (*right*), born of a rich New England family, was concerned with the early development of Colonial Airlines before taking over the fortunes of Pan American Airways from its foundation in 1927. Showing a masterly grasp of international affairs, both business and political, he built a globe-circling airline in less than 20 years. His vision of the ultimate possibilities of transport aircraft was ahead of his time, and he turned the name Pan American into a household word around the world, before handing over the presidency in 1964.

Except for Hughes, none of these great men had a substantial financial interest in the airline they served so well. With advancing years, their touch was still sure, although eventually age and change began to overtake them. In their own way they were benevolent dictators—although their benevolence was not always obvious to some of their employees—but gradually their unilateral way of doing things became an anachronism as the vast problems of finance, operational complexity, and technological diversity became too much for individual men to comprehend or manage in full.

Characteristically, Eddie Rickenbacker made a clean break. He was never a proponent of a policy of gradualness, least of all when it concerned himself. On 31 December, 1963, he resigned as chairman and general manager, and Floyd D. Hall joined the airline as president. Hall immediately gathered around him a nucleus of new blood in the top echelons of Eastern and set about the task of giving the company a complete new image, ranging from the appearance of its aircraft to the courtesy of its stewardesses.

Bill Patterson had already retired as president of United Air Lines on 28 September, 1963, to be succeeded by George Keck; but he remained as chairman until final retirement on 28 April, 1966, after 37 years with United or its predecessor company. C. R. Smith became chairman of American Airlines—paralleling Patterson's elevation—in February 1964, finally retiring in January 1968 when President Johnson asked him to take over as United States Secretary of State for Commerce. Marion Sadler took over as president of American in 1964, to be succeeded by George Spater in January 1968 because of ill health. Juan Trippe remained coolly at the helm of Pan American, autocratic as ever in major decision-making, but gradually handing over control to his heir, Harold Gray, who had been one of the pilots of the Boeing flying-boats which inaugurated the world's first transatlantic scheduled air services.

Gray's tenure was quite short, for in 1969 Najeeb Halaby, former F.A.A. Administrator who had been prominently associated with such projects as the supersonic airliner in addition to his more routine responsibilities, took over the helm of Pan Am. Halaby faced a formidable set of problems, not the least of which was to put into service the revolutionary Boeing 747, which Trippe had sponsored, apparently following his old maxim that each generation of aircraft should have twice as many seats as its predecessor.

The changing of the old order by the retirement of Patterson, Smith, Rickenbacker, and Trippe resulted in no revolutions, no board room battles or administrative upheavals—although there was a certain amount of reshuffling here and there. It was all done very politely, even ceremoniously, accompanied by much mutual praise and tribute, which was no more than their due.

In the case of Howard Hughes, however, the withdrawal of his interest from TWA was the very antithesis of evolution, and forms a unique episode in the case history of a man and his company which has no parallel in the history of civil aviation.

Howard Hughes

The heir to the Hughes Tool Company fortune is one of the most enigmatic personalities that the world of air transport, or indeed any other industry, has ever encountered. He was much younger than the other great men of the airlines when he acquired the majority shareholding in TWA in 1938. At that time he was adventurous, extrovert, daring and determined.

Already famous as a round-the-world pilot, loving aeroplanes and aviation passionately, his interest in TWA might have been no more than a multi-millionaire's hobby. Hughes' relationship with TWA was much more. He stimulated the company—which already had an enviable record of innovation and pioneering—to even greater heights. Having been the sponsor of the Lockheed Constellation, the first civil airliner to challenge Douglas' supremacy, he emerged from World War 2 with a magnificent route award which gave TWA the enviable distinction of being the only airline with both transcontinental and transatlantic traffic rights. (American relinquished the privilege by selling out to Pan American.)

Howard Hughes (*left*), heir to a large fortune which his father amassed in the Hughes Tool Company, was a famous record-breaking pilot during the 1930s. He bought 87 per cent of the TWA stock in 1937 and controlled the airline's fortunes with spectacular success for more than 30 years. Forced to surrender absolute control in 1960 he eventually sold his stock for $566 mn in 1966. Ralph Damon (*right*), one of the most respected airline leaders, became president of Curtiss-Wright in 1932; vice-president of operations, American Airlines in 1936; president of Republic Aviation in 1941; president of American Airlines in 1945; and finally president of TWA in 1949. Damon worked closely with Howard Hughes for seven years in a remarkably successful partnership.

During the post-war decade, Hughes concentrated on the most important broad aspects of company policy vital to competitive survival against rivals such as American, United, and Pan American. When in 1950 the C.A.B. agreed to his raising the Hughes Tool Company's (Toolco's) stockholdings to 73 per cent, it warned against further extension of indebtedness, but commented favourably on 'the contributions of Toolco's aircraft division and Mr Hughes to the science of aeronautics . . . and financial support to the carrier, in the selection and purchase of its equipment, and their advice and guidance to the engineering and operations departments of the carrier'.

Hughes' participation in major policy decision-making was highly successful during the whole period of the presidency of Ralph Damon, who joined Hughes from American Airlines on 25 January, 1949, as a strong advocate of regulated competition, and disillusioned by American's withdrawal from the Atlantic market with its sale of AOA to Pan American. Like Jack Frye, Hughes' companion and TWA president until February 1947, Damon's attributes complemented those of Hughes, who appears throughout his life to have needed a partner of equal stature and character to put practical polish on the raw gems of his own agile intellect. Damon's death in January 1956 could not have come at a worse time. Since the Toolco takeover in 1947, Warren Lee Pierson had been chairman of the Board, and Damon and he had, with Hughes' co-operation and inspiration, steered TWA successfully, but when the vital decisions were required in 1956 and 1957 to order the big jet airliners which were to be the backbone of TWA's fleet for the next ten years, Damon's steady hand was missing, and what was more, the whole industry was beginning to suffer from a minor economic recession in 1958–1959.

Whether Hughes was deeply moved by the loss of Damon at such a time is hard to judge, as few people have ever set eyes on him since the late 1940s. During this period Hughes became more and more a recluse, seeking privacy to the point where he was regarded as eccentric. There was some reason, if not factual evidence, for this deduction. Although Carter Burgess became president of TWA on 25 January, 1957, he never once met Hughes, and left before the end of the year, after which the office remained vacant for far too long.

Law Suit Extraordinary

The events which followed Hughes' and TWA's difficulties in financing the new big jets developed into what *Fortune* magazine has described as the largest private civil suit in the history of U.S. business. The contest raised important questions about the relationship of owners, lenders, and managers of large businesses, neatly crystallized by *Fortune*:

'(A) What is the justification for preventing a man who owns 77 per cent of a company, however unorthodox he happens to be, from voting his stock and controlling his business?

(B) How far into the control of a large-scale business are big institutional lenders entitled to protect their loans?

(C) What is the public interest in these matters, particularly the unique public interest that arises in a quasi-public utility such as an airline?'

As the only individual equity owner in any of the five major airlines with more than a five per cent stockholding, Hughes had a definite interest to defend. The banks and financiers were apprehensive of their investment and, when danger threatened in the direction of their dollars, the fight began.

Originally, when TWA was in trouble in 1946 through crashes, a pilot strike, and the grounding of its Constellation fleet, Hughes Tool Company put $10 million cash into the airline and took back convertible notes and the power to name the majority of TWA's directors. Equitable Life, holding

$40 million of loan debentures, agreed on condition that if TWA defaulted on payments, the Tool Company's stock could be put into an Equitable-controlled voting trust. This clause was to become the key issue in the whole history of the litigation, with Hughes fighting every inch of the way to retain financial control.

When TWA ordered 63 new jet aircraft in the spring of 1956, worth $300 million, the prospect of long-term lending arrangements during the delivery period of 1959-1960 became inevitable. When, because of the shortage of cash during the first quarter of 1958, TWA had to go to the Bank of America and Irving Trust for $12 million on a 90-day note guarantee by the Tool Company, Equitable insisted that long-term financing must be arranged quickly. Otherwise it would invoke the voting trust clause of the 1946 agreement.

Hughes used all his ingenuity to escape from the clutches of Equitable. He tried to set up a leasing plan whereby a separate company would be created as a wholly-owned subsidiary of Hughes Tool. He released Boeing 707s off the line to Pan American and reduced the Convair 880 order. He tried to persuade the aircraft manufacturers to participate in financing Hughes Tool. But all this was to no avail and, when Irving Trust stopped credit in March 1960, Hughes was obliged to come to an understanding with all parties on a long-term financing plan covering the necessary $300 million. On 19 May, Hughes Tool agreed to guarantee certain obligations covering interim credit for immediate aircraft deliveries and the converting of Equitable's old long-term loan to a short-term one.

Equitable Life qualified its commitment to the long-term financing plan by a condition that if there was any change of management thought to be adverse, it could demand a voting trust of Hughes' stock. On 27 July, 1960, 24 hours before the scheduled closing of the whole deal, TWA's president, Charles S. Thomas, who had succeeded Burgess on 15 July, 1958, resigned. The lenders chose to regard this move as the ultimate proof that Hughes' management policy was unsound and hardened their attitude, playing as hard to get in financial negotiation as Hughes had in his withdrawal from public life.

On 31 December, 1960, Hughes had to capitulate to Equitable and the banks on their own terms, and reluctantly agreed to accept the loss of control of TWA by having his entire stockholding placed in the hands of a voting trust controlled by the lending institutions.

Soon afterwards, TWA appointed two new leaders, Ernest Breech, formerly chairman of Ford Motors, as chairman; and Charles Tillinghast, formerly with Bendix, as president. In addition to directing the day-to-day policies of TWA, one of their first decisions was to file, on 30 June, 1961, an anti-trust suit against the Hughes Tool Company, on the basis that as both supplier and financier of aircraft for TWA, it had excluded other suppliers.

Hughes offered to subscribe to and guarantee a $100 million issue of new TWA stock, on condition the voting trust was terminated. The TWA

Board rejected this offer and furthermore filed suit in the Southern District of New York, asking not only for damages but for divestiture of Hughes' stock.

This could hardly be construed as a friendly act, and predictably Hughes counterclaimed vigorously and a protracted period of high-level litigation, lasting many years, was set in motion.

In May 1963, the Federal District Court judged Toolco to be in default, for intentional refusal to produce Howard Hughes as a witness, and to deliver documents. It also assessed TWA's damage claim at $145 mn, an increase of $30 mn. This decision was subsequently confirmed by the Court of Appeals on 2 June, 1964.

The situation was complicated by support for Hughes from the Civil Aeronautics Board. On 19 June, 1962, it granted Hughes permission to control Northeast Airlines; and later, on 10 July, 1964, declared that he could resume control of TWA provided that he disposed of his interest in Northeast. TWA protested against this latter decision and appealed to the Circuit Court, citing Hughes' default in the anti-trust suit. Also on 7 December the Court of Appeals for the Second Circuit reversed the C.A.B. decision of 10 July on the legal grounds that there should have been a public hearing.

The sands were running out. On 8 March, 1965, the Supreme Court upheld the Court of Appeals' opinion, and on 11 October refused to hear Toolco's appeal. On 5 January, 1966, the District Judge denied Toolco's motion for a preliminary ruling which would have had the effect of restricting the scope of the default judgement, and directed that the proceedings continue before the Special Master, Herbert Brownell, who, in September 1968, decided that TWA was entitled to $137,611,435 (and 95c) in treble damages against the Hughes Tool Company (Toolco).

Another dramatic contribution to the wretched affair occurred on 3 May, 1966, when the Hughes Tool Company sold its entire trustee-held stock through a secondary offering to the general public. A total of 6,584,937 shares, valued at $86 each, changed hands—in twenty minutes—for $566,304,582.

The British commentator, Richard Worcester, paid this tribute to the former TWA chief: 'This may lay the foundations of a new TWA structure that will enable it to survive and justify the dreams that Jack Frye and Howard Hughes had for the airline before the war when they conceived the Constellation. Whatever Hughes has done or not done, he will always be a great son of American commercial aviation for brilliance in sponsoring an aircraft so prescient in conception that the delay in its fruition of several years due to the war did not prevent it from going on to become a great intrinsic source of U.S. world prestige and wealth.'

The airline world has not heard the last of Howard Hughes. He kept in practice, as it were, by taking over a merged Local Service airline, Air West, on 21 July, 1969. At this time, the company seemed bent on self-destruction, through the inability to reconcile the conflicts of a three-way merger.

Hughes' association, to the extent of adding his name officially to the airline (as Hughes Air West), is perhaps the portent of dramatic revival.

They Also Served

To select names among the captains of the U.S. airline industry in the sense of placing them on some kind of pedestal would be invidious. The leaders of the Big Four and Pan American of course stand out but the passing of an Age and of a Style was associated with the disappearance of other personalities in the domestic field.

The first casualty was Thomas E. (Tom) Braniff, co-founder of the only trunk airline which bears its founder's name, and who was killed in an aircraft crash on 10 January, 1954. A typical self-made man, high-principled, determined, he rose from selling insurance to the first settlers in Oklahoma at the turn of the century to become a senior pillar of business in the Midwest. His airline was noted for unspectacular but steady progress; but his foresight was such that, just before his death, he publicly predicted that his employees would witness flights to the moon.

In complete contrast with Tom Braniff, Ted Baker had founded National Airlines in 1934 and ran it with the rugged individuality which had characterized his early life. A complete autocrat, he was supported by resilient men able to tolerate his unpredictable methods. He conducted a life-long feud with Eddie Rickenbacker, and withstood the formidable poker play of Juan Trippe. Yet Baker's withdrawal from the scene was almost an anticlimax. Lewis B. (Bud) Maytag, Jr, former owner of Frontier Airlines, bought National Airlines from Baker for $6.5 million in April 1962. After revelling in the tough in-fighting which characterizes the rivalry between the domestic trunk airlines, Baker's aggressive zeal evaporated. Refusing to be humbled with a non-influential appointment, he resigned from National, went for an extended vacation in Europe, and died suddenly of a heart attack.

While National's fortunes ebbed and flowed, partly because of Baker's genius for precipitating crises, a neighbour airline, Delta, went steadily from strength to strength under the benevolent and energetic leadership of C. E. Woolman. Woolman had founded the world's first commercial aerial crop-dusting company in 1925, had suffered under W. F. Brown, and had entered the airline scene alongside Baker in 1934. He died on 11 September, 1966, two days after signing his Report to Stockholders which showed the gratifying increases on all counts which were to continue for many years. Charles H. Dolson, who succeeded Woolman, inherited a gilt-edged investment, and by the early 1970s Delta's outstanding prosperity was threatening to cause a revision in the familiar term Big Four.

Of the other trunk airlines, Northeast and Western have not enjoyed continuous leadership by their founders, although the record of Terrell C. Drinkwater deserves mention. Drinkwater saved Western from almost certain extinction by keeping his nerve when he took over the airline on

Robert F. Six (*left*) has guided Continental Airlines since 1938 when it was still one of the smallest of the certificated airlines. In spite of the deficiencies of a small route network and low traffic density, Six has refused to be overawed by formidable competition from the Big Four. Donald W. Nyrop (*right*) was trained as a lawyer, and his early career included important posts at the C.A.B. from 1942, whose chairman he was in 1951–52 after spells with Air Transport Command and the ATA. He took over the presidency of Northwest Orient Airlines in 1954.

1 January, 1947. Selling its best route was a hard decision to make but it kept Western alive. Drinkwater patiently restored Western to health before resigning in July 1970 when the Kerkorian interests moved in.

Without underrating the abilities of the new generation of top executives who administer the great U.S. domestic airlines in the 1970s, their power as individuals is not as dominant as their illustrious predecessors'. One of the younger pioneers is still in control, Robert F. Six, of Continental Airlines, still displaying a welcome tendency for creative marketing. But in general the chairmen and presidents are not the autocrats of old. One exception is perhaps Harding Lawrence, who left Continental to take over the presidency of Braniff on 5 April, 1965, assumed firm control from the start, and demonstrated that decision-making can still be a single-minded —and almost single-handed—affair.

A different personality was Donald W. Nyrop, who, unlike most airline leaders, came from a legal and government background, specializing in aviation law and administration. A true believer in thrift, his arrival as president of Northwest Orient Airlines on 16 October, 1954, heralded a sustained run of outstanding financial success which was the envy of the entire airline industry.

And so, 'The Kings are Dead, Long Live the Kings' applies as much to the aristocrats of the air transport world as it does to those of any other commercial activity. The late 1960s witnessed the withdrawal or demise of colourful characters; but their responsibilities continue to lie in capable, though widely different, hands.

Although Eastern Air Lines pioneered the Air-Shuttle, the air bus idea was old. Seen here is the Bellanca P-200 Airbus NC785W (c/n 702) operated during the 1930s by New York and Suburban Airlines. This aircraft had a large cargo door. (*Gordon S. Williams*)

CHAPTER TWENTY-TWO

Fresh Horizons

The Eastern Shuttle

Due credit has already been given to Allegheny Airlines for being first off the mark with the idea of a no-reservations service, although for a number of reasons, it was not a complete success. It was left therefore to Eastern Air Lines to fashion a formula, then to persevere throughout an experimental but uncertain period, and finally to emerge with a successful operation which gave a new dimension to air travel.

The need for improvements in providing a prospective passenger with a guaranteed seat was greatest, by definition, on the busiest routes. Eastern shared the sitting tenancy on two of the biggest three of these routes, New York—Boston and New York—Washington. The distances are extremely short, well below the average stage length of major air routes—Newark Airport, one of the three serving New York, is almost exactly 200 miles from both Boston and Washington Airports. By the late 1950s the problem of obtaining a reservation on either route had reached intolerable proportions and was becoming a deterrent to air travel in the Northeast Corridor, as the populated coastal strip from Washington to Boston had become known.

At this time, Eastern was going through a tense period. Because of its lack of long-distance routes and consequent relatively high cost levels, it was suffering more than most airlines from the coincidence of large expenditures on new jet equipment and a minor economic recession which depressed traffic demand. It was also meeting stiff competition from rival airlines to whom the C.A.B. had given a fair number of routes overlapping or competing directly with some of Eastern's best revenue earners.

Eastern's first exploratory efforts directed towards improving its traffic share was an Air-Bus service from Cleveland, Pittsburgh and St Louis to Miami begun on 13 October, 1960. The objective was to reduce amenities to a bare hygienic minimum on old, depreciated aircraft, and thereby correspondingly reduce fares. The resultant $40 fare was 26 per cent less than the day tourist and 15 per cent less than the night tourist air fares. More important, it was the same as the Greyhound Bus fare which, however, applied to a tiring 25-hr journey. The rail fare was $46 for a 31-hr trip, and Eastern estimated that the per capita cost of driving by car would be $45, assuming a three-day itinerary, including meals and motels.

Market surveys taken after the first year of Air-Bus operations showed that 17 per cent of the patrons were taking their first air trip, and 31 per cent would otherwise have gone by surface transport. The Air-Bus concept was extended on 29 April, 1962, to a few other city pairs serving the Great Lakes—Florida market but the initial promise was not sustained. Basically it appeared that a few dollars reduction on a fare which was already a good bargain was not the major factor in creating new traffic, and after a few years the tariff structure reverted to the standard categories based on seat pitch and aircraft type.

Eastern tried another variation on the Air-Bus theme—when it inaugurated, on 30 April, 1961, its historic Air-Shuttle service on the Washington—New York (LaGuardia)—Boston route. The Air-Shuttle introduced a no-reservations system, with passengers purchasing tickets on the aircraft, and dispensing with the ponderous standard airline ticket. But the key to the astounding success that followed was the positive guarantee of a seat, a unique feature which involved a considerable amount of organization of reserve aircraft to take care of the need to operate additional sections of a single flight schedule.

The Air-Shuttle began with flights every two hours, using 95-seat Constellation aircraft which had been relegated from Eastern's main routes by the rapid introduction of large jet fleets. On 12 June came the first instance of the necessity of providing a second section to carry one passenger; Eastern lost money on the flight but reaped its reward in the publicity and news coverage generated by the event. On 1 August the New York—Boston service was increased to hourly frequency, and New York—

Main base for Eastern Air Lines' Air-Shuttle operation, LaGuardia Airport, New York. This 1967 photograph shows the new curved terminal building and the runway extensions. The control tower is centred on the left-hand traffic pier. American Airlines hangars are on the left and that on the right belongs to United Air Lines. (*The Port of New York Authority*)

Washington quickly followed the pattern on 15 September. On 26 November there were seven sections for one scheduled departure from LaGuardia to Boston. By 11 June, 1962, only 13½ months after the inaugural Air-Shuttle flight, one million passengers had been carried. On this occasion, Alan Boyd, then the chairman of the C.A.B., described the achievement as '. . . the greatest experiment I know of in recent times . . . the Air-Shuttle is the greatest thing that has happened in air transportation in years . . . I would like to see a lot more of this kind of thinking in air transportation'.

During the first few years the Air-Shuttle lost money for Eastern. The management admitted that they had miscalculated the full effect of the guaranteed-seat factor. Originally sixteen Constellations were allocated to the service, but more had to be added to maintain the enviable record of never refusing a passenger. Because of the severe peaking of traffic at the beginning and end of the day, many aircraft and crews would be inactive all day, so that some stand-by aircraft averaged only two revenue flying hours per day, leading to an Air-Shuttle average of four, compared with an Eastern system average of ten hours per day. Another wasteful procedure was the continual positioning of empty stand-by aircraft—the magnitude of which operation was unforeseen—to ensure constant availability of extra seats when needed—as when, for example, the entire Boston Symphony Orchestra turned up for a no-reservations Air-Shuttle to return home late one night.

Losing money or not, the service made Eastern a new force in the North-east Corridor market, and its share of the total traffic increased to almost monopoly proportions. The unreserved guaranteed seat was a winning formula. Quality of equipment did not matter, neither did the fare. Although passengers made unkind remarks about the old Constellations these were more affectionate than abusive; and Eastern was to discover that the clientèle would not complain too severely if the fare was actually raised. In fact, by 1969, the initial $12 one-way New York—Boston ticket had increased to almost $20, with no apparent adverse effect on the traffic trend—and more increases were to follow.

Possibly more significant than Eastern's renewed penetration of the existing market was some evidence that the new type of service had actually stimulated additional travel. Before the introduction of the Air-Shuttle, the market had lagged behind the national average air traffic growth. During the next four years the shuttle routes grew faster than the national average—a remarkable achievement where the attraction of travelling by surface means was considerable.

The Air-Shuttle rocketed in popular esteem. Newark, New York's second domestic airport, was added to the Shuttle system on 29 April, 1962. Frequencies were continually augmented and records continually broken, with 20,000 passengers carried in one day for the first time on 1 December, 1963. Lockheed Electras were introduced on the New York—Boston route on 1 August, 1965, and all first sections of Air-Shuttles from LaGuardia Airport used this equipment from 31 October. Ten million passengers had been carried by 28 December, 1965.

There was one shortlived operation in the Air-Shuttle system: the direct Washington—Boston service, originally added on 1 February, 1962, was given special treatment on 1 October, 1964, by being named the *Executive Shuttle*, with attendant extra amenities; but it was withdrawn on 25 April, 1965, in favour of normal reservations-type scheduled service.

Eastern Air Lines kept up the pace of introducing new and faster aircraft and quickly eliminated any trace of a relegated-aircraft image by starting 118-seat Boeing 727 trijet service on 24 April, 1966, and 110-seat Douglas DC-9-30 service on 1 February, 1967. Constellations were withdrawn progressively and on 14 February, 1968, the last one was put out to grass in some meadow in Florida, while Electras provided only extra section flights beyond the capacity of the jets.

By this time the Air-Shuttle was as much a part of the New York, Boston, or Washington transport scene as the Triboro Bridge or the Jersey Turnpike. There were sixteen flights daily on LaGuardia—Boston, LaGuardia—Washington, and Newark—Boston, and eight on Newark—Washington. An inspired idea had resulted in a great public benefit, consistent with the C.A.B.'s best ideals. If identified as a separate, autonomous, airline—which effectively it was—the Air-Shuttle ranked as the 16th largest airline in the world, measured in passenger boardings.

Eastern displaced American Airlines from its dominant position in the busy commuter markets of the Northeast Corridor. Eventually American responded to the threat of virtual elimination from the market altogether by inaugurating, on 12 February, 1967, its *Jet Express* service on the New York—Boston route. Using BAC One-Elevens, this was, however, little different from a normal airline scheduled service, with the usual frustrations of booking procedures and the need for advance reservations for the peak-hour services. The addition of more frequencies, matching Eastern's, did enable American to recover some lost ground, but there was no sign of a mass desertion of the popular Air-Shuttle, which continued to constitute a dangerously 'un-American activity'.

A Douglas DC-9-31 of Eastern Air Lines.

Northeast Airlines too, which had survived many a competitive battle on the New York—Boston route, entered the fray as, backed by the new ownership by the Storer Broadcasting Company, it completely revolutionized its staid image of northeastern conservatism. Northeast more than matched American's frequency with 33 Boston—New York services per day, all except one serving LaGuardia, and all except seven of which were jets, normally DC-9-30s with occasional Boeing 727s, either the -100 series or the longer-bodied -200. Northeast was the first airline in the world to put into service the trijet Boeing 727-200 which could accommodate 141 passengers in mixed-class layout, or about the same as that of the earlier four-engined Boeing 707.

No less of an innovation was the striking—almost alarming—new paint scheme adopted by Northeast for all its aircraft. The imaginative yellow and white aircraft markings of the *Yellowbirds* were a dramatic change from the traditional subdued colours of the pre-Storer days. A similar revolution had taken place at Eastern which by mid-1965 had completed the repainting of its entire fleet with bold light and dark blue lines, replacing the previous fussy scheme with the Falcon motif and the exhortation to Fly Eastern prominently displayed along the fuselage.

American Airlines made a point in its publicity for the *Jet Express* that it had been serving the New York—Boston route for about 40 years. One disturbing feature was the consistency in journey times between city centres. Allowing about 60 min for traffic and passenger processing at each end, the scheduled time from the centre of New York

The new
Air-Shuttle Schedule
featuring Eastern's
fleet of DC-9-30's

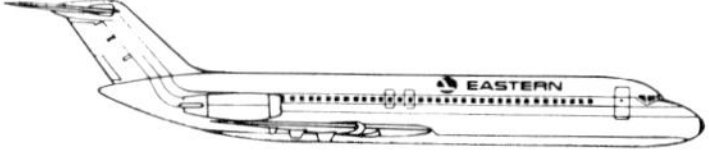

EASTERN
We want everyone to fly.

LaGuardia to Boston

Effective September 1, 1967.

Departs	Arrives	Frequency	Equipment
7:00 am	7:53 am	Ex. Sat., Sun.	DC-9-30
8:00 am	8:53 am	Ex. Sun.	DC-9-30
9:00 am	9:53 am	Daily	DC-9-30
10:00 am	10:53 am	Daily	DC-9-30
11:00 am	11:53 am	Daily	DC-9-30
12:00 n	12:53 pm	Daily	DC-9-30
1:00 pm	1:53 pm	Daily	DC-9-30
2:00 pm	2:53 pm	Daily	DC-9-30
3:00 pm	3:53 pm	Daily	DC-9-30
4:00 pm	4:53 pm	Daily	DC-9-30
5:00 pm	5:53 pm	Daily	DC-9-30
6:00 pm	6:53 pm	Daily	DC-9-30
7:00 pm	7:53 pm	Daily	DC-9-30
8:00 pm	8:53 pm	Daily	DC-9-30
9:00 pm	9:53 pm	Ex. Sat.	DC-9-30
10:00 pm	10:53 pm	Daily	DC-9-30

Air-Shuttle Fares

Between Cities	Regular (one way)	Off Peak (one way)	Excursion (week-end round-trip)	Family* (one way)	Youth and Military (one way)
LaGuardia—Boston	$15.24	$12.38	$22.86	$31.35	$8.20
LaGuardia—Washington	17.14	14.28	25.71	35.55	9.10
Newark—Boston	15.24	12.38	22.86	31.35	8.20
Newark—Washington	17.14	14.28	25.71	34.55	9.10

All fares plus tax. Subject to change without notice.
Check with Eastern for times when fares apply.
*Family (Husband, Wife and Child).

BOSTON TO NEW YORK

AM—Light Type Effective February 12, 1967 PM—Heavy Type

Leave BOSTON	Arrive NEW YORK	At Airport	Fre-quency	Type Aircraft	Flight No. & Class
7:15	8:07	Kennedy	Ex. Sun.	707 Astrojet	295 F/Y
7:30	8:16	LaGuardia	Ex. Sun.	727 Astrojet	371 F/Y
8:30	9:22	LaGuardia	Daily	400 Astrojet	543 F/Y
9:30	10:22	LaGuardia	Daily	400 Astrojet	545 F/Y
10:30	11:22	LaGuardia	Daily	400 Astrojet	547 F/Y
11:30	**12:22**	LaGuardia	Daily	400 Astrojet	549 F/Y
12:30	**1:22**	LaGuardia	Daily	400 Astrojet	551 F/Y
1:30	**2:24**	LaGuardia	Daily	400 Astrojet	553 F/Y
2:30	**3:21**	LaGuardia	Daily	400 Astrojet	561 F/Y
3:30	**4:23**	LaGuardia	Daily	400 Astrojet	411 F/Y
4:30	**5:23**	LaGuardia	Daily	400 Astrojet	555 F/Y
5:30	**6:25**	LaGuardia	Daily	400 Astrojet	559 F/Y
6:30	**7:22**	LaGuardia	Daily	400 Astrojet	563 F/Y
7:30	**8:22**	LaGuardia	Daily	400 Astrojet	565 F/Y
8:30	**9:22**	LaGuardia	Daily	400 Astrojet	567 F/Y
9:30	**10:20**	LaGuardia	Ex. Sat.	400 Astrojet	571 F/Y
9:45	**10:39**	Kennedy	Ex. Sat.	727 Astrojet	599 F/Y
10:30	**11:20**	LaGuardia	Ex. Sat.	400 Astrojet	573 F/Y

ALL FLIGHTS NONSTOP

JET ONE WAY — (First Class) $18.09 — (Coach) $15.24 (Plus Tax)
fares subject to CAB approval

Major Credit Cards Accepted

F/Y—First Class/Coach (Jet)

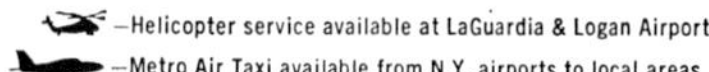

—Helicopter service available at LaGuardia & Logan Airports
—Metro Air Taxi available from N.Y. airports to local areas

CALL RESERVATIONS
in BOSTON: LI 2-6700
in WORCESTER: 754-4478

Effective February 12
American Airlines will inaugurate

JET EXPRESS

Service Between

NEW YORK & BOSTON

TIME TABLE

Effective April 26, 1931—Schedule and Rates Subject to Change without Notice.

DAILY — EXCEPT WHERE NOTED

All times given are EASTERN STANDARD TIME except as otherwise noted

NEW YORK • HARTFORD • BOSTON

Via Schedule No. . .	1004 Daily	1008 Daily Exc. Sun.	1000 Daily Exc. Sun.	1006 Daily Exc. Sun.	1002 Daily Exc. Sun.	1010 Daily
Bus Lv. Hotel Pennsylvania*	7.30 a.m.	9.30 a.m.	11.30 a.m.	1.30 p.m.	3.30 p.m.	5.30 p.m.
Plane Lv. NEWARK Airport	8.15 a.m.	10.15 a.m.	12.15 p.m.	2.15 p.m.	4.15 p.m.	6.15 p.m.
Plane Lv. Hartford Airport	9.10 a.m.	11.10 a.m.	1.10 p.m.	3.10 p.m.	F5.10 p.m.	F7.10 p.m.
Plane Ar. BOSTON Airport	10.05 a.m.	12.05 p.m.	2.05 p.m.	4.05 p.m.	6.00 p.m.	8.00 p.m.
Bus Ar. Parker House	10.30 a.m.	12.30 p.m.	2.30 p.m.	4.30 p.m.	6.25 p.m.	8.20 p.m.
Bus Ar. Hotel Statler	10.35 a.m.	12.35 p.m.	2.35 p.m.	4.35 p.m.	6.30 p.m.	8.25 p.m.

NOTE:—"F" indicates stop to leave from New York, Newark or beyond

*Bus stops at Irvington Cafeteria, 121 Varick St.—N. Y. end of Holland Tunnel, 10 minutes after leaving Hotel Pennsylvania.

BOSTON • HARTFORD • NEW YORK

Via Schedule No. . .	1005 Daily Exc. Sun.	1007 Daily Exc. Sun.	1001 Daily	1009 Daily Exc. Sun.	1003 Daily Exc. Sun.	1011 Daily
Bus Lv. Hotel Statler	7.00 a.m.	9.00 a.m.	11.00 a.m.	1.00 p.m.	3.00 p.m.	5.00 p.m.
Bus Lv. Parker House	7.05 a.m.	9.05 a.m.	11.05 a.m.	1.05 p.m.	3.05 p.m.	5.05 p.m.
Plane Lv. BOSTON Airport	7.30 a.m.	9.30 a.m.	11.30 a.m.	1.30 p.m.	3.30 p.m.	5.30 p.m.
Plane Lv. Hartford Airport	8.20 a.m.	10.20 a.m.	12.20 p.m.	2.20 p.m.	4.20 p.m.	X6.20 p.m.
Plane Ar. NEWARK Airport	9.35 a.m.	11.35 a.m.	1.35 p.m.	3.35 p.m.	5.35 p.m.	7.30 p.m.
Bus Ar. Hotel Pennsylvania	10.20 a.m.	12.20 p.m.	2.20 p.m.	4.20 p.m.	6.15 p.m.	8.00 p.m.

NOTE: "X" indicates stops to take for New York, Newark and beyond.

DIRECT CONNECTIONS FOR Philadelphia, Baltimore, Washington and the South — Cleveland, Toledo, Chicago—Pittsburgh, St. Louis, Kansas City and Los Angeles. Shown on INSIDE PAGES.

AMERICAN AIRWAYS

COLONIAL  **DIVISION**

122 East 42nd St., New York **Boston Airport, Boston**

Eastern Air Lines pioneered the Air-Shuttle. Opposite (*above*) is part of Eastern's Air-Shuttle timetable effective 1 September, 1967. It shows an hourly service, from 7 a.m. until 10 p.m., between LaGuardia and Boston with all flights being operated by DC-9-30 jet aircraft. The lower illustration shows American Airlines' timetable, effective 12 February, 1967, for its *Jet Express* Boston—New York services. The BAC One-Eleven, known to American as the 400 Astrojet, is featured on the cover. The timetable above shows American Airways (Colonial Division) schedules for the New York—Boston route effective 26 April, 1931.

to the centre of Boston in 1967 was only 20 min shorter than it was in 1931. Bearing in mind that the old American Airways (Colonial Division) Stinson Tri-motors stopped at Hartford, and that an additional 15 min is now recommended for rush-hour access to the New York airports, progress in one sense of the word would appear to have been minimal.

The airlines, at least, are looking into the matter, which is the familiar one of increased urban congestion as the motor-car takes over the occupation of city streets. Faced with an apparent impasse in solving the airport accessibility problem, both Eastern and American embarked on a joint programme with the McDonnell Douglas aircraft company towards the end of 1968 and conducted experimental flights with the Breguet 941 leased by McDonnell for the purpose.

The Breguet was a STOL (short take-off and landing) aircraft whose unique characteristics permitted it to (a) take-off and land at speeds much slower than those of a conventional jet, thus allowing it to operate from separate, shorter, runways and taxiways; (b) achieve flying altitude much more quickly because of its faster ascent and descent, thus reducing noise in areas near its runways; and (c) fly in its own air corridor, avoiding congested air and ground traffic near major terminals. The experiments have so far been confined to using special STOL strips at the conventional airports, where the STOL characteristics have been effectively (and almost unbelievably) demonstrated, but the ultimate aim is to operate from special STOL airports close to the centre of the cities, possibly on the water's edge of the riversides in the downtown areas. If these airports could be established, much of the tedious ground journey to the edge-of-town airports could be eliminated.

Intra-State and the California Corridor

A distinguishing feature of the United States political system is the comparative autonomy enjoyed by the individual States in many fields of government and public service, ranging from criminal law to highway regulation and the consumption of alcohol. Two States which, by virtue of their population, size, and wealth, assert their autonomy rather more vigorously than the others are Texas and California. California, particularly, has among its other expressions of independence, gone so far as to establish an important regulatory authority, the California Public Utilities Commission (P.U.C.) at Sacramento.

One of the first, and certainly the most famous, of its protégés was Pacific Southwest Airlines (PSA). It was originally founded in 1945 as a fixed-base and charter operator from San Diego, specializing in training ex-servicemen. After a few years this business declined, but Kenneth G. Friedkin, the founder, was so convinced of the need for additional airline service between the major cities of California that on 6 May, 1949, he started a San Diego—San Francisco scheduled service with a single DC-3. J. Floyd Andrews, who became president in 1963, recalls that 'we had no facilities . . . we checked people in through the lobby of our old flying school and bought a set of bathroom scales to weigh the baggage'. Nevertheless, charging $10 against the $25 regular fare, PSA carried 15,000 passengers in the first year, and there seemed to be a strong indication that low fares could overcome all other handicaps.

By 1952 the fleet had grown to four DC-3s and in January 1955, PSA ventured to add a new service, from Los Angeles to Oakland. So great was its popularity that the 31-seat DC-3s had to be replaced by 70-seat DC-4s, purchased from Capital Airlines in November 1955. Largely ignored, and somewhat despised by the certificated airlines, against whom the competition was intense, PSA was popular with its public, who patronized the airline to such an extent that it was emboldened to lease three 98-seat propeller-turbine Electras in November 1959, much to the astonishment

N93057 *City of Los Angeles* was one of the Martin 2-0-2s which California Central Airlines, a Californian intra-state carrier, purchased from Northwest Airlines in 1951.

of some experts who regarded PSA as a transient phenomenon which could not long withstand the superior might of Western Airlines or United Air Lines.

There was some justification for this assumption. There had already been a maverick airline which had tried to fight the Establishment, and lost the battle. In 1947 California Central Airlines (CCA) had been formed by Col Charles Sherman and on 21 December, 1948, had filed a tariff with the California P.U.C., undercutting substantially the fares of the certificated airlines. One of the Large Irregular Carriers, Airline Transport Carriers Inc (ATC), an associate of CCA, had operated between San Francisco and Los Angeles (Oakland to Burbank Airports) on a schedule which was far from irregular, and was one of the major reasons why the Civil Aeronautics Board, in its Order of December 1948, curtailed such flights to eight per month.

CCA took over the route from ATC on 2 January, 1949, operating under the jurisdiction of the P.U.C., and was thus free from Washington control as long as it operated strictly within the borders of California. At this time, CCA's fare was $9.99 for the one-way trip, which compared handsomely with the cheapest train fare of $7.50 (Southern Pacific), which took

N93045 *City of Burbank*, seen with ventral airstairs lowered, was another California Central Airlines Martin 2-0-2. It later became Allegheny Airlines N171A *The New Yorker*.

between 10 and 14 hr for the trip; the $5.15 bus fare (Pacific Greyhound) for 11 to 15 hr on the road; or $20 on Western Airlines. Naturally, many people were attracted by this bargain and in 1951 CCA had to acquire five Martin 2-0-2s from Northwest Airlines in exchange for its DC-3s and DC-4s, in order to provide adequate service.

In 1952 California Central carried 137,000 passengers, an impressive total in the face of severe competition. The trouble was that the $9.99 fare was just too low for the airline to be economically viable if its affairs suffered a setback, which in due course they did. Its re-equipment costs did not allow enough return and in 1953 CCA incurred a substantial deficit, amounting to almost $1,000,000. The end came quite suddenly. The Martin fleet was offered for sale and in February 1954 the airline went into voluntary bankruptcy. During its brief career, CCA had reached the dizzy heights of leasing a Constellation from Los Angeles Air Services, the company which was to become Trans International Airlines, one of the most successful of the Supplemental airlines of the 1960s.

Pacific Southwest did not suffer the same fate, although many expected it. By pursuing its policy of low fares (but not so low as CCA's) and combining this with high frequency and reliable service, PSA prospered to the extent that United Air Lines was compelled to introduce 113-seat Boeing 727s on a new *Jet Commuter* service on 27 September, 1964, in order 'to restore United's strong position in this California market'. United's one-way fare was $14.50 (plus tax) for the Los Angeles—San Francisco route, compared with PSA's $11.43 for its Electra service.

PSA did not wait to be swamped by the superior might of United. Before the *Jet Commuter* even started, it had ordered five Boeing 727s. So strong was its financial position by this time that no equity capital was required for the financing of the $27 million purchase. PSA's Boeings began operation on 9 April, 1965, at a one-way fare of $13.50.

In October 1965, PSA announced plans to open service from Los Angeles to San Jose at a fare of $12, compared with the incumbent carrier's—Pacific's—fare of $24. Pacific Air Lines, a Local Service carrier, severely restricted by C.A.B. regulations and mainly concerned with providing feeder services to small communities, was no match for PSA, which obliterated its opponent. Furthermore, it released a latent air travel potential from the fast-growing urban concentration of population at the southern end of San Francisco Bay, hitherto undeveloped by Pacific, whose modest F-27 propeller-turbine aircraft had not been sufficiently attractive to lure passengers away from the jets serving San Francisco.

In February 1967, PSA opened a new route from Los Angeles to Sacramento. In September 1968 the timetables showed a total of 73 services on the northbound schedule between Southern California and the San Francisco Bay area. Eighteen of these provided nonstop connections between Los Angeles and San Francisco International Airports, with many others linking satellite airports such as Burbank, Oakland, San Jose, and Sacramento. This astonishing effort, which resulted in PSA being listed among the world's leading airlines in terms of passengers carried, was due to a sustained campaign to give the public what it wanted, essentially the lowest possible fare and almost unlimited frequency. Not a little of the success also was perhaps due to the consistent charm of the stewardesses who enabled PSA to reverse the common practice of emphasizing the desirability of window seats.

The other airlines serving the market had not exactly welcomed PSA's intrusion on their traditional markets. Western Airlines, for example, had been serving the route since 26 May, 1928. In 1962 it supplemented normal

Three turbojet types in Pacific Southwest Airlines' service. *Top*: The Boeing 727-14 N970PS; *centre*: the Boeing 727-214 N532PS; and *bottom*: N378PS, first of the airline's Boeing 737-214 twin-jets. Markings are red and white. (*The Boeing Company*)

service with a *Thriftair* economy service, charging $12.95 for the one-way trip, using DC-6Bs retired from front-line service, and providing 'no frills'. On 25 February, 1963, the fare was reduced even further to $11.43, plus tax, which matched anything which PSA had to offer.

United could trace its history on the route back to Pacific Air Transport's service which started on 15 September, 1926—even earlier than Western. It brought in its *Jet Commuters* in 1964—and built up the frequency from nine to 20 round trips by 1965, Western came back belligerently with the lowest jet fare ever offered. On 1 April, 1965, it converted part of its Boeing 720B fleet to a 146-seat all-economy layout and introduced the *Fanjet Commuter* at a fare of $13.50. This was actually ahead of PSA's Boeing 727 service at the same fare.

Although TWA had been granted turn-round authority on the Los Angeles—San Francisco route in January 1962, replacing a previous long-haul restriction which required flights to originate or terminate east of Albuquerque, this airline did not see fit to pursue the California commuter market with enthusiasm, deciding presumably that three contestant carriers were enough, and that in any case there were far more important matters to attend to.

Thus the next challenge came not from a United States certificated airline, but from a completely new company which, by most of the previous criteria of competition, should never have got past first base.

Air California was launched on the faith of a few people who believed in market research. In mid-December 1965, Bill Myers, Wm. L. Pereira, and a group of other young enthusiasts, gathered together to discuss their firm belief in the traffic potential of their local airport at Santa Ana, or Orange County Airport, as it was called in deference to its catchment area. Survey results concluded that there was a big untapped market waiting for an airline which provided direct service to San Francisco from Orange County, the fastest-growing metropolitan area in the U.S.A., with well over a million people. Quite apart from the business traffic which, they calculated, could be drained from Los Angeles International Airport, with its access problem, there was the special tourist attraction of Disneyland close by.

Having acquired financial support, the founders of Air California applied to the Public Utilities Commission for a Certificate of Convenience and Necessity. This was in April 1966. The hearing was in June, the P.U.C. granted the route in September, and Air California started service on 16 January, 1967. The first services were with ex-Qantas Lockheed Electras, resplendent in a yellow, black, and red paint scheme. The traffic diversion experienced by the airlines serving Los Angeles amounted to 300,000 passengers in the first year of Air California's operations.

Before the year was out, Air California had uspplemented its Electra flights—seven a day each way from 1 April—with DC-9s, having overcome objections to operating jets out of the comparatively small airport at Santa Ana, surrounded by residential areas. On 23 October, 1967, it opened

One of Air California's fleet of Boeing 737-293s. Markings are predominantly yellow, with black and red detail and fuselage top and lower surfaces painted white. (*The Boeing Company*)

a service to San Jose and Oakland—and then began to suffer from growing pains. Its passenger boardings had leaped forward at such a pace that the need to acquire equipment began to outstrip the resources available to buy it. On 11 June, 1968, the P.U.C. granted a new route from Ontario to the Bay area, but two weeks later Air California announced a trading loss of almost $1,000,000 on an earned revenue of $6,650,000.

The airline managed to find a solution to its twin problems, the need for bigger aircraft and financial aid, by leasing six 115-seat Boeing 737s from the GATX/Boothe Aircraft Corporation, which purchased Air California's two DC-9s and four Electras. The 737's performance was described as 'highly compatible' with operating requirements at Orange County Airport, its improved rate of climb assisting noise abatement procedures.

On 3 December, 1968, another commuter service was started from Hollywood/Burbank to San Jose and Oakland. The passenger total for 1968 was 650,000 which undoubtedly gave Air California the first prize as the quickest-growing airline in the history of civil aviation.

Success in California for more than one airline had consolidated the term Intrastate as a class of air carrier, although not figuring in the C.A.B.'s traditional classification lists. PSA and Air California had profited by the happy circumstance of there being two or more metropolitan areas in one state large enough and distant enough to justify air transport services. Few other states in the U.S.A. were so fortunate.

Texas alone seemed to qualify, and, sure enough, in 1967 Southwest Airlines applied to the Texas Aeronautics Commission for permission to operate low-fare services between the major Texan cities. A certificate was granted, and although Braniff and Texas International staged delaying tactics, full legal clearance was finally obtained in 1971.

Learning the lessons of PSA, Southwest Airlines launched its 112-seat Boeing 737-200 *Love Bird* service on 18 June, 1971. It scheduled twelve round-trips daily, Dallas—Houston, and six daily, Dallas—San Antonio. Fares were $40 round-trip, undercutting the competition by $14 and $16 respectively. Innovations were pre-punched IBM-card packets of tickets for commuters, monthly billing, and stewardess uniforms which included red hot-pants and orange vinyl hot-skirts. The competitors increased flights, reduced fares, and improved amenities. Texan air commuters were delighted on all counts.

Importance of Route Cases

The development history of the United States airline industry has, since 1938, been inextricably associated with route expansion policy as decided by the Civil Aeronautics Board. Even more than its control over fares, which in general applied to the industry as a whole, the C.A.B. has always been able to exert great power over individual operators by its allocation of routes. The process between the first application for new route authority by an airline, and ultimate irrevocable granting of such authority by the Board (excepting in the recent Sub-Part M clause relating to the Local Service carriers) has always been time-consuming, often the subject of bitter argument, and inevitably either disappointing or stimulating to the airlines involved, depending on the outcome for each.

A soundly-based route structure is essential to airline success. In many countries this has been achieved by the simple expedient of creating a monopoly company, either state-owned or state-sponsored. In very few countries does competition exist in the free sense of the word. Even in Australia, for example, where apparently two major domestic airlines compete, the regulations are so restrictive on route sharing and selection of aircraft type that a passenger's choice is reduced almost to a preference for the colour of the paint scheme or the cut of the stewardesses' uniform. In the United States a unique situation prevails in which, over all the main trunk routes, and over an increasing number of secondary routes, competition prevails as a facet of C.A.B. policy and therefore as a dominant marketing factor. The competing airlines can decide their own frequencies, schedules, and equipment, and—within normal criteria of economic good sense and C.A.B. blessing—fares. But their participation in the route at all stems either from time-honoured Grandfather Rights or from subsequent additions, modifications, or redeployment, granted by the C.A.B., and subject to Presidential approval in international cases.

During its thirty years of existence, the Board has dealt with thousands of applications from airlines for route changes. They have ranged from modest requests for the elimination of a minor point on a poorly-patronized local service route to a major application from a trunk carrier for a group of new routes to new countries. The airlines have been motivated by the urge to expand and to improve their route structures in an effort to become more efficient. The spirit of aggressive rivalry has also entered into the matter. At times, an application has been a symptom of a struggle for existence, and there have been occasions when, in dealing with an important case, the C.A.B. has held the fate of an airline in the balance.

The route-awarding process has been one of constant evolution, punctuated by periods of intensive activity in consolidated route cases, where overlapping applications covering the same geographical area have been dealt with together and a wide-ranging decision made by the Board involving several airlines. Many of the more prominent cases have passed into airline history as landmarks in route development. In the international field, for example, the North Atlantic, Pacific, and Latin American Cases, decided immediately after World War 2, set the pattern for two decades; while such actions as the Denver Case, the Great Lakes—Southeast Case, and the Southern Transcontinental Case had a profound effect on the fortunes of the airlines concerned. But probably none of these famous Cases has generated so much effort, or provoked so much controversy, as the Transpacific Route Investigation which was finally decided in the spring of 1969.

Preliminary Sparring in the Pacific

When in 1946 the C.A.B. added Northwest Airlines to Pan American as the second U.S. flag carrier across the Pacific Ocean, and both Northwest and United Air Lines to provide additional service to Hawaii, the consensus of opinion was that the package was fair and reasonable. Of the other giant airlines which might have wanted a larger share of that cake, Eastern was considered to be geographically irrelevant, and TWA was well satisfied with its entry into the transatlantic market.

The Pacific Ocean therefore lived up to its name for the first post-war decade as far as route applications were concerned. Pan American continued to be the dominant carrier, and its eventual consolidation of a round-the-world service in 1947 did not excite a great deal of envy in the airline industry. There were good reasons for this: the antagonism of Communist China towards the U.S.A., and later the Korean War, together with the initially slow rate of international involvement by Japan, all combined to dissuade airline managements from becoming too ambitious in the Orient.

Thus, after TWA obtained a permanent certificate to operate eastwards to Bombay from June 1952, it did not move effectively to challenge Pan American in East Asia. In 1953, the route reached Colombo, but further extension to Shanghai was impracticable because of Chinese intransigence. TWA therefore applied in 1954 for substitution of Tokyo as a terminal, but this was denied. In 1956, the C.A.B. did approve a service to Bangkok and Manila, where a connection with Northwest Airlines provided a second all-American round-the-world airline route. Such lines drawn on the map, however, were largely academic, and although TWA began service to Manila on 1 October, 1957, this was withdrawn on 13 April, 1959, and even Bangkok was removed from the timetables in 1961, because of low load factors. For several years, TWA's eastern service terminated at Bombay and flights were not resumed to Bangkok until the summer of 1966. This seems to have been a turning point for TWA, as shortly afterwards, late in October, it was able to fly into Hongkong, the rights for which had finally been conceded by the British authorities, after many years of negotiation.

If TWA's attempt to penetrate into the Pacific was difficult, that of another aspirant, Western Airlines, was even more frustrating. On 12 March, 1959, it had applied to the C.A.B. for routes to Hawaii, in the same year the Islands had achieved Statehood. Western's proposals were for service between both Honolulu and Hilo to seven major western metropolitan centres, covering an area from California to Minneapolis. Continental Airlines asked for a similar selection of western points as far east as Chicago, but competing with Western in California; whilst Northwest also requested California—Hawaii rights, together with a route across the central Pacific. Hawaiian Airlines asked to be considered for a mainland connecting route.

On 7 December, 1960, the C.A.B. decided that Western be certificated to operate jet routes linking the specified cities through the Californian gateways—exactly as Western had wished. But when the decision was announced on 19 January, 1961 (following a strike dispute at Western), it was accompanied by a temporary stay order pending further study. The Board explained that its international route recommendation in the Case, which required Presidential approval because of its relation to foreign policy, had been largely disapproved by President Eisenhower, who had at the same time suggested that the C.A.B. reconsider its mainland—Hawaii domestic awards as part of the overall Transpacific Case. This was a severe blow to Western, whose hopes for an exciting new route development evaporated at the eleventh hour.

On 27 July, 1961, the C.A.B., working under the new Kennedy administration, reopened the international phase of the Transpacific Case and hearings were held in November. Award of the domestic routes between California and Hawaii was specifically excluded. Western's disappointment was extreme. In its 7 December, 1960, decision, all five C.A.B. members had agreed that new and improved service was required to Hawaii; a majority had selected Western. Now the Board appeared to be procrastinating on the whole affair.

The denial of route extension went deeper than the question of Hawaii alone. To Western it represented the first stage of expansion on a route network whose route mileage had remained unchanged for many years; longer routes were necessary to attain full utilization of the new jet equipment—a benefit which other airlines had received from Board decisions.

On 8 June, 1962, the C.A.B. lifted the stay order on the domestic phase of the Case, thus permitting other carriers to file petitions for reconsideration. Not until 8 November, 1963, did the Board make its decision and then, almost unbelievably, by a 3:2 vote, both the domestic and international phases of the Transpacific Route Case were terminated. Western's long-standing application was thus neither granted nor denied, and on 29 November it asked the C.A.B. for reconsideration. Believing further that the C.A.B.'s procrastination was not within the legal framework of the regulatory agency's powers, Western filed a petition to that effect with the U.S. Court of Appeals for the District of Columbia on 6 January, 1964.

On 3 March, 1964, the C.A.B. denied Western's request for reconsideration. On 12 May Western argued its case before the court, desperately seeking an order that the Board should make a decision of some kind. Ultimately, on 7 February, 1966, it was informed that the U.S. Court of Appeals had affirmed an order by the C.A.B., issued on 14 December, 1965, denying application to serve Hawaii.

Western's sad story has been chronicled here at some length to illustrate the lengthy and complex procedures which have become necessary as the result of built-in safeguards in the law to prevent abuse. This was an extreme case of a legitimate and straightforward application dragging on for seven years before a final decision was made—which was to decide not to make a decision. The unfortunate airline concerned must have had good reason for believing that the responsible civil servants and politicians kept on tossing the proverbial penny until it came down heads. Effectively, Western was back to where it started in 1959, but whereas in that year the issue was comparatively simple, with the C.A.B. having to decide on the relative merits of a few airlines, the new Transpacific Route Case was to be one of the most comprehensive ever to be undertaken.

The Transpacific Route Investigation

During the period when TWA was unsuccessfully trying to complete its encirclement of the world by extension eastwards, and Western Airlines was trying to legalize its Hawaii route award, the Pacific Ocean area, in terms of economic wealth and trade, changed beyond recognition. The scars of World War 2 were almost completely healed and Japan was asserting itself as one of the world's leading trading nations, particularly with the U.S.A. In spite of the Korean War, the countries of East Asia generally were developing their industries and improving standards of wealth. Exports and imports, together with associated business travel, were booming. Tourism was beginning to emerge as a potential activity of some magnitude.

Between 1959 and 1965, air travellers between the United States and the Far East and Oceania increased from less than 300,000 to more than 900,000, a rate of growth far exceeding that of other major world routes. The most spectacular feature was the remarkable explosion of Japanese airline activity, although every country in the area shared in the phenomenal growth. Most important, every forecast made for the future predicted improved economic, cultural, and social ties between the two sides of the Pacific Ocean, and confidently foresaw even higher rates of expansion in the future.

The message was not lost on the United States airline industry. When the C.A.B. reopened the Transpacific Case in February 1966 (immediately after the Court of Appeals had ruled against Western) it set in motion unprecedented activity on the part of interested airlines. There were eighteen applicants, ranging from incumbents such as Pan American, United, and Northwest, which asked for substantial route extensions; old hands like Western, Hawaiian, and Continental, which brought their former applications up to date; and a number of newcomers. American Airlines' publicity included maps covering the Pacific so comprehensively that its domestic trunk routes looked like a feeder network. Every U.S. Trunk carrier got into the act, although the prospect of Northeast Airlines, hitherto operating no further west than Florida, obtaining trans-Pacific authority appeared so bizarre that its application was tactfully withdrawn.

Some idea of the scope of the Case was indicated by the American Airlines exhibit, whose 325 four-volume tomes alone weighed three tons. The time, effort and cost expended, however, was a good risk in terms of the possible dividends: a stake in a burgeoning world market, with guaranteed long average stage distances, resulting in certain high profit margins. The C.A.B.'s task was no sinecure; for almost every airline asked for almost everything, encompassing every major city, and many minor ones, from New York and Boston in the east to the whole of East Asia, Australasia, and the Pacific islands—roughly half the world.

The C.A.B. started to hear evidence in February 1967, and in accordance with normal C.A.B. procedure, the Examiner, Robert L. Park, made his recommendations to the Board late in April 1968. In broad terms, Pan American and Northwest lost their monopolies over the central and north Pacific routes to each other respectively; United's authority to Hawaii was strengthened by the addition of many Midwest, Great Lakes, and Northeast cities; TWA gained trans-Pacific routes, both central and northern; Eastern Air Lines gained direct routes from almost all points east of the Mississippi to almost all points in the South Pacific, including Hawaii and via Mexico; and Western—at last—was granted its Hawaii route; The Flying Tiger Line gained a trans-Pacific all-cargo route to Tokyo.

This seemed to be a sensible enough package and President Johnson's approval was expected to contain only minor changes. Considerable consternation was aroused in some quarters, therefore, when, on 19 December, 1968, he qualified his approval with some amendments which were anything but minor. Chief amongst these were the substitution of Continental Airlines for Eastern on the South Pacific routes, plus a route to Okinawa, with a change of emphasis from eastern U.S. cities to western points; the award to Braniff International of a group of routes from the Southeast to Hawaii via Mexico City and Acapulco; and the removal of Tokyo from TWA's new trans-Pacific and round-the-world route. On 4 January, 1969, the President followed this with approval of Western for its long-awaited Hawaii routes, plus Hawaii—Anchorage (to link with

Western's Northern Division, formerly Pacific Northern Airlines' network); also of Continental, and Northwest, to Hawaii from western points, and of United from eastern cities.

President Johnson's term of office ended on 4 January, 1969, and according to the letter of the law he had allowed the new President, Richard Nixon, only a few hours in which to rescind the awards after being sworn in, a course thought to be extremely unlikely. But Nixon dealt firmly with what was alleged to be a politically-inspired allocation of the Pacific spoils. On 24 January he announced a deferment of the Pacific Route Awards, pending further review, and postponed the Hawaii awards, as these were closely tied with the international routes.

On 11 April the text of a letter from the President to John H. Crooker, Jr, chairman of the C.A.B., was published. It modified President Johnson's awards by removing all Great Circle routes to the Orient from California and Pan American's route from the Pacific Northwest; and deleted all routes awarded to Continental and Braniff, recommending that the South Pacific should be served by a carrier serving the Midwest and East Coast. It also deferred Continental's American Samoa—Okinawa segment, pending further review in the Pacific Islands Local Service Investigation.

A significant, and possibly far-reaching feature of the Nixon decision was (on the advice of Professor Paul Cherrington, of the Department of Transportation) the complete elimination of the use of satellite airports in the Californian areas concerned in the case. In a year when the F.A.A. had to impose frequency restrictions on airlines serving the New York airports because of excessive airway congestion, this seems to have been a retrograde step, as Johnson's recommendation was an attempt to forestall an inevitable future problem.

When the C.A.B. finally confirmed these modifications on 24 April, 1969, effective 28 May, this left substantially TWA and Flying Tiger with new trans-Pacific authority, and Northwest and Pan American with amended authority. Later, on 22 July, 1969, Western, United, Continental, Braniff, and Northwest received modified confirmation of the Hawaii routes. Almost all the route awards were characterized by a complex pattern of restrictions involving beyond and co-terminal rights.

On the same day, the C.A.B. and the President had reached a compromise on the southern portion of the Pacific Route Case. In place of Johnson's preferred airline (Continental) and Nixon's (Eastern), the C.A.B. chose American Airlines to serve Australia, New Zealand, Fiji, and American Samoa, from four designated points in the East. Certain restricted authority to Hawaii was also granted as compensation for what was commonly believed to be a difficult and costly programme. Also, the restrictions on frequency expected to be imposed by Australia and New Zealand, in defence of what they considered to be fair market shares, was a handicap to operating the route at maximum efficiency.

But the controversy and litigation over the Pacific Ocean routes was far from ended. Just as in 1946 the North Atlantic route awards represented only the first round in a continuous contest for shares of the world's most productive airway, so in 1969 the airlines which emerged triumphantly from the desperate days of the Transpacific Investigation were on the threshold of a new rivalry for a fast-growing market of similar magnitude.

The airlines got quickly off the mark during the summer of 1969. Western was first, with Minneapolis—Honolulu and Phoenix—Honolulu flights, both stopping at Los Angeles (in compliance with its certificate restriction) starting on 25 July. Poor Western, plagued with problems ever since 1959, then suffered a mechanics' strike which grounded the fleet and set back the programme by several weeks. TWA began its round-the-world service on 1 August, with two flights daily, one westbound starting at New York, and the other eastbound starting at Los Angeles. On the trans-Pacific portion of the route, stops were made at Honolulu, Guam, Okinawa, Taipei, and Hongkong. Northwest also began service from San Francisco to Tokyo via Honolulu on 1 August, and United put its long-range DC-8-62s to good use on the 4,340-mile Chicago—Honolulu segment. Braniff began on 14 August, and Continental on 9 September by introducing five-abreast coach-class seating on its Chicago—Los Angeles—Hawaii route, as well as setting the pace with a new $85 single off-peak fare, believed to be the lowest daytime rate per mile anywhere in the whole U.S. route system.

These were the immediate, visible, results of the Pacific Route Case. By the introduction of substantial additional carrier participation, together with greatly improved nonstop route availability, the public will undoubtedly benefit; and this is one of the main planks in the C.A.B.'s platform. But in its relationship with the supreme governmental seat of power, the Presidency, some eyebrow-raising issues have been joined. Hitherto, the President's intervention in a foreign route case was invoked because of implications on United States foreign policy. In the Pacific Case, however, the whole affair became a political football, reaching a point where President Nixon over-rode the C.A.B. on its recommendations of route pattern, and on its selection of carrier. His action was taken on the advice of the Department of Transportation, whose experience in reviewing the Case cannot have been exhaustive. On the other hand, perhaps a clean broom was needed to sweep the dust from the C.A.B. files. Either way, the event raises serious questions as to the future rôle of the C.A.B. in the examination of foreign route cases, and in particular throws doubt on the usefulness of the prolonged system of Examiner's recommendations and subsequent C.A.B. decision without prior consultation with the President.

As a postscript to the Pacific route awards, which provided the participating airlines with a package of problems to keep them busy for several years, President Nixon himself opened up new possibilities by the overtures to mainland China announced in April 1971. The easing of political tension would reopen the possibility of TWA serving Canton and Shanghai, via India, Burma and Hanoi, together with a new trans-Pacific route via Tokyo; and Pan American serving Shanghai and Peking, from Hongkong.

Northwest, equally, still holds the U.S. certificate to serve a number of points in China—Harbin, Mukden, Darien, Peking, Shanghai, and Nanking—and had operated to Shanghai between 1947 and early 1949. These route authorities should be sufficient to serve United States interests in the foreseeable future.

More Routes and Mergers

Compared with the Pacific Route Case, additions to the route networks of the larger United States airlines during the latter 1960s seemed almost trivial by comparison. Changes made to basic route structures were very small, except by mergers, and companies continued to operate within the same geographical boundaries. The three major transcontinental trunk lines hardly changed at all, but accounting as they did for a steady 55 per cent share of the total domestic trunk market, any improvement would have encouraged charges of monopoly by their competitors. Other Domestic Trunks continued to press for route extensions but the change in actual routes operated was in striking contrast with the optimistic maps of routes applied for, as featured in the glossy annual reports.

Eastern Air Lines was in need of route strengthening, as its average stage distance was low, compared with the transcontinentals. In 1967 it was successful in two important directions: to the vacation area of the Bahama Islands, rapidly taking its place with Florida as a major tourist attraction, and to the Pacific Northwest. Two days after Eastern's merger with Mackey Airlines, a small international carrier based in Miami, on 8 January, Eastern began to schedule through-plane services to Nassau from many points on the network. In April 1967 the C.A.B. awarded to Eastern a route from St Louis to Seattle, and service was inaugurated on 13 June with a through flight from Seattle to Cape Kennedy, via St Louis and Huntsville. Eastern thus gained a tiny foothold in the transcontinental market.

Eastern also grasped an opportunity to expand into an important growing traffic area, the Caribbean, when, in 1971, it took steps to acquire the Puerto Rico based Caribair. The C.A.B. Examiner recommended what amounted to an outright purchase on 21 May, 1971 (*see also page 320*).

Having been virtually saved from extinction by the Storer purchase in 1965, Northeast Airlines was assisted in profiting from the new investment by C.A.B. support in consolidating and expanding its meagre route network. On 2 March, 1967, the Northeast—Florida routes were renewed indefinitely, thus removing a constant source of apprehension; and on 19 December, 1968, the airline received a batch of important routes to Bermuda. Later an extension to the Great Lakes area heralded Northeast's first step towards breaking away from confinement to Atlantic coastal cities.

Western Airlines appeared to have despaired of obtaining reinforcement to its existing route network, but made a significant move by negotiating a merger with Pacific Northern Airlines, authorized by the C.A.B. on

1 July, 1967. This effectively gave Western a north–south area coverage from Alaska to Mexico to augment its hopes for an east–west coverage from the Mississippi to Hawaii. Curiously, Arthur Woodley, owner of PNA, became the largest single stockholder of Western for a short while, until Kirk Kerkorian, former owner of the Supplemental Carrier, Trans International Airlines, bought 22 per cent of Western's stock in December 1968. Meanwhile, minor improvements had been made to Western's routes by the opening of nonstop services between California and the Twin Cities, on 1 October, 1966, and a direct Denver—Calgary link on 1 December, 1968.

Braniff International Airways, under the new aggressive presidency of Harding Lawrence, formerly of Continental Airlines, achieved a notable landmark in its progress by completing all stages of the acquisition of Pan American-Grace Airways on 8 January, 1967. This gave Braniff a half-share in the U.S. international routes in South America, a continent where Pan American had hitherto been the dominant carrier. Braniff consolidated its position late in 1968 when the C.A.B. awarded a wide range of nonstop routes linking the continental U.S.A. with major cities of South America.

For the first time since 1946, a new passenger airline was designated as a transatlantic carrier. National Airlines was awarded a route from Miami to London, thus offering not only direct service between Europe and Florida, but offering interesting possibilities of domestic interchanges from as far west as California. National's entry into this potentially lucrative market was delayed by labour troubles at both ends of the line, the whole airline being close to a complete shut-down for three months until a settlement was negotiated on 27 May, 1970.

In 1965 both TWA and Pan American were awarded extensions to their European and African routes respectively to serve East Africa, while Pan American gained, after many years of patient negotiation, the right to serve Moscow on a reciprocal basis with the Soviet airline, Aeroflot. Pan Am began service on 15 July, 1968, on this important link between New York and Moscow, the leading commercial cities of the world's most powerful nations respectively.

Both of these U.S. international airlines recognized that there was more to providing air travel than merely to offer an airline flight. Becoming more critical as the proportion of tourists increased, the provision of hotel accommodation developed into a major factor in developing the airline business. Thus both Pan Am and TWA became hotel keepers. Pan Am had established the Intercontinental Hotels Corporation (I.H.C.) in 1946 at the instance of the U.S. Government and by 1965 there were more than 30 big establishments owned and operated by this subsidiary at strategic points throughout the carrier's world-wide network. TWA eventually met this indirect competition by acquiring, on 9 May, 1967, the Hilton International Company, then operating 39 hotels in 25 countries. Both I.H.C. and Hilton continue to expand their activities throughout the world.

Another activity in which both Pan American and TWA were involved was a possible merger of the two giant airlines. Arising partly out of serious financial difficulties following the litigation with the Hughes Tool Company, TWA's new management faced a heavy loss in 1962 and seriously considered association with its lifetime rival, Pan American. Improving fortunes, however, plus an expectation of strong industry and government opposition, led to the abandonment of this monolithic proposal in October 1963.

During the same period, two other mighty airlines, American and Eastern, took steps towards amalgamation, which, had they been successful, would have made even the United/Capital merger of 1961 look small by comparison. On 23 January, 1962, the two airlines made a joint application to the C.A.B., claiming an annual saving of more than $50 million, elimination of duplicated facilities, and reducing future capital requirements by $100 million. Eastern Air Lines badly needed the merger at the time, as it was going through a severe financial crisis. It complained about 'aggressive opposition from those carriers favoured with monopolies or with routes granted at Eastern's expense'. Coming from an airline which had once protested vigorously at the idea of any other carrier entering the Northeast—Florida market, this seemed an odd display of self-righteousness. The merger was opposed by the C.A.B. Examiner and the Department of Justice, both of whom, Eastern claimed, 'ignored compelling economic evidence and applied anti-trust principles which . . . do not apply to regulated airline mergers'. Such protests did not impress the C.A.B., which rejected the application in April 1963. In one respect, Eastern had cause to complain. Partly because of a route structure dominated by short-haul—and therefore potentially unprofitable—routes, it began to lose money from 1960 onwards and reached a crisis figure of $37·8 million in 1963, offering a tremendous challenge to the new management which took over from the Rickenbacker regime.

Since the United/Capital merger of 1961, the number of U.S. Domestic Trunk airlines had remained constant at eleven companies. Minor changes in 1967 such as Western's acquisition of Pacific Northern, Braniff of Panagra, and Eastern of Mackey enabled the C.A.B. to tidy up its list of airlines in other categories, particularly in Alaska. But in 1969 rumours of possible mergers between two or more Trunk airlines were common. The cause was a severe decline in earnings which swept the whole industry into a state of mild despondency. Few companies escaped financial problems which in some cases approached crisis level.

One merger was quickly disposed of. This involved only one trunk carrier, American Airlines, and brought about the demise of one of the companies, Trans Caribbean (TCA), whose place in affairs had always been peripheral. Although it had enjoyed a period of exciting success, when it threw down the gauntlet to Pan American and Eastern Air Lines on the routes from the northeast to Puerto Rico, TCA had fallen on hard times, in spite of acquiring DC-8s to maintain competitiveness.

It was a case of sheer corporate depth providing the industrial stamina which ensured survival of the strong. Consequently, when American Airlines moved to acquire TCA in 1970, agreement by all parties was soon forthcoming, with Presidential approval coming on 30 December of that year. American began flying the routes of TCA on 2 March, 1971, technically six days before the C.A.B. formally transferred the operating certificate. The merger produced immediate results. Routes to the Caribbean, combined with an existing solid trunk route structure, enabled American to achieve a leading position on the New York—San Juan sector within six months of the take-over.

Simultaneously with the TCA merger, American announced a far more important association on 2 November, 1970, no less than a plan to merge with Western Airlines. On 19 March, 1971, the shareholders of both companies agreed simultaneously to the merger, although, predictably, Continental Airlines, among others, protested vigorously. Western blamed its predicament on the cost of new equipment, but its finances were, in fact, relatively healthy. According to the guidelines set by the Department of Transportation governing mergers, the American/Western proposal came dangerously close to some of the disqualifying clauses, including those relating to excessive market shares and the danger of extensive reaction and defensive merger proposals by competitive carriers. As a safeguard against all eventualities, Western ordered four DC-10s in September 1971, under a contract which permitted transfer to American if the merger went through. Western's DC-10 was an overwater version of the Series 10, permitting nonstop Minneapolis—Hawaii operations.

During the late 1960s, Eastern made a steady recovery through good management, employing unspectacular but methodical principles to restore a somewhat tarnished reputation. The struggle was an uphill fight, now that the major revenue runs to Florida and San Juan, which formerly had compensated for the handicaps of short-stage average hauls, had been eroded as revenue earners by continuous fare competition. The route to Seattle, referred to above, was small compensation; but at last, in August 1969, Eastern was an important beneficiary from the Southern Tier Competitive Non-stop Investigation. The C.A.B. awarded the airline its first truly transcontinental route, from the East to Los Angeles through the domestic 'gateway' of Atlanta, one of the most important hub airports in the country. Eastern started service on 21 September, 1969.

The Southern Tier case was perhaps the last major route case to be decided for a considerable period. With its completion, involving a network of city-pair links across the southern United States, every one of the eleven Trunk airlines had access to Los Angeles. Additionally, a Local Service carrier, Texas International (formerly Trans-Texas), gained a Dallas—Albuquerque—Los Angeles route, so that it became theoretically possible to cross the continent by using only two Locals, now that Piedmont had access to New York, linking at Memphis.

The C.A.B. stoutly defended its position by some forthright statements about the virtues of competition and the rights of all carriers, including the smaller ones, to share the spoils. But in the Southern Tier, there were justifiable headshakings on the route given to Northeast, from Miami to Los Angeles nonstop. Northeast was unknown in the West; Delta and National were firmly established; and Northeast appeared to torpedo its own case by operating Boeing 727s, aircraft designed primarily for much shorter ranges.

Northeast, in fact, was in trouble. The little New England airline which had defied all industrial logic by surviving at all, was severely strained during 1969, with a general recession in revenues coupled with mounting costs hitting it much harder than its bigger brothers. Sensible economy measures were taken: the C.A.B. authorized the transfer of several short unprofitable routes in the northeast to selected Third Level companies. There were staff reductions and some schedules were cut. Finally, however, in November, came the announcement that Northwest Airlines had made a serious bid to absorb Northeast. It was serious for two reasons. The terms of the offer were made public and in detail. And it met most of the 'guidelines' recommended by the C.A.B. and the Department of Transportation on the suitability of merger candidates.

On 31 December, 1970, the C.A.B. approved the merger but excluded Northeast's recently-awarded Miami—Los Angeles route. Unable to change the Board's mind, Northwest abruptly withdrew the offer on 10 March, 1971, and Delta Air Lines promptly substituted its claims, which were approved by both boards of directors within two months. The case dragged on into 1972, with problems over the continuance of New England services. The end seems near for Northeast, as without a merger partner, it can hardly survive on its own.

Northwest, meanwhile, transferred its attention to National, and proposed a merger on 3 September, 1971.

Another epoch-making break with tradition occurred in 1971. Throughout its entire existence the C.A.B. had been dedicated to encouraging competition, within the framework of its complete control over the allocation of carriers to routes through the certification process. Indeed, along with the airlines themselves, it had viewed with disfavour the custom of pooling arrangements—mutual agreements on scheduling, equipment, and revenue shares—common in Europe.

But special problems demanded special solutions. In 1970–71 three marketing factors combined to produce an intolerable situation: (a) a new wave of equipment augmentation (Boeing 747s) produced a sharp rise in seat capacity, especially on major trunk routes; (b) an economic recession dampened traffic growth and thus lowered load factors to a dangerous level; (c) the C.A.B.'s policy of encouraging competition had resulted in three or more participating carriers on most routes.

Certain airline economists among the Big Four, in particular those engaged in transcontinental operations, had become alarmed at the plummeting load factors on their most lucrative routes. After they had submitted a well-argued case to the C.A.B., the Board approved a capacity reduction programme on selected long-haul routes. American, TWA, and United agreed to control schedules on New York—Los Angeles. One objecting airline described the move as a 'classic violation of the anti-trust laws', while the dissenting Board member, Joseph Minetti, said 'it represents a highly repugnant departure from anti-trust principles'. The C.A.B., in fact, kept within the letter of its law which required 'competition *to the extent necessary* to assure the sound development of a national air transport system'.

When the dust had settled, the public found that the reduction of 185 weekly nonstop round-trips to 132 on the New York—Los Angeles route was tolerable. The airlines, relieved of the ruthless necessity to schedule identical flights at identical times, set about raising average load factors from the intolerable levels which had at times fallen to below 30 per cent.

Although schedule control gave the U.S. airlines their 'first dose of cartelism'—to quote one commentator—there were grounds for equanimity, indeed optimism. The economic factors listed jeopardized the industry's financial stability, and came close to bringing one or two illustrious companies to their knees. The schedule limitation experiment was no more than the application of common sense in a situation when rigorous adherence to dogma could have brought ruin. The downfall of one of the United State's biggest airlines would have been a heavy price to pay for the upholding of diehard principles.

The domestic trunk industry survived the economic crisis of 1970–71 comparatively unscathed. There were no absolute casualties, although many emerged with permanent scars. Significantly, with the exception of the Delta/Northeast merger (and this is dragging its feet into 1972) none of the rumoured mergers came to anything, and *Fortune* magazine's speculation of a six-airline trunk industry seems as remote today as it did in 1938.

Safety

Paradoxically, in an age of realism, air safety is still a delicate subject among the airline fraternity, which retains an element of superstition strangely out of keeping with the ultra-modern image it otherwise tries so diligently to preserve. Yet the airlines have little cause for reticence. Although experts argue about which particular unit should be used as the ultimate criterion, the safety record by any measure is a creditable one.

The chances of being killed while travelling by airline, trunk or local, scheduled or charter, are now so slight that they may be regarded as negligible, needing no further statistical proof. There was one year soon after World War 2 when an observer remarked that more people in the U.S.A. were kicked to death by animals than were killed in aeroplanes. Leaving to one side this example of hyperbole, there are certainly many activities—driving down the Los Angeles freeways, swimming off the coast of Florida, or crossing the streets of New York, for example—where the chances of injury or death are probably as great. Nevertheless this achievement has been dearly bought.

The jet age had swept across the U.S.A. for barely more than a year when civil aviation experienced one of its worst fatal accidents. Bringing harsh reality to the sad humour of the aviation insurance underwriter: 'Remember, a mid-air collision can ruin your whole day', on 16 December, 1960, a United Air Lines DC-8 collided with a TWA Super Constellation over New York. 128 passengers and crew were killed, plus eight people on the ground. The incident provoked a flurry of discord between the C.A.B. and F.A.A., with the pilots' union ALPA also defending its position, on the issue of observance of traffic control procedures. Damages were eventually settled on the basis of 61 per cent by United, 15 per cent by TWA, and 24 per cent by the government (F.A.A.). This salutary experience threw into relief the critical situation which faced the F.A.A. in providing adequate air traffic control in a congested area such as New York.

After this inauspicious start to the jet era, each year's crop of accidents was thereafter kept within tolerable limits. Passenger fatalities in any single year during the 1960s seldom exceeded in total that of the early disaster. Reflecting the laws of probability surprisingly well, Fate seems to have been no respecter of airlines or manufacturers, and tragedies have occurred in all categories of airline operation. Predictably from the section of the industry accounting for the greatest percentage of flights, the Big Four Domestic Trunk airlines and Pan American appear in statistics; but most of the other Trunk airlines, the Local Service, Third Level, and Helicopters have all had their proportionate share of headline news. Valiantly struggling to maintain a good safety record for a sustained period, the Supplemental airlines, particularly, have done much to wipe out a reputation for unreliability inherited from a previous generation.

The causes of accidents have been legion, and, as no airline has yet become fully automatic, human factors of some kind have been at the root of many problems. A momentary mistake on the part of a crew member, air traffic controller, or maintenance engineer, has sometimes proved fatal. Sometimes a procedural shortcoming in flying technique or training has led to a series of crashes; but seldom has negligence been judged to be a factor.

Not all crashes are the result of human failure. There have been lightning strikes, bird strikes, and isolated examples of passengers running amok. Sabotage has been cited as a possible cause in some cases, and on 1 May, 1961, came the first case of a phenomenon which, though not necessarily causing loss of life, added to the hazards of flying. This was when an airliner was subjected to the ignominy of being literally kidnapped—or hi-jacked—by a passenger or group of passengers forcing the pilot at the point of a gun to fly to a destination other than the scheduled one. These incidents gradually became so frequent that they almost ceased to excite journalistic comment, except in cartoons. Normally Cuba, deprived of direct service to and from the U.S.A. since the Castro revolution of 1959, was the non-scheduled alternative destination for the hijacked aircraft which were promptly returned, with passengers, by the Cuban authorities after extraction of the landing fee and tax.

United States domestic carriers were the main victims of these incidents, with the airlines serving Miami or Florida points the most frequent sufferers. But other world trouble-spots also endangered U.S. aircraft overseas. The most dramatic incidents occurred in the Middle East, casualties of the Arab-Israeli conflict. On 6 September, 1970, a new Boeing 747 of Pan American was destroyed by terrorists at Cairo Airport, while a TWA Boeing 707 (along with a BOAC VC10 and a Swissair DC-8) were blown up after being forced to land in the Syrian desert. Fortunately, in these cases, there were no fatalities, although many passengers were severely inconvenienced by being forced to camp out in the desert for several days.

Passenger Standards

During the 1960s, airline jet fleets had become so much an accepted part of the U.S. travel scene, and of a way of life generally, that performance and safety were taken for granted, with no one airline enjoying a special public preference on the grounds of reliability, punctuality, or quality of equipment. Only a minority even thought to enquire about the identity of the aircraft manufacturer, or to bother about the technical

William E. Boeing (*left*) started in the lumber industry and built his first two-seat aeroplane in 1916. Keenly interested in air transport, he combined with a pilot, Eddie Hubbard, to start a mail service from Seattle to Victoria in 1919. In 1926, he produced the Boeing 40A mailplane which was able to carry two paying passengers in addition to mail and was thus able to undercut rival bidders for the transcontinental mail contract, and Boeing Air Transport was formed. This led to the founding of United Air Transportation. Donald W. Douglas (*right*) graduated from M.I.T. in 1914, and worked as chief engineer of the Martin Company before forming his own company in 1920 in association with a millionaire sportsman, David R. Davis. After building primarily military aircraft, Douglas rocketed to aviation fame by winning TWA's famous competition, in 1932, for a commercial passenger aircraft to beat the Boeing 247.

merits of, for example, the number or position of the engines; although there were many experienced travellers who had acquired a preference for a certain airline, for diverse and often illogical reasons. Between 1961 and 1963 American Airlines even adopted the collective term Astrojet and ceased to identify aircraft types on its timetables.

This state of high-class equality was satisfactory from the point of view of the industry as a whole, which could regard the situation as an effective though unpublicized recognition that it had come of age. In another sense however, it raised a problem. In a world which by philosophy and regulatory direction, was motivated by competition, the field open to competitive practices had narrowed considerably.

Passenger seating standards had settled down to measures of pitch, width, and number abreast which were generally agreed upon by airlines and the C.A.B. Typical layouts were four abreast at about 40-inch pitch in first class, six abreast at 34-inch pitch in coach class. There were a few exceptions: United Air Lines introduced one-class *Red Carpet* service on some flights on 10 March, 1963, then tried three levels, at four, five, and six abreast, in August 1964, but this was unsuccessful, just as on the North Atlantic route, three classes (first, tourist, and economy) had not lasted long. Continental Airlines persevered with five abreast in coach class, risking the inevitable higher turnaway risk in busy periods so as to attract higher average loads. But these were exceptions to the general rule on seating standards and the public did not normally choose its airline on that basis alone.

The year 1971, however, was far from normal, and in addition to reducing transcontinental schedules, in an effort to mitigate an excess capacity situation, the airlines also took steps to make a virtue out of necessity. On 2 March, 1971, American Airlines replaced otherwise empty seats with a *Coach Lounge*, a separate area in the coach-class section devoted to promoting casual conviviality. The C.A.B. did not insist that American should charge extra for this example of coach-class luxury, a point which raised protests from Bob Six of Continental Airlines, who was threatened with a higher charge for his five-abreast coach-class seating.

TWA quickly copied American, with its *Ambassador Lounge* on 26 May, 1971, and United's *Friendship Room* appeared on the scene in June. American's enterprise reaped temporary dividends in increased load factors, but the installation of Wurlitzer piano bars in its 747s towards the end of the year added a ludicrous touch to an ironic situation in which the real purpose of air transport seemed to be forgotten.

Passenger amenities thus continued to be a competitive factor. The idea of air travel as a luxury and the privilege of the affluent, with attendant perquisites such as a high-class cuisine, was outmoded. Nevertheless, meal service is essential on flights lasting more than an hour or so. Even in coach-class travel, meals of a good standard continue to be served neatly on trays and dishes specially designed to provide maximum convenience both to passenger and hard-working stewardess. The incorporation of galleys to supply hot meals has long become an essential design feature on all mainline aircraft.

Supplementing meals as a way of occupying the tedious hours of transcontinental or transatlantic flights, most airlines now provide inflight films, using a variety of methods. TWA first seriously promoted the idea on 19 July, 1961, in conjunction with Inflight Motion Pictures Inc, and did most of the initial work in gaining public and official acceptance. American Airlines introduced Astrovision in 1964, incorporating television and enroute pictures of terrain in addition to films, but this was superseded in February 1967 by a far superior system, Astro-Color, perfected by Bell & Howell. The advantage of Astro-Color was that it provided fourteen smaller screens in place of the usual two or three large ones, and they were placed at the side of the cabins so that stewardesses and passengers could move about freely without obstructing the view of the screens. Not to be outdone, United Air Lines, the other main transcontinental airline, installed a wide-screen colour system on its Hawaii flights in November 1964 and quickly expanded its Jetarama Theater to other long-distance flights.

So, with an almost universal standard of seating, reasonable meal service, films on long-distance flights, and free drinks for first-class passengers, each airline turned to the other problem in promotion: to portray itself to the would-be passenger as the best-looking—and therefore by association, the best—airline.

The New Image

From time to time airlines have revised their public image by adopting completely new styling in publicity literature, uniforms, advertising, and aircraft markings. In the 1960s most of the major companies went through the process once again, with special emphasis on extravagant paint schemes to identify their new jet fleets, as a means of obliterating memories of a prosaic piston-engined past.

Pan American and TWA ushered in their jets with new emblems departing from long-held tradition and keeping abreast of modern mid-century commercial design trends. Continental Airlines used gold extensively to support symbolically its quest for quality. Eastern's new management demonstrated its complete break with the past by adopting brighter colours with an accent on simplicity.

Boldest of all the colourful innovations was Braniff International's announcement of 'The End of the Plain Plane'. It took the unprecedented step of painting the entire fuselage of each of its aircraft from a selection of different colours, yellow, beige, orange, green, ochre, and two shades of blue—a striking departure from the traditional horizontal stripes—and the wings, tail, and engine pods were white. Braniff also engaged the services of Emilio Pucci, the famous Italian designer of haute couture, to give its stewardesses an exotic appearance, ranging from multi-coloured miniskirts to space helmets for use in inclement weather. Braniff's new look drew much satirical comment, but it achieved its main objective. People began to discuss Braniff more than ever before, and the renewed interest was reflected in handsome traffic increases.

Possibly the most successful of the new paint schemes was Northeast's *Yellowbird* look. Conceived by the famous industrial designer, Raymond Loewy, Northeast employed a colour never previously used, and its dramatic impact helped considerably to demonstrate that its sphere of interest had developed beyond the sheltered confines of the colonial northeast. National Airlines, too, adopted bright colours and motif depicting the sunshine for which Florida (its home base) was famous.

United Air Lines remained aloof from these violent breaks from tradition—although its other activity in promotion was anything but placid—but American Airlines finally succumbed to the new trend by abandoning its old aircraft styling which was so austere that the main objective seemed to be to save paint. While still leaving large areas of the aircraft unpainted, the new broad red, white, and blue horizontal stripes and enormous caption *American* was as effective as any of the other airlines' new colour schemes.

To draw further attention to the bright new aircraft, the airlines went to new lengths of lyricism in portraying their virtues in slogans and songs. The public was persuaded to sample the pleasures of Fastback Jets, Whisperjets, Pamperjets, and Funjets. Radio and television commercials constantly reminded the eager traveller of the Friendly Skies of United, or that Pan Am Made The Going Great, or that Western was the Only Way to Fly. Pride of place in the song-plugging contest went to the airline which promptly adapted an already popular tune to invite people to fly exhilaratingly Up Up And Away With TWA.

Threshold of a New Era

The popularity of TWA's theme song may have had something to do with its astonishing success on the world's number one route, the North Atlantic. Other, less fanciful, factors were the consolidation of TWA's immense advantage inherent in its dual domestic/international route certificate, permitting single-plane service to Europe from many more cities in the U.S.A. than by any other airline; and an indefinable human sympathy for 'Number Two'. Whatever the reasons, the air transport world noted with surprise that, in July 1969, Pan American lost its position to TWA as leading carrier on the transatlantic route for the first time in history.

The year 1969 was a sad one for Pan Am in many ways. Once enjoying a virtual monopoly of U.S. international routes, its dominating rôle had been gradually eroded in the post-war period, by TWA on the Atlantic, and by Northwest on the Pacific. During the 1960s Braniff International climbed up from a comparatively insignificant foothold in Latin America; and in Mexico and the Caribbean area, many other carriers vied for an airline place in the sun. The substantial inroads made into the Pacific by the 1969–70 Route Case awards had been preceded by another challenge on the Atlantic, when in July 1969—the month of TWA's success—National Airlines was given authority to operate directly from Miami to London.

In one field of endeavour, however, Pan American still reigned supreme: the sponsorship of a new generation of long-range civil airliners. In the early days of civil jets, it had secured itself against possible future British competition by ordering the Comet 3. The Comet did not develop to be the powerful threat which its pioneering efforts deserved. But this did not destroy Pan American's belief in insuring against the risk of losing technical leadership, and in another delicately-balanced competitive situation, it ordered six Anglo-French Concordes on 4 June, 1963. Hedging its bets all ways, it then proceeded to reserve delivery positions for 15 U.S. supersonic transports.

The development contract for the SST, as the U.S. supersonic project became known, had been awarded to Boeing in 1965, following the recommendations of the Project Horizon Report undertaken at the request of President Kennedy, and released by the White House on 10 September, 1961. The SST campaign was sustained with the help of the F.A.A., which assumed overall leadership of a Steering Group, under Najeeb Halaby's chairmanship, to guide the progress of this revolutionary development. As time went on, however, the formidable magnitude of the technological problem of Mach 3 flight, coupled with financial stringency, combined to delay the project, and it was eventually cancelled by Congress after a desperate and emotion-filled battle on Capitol Hill on 24 March, 1971.

Although both the Concorde and the U.S. SST are supersonic designs, there is a marked difference between the two. The Concorde is intended to cruise at about 1,250 mph, carrying about 130 passengers; whereas the American aircraft would have been half as fast again, and would have carried more than 300 passengers. To be absolutely factual, neither of Pan Am's supersonic orders can be treated as firm in the orthodox sense, as the Concorde is still awaiting the complete go-ahead, and the U.S. SST is not yet launched. Nevertheless progress continues, and the Concorde prototype made its maiden flight on 2 March, 1969—two months after the U.S.S.R.'s Tupolev 144 supersonic airliner had reached the same stage of development, on 31 December, 1968.

Wide-Bodied Jets

Although the Anglo-French Concorde began to demonstrate commendable performance and reliability—recalling the Comet 1 of an earlier age—considerable doubt remains as to its potential economic viability. Without special operational privilege, combined with artificial price support and the benefit of surcharge fares, its prospects of success in the mainstream of airline activity appear dim.

While Pan American was determined not to be left behind in any race

Passengers disembarking at New York International Airport from the Pan American World Airways Boeing 747 *Clipper Young America* at the completion of the inaugural London—New York Boeing 747 service on 22 January, 1970. The first Boeing 747 service took-off from New York very early (just after midnight) on 22 January.

towards supersonic air transport, its main preoccupation was to seek further directions of improving its economic operating base by aircraft which offered the prospect of lower operating costs. As most of the previous avenues of development—higher block speeds, higher aircraft utilization, higher load factors—had been fully explored, and found to be close to their top limits, the only direction left was to face the inevitability of bigger aircraft. Accordingly, Pan American Airways, in conjunction with the Boeing Aircraft Company, repeated the history of the first jet procurement story. On 13 April, 1966, an order was placed for 25 Boeing 747s, huge airliners which could carry 360–450 passengers, according to seating layout, which were twice as big as the previous Boeing generation, and 80 per cent bigger than the largest commercial aircraft then designed, the Douglas DC-8-63.

Boeing built a complete new factory and construction of the 350-ton giant proceeded to break all previous records to make possible its maiden flight on 19 February, 1969. Pan American originally intended to start scheduled services across the North Atlantic before Christmas of the same year, but some irritating engine problems postponed this notable historical event until 21 January, 1970. Pan Am was plagued with ill luck even then, for an engine overheated at John F. Kennedy Airport before take-off, and the start was delayed for a few more hours, until 1.52 a.m. on 22 January to be exact. Pan American was paying an unfair price for its pioneering advance.

Other airlines followed Pan American's lead. TWA opened transcontinental New York—Los Angeles Boeing 747 service on 25 February, 1970, followed by American (with aircraft leased from Pan Am) on 2 March. Continental, always prominent in the equipment race, began

N4703U, United Air Lines' first Boeing 747. The aircraft is seen carrying a spare engine beneath the port wing root.

through-plane service Chicago—Los Angeles—Honolulu on 26 June, and Northwest on a Chicago—Seattle—Tokyo route, on 1 July. United, on 23 July, to Hawaii, and Delta and National, on 25 October, followed, while Eastern and Braniff brought the total of U.S. domestic 747 operators to nine, within a year of Pan Am's first service.

Illustrating the consistent momentum which characterizes the American air transport scene, the giant Boeing airliner, regarded during its development stage by hardened airline executives with awe and apprehension, thus quickly established itself as a familiar visitor to the nation's leading airports, as a distinguished flagship of the domestic airline industry.

There were many experts who disagreed with the industry's claims to have launched a new era of airliner service. After all, the aircraft were no faster, or only slightly so; the fares were the same, or nearly so; and feelings were mixed as to the advantages of a wide body which permitted ten seats abreast, with two aisles. New era or not, the commercial aviation industry, airlines and manufacturers alike, recognized that the only way to go was bigger; and both Douglas, with the 250-seat DC-10, and Lockheed, with

First of the wide-bodied trijets, the McDonnell Douglas DC-10-10. American Airlines introduced the DC-10 on the Los Angeles—Chicago route on 5 August, 1971. One of American's DC-10s is seen here with a United aircraft in the background.

United Air Lines was the second DC-10 operator, introducing the type between San Francisco and Washington, D.C., on 14 August, 1971.

a similarly sized L. 1011 TriStar, launched their trijet wide-bodied contenders early in 1968. In Europe, a Franco-German venture, with Hawker Siddeley participation, resulted in a twin-engined short-haul wide-body design, the A-300B. Aircraft with between eight- and ten-abreast seating thus appear to be destined to cover the whole spectrum of demand as the airline industry moves further into the Seventies.

First of the new trijets to go into service was the DC-10-10. Following a tradition of inexorable production reliability, once a project was underway, McDonnell Douglas kept ahead of its original delivery schedules to such good effect that American Airlines was able to put the first aircraft into service on the Los Angeles—Chicago route on 5 August, 1971, less than a year after the first flight on 24 October, 1970. United Air Lines followed shortly afterwards, on the San Francisco—Washington route, on 14 August, with National, the third DC-10 operator, on the New York—Florida routes on 15 December.

Douglas had built the DC-10 as a versatile wide-bodied airliner which could combine long-range with flexible airport requirements. Bigger than

Second type of wide-bodied trijet is the Lockheed L.1011 TriStar. The example illustrated, in TWA's white and red livery, is seen during the test programme following the first flight on 16 November, 1970.

the DC-8-63, but smaller than the Boeing 747, it seemed to fit perfectly the traffic demands of all except the densest routes. Like the DC-9, it had been built to exacting standards for maintenance, and an American Airlines spokesman referred to its 'unprecedented dependability'.

Lockheed, with an aircraft almost identical in specification, ran into serious trouble. The British company Rolls-Royce had won the power-plant competition for the L.1011 TriStar with its RB.211, of advanced design, incorporating three compressor stages (the General Electric CF-6 in the DC-10 had only two) and sophisticated metallurgy. But in cutting prices to match the intense competition, Rolls-Royce had miscalculated the costs, and, to the astonishment of the world, the illustrious company went bankrupt on 4 February, 1971.

After agonizing reappraisal of the entire project, during which time the British Government took over Rolls-Royce, appointed a new management, and underwrote continuing costs to keep the project alive, a solution was eventually found to save Lockheed—which was itself in dire financial straits—and the L.1011. The banks were prepared to loan $250 mn, with a government guarantee. After a bitter controversy involving bankers, airlines, governments and industry, the U.S. Government finally agreed, the Senate approving the Emergency Loan Guarantee Act, by a margin of one vote, on 2 August, 1971.

The TriStar made its first flight on 16 November, 1970, is in full production, and entered scheduled service on 26 April, 1972, with Eastern Air Lines. Delta and TWA also have TriStars on order.

Oddly, the development of each successive major generation of transport aircraft has occurred when either the economic or political climate in the world has been far from auspicious. The Boeing 247/Douglas DC-2 generation came when the United States was fighting its way out of the biggest economic depression in history. The Boeing 307/Douglas DC-4/ Lockheed Constellation types were just in time for World War 2. The Boeing 707/Douglas DC-8 jets entered service when the world air traffic growth curve experienced a distinct hiccup. Now the Boeing 747, DC-10, L.1011, and A-300B are entering service when the experts are looking gloomily at the air traffic curve once again.

In the United States, the economy took a downward turn in 1970, and the declining gross national product (GNP) was reflected in the decrease in consumer incomes and expenditures. There was an immediate effect on domestic travel, and all the airlines felt the economic pinch.

For a period of about a year in 1970–71, financial results of disastrous proportions were announced by many airlines. These resulted, as has been explained above, from the introduction of a substantial volume of additional capacity at a time when traffic growth almost stagnated. The airlines' reaction was to apply to the C.A.B. for a general increase in fares, which was granted, at 6 per cent, effective from 3 May, 1971. Although revenues increased from the captive business market, higher fares further depressed total traffic growth during a period of declining real personal incomes. The net result was traffic stagnation in 1971, the first such occurrence for more than a decade. One other significant effect of the recession was the destruction of confidence in high air freight potential.

Internationally, the picture was a little brighter, but Pan American and TWA, along with the leading European scheduled airlines, were beginning to feel the impact of the powerful threat from low-fare charter operators on the North Atlantic routes. Eventually, after much preliminary sparring behind the scenes, the IATA carriers met in Montreal on 28 June, 1971, to discuss lowering all transatlantic fares. Unable to agree, an 'open-rate' situation was threatened by a unilateral stand taken by Lufthansa, the German national airline; but after more wrangling, at another emergency meeting at the Annual IATA Conference in Honolulu, in November, agreement was reached. In 1972 scheduled transatlantic fares were the lowest in history, with a round-trip excursion off-peak New York—London fare of $204 opening up new prospects of traffic growth derived from a new income stratum.

Though much has been made of the air-mindedness of the U.S. travelling public, many air journeys (statistically recorded as individual passengers) are in fact made by the same frequent travellers, mostly businessmen. Led by the innovative Supplemental airlines, there was a rising tide of opinion to widen the entire air travel market by several experiments in lowering fares.

These efforts were successful and during the 1970s, most of the airlines met the growing demand for lower fares within the U.S.A. And although he was not the first to introduce low fares, England's Sir Freddie Laker's influence reverberated throughout the industry when he introduced a no-reservation, no-frills, *Skytrain* service between New York and London at incredibly low fares on 26 September, 1977.

On the other hand, the airlines had been obliged to raise their fares in 1973/74 because the worldwide increase in the price of oil led to a quadrupling of the price of aviation fuel. Other inflationary forces affecting the cost of labour, and higher interest rates which placed an additional burden on fleet acquisition costs, combined to reduce airline profit margins and bring return-on-investment ratios to a low ebb.

Nevertheless the airlines survived gallantly, by a variety of cost-saving methods; and although there were predictions of widespread disaster, only one major airline disappeared from the lists during the 1970s (Northeast; see page 566). In general, the annual rate of total U.S. air traffic growth slowed down considerably, but in no year of the decade was there an actual decline. Traffic volume even grew modestly during the years of the fuel-related fare increases, thus revealing a public determination to fly, even in defiance of the predictions of computerized econometric models.

Undoubtedly, the main event of the 1970s was the Deregulation Act of 1978. This legislation, so far-reaching in scope and revolutionary in effect, is discussed in a separate appendix essay (pages 675–78).

Bibliography

(A) BOOKS ON AIR TRANSPORT (Listed chronologically according to publication date)

An Introduction to the Economics of Air Transportation, by Hart Kennedy (The Macmillan Company, New York, 1924)

Civil Aviation—Report by the Joint Committee on Civil Aviation of the U.S. Department of Commerce and the American Engineering Council (McGraw-Hill, New York, 1926)

Airplane Transportation, by James G. Woolley and Earl W. Hill (Hartwell Publishing Corporation, Hollywood, 1929)

Aviation's Place in Tomorrow's Business, by Earl Reeves (B. C. Forbes, New York, 1930)

North to the Orient, by Anne Morrow Lindbergh (Harcourt, Brace, New York, 1935)

The Early History of Air Transportation, by E. P. Warner (Norwich University, Northfield, Vermont, 1937)

The Aviation Business, by Elsbeth E. Freudenthal (Vanguard Press, New York, 1940)

Airways, by Henry Ladd Smith (Alfred A. Knopf, New York, 1942)

International Air Transport and National Policy, by O. Lissitzyn (Council on Foreign Relations, New York, 1942)

The Struggle for Airlines in Latin America, by William H. Burden (Council on Foreign Relations, New York, 1943)

Empire of the Air, by Matthew Josephson (Harcourt Brace, New York, 1943)

Wings Over America, by Harry Bruno (Halcyon House, New York, 1944)

Air Transport At War, by Reginald M. Cleveland (Harper and Brothers, New York, 1946)

Airline Competition, by F. W. Gill and G. L. Bates (Harvard University, 1949)

Airways Abroad, by Henry Ladd Smith (University of Wisconsin Press, 1950)

Transocean, by Richard Thruelson (Henry Holt and Company, New York, 1952)

United Air Lines and its Predecessors and Subsidiaries, 1925–1945 (United Air Lines Corporate and Legal History, Chicago, 1953)

High Horizons, by Frank J. Taylor (McGraw-Hill, New York, 1955)

Glacier Pilot, by Beth Day (Henry Holt and Company, New York, 1957)
The Challenge, by Harold Mansfield (Allan Wingate, London, 1958)
This Was Air Travel, by Henry R. Palmer Jr (Superior Publishing Company, Seattle, 1960)
Big Eight, by Richard G. Hubler (Duell, Sloan and Pearce, New York, 1960)
The Modern Airliner, by Peter W. Brooks (Putnam, London, 1961)
Saga of the U.S. Air Mail Service, 1918–1927, edited by Dale Nielson (Air Mail Pioneers, Inc, 1962)
The World's Airliners, by Peter W. Brooks (Putnam, London, 1962)
The Sky's The Limit, by Charles J. Kelly Jr (Coward-McCann, New York, 1963)
A History of the World's Airlines, by R. E. G. Davies (Oxford University Press, London and New York, 1964)
Revolution in the Sky, by Richard Sanders Allen (The Stephen Greene Press, Brattleboro, Vermont, 1964)
Hungry Tiger, by Frank Cameron (McGraw-Hill, New York, 1964)
United Air Lines, Inc., and its Subsidiaries, 1946–1955 (United Air Lines Corporate and Legal History, Chicago, 1965)
Safer Skyways, by Donald R. Whitnah (Iowa State University Press, Ames, Iowa, 1966)
Flight Plan for Tomorrow, edited by Crosby Maynard (Douglas Aircraft Company, Santa Monica, California, 1966)
Above The Pacific, by William J. Horvat (Aero Publishers, Fallbrook, California, 1966)
Boeing Aircraft since 1916, by Peter M. Bowers (Putnam, London, 1966)
The Ford Tri-Motor, by William T. Larkins (Profile Publications, London, 1967)
Rickenbacker, by Edward V. Rickenbacker (Prentice-Hall, Englewood Cliffs, New Jersey, 1967)
The Technical Development of Modern Aviation, by Ronald Miller and David Sawers (Routledge and Kegan Paul, London, 1968)
Birth of an Industry, edited by The Official Airline Guide (Ruben H. Donnelley Corporation, Oak Brook, Illinois, 1969)
Adventures of a Yellowbird, by Robert W. Mudge (Branden Press, Boston, 1969)
The Anatomy of an Airline, by Brad Williams (Doubleday, Garden City, New York, 1970)
Legacy of Leadership, by Trans World Airlines Flight Operations Department (Walsworth Publishing Company, Marceline, Mo., 1971)

(B) REFERENCE BOOKS

The Aircraft Yearbook, compiled by the Aeronautical Chamber of Commerce of America, and published annually from 1919 onwards (by various publishers). Now discontinued

Jane's All The World's Aircraft, edited by C. G. Grey, later by Leonard Bridgman, and John W. R. Taylor, and published by Samson, Low and Marston, London, annually, from 1911 onwards

World Airline Record, edited by Roy R. Roadcap, and published at intervals by Roadcap and Associates, Chicago. Last edition 1965

World Aviation Annual, edited by J. Parker Van Zandt, and published by the Aviation Research Institute, Washington, 1948

The Official Airline Guide, originally published by John R. Fletcher, Chicago, 1929, and published monthly ever since by the Official Airline Guide Company

Handbook of Airline Statistics, compiled by the Civil Aeronautics Board, and published annually since 1960 by the U.S. Government Printing Office. Format devised by William Weinfeld

Historical Fact Book, a Chronology, 1926–1963, prepared by Arnold E. Briddon, Federal Aviation Agency, and published by the U.S. Government Printing Office, 1966

Civil Aeronautics Board Annual Reports to Congress, published annually by the U.S. Government Printing Office since 1938

The FAA Statistical Handbook of Aviation, published annually since 1944 by the U.S. Government Printing Office

(C) MAGAZINES AND PERIODICALS

Esso Air World, published six times per year by Esso International Inc, 15 West 51st Street, New York, N.Y., 10019

Flight Magazine, published monthly by the Air Review Publishing Corporation, 2700 North Haskell Avenue, Dallas, Texas, 75204

Airline Management and Marketing, including American Aviation, published monthly by the Ziff-Davis Publishing Company, 1156 15th Street N.W., Washington, D.C., 20005

Aviation Week and Space Technology, published weekly by the McGraw-Hill Publishing Company, 330 West 42nd Street, New York, N.Y.

Air Transport World, published monthly by World Aviation Publications Inc, 916 Shoreham Building, Washington, D.C., 20005

Flight International, incorporating The Aeroplane, published weekly by Iliffe Transport Publications, Ltd., Dorset House, Stamford Street, London, S.E.1, England

Tables

TABLE 1

SUMMARY OF PIONEER AIRLINES
1914 - 1924

Date of First Service	Airline	Service	Routes	Initial Fleet	Remarks	Date of Last Service
1 Jan. 1914	St Petersburg-Tampa Airboat Line	P	St Petersburg-Tampa	1 Benoist XIV	World's first regular service	Apr. 1914
3 Mar. 1919	Seattle-Victoria Air Mail Line	M	Seattle-Victoria (FAM-2)	1 Boeing C-700	Also called Hubbard Air Transport and (in 1928) Northwest Air Service	To Barnes & Gorst, July 1928
4 Jul. 1919	Syd Chaplin Airlines	P	San Pedro-Avalon	1 Curtiss MF	Route taken over by Pacific Marine Airways 1920	15 Sep. 1919
Aug. 1919	Aero Limited	P	New York-Atlantic City	HS-2L		Sep. 1919
15 Oct. 1920	Florida West Indies Airways	M	Key West-Havana (FAM-1)	HS-2L		Taken over by Aeromarine. Winter 1920-21
Winter 1920	Aeromarine Airways	PME	Key West-Havana (FAM-1)	F-5L	Regular passenger services begun 1 Nov. 1921	Sep. 1923
End 1920	Pacific Marine Airways	P	San Pedro-Avalon	2 HS-2L		Bought by WAE 29 June, 1928
Summer 1922	New York-Newport Air Service	P	New York-Newport, R.I.	3 Loening Air Yacht		July 1923
Summer 1922	Balsam's Air Service	E	Garden City, L.I.-Dixville Notch, N.H.	3 Curtiss Oriole	Newspaper Service	-
19 June 1922	United States Army "Model Airway"	P	Anacostia, D.C.-Dayton; later New York-San Antonio, extended 1926 to Los Angeles	DH-4	Military or gov't. personnel only	1926
9 Apr. 1923	The Gulf Coast Airline	M	New Orleans-Pilottown (FAM-3)	HS-2L	Known as Johnson Airways, 1932	1933
Winter 1923	Curtiss Metropolitan Airplane Company	E	Miami-West Palm Beach	HS-2L	Newspaper Service	-

P = Passenger; M = Mail; E = Express

U.S. POST OFFICE AIR MAIL SERVICE — TABLE 2

SUMMARY OF EXPENSES AND OPERATING REPORT, AUGUST 1918

TOTAL OF 14 AIRCRAFT (8 CURTISS JN-4H, 6 STANDARD)

EXPENSES	($)		($)
Fuel	1075	**Mechanics:**	
Grease and Oil	290	On plane	1564
Office Force	208	Shop Time	183
Motorcycles, Trucks	340		
Rent, Light, Fuel		Repairs and Accessories	1320
Power, Telephone, Water	415		
Miscellaneous	134	Interest on Investment	1122
Pilots:		Department Overheads	861
Actual Time	1369		
Dead Time	223		
Hangar Men:		**TOTAL**	$9556
On plane	348		
Miscellaneous	104		

UNIT COST ANALYSIS	
Gallons of Fuel	3510
Hours Flown	203
Miles Flown	15120
Miles per Gallon	4.3
Cost per Hour	$47.06
Cost per Mile	63.2¢

U.S. AIR MAIL SERVICE – STATISTICAL SUMMARY

TABLE 3

Year (Ending 30 June)	Mail Trips Flown (miles)	Percentage of Scheduled Miles Flown	Forced Landings		Crashes	No. of Letters Carried (40 per lb)	Casualties			Total Amount of Appropriation Expended $
			Mechanical	Weather			Minor Injuries	Seriously Injured	Killed	
1918	16,009	84	6	6	0	713,240	0	0	0	13,604
1919	160,066	96	37	56	13	9,210,040	2	1	3	717,177
1920	549,244	84	155	105	33	21,063,120	12	2	9	1,264,495
1921	1,554,985	86	810	954	56	44,834,080	33	3	17	2,653,882
1922	1,537,927	94	281	479	17	48,988,920	33	4	1	1,418,146
1923	1,590,637	96	176	279	12	67,875,840	27	2	4	1,897,151
1924	1,522,763	95	154	353	14	60,001,360	41	6	4	1,498,674
1925[1]	2,076,764	96	174	586	12	9,300,520	46	5	2	2,743,750
1926[1]	2,256,137	94	155	707	9	14,145,640	59	2	2	2,782,422
1927[1]	2,329,553	95	140	881	33	22,385,000	51	11	1	2,255,919
1928[2]	173,987	97	7	31	1	3,338,680	4	0	0	166,314
TOTAL	13,768,072	93	2,095	4,437	200	301,855,840	308	36	43[3]	17,411,534

NOTES: [1] From 1925 onwards, mail volumes reduced when only higher rated mail carried
[2] July–August, New York–Chicago only
[3] 32 fatal crashes. Number includes 32 pilots, 9 employes killed in air, 2 on ground

POST OFFICE DEPARTMENT MAIL CONTRACTS TABLE 4

(Dates of Inaugural Service)

Mail Contract Number	Route	Airline	Date of Service Inauguration
CAM 1	New York-Boston	Colonial	18 June 1926
2	St Louis-Chicago	Robertson	15 April 1926
3	Chicago-Dallas	NAT	12 May 1926
4	Los Angeles-Salt Lake City	WAE	17 April 1926
5	Pasco-Elko	Varney	6 April 1926
6	Detroit-Chicago	Ford	3 April 1925
7	Detroit-Cleveland	Ford	31 July, 1925
8	Seattle-Los Angeles	Pacific	15 Sept 1926
9	Minneapolis-Chicago	Dickenson	7 June 1926
10	Atlanta-Miami	Florida	1 June 1926
11	Cleveland-Pittsburgh	Ball	21 April 1927
12	Cheyenne-Pueblo	Colorado	31 May 1926
13	Philadelphia-Washington	P.R.T.	6 July 1926
14	Detroit-Grand Rapids	Stout	2 Aug 1926
15	Philadelphia-Norfolk	P.R.T	10 Oct 1926
16	Louisville-Cleveland	Continental	1 Aug 1928
17	New York-Chicago	NAT	1 Sept 1927
18	San Francisco-Chicago	Boeing	1 July 1927
19	New York-Atlanta	Pitcairn	1 May 1928
20	Cleveland-Albany	Colonial Western	17 Dec 1927
21	Dallas-Galveston	Texas	6 Feb 1928
22	Dallas-Brownsville	Texas	6 Feb 1928
23	New Orleans-Atlanta	St Tammany-Gulf	20 Aug 1927
24	Cincinnati-Chicago	Embry-Riddle	17 Dec 1927
25	Atlanta-Miami	Pitcairn	1 Dec 1928
26	Great Falls-Salt Lake City	National Parks	1 Aug 1928
27	Chicago-Pontiac	Thompson	17 July 1928
28	St Louis-Omaha	Robertson	1 May 1929
29	New Orleans-Houston	St Tammany-Gulf	23 Jan 1929
30	Atlanta-Chicago	Interstate	1 Dec 1928
31	Chicago Loop-Municipal	Curtiss Flying Service	June 1929
32	Spokane -Seattle	Varney	23 Sept 1929
33	Atlanta-Los Angeles	Southern Air Fast Express	15 Oct 1930
34	New York-Los Angeles	TWA	25 Oct 1930

TABLE 5

SUMMARY OF U. S. DOMESTIC AIRLINES 1925 - April 1927
(First 15 P. O. Mail Contracts)

Date of First Service	Airline	Service	Routes	Initial Fleet	Remarks	Date of Last Service
1 Mar. 1925	Ryan Airlines	P	San Diego-Los Angeles	6 Ryan-Standard then Douglas Cloudster	5,600 passengers carried in 1926	1927
3 Apr. 1925	Ford Motor Company	E	Detroit-Chicago (CAM 6); later Detroit-Cleveland (CAM 7)	Ford 2-AT, later Ford 4-AT Tri-Motor	Private express service, then contract mail and passenger, finally private express again.	1931
1 Apr. 1926	Florida Airways Corp	P	Atlanta-Jacksonville-Miami (CAM 10 from 1 June)	Ford 2-AT	Route taken over by Pitcairn	End 1926
6 Apr. 1926	Varney Air Lines	M	Pasco-Boise-Elko (later Salt Lake City)(CAM 5); later Spokane-Seattle (CAM 32) 23 Sept. 1929	6 Swallow biplane	One flight made; service resumed on 6 June	to United 30 June, 1930
15 Apr. 1926	Robertson Aircraft Corp	M	St Louis-Chicago (CAM 2); later St Louis-Kansas City-Omaha 1 May 1929 (CAM 28)	4 DH-4M		To Universal 31 Dec. 1928
17 Apr. 1926	Western Air Express (WAE)	MPE	Los Angeles-Salt Lake City (CAM 4)	6 Douglas M-2 3 DH-4M	Passenger Service 23 May, 1926	-
12 May, 1926	National Air Transport (NAT)	MPE	Chicago-Dallas (CAM 3), later Chicago-New York (CAM 7) 1 Sept. 1927	10 Curtiss Carrier Pigeon	Passenger service 1 Feb. 1928	To United 7 May, 1930
31 May, 1926	Colorado Airways	M	Cheyenne-Denver-Pueblo (CAM 12)	Standard biplane, later Ryan M-1		To WAE 10 Dec. 1927

P = Passenger; M = Mail; E = Express

Date of First Service	Airline	Service	Routes	Initial Fleet	Remarks	Date of Last Service
7 June, 1926	Charles Dickenson	M	Minneapolis-Chicago (CAM 9)	Laird biplane	Route taken over by Northwest Airways (q.v.)	Nov. 1926
18 June, 1926	Colonial Air Transport	MPE	New York-Boston (CAM 1)	Curtiss Lark	Passenger service 4 Apr. 1927. Became division of Colonial Airways Corporation.	to AVCO May 1929
6 July, 1926	Philadelphia Rapid Transit Service (P.R.T.)	P	Philadelphia-Wash. (CAM 13), later Philadelphia-Norfolk (CAM 15)	Fokker F.VIIa-3M		30 Nov. 1926
2 Aug. 1926	Stout Air Services	PM	Detroit-Grand Rapids (CAM 14), later Detroit-Cleveland	4 Ford-Stout 2-AT 2 Ford 4-AT Tri-Motor	Took over Ford Motor Company's routes but relinquished mail contracts	To United 30 June, 1929
15 Sept. 1926	Pacific Air Transport	MPE	Seattle-S. Francisco Los Angeles (CAM 8)	10 Ryan M-1		To Boeing 1 January, 1928
1 Oct. 1926	Northwest Airways	MPE	Minneapolis-Chicago (CAM 9)	3 Stinson Detroiter	Took over route from Dickenson	-
21 Apr. 1927	Clifford Ball	MPE	Cleveland-Pittsburgh (CAM 11)	2 Waco 9	Became Pennsylvania Airlines, eventually Capital Airlines	To United 1 June, 1961

P = Passenger; E = Express; M = Mail

TABLE 6

SUMMARY OF U. S. DOMESTIC AIRLINES - July 1927
(First Transcontinental Mail Contract) -End 1928
(Inc. Second Mail Contracts)

Date of First Service	Airline	Service	Routes	Initial Fleet	Remarks	Date of Last Service
1 July 1927	Boeing Air Transport	PME	San Francisco-Chicago (CAM 18)	25 Boeing 40A		Became Division of United Aircraft 30 Oct. 1928
21 July 1927	Maddux Air Lines	PE	Los Angeles-San Diego, later Los Angeles-San Francisco	2 Ford 4-AT Tri-Motor	1400 Pass. in 1927; 9440 in 1928	To TAT, 16 November, 1929
20 Aug. 1927	St. Tammany-Gulf Coast Airways	PM	New Orleans-Atlanta (CAM 23) New Orleans-Houston (CAM 29)	Fokker	Became Gulf Air Lines in Oct. 1928	Merged with Texas Air Tpt (q.v.)
28 Nov. 1927	Standard Air Lines	PE	Los Angeles-Tuscon, later El Paso	Fokker F.VII		To WAE, May 1930, later American
17 Dec. 1927	Embry-Riddle	PME	Cincinnati-Chicago (CAM 24)	6 Waco 10		To AVCO, Sept. 1929
17 Dec. 1927	Colonial Western Airways	PME	Cleveland-Albany (CAM 20)	3 Fairchild FC-2	Became division of Colonial Airways Corporation	To AVCO, May 1929
6 Feb. 1928	Texas Air Transport	PM	Dallas-Galveston(CAM 21) Dallas-Brownsville (CAM 22)	7 Pitcairn Mailwing	Merged with Gulf (q.v.) on Feb. 1929	To AVCO, Jan. 1930
5 March 1928	West Coast Air Transport	PE	San Francisco-Seattle	8 Bach Air Yacht	5,000 passengers in first year. Subsidiary of Union Air Lines	To WAE, late 1929

P - Passenger; M - Mail; E - Express

Date of First Service	Airline	Service	Routes	Initial Fleet	Remarks	Date of Last Service
1 May, 1928	Pitcairn Aviation	M	New York-Atlanta (CAM 19) later, Atlanta-Miami (CAM 25)	8 Pitcairn Mailwing	Sold to N.American Aviation 10 July 1929, renamed Eastern Air Transport 17 Jan. 1930	
1928	Wichita Air Service Provision Company	P	Kansas City-Wichita			
June 1928	Mutual Aircraft Corp	PE	Los Angeles-Oakland	4 Ryan Brougham	2350 Passengers carried in 1928	1929?
15 June, 1928	United States Air Tpt	P	Washington-New York			1932?
20 June, 1928	Paul R. Braniff	P	Tulsa-Oklahoma City	4 Stinson Detroiter	3000 Passengers carried in 1928	To Universal May 1929
17 July, 1928	Thompson Aeronautical Corporation	M	Chicago-Muskegon-Bay City-Pontiac (CAM 27)	6 Stinson Detroiter		To American Jan. 1933
19 July, 1928	Royal Airways	P	Chicago-Madison			Feb. 1929
July 1928	Rapid Air Lines	P	Watertown-Rapid City	1 Ford 4-AT		Aug. 1929
1 Aug. 1928	National Parks Airways	MP	Salt Lake City-Great Falls (CAM 26)	3 Fokker Super Universal	Name changed to Alfred Frank June 1934	To W A E 1 Aug. 1937
1 Aug. 1928	Continental Airlines	MP	Louisville-Cleveland (CAM 16)	3 Travel Air 6000		To Universal 31 Dec. 1928
16 Aug. 1928	Northern Air Lines	P	Chicago-Minneapolis			To Universal 31 Dec. 1928
15 Sept. 1928	Universal Aviation Corp	PE	Cleveland-Chicago		Became Universal	To AVCO

Date of First Service	Airline	Service	Routes	Initial Fleet	Remarks	Date of Last Service
1928	Central Airlines	P	Tulsa-Wichita			To Universal
1 Oct. 1928	Canadian Colonial Airways	MP	New York-Montreal(FAM-1)		Became Division of Colonial Airways Corp	To AVCO, May 1929
22 Oct. 1928	Capitol Air Lines	P	Louisville-Chicago Detroit	4 Ryan Broughams 3 Alexander Eaglerock		1929
12 Nov. 1928	Midwest Airways	P	Waterloo-Des Moines	2 Ryan Broughams		1929
1 Dec. 1928	Interstate Airlines	MP	Atlanta-Chicago (CAM 30)	7 Fairchild		To AVCO end of 1928
1928	Comercial Air Transport	P	Seattle-Vancouver	Ryan Brougham		1930
1928	Jefferson	P	Minneapolis-Rochester	1 Ford 4-AT Tri-Motor		1928

TABLE 7

SPANNING THE CONTINENT
REDUCTION IN TRANSCONTINENTAL AIR TIMES, 1920–1931

Date	Airline	Route (Not All Stops Listed)	Mail (M) or Passenger (P)	Aircraft Used	Coast-to-Coast Time (hrs)
8 Sept 1920	Post Office Department	New York–Chicago–Omaha–Cheyenne–Salt Lake City–San Francisco (Daytime service, in relays)	M	DH–4B	78
1 July 1924	Post Office Department	(Same route, including night flying)	M	DH–4B	29–34
1 July 1927	Boeing Air Transport	New York–Chicago (rail); Chicago–Omaha–Cheyenne–Salt Lake City–San Francisco (BAT)	MP	Boeing 40A	48
1 Sept 1927	Boeing Air Transport National Air Transport	New York–Chicago (NAT); Chicago–San Francisco (BAT)	M	Curtiss Carrier Pigeon (NAT) Boeing 40B (BAT)	32
1 June 1929	Western Air Express	Los Angeles–Albuquerque–Kansas City–(various railroads)– East Coast	MPE	Fokker F–X	70–80
14 June 1929	Universal Aviation Corporation	New York–Cleveland (N.Y. Central R.R.); Cleveland–Chicago–Kansas City–Garden City (UAC); Garden City–Los Angeles (A.T. & Santa Fe R.R.)	P	Fokker F–XA	67
7 July 1929	Transcontinental Air Transport (T A T)	New York–Columbus (Pennsylvania R.R.); Columbus–Waynoka, Okla. (T A T); Waynoka–Clovis, N.M. (A.T. & Santa Fe R.R.); Clovis–Los Angeles (T A T)	P	Ford 5–AT	48

E = Express

Date	Airline	Route (Not All Stops Listed)	Mail (M) or Passenger (P)	Aircraft Used	Coast-to Coast Time (hrs)
August 1929	Standard Airlines Southwest Air Fast	New York-St. Louis (N.Y. Central R.R.); St. Louis-Sweetwater, Texas (SAFE); Sweetwater-El Paso (Texas & Pacific Ry.); El Paso-Los Angeles (Standard)	P	Ford 5-AT (SAFE) Fokker F-VII (Standard)	67
25 Oct 1930	Transcontinental & Western Air (T W A)	New York-Pittsburgh-Columbus-Indianapolis-St. Louis-Kansas City-Albuquerque-Los Angeles (Night stop at Kansas City)	PM	Ford 5-AT	36
1 Dec 1930	United Aircraft & Transportation Corporation	New York-San Francisco (One carrier service after purchase of N A T by United) (Night stop at Chicago)	PM	Ford 5-AT Boeing 80A	48
15 June 1931	American Airways	New York-Columbus (Pennsylvania R.R.); Columbus-Louisville-Nashville-Memphis-Dallas-El Paso-Phoenix-Los Angeles	P	Ford 5-AT	53

TABLE 8

SUMMARY OF U. S. DOMESTIC AIRLINES
1929 - 1933

Date of First Service	Airline	Service	Routes	Initial Fleet	Remarks	Date of Last Service
Jan. 1929	Amarillo Airport Corporation	P	Amarillo-Oklahoma City	4 Lockheed Vega		To Universal July 1929
29 March, 1929	Pickwick Airways	P	Los Angeles-San Diego, later San Francisco and Mexico City	Bach Tri-motor Fairchild, etc.		May 1930
2 April, 1929	Southwest Air Fast Express (SAFE)	PE	Tulsa-Dallas, Tulsa-Kansas City	9 Ford 5-AT Tri-Motor	Participated in Air-rail transcontinental Service	October 1930
15 April, 1929	Mamer Air Transport	PE	Portland-Spokane	2 Ford 4-AT Tri-Motor	Participated in Air-rail Chicago-Seattle Service	October 1932
15 April, 1929	Alaska-Washington Airways	PE	Ketchikan-Sitka; Seattle-Olympia; Wenatchee-Pasco; Victoria-Nanaimo		Company sold to Seattle-Wenatchee-Yakima Airways, 1 July, 1930	1930?
1 May, 1929	Nevada Air Lines	P	Reno-Los Angeles	4 Lockheed Vega		Feb. 1930
6 May, 1929	Yellow Cab Airways	PE	Kansas City-Minneapolis	Fairchild 71		Sept. 1929
28 May, 1929	Coastal Airways	P	New York-Albany	Fairchild 71		Nov. 1929
15 June, 1929	Gorst Air Transport	P	Seattle-Bremerton	2 Loening Amphibian		1935?
16 June, 1929	Delta Air Service	P	Dallas-Birmingham			To American 16 Sept. 1930
June 1929	Curtiss Flying Service of the Middle West	P P	Chicago Loop-Municipal Airport (CAM 31)	Sikorsky Amphibian		Sept. 1929
June 1929	Middle States Airlines	P	Akron-Detroit	2 Lockheed Vega		Sept. 1929

P = Passenger; E = Express; M = Mail

Date of First Service	Airline	Service	Routes	Initial Fleet	Remarks	Date of Last Service
7 July, 1929	Transcontinental Air Transport (TAT)	P	Columbus, Ohio-Waynoka, Ok.;Clovis, N.M.-Los Angeles	10 Ford 5-AT Tri-Motor	Air-rail service in conjunction with Penn. and Santa Fe Railroads	Merged with W A E and P.A.I.C. to form T W A 25 Oct. 1930
29 July, 1929	United States Airways	P	Kansas City-Denver	Flamingo	Associated with Pittsburgh Airways in forming United Avigation	June 1934
July 1929	Mason & Dixon Air Lines	P	Detroit-Cincinnati	Flamingo		January 1931
July 1929	Curtiss Flying Service	P	Boston-Nantucket; Boston Bar Harbor			1932
July 1929	New York-Asbury Park Air Line	P	New York-Asbury Park	Bellanca		Sept. 1929
July 1929	Southern Air Express	P	Montgomery-Jackson; Montgomery-Atlanta			Jan. 1930
July 1929	Airvia Transportation Company	P	New York-Boston	Savoia Marchetti S.55		Dec. 1929
July 1929	Cape Cod Airway	P	Philadelphia (Camden)-Woods Hole, Mass.	2 Travel Air 6000	Also known as Ludington Flying Service	Sept. 1929
Aug. 1929	Scenic Airways	P	Grand Canyon Service North Rim-South Rim	2 Ford 4-AT Tri-Motor		1930?
Aug. 1929	Canadian-American Airlines	P	St Paul-Winnipeg	Travel Air 6000		Jan. 1930
1 Sept. 1929	Kohler Aviation Corp	PE	Milwaukee-Grand Rapids, later Detroit-Grand Rapids, 6 Oct. 1930	Keystone-Loening Amphibian	Sold route to Northwest, who sublet back to Kohler	To Pennsylvania 1934

Date of First Service	Airline	Service	Routes	Initial Fleet	Remarks	Date of Last Service
1 Sept. 1929	Continental Air Express	PE	Los Angeles-San Diego, later Los Angeles-San Fran.			October 1930
Sept. 1929	Atlantic Coast Airways Corp	P	Atlantic City-New York	Keystone-Loening Amph.		Nov. 1929
21 Sept. 1929	Mid-Continent Air Express	PE	Denver-El Paso	13 Fokker Super Universal		To W A E Oct. 1931
Sept. 1929	Seagull Air Lines	P	Salt Lake City-Ely	Curtiss Robin		Nov. 1930
29 Sept. 1929	The Brower's Air Service Corp	P	Wichita-Omaha	Curtiss Robin Stinson Detroiter	Taken over by Western Air Service Corp on 15 June, 1930	End 1930
1 Nov. 1929	Pittsburgh Airways	P	Pittsburgh-Philadelphia-New York	2 Travel Air	Joined U.S. Airways in forming United Avigation	Oct. 1931
11 Nov. 1929	Inter-Island Airways	P	Honolulu-Hilo; Honolulu-Kauai	2 Sikorsky S-38	Name changed to Hawaiian Airlines, Ltd, 1 Oct. 1941	
Nov. 1929	Cromwell Air Lines	P	Dallas-San Angelo	Stinson		Oct. 1931
30 Nov. 1929	Wedell-Williams Air Service Corp	P	New Orleans-Shreveport-Ft. Worth; New Orleans-Houston; N.O.-Grand Isle		Ceased operations, end 1929; new route N.O.-Laredo, summer 1933; Mail contract N.O.-Houston 1934	To Eastern 1937

Date of First Service	Airline	Service	Routes	Initial Fleet	Remarks	Date of Last Service
Jan. 1930	Inter Citiair Express	P	Seattle-Yakima			To Alaska-Washington, April 1930
1 Feb. 1930	Air Ferries	P	San Francisco-Oakland	2 Keystone-Loening Amph.	60,000 Passengers carried in 1930	1933
Feb. 1930	Davis Air Lines	P	Atlanta-Birmingham	Travel Air		June 1930
March 1930	Apache Airlines	P	Phoenix-Globe			July 1930
31 March, 1930	Rapid Air Transport	P	St Louis-Omaha		In association with Braniff 1931	Merged with Hanford, Dec. 1933
April 1930	Eastern Air Express	P	New York-Providence			October 1930
27 April, 1930	Robertson Airplane Service Company	P	St Louis-New Orleans	Ryan Brougham		1933
May 1930	Michigan Air Express	P	Grand Rapids-Petoskey		Operated jointly with Kohler Aviation Corp.	Feb. 1931
May 1930	New England & Western Air Transportation Co Inc	P	Springfield, Mass.-New York;-Boston; -Albany			Nov. 1930
1 June 1930	New York Airways	P	New York-Atlantic City	Ford Tri-Motor Fokker F-X, Sikorsky S-38	Subsidiary of Pan American	To Eastern 15 July, 1931
June 1930	General Aviation	P	Elmira-Syracuse	Ryan Brougham		July 1930
June 1930	Continental Airways	P	Chicago-Columbus, later Chicago-Washington, 18 July, 1931	Travel Air		March 1932
July 1930	Montana Devt. & Air Transport Co	P	Missoula-Kalispell	Lockheed		Nov. 1930

Date of First Service	Airline	Service	Routes	Initial Fleet	Remarks	Date of Last Service
July 1930	Oklahoma Short Line Airways	P	Tulsa-Memphis			Oct. 1930
Aug. 1930	Eagle Airlines	P	Kansas City-Minneapolis	American Eagle		Nov. 1930
Aug. 1930	Sky View Air Lines	P	Pittsburgh-Niagara Falls	Ford 4-AT Tri-Motor		Oct. 1930
1 Sept. 1930	New York, Philadelphia, and Washington Airway	P P	New York-Philadelphia-Washington	Lockheed Vega Stinson Tri-motor Cons. Fleetster	Probably first profit-making passenger airline	To Eastern 15 Feb. 1933
Sept. 1930	Frank Martz Airline	P	New York-Wilkes Barre, later to Buffalo, 15 July, 1931	2 Bellanca Air-bus; 1 Ford Tri-Motor		To American end 1932
1 Oct. 1930	Bowen Air Lines	P	Fort Worth-Houston, later F.W. - Oklahoma City 1931, St Louis, Brownsville 1934	Lockheed Vega	In association with Braniff, 1931	March 1936
15 Oct. 1930	Southern Air Fast Express (SAFE)	PME	Atlanta-Los Angeles (CAM 33)	Ford Tri-Motor	Formerly Southwest Air Fast Express (part)	To American Sept. 1931
Oct. 1930	Arrow Airways	P	Memphis-Little Rock	Stinson		Nov. 1930
Oct. 1930	Clarksburg Airways	P	Clarksburg, W.V.-Pittsburgh			Nov. 1930
25 Oct. 1930	Transcontinental and Western Air	PME	New York-Los Angeles (CAM 34)	Ford Tri-Motor	Merger of W A E T A T & P.A.I.C.	

Date of First Service	Airline	Service	Routes	Initial Fleet	Remarks	Date of Last Service
1 Nov. 1930	Main Flying Service	P	Pittsburgh-Cinn-cinnati	Ryan		1 Oct. 1931
6 Nov. 1930	Dixie Flying Service	P	Charlottesville-Washington		In association with Ludington	May 1932
Nov. 1930	Indiana Airways	P	Indiana, Penn.-Pittsburgh	Ryan		1931
13 Nov. 1930	Braniff Airways	P	Tulsa-Oklahoma City-Wichita	2 Lockheed Vega		
8 Dec. 1930	Gilpin Air Lines	P	Los Angeles-San Diego		Became known as G.&.G. Air Lines Company, Ltd	Feb. 1934
23 March, 1931	Tuxhorn Airlines	P	Kansas City-Springfield, Mo			Jan. 1932
23 March, 1931	Century Air Lines	P	St Louis-Chicago-Detroit-Cleveland	14 Stinson	Associated with Braniff	To American April 1932
16 April, 1931	Wyoming Air Service	P	Denver-Billings		Also known as Wyoming-Montana Air Service; Re-organized April 1938 as Inland Air Lines	To Western 7 October, 1943
May 1931	Overland Airways	P	San Francisco (Alameda)-Sacramento	Travel Air		July 1931
May 1931	Port Angeles Air Transport	P	Port Angeles-Seattle			July 1931

Date of First Service	Airline	Service	Routes	Initial Fleet	Remarks	Date of Last Service
May 1931	Richmond A.T. & Sales Corp	P	Richmond-Washington			Sept. 1931
1 June, 1931	Chicago-Detroit Airways	P	Chicago-Detroit			Sept. 1931
6 June, 1931	Wilmington-Catalina Air Lines	PE	Wilmington-Catalina	Douglas Dolphin	Renamed Catalina Air Transport 29 March, 1941	3 Sept. 1942
15 June, 1931	Oklahoma-Texas Air Line	P	Wichita Falls-Lawsor-Oklahoma City	Ryan	Associated with Braniff	Early 1932
3 July, 1931	Century Pacific Lines	P	San Francisco-Los Angeles-San Diego-Phoenix	Stinson		To American April 1932
Aug. 1931	Midland Air Express	P	Kansas City-Cheyenne	Lockheed Vega	Associated with Braniff	Aug. 1932
28 Aug. 1931	Tramp Airways	P	Tulsa-Little Rock			Feb. 1932
1 Sept. 1931	Reed Airline	P	Wichita Falls-Oklahoma City	2 Travel Air	Associated with Braniff	30 April, 1934
4 Sept. 1931	Metropolitan Air Ferry Service	P	Glenn Curtiss Airport-Newark-Floyd Bennett Field	Ford Tri-Motor		Dec. 1931
15 Oct. 1931	Varney Air Service	PE	San Francisco-Los Angeles, later route to Mexico as Lineas Areas Occidentales	Lockheed Orion	Changed name to Varney Speed Lines Air Service	1934
1931	Coast Airways	P	Santa Barbara-Los Angeles	Stinson		July 1932

Date of First Service	Airline	Service	Routes	Initial Fleet	Remarks	Date of Last Service
Nov. 1931	Skyway	P	Wichita-Kansas City	Ford Tri-Motor		Jan. 1932
Nov. 1931	Knollwood Airport	P	Pinehurst-Raleigh			Jan. 1932
11 Jan. 1932	Hunter Airways	P	Tulsa-Little Rock	Fokker Super Universal		Dec. 1932
March 1932	Maine Air Transport	P	Rockland-Islands	Fairchild		Feb. 1933
April 1932	Hanfords Tri-State Air Lines	P	Sioux City-St Paul	Lockheed Vega	Became Hanford Airlines, 1 July, 1936, changed name to Mid-Continent Airlines August 1938	To Braniff 15 Aug. 1952
28 July, 1932	Seattle-Vancouver Airways	P	Seattle-Vancouver			
1932	Commuters Air Service	P	Springfield-Hartford			Oct. 1932
1932	Inter-City Air Lines	P	Springfield-Boston			April 1933
Oct. 1932	Portland Airways	P	Portland-Walla Walla	Stinson Junior		Jan. 1933
Dec. 1932	Air Express Corp	E	New York-Los Angeles	Lockheed Orion		March 1933
1932	Ozark Airways	P	Kansas City-Springfield, Mo	Stinson		March 1933
Feb. 1933	Southwest Airways	P	Tulsa-Salina	Travel Air		March 1933
(Early) 1933	Cardiff & Peacock Air Lines	P	Bakersfield-Los Angeles; Fresno-San Francisco			Early 1934
(Early) 1933	Champlain Air Transport	P	Pittsburgh-Burlington			Early 1934

Date of First Service	Airline	Service	Routes	Initial Fleet	Remarks	Date of Last Service
(Early) 1933	New York & New England Airways	P	Hartford-New York			Early 1934
23 June, 1933	Pacific Seaboard Airlines	P	San Francisco-Los Angeles	Bellanca Pacemaker	Changed to Chicago & Southern Air Lines	To Delta 1 May, 1953

P = Passenger; E = Express; M = Mail

TABLE 9

AIRLINE MAIL REVENUES, EXPENSES, PROFITS, AND SUBSIDIES, 1931–1933
(DOLLARS)

(A) ESTIMATED BY POST OFFICE DEPARTMENT, 1934

Year	(A) Airline Air Mail Revenue	(B) Post Office Revenue	(C) Subsidy (A) – (B)	(D) Post Office Handling Costs	(E) Total Cost to Public (C) + (D)
1931	16,943,606	6,210,345	10,733,261	649,804	11,383,065
1932	19,938,123	6,016,280	13,921,843	3,833,244	17,755,087
1933	19,400,265	6,116,442	13,283,823	3,633,591	16,917,414
1931–33	56,281,994	18,343,067	37,938,927	8,116,639	46,055,566

(B) ESTIMATED BY PAUL T. DAVID, 1934*

Year	(A) (See Above)	(F) Airline Expenses	(G) Estimated Fair Profit, at 7-1/2%	(H) Total Airline Expenses (F) + (G)	(I) Total Cost to Public (A) – (H)
1931	16,943,606	8,814,438	661,083	9,475,521	7,468,085
1932	19,938,123	7,121,785	534,134	7,655,919	12,282,204
1933	19,400,265	4,320,111	324,008	4,644,119	14,756,146
1931–33	56,281,994	20,256,334	1,519,225	21,775,559	34,506,435

* Economics of Air Mail Transportation' Brookings Institution

Route Number	Contractor	Route	Mileage	Rate Per Mile ¢	Former Rate ¢
1	United Air Lines	Newark–Oakland	2720	38.00	42.65
2	T W A	Newark–Los Angeles	2609	24.00	44.00
3	Northwest Airlines	Fargo–Seattle	1286	28.80	45.00
4	American Airlines	Fort Worth–Los Angeles	1328	39.50	45.00
5	Eastern Air Lines	Newark–New Orleans	1305	19.00	44.33
6	Eastern Air Lines	Newark–Miami	1195	29.00	44.00
7	American Airlines	Newark–Chicago	794	39.50	44.00
8	Pacific Seaboard Airlines	Chicago–New Orleans	903	17.50	45.00
9	Braniff Airways	Chicago–Dallas	955	22.50	45.00
10	Eastern Air Lines	Chicago–Jacksonville	928	19.00	45.00
11	United Air Lines	Seattle–San Diego	1224	39.50	44.00
12	United Air Lines	Salt Lake City–Seattle	1029	39.50	44.33
13	General Air Lines	Salt Lake City–San Diego	778	24.00	45.00
14	Central Airlines	Washington–Detroit	457	23.80	44.00
15	Long & Harman Airlines	Amarillo–Brownsville	1125	19.75	45.00
16	Hanford's Tri-State Airlines	Chicago–Pembina	772	19.60	44.33
17	Wyoming Air Service	Cheyenne–Pueblo	201	35.00	44.33
18	American Airlines	Boston–Newark	201	33.33	44.00
19	Alfred Frank	Salt Lake City–Great Falls	517	39.00	45.00
20	Robertson Airplane Service	New Orleans–Houston	337	16.70	45.00
21	American Airlines	Boston–Cleveland	612	24.50	43.00
22	American Airlines	Cleveland–Nashville	470	14.87	43.00
23	American Airlines	Newark–Fort Worth	1460	13.00	43.00
24	Delta Air Lines	Charleston–Fort Worth	1087	24.80	43.00
25	American Airlines	Washington–Chicago	679	29.00	–
26	Hanford's Tri-State Airlines	St Paul–Omaha	902	18.90	–
27	National Airways	Boston–Burlington/Bangor	410	29.50	–
28	Wyoming Air Service	Billings–Cheyenne	405	28.50	–
29	Varney Speed Lines	Pueblo–El Paso	530	24.00	41.00
30	American Airlines	Chicago–Fort Worth	914	8.00	41.50
31	Franklin & Baker Airlines	Daytona Beach–St Petersburg	158	17.00	43.00
32	Pennsylvania Airlines	Detroit–Milwaukee	265	38.90	38.00

TABLE 11

U. S. AIRLINES, 1934

(In Alphabetical Order)

*	American Airlines (A A)	- Formerly American Airways (A A); reorganized 11 April, 1934 under new name
	Boston-Maine Airways	- Formerly Boston-Maine Airway; acquired National Airways, 1 March 1937; renamed Northeast Airlines (N E A) November 1940
	Bowen Air Lines	- Absorbed by Braniff Airways, 1935
*	Braniff Airways	- Acquired Long & Harman Airlines, 1 January 1935; Bowen Airways, 1935; Mid-Continent Airlines, August 1952
*	Central Airlines	- Merged with Pennsylvania Airlines, 1 November 1936
	Canadian Colonial Airways	- Formerly Colonial Division of American Airways; retained New York-Montreal route as Canadian Colonial; renamed Colonial Airlines, 1 May 1942; absorbed by Eastern Air Lines 1 June 1956
*	Delta Air Corporation	- Renamed Delta Air Lines (D A L).
*	Eastern Air Lines (E A L)	- Formerly Eastern Air Transport (E A T) reorganized 31 April 1934 under new name
*	General Air Lines	- Renamed Western Air Express (W A E) 29 December 1934 Renamed Western Air Lines(W A L) 17 April 1941
	Gorst Air Transport	
*	Hanford Airlines	- Formerly Hanford's Tri-State Airlines renamed Mid-Continent Airlines, August 1938; absorbed by Braniff Airways, August 1952
	Inter-Island Airways	- Renamed Hawaiian Airlines, 1 October 1941
	Kohler Aviation Corporation	- Absorbed by Pennsylvania Airlines, June 1934
*	Long & Harman Airlines	- Absorbed by Braniff Airways, 1 January 1935
*	National Airline System (Franklin & Baker, Inc)	- Renamed National Airlines
*	National Airways	- See Boston-Maine

*	National Parks Airways (Alfred Frank)	- Absorbed by Western Air Express 1 August 1937
*	Northwest Airlines (N W A)	- Formerly Northwest Airways (N W A); absorbed Northern Air Transport 1934
*	Pacific Seaboard Air Lines	- Formed in 1933 to carry passengers Los Angeles-San Francisco; successfully bid for Mississippi Valley route and renamed Chicago & Southern Air Lines (C & S), summer 1934; merged with Delta Air Lines 1 May 1953
*	Pennsylvania Airlines	- Subsidiary of P.A.I.C.; absorbed Kohler Aviation Corporation 1934; merged with Central Airlines, 1 November 1936 and joint airline named Pennsylvania-Central Airlines (P C A); renamed Capital Airlines, 21 April 1948; absorbed by United Air Lines, 1 June 1961
	Reed Airline	- Ceased operations June 1934
*	Robertson Airplane Service Company	- Absorbed by Wedell-Williams Air Service Corp. (see below)
*	Transcontinental & Western Air (T W A)	- Organized TWA Inc. on 17 April 1934 as operating subsidiary. Both corporations consolidated under former name in December 1934
*	United Air Lines (U A L)	- Reorganized 1934
	U.S. Airways	- Ceased operations June 1934
*	Varney Speed Lines	- Renamed Varney Air Transport 17 December 1934; Renamed Continental Air Lines (C.A.L.) 1 July 1937
	Wedell-Williams Air Service Corporation	- Absorbed by Eastern Air Lines, 1937
	Wilmington-Catalina Airline	- Continued operation of single route sold by Western Air Express, 1932; renamed Catalina Air Transport 22 July 1941; ceased operations 13 September 1955
*	Wyoming Air Service	- Renamed Inland Air Lines, 1 July 1938; absorbed by Western Airlines 23 May 1944; operated as antonomous division of Western until complete elimination of identity 9 April 1952

----

* New Domestic Air Mail Route Contractors

TABLE 12

SUMMARY OF U. S. DOMESTIC
AIRLINES 1934 - 1938

Date of First Service	Airline	Service	Routes	Initial Fleet	Remarks	Date of Last Service
31 May, 1934	Central Airlines	P	Washington-Pittsburgh-Cleveland-Detroit		Merged with Penn. Airlines on 1 Nov. 1936, to form Penn.-Central Airlines (P C A). Name changed to Capital Airlines 21 April, 1948	To **United Air Lines** 1 June 1961
1 June, 1934	Long & Harman Airlines	MPF	Amarillo-Dallas-Brownsville			To Braniff Airways 1 Jan. 1935
1934	Delta Air Lines	MPF	Fort Worth-Atlanta-Charleston	Travel Air		
15 July, 1934	Varney Speed Lines (S.W. Division)	MPF	Denver-Albuquerque-	Lockheed Vega	Became Varney Air Transport 17 Dec. 1934; changed name to Continental Air Lines 1 July, 1937	
Sept. 1934	Robertson Air Lines	MPF	Houston-New Orleans			Route taken over by Wedell-Williams
15 Oct. 1934	Franklin & Baker	MPF	St Petersburg-Daytona Beach	3 Ryan	Name changed to National Airline System 1934, then National Airlines	
Summer 1935	Grand Canyon Airlines	P	Winslow-Grand Canyon			
Aug. 1935	Watertown Airways	P	St Paul-Watertown-Pierre-Rapid City-Spearfish		Served Mount Rushmore	Early 1936
Sept. 1935	Columbia Airlines	P	Chicago-Detroit-Cincinnati-St Louis			March 1936

Date of First Service	Airline	Service	Routes	Initial Fleet	Remarks	Date of Last Service
Sept. 1935	Consolidated Airlines	P	Alameda-Sacramento	Fokker Super Universal		December 1936
Aug. 1936	Condor Air Lines	P	Alameda-Salinas			November 1936
Oct. 1936	Capital Airlines	P	Pocatello-Twin Falls-Boise	Beechcraft		April 1937
Nov. 1936	Keystone Airline	P	New York-Philadelphia	Sikorsky		Feb. 1937
Dec. 1936	Palm Springs Airlines	P	Los Angeles-Palm Springs			July 1937
2 Jan. 1937	Florida Airlines	P	Jacksonville-Tampa-Sarasota	Ford Tri-Motor		March 1937
Mar. 1937	Miami-Key West Airways	P	Miami-Key West	Commodore		July 1938
May 1937	Atlantic & Gulf Coast Airline	P	Savannah-Jacksonville	Stinson Tri-motor		August 1937
July 1937	Mayflower Airlines	P	Boston-Cape Cod Area-Nantucket			To Northeast 1944
4 Oct. 1937	Airline Feeder System	P	Springfield-Hartford-New Haven-Bridgeport-New York			October 1939
20 April, 1938	Marquette Airlines	PM	St Louis-Cincinnati-Detroit	Stinson Tri-motor		To TWA 5 Dec. 1941

UNITED STATES DOMESTIC AIRLINE FLEETS
1942

TABLE 13

Airline	Boeing 247D	Lockheed L.10 Electra	Lockheed L.18 Lodestar	Douglas DC-2	Douglas DC-3	Total
American Airlines					74	74
Braniff Airways				5	10	15
Chicago & Southern Air Lines					6	6
Colonial Airlines					4	4
Continental Air Lines			6			6
Delta Air Lines		4			5	9
Eastern Air Lines					39	39
Mid-Continent Airlines		5	4			9
National Airlines		2	3			5
Northeast Airlines		1			3	4
Northwest Airlines		4			10	14
Pennsylvania-Central Airlines (P C A)	2				16	18
Transcontinental & Western Air (T W A)				3	37	40
United Air Lines	13				49	62
Western Airlines/Inland Air Lines	10				7	17
Total	25	16	13	8	260	322

PAN AMERICAN ANCESTORS, ASSOCIATES, AND SUBSIDIARIES IN LATIN AMERICA 1927 – 1928

TABLE 14

Airline	Date Founded	Date Acquired by Pan American	Remarks	
A. Formation, 1927 – 1928				
Atlantic, Gulf and Caribbean Airways	11 Oct 27	28 June 28	Founded as Southeastern Air Lines July 1927, by Reed Chambers Group. Formerly Florida Airways, 1926	Aviation Corporation of the Americas
Pan American Airways	14 March 27	23 June 28	Montgomery Group	
Aviation Corporation of America	2 June 27	23 June 28	Trippe Group	
B. Latin American Expansion, 1928 – 1932				
West Indian Aerial Express	3 Dec 27	15 Dec 28	Dissolved 22 Dec 1928	
Peruvian Airways	4 Sept 28	16 Sept 28	Originally Huff-Daland Dusters, formed 1927	
Chilean Airways	21 Dec 28	31 Dec 28	'Paper' airline only. Dissolved 30 July 36	
Cia Mexicana de Aviacion (C M A)	20 Aug 24	23 Jan 29	Stockholding progressively reduced to nil in June 1968.	
Pan American Grace Airways (PANAGRA)	24 Jan 29	25 Jan 29	Formed jointly (50% each) with Grace Shipping Company. Sold to Braniff	
New York, Rio and Buenos Aires Line (NYRBA)	17 March 29	15 Sept 30	A subsidiary, NYRBA do Brasil, formed 22 Oct 29, became Panair do Brasil, 17 Oct 30. Stockholding progressively reduced to nil by 28 Sept 61	
Sociedad Colombo-Alemana de Transportes Aereos (SCADTA)	5 Dec 19	10 Feb 30– 10 Apr 31	Name changed to AVIANCA 8 June 1940 Stockholding progressively reduced from 84.4% to 38% by 1969.	
Uraba, Medellin and Central Airways (UMCA)	24 Aug 31	13 Apr 32	53.85%. Stockholding progressively increased to 100% by 2 Dec 1947. Dissolved 15 June 1961.	
Aerovias Centrales, S.A.	26 Feb 32	26 Feb 32	Formed as Corporation de Aeronautica de Transportes. (CAT), Spring 1929. Dissolved 18 Dec 1935.	
Cia Nacional Cubana de Aviacion, S. A.	8 Oct 29	6 May 32	Formerly Cia Nacional Cubana de Aviacion Curtiss. Name changed to Cia Cubana de Aviacion 1 Feb 44. Stockholding progressively reduced to nil by 23 July 1954	

PAN AMERICAN ASSOCIATES AND SUBSIDIARIES
ACQUIRED DURING PERIOD OF OCEAN CONQUEST

TABLE 15

Airline	Date Founded	Date Acquired by Pan American	Remarks
A. NORTH ATLANTIC			
New York Airways, Inc	8 July 27	27 June 28	Incorporated as Southern Air Lines Inc Sold to Eastern, 15 July 31
Boston-Maine Airways, Inc	20 July 31	27 June 28	Pan Am contracted to operate Service Boston-Bangor, Summer 1931
Pan American-Imperial Airways Company	14 May 30	14 May 30	Pan Am 50%; dissolved 11 June 40
B. PACIFIC			
Alaskan Airways Inc	1929	1 Sept 32	Formerly owned by American Airways
Pacific International Airways of Alaska, Inc	1931	15 Oct 32	Merged with Alaskan to form Pacific Alaska Airways Inc
Alaska Southern Airways Inc	1933	13 Nov 34	
China National Aviation Corporation (C N A C)	8 July 30	31 March 33	45% of stock held by North American Aviation Inc through China Airways Federal Inc. Pan Am bought latter. Dissolved 20 Dec 1945

PAN AMERICAN ASSOCIATES AND SUBSIDIARIES
FOUNDED IN CARIBBEAN REGION
1936 – 1944

TABLE 16

Airlines	Date Founded	Date Acquired by Pan American	Remarks
Panama Airways, Inc	7 Nov 36	7 Nov 36	Wholly-owned subsidiary. Dissolved 30 April 41
Aerovias de Guatemala, S. A	10 Oct 44	10 Oct 40	Pan Am 40%, reduced to 20%, then sold 30 Nov 45
Aeronaves de Mexico, S.A.	7 Nov 34	18 Dec 40	Pan Am 40%, progressively reduced to nil by 26 Dec 59
Aerovias Venezolanas, S.A (AVENSA)	13 May 43	14 July 43	Pan Am 30%
Bahamas Airways Ltd	1936	10 Dec 43	Pan Am 45%; sold 23 Oct 48
Cia Dominicana de Avacion, C. pro A. (C. D. A.)	26 Apr 44	26 Apr 44	Pan Am 40%; sold 26 July 57
Cia Panamena de Aviacion, S.A. (COPA)	21 June 44	30 Aug 44	Pan Am 40%; reduced to 33% 18 Sept 46; to 26% 31 Dec 1968
Servicio Aereo de Honduras, S.A. (SAHSA)	16 Nov 44	16 Nov 44	Pan Am 40%; reduced to 38% 5 April 57
Lineas Aereas de Nicaragua, S.A. (LANICA)	17 Nov 44	17 Nov 44	Pan Am 40%; reduced to 13% 14 Oct 57
Lineas Aereas Costarricenses, S.A. (LACSA)	17 Oct 44	17 Oct 44	Pan Am 40%; reduced to 34% by June 64

ACTIVE AIRLINES IN ALASKA, 1960

(In Alphabetical Order)

TABLE 17

Airline	Scheduled Service Started*	Area of Operations	Mergers and Acquisitions
Alaska Airlines	Approx 1932 17 Aug 1951	Local services in SW Alaska (most transferred to PNA and Wien in 1960) Trunk route Fairbanks–Seattle	Acquired Cordova 1 Feb 1968 Acquired Alaska Coastal 1 April 1968
Alaska Coastal Airlines	Approx 1935	Local services in SE Alaska	Acquired Alaska Island Airways 1954 merged with Ellis 1 April 1962 acquired by Alaska Airlines 1 April 1968
Cordova Airlines	Approx 1936	Local services in Cordova–Anchorage region	Acquired Christensen Air Service 3 March 1956 acquired by Alaska Airlines 1 Feb 1968
Ellis Air Lines	Approx 1936	Local services in SE Alaska	Merged with Alaska Coastal 1 April 1962
Kodiak Airways	6 Dec 1960	Local services on Kodiak Island	--
Northern Consolidated Airlines (NCA)	Approx 1945	Local services in SW Alaska south of Yukon and Tanana Rivers	Merged with Wien Air Alaska 1 April 1968
Pacific Northern Airlines (PNA)	Approx 1934 Oct 1951	Local Services in Southern Alaska Trunk route Anchorage–Seattle	Acquired by Western Airlines 1 October 1967
Reeve Aleutian Airways	April 1946	Local services SW of Anchorage and throughout Aleutian Islands	--
Western Alaska Airlines	27 Feb 1960	Local services in Bristol Bay area	--
Wien Alaska Airlines	1 July 1934	Local services throughout northern Alaska, north of Yukon and Tanana Rivers	Acquired Ferguson Airways 25 June 1949, Byers Airways 9 July 1956, changed name to Wien Air Alaska Feb 1966. merged with Northern Consolidated 1 April 1968

*The nature of airline activity in Alaska in the pioneer period of the early 1930s prevents precise interpretation of the term 'scheduled'

TABLE 18

DOMESTIC TRUNK INTERCHANGE ROUTES

1948 - 955

Service Started	Airlines	Route (Transfer point underlinec)	Service Terminated	Remarks
1 June, 1948	TWA - Delta	Detroit-Cincinnati-Atlanta	11 June, 1961	Terminated following Great Lakes-Southeast case route awards 1958
25 Sept. 1949	Delta - American	Atlanta-New Orleans-Dallas-California	11 June, 1961	Terminated with Southern Transcontinental route awards 1961
16 March,1951	Capital - National	Detroit-Cleveland-Pittsburgh-Washington-Miami	14 Dec. 1958	Terminated with Great Lakes-Southeast case route awards 1958
1 May, 1951	National - Delta - American	Miami-Tampa-New Orleans-Dallas-California	11 June, 1961	Terminated with Southern Transcontinental route awards 1961
26 July, 1951	Continental - American	Houston-San Antonio-El Paso-California	11 June, 1961	Terminated with Southern Transcontinental route awards 1961
1 Dec. 1951	Braniff - Eastern	Denver-Memphis-Miami	-	Cut back to Tulsa-Memphis-Atlanta 1964, amended to Okla/Ark cities
10 Jan. 1952	Eastern - Mid-Continent	Kansas City-St Louis-Miami	9 Sept. 1963	TWA granted direct service
1 Feb. 1952	Continental - Mid-Continent	Denver-Kansas City-St Louis	13 June, 1967	Frontier granted direct service
1 April, 1953	TWA - Delta - C&S	New York-Pittsburgh-Indianapolis-Houston	1 Feb. 1958	Terminated following award of New York route to Delta 1956
15 Sept. 1953	United - Continental	Seattle-Denver-Tulsa	1 July, 1967	Terminated when Braniff granted route to Seattle in 1966
27 Sept. 1953	United - Braniff	Seattle-Denver-Dallas-Houston	13 June, 1967	(see above)
15 Dec. 1955	Northwest - Eastern	St Paul-Chicago-Miami	6 Dec. 1958	Terminated with Great Lakes-Southeast case route awards 1958
14 Jan. 1955	Braniff - TWA	Houston-Dallas-Amarillo-California	1 March, 1956	Suspended after one year

UNITED STATES AIRLINE FLEETS AUTUMN 1958

TABLE 19

AIRLINE	BOEING 377	DOUGLAS[4] DC-3	DC-4	DC6, 6B	DC7/7B	DC7C	LOCKHEED Twins	L049/749	L1049	L1649	CONVAIR 2/3/440	MARTIN 2-0-2/4-0-4	CURTISS C-46	VICKERS VISCOUNT	OTHERS	TOTAL
TRUNKS[1]																
American				85	58						58					201
Braniff		22		10		6		2			31		2			73
Capital		18	12					11						58		99
Continental		13		5	4						9			15		46
Delta		12		7	21			4			28		5			77
Eastern				7	48			18	38		20	56				187
National				12	8		10		4		18					52
Northeast		11		10							6			9		36
Northwest	9		12	20		14										55
T W A			8					71	41	29		48			1	198
United				90	55						53					198
Western		2		24							6					32
	9	78	32	270	194	20	10	106	83	29	229	104	7	82	1	1254
FREIGHT																
AAXICO			1	1									35			37
Flying Tiger									13				9			22
Riddle			3										31			34
Seaboard & Western			3						10							13
	—	—	7	1	—	—	—	—	23	—	—	—	75	—	—	106
LOCAL SERVICES[2]																
Allegheny		15										8				23
Bonanza		10														10
Central		13														13
Frontier		15														15
Lake Central		10														10
Mohawk		8									11					19
North Central		31														31
Ozark		20														20
Pacific		11					1					8				20
Piedmont		21														21
Southern		13														13
Trans-Texas		20														20
West Coast		14														14
	—	201	—	—	—	—	1	—	—	—	11	16	—	—	—	229

INTERNATIONAL																
Pan-American[3]	23	4	23	48	7	26										131
Panagra		4	2	9	5											20
	23	8	25	57	12	26	—	—	—	—	—	—	—	—	—	151
ALASKA, HAWAII, PUERTO RICO																
Alaska		1	2	2									3		12	20
Alaska Coastal															17	17
Cordova		2											1		3	6
Ellis															13	13
Hawaiian		8		1							5					14
Pacific Northern		4	2					4							2	12
Reeve Aleutian		2	1										1		6	10
Caribair			3	3									2			8
Trans-Pacific (Aloha)		8														8
Wien Alaska		3											4		17	24
	—	28	8	6	—	—	—	4	—	—	5	—	11	—	70	132
HELICOPTER																
Chicago Helicopter															8	8
Los Angeles															7	7
New York															6	6
	—	—	—	—	—	—	—	—	—	—	—	—	—	—	21	21
OTHER CARRIERS OPERATING SCHEDULED ROUTES																
Apache															3	3
Avalon															7	7
Mackey		4	2												2	8
Pacific Southwest			4													4
Provincetown-Boston															4	4
TAG															4	4
Transocean			6					1	2						3	12
U.S. Overseas			9						2							11
	—	4	21	—	—	—	—	1	4	—	—	—	—	—	23	53
TOTAL U.S.A.	32	319	93	334	206	46	11	111	110	29	245	120	93	82	115	1946

Notes 1. Several United States Domestic Trunk operators, notably Northwest, T W A and Braniff, also operate International services
2. Initial deliveries of Fairchild F-27 began in Autumn 1958
3. Six Boeing 707-121s delivered during Autumn 1958
4. **Total** Douglas 998 (51% of United States total)

UNITED STATES DOMESTIC AIRLINE PARTICIPATION IN INTERNATIONAL ROUTES 1939 – 1949

(IN ALPHABETICAL ORDER)

TABLE 20

AIRLINE	ROUTE	DATE AWARDED	DATE OF FIRST SERVICE	REMARKS
AMERICAN AIRLINES	NEW YORK–TORONTO		24 JUNE 41	
	NORTH ATLANTIC ROUTE	10 FEB 42	20 JUNE 42	OPERATED BY AMERICAN EXPORT AIRLINES (AEA) AMERICAN ACQUIRED 62% STOCK 1 JUNE 45; NAME CHANGED TO AMERICAN OVERSEAS AIRLINES (A O A); SOLD TO PAN AM 25 SEPT 50
	DALLAS/EL PASO – MEXICO CITY	14 APR 42 17 MAY 46	3 SEPT 42 ——	TEMPORARY CERTIFICATE PERMANENT CERTIFICATE BUT SERVICES DELAYED PENDING BILATERAL NEGOTIATIONS.
BRANIFF AIRWAYS	NUEVO LOREDO – MEXICO CITY	LATE 43	4 APR 45	TEMPORARY AUTHORIZATION AS AEROVIAS BRANIFF, S.A. REVOKED 26 OCT 46
	HOUSTON – ARGENTINA AND BRAZIL, VIA S.A. PACIFIC COAST	22 MAY 46	4 JUNE 48	SERVICE DATE TO LIMA, FURTHER EXTENSIONS IN 49 – 50
CHICAGO & SOUTHERN AIR LINES	HOUSTON/NEW ORLEANS– HAVANA SAN JUAN, CARACAS	22 MAY 46	1 NOV 46	SERVICE DATE TO HAVANA, FURTHER EXTENSIONS 48
COLONIAL AIRLINES	NEW YORK–MONTREAL	(GRANDFATHER ROUTE)		
	NEW YORK–BERMUDA	22 MAY 46	1 AUG 47	
EASTERN AIR LINES	NEW ORLEANS– MEXICO CITY	17 MAY 46		SERVICES DELAYED PENDING BILATERAL NEGOTIATIONS, UNTIL 57
NATIONAL AIRLINES	MIAMI/TAMPA–HAVANA	22 MAY 46	15 DEC 46	
NORTHEAST AIRLINES	BOSTON–MONTREAL	(GRANDFATHER ROUTE)		
NORTHWEST AIRLINES	TRANS–PACIFIC ROUTE VIA ALASKA	20 JUNE 46	15 JULY 47	SEATTLE–ANCHORAGE SERVICE 1 SEPT 46
TRANSCONTINENTAL & WESTERN AIR (TWA)	NORTH ATLANTIC ROUTES INC. EXTENSIONS TO CHINA, VIA MIDDLE EAST	5 JULY 45	5 FEB 46	FIRST SERVICES TO EUROPE ONLY EXTENSION TO BOMBAY 1947
UNITED AIR LINES	SEATTLE–VANCOUVER	GRANDFATHER ROUTE		
	NOGALES–MEXICO CITY AND OTHER MEXICAN SERVICES	17 SEPT 46	OCT 46	THROUGH MEXICAN SUBSIDIARY, LAMSA; SOLD JULY 52

Airline	Date of Initial Interest	T W A Affiliation
TACA Airways, S.A (Panama)	5 October 1943	Company purchased substantial stock holding in association with other U.S. interests. T W A 's share equivalent to approximately 22% of outstanding stock. T W A interest reduced in February 1949, and subsequently withdrawn in 1951 when Waterman Steamship Company assumed control of TACA and set up new corporations (TACA owned Aerovias Brasil, British West Indies, and other small subsidiaries.)
Aerovias Brasil	5 October 1943	Acquired with TACA. T W A interest reduced to 9% on 11 January 1947 when TACA sold most of its stock to Brazilian investors. T W A interest severed completely by 1950.
British West Indies Airways (B W I A)	5 October 1943	Acquired with TACA. T W A interest reduced early in 1947 and finally sold to Trinidad Government when British interests bought substantial shareholding.
Philippine Air Lines (P A L)	August 1945	Colonel Soriano of P A L confirmed agreement made with T W A in 1944 for minority stockholding and cooperation. This amounted to 6% in 1952.
Hawaiian Airlines	May 1944	T W A purchased 20% stock. Sold in 1948.
Technical and Aeronautical Exploitation Company (T A E) (National Greek Airlines)	6 April 1946	T W A helped form airline, with 35% share of initial stock. Provided technical and supervisory assistance. Interest reduced to 15.4% in July 1951. Greek government took control of airline on 1 June 1955 and shares sold to Aristotle Onassis on 1 January 1957.

Continued overleaf

Airline	Date of Initial Interest	T W A Affiliation
Ethiopian Airlines	26 December 1945	T W A assisted in organizing airline by providing technical and management assistance. No financial interest but initially provided two board members. Agreement renewed in 1953 and T W A continues to provide main senior management and has close working relationship, including special arrangement for interline traffic.
Saudi Arabian Airlines	20 September 1946	T W A helped Saudi Arabian Government to organize airline. Provided technical and supervisory assistance but held no shareholding. Has managed company ever since.
Linee Aeree Italiane (L I A)	16 September 1946	Company formed with 40% T W A shareholding. Reduced to 30% in 1952; withdrawn on merger of L I A and Alitalia on 1 September 1957.
Iranian Airways	26 October 1946	Company formed with 10% T W A shareholding; 5-year management contract withdrawn in 1949 when Iranian Government re-organized airline.
Trans Mediterranean Airways (T M A)	4 August 1964 12 November 1966	1 - Organization of Engine Overhaul Shop. 2 - Technical Management Contract.

TABLE 22

UNITED STATES LOCAL SERVICE OPERATORS

(In order of date of first service under Local Service certificate)

Airline and Base	Date Founded	Date Certificated	Date First Service	Original Route and Area of Early Development	First Aircraft	Remarks
Pioneer Air Lines (Dallas)	Jan 39	5 Nov 43 re-issued Apr 45	1 Aug 45	Houston–Amarillo, via Abilene, Extensions to Dallas, Midland and Albuquerque, covering N. Texas and New Mexico	Lockheed 10A	Founded as Essair, Services suspended July 1939 because of objections from Braniff Airways. Airline renamed Nov 1943. DC–3 in 1946. Martin 2–0–2 June 1952, but suspended March 1943. Merged with Continental Airlines 1 April 55.
Empire Air Lines (Boise)	1 Apr 44	22 May 46	28 Sept 46	Pocatello–Boise–Coeur d'Alene Extensions to Seattle, Spokane and Portland	Boeing 247D	Founded as Zimmerly Air Lines. Began operations Boise–Lewiston 1 April 1944 with single-engined Cessnas Three Boeing 247Ds on 24 July 1945. Taken over by Empire Air Lines 1 March 1946. DC–3 on 10 March 1948. Absorbed by West Coast Airlines 4 Aug 1952.
● Monarch Air Lines (Denver)	Early 46	28 Mar 46	27 Nov 46	Denver–Durango–Grand Junction–Salt Lake City–Albuquerque.	DC–3	Acquired Challenger Air-lines Dec 49. Merged with Arizona Airways April 50. Became Frontier Air-lines 1 June 50.

● Airline still in existence 1971

Airline and Base	Date Founded	Date Certificated	Date First Service	Original Route and Area of Early Development	First Aircraft	Remarks
Southwest Airways	Early 41	22 May 46	2 Dec 46	San Francisco–Los Angeles – San Francisco–Medford	DC–3	Specialized in one-minute stops at minor stations, with built-in stairs etc. Martin 2-0-2 late 1952. Changed name to Pacific Air Lines on 6 March 58. Merged with Bonanza and West Coast to form Air West 17 April 68.
• West Coast Airlines (Seattle)	14 Mar 41	22 May 46	5 Dec 46	Seattle–Portland Portland–Medford	DC–3	Commuter ticketing Feb 1948. Absorbed Empire Air Lines 4 Aug 52. Merged with Bonanza and Pacific to form Air West 17 April 1968.
Florida Airways (Orlando)	Early 43	28 Mar 46	Jan 47	Orlando–Jacksonville–Orlando–Tallahassee	Beech D–18	Founded as Orlando Air-Lines. Operations terminated 29 Mar 49.
Challenger Airlines (Denver)	Early 46	29 Mar 46	5 May 47	Denver–Salt Lake City	DC–3	Founded as Summit Air-ways. Name changed Jan 47. Acquired by Monarch Air Lines Dec 49.
• Trans-Texas Airways (Houston)	14 Nov 44	12 May 47	11 Oct 47	Houston–San Antonio–Dallas–Houston–Extensions mainly in South Texas	DC–3	Founded as Aviation Enterprises. Name changed 21 June 47. Now Texas International Airlines

Airline and Base	Date Founded	Date Certificated	Date First Service	Original Route and Area of Early Development	First Aircraft	Remarks
• Piedmont Airlines (Winston-Salem)	1 Jan 48	4 Apr 47	20 Feb 48	Wilmington, N. C.–Cincinnati, Extensions throughout North Carolina, Virginia and Eastern Kentucky	DC-3	Company, a division of Piedmont Aviation, formed on 2 July 1940 as a charter and general aviation company.
• Wisconsin Central Airlines	15 May 44	19 Dec 46 re-issued 3 Oct 47	24 Feb 48	Large network of routes covering Wisconsin State and linking Twin Cities with Chicago	Lockheed 10A	DC-3 in 1951. Renamed North Central Airlines 16 Dec 1952
• Robinson Airlines (Ithaca)	6 Apr 45	20 Feb 48	19 Sept 48	Ithaca–New York Extensions throughout New York State	Fairchild F-24	Originally Airline Div. of Robinson Aviation. Began Intra-state passenger service on 6 April 1945 with Fairchild F-24. Services continued under Local Service Certificate. Named changed to Mohawk Airlines 23 Aug 1952.
• All American Airways (Washington)	5 Mar 37	11 Jan 49	7 Mar 49	Pittsburg–Washington extensions throughout Pennsylvania, Maryland, New Jersey to Buffalo New York, and Cincinnati	DC-3	Founded as All American Aviation. Began experimental mail pick-up service 13 Sept 38 over network of routes radiating from Pittsburgh. These routes permanently certificated 12 Aug. 1940. Operations begun 12 Aug 1940. Mail pick-up services ended June 1949. Name changed to Allegheny Airlines on I Jan 53.

Airline and Base	Date Founded	Date Certificated	Date First Service	Original Route and Area of Early Development	First Aircraft	Remarks
Purdue Aeronautics Corp. (Lafayette)	5 May 42	1949	1949	Lafayette–Chicago		Temporary certificate expired 30 JAN 50 on inauguration of service by Turner Airlines.
• Southern Airways (Atlanta	July 43	Apr 47 re-issued 8 Feb 49	10 June 49	Memphis–Atlanta Charlotte–Charleston S. C.–Jacksonville	DC–3	DC–3 late 1950. Merged with Frontier 1 October 1967.
Central Airlines (Fort Worth)	Mar 44	14 Nov 46	15 Sept 49	Fort Worth–Dallas–Wichita various routes mainly in Oklahoma State	Beech Bonanza	DC–3 late 1950. Merged with Frontier 1 October 1967.
E. W. Wiggins Airways (Norwood)	1930	13 June 46	19 Sept 49	Boston–Albany by four routes	Cessna T–50	Founded in 1930 as a fixed based operator. Operations terminated 1 Aug 53. Routes taken over by Mohawk and Northeast.
Turner Airlines (Indianapolis)		3 Sept 47 re-issued 8 Feb 48	12 Nov 49	Routes radiating from Indianapolis	Beech 18	Founded as Roscoe Turner Aeronautical Corp. Name changed 31 May 49 to Turner, then in Dec 50, to Lake Central Airlines Merged with Allegheny 1 July 1968.
Mid–West Airlines	1933	19 Dec 46	12 Nov 49	Omaha–Twin Cities–Huron	Cessna 190	Name changed 1949. Founded as Iowa Airplane Co. Acquired Nov 51 by Purdue Research Foundation but ceased operations 16 May 52.

Airline and Base	Date Founded	Date Certificated	Date First Service	Original Route and Area of Early Development	First Aircraft	Remarks
Bonanza Air Lines (Las Vegas)	31 Dec 45	15 June 49	19 Dec 49	Reno–Las Vegas–Phoenix. Later extensions to Los Angeles	DC–3	Originally charter operator. Started intra-state services 5 Aug 46. Las Vegas–Phoenix route transferred from T W A. Merged with West Coast and Pacific to form Air West 17 Apr 60.
•Ozark Air Lines (St. Louis)	1 Sept 43	July 50	26 Sept 50	Routes radiating from St. Louis–Chicago–Tulsa and Memphis	DC–3	Originally operated intra-state services from Springfield, Mo. Acquired most of routes awarded to Parks Air Transport.
(Mid-Continent Airlines) (Kansas City)	6 May 36	July 50	Sept 50	Sioux City–Chicago	DC–3	Mid-Continent was a Domestic Trunk operator which applied to acquire Parks Air Transport. C.A.B. refused, but awarded local service certificate to M C A on some routes, others to Ozark.
Air Commuting (New York)		7 May 47		New York Area		Never operated. Certificate cancelled 7 Nov 50.

Airline and Base	Date Founded	Date Certificated	Date First Service	Original Route and Area of Early Development	First Aircraft	Remarks
Yellow Cab Company of Cleveland (Cleveland)		3 Sept 47		Cleveland area		Never operated. Certificate cancelled 3 March 1951.
Parks Air Transport (East St. Louis)		Dec 47		Network in Missouri and Illinois states		Certificate cancelled 28 July 50. Routes taken over by Ozark Air Lines and Mid-Continent Airlines.
Arizona Airways (Phoenix)	Mar 46	13 Jan 48		Phoenix–El Paso		Routes only operated after merger with Frontier Airlines, see Monarch Air Lines
Island Air Ferries	19 Feb 48	19 Feb 48		New York–Long Island		Never operated.

TABLE 23

UNITED STATES FREIGHT AIRLINES
1946 – 1947
(In Order of First Service Date)

Airline (and base)	Date of First Service	Route Pattern	Remarks
Airborne Cargo	1945		Ceased operations 1947
Air Cargo Transport Corporation (Newark)	1945	Transcontinental	Ceased operations 1948
American Air Express	1945		Ceased operations 1947
Calasia Airlines	1945	Trans-Pacific	Ceased operations 1947
Flamingo Air Service Inc (Aron Park, Florida)	1945	Great Lakes Northeast–Florida	Ceased operations 1948
The Flying Tiger Line	July 1945	Transcontinental	Founded 25 June 1945 as National Skyway Freight Corporation. First fleet 14 Budd RB-1 Conestogas. (Full history in text)
Globe Freight Airline Inc. (Hartford)	1945	Northeast – Southeast	Ceased operations 1948
Lone Star Airline	1945		Ceased operations 1947
Mutual Aviation Inc	1945	New York–Buffalo	Ceased operations 1948
Trans-Air Hawaii Ltd (Honolulu)	1945	Local Hawaii	Ceased operations 1948
U.S. Airlines Inc (St Petersburg)	5 Dec 1945	Transcontinental, Southeast and Texas	Incorporated 9 June 1944, first scheduled operations in January 1946 with C-47s. Received first nonscheduled air carrier operating permit 10 October 1946 and first Letter of Registration 30 July 1947. (Full history in text)
Willis Air Service Inc (Teterboro, N.M.)	23 Dec. 1945	Transcontinental and Florida	Founded by C.E. Willis October 1945 with ex-NATS personnel. Known as The Commander Airline. Increased fleet from 1 C-47 to 5 C-47s and 2 C-54s, but suspended operations in 1949.

Continued overleaf

Airline (and base)	Date of First Service	Route Pattern	Remarks
Riddle Airlines Inc (Coral Gables, Fla)	1946	New York–Puerto Rico	Founded by John P. Riddle as commercial extension of wartime ferrying service to Brazil. Acquired route certificate of U.S. Airlines in 1951. Eventually became Airlift International. (Full history in text)
Slick Airways Inc (San Antonio)	4 March 1946	Transcontinental	Founded January 1946 by Earl F. Slick, former ATC pilot. First fleet 10 C–46E, purchased from Reconstruction Finance Corporation. Became largest freight operator before attempted merger with Flying Tigers.(full history in text)
Pacific Overseas Airlines Corporation (Ontario, Calif.)	18 March 1946	Trans–Pacific	Formed October 1945 as Industrial Air Transport by former key members of Consair Way Division of Consolidated Vultee Aircraft Corp. Operated 3 trans–Pacific daily services under United Air Lines subcontract, using 15 Army–owned C–54s. Other contracts worldwide, then became certified air repair station in September 1947.
California Eastern	May 1946	Transcontinental	Pioneered long–haul air freight service with 5 C–54 Freightmasters. Frequency increased to 4 coast–to–coast flights daily, but ceased operations in May 1948 and equipment sold to Slick Airways.
Seaboard & Western	10 May 1947	Trans–Atlantic	Organized 16 September 1946. Began operations to Luxembourg with 1 C–54. Eventually became certificated international scheduled cargo operator. (Full history in text)
Aerovias Sud Americana	17 Oct 1947	Caribbean area	Founded Summer 1947 by group of ex–U.S. Airlines employees. Certificated as large Irregular Carrier (full history in text)

THE 15 SUPPLEMENTAL CARRIERS 1962

TABLE 24

(LISTED ALPHABETICALLY, EXCEPT THE LAST TWO, NOW DEFUNCT)

AIRLINE	BRIEF HISTORY	OVERSEAS OPERATING AUTHORITY
AMERICAN FLYERS AIRLINE CORPORATION (ARDMORE, OK.)	FORMED 1949 BY REED PIGMAN; BOUGHT BY PITTSBURGH COKE & CHEMICAL CO., 1968, AND BASE MOVED TO HARRISBURG, PA., 1969. OPERATED ELECTRAS 1966, B-727 1968, DC-6-63 1969. BOUGHT BY UNIVERSAL, 4 JUNE 1971.	TRANSATLANTIC 5 APRIL 1966 CARIBBEAN & MEXICO 30 SEPTEMBER 1965
CAPITOL INTERNATIONAL AIRWAYS INC. (NASHVILLE)	FOUNDED 11 JUNE 1946 BY JESSE STALLINGS AS CAPITOL AIRWAYS; CHANGED NAME 22 MARCH 1967 AND BECAME PUBLIC COMPANY; VIGOROUS PROMOTION IN EUROPEAN CHARTERS. BEGAN WITH LARGE C-46 FLEET, THEN CONSTELLATIONS, AND INTRODUCED DC-8S IN 1964, DC-10S IN 1981. CHANGED NAME TO CAPITOL AIR ON 6 JANUARY 1982.	TRANSALTLANTIC 24 FEBRUARY 1964 CARIBBEAN 30 SEPTEMBER 1966
JOHNSON FLYING SERVICE (MISSOULA, MONTANA)	INCORPORATED 6 MARCH 1929 BY BOB JOHNSON; BECAME EXPERT IN FOREST FIRE CONTROL WITH VERSATILE FLEET SPECIALIZING IN FIRE-FIGHTING DEVICES; STILL OWNED FORD TRI-MOTOR AND OPERATED DC-2 IN 1970. BECAME EVERGREEN INTERNATIONAL AIRLINES ON 28 NOVEMBER 1975 WHEN CERTIFICATE ACQUIRED BY EVERGREEN HELICOPTERS, INC., IN OREGON.	CANADA 26 NOVEMBER 1966
MODERN AIR TRANSPORT (MIAMI)	INCORPORATED IN 1946 AT HEMPSTEAD, LONG ISLAND; ACQUIRED BY GULF AMERICAN LAND CORPORATION 1966; BOUGHT 5 CV-990 FROM AMERICAN AIRLINES JANUARY 1967. TRANSFERRED ALL OPERATIONS TO W. BERLIN, GERMANY, 1972. AIRLINE GRADUALLY DISBANDED DURING THE LAST QUARTER OF 1975.	CANADA, MEXICO 30 SEPTEMBER 1966
OVERSEAS NATIONAL AIRWAYS (ONA) (NEW YORK)	FORMED JUNE 1950 BY GEORGE TOMPKINS; LARGE AIR FORCE CONTRACTS, USING DOUGLAS DC-6/7S UNTIL OPERATIONS SUSPENDED 29 OCTOBER 1963 THROUGH UNECONOMICAL PRICE SETTING. RESUMED SERVICE 4 OCTOBER 1965 AFTER RE-FINANCING BY GROUP HEADED BY STEADMAN HINKLEY. PUBLIC CORPORATION 28 JUNE 1967; DC-8S JUNE 1966, DC-10S MAY 1973. CERTIFICATE WITHDRAWN 19 MAY 1982. COMPANY DISSOLVED 7 SEPTEMBER 1978.	TRANSATLANTIC 5 APRIL 1966 CARIBBEAN 30 SEPTEMBER 1966
PURDUE AERONAUTICS CORPORATION (LAFAYETTE)	FORMED 12 MAY 1942 AS AFFILIATE OF PURDUE UNIVERSITY; ACTIVITIES IN SUPPORT OF SCHOOL OF AVIATION TECHNOLOGY; OPERATED TEMPORARY LOCAL SERVICE TO CHICAGO 1949. STEPHENS INC. BOUGHT MAJORITY SHAREHOLDING 23 FEBRUARY 1968. SUSPENDED OPERATIONS, 1 MAY 1971.	CANADA 30 SEPTEMBER 1966
SATURN AIRWAYS INC. (OAKLAND)	FOUNDED IN MIAMI IN 1948 AS ALL AMERICAN AIRWAYS INC; MERGED WITH AAXICO AIRLINES 1 NOVEMBER 1965; HOWARD KORTH OF AAXICO TOOK CONTROL; PUBLIC CORPORATION EARLY 1967; DC-8S INTRODUCED 1967. BECAME CARGO SPECIALISTS, OPERATING LOCKHEED L-100S. ACQUIRED BY TIA (NOW TRANSAMERICA) ON 30 NOVEMBER 1976.	TRANSATLANTIC 24 FEBRUARY 1964 CARIBBEAN 30 SEPTEMBER 1966
SOUTHERN AIR TRANSPORT (MIAMI)	FOUNDED 1946; SPECIALIZES IN CARRIAGE OF LIVESTOCK; MILITARY CONTRACT OPERATIONS BASED IN OKINAWA. CERTIFICATE REVOKED ON 28 DECEMBER 1982, BUT PREVIOUSLY ACQUIRED AUTHORITY ON 1 OCTOBER 1962 FOR MILITARY CONTRACTS.	CARIBBEAN, PACIFIC 30 SEPTEMBER 1966

continued overleaf

STANDARD AIRWAYS (SEATTLE)	FOUNDED 1946 AS STANDARD AIR CARGO; SUSPENDED OPERATIONS 31 JANUARY 1964. RESUMED 17 JULY 1966 UNDER DIRECTION OF FRANK B. LYNOTT, USING EX-QANTAS B-707-138S. CEASED OPERATIONS, 24 SEPTEMBER 1969.	CANADA, MEXICO 15 DECEMBER 1966
TRANS INTERNATIONAL AIRLINES (TIA) (OAKLAND)	FORMED ON 20 DECEMBER 1948 AS LOS ANGELES AIR SERVICE; CAB CERTIFICATE 8 JULY 1949; NAME CHANGED 18 JULY 1960 TO AVOID CONFUSION WITH LOS ANGELES AIRWAYS; CEASED INDIVIDUAL TICKETING OCTOBER 1961. FIRST SUPPLEMENTAL JET OPERATOR, ON DELIVERY OF DC-8-51 ON 22 JUNE 1962; PURCHASED BY STUDEBAKER CORPORATION OCTOBER 1962; THEN BY KIRK KERKORIAN SEPTEMBER 1964; PUBLIC CORPORATION 28 JUNE 1967; TRANSAMERICA CORPORATION ACQUIRED CONTROL 23 FEBRUARY 1968; DC-10S INTO SERVICE 27 APRIL 1973; CHANGED NAME TO TRANSAMERICA ON 1 OCTOBER 1979. BOEING 747 SERVICE IN DECEMBER 1979. BEGAN SCHEDULED SERVICES IN NOVEMBER 1979.	TRANSATLANTIC 5 APRIL 1966 PACIFIC AND LATIN AMERICA 30 SEPTEMBER 1966
UNIVERSAL AIRLINES INC. (DETROIT)	FOUNDED AS ZANTOP AIR TRANSPORT BY ZANTOP BROTHERS ON 6 JULY 1956; TOOK OVER CERTIFICATE OF COASTAL CARGO COMPANY, INC. (FOUNDED 1947) ON 9 MAY 1962. SPECIALIZES IN SHIPMENT OF AUTO PARTS FROM DETROIT TO ASSEMBLY PLANTS THROUGHOUT USA; FORMERLY LARGE C-46 OPERATOR, THEN AW ARGOSIES; SOLD AS WHOLLY-OWNED SUBSIDIARY TO UNIVERSAL AIR-LINES COMPANY ON 21 SEPTEMBER 1966; ACQUIRED DC-6-61S IN 1968 AND BECAME PUBLIC CORPORATION. BOUGHT AMERICAN FLYERS AIRLINE, 4 JUNE 1971. CEASED OPERATIONS ON 4 MAY 1972. ZANTOP CONTINUED AS A CONTRACT CARRIER AND OBTAINED A SUPPLEMENTAL CERTIFICATE ON 15 SEPTEMBER 1981.	CANADA, MEXICO 30 SEPTEMBER 1966
VANCE INTERNATIONAL AIRWAYS (SEATTLE)	FOUNDED 1949 AS VANCE AIRWAYS BY VANCE ROBERTS; AIR TAXI EXEMPTION 19 DECEMBER 1962. BECAME MCCULLOCH INTERNATIONAL AIR-LINES (LONG BEACH, CALIFORNIA) IN 1971, WHEN MCCULLOCH BOUGHT AIRLINE FROM ROBERTS. AIRLINE CEASED OPERATIONS IN 1979.	CANADA, MEXICO 15 DECEMBER 1966
WORLD AIRWAYS (OAKLAND)	INCORPORATED 29 MARCH 1948; BOUGHT BY EDWARD J. DALY IN 1950; INTERIM CERTIFICATE 15 NOVEMBER 1955; WON LOGAIR TRANSCON-TINENTAL CONTRACT 15 JUNE 1960. ORDERED B-707-320C MAY 1962. PUBLIC CORPORATION 18 APRIL 1966. DC-8-63S IN 1971, B-747S IN 1973, DC-10S IN 1978. BEGAN SCHEDULED SERVICES ON 11 APRIL 1979.	TRANSATLANTIC 5 APRIL 1966 PACIFIC AND LATIN AMERICA 30 SEPTEMBER 1966
AAXICO AIRLINES INC. (MIAMI)	FOUNDED 1945 AS AMERICAN AIR EXPORT & IMPORT COMPANY; SCHEDULED CARGO OPERATIONS NEW YORK-ATLANTA 15 NOVEMBER 1956. ADOPTED NEW NAME 31 DECEMBER 1956; LARGE C-46 OPERATOR; MERGED WITH SATURN 1 NOVEMBER 1965 (SEE ABOVE).	
UNITED STATES OVERSEAS AIRLINES (USOA) (CAPE MAY, N.J.)	FOUNDED 1946; INTERNATIONAL CERTIFICATE AS IRREGULAR CARRIER 1 JANUARY 1956; TOOK OVER OPERATIONS OF TRANSOCEAN AIR LINES 11 JULY 1960. CEASED OPERATIONS 30 NOVEMBER 1964.	

NOTE: ALL 15 CARRIERS (PLUS 8 OTHERS) AWARDED INTERIM INTERSTATE CERTIFICATES, 29 JANUARY 1959: ALL EXCEPT AAXICO AND U.S.O.A. AWARDED PERMANENT DOMESTIC (INCLUDING HAWAII) CERTIFICATES 14 MARCH 1966.

SPECIAL NOTE ON TABLE 25 A AND B (THIRD LEVEL CARRIERS)

The Third Level, Scheduled Air Taxi, or Commuter Airline industry (the last term is now popularly accepted) has been one of phenomenal growth since the mid-1960s. As noted on page 494, airline numbers in this category have grown from 12 in 1964 to an average of 180 immediately prior to deregulation, and are estimated to be 270 in 1981.

To record the history of all but a few individual companies, which merit inclusion because of their pioneering role, would be impossible in a book of this size. Indeed, an entire book on the U.S. Commuter airlines will no doubt be written as they mature towards two decades of vigorous existence. The leaders of the industry deserve to be recognized, however, and this is done in Table 25a by ranking in two ways the top twenty commuter airlines in selected years. Because of the inadequacies of statistical reporting, the lists for 1968–76 are based on F.A.A. reports of aircraft fleets, but the tabulation for 1981 is based on published traffic results.

Table 25b is a chronological listing of the earlier Commuter airlines, up until the end of 1967. Although a substantial percentage of these airlines no longer exist, the list contains all the pioneers in this category of airline, and it is satisfactory to record that many of the same names are still to be found among the higher ranks today.

The compilation was made from many sources, including published data (either in aviation periodicals or in government agency reports), personal correspondence, and extensive interviewing. Following the format adopted throughout this book, the carriers have been listed in chronological order according to the start of scheduled services, as far as can be ascertained.

Some discrimination has been applied to the selection. Although there are records for air taxi operators which conducted quasi-scheduled services on an experimental basis, many of these were short-lived. A qualification period of one complete year's continuous scheduled operations has therefore been applied as a requirement for inclusion in the table (25 a and b).

The brief descriptions of route network and aircraft fleet are not intended to be exhaustive. With the continuously changing nature of commuter operations, routes and fleets are seldom the same from one year to another. The intention is simply to indicate the main area of airline activity and the aircraft types commonly used during the formative years of the Commuter airline industry.

20 LEADING SCHEDULED AIR TAXI (COMMUTER) OPERATORS
RANKED BY FLEET NUMBERS, 1968-1976

RANK	1968		1970		1972		1974		1976	
1	Sun Airlines	23	S-M-B Stage Lines	40	S-M-B Stage Lines	43	S-M-B Stage Lines	47	S-M-B Stage Lines	46
2	Cable Flying Serv.	20	Ross Aviation	29	Buckeye Air Serv.	34	Federal Express	32	Skyway Aviation	45
3	Commuter (Chicago)	20	Executive Airlines	27	Golden West	20	Air New England	19	Great Western	34
4	Horizon Aviation	20	Golden West	25	Prinair	18	Cumberland Airlines	17	Federal Express	29
5	Catalina Airlines	16	Keystone Aero.	15	Hankins Airways	16	Hankins Airways	17	Prinair	22
6	Provincetown-Boston	14	Suburban Airlines	14	Keystone Commuter	16	North Cay Airways	17	Provincetown-Boston	20
7	Midwest Aviation	13	Provincetown-Boston	14	Capital Airlines	15	Provincetown-Boston	16	Capital Air Service	16
8	Newport Airpark	13	Skyway Aviation	14	North Cay Airways	15	Skyway Aviation	15	Corporate Air	16
9	Buker Airways	12	Prinair	14	Provincetown-Boston	14	Antilles Air Boat	14	Scenic Airlines	16
10	Florida Air Taxi	12	Hub Airlines	13	Skyway Aviation	13	Capital Air Serv.	14	Combs Airways	15
11	Prinair	11	Monarch Airlines	12	Mackey Int'l	12	Commuter (B'h'pton)	13	Polar Airways	15
12	Richmond Aviation	11	Mackey Int'l	12	Air New England	12	Gross Aviation	13	Antilles Air Boat	14
13	Viking Airways	11	Air San Juan	12	Shawnee Airlines	11	Mackey Int'l	13	Commuter (B'h'pton)	13
14	Cape and Island	10	Buckeye Air Serv.	10	Antilles Air Boat	11	Trican Int'l	12	Florida Airlines	13
15	Commuter (B'h'pton)	10	Commuter (B'h'pton)	10	Commuter (B'h'pton)	11	Apollo Airways	11	Altair Airlines	13
16	Royal Hawaiian A.S.	10	Wright Airlines	10	Executive Air Trvl	11	Sun Valley Key	11	Golden West	12
17	Safeway Airways	10	Air Midwest	9	Nicholson Air	10	Altair Airlines	10	L.A.B. Flying Serv.	11
18	Wright Airlines	10	Combs Airways	9	Altair Airlines	10	Coast Air	10	Royal Hawaiian	11
19	Carco Air Services	9	Royal Hawaiian A.S.	9	Scenic Airlines	9	Hamilton Aviation	10	Air South	10
20	Combs Airways	9	Shawnee Airlines	9	Apollo Airways	9	Royal Hawaiian A.S.	10	Dorado Wings	10

COMMUTER AIRLINES 1981
THE TOP TWENTY AIRLINES RANKED BY TRAFFIC VOLUME

RANK	AIRLINE	PASSENGERS CARRIED	AIRLINE	PASSENGER-MILES MILLIONS	AVERAGE TRIP LENGTH (MILES)
1	Ransome Airlines	730,908	*Altair Airlines	135.0	337
2	*Air Wisconsin	705,265	*Air Wisconsin	108.9	154
3	Prinair	658,475	Ransome Airlines	91.4	125
4	*Golden West	651,143	*Empire Airlines	90.9	222
5	Metro Airlines	609,071	*Golden West	69.3	106
6	Henson Aviation	495,945	Metro Airlines	66.1	108
7	Provincetown-Boston	479,802	Henson Aviation	62.4	126
8	*Empire Airlines	409,056	Prinair	62.1	94
9	*Altair Airlines	400,878	*Air Midwest	56.7	200
10	Pennsylvania Airlines	370,374	Provincetown-Boston	56.3	117
11	*Mississippi Valley	352,784	*Mississippi Valley	54.9	156
12	*Air Midwest	283,874	Cape Smythe Air	45.5	193
13	Suburban Airlines	257,782	Pennsylvania Airlines	42.3	114
14	*Aspen Airways	246.000	Scheduled Skyways	37.7	221
15	Cape Smythe Air	235,268	Inland Empire	35.3	73
16	Bar Harbor	225,670	Air Oregon	30.7	190
17	Pilgrim Airlines	219,372	Pilgrim Airlines	30.0	137
18	Aero Mech Airlines	191,148	Scenic Airlines	29.8	181
19	Imperial Airlines	189,910	Air Illinois	28.7	157
20	Air Illinois	182,806	Royale Airlines	26.9	147

Notes: Airlines underlined founded before 1968. *Classified by C.A.B. as Regionals.

TABLE 25B

THIRD LEVEL AIRLINES

(Listed chronologically by date of FAA certification, or de facto start of scheduled service, if earlier)

Date	Airline	Base	Route Network	Aircraft	Remarks
47	Island Air Lines	Port Clinton, Ohio	Port Clinton-Bass Islands	3 Ford Tri-Motor	Founded by Ralph Dietrick at Sandusky as Sky Tours. Took over Air Tours, Inc , in 1953, and moved to Port Clinton, 1961
Aug 47	Reading Aviation Service	Reading, Pa.	Reading-Allentown-Philadelphia and New York	Beech 18, DH Dove	Merged with Air Taxi Company (Red Bank) 29 July, 1968, to form Suburban Airlines. Agreement with Eastern 13 Aug 1969
21 Nov 47	Chalk's Flying Service	Miami, Fla.	Miami-Bimini, Nassau, etc.	Grumman (flying boat)	Founded by Arthur Chalk as charter service in the 1920s
48	Carco Air Service	Albuquerque, N. M.	Albuquerque-Los Alamos	Beech Twin Bonanza	Certificated July 1964
Apr 51	Cape & Islands Flight Service	Hyannis, Mass.	Hyannis-Nantucket	Beech 18	Founded by George Parmenter. Agreement with NEA, 16 June, 1969, for local routes
51	G.C.S. Air Service (Galion Commuter Service)	Galion, Ohio	Galion-Marion-Mansfield-Cleveland	Piper Aztecs	Founded by Fischer Brothers Aviation. Agreement with Allegheny 1969
27 Aug 53	Avalon Air Transport	Long Beach, California	Long Beach-Catalina Island	Grumman Goose (amphibian)	Took over service from United Air Lines; operated Sikorsky VS-44 1957-1967; changed name to Catalina Airlines 1963; linked with Aero Commuter 1968, which became Golden West 1969
1 Sep 53	Fayetteville Flying Service	Fayetteville, Arkansas	Fayetteville-Little Rock	Various Piper and Cessna	Also known as Scheduled Skyways
27 Nov 53	Provincetown-Boston Airline	Provincetown, Massachusetts	Provincetown-Boston	Lockheed 10A and various small types	Founded Feb. 1946 as Cape Cod Flying Service by John van Arsdale. Founded subsidiary in Naples, Florida, 1 Jan 60

Date	Airline	Base	Route Network	Aircraft	Remarks
1 May 55	Catalina Air Lines	Long Beach, California	Long Beach-Catalina Island	DC-3, DH Dove	Ceased operations 1 Nov, 1959 (Note: different company from Avalon, founded 27 Aug,1953)
55	Command Airways	Poughkeepsie, New York	New York airports-Poughkeepsie	Beech 18 s, various small types	Founded as Mid-Hudson Airline in 1951
Jun 56	Holiday Airlines	Oakland, California	Oakland-Lake Tahoe, etc.	DH Dove	Has also operated four-engined equipment under special exemption from California P.U.C.
12 Nov 57	Apache Airlines	Phoenix, Arizona	Phoenix-Tucson, Lake Havasu, Las Vegas, Show Low, etc.	DH Dove DH Heron	Arranged first route replacement of certificated airline (American, Douglas-Tucson) 21 Sept, 1964
1 Oct 58	TAG Airlines (Taxi Air Group)	Detroit, Michigan	Detroit-Cleveland	DH Dove DH Heron Piper Aztec	Subsidiary of Miller Oil Company
2 Dec 58	Aeroflex Corporation	Andover, New Jersey	Andover-New York	Beech	Ceased operations 1968
26 Dec 58	Catalina Seaplanes	San Pedro, California	San Pedro-Catalina Island	Grumman Goose	Started as Catalina Channel Airlines at Long Beach; moved to San Pedro 1965
12 May 59	Air Transit	Show Low, Arizona	Show Low-Phoenix and local	Beech types	Ceased operations 1968
15 Jun 59	Trade Winds Airways	San Juan, Puerto Rico	San Juan-St Thomas-St. Croix, etc.	Various small types	Acquired Western Airways, 1968
1 Jan 60	Naples Airlines	Naples, Florida	Naples-Miami, Tampa-Fort Myers	Lockheed 10A	Subsidiary of Provincetown-Boston (27 Nov, 1953)
14 Mar 60	Des Moines Flying Service	Des Moines, Iowa	Local services	Piper types	

Date	Airline	Base	Route Network	Aircraft	Remarks
18 Mar 60	Skyway Aviation	Fort Leonard Wood, Mo.	Fort Leonard Wood-St Louis	Piper	Semi-scheduled until 1968
May 60	Princeton Aviation Corp.	Princeton, New Jersey	Princeton-New York	Various small types	Participated in Metro Air Service, in association with American Airlines, September 1965
6 July 60	American Air Taxi	Miami, Florida	Miami-Key West	Piper Aztecs, etc.	Operates as Key West Airlines
8 Dec 60	Air Taxi Company	Red Bank, New Jersey	Red Bank-New York	Various small types	September 1965 was part of Metro Air Service, in association with American Airlines. Merged with Reading Aviation on 29 July 68 to form Suburban Airlines
Jun 61	Executive Airlines	Boston, Massachusetts	Boston-Martha's Vineyard, Nantucket and many points in New England states	Aero Commander	Founded by Joseph Whitney in 1959 as National Executive Flight Service. Founded subsidiary at Sarasota, Florida, 1 Dec 1964. Agreement with NEA, 1969
19 Mar 62	Yankee Airlines	Pittsfield, Massachusetts	Pittsfield, Mass.	DH Dove	Division of Grey Lock Airways
28 Mar 62	Mac-Aire Aviation Corp	Ronkonkoma, New York	East Hampton, Islip, Bridgeport, New Haven-New York	Various small types	Participated in Metro Air Service, in association with American Airlines, Sep 1965; ceased operations 1968
Jul 62	Pocono Airlines	Mt. Pocono, Pennsylvania	Mt Pocono-New York	Beech 18	Became Allegheny Commuter in 1968, under associate agreement with Allegheny Airlines
16 Aug 62	Pilgrim Airlines	New London, Connecticut	New London-New York	Beech 18, later Twin Otter	Founded by Joe Fugere. Began Twin Otter service November 1966
25 Sep 62	Southeast Airlines	Miami, Florida	Miami-Cape Kennedy-Orlando and Key West	Beech 18, Fairchild F-27	Agreement with National to serve Marathon/Key West

Date	Airline	Base	Route Network	Aircraft	Remarks
12 Nov 62	Hulman Field Aviation	Terre Haute, Indiana	Terre Haute-Indianapolis, Chicago	Cessna types	Changed name to Hulman Airlines 1968
May 63	General Aviation Service	Allentown, Pennsylvania	Reading-Allentown-Baltimore	Beech 18	
10 May 63	Virgin Islands Airways	St Croix, Virgin Islands	St Croix-St Thomas-San Juan	Aero Commander	Ceased operations 1968
14 Jul 63	Montauk-Caribbean Airways	Montauk, New York	Montauk-New York, and to islands in Long Island Sound	Various small types	
6 Aug 63	Altus Airlines	Altus, Oklahoma	Local services in southwest Oklahoma	Cessna types	Founded as Altair; changed name 1967
Aug 63	Nevada Airlines	Hollywood, California	Long Beach-Burbank-Hawthorne	DC-3	Successor to Blatz Airlines, a large irregular carrier; ceased operations Dec 1963; succeeded by Hawthorne-Nevada Airlines, Jan 1964
23 Oct 63	Antilles Air Boats	St Croix, V.I.	Local services throughout U.S. and British Virgin Islands	Grumman Goose and Sikorsky VS-44	Started VS-44 service in January 1968
12 Nov 63	East Coast Air Taxi	Washington, D.C.	Washington - Ocean City-Wallops Station, etc.	Various small types	Operates as East Coast Commuter
Jan 64	Hawthorne-Nevada Airlines	Burbank, Ca.	Long Beach-Burbank-Hawthorne	DC-3	Successor to Nevada Airlines; registered as Mineral County Airlines.

Date	Airline	Base	Route Network	Aircraft	Remarks
2 Feb 64	Crowther Flight Center (Bremerton Air Taxi)	Bremerton, Wash.	Bremerton - Seattle	Piper types	Became part of Puget Sound Airlines, 28 August, 1967
17 Feb 64	Mid-State Air Commuter	Marshfield, Wis.	Marshfield - Chicago	Beech 18	Registered as Marshfield Airways
27 Apr 64	Hood Airlines	Killeen, Texas	Killeen - Dallas and Houston	Beech 99 and various small types	Merged with DAL Airlines, 23 May, 68
11 May 64	Empire State Airlines	Syracuse, N.Y.	Syracuse - Ithaca - Elmira - Binghampton	Beech 18	Founded as Flight Service 1953; used Learjet from 28 March, 66 on experimental basis
4 Jul 64	Puerto Rico International Airlines (Prinair)	San Juan, P.R.	San Juan - Ponce, Mayaguez, St Croix, St Thomas	DH Heron	Founded as Ponce Air and changed name in 1965
1 Sep 64	Tennessee Airmotive	Chattanooga, Tenn.	Chattanooga - Nashville	Piper Aztec	
8 Sep 64	Angeles Flying Service	Port Angeles, Wash.	Port Angeles - Seattle	Various small types	Became part of Puget Sound Airlines, 28 August, 1967
15 Sep 64	Southern Aviation	Lawton, Ok.	Lawton - Ardmore - Dallas	Cessna types	
16 Sep 64	Mid-States Aviation Corp.	Chicago, Illinois	Local services around Chicago	Cessna types	
18 Sep 64	Thunderbird Airlines	Ogden, Utah	Ogden - Salt Lake City, Logan	Various small types	Established as division of Thunderbird Flying Services; changed name to Key Airlines, 1 Jan. 69
24 Sep 64	Bellingham - Seattle Airways	Bellingham, Wash.	Bellingham - Seattle	Beech and Piper types	Became part of Puget Sound Airlines, 28 August, 1967

Date	Airline	Base	Route Network	Aircraft	Remarks
24 Sep 64	Island Sky Ferries	Friday Harbor, Wash.	Friday Harbor - Seattle	Cessna types	Became part of Puget Sound Airlines, 28 August, 1967
1 Oct 64	Swift Air Service	San Diego, California	San Diego - Catalina I. and Las Vegas	Various small types	
1 Oct 64	Hagerstown Commuter	Hagerstown, Md.	Hagerstown - Washington	Beech 18 and various small types	Started by R. A. Henson as division of Henson Aviation; became Allegheny Commuter, August 67, under associate agreement with Allegheny Airlines
10 Oct 64	Coastal Aviation	Orlando, Florida	Orlando - Tallahassee, Tampa, Nassau	Grumman	
10 Oct 64	Imperial Commuter Airlines	El Centro, Calif.	El Centro - San Diego	Various Beech types	Founded as Visco Flying Co.; changed name 30 August, 67
12 Oct 64	Commuter Airlines	Binghamton, N. Y.	Binghamton - Washington	DH Dove, Piper etc.	
15 Oct 64	Hub Air Service	McGrath, Alaska	McGrath - Tatalina	Various small types	
20 Oct 64	Air General	Boston, Mass.	Local services in Boston metropolitan area	Bell helicopters	Began services as Massachusetts Helicopter Airlines
28 Oct 64	Vercoa Air Service	Danville, Illinois	Danville - Chicago	Beech and Aero Commander	Became Allegheny Commuter Service 20 Sept. 1968
30 Oct 64	Florida Air Taxi	Tampa, Florida	Tampa - Fort Myers-Gainesville	Beech and Pipers	
5 Nov 64	Trans East Airlines	New York City	Manchester, N.H. - New York	DH Dove, Twin Otter	Founded as Statewide Airlines; changed name 1967
9 Nov 64	Safeway Airlines	Anchorage, Alaska	Services around Anchorage	Piper types	

Date	Airline	Base	Route Network	Aircraft	Remarks
9 Nov 64	Alpena Flying Service	Alpena, Michigan	Alpena - Detroit	Beech 18, etc.	Operates as Detroit Northern Air Service
17 Nov 64	Massachusetts Air Industries	New Bedford, Mass.	New Bedford - Nantucket	Various small types	Founded by E. Anthony & Sons; bought by Ottaway Newspapers, 1 Feb.66
20 Nov 64	Rockford Air Charter	Rockford, Illinois	Rockford - Chicago	Cessna	Cargo only; ceased operations early 1966
21 Nov 64	Maryland Airlines	Easton, Maryland		Various small types	
23 Nov 64	Owensboro Aviation	Owensboro, Ky.	Owensboro - Evansville - Chicago	Beech	
23 Nov 64	Air Taxi Associates (Eastern Air Taxi)	Monmouth County Airport, N.J.		Pipers	Acquired by Castanea Corp. (see 23 Feb. 1965) in 1966
Nov 64	Chatham Aviation	Morristown, N. J.	Morristown - New York	Cessnas	Founded as Lemco Flying Service at Teterboro Airport; part of Metro Air Service, Sept. 65, in association with American Airlines
1 Dec 64	Executive Airlines	Sarasota, Florida	Sarasota - Tampa	Aero Commander	Branch of Executive Airlines, Boston (June 61)
14 Dec 64	Newport Air Park	Newport, R. I.	Newport - Providence	Aero Commander and various small types	
17 Dec 64	Whidbey Flying Service	Oak Harbor, Wash.	Oak Harbor - Seattle	Piper	Became part of Puget Sound Airlines, 28 August, 1967
18 Dec 64	Mid-Continent Airlines	Morris, Illinois	Chicago - International Falls - Winnipeg	DH Dove Beech 18	

Date	Airline	Base	Route Network	Aircraft	Remarks
27 Dec 64	Viking Airways	Westerly, R.I.	Westerly - Block Island	Various small types	Formed as Travel Air Service; changed name 24 Feb.67
28 Dec 64	Sun Valley Airlines	Gooding, Idaho	Gooding - Sun Valley - Salt Lake City	Beech 18	
7 Jan 65	Southwest Airlines	San Antonio, Texas	Del Rio - Eagle Pass - Kerrville	Beech 18	Ceased operations, 1967
8 Jan 65	Ortner Air Service	Cleveland, Ohio	Local services around Cleveland	Beech 18	
16 Feb 65	Fairbanks Air Service	Fairbanks, Alaska	Local services around Fairbanks, and to Anchorage	Cessna types	Company originally founded during World War 2
22 Jan 65	Pennsylvania Commuter Airlines	State College, Pa.	State College - Harrisburg - Washington, Baltimore	Beech and Cessna	Subsidiary of L.B. Smith Aircraft Corp. Agreement with Eastern, 8 Oct 1968, to operate to Lancaster
18 Feb 65	King Flight Service	Wichita Falls, Texas	Wichita Falls - Abilene	Beech and Piper	Operates as King Airlines
23 Feb 65	Eastern Air Taxi	Monmouth County, N.J.	Monmouth County - New York	Piper	Formed by Castanea Corp. Bought Air Taxi Associates (Eastern Air Taxi) 1966; set up Piper Twinair 1 May 66
1 Mar 65	Miller Aviation Center	Pittsburgh, Pa.	Shuttle service between Pittsburgh's two airports	Pipers	
1 Mar 65	Munz Northern Airlines	Nome, Alaska	Local services throughout Seward Peninsula	Various small types	Originally founded in 1938 and has operated bush services ever since
2 Mar 65	Green Bay Aviation	Green Bay, Wisconsin	Local services in Wisconsin	Cessnas	

Date	Airline	Base	Route Network	Aircraft	Remarks
27 Mar 65	Aspen Airways	Denver, Colorado	Denver - Aspen	DH Heron and various	Has operated DC-3 and F-27
30 Mar 65	International Air Taxi	Anchorage, Alaska	Local services around Anchorage	Cessna	
31 Mar 65	ABC Airlines	Ontario, California		Piper, Beech	Ceased operations 1966
1 Apr 65	Andrew Flying Service	Honolulu, Hawaii	Local services in Hawaii	Cessna	Absorbed by Sky Tours Inc , 1966
6 Apr 65	Pacific Flight Service	Honolulu, Hawaii	Local services in Hawaii	Various small types	Ceased operations 1967
8 Apr 65	Hawaiian Air Tour Service (HATS)	Honolulu, Hawaii	Tour services throughout Hawaiian Islands	DH Doves and Herons	Absorbed Resort Airways, 1969
12 Apr 65	Interior Air Taxi	Fairbanks, Alaska	Local services around Fairbanks	Various small types	Operates as Interior Airways
13 Apr 65	Royal Hawaiian Air Service	Kona, Hawaii	Local services around 'Big Island' and to Honolulu	Cessna types	
3 May 65	Aroostock Airways	Presque Isle, Maine	Presque Isle - Augusta - Portland Boston	Pipers	Founded as P.& M. Flying Service by John C. Philbrick. Changed name 1968
5 May 65	Resort Airways	Honolulu, Hawaii	Honolulu - Kannapali	Aero Commander	Absorbed by HATS, 1969
19 May 65	Aviation Services	Wichita, Kansas	Local services to various points in Kansas and Colorado	Cessnas	Agreement with Frontier 31 Oct. 1968 to operate Dodge City - Kansas City

Date	Airline	Base	Route Network	Aircraft	Remarks
30 June 65	Air Wisconsin	Appleton, Wisconsin	Chicago - Milwaukee Appleton - Minneapolis	Twin Otter and Beech 99	Replaced North Central at points in Wisconsin
29 Jul 65	Casement Aviation	Painesville, Ohio	Painesville - Cleveland	Cessnas	
17 Aug 65	Henry's Charter Service	Concordia, Kansas	Concordia - Kansas City	Cessna	Ceased operations 1968
29 Sep 65	Lisle Air Service	Fresno, California	Fresno - Sacramento	Cessna	Ceased operations 1967
21 Oct 65	Longhorn Airlines	Lafayette, La.	Houston - Lafayette New Orleans	Piper and Cessna	Ceased operations 1967
31 Oct 65	Beeson Aviation	Topeka, Kansas	Concordia - Topeka-Kansas	Cessnas	Ceased operations 1967
17 Nov 65	Commuter Airlines	Chicago, Illinois	Chicago - Detroit, Springfield, Sheboygan, etc.	Beech Queen-Air	Founded at Sioux City, Iowa
19 Nov 65	Walter Faryniak	Allentown, Pa.		Piper	Ceased operations 1968
3 Dec 65	Sky Tours Hawaii	Honolulu, Hawaii	Tour and local services east of Honolulu	DH Dove, etc.	Absorbed Andrew Flying Service and Pan Pacific Aero in 1966. Scheduled service operated as Trans-Isle Airlines
15 Dec 65	Davis Airlines	College Station, Texas	College Station - Dallas, Houston	Piper	
1 Jan 66	Island Mail	Anacortes, Wash.	Northern Puget Sound	Cessna 206	Mail service only
3 Jan 66	Cannon Aviation	Tulsa, Oklahoma	Tulsa - Muskogee - McAlester	Piper, etc.	Ceased operations 1968

Date	Airline	Base	Route Network	Aircraft	Remarks
19 Jan 66	Midwest Aviation	Jamesville, Wisconsin	Jamesville - Chicagc	Beech 18	
27 Jan 66	Janss Airways	Salt Lake City, Utah	Salt Lake City - Sun Valley - Boise	Piper	
10 Feb 66	Air Enterprises	Huntington, W. Va.	Huntington - Columbus	Piper	Operated as Tag Commuter; ceased operations 1968
15 Feb 66	General Aviation Service	Reading, Pa.	Reading - Baltimore Washington	Beech 18	
25 Feb 66	Air Shannon	Fredericks-burg, Va.	Fredericksburg - Washington	Piper	Ceased operations 24 April, 67
16 Mar 66	Nicholson Air Services	Cumberland, Md.	Cumberland - Washington	Piper	
22 Mar 66	Ambassador Airlines	Palm Springs, Calif.	Palm Springs - Las Vegas	Various small types	
22 Mar 66	Trans Central Airlines	Denver, Col.	Denver - Pueblo - Trinidad - Albuquerque	Cessna 402	
16 Apr 66	Philips Michigan City Flying Service	Michigan City, Ind.	Michigan City - Chicago	Piper	
18 Apr 66	Buker Airways	North Spring-field, Vermont	Boston - New York - Pittsburg - Cincinnati	Learjet, Beech 18	Mail services
1 May 66	Piper Twinair	Belmar, N.J.	Belmar - New York - Bridgeport	Piper	Formed by Castanea Corp , Monmouth County Airport. (23 Feb. 65); ceased operations 1968
6 May 66	Catskill Airways	Oneonta, N.Y.	Oneonta - New York	Beech	

Date	Airline	Base	Route Network	Aircraft	Remarks
13 May 66	Rocky Mountain Airways	Denver, Colorado	Denver - Eagle - Aspen	Aero Commander	Founded as Vail Airways; changed name late 1968
25 May 66	Wright Airlines	Cleveland, Ohio	Cleveland - Detroit, Columbus, Dayton, Pittsburgh	Twin Otter, Beech 18, Cessna 402	
1 Jun 66	Miller Airmotive	Reed City, Mich.	Reed City - Grand Rapids	Various small types	Operates as Miller Airlines
8 Jun 66	Raritan Valley Air	Manville, N.J.	Manville - New York	Beech, Piper	Ceased operations 1968
9 Jun 66	Sedalia - Marshall - Boonville Stage Lines (S.M.B. Stage Line)	Des Moines, Iowa	Tulsa - Muskogee - Dallas, plus expensive mail routes throughout Midwest States	Beech 18	Largest air taxi mail operator. Agreement with Frontier 31 Oct 1968 to operate to points in Oklahoma and Texas
20 Jun 66	Pioneer Airlines	Springfield, Mo.	Local services in Missouri	Cessna	Ceased operations 1968
11 Jul 66	Trans-Mo Airlines (T.M.A.)	Jefferson City, Mo.	St Louis - Jefferson City - Kansas City - Topeka	Cessna 402	
18 Aug 66	DAL Airlines	Killeen, Texas	Killeen - Dallas	Beech 18	Merged with Hood Airlines (the surviving name) 23 May, 68
7 Sep 66	Aztec Airlines	El Paso, Texas	El Paso - Los Cruces - Douglas	Beech, Piper	Ceased operations 1967
15 Sep 66	Eugene Aviation Service	Eugene, Oregon	Eugene - Roseburg	Piper Aztec	Operated on behalf of West Coast Airlines for one year ending Aug. 67
3 Oct 66	West - Central Airlines	Lincoln, Nebraska	Local services in Nebraska	DH Dove, etc.	Ceased operations 1968

Date	Airline	Base	Route Network	Aircraft	Remarks
16 Oct 66	Trojan Airways	Kansas City, Kansas		Aero Commander	
20 Oct 66	Gold Coast Air Taxi	West Palm Beach, Fla.	Fort Lauderdale - West Palm Beach - Miami	Beech 18	Operates as Gold Coast Airlines
25 Oct 66	Trans-Aire	Detroit, Michigan		Piper	Ceased operations 1968
4 Nov 66	Altair Airlines	Philadelphia, Pa.	Philadelphia - Scranton, etc, Richmond, White Plains	Beech Queen Air	
21 Nov 66	Cable Commuter Airlines	Ontario, Cal.	Ontario - Los Angeles, Ventura, Santa Ana	Cessnas, Twin Otters	Founded as Cable Flying Service and became largest Third Level carrier. Merged with Aero Commuter, May 1969 to become Golden West Airlines
21 Dec 66	Hub Airlines	Fort Wayne, Indiana	Fort Wayne - Chicago	Beech 99	
13 Jan 67	Vermont International Airways	Morrisville, Vermont	Local services in Vermont	Beech 18	
14 Feb 67	Amistad Airline	San Antonio, Texas	San Antonio - Del Rio	Piper, Cessna	
16 Feb 67	Skyline Air Service	Anacortes, Wash.	Seattle - Everett - Anacortes	Cessna	Became part of Puget Sound Airlines, 28 August, 1967
17 Feb 67	Ransome Air	Philadelphia, Pa.	Philadelphia - New York, Washington, Norfolk	Beech 18	
3 Mar 67	Mackey Air Taxi	Ft Lauderdale Florida	Ft Lauderdale - West Palm Beach - Miami - Bahamas	Piper and Beech 99	Set up local third level service after selling airline to Eastern Air Lines

Date	Airline	Base	Route Network	Aircraft	Remarks
15 Apr 67	Commute Air	Spokane, Wash.	Spokane - Seattle, Everett, Missoula, Kalispell	Cessna 402	
30 Mar 67	Sun Airlines	St Louis, Missouri	Local service in Missouri, then extensive network throughout southern states	Learjet Beech 18	Operated most widespread third level network in U.S.A.
11 Jun 67	Horizon Airlines	Lynchburg, Va.	Lynchburg - Richmond and local services in Virginia	Piper	
20 Jun 67	Midwest Commuter	Indianapolis, Ind.	Local services in Indiana	Piper	
12 Jul 67	Fleetway Airlines	Tyler, Texas	Austin - Houston - Tyler - Dallas	Various small types	
2 Aug 67	Delaware Air Freight	Wilmington, Del.		Cessna	
3 Aug 67	Pitt Airlines	Pittsburgh, Pa.		Various small types	
26 Aug 67	Fleet Airlines	Hopkins, Minn.	Duluth - Minneapolis - Fargo	Piper, Beech	Agreement with North Central to serve Mankato 27 Jan 1969
28 Aug 67	Puget Sound Airlines	Seattle, Wash.	Network of services throughout Puget Sound	Various small types	Merger of 6 airlines in Puget Sound Area - viz. Bremerton Air Taxi, Angeles Flying Service, Island Sky Ferries, Whidbey Flying Service, Skyline Air Service, Bellingham - Seattle Airways
31 Aug 67	Central Texas Airlines	Killeen, Texas	Killeen - Temple - Waco - Dallas	Cessna	

Date	Airline	Base	Route Network	Aircraft	Remarks
11 Sep 67	Northern Airways	Burlington, Vermont	Network of routes throughout upper New York State and to Boston	Twin Otters, Beech, Piper	Operates in association with Mohawk Airlines and NEA
12 Sep 67	Dover Air Transport	Dover, Delaware	Dover - Washington	Cessna	
29 Sep 67	Combs Airways	Billings, Montana	Billings - Williston, Cody, Lewistown, Spokane, etc.	Aero Commander	Originally Combs-Pickens Montana Aircraft Co. Agreements with Frontier to Cody and Lewistown, 1969
29 Sep 67	Lynch Flying Service	Billings, Montana		Cessna	
11 Oct 67	Air Hawaii	Honolulu, Hawaii	Network throughout Hawaii	Twin Otter	
7 Dec 67	Air South	Atlanta, Georgia	Atlanta - Birmingham - Nashville, and local points in Georgia	Beech 99	Agreements with Eastern 1969 to serve Waycross and Bowling Green
Dec 67	Aero Commuter	Long Beach, California	Long Beach - Los Angeles - Catalina Island	Twin Otter	Merged with Catalina Airlines, then with Cable Commuter, May 69; then acquired Golden West and Skywark to form Golden West Airlines, largest Third Level carrier in U.S.A.

TABLE 26

UNITED STATES AIRLINE FLEETS
31 December 1969

	BAC	Boeing							Convair		Douglas						Fairchild		Lockheed		Nihon	Sud		
	1-11	707-100	707-300	720	727-100	727-200	737	747	580/660	880/990	DC3	DC4/7	DC8-10/50	DC8-61/3	DC9-10	DC9-30	FH-27	FH-227	Electra	L.100	YS11	Caravelle	Other	Total
TRUNKS																								
American	27	54	46	22	57	41																		247
Braniff	13	8	9	5	34									7										76
Continental			13	8		14									19									54
Delta										16			32	13	15	53								129
Eastern				9	75	11							17	23	15	66			24					240
National					13	21							14	2										50
Northeast					8	13												6						27
Northwest			36	16	31	24													11					118
TWA		59	65		35	29				25					19									232
United				29	122	28	73						74	40								20		386
Western			5	29		6	30												12					82
SUB TOTAL	40	121	174	118	375	187	103			41			137	85	68	119		6	47			20		1641
INTERNATIONAL																								
Caribair									6							3							2	11
Pan Am		5	117	9	24			2					1											158
Trans-Caribbean					1	2							2	3										8
SUB TOTAL		5	117	9	25	2		2	6				3	3		3							2	177
LOCALS																								
Air West															4	15	33							52
Allegheny									42							24								66
Frontier						4	8		41															53
Mohawk	20																	17						37
North Central									33							13								46
Ozark											4				5	7		21						37
Piedmont							12														21		19	52
Southern															7	3							24	34
Texas Intl									27						13	4								44
SUB TOTAL	20					4	20		143		4				29	66	33	38			21		43	421
TERRITORIAL																								
Alaska					6															3			5	14
Aloha							6																4	10
Hawaiian									7						2	5								14
Reeve-Aleutian											2	3							1				4	10
Wien-Consol'd							3				2						5						7	17
SUB TOTAL					6		9		7		4	3			2	5	5		1	3			20	65

	BAC	Boeing							Convair		Douglas						Fairchild		Lockheed		Nihon	Sud		
	1-11	707-100	707-320	720	727-100	727-200	737	747	580/640	880/990	DC3	DC4/7	DC8-10/50	DC8-61/3	DC9-10	DC9-30	FH-27	FH-227	Electra	L. 100	YS11	Caravelle	Other	Total
SUPPLEMENTAL																								
American Flyers					2									2					5					9
Capitol													4	4									29	37
Johnson F/S											3	1												4
Modern Air										6														6
Overseas Natl													1	4		7			8					20
Purdue											4	3				3								10
Saturn												22	2	2										26
Southern Air Tpt.					2							6								2			3	13
T I A					2									8										10
Universal												21	1	2					13				13	50
Vance Intl											1	2											1	4
World			9		4																			13
SUB TOTAL			9		10					6	8	55	8	22		10			26	2			46	202
CARGO																								
Airlift Intl			3		4							5		3						3			5	23
Flying Tiger														14										14
Seaboard World														11									1	13
SUB TOTAL			3		4							5		28						3			6	50
OTHERS																								
Aspen											3												1	4
Fairways									1		1													2
Galaxy											6													6
Holiday												1							2					3
Flying W																				2				2
Interior					1						2	1					2			7			7	20
Southeast											2						1							3
McCulloch																			3					3
Air California							6																	6
P S A						14	9																	23
SUB TOTAL					1	14	15		1		14	2					3		5	9			8	72
TOTALS	60	126	303	127	421	207	147	2	157	47	30	65	149	138	99	203	41	44	79	17	21	20	125	2628

DATE OF FIRST JET SERVICE BY U.S. DOMESTIC TRUNK AIRLINES

Date	Airline	Route	Aircraft	Remarks
10 December, 1958	National	New York - Miami	B-707	Leased from Pan American. Own DC-8 on 18 February, 1960
25 January, 1959	American	New York - Los Angeles	B-707	
20 March, 1959	TWA	New York-San Francisco	B-707	
8 June, 1959	Continental	Los Angeles - Chicago	B-707	
18 September, 1959	United	New York-San Francisco	DC-8	
18 September, 1959	Delta	New York - Atlanta	DC-8	
17 December, 1959	Northeast	New York - Miami	B-707	Leased from TWA. Own Convair 880 on 15 December, 1960
20 December, 1959	Braniff	Dallas - New York	B-707	
24 January, 1960	Eastern	New York - Miami	DC-8	
1 June, 1960	Western	Los Angeles - Seattle	B-707	Leased from Boeing. Own B-720 June 1961
16 September, 1960	Northwest	New York - Seattle	DC-8	
8 January, 1961	Capital	New York - Chicago	B-720	Leased by United, which acquired company and integrated own services

Special Note on Appendices

The appendices which follow are intended to supplement other factual material contained in this book, and to provide a quick reference on certain data. The comprehensiveness of selection and the standard of accuracy take into account that this book is primarily about operators and their history rather than aircraft and their characteristics.

In addition to these general criteria the following notes are also appropriate:

1. *Main Characteristics of Commercial Airliners used by U.S. Airlines*
This tabulation is divided into the following categories of airliners:

a. Flying-boats
b. Piston-engine powered (pre-1933)
c. Piston-engine powered (post-1933)
d. Propeller-turbine powered
e. Turbojet-powered
f. Helicopters
g. Representative Third Level aircraft

The 162 aircraft listed include most of those mentioned in this book. The data reflect a sensible interpretation of accuracy standards which should be valuable to most readers.

Especially in the case of earlier types, the engines quoted are those normally used, although there were often many substitutes. Information on numbers built is often qualified in the 'remarks' column, but a complete analysis of all civil and military variants is impossible, indeed inadvisable, in this context. For the specialists there are many excellent books available on this subject.

2. *Development of Airliner Productivity*
This takes the form of a set of three charts, tracing the development of airliner weight, speed, and seat-mile productivity. The aircraft selected for inclusion are considered to be the most significant in terms of technical development and/or representative of an aircraft generation.

3. *Passenger-miles Flown by U.S. Airlines 1926–1969*
This table contains passenger-mile statistics of every class of airline which has provided public service since the passing of the 1925 Air Mail Act. These include (possibly for the first time) data not normally included in C.A.B. Statistics, e.g., Intra-state, Supplemental and Third Level (Commuter) airlines.

4. *Passengers Carried by U.S. Domestic Trunk Airlines, 1950–1970*
This chart shows the passenger traffic growth at 10-year intervals.

5. *U.S. Transcontinental Route: Reduction in Journey Time, 1850–1960*
This chart shows the major developments which have reduced the 24-day surface journey to a flight of a few hours.

6. *U.S. Intercity Travel by Modes, 1950–1970*
This shows passenger-miles in U.S. billions for air, bus and rail transport from 1950 to 1970, with air overtaking buses in 1956 and rail by 1958.

7. *The USA in Perspective*
This series of charts provides a postscript which relates the United States airline industry to world air transport and to other U.S. transport media.

Appendix 1

MAIN CHARACTERISTICS OF COMMERCIAL AIRLINERS USED BY U. S. AIRLINES
(A) FLYING-BOATS

AIRCRAFT		ENGINES				CHARACTERISTICS				PERFORMANCE			FIRST SERVICE		REMARKS
MANUFACTURER	TYPE	NO.	MANUFACTURER	TYPE	TAKEOFF POWER (EHP)	LENGTH (FT)	SPAN (FT)	GROSS WEIGHT (LB)	MAX SEATS	CRUISE SPEED (MPH)	RANGE (ST MI)	NO. BUILT	DATE	AIRLINE	
AEROMARINE	50C	1			150	28	48	3,276	4	75	300		EARLY 1920	AEROMARINE	AEROMARINE DESIGNS. ALSO BUILT BY OTHER MANUFACTURERS UNDER MILITARY CONTRACT
	F-5 L	2	–	LIBERTY	800	49	104	13,600	14	75	830		LATE 1920	AEROMARINE	
BENOIST	XIV	1	ROBERTS	–	75	26	36	1,404	2	80	50	(10)	1 JAN 1914	ST PETERSBURG – TAMPA	WORLD'S FIRST SCHEDULED AIRLINE SERVICE
BOEING	C-700	1	HALL-SCOTT	A-7A	100	27	44	2,395	1	70	200	53	3 MAR 1919	SEATTLE-VICTORIA	FIRST U.S. MAIL SERVICE (NAVY TRAINER)
	B-1	1	HALL-SCOTT	L-6	200	31	50	3,850	4	80	400	1	15 OCT 1920	SEATTLE-VICTORIA	FIRST PRIVATE CONTRACT AIR MAIL SERVICE
	B-314	4	WRIGHT	CYCLONE	6,200	106	152	8[illegible],480	70	145	2,400	12	20 MAY 1939	PAN AM	FIRST 6 AIRCRAFT SERIES 314. SECOND 6, 314A. FEWER PSGR. ON LONG STAGES. OPENED WORLD'S FIRST TRANSATLANTIC SCHEDULED SERVICE
CONSOLIDATED	COMMODORE	2	PRATT & WHITNEY	HORNET	1,150	68	100	1[illegible],650	22	102	650	14	18 FEB 1930	NYRBA	
	CATALINA	2	PRATT & WHITNEY	R1830-92	2,400	64	104	3[illegible],000	12	130	2,000				DEVELOPED FROM BASIC MODEL 28, USED BY AMERICAN EXPORT. LATER MODELS MAINLY NAVAL DESIGNATIONS E.G. PBY-5A
CURTISS	MF	1	CURTISS	C-6	150	31	50	[illegible],488	4	60	288	16	4 JULY 1919	SYD CHAPLIN	CURTISS DESIGNS/ALSO BUILT BY OTHER MANUFACTURERS UNDER MILITARY CONTRACTS
	HS-2L	1	–	LIBERTY	330	40	74	5,223	4	91	517	1,101	LATE 1919	AERO	
DOUGLAS	DOLPHIN	2	PRATT & WHITNEY	WASP	900	44	60	9,500	8	150	740	59	JULY 1931	WILMINGTON CATALINA	AMPHIBIAN. NUMBER INCLUDES 47 MILITARY. ALSO USED IN CHINA
FAIRCHILD	91	1	PRATT & WHITNEY	HORNET	750	43	56	9,700	8	154	750		APR 1936	PANAIR DO BRASIL	AMPHIBIAN. USED ON AMAZON RIVER SERVICE

Aircraft Manufacturer	Aircraft Type	Engines No.	Engines Manufacturer	Engines Type	Takeoff Power (ehp)	Length (ft)	Span (ft)	Gross Weight (lb)	Max Seats	Cruise Speed (mph)	Range (st mi)	No. Built	First Service Date	First Service Airline	Remarks
Ireland	N-2-B	1	Wright	R-975	300	31	40	4,400	4				1929	Curtiss Flying Service	
Loening	23 L Air Yacht	1	–	Liberty	400	34	45	5,560	2	100	200		1922	N.Y. Newport – A.S.	Amphibian
	C-2	1	Wright	Cyclone	525	35	47	5,900	6	120	400		1929		Amphibian
Martin	M.130	4	Pratt & Whitney	Wasp	3,320	91	130	52,250	32	130	2,400	3	22 Nov 35	Pan Am	Max. passenger load indicated. Fewer passengers on long stages. Opened world's first trans-Pacific scheduled service
Savoia-Marchetti	S-55	2	Isotta-Fraschini	Asso	1,000	79	54	16,100	14	106	650		July 1929	Airvia Transportation Co	Licence-built by American Aeronatical Corp. from Italian design
Sikorsky	S-36	2	Wright	Whirlwind	400	34	72	6,000	7	90	200	1	–	Pan Am	Amphibian. Never entered regular services
	S-38	2	Pratt & Whitney	Wasp	850	41	72	10,480	8	105	300	115	31 Oct 1928	Pan Am	Amphibian
	S-40	4	Pratt & Whitney	Hornet	2,300	77	114	34,600	40	100	800	3	19 Nov 1931	Pan Am	
	S-41	2	Pratt & Whitney	Hornet	1,150	45	79	13,800	11	105	400	3	1 Aug 1931	Pan Am	Amphibian
	S-42	4	Pratt & Whitney	Hornet	2,800	69	118	43,000	32	140	750	10	16 Aug 1934	Pan Am	S-42B modification gave greater range in exchange for smaller payload
	S-43	2	Pratt & Whitney	Wasp	1,500	52	86	19,500	18	150	500		Apr 1936	Pan Am	Amphibian
Vought-Sikorsky	VS-44	4	Pratt & Whitney	R-1830	4,800	79	124	57,500	16	160	3,000	3	20 Jun 1942	A O A	

(B) PISTON-ENGINED (PRE - 1933)

AIRCRAFT		ENGINES				CHARACTERISTICS				PERFORMANCE			FIRST SERVICE		
Manufacturer	Type	No.	Manufacturer	Type	Takeoff Power (EHP)	Length (ft)	Span (ft)	Gross Weight (LB)	Max Seats	Cruise Speed (MPH)	Range (ST MI)	No. Built	Date	Airline	Remarks
Boeing	B-40A	1	Pratt & Whitney	Wasp	425	33	44	6,000	2	110	300	82 (B-40A and B-40B)	1 July 1927	Boeing A.T.	
	B-40B	1	Pratt & Whitney	Hornet	525	33	44	6,079	3	125	535		15 Sept 1929	Varney A.L.	
	B-80	3	Pratt & Whitney	Hornet	1,575	57	80	17,500	20	115	460	11	30 Oct 1928	Boeing A.T.	
	B-95	1	Pratt & Whitney	Hornet	525	32	44	6,840	-	120	520	25	Apr 1929	Western A.E.	
	B-200 Monomail	1	Pratt & Whitney	Hornet	575	41	59	8,000	-	140	575	2	1933	United	Mail only. Built by Boeing as experimental high-speed mail carrier, converted later to Model 221A for passengers
Buhl	CA-3 Air Sedan	1	Wright	Whirlwind	220	25	36	3,200	4	110	800	50			
Bach	3-CT-6	1	Pratt & Whitney	Hornet	525	37	58	8,000	10	133	500		5 Mar 1928	West Coast A. T.	
		2	Wright	Whirlwind	165										
Bellanca	Pacemaker CH-300	1	Wright	Whirlwind	220	28	46	4,050	6	122	675	118	Aug 1929	New York-Asbury Park	
Consolidated	Fleetster 17	1	Pratt & Whitney	Hornet	575	32	45	5,300	6	150	750	3,290	Late 1930	NYRBA	Not including Russian-built
Curtiss	JN-4 H	1	Wright-Hispano	-	150	27	44	2,150	-	75	250	929	15 May 1918	U.S. Army	Under contract to U.S. Post Office. 7591 Jennies of all types
	H-A	1	Curtiss	C-6	160	25	33	2,524	-	90	450	6	1920	U.S. Post Office	Mail only
	Lark	1	Wright	Whirlwind	200	21	31	2,708	2	97	380	3	18 June 1926	Colonial A.T.	
	Carrier Pigeon	1	Curtiss	Conqueror	635	35	48	7,600	-	128	650	15	12 May 1926	National A.T.	Mail only. Number includes earlier model with Liberty engine
	Falcon	1	-	Liberty 12	425	27	38	5,110	1	124	500	20	1929	National A. T.	Also 450 military and export

AIRCRAFT		ENGINES				CHARACTERISTICS				PERFORMANCE			FIRST SERVICE		
Manufacturer	Type	No.	Manufacturer	Type	Takeoff Power (EHP)	Length (FT)	Span (FT)	Gross Weight (LB)	Max Seats	Cruise Speed (MPH)	Range (ST MI)	No. Built	Date	Airline	REMARKS
Curtiss (Cont'd)	Robin	1	Curtiss	Challenger	170	25	41	2,600	2	100	300	773		Robertson Air Service	
	Kingbird J-2	2	Wright	Whirlwind	440	35	55	5,870	6	115	450	15	10 Dec 1930	Eastern A.T.	
	Condor C0 (1929)	2	Curtiss	Geared Conqueror	1,200	58	92	17,678	18	118	500	6	10 Dec 1930	Eastern A.T.	
	Condor 32 (1933)	2	Wright	R-1320F Cyclone	1,400	49	82	17,500	14	145	650	45	5 May 1934	American	
De Havilland	DH-4B	1	-	Liberty	400	30	42	4,595	-	115	350	100	Late 1918	U.S. Post Office	Built in USA under Licence from De Havilland, England, and modified from original DH-4 design. Mail only
Douglas	M-2	1	-	Liberty	400	29	40	4,968	2	110	650	6	17 Apr 1926	Western A.E.	
	M-3 and 4	1	-	Liberty	400	29	45	4,855	-	120	700	52	1926	U.S. Post Office	Mail only
Fairchild	FC-2	1	Wright	Whirlwind	220	50	31	3,600	4	115	150	} 100	19 Oct 1927	Pan Am	All Fairchild models built also as floatplanes
	FC-2W	1	Pratt & Whitney	Wasp	450	33	50	5,500	6	115	150		17 May 1929	Panagra	
	71	1	Pratt & Whitney	Wasp	450	33	50	5,500	7	103	900	90	17 May 1929	Panagra	
Fokker	Universal (Model 4)	1	Wright	Whirlwind	220	33	48	4,000	4	100	535	44	1926	Colonial A.T.	
	Super Universal (Model 8)	1	Pratt & Whitney	Wasp	420	37	51	5,550	6	118	740	123	31 Aug 1929	Western A.T.	Number includes 14 built in Canada, 29 in Japan
	F-VIIA/3M(C-2)	3	Wright	Whirlwind	660	48	63	7,650	8	110	600	25	6 July 1926	P.R.T Line	P.R.T's aircraft imported F-VII s. Number indicates U.S. - built only
	F-10	3	Pratt & Whitney	Wasp	1,275	50	71	12,500	12	120	900	65	26 May 1928	Western A.E.	
	F-10A	3	Pratt & Whitney	Wasp	1,275	50	79	13,100	14	120	800	59	13 Nov 1928	Western A.E.	

Aircraft		Engines				Characteristics				Performance		No. Built	First Service		Remarks
Manufacturer	Type	No.	Manufacturer	Type	Takeoff Power (EHP)	Length (FT)	Span (FT)	Gross Weight (LB)	Max Seats	Cruise Speed (MPH)	Range (ST MI)		Date	Airline	
Fokker (Cont'd)	F-14	1	Pratt & Whitney	Hornet	525	43	59	7,200	8	116	730	35	12 Dec 1929	Western A.E.	
	F-32	4	Pratt & Whitney	Hornet	2,300	70	99	24,250	32	123	500	10	1 Apr 1930	Western A.E.	
Ford	4-AT Tri-Motor	3	Wright	Whirlwind	660	50	74	10,130	14	100	570	78	2 Aug 1926	Ford Motor Co	
	5-AT Tri-Motor	3	Pratt & Whitney	Wasp	1,350	50	78	13,500	16	110	510	116	1 Sept 1926	Northwest Airways	
	8-AT	1	Wright	Hispano	525	51	78	11,000	2	110	500	1	July 1934	Pacific Alaska	Used mainly for freight
Hamilton	H-45	1	Pratt & Whitney	Wasp	425	35	54	5,750	8	115	600		7 June 1928	Northwest	
Junkers	J L 6 (F-13)	1	B M W	IIIA	240	32	59	3,850	-	85	250	350	1919	U.S. Post Office	Mail only. Imported from Germany. Used extensively world-wide
Keystone	K-78 D Patrician	3	Wright	Cyclone	1,575	62	86	16,600	20	115	400	3	Late 1929	W. Indies Air Express	
Lockheed	Vega	1	Pratt & Whitney	Wasp	420	28	41	4,217	6	135	600	130	17 Sept 1928	Intern'l Airlines	Converted Vega known as Air Express
	Orion	1	Pratt & Whitney	Wasp	500	28	43	5,200	6	191	750	36	May 1931	Bowen Air Lines	
Laird	LC-B	1	Wright	Whirlwind	220	24	34	2,850	3	110	600	35	7 June 1926	Ch. Dickenson	
Martin	70	1	Wright	E-4	200	28	38	3,235	-	90			1923	U.S. Post Office	Mail only

Aircraft: Manufacturer	Aircraft: Type	Engines: No.	Engines: Manufacturer	Engines: Type	Takeoff Power (EHP)	Length (ft)	Span (ft)	Gross Weight (lb)	Max Seats	Cruise Speed (mph)	Range (st mi)	No. Built	First Service: Date	First Service: Airline	Remarks
Northrop	Alpha	1	Pratt & Whitney	Wasp	420	28	42	4,500	5	140	700	17	Early 1931	National Air Tpt	Mail only
	Gamma	1	Wright	SR1820F3	710	30	48	7,350	-	178	1,550	9	May 1934	T W A	Also used for high altitude experimental programme
	Delta	1	Pratt & Whitney	Hornet	725	33	48	7,000	8	175	1,550	11	Sept 1933	T W A	
Pilgrim	100-A	1	Pratt & Whitney	Hornet	575	38	57	6,500	8	110	440	26	1 Nov 1935	Pacific Alaska	Formerly Fairchild Company. Aircraft marketed under Pilgrim name
Pitcairn	PA-5 Mailwing	1	Wright	Whirlwind	240	22	33	2,812	-	135	500	120	6 Feb 1928	Texas A.T.	
Ryan	(Standard J-1 conversion)	1	Hispano Suiza	-	150	27	40		4	90	400	6	1 Mar 1925	Los Angeles-San Diego Air Line	
	(Douglas Cloudster conversion)	1	-	Liberty 12	425	37	56	9,600	10	90	550	1	Mid 1925	Los Angeles-San Diego Air Line	
	M-1	1	Wright	Whirlwind	200	22	36		2	115		25	15 Sept 1926	Pacific Air Tpt	
	B-5 Brougham	1	Wright	Whirlwind	220	28	42	4,000	5	120	750		June 1928	-	Mutual aircraft company
Standard	JR-1 B	1	Hispano Suiza		150	27	44	2,200	-	94	280	7	12 Aug 1918	U.S. Post Office	Mail only
Stearman	Speedmail	1	Pratt & Whitney	Hornet	525	32	46	2,750	-	126	780	27	1928	Varney	Mail only
Stinson	SM-1 Detroiter	1	Wright	Whirlwind	200	29	36	3,280	4	105	550	96	1 July 1927	Northwest Airways	
	Tri-Motor SM-6000	3	Lycoming	R-680	645	43	60	8,500	10	110	400	55	1 Sept 1930	NY, Phil, Wash Airways	

Aircraft		Engines				Characteristics				Performance			First Service		
Manufacturer	Type	No.	Manufacturer	Type	Takeoff Power (EHP)	Length (FT)	Span (FT)	Gross Weight (LB)	Max Seats	Cruise Speed (MPH)	Range (ST MI)	No. Built	Date	Airline	Remarks
Stout	2-AT	1	-	Liberty 12	400	46	58	6,000	8	100	400	11	3 Apr 1925	Ford Motor Company	
Swallow	Swallow	1	Curtiss	K-6	150	24	36	2,700	-	90	500		6 Apr 1926	Varney	Mail only
Travel Air	6000	1	Wright	Whirlwind	220	31	49	4,100	6	100	600	135	Early 1929	National Air Tpt	
Waco	9 and 10	1	Curtiss	OX5	90	23	30	2,100	2	90	400	1350	21 Apr 1927	Clifford Ball	

MAIN CHARACTERISTICS OF COMMERCIAL AIRLINERS USED BY U. S. AIRLINES
(C) MODERN PISTON-ENGINED (POST - 1933)

Aircraft		Engines				Characteristics				Performance			First Service		Remarks
Manufacturer	Type	No.	Manufacturer	Type	Takeoff Power (EHP)	Length (FT)	Span (FT)	Gross Weight (LB)	Max Seats	Cruise Speed (MPH)	Range (ST MI)	No. Built	Date	Airline	Remarks
Boeing	247D	2	Pratt & Whitney	R1340-53	600	54	74	13,650	10	160	500	75	22 May 1933	Boeing A.T	
	307 Stratoliner	4	Wright	R1320-G102A	1,100	74	107	42,000	33	200	1,200	10	8 July 1940	TWA	
	377 Stratocruiser	4	Pratt & Whitney	R4360-86	3,500	110	141	145,800	60	300	3,000	56	7 Sept 1948	United	
Convair	240	2	Pratt & Whitney	R2800-CA18	1,200	75	92	42,000	40	285	750		1 June 1948	American	Number includes 340 & 440 (some
	340	2	Pratt & Whitney	R2800-CB16	2,400	79	106	45,000	44	284	685	553	16 Nov 1952	United	340s rebuilt as 440s)
	440 Metropolitan	2	Pratt & Whitney	R2800-CB17		79	106	49,100	52	289	650		1 Apr 1956	Continental	
Curtiss	C-46	2	Pratt & Whitney	R2800-CB16	2,400	76	108	45,000	40	227	2,300	3,180	1 Oct 1942	Eastern	Number includes military.
Douglas	DC-1	2	Wright	SCR-1820-3	875	60	8	17,500	14	180	500	1	-	TWA	Prototype. In limited operation with TWA
	DC-2	2	Wright	R-1820-F3	875	62	8	18,080	14	170	500	220	18 May 1934	TWA	
	DC-3	2	Pratt & Whitney	R-1830-92	1,200	64	9	25,200	28	180	500	13,500	25 June 1936	American	Number includes military & foreign built, and DSTs.
	DC-4	4	Pratt & Whitney	R-2000-3	1,450	94	118	73,000	40	205	2,500	2,300	7 Mar 1946	American	Number includes military production
	DC-6	4	Pratt & Whitney	R-2800-CB	2,400	101	118	97,200	56	310	2,750	175	27 Apr 1947	United	
	DC-6B	4	Pratt & Whitney	R-2800-CB	2,500	107	118	107,000	66	315	3,000	362	11 Apr 1951	United	Number includes DC-6A & 6C, but not military
	DC-7	4	Wright	R-3350	3,250	109	118	122,000	99	360	2,800	106	29 Nov 1953	American	
	DC-7B	4	Wright	R-3350	3,250	109	118	126,000	99	360	2,760	109	13 June 1955	Pan Am	
	DC-7C	4	Wright	R-3350	3,250	112	128	143,000	110	355	4,250	121	1 June 1956	Pan Am	
Lockheed	L-10 Electra	2	Pratt & Whitney	R-985-13	450	39	55	10,500	8	185	500	148	11 Aug 1934	Northwest	
	L-12	2	Pratt & Whitney	WASP SB-3	400	36	50	8,650	8	212	824	114			
	L-14	2	Wright	GR1820-G205A	1,000	44	66	20,000	12	255	2,160	112	Sept 1937	Northwest	
	L-18 Lodestar	2	Wright	GR1820-G107A	900	50	66	18,500	17	229	1,800	624	Mar 1940	Mid-Continent	Number includes military variants

AIRCRAFT		ENGINES				CHARACTERISTICS				PERFORMANCE			FIRST SERVICE		REMARKS
Manufacturer	Type	No.	Manufacturer	Type	Takeoff Power (EHP)	Length (FT)	Span (FT)	Gross Weight (LB)	Max Seats	Cruise Speed (MPH)	Range (ST MI)	No. Built	Date	Airline	
Lockheed (Cont'd)	L-049 Constellation	4	Wright	R3350-C18	2,200	95	123	98,000	54	310	3,000	88	1 Mar 1946	TWA	Number includes military models
	L-749 Constellation	4	Wright	749C-188D1	2,500	95	123	107,000	64	300	3,000	145	17 June 1947	Pan Am	Number includes military models
	L-1049A Super-Const.	4	Wright	C18CA1	2,700	114	123	120,000	88	279	2,450	104	17 Dec 1951	Eastern	Number includes C, D & E models
	L-1049G Super-Const.	4	Wright	972TC18DA3	3,250	114	123	137,500	99	335	4,620	157	1 Apr 1955	TWA	Number includes H model
	L-1649 Starliner	4	Wright	998TC18EA2	3,400	116	150	156,000	99	350	5,280	44	1 June 1957	TWA	
Martin	M-202	2	Pratt & Whitney	R-2800-CB16	2,400	71	93	42,750	36	286	1,380	31	15 Nov 1947	Northwest	
	M-404	2	Pratt & Whitney	R-2800-CB16	2,400	75	93	43,650	40	280	1,080	160	5 Oct 1951	TWA	
Vultee	V-1A	1	Wright	Cyclone F2	735	37	50	8,500	8	215	1,000		9 Sept 1934	American	

(D) TURBOPROP

AIRCRAFT		ENGINES				CHARACTERISTICS				PERFORMANCE		No. Built	FIRST SERVICE		REMARKS
Manufacturer	Type	No.	Manufacturer	Type	Takeoff Power (ehp)	Length (ft)	Span (ft)	Gross Weight (lb)	Max Seats	Cruise Speed (mph)	Range (st mi)		Date	Airline	
Fairchild Hiller	F-27	2	Rolls-Royce	RDa6-511	1,670	77	95	39,400	40	258	343	529	28 Sept 1958	West Coast	Number includes all models & Fokker-built still in production
	F-27J	2	Rolls-Royce	RDa7-523	1,815	77	95	42,000	40	276	910		1 Dec 1965	Allegheny	
	F-227B	2	Rolls-Royce	RDa7-523	1,815	84	95	45,500	46	276	614	69	1 July 1966	Mohawk	
Convair	580	2	Allison	501-D13	3,750	82	105	53,200	52	342	645	170	1 June 1964	Frontier	Conversion of 340/440
	600	2	Rolls-Royce	RDa10-542	3,025	75	92	46,200	52	309	450	34	1 Dec 1965	Central	Conversion of CV-240
	640	2	Rolls-Royce	RDa10-542	3,025	82	105	55,000	56	300	450	22	23 Dec 1965	Caribair	Conversion of CV-340/440
Nihon	YS-11A	2	Rolls-Royce	RDa10-542	3,025	86	105	54,000	60	294	690	136	19 May 1968	Piedmont	Still in production
Lockheed	L188A Electra	4	Allison	501-D15	4,050	105	99	116,000	98	405	2,770	171	12 Jan 1959	Eastern	
Vickers	V700D Viscount	4	Rolls-Royce	RDa6-510	1,650	82	94	64,500	48	312	2,080	459	26 July 1955	Capital	Number includes all models
Nord	262	2	Turbomeca	Bastan VI c	1,065	63	72	22,700	27	226	200	95	31 Oct 1965	Lake Central	

(E) JETS

Aircraft Manufacturer	Aircraft Type	Engines No.	Engines Manufacturer	Engines Type	Takeoff Thrust (lb)	Length (ft)	Span (ft)	Gross Weight (lb)	Max Seats	Cruise Speed (mph)	Range (st mi)	No. Built	First Service Date	First Service Airline	Remarks
British Aircraft Corp	BAC1-11-200	2	Rolls-Royce	RB163-2	10,600	94	89	74,500	79	507	1,767	55	25 Apr 1965	Braniff	Also 70 BAC111-500 s sold
	BAC1-11-400	2	Rolls-Royce	RB163-25	11,000	94	89	78,500	84	507	1,767	75	6 Mar 1966	American	Still in production in 1970.
Boeing	707-120	4	Pratt & Whitney	JT3C-6	13,500	145	131	248,000	181	600	3,000	146	28 Oct 1958	Pan Am	120B JT3D fans. Range 4,900 mi.
	707-320C	4	Pratt & Whitney	JT3D	18,000	153	146	336,000	202	600	4,000	548	3 June 1963	Pan Am	Number includes 320, 320B & 420 (RR Conway)
	720	4	Pratt & Whitney	JT3C-7	12,500	137	131	230,000	167	600	3,000	154	5 July 1960	United	Number includes 720B JT3D fans. Range 4,150 mi
	727-100	3	Pratt & Whitney	JT8D-7	14,000	133	108	170,000	131	600	2,500	563	1 Feb 1964	Eastern	Number includes 100 QC version
	727-200	3	Pratt & Whitney	JT8D-9	14,500	153	108	173,000	189	600	1,750	277	14 Dec 1967	Northeast	
	737-200	2	Pratt & Whitney	JT8D-7	14,000	100	93	111,000	119	575	1,760	270	28 Apr 1968	United	Number includes 29 737-100s. (None used by US airlines)
	747	4	Pratt & Whitney	JT9D	47,000	231	196	713,000	490	625	5,800	190	22 Jan 1970	Pan Am	Number at 30 June 1970
Convair	880	4	General Electric	CJ-805-3	11,200	129	120	184,500	124	605	2,845	65	15 May 1960	Delta	
	990A Coronado	4	General Electric	CJ-805-23	16,100	139	120	239,200	159	625	5,460	37	18 Mar 1962	American	
Douglas	DC-8-10	4	Pratt & Whitney	JT3C-6	13,500	151	142	273,000	179	542	4,300	294 (DC-8-10, -30, -50)	18 Sept 1959	United/Delta	
	DC-8-30	4	Pratt & Whitney	JT4A-11	17,500	151	142	315,000	179	592	5,970		27 Apr 1960	Pan Am	
	DC-8-50	4	Pratt & Whitney	JT3D-3B	18,000	151	142	325,000	179	580	5,720		30 Apr 1961	United	
	DC-8-61	4	Pratt & Whitney	JT3D-3B	18,000	187	142	328,000	250	580	5,300	88	24 Feb 1967	United	
	DC-8-62	4	Pratt & Whitney	JT3D-7	19,000	157	148	350,000	189	586	5,800	61	4 Sept 1967	Braniff	
	DC-8-63	4	Pratt & Whitney	JT3D-7	19,000	187	148	355,000	250	583	5,700	104	30 June 1968	Seaboard	Still in production in 1970
	DC-9-10	2	Pratt & Whitney	JT8D-1	14,000	104	89	91,500	80	557	1,700	137	8 Dec 1965	Delta	Also 34 DC-9-20/40 Sold
	DC-9-30	2	Pratt & Whitney	JT8D-9	14,500	119	93	109,000	105	557	1,600	440	1 Feb 1967	Eastern	Still in production in 1970
	DC-10-10	3	General Electric	CF6-6D	40,000	181	155	430,000	345	600	2,760		5 Aug 1971	American	In production (DC-10-10, -20, -30)
	DC-10-20	3	Pratt & Whitney	JT9D-15	47,000	182	161	555,000	345	600	5,900		(1972)	Northwest	
	DC-10-30	3	General Electric	CF6-50A	49,000	182	161	555,000	345	600	6,100		(1973)	National	
Lockheed	L.1011-1	3	Rolls-Royce	RB211-22	40,600	178	155	409,000	345	600	3,280		(1 July 1972)	Eastern	In production
Sud Aviation	SE-210 Caravelle VI R	2	Rolls-Royce	RA29-533R	12,600	105	113	110,231	70	488	1,450	269	14 July 1961	United	Number includes all types of Caravelle.

(F) HELICOPTERS

AIRCRAFT		ENGINES				CHARACTERISTICS				PERFORMANCE			FIRST SERVICE		REMARKS
Manufacturer	Type	No.	Manufacturer	Type	Takeoff Power (ehp)	Length (ft)	Rotor Diam. (ft)	Gross Weight (lb)	Max Seats	Cruise Speed (mph)	Range (st mi)	No. Built	Date	Airline	
Bell	47D	1	Lycoming	VO-435-23	260	41	37	2,450	2	80	170	2,500	20 Aug 1949	Chicago	Number includes military still in production
Sikorsky	S-51	1	Pratt & Whitney	R985-584	450	59	49	5,300	3	90	220	500	1 Oct 1947	Los Angeles	Number includes military
	S-55	1	Pratt & Whitney	R1340-40	600	63	53	7,500	7	80	110	1,600	8 July 1953	New York	Number includes military
	S-61	2	General Electric	T58-8	1,250	73	62	18,700	25	135	150	150	1 March 1962	Los Angeles	Number includes military
	S-62	1	General Electric	CT-58-100-1	730	62	53	7,500	9	98	90		21 Dec 1960	Los Angeles	
Vertol	V-44B	1	Wright	R1820-103	1,425	86	44	14,350	15	100	180	800	21 Apr 1958	New York	Number includes military
	V-107	2	General Electric	T58-8	1,250	84	50	18,400	25	1377	180	40	1 July 1962	New York	Number includes USCG

(G) REPRESENTATIVE THIRD LEVEL

Aircraft		Engines				Characteristics				Performance		No. Built	First Service		Remarks
Manufacturer	Type	No.	Manufacturer	Type	Takeoff Power (EHP)	Length (ft)	Span (ft)	Gross Weight (lb)	Max Seats	Cruise Speed (mph)	Range (st mi)		Date	Airline	
Beech	D-18 Expediter	2	Pratt & Whitney	R985-AH14B	450	34	48	8,750	7	185	280	7,020	Feb 1940	Wiggins	Number includes military. Also 2044 rebuilt
	B-99A	2	Pratt & Whitney	PT6A-20	579	45	46	10,445	17	250	650	142	May 1968	Commuter Air Lines	Still in production
Britten-Norman	Islander	2	Lycoming	0-540E4C5	260	36	49	5,995	9	150	220	184	Jan 1968	La Posada	Still in production
Cessna	C-402	2	Continental	TS10-520	300	36	40	6,300	10	220	900	1,419	Jan 1967	Peninsula Air Tpt	Still in production. Number includes all 400 series
De Havilland	DH104 Dove Mk 2	2	De Havilland	Gipsy Queen 70 Mark 3	400	39	57	8,500	8	210	1,000	543	1955	Midway	Number includes all versions
	DH114 Heron Mk 2	4	De Havilland	Gipsy Queen 30 Mark 2	1,000	49	72	13,500	22	195	500	149	Jun 1957	Illinois Air Lines	
De Havilland	DHC6-300	2	Pratt & Whitney	PT6A-20	579	52	65	12,500	20	210	100	289	Oct 1966	Air Wisconsin	Still in production
Piper	Aztec	2	Lycoming	O-540	250	28	37	4,800	5	200	1,200	3,014			
	Navajo	2	Lycoming	T10-540	310	33	41	6,500	8	180	650	598	1966	West Coast	Still in production
	Cherokee Six	1	Lycoming	O-540-B2B5	235	24	32	2,900	4	156	1,130	2,131	Late 1965	East Coast Air Taxi	

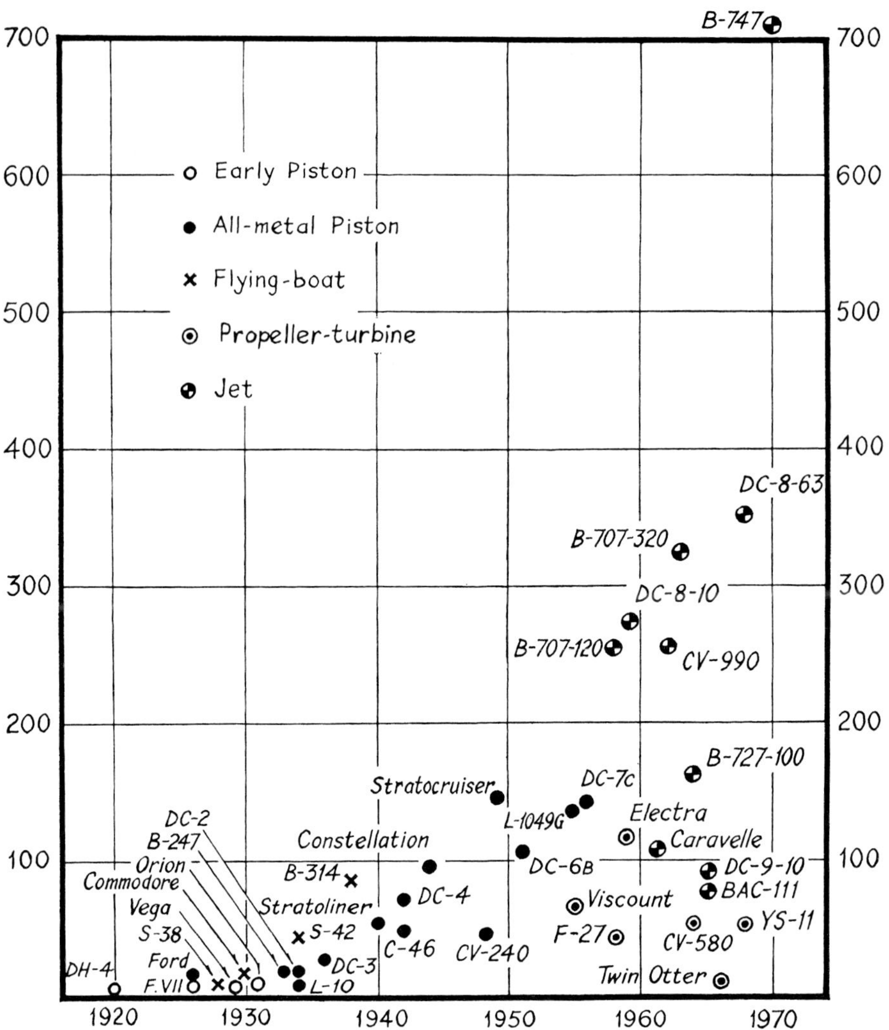

Appendix 2. Development of Airliner Productivity—Growth of gross weight, lb times 1,000.

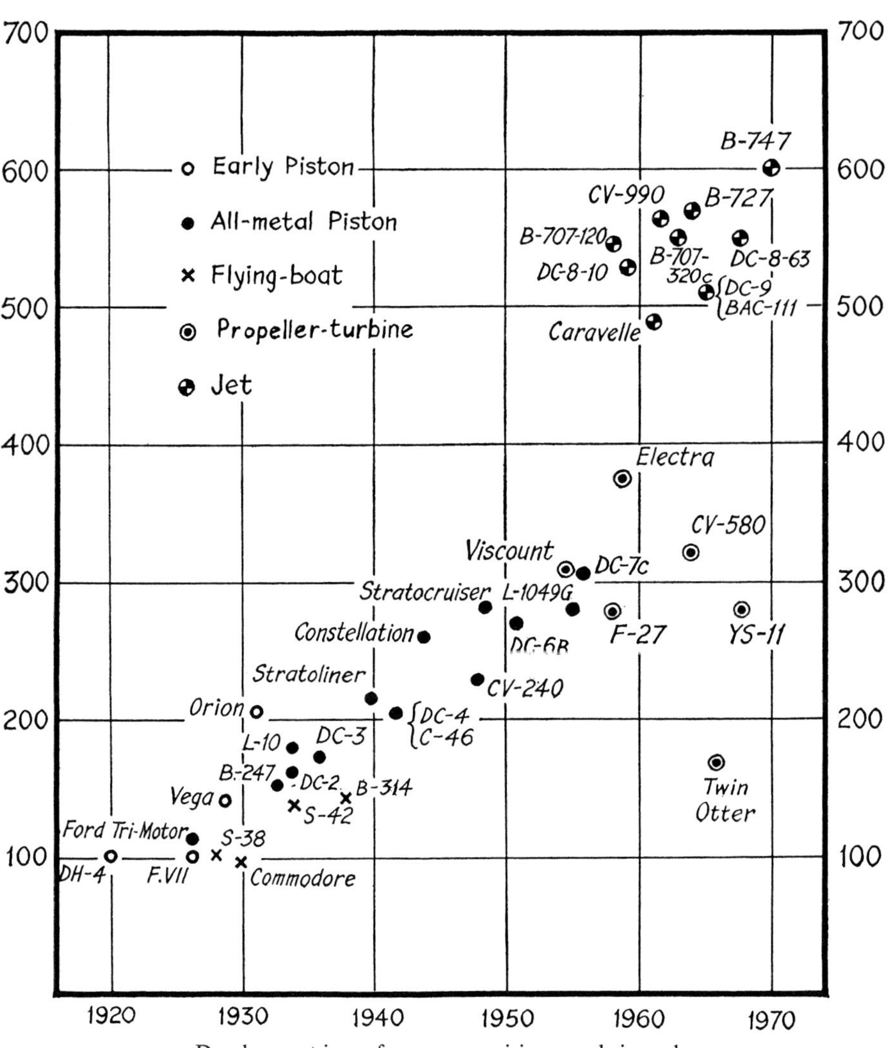

Development in performance, cruising speeds in mph.

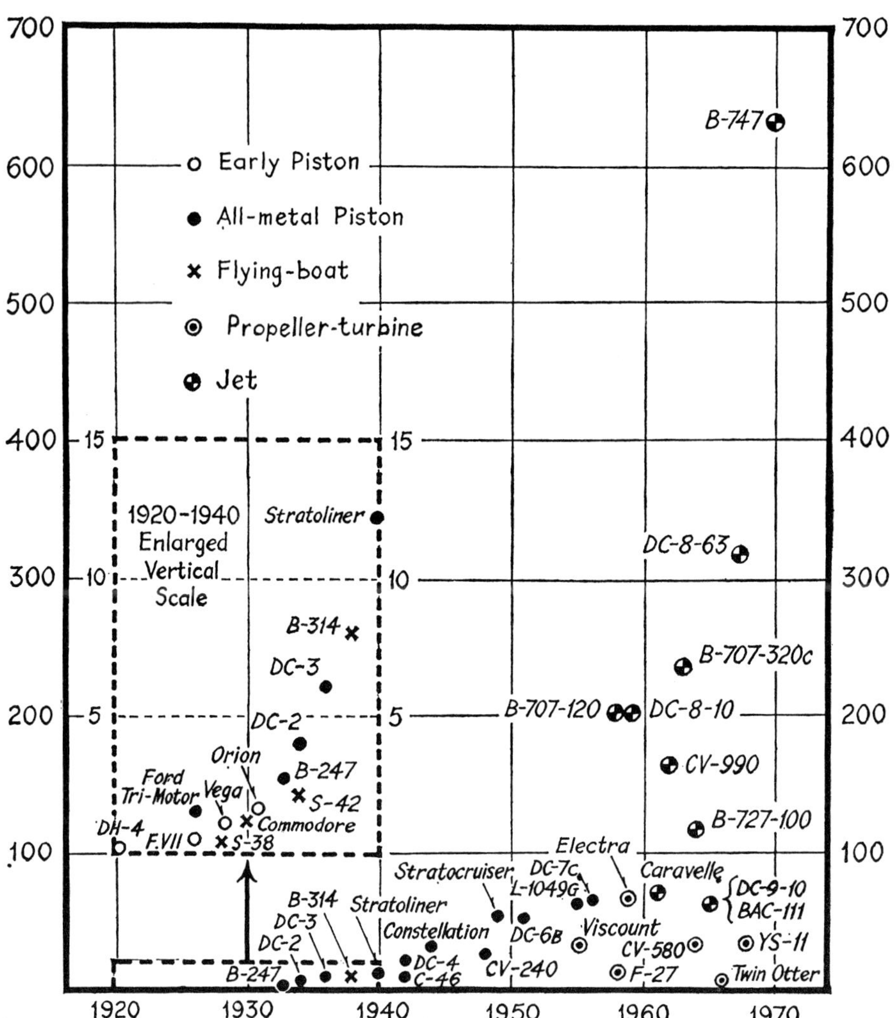

Development in productivity, seat-miles per year in millions.

Appendix 3

PASSENGER-MILES FLOWN BY U. S. AIRLINES, 1926–1969

(ALL FIGURES IN MILLIONS)

YEAR	BIG FOUR				OTHER TRUNKS											
	AMERICAN	EASTERN	TWA	UNITED	BRANIFF	C & S	COLONIAL	CONTINENTAL	DELTA	INLAND	MID-CONTINENT	NATIONAL	NORTHEAST	NORTHWEST	P.C.A.	WESTERN
	(STANDARD) 28 NOV 1927	(PITCAIRN) 18 AUG 1930	7 JULY 1929	(STOUT) 2 AUG 1926	20 JUNE 1928	(PACIFIC SEABOARD) 17 JULY 1934	4 APRIL 1927	(VARNEY) 15 JULY 1934	1934	(WYOMING) 16 APRIL 1931	(HANFORD) APRIL 1932	15 OCT 1934	(BOSTON-MAINE) 11 AUG 1933	7 JUNE 1928	(CLIFFORD BALL) 1930	(W.A.E.) 23 MAY 1926
1926	–	–	–	+	–	–	–	–	–	–	–	–	–	–	–	+
	–	–	–	+	–	–	+	–	–	–	–	–	–	–	–	+
	–	–	–	1	+	–	+	–	–	–	–	–	–	–	–	1
	1	–	4	2	+	–	+	–	–	–	–	–	–	2	–	2
1930	3	+	8	6	+	–	+	–	–	–	–	–	–	2	+	5
	6	2	16	19	1	–	+	–	–	+	–	–	–	4	1	1
	15	7	13	40	2	–	+	–	–	+	–	–	–	4	1	1
	22	13	19	70	2	–	+	–	–	+	+	–	+	4	2	2
	20	13	30	71	1	+	1	+	+	+	1	+	1	4	5	2
1935	70	20	61	83	4	2	1	+	1	+	1	+	1	10	8	5
	100	40	76	102	10	4	2	+	2	+	2	+	1	17	10	7
	123	60	67	93	10	5	2	+	3	+	2	+	1	17	13	8
	141	71	72	104	14	7	2	1	5	1	3	1	2	21	16	11
	207	103	100	143	20	9	3	2	6	2	3	1	2	35	21	11
1940	312	158	155	213	36	16	7	5	10	3	6	4	3	51	38	16
	409	211	203	261	46	23	9	6	22	3	9	9	7	60	66	25
	402	218	202	279	50	28	8	10	33	3	8	15	5	52	55	28
	436	215	242	343	67	34	11	15	43	4	11	23	9	64	52	37
	549	258	348	434	95	49	17	22	65	8	21	38	13	116	87	62
1945	762	446	514	571	147	87	28	48	103	18	44	66	39	208	184	111
	1,308	805	853	1,074	213	139	46	76	210	22	76	174	84	385	373	214
	1,438	901	1,044	1,231	200	120	41	59	201	28	82	167	62	383	288	195
	1,353	983	1,113	1,217	194	119	52	59	183	27	94	98	52	386	276	136
	1,573	1,015	1,227	1,340	229	162	60	67	209	31	100	186	62	497	362	156
1950	1,814	1,247	1,464	1,495	262	172	68	74	280	36	104	265	71	618	430	174
	2,553	1,637	1,895	1,869	335	200	82	112	402	41	130	437	88	605	616	216
	2,927	2,022	2,324	2,403	429	239	100	139	443	11	88	484	84	722	638	288
	3,306	2,528	2,888	2,717	557	83	135	149	737	–	–	623	92	855	717	360
	3,457	3,073	3,213	3,327	623	–	132	167	836	–	–	747	104	910	765	402
1955	4,360	3,600	3,503	3,986	684	–	130	222	1,009	–	–	908	117	1,019	804	515
	4,900	4,129	3,977	4,518	791	–	40	260	1,189	–	–	1,012	119	1,103	1,022	458
	5,143	4,835	4,396	4,868	963	–	–	363	1,394	–	–	953	246	1,209	1,514	703
	5,021	4,290	4,593	5,214	1,008	–	–	423	1,467	–	–	1,070	407	1,435	1,414	533
	5,737	5,056	5,673	5,161	1,033	–	–	677	1,616	–	–	1,169	519	1,751	1,612	982
1960	6,371	4,776	5,660	5,794	1,196	–	–	891	1,870	–	–	1,074	565	1,676	1,492	1,034
	6,058	4,757	5,243	7,357	1,235	–	–	902	2,203	–	–	1,139	751	1,402	600	958
	6,518	4,131	5,681	8,453	1,282	–	–	943	2,781	–	–	1,539	736	1,977	–	1,307
	7,205	5,612	7,016	9,191	1,385	–	–	1,210	3,113	–	–	1,726	648	2,367	–	1,615
	8,159	6,474	8,875	10,061	1,544	–	–	1,421	3,608	–	–	2,063	596	3,045	–	1,965
1965	9,243	8,003	10,564	12,385	1,819	–	–	2,149	4,336	–	–	2,666	674	4,008	–	2,045
	11,867	7,887	11,328	13,388	3,060	–	–	3,380	6,050	–	–	2,784	940	4,985	–	2,643
	13,449	11,224	15,524	18,766	4,766	–	–	4,934	6,578	–	–	3,600	1,187	6,668	–	3,218
	15,526	12,513	16,905	22,183	5,598	–	–	5,058	7,635	–	–	4,165	1,806	7,127	–	3,842
	16,296	14,002	19,150	25,485	5,999	MERGED, DELTA 1 MAY 1953	MERGED, EASTERN 1 JUNE 1955	5,729	8,875	MERGED, WESTERN 9 APRIL 1952	MERGED, BRANIFF 15 AUG 1952	4,276	1,878	7,481	MERGED, UNITED 1 JUNE 1961	3,721

NOTES:

1. DATE AT HEAD OF COLUMN SHOWS FIRST SERVICE DATE (AND ORIGINAL AIRLINE NAME, WHERE APPROPRIATE).
2. PASSENGER-MILE FIGURES LESS THAN 500,000 SHOWN THUS: +

Continued overleaf

Year	International: Pan Am	Panagra	Alaska	P.N.A.	Caribair (Powelson)	T.C.A.	Other	Feeder: Local Service (Pioneer)	Intra-Hawaii (Inter-Island)	Intra-Alaska	Helicopter (New York)	All Cargo	Supplementals	Intra-State	Third Level	Total
	16 Jan 1928	17 May 1929	17 Aug 1951	Oct 1951	Oct 1938	8 Mar 1958		25 Aug 1925	11 Nov 1929		8 July 1953					
1926	–	–	–	–	–	–	–	–	–	–	–	–	–	–	–	+
	–	–	–	–	–	–	–	–	–	–	–	–	–	–	–	+
	+	–	–	–	–	–	–	–	–	–	–	–	–	–	–	2
	3	+	–	–	–	–	–	–	+	–	–	–	–	–	–	14
1930	7	1	–	–	–	–	–	–	1	–	–	–	–	–	–	32
	12	2	–	–	–	–	–	–	1	–	–	–	–	–	–	65
	18	3	–	–	–	–	–	–	+	+	–	–	–	–	–	104
	21	4	–	–	–	–	–	–	1	+	–	–	–	–	–	160
	31	6	–	–	–	–	–	–	1	+	–	–	–	–	–	187
1935	40	7	–	–	–	–	–	–	2	+	–	–	–	–	–	316
	47	9	–	–	–	–	–	–	3	+	–	–	–	–	–	432
	44	8	–	–	–	–	–	–	3	+	–	–	–	–	–	459
	45	8	–	–	+	–	–	–	4	+	–	–	–	–	–	529
	64	8	–	–	+	–	–	–	3	+	–	–	–	–	–	743
1940	87	13	–	–	1	–	–	–	4	1	–	–	–	–	–	1,139
	146	17	–	–	1	–	–	–	7	1	–	–	–	–	–	1,541
	225	22	–	–	+	–	–	–	11	2	–	–	–	–	–	1,656
	195	51	–	–	+	–	–	–	15	2	–	–	–	–	–	1,869
	250	62	–	–	1	–	–	–	16	4	–	–	–	–	–	2,515
1945	359	87	–	–	2	–	–	1	23	5	–	–	50	–	–	3,903
	775	126	–	–	3	–	–	7	35	19	–	–	300	–	–	7,317
	1,142	107	–	–	4	–	–	46	43	18	–	–	200	–	1	8,001
	1,134	104	–	–	5	–	–	88	48	24	–	–	350	–	2	8,097
	1,190	106	–	–	6	–	–	139	47	18	–	–	536	6	2	9,326
1950	1,258	104	–	–	6	–	40	191	52	27	–	–	774	17	2	11,045
	1,572	128	2	4	7	–	98	300	61	39	–	–	1,069	24	3	14,525
	1,807	133	11	32	9	–	83	347	72	34	–	+	1,252	30	6	17,157
	2,015	137	16	47	10	–	91	398	72	37	+	6	1,378	38	7	19,999
	2,285	151	9	48	10	–	77	473	73	37	+	66	1,300	41	7	22,333
1955	2,818	164	8	71	11	–	13	549	83	41	1	115	1,774	52	7	26,564
	3,386	172	9	92	13	–	20	648	86	52	2	651	955	64	8	29,676
	3,876	174	8	106	16	–	32	766	91	53	3	1,072	743	75	9	33,611
	3,894	163	39	106	18	125	20	844	113	38	5	717	1,131	96	11	34,195
	4,594	188	91	113	23	151	24	1,057	130	47	7	366	1,512	119	12	39,420
1960	5,126	198	108	116	27	216	32	1,171	170	50	9	376	2,019	204	14	42,235
	6,191	230	83	123	31	171	30	1,366	128	53	9	762	1,599	231	16	43,628
	7,267	238	72	129	41	358	29	1,627	129	56	8	946	1,824	332	18	48,422
	8,069	239	63	138	53	493	44	1,891	148	56	13	919	1,534	418	20	55,186
	9,027	251	92	160	63	736	37	2,276	173	63	16	1,088	1,502	490	25	63,810
1965	9,871	278	130	199	75	897	46	2,651	199	70	19	886	2,489	585	110	76,397
	13,224	284	140	256	82	908	53	3,514	227	76	26	1,042	4,125	834	175	93,278
	14,900	26	254	–	87	905	–	4,205	275	84	30	986	6,056	1,136	250	119,108
	16,484	–	298	–	110	1,662	–	5,558	301	86	25	3,102	8,887	1,577	353	140,801
	17,058	Merged, Braniff 31 Jan 1967	346	Merged, Western 10 Nov 1966	115	1,234	–	6,474	327	106	17	3,825	11,145	1,678	636	155,853

Notes:

3. Figures in "All Cargo" column are military contract passengers.
4. Figures in "Other" column include Mackey, Midet, Resort, Samoan, South Pacific, and UMCA.

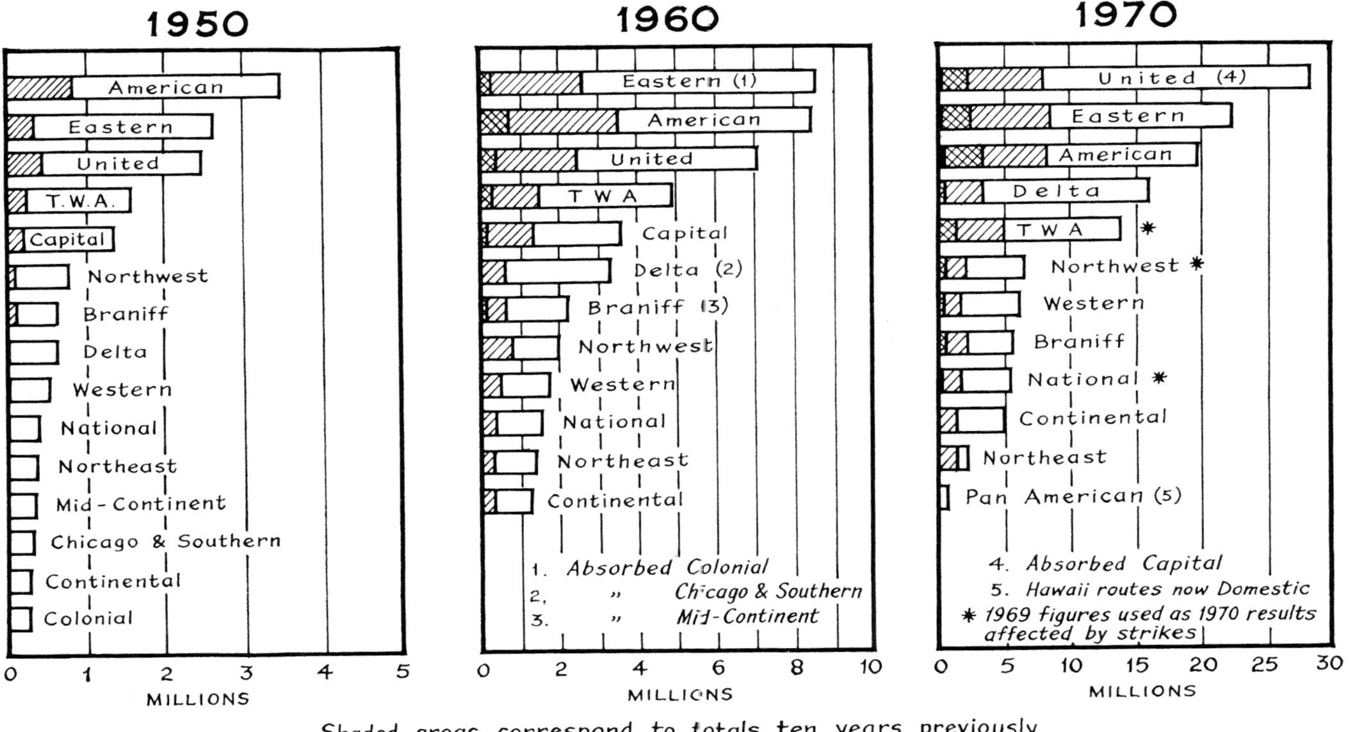

Appendix 4. Passengers Carried by U.S. Domestic Trunk Airlines, 1950–1970. Growth by 10-year intervals.

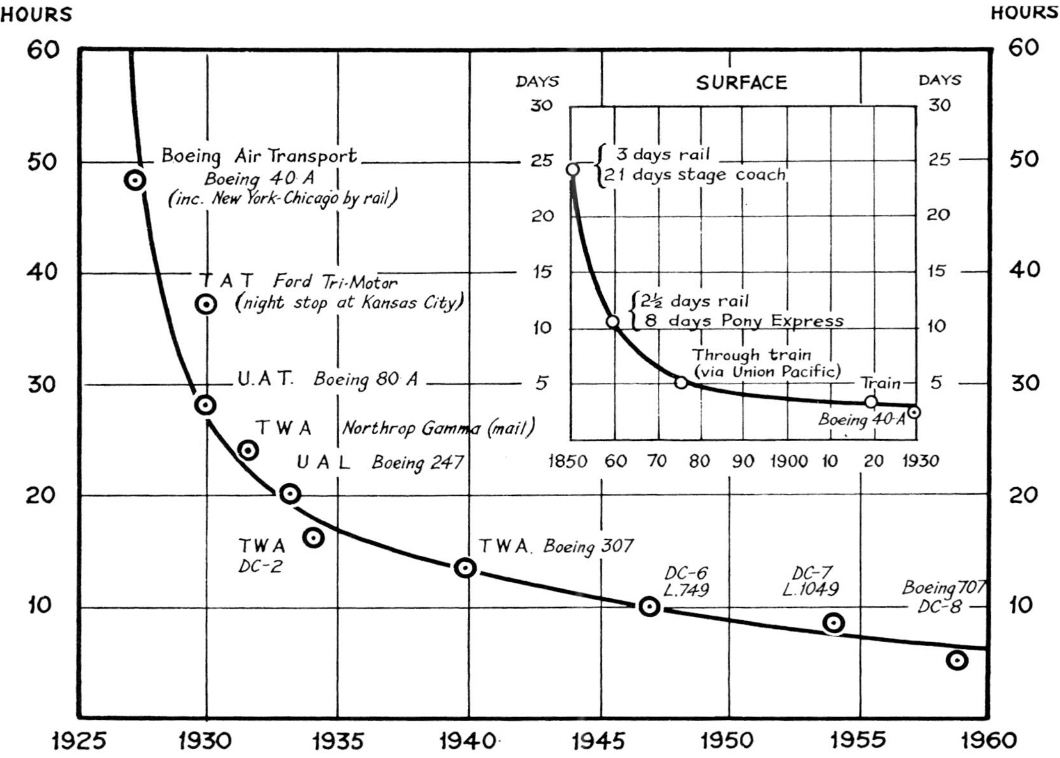

Appendix 5. U.S. Transcontinental Route: Reduction in Journey Time, 1850–1960.

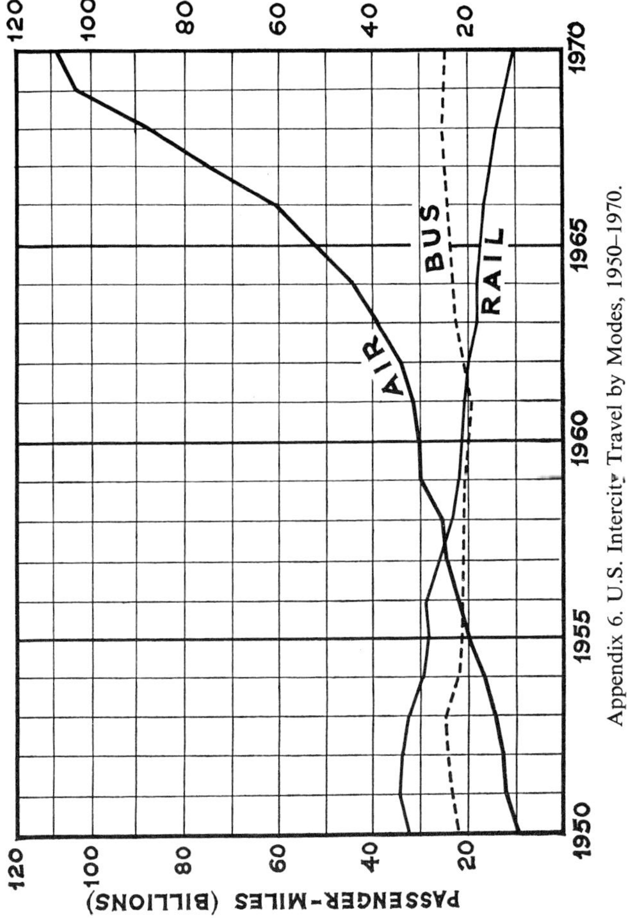

Appendix 6. U.S. Intercity Travel by Modes, 1950–1970.

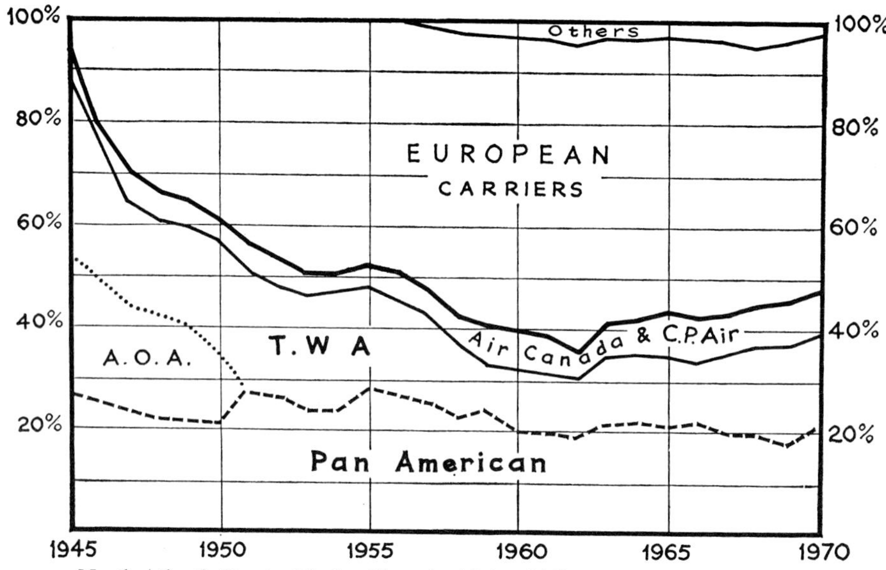

North Atlantic Route: Market Share by Major Airlines or Groups, 1945–1970.

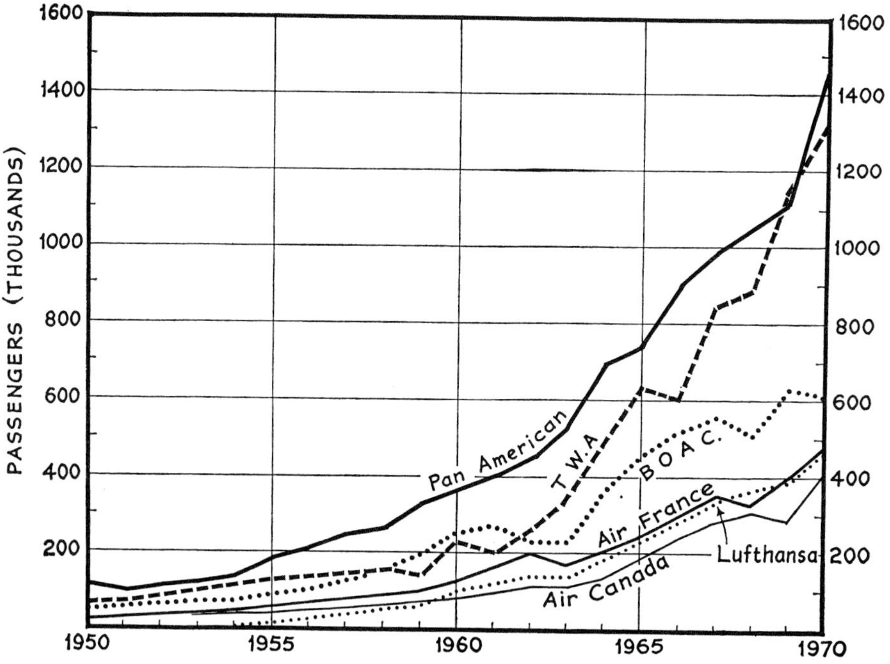

North Atlantic Route: Passengers carried by Six Leading Airlines, 1950–1970.

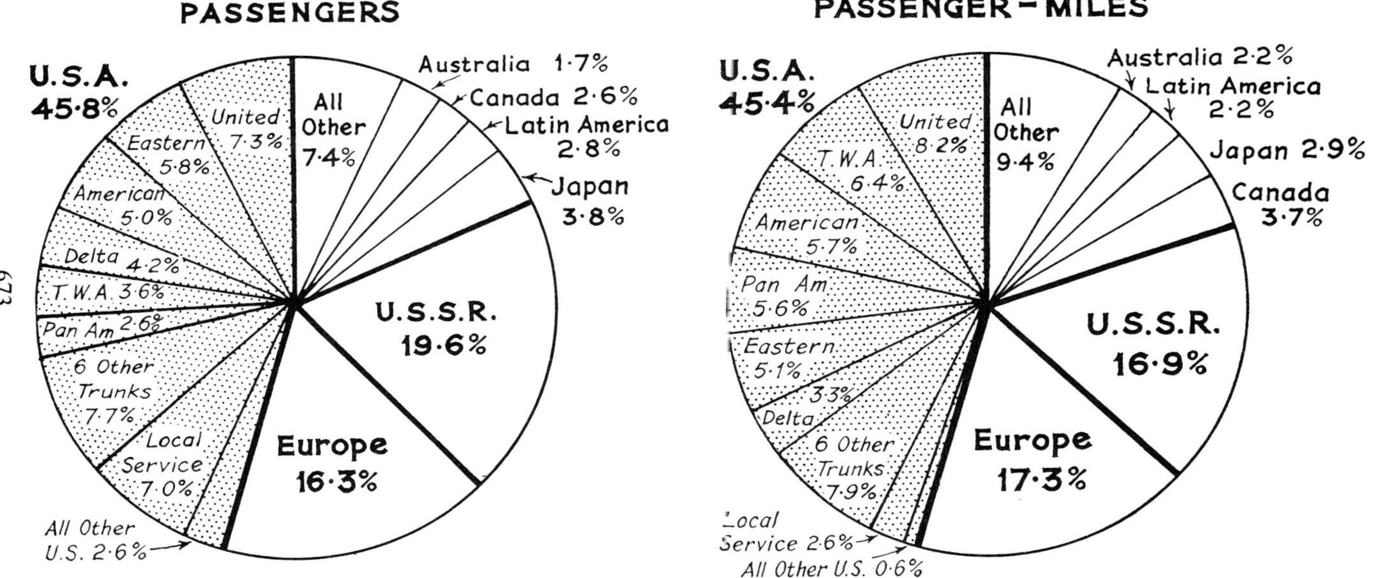

Percentage Share of World Airline Traffic 1970 by Major Airlines and Groups.

These three charts show the top ranking world airlines in 1970, illustrating the importance of the U.S. carriers. TOP: passengers carried. CENTRE: passenger-miles. BOTTOM: cargo ton-miles.

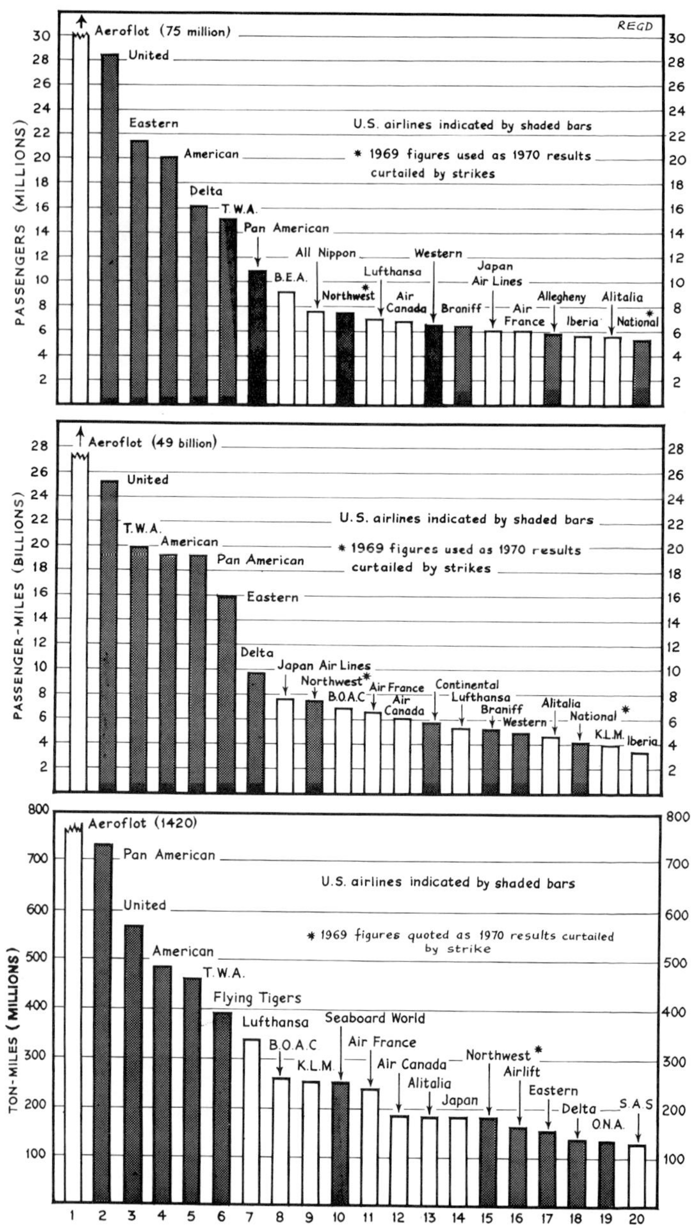

Essay on Deregulation

Checks and Balances In a democratic society, the people's well-being is dependent upon a code of justice, achieved by the enactment of legislation containing a substantial element of what is popularly termed the system of checks and balances. These include regulatory institutions, working in harmony with the civil service and local government, to watch over those areas of industry vital to daily life, such as heat, light, power, and communication. Such agencies tread a delicate tightrope. On the one hand, they must protect the public from the predatory greed of those who aim to pervert the machinery of a capitalist society; and on the other hand, they must guard against the evils of a faceless, self-serving bureaucracy.

The United States Civil Aeronautics Board, set up in 1938, has been such an institution, charged with regulating a confident, ambitious, and expanding industry. From the outset, the C.A.B., with fewer than a thousand administrators, has controlled roughly half of the world's airline activity. The United States airlines have led the world throughout the entire period, and this might suggest that those who controlled it must have done some things correctly.

This is not to state that everything was right at the C.A.B., where lawful adherence to a rigid system, designed for a less frantic era, failed to keep pace with the jet age. To its credit, the C.A.B. recognized the problem in the early 1970s, and moved to put its house in order.

Erosion of a Regulatory System The C.A.B. had observed, somewhat aloofly, the low fare, high volume activity of Pacific Southwest Airways (PSA), which operated in a free market environment within the state of California, and therefore free of C.A.B. control (see pages 548–52). PSA helped to make the Los Angeles–San Francisco air corridor both the densest travel market in the world, and the cheapest. Also during the early 1960s, European nonscheduled airlines had demonstrated that significant fare savings were possible by filling all the aircraft seats rather than accepting the 55 percent load factor which had become customary during the jet age. The C.A.B. progressively eased the dampening effect of the ponderous air charter regulations, by authorizing first the Supplementals to operate Inclusive Tour Charters (ITC) in 1966 (pages 460–61); then in 1972 Travel Group Charters (TGCs) which were unsuccessful; and in August 1975, One-Stop Inclusive Tour Charters (OTCs). Significantly, and for the first time, large establishment airlines such as Pan American and United publicly favoured OTC rules.

In February 1976, the Board moved even further, with Advance Booking Charters (ABCs), partly in an effort to match the British innovation, Advance Purchase Excursion (APEX) fares. By the winter of 1976/77, it was possible to fly between New York and Florida for $99.

While the airlines were recovering from a mild recession, they were faced with an almost crippling increment in the price of fuel. During the early 1970s, the international oil companies put up their prices. A gallon of kerosene went up to almost a dollar, from about 25 cents two years previously, and a far cry from the 11 cents of the early 1960s.

There were apparent inconsistencies in the C.A.B.'s policy. In January 1976 it denied World Airways' application for a transcontinental scheduled one-way fare of $89, because World was a Supplemental, and therefore ineligible to operate a scheduled route. Here was an airline, fit, willing, and able to offer the public a bargain, but being prevented from doing so because of a legal technicality. As the British lawyers have it: justice not only must be done, but must be seen to be done. And in due course, so it was.

The First Price War Looking over their shoulders at the Atlantic price war, the U.S. domestic airlines began the infighting. The charter airlines invaded the scheduled preserves, and vice versa. Discount fares were followed by deep discounts, with tempting packages such as American Airlines *Super-Saver* ($227 transcontinental round trip) introduced on 25 April, 1977. Eastern offered low cost New York–Florida packages. TWA matched American's *Super-Saver. Super-Coach*, *Simple Saver* and *Super No Frills* followed. Then, on 6 June, 1977, the Board approved the Laker *Skytrain*, to open a new chapter in international fares and scheduling practice. The old established edifice of controlled routes, schedules, pricing, and time-honoured procedures was creaking.

Regulatory Reform The question seemed to be: was the structure worth reinforcing, should it be completely rebuilt, or, as an extreme measure, should it be pulled down altogether? The C.A.B. had already sought architectural advice. Late in 1974 (far earlier than is now remembered) it ordered a study to be conducted by selected members of its staff, including an independent consultant. The report of this Special Staff on Regulatory Reform, directed by Roy Pulsifer, issued its report on 22 July, 1975. It contained recommendations which were in many ways prophetic. With minor exceptions, most were later adopted as the basic framework of the Deregulation Act of 1978. To quote the C.A.B.'s unofficial historian, Dr. Samuel R. L. Brown: "The Civil Aeronautics Board thus became the first regulatory agency to . . . recommend essentially doing away with the main business of the agency."

The Deregulation Act of 1978 Alfred E. Kahn was sworn in on 10 January, 1977, as the new C.A.B. chairman, replacing John E. Robson, under whose authority, however, had been established the Advisory Committee on Procedural Reform, on 21 June, 1975, concurrently with the workings of Pulsifer's special staff. Speeding up rule-making procedures, an airline would no longer have to wait ten years for a decision (see page 556). The effects of free market entry and exit, and freedom to manipulate fares within certain limits, had also been closely studied. When deregulation came, therefore, the C.A.B. staff were ready for the onslaught. On 15

October, 1978, the U.S. Congress enacted into law the Airline Deregulation Act of 1978, signed by President Carter on 24 October. Marvin S. Cohen was appointed to succeed Alfred Kahn as C.A.B. Chairman and Michael Levine was named General Director, an unprecedented position of influence and authority. Suddenly, the airlines could fly almost where they wanted to, and to charge almost any fare they liked.

The Floodgates Open Each domestic airline, including Supplementals and Intra-State operators, could select one new route each year, without C.A.B. approval, and could equally protect one of its own routes from new entry. Additionally, on 18 October, 1978, at 8:30 A.M., the airlines stood in line outside the C.A.B. in Washington, to claim dormant nonstop-route authority. Seven hundred routes out of an estimated 10,000 were applied for. The effect upon the airline map was revolutionary. Old geographically oriented names like Western, Eastern, or Northwest ceased to have much meaning.

Both dormant authority and automatic entry were superseded by the Board's policy decision (under the new law) to open city pair entry to all fit carriers in the spring of 1979. Hence, when C.A.B. route authority ceased to be mandatory on 31 December, 1981, open entry had already been achieved in practice throughout the U.S. domestic market.

The liberal effect of a new international policy was also evident. Airlines invaded spheres of influence which had been closely guarded privileges for decades. At London's Gatwick Airport, reservation counters opened for Braniff, Northwest, Western, Air Florida, Northwest, and Capitol.

Under Section 10 of the Deregulation Act, governing new entrants, almost thirty new airlines joined the Regional airline ranks during the first year. These included former Intra-State airlines, the larger Commuters, and a growing number of new companies. Names such as Muse Air, New York Air, and People's Express, well capitalized, well equipped, and effectively promoted, quickly became as familiar in some market areas as the traditional giants of the industry.

The Second Price War The airlines started a new price war as soon as deregulation came into effect. Throughout 1979, there was a plethora of special fare promotions. Airlines offered transcontinental flights at $99.99 one way, New York to Florida for $55. Taking full advantage of the freedom of exit provisions, carriers quickly suspended service over many routes, but significantly, these were almost entirely on short haul segments.

There were some curious side effects. High volume traffic over city pairs such as Los Angeles–New York permitted low fares with internal cross-subsidization, whereas low volume traffic did not allow such flexibility. Thus, in 1980, the cheapest way to fly from Los Angeles to Philadelphia was via New York, even including taxi fare.

The Aftermath But after the feast came the reckoning. From record profits in 1978 many airlines plummeted into deep deficits, and by 1981 their situation was desperate. Advocates of deregulation claimed that the cream would rise to the top, and the inefficient would rightly pay the ultimate price. Was it not better to have an airline like Southwest, with a cost structure half the level of Braniff's? But experienced analysts like Melvin Brenner, an old TWA hand, dissected the fares structures with surgical precision, revealing fundamental deficiencies of so-called sixth freedom discounting by false applications of marginal cost formulae.

Some airline managements, bemused by deregulation, were responsible for much of the airlines' problems. Another economic recession played its part, and a strike by the air traffic controllers, called in the summer of 1981, did not help. But cutthroat fare competition, and cardinal errors of misjudgment by management, were no longer monitored by a watchful agency, nor were excesses kept in check. Pan American Airways purchased National Airlines on 26 October, 1980, almost as a conditioned reflex action stemming from the days when a plausible case could have been made for linking its international gateways. Harding Lawrence, of Braniff, possibly seeing himself as Juan Trippe's natural successor, launched his airline into an orgy of route expansion in 1979, including Europe and the Far East, dozens of new domestic segments, and a short-lived Concorde interchange service from Dallas to London/Paris between 12 January, 1979, and 31 May, 1980.

The irony is that the C.A.B., given its traditional powers, would not have authorized the Pan American purchase of National, nor countenanced Braniff's illusions of grandeur. The C.A.B. was always conscious of its mandate to regulate the airline industry ". . . in the public convenience and necessity," taking the view that this embraced the travelling public, the investors, and the employees.

Howard Putnam had replaced the spendthrift Harding Lawrence as chairman when Braniff filed for bankruptcy on 12 May, 1982. Its private debt amounted to an unbelievable $733 million. Such was the fate of an airline that had been founded by a true pioneer and a respected name in industry. The public will now have to decide whether it is better served by those whom one abrasive writer described as the "entrepreneurial vultures, each gathering to pick the bones of the carcass conveniently anesthetized by Washington edict."

On 31 December, 1981, the C.A.B. lost control over domestic routes; on 31 December, 1982, it will cease to control fares; and by the end of 1983 it may cease to exist. Already, its powers are so emasculated as to reduce a once-powerful agency to a faded shadow of its former self. As for the airlines, not one has yet publicly gone on record in support of a return to regulation, partial or otherwise. If nothing else, deregulation has brought sharply into focus the basic issue: is air transport simply a means of making money, or is it a public service, in the conduct of which the public must be protected?

Index

Main entries and main page references are in bold type.
Illustrations are indicated by italics.
A finding list for new material appears on pages 745–46.

Finding List for New Material

The most influential of the Commuter airlines tabulated in rank order on page 630 are listed alphabetically below:

Aero Mech
Air Illinois
Air Midwest
Air Oregon
Air Wisconsin
Altair Airlines
Antilles Air Boats
Aspen Airways
Bar Harbor
Cable Flying Service
Cape & Islands Air Service
Cape Smythe Air
Catalina Airlines
Combs Airways
Commuter Airlines
Empire Airlines
Executive Airlines
Golden West Airlines
Henson Aviation
Imperial Airlines
Inland Empire
Mackey International
Metro Airlines
Mississippi Valley Airlines
Pennsylvania Airlines
Pilgrim Airlines
Prinair
Provincetown-Boston Airline
Ransome Airlines
Royale Airlines
Royal Hawaiian Air Service
Scenic Airlines
Scheduled Skyways
Skyway Aviation
S-M-B Stage Lines
Suburban Airlines
Sun Airlines
Wright Airlines